SHAN S. KUO
Massachusetts Institute of Technology
and University of New Hampshire

Assembler Language for FORTRAN, COBOL, and PL/I Programmers

IBM 370/360

▲
▼▼
ADDISON-WESLEY PUBLISHING COMPANY
Reading, Massachusetts
Menlo Park, California · London · Amsterdam · Don Mills, Ontario · Sydney

Second printing, March 1977

Copyright © 1974 by Addison-Wesley Publishing Company, Inc. Philippines copyright 1974 by Addison-Wesley Publishing Company, Inc.

ISBN 0-201-03954-0
BCDEFGHIJ-HA-798

To my parents

Preface

The objective of this book is to help the student in programming the IBM System/370 or System/360 in assembler language. Study of assembler language is intimately tied to a particular computer organization. A *byte* computer (such as the IBM System/370, IBM System/360, the Univac Series 90, and the former RCA Spectra 70, for example) was chosen for two main reasons: (1) it is the largest selling type of machine; (2) it offers a more representative view of the many types of programming features available on recent computer systems.

This book is written from the viewpoint of a student who has experience in one of the high-level languages, such as FORTRAN, PL/I, *or* COBOL but finds this high-level language not flexible enough to describe some parts of his or her problem in an efficient manner.

It is an outgrowth of a set of class notes used at the University of New Hampshire. This set of notes has been used also as a self-study text for personnel in several computing centers, who are familiar with data processing methods and basic programming but not yet versed in assembler language.

One of the most important, yet difficult, topics in any programming language is how to handle the class of statements or instructions for input and output. This is certainly true for the assembler language programming. When I began teaching the course, I found that the student had to deal with approximately one-foot thickness of extensively cross-referenced manuals, if he or she wished to learn every detail of a program ready to run on an IBM System/360 computer. Several excellent texts have since become available and two approaches are suggested to handle the input/output programming. First, the input/output feature is completely omitted and students learn to write only the manipulative portions of a program. Second, a limited treatment of input/output appears near the end of the book and is often restricted to a particular operating system. As a consequence, students are not able to actually *run* a program on a computer until the latter part of the course.

In order to help alleviate this unhappy situation, the input/output is handled in this book largely through the use of a main program written in one of the high-level languages, such as FORTRAN, COBOL, or PL/I, *which calls a subroutine written in the assembler language*. The author has found that the students already have some background in one of the high-level languages, and that they are eager to utilize their knowledge and experience.

This procedure has several advantages. First, it allows the student to write and *run* a complete program as quickly as possible. Second, it provides the student with strong motivation to learn well the bridges to and from a program written in a high-level language. Third, the reliance of a main program written in a high-level language often makes life easier for a professional programmer. For example, an assembler language programmer using floating-point arithmetic has a tough task to convert numbers from one format to another. An advantage of a main program in a high-level language is that it does the job with much less work on the part of the programmer.

This book is divided into three parts. Part I deals with the fixed-point binary programming, the logical instructions, save-area chaining, macro programming, and conditional assembly. Part II presents decimal programming, editing operations, and floating-point programming. Part III is, in general, based on the System/360 Operating System (OS). It introduces the job control language and input/output through OS. It also introduces a number of sophisticated topics commonly used by systems programmers. The prerequisite is a short introduction to programming in a high-level language, such as COBOL, FORTRAN, or PL/I.

An important feature of the book is that it contains a large number of programming examples. They are completely worked out, including statement of the problem, sample input, listing for main program, subroutine listings (or assembly listings), and the associated output. Each programming example is *tested* on an IBM System/370 or System/360. An integral part of the book is the problems and the laboratory work listed at the end of each chapter. It is desirable that the laboratory assignments be programmed and run on a computer.

As a text, this book is suited for the courses on programming languages which are normally included as a "second" course in the computing curricula of most colleges and universities. The student is advised to refer to the manuals for a particular computer system for additional information if such need arises.

It is with pleasure that I gratefully acknowledge the help and encouragement of my friends, colleagues, and students. In particular, my thanks go to A. Clark, J. Davids, E. G. Fisher, A. Hayes, M. A. Lamson, J. P. Morency, C. L. Richardson, and P. Wong for their comments, criticisms, and help in eliminating errors. Numerous ideas were drawn from the internal publications of Computation Centers at Brown University, Massachusetts Institute of Technology, University of New Hampshire, and University of Waterloo.

I am also grateful for the expert typing and key-punching by A. Beaudet, K. J. Duh, L. M. Hsu, and K. F. Tsai. Finally, I wish to thank the staffs of Addison-Wesley Publishing Company and William Clowes & Sons Composition Company for their continuous cooperation.

Durham, New Hampshire   S. S. K.
April 1974

Contents

FIXED-POINT BINARY PROGRAMMING

There are four ways to represent a piece of data in the IBM System 370/360; one of them uses the fixed-point binary format. The subject matter of Part I is centered around this type of data and its associated instructions. It is divided into nine chapters.

Chapter 1 is introductory while Chapter 2 presents number systems and fixed-point arithmetic. Chapter 3 deals with some basic instructions for addition, subtraction, multiplication, and division of two fixed-point numbers. Nine most frequently used instructions are discussed in Chapters 4 and 5.

As an illustration of usage of these common instructions, Chapter 5 also discusses the convention of linkage between a main program written in a high-level language and its subroutine. When finishing this chapter, students should have no difficulty in writing complete programs for an actual computer run: subroutine in assembler language and the main program in any one of several high-level languages.

Chapter 6 gives an overview of the assembler language instructions. Chapter 7 discusses bit manipulations, which is an important topic in nonnumerical applications. Additional instructions in logical operations are also introduced. Chapter 8 deals basically with linkage between a subroutine and its own subroutine. The concept of control sections is introduced and section-to-section relationship discussed.

Chapter 9 is concerned with basics of macroprogramming. How to write macro definitions for conditional assembly is an important and sophisticated subject. It is discussed with many illustrative examples.

CHAPTER 1

Computer Hardware and Software

1.1 INTRODUCTION

Since the first vacuum tube computer was designed in 1947, digital computers have reached into nearly every realm of human endeavor to alter dramatically the shape of today's society. The essence of a modern computer is its simplicity: It takes but a single step at a time to obtain final answers. Each step is dictated by an instruction. A collection of instructions in a specified sequence plus the required data is called a program. A modern digital computer can store a program in its memory and execute it without human intervention; it is thus known as *stored-program* computer.

Today we write a program in a programming language (such as FORTRAN, PL/I, COBOL, or assembler language), not in machine language (the only language understood by a computer). To use assembler language effectively, a programmer has to know some technical terminologies related to computer hardware and system software. They are briefly discussed in Sections 1.2 through 1.5. Section 1.6 includes a sample program written in assembler language which gives orientation and motivation for much of the material in this book. Finally, Section 1.7 contains a check list which helps establish communication between you and your installation.

1.2 COMPUTER HARDWARE

A digital computer comprises several basic elements that provide five essential functional capabilities: memory, arithmetic-logic, control, input, and output as shown in Fig. 1.1. The arithmetic-logic unit and control are often called Central Processing Unit (CPU). In this section, we shall review the memory units, leaving CPU and input/output (I/O) devices in the next section.

There are two classes of memory units: main memory and auxiliary memory units. The outstanding difference between these two lies in the *access time*, the time

3

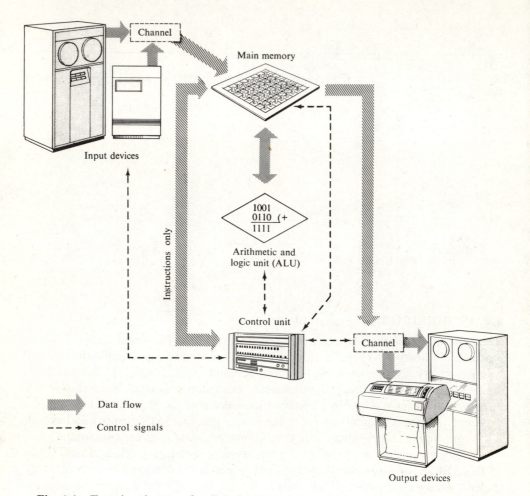

Fig. 1.1   Functional parts of a digital computer. Channels are used in large systems.

needed to locate a particular item of information and to transmit it to and from the memory unit. A memory unit is also called a storage unit.

The main memory unit (or main storage) is the seat of immediate "memory" of a computer system. Instructions or data must be stored in main storage if they are to be processed. The magnetic core memory has been the major main storage unit up to the present time. Some computers today use semiconductors (monolithic "chips") as the main memory. Plated wire is also in use.

A magnetic core is a doughnut-shaped piece of ferromagnetic material about 0.02 to 0.1 inch in diameter. It can be magnetized in either a clockwise or a counterclockwise direction. The cores are strung by pairs of wire at right angle to each other, called a *core plane*. A number of core planes is stacked. We can consider the corresponding cores in each core plane as one distinct group (see Fig. 1.2). Such a group is usually identified with a unique number commonly known as an *address* or a *location*. For example, in location 7164 which contains 8 cores, the information stored may be 10110101.

The basic building block of a monolithic memory is a silicon "chip," less than $\frac{1}{8}$-in. square. Each chip contains several thousands of microscopic circuit elements, such as resistors, transistors, and diodes, which are interconnected to form a few hundreds of complete memory and support circuits. There are two basic types: metal-oxide-silicon (MOS) type and bipolar type. MOS devices are more compact than bipolar ones (eight times as much) and for that reason are used in the main storage where more capacity is required. The high density of the monolithic circuits makes it possible to provide users with faster main memories. For example, the internal operating speed of System/370 Model 168, which has the monolithic main memory, is up to 30 percent faster than Model 165, which uses the conventional core-memory unit. Figure 1.3 shows two silicon chips. They are mounted on a single substrate, and two substrates are stacked to form a storage array module of 64 characters.

Auxiliary Memory Units

The main storage has relatively limited storage capacity and is very expensive. The auxiliary memory units enable a larger capacity, at the expense of a somewhat longer

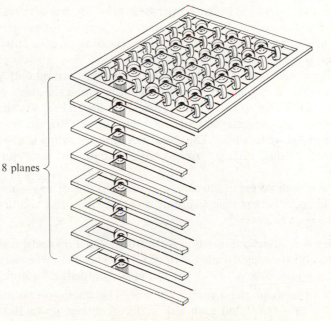

8 planes

Fig. 1.2   Core array.

Fig. 1.3 Monolithic technology—two silicon chips are mounted on a single substrate. Each chip is about ⅛ inch square.

access time. In ascending order of the access time, the major types of auxiliary memories are magnetic drums, direct access devices such as magnetic disk packs, data cells, and magnetic tapes. Thus the access time of a magnetic drum is less (faster) than that of a disk pack, but by far greater (slower) than that of cores. All auxiliary memory units are used mainly for temporary storage, or for programs or data to which no immediate access is required. All instructions or data must first be transferred to main storage if they are to be processed.

Disks, tapes, and data cells are probably the most commonly used auxiliary storage units. The removable disk pack, which resembles a stack of phonograph records, enables the user to easily change packs as he wishes. As the disks spin at about 2,500 rpm, data are magnetically recorded on or retrieved from the surfaces of disks by the read-write heads. The density of data recording is about 200,000 bits per square inch of disk surface. Access time to data on disks can be as fast as 1/30,000 sec.

A disk pack with access mechanism in a disk storage drive is shown in Fig. 1.4. The basic differences between the recording on a magnetic disk and that on a phonograph record are as follows:

1. The methods by which information is recorded. On a magnetic disk, information is recorded on the magnetizable surface of a metal disk, whereas a phonograph record is a plastic disk on which the sound is recorded in a spiral groove.

2. Each side of a phonograph record has only one track—one continuous groove in the form of a spiral, but each disk surface contains up to 1000 tracks in the form of concentric circles.

The information is usually recorded on or retrieved from consecutive vertical tracks

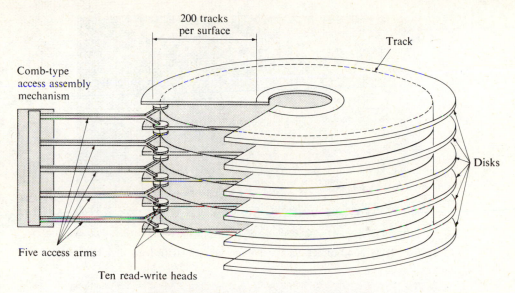

200 tracks
per surface

Track

Comb-type
access assembly
mechanism

Disks

Five access arms

Ten read-write heads

Fig. 1.4 Disk pack with access mechanism.

rather than consecutive horizontal tracks. The reason: All vertically aligned tracks
can be used for recording or retrieval without any movement of the access mechanism,
which saves time. These tracks have equal distance from the center of disk and are
collectively called a *cylinder*. Figure 1.5 shows ten tracks and 203 cylinders. The
popular IBM/2311 disk pack, for example, contains 3625 bytes per track. (Each byte
has eight bits, as discussed in Section 2.4). There are ten tracks per cylinder, and 200
cylinders per pack.

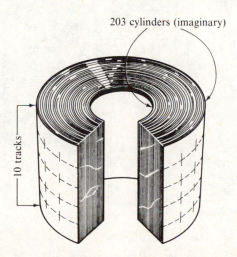

203 cylinders (imaginary)

10 tracks

Fig. 1.5 Tracks and cylinder. (Ten tracks are shown.)

Fig. 1.6   IBM 3340 direct-access storage facility (with four disk drivers).

Fig. 1.7   IBM 2321 data cell drive.

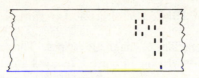

Fig. 1.8 Information recorded on a nine-track magnetic tape. Across the width of the tape, each of the nine small areas can be either magnetized or not.

Fig. 1.9 IBM 3420 magnetic tape drive.

Figure 1.6 shows an IBM 3340 direct-access storage facility with four disk drives.

Data cells contain magazines of magnetic stripes. The drive unit can address one of the stripes for reading or writing. Figure 1.7 shows an IBM 2321 data cell drive. Finally, the magnetic tape is a storage medium which costs the least, but the data on tape can be retrieved only sequentially, and this causes delay which results in slowing down computer operation. The magnetic tape in a computer system is of the same type one uses for home tape recorders. Across the tape width (about 0.5 in.) several small areas can be either magnetized or nonmagnetized. If nine small areas are used, thus forming nine bits across the width of the tape (see Fig. 1.8) and nine tracks along the length of the tape, the tape is known as a nine-track one. Each nine-bit group—eight data bits and one check bit (or parity bit)—is used to represent a character. Similarly, on a seven-track tape, data are written by magnetizing seven parallel tracks along the length of the tape. If a density of 800 characters per inch of tape is used, millions of characters can be stored on one reel of tape. Other typical tape densities are 200, 556, 1600, and 3200 characters per inch. The tape moves past the read head or write head in a tape drive at typical speed 36, 75, or 112.5 inches per second. An IBM 3420 magnetic tape drive is shown in Fig. 1.9.

1.3 CENTRAL PROCESSING UNIT (CPU), INPUT/OUTPUT DEVICES, AND CHANNELS

The central processing unit (CPU) contains mainly the arithmetic and logic unit (ALU), and the control unit. The ALU performs arithmetic on receiving information on (1) the required operation and (2) the operand(s) to be operated on. The basic arithmetic operations are addition and subtraction. Multiplication and division are carried out, respectively, by repeated addition and repeated subtraction. The ALU can also compare two operands and indicate the result.

To a programmer, the ALU unit may be idealized as a set of *registers*, as shown in Fig. 1.10. Like an accumulator in a desk calculator, each register holds information for future processing or information already processed. A piece of data can be

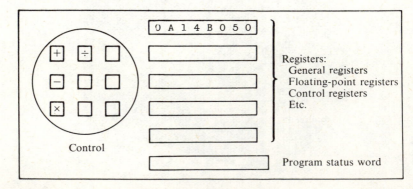

Fig. 1.10 Idealized CPU.

transferred between two registers, from a register to main storage, or from main storage to a register.

In IBM System/370 or System/360, there are 16 *general registers* available, which are numbered 0,1,..., 15 in larger models. Although a register is used primarily as an accumulator (see Section 3.4), it often enables efficient specification and modification of memory addresses. It is then called a *base register*. Finally, a register which merely serves as a counter is known as an *index register*. Both base and index registers are discussed in Chapter 3.

Floating-point computation is a very useful arithmetic method with many scientific applications. In IBM System/370 or System/360, floating-point hardware with four floating-point registers is an option. This method is discussed in Chapter 12.

Each computer operation is divided into two cycles:

a) Instruction cycle—fetching and decoding the next instruction; and

b) Execution cycle—execution of the instruction.

These two cycles are typically completed in sequence, that is, instruction cycle is followed by an execution cycle, but in more advanced systems such as IBM System/370, instruction execution is overlapped with instruction fetching. The control unit supervises the fetching, decoding, and execution of each instruction. It has the following components:

1. Location counter—containing the location of the current instruction being executed;

2. Instruction register—containing the current instruction;

3. Instruction decoder—analyzing the instruction.

During the instruction cycle, the interaction between the control unit and the main storage is shown in Fig. 1.11.

An assembler language programmer should know a part of CPU in System/370 or System/360, the so-called program status word (PSW). Its major functions are as follows:

1. Gives location of the next instruction.

2. Indicates the status of the program currently being executed.

3. Serves as interrupt control, which is useful to handle input/output (I/O) or unusual situations.

4. Signifies whether a part of software—the supervisor—is being run, or a user's program processed.

Channels and Input/Output Devices

The central processing unit and main storage are often referred to as the *main frame*. All units outside the main frame are collectively known as *peripheral equipment*. They

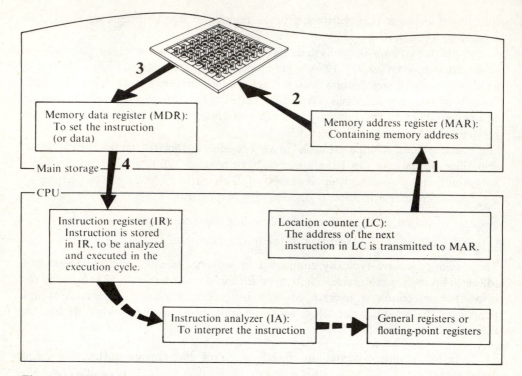

Fig. 1.11   Interaction between the main storage system and the control in CPU during the instruction cycle.

include the auxiliary memories and a wide assortment of input/output devices: card readers, printers and plotters, optical scanning devices, and terminals with keyboards and TV-like screens. More sophisticated input/output devices are also commercially available: Printers that record output on microfilm at high speed (about 100,000 characters per sec) and portable terminals which enable the user to have a direct contact with a remote computer through a keyboard and telephone. Also graphic devices of great versatility are growing in number and variety. An IBM 3211 printer with 3811 printer control unit is shown in Fig. 1.12.

The continuing demand for new peripherals stems from the fact that a CPU can process data in the nanosecond range, whereas the electromechanical peripheral devices still work relatively slowly. Specifically, the speed ratio between the fastest card reader and the slowest core memory is about 1/500. Much CPU time would be wasted if a card reader were attached directly to the CPU, because the CPU has to wait when a card is being read into the main memory. In order to enable the CPU to do more computing, *channels* are installed between the CPU and peripheral equipment.

Each channel is in fact a mini-computer. In IBM System/370 or System/360, two types of channels are in use: selector channels and multiplexor channels. The former

Fig. 1.12   IBM 3211 printer with 3811 printer control unit.

is positioned between the CPU and high-speed devices such as drum or disk drives, and the latter, between the CPU and low-speed devices such as the card reader or printers.

1.4 THE IBM SYSTEM/370 VERSUS SYSTEM/360

The System/370 seems to be the eventual successor of System/360. Each system has several models which differ in the size of main storage, the cycle time of CPU, and the number of channels. They are shown, respectively, in Figs. 1.13 and 1.14, and Table 1.1. The IBM System/370 is known to be "upward compatible" with System/360, which means that the program written for the System/360 runs in same way in the System/370. However, the reverse is not true, primarily because System/370 has a larger instruction set than System/360. The word "compatible" does not mean "exact," and certainly not "optimum." Some rare cases of incompatibility do exist. For example, programs requiring special I/O devices which are not available in the System/370 (such as 2302 disk pack) must be modified. A less expensive model of the IBM System/370, Model 135, is shown in Fig. 1.15.

All hardware differences between the System/370 and System/360 are "transparent" to a programmer, that is, they are not visible to him or her. Perhaps the most important difference is the high-speed *buffer storage* which is used in all models of System/370. It is located between main storage and CPU, providing high-speed data access for the CPU. The portion of program currently being run is stored in two

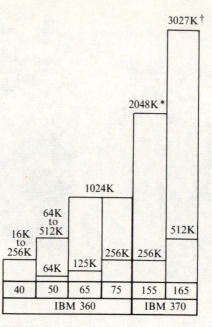

*With intermediate sizes of 384K, 512K, 768K,
1024K, and 1536K.

† With intermediate sizes of 1024K, 1536K,
and 2048K.

Fig. 1.13 Minimum/maximum sizes for the main storage with selected models in System 370/360.

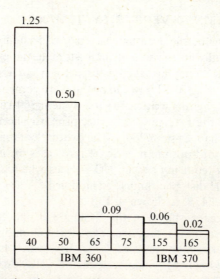

Fig. 1.14 CPU cycle time in nanoseconds for selected models in System 370/360.

Table 1.1 Channel numbers in selected models of IBM System/370 or System/360

Computer model	360/40	360/50	360/65	360/75	370/155	370/165
Number of channels	3	4	7	7	6	12
Buffered memory	No	No	No	No	Yes	Yes

places: in main storage and—whenever possible—in high-speed buffer. If the required instruction or data is in the buffer, it is fetched and sent along to the CPU at the buffer speed (e.g., 160 nanoseconds per eight bytes in Model 165). If not in the buffer, it is fetched from the main storage. It is known that in about 90 percent of cases the required instruction or data is already in the buffer storage. As a result, the System/370 operates most of the time at fast buffer speed rather than the slower main-storage speed. Similarly, the immediate or final results are placed (stored) in main storage as well as in the high-speed buffer.

The System/370 keeps right on processing even when the buffer storage is out of service. In this case the CPU time is considerably greater than that in a comparable run when the buffer storage is working. Buffer control is done by hardware; it increases performance without adding new chores for a programmer.

Next to the high-speed buffer, the most important difference between System/370 and System/360 is the reliability of hardware. This is due to the following features:

1. More reliable components are used.

Fig. 1.15   IBM System/370. Model 135.

2. Recovery facilities (hardware as well as software) are available to reduce the number of failures that cause a crash.

3. Repair of programs is possible while the system is running.

1.5 COMPUTER SOFTWARE

A complete set of instructions of operation which direct a computer to perform a given task is called a program. There are two types of programs—*application programs* and *systems programs*. An application program is a set of complete instructions used to produce results for a specific application, such as a payroll problem or a matrix inversion; whereas a systems program is devised to ease the programmer's burden. Compilers, assemblers, utility routines, various control programs, and diagnostic routines are examples of the systems programs. The collection of all systems programs, which may make it easier to use the hardware capabilities, is loosely called *software*.

An operating system is a major component of software. It increases the system *throughput*, which is a measure of system efficiency, the rate at which work can be handled by a computing system. It also supervises internal activities in hardware, connects each job to the required compiler or assembler, and reduces the chances of undetected errors.

The performance of a medium or large computer installation is strongly affected by the operating system selected. For example, an installation can implement an operating system under which one program is processed at a time. Alternatively, it can select one under which more than one program is running—the so-called multiprogramming. In multiprogramming environment, a preset time slice is allotted to each program. One program is interrupted when it exhausts its time slice, and the CPU immediately switches to another program.

A large number of programs can be simultaneously active under an operating system with *time sharing*. The time slice is now much shorter and a priority scheme is often built in this system. The number of active programs is not limited to how many can fit in main storage at one time. It rather operates in the following way: Active programs currently not being processed are stored in disk storage; when the turn of a slice of CPU time comes for some given programs, they simply swap with the ones already placed in main storage.

A program must be stored in main storage if it is to be processed by CPU and yet only part of a program is in use at a given time. In multiprogramming or time-sharing techniques, CPU can process several jobs at the same time, but much of their main storage is idled by portions of programs that are not being used. To alleviate this situation, we use the *virtual storage* method. Essentially, a program is broken into many sections, called *pages*. It makes use of slower, but less costly secondary storage (e.g., disks) that is in constant touch with main storage. If CPU is processing, say, ten jobs, the virtual-storage control system constantly turns over the pages, the required pages for the ten programs (now in secondary storage) are swapped with those pages already processed in main storage. The continuous turnover of pages is automatically handled by software. As a result, a computer with, say, 64,000 bytes of main storage may appear to have up to two million bytes.

In many large-scale computers, the concept of virtual storage can further be extended. Just as an image of storage can be created by software, so can be the image of an entire computer. A single real computer can provide functional simulation of one or more *virtual machines*, each with its own virtual storage, virtual CPU, virtual I/O devices, and virtual console. The main point is: Each user of a virtual machine is insulated from the others.

Software for System/370 and System/360

One of the most important aims of operating systems is to separate the user's program as much as possible from the programs used to manage the computer systems. The most common operating systems for System/360 are as follows:

    Operating System (OS)
        Operating System/Multiprogramming with Fixed Tasks (OS/MFT)
        Operating System/Multiprogramming with Variable Tasks (OS/MVT)
    Disk Operating System (DOS)
    Tape Operating System (TOS)
    Basic Operating System (BOS)

Systems available to System/370 are:

    Operating System (OS): OS/MFT and OS/MVT
    Disk Operating System (DOS)

System control programs for virtual storage:

    OS/VS1: Virtual storage is divided into static partitions. Up to 15 user jobs can be handled simultaneously.
    OS/VS2: Virtual storage is divided into dynamic regions. Up to 63 user jobs can be handled. The Time-Sharing Option (TSO) can provide for conversational program development and execution from remote terminals.
    DOS/VS: Extensions of DOS. Maximum number of partitions is five.
    VM/370: Supporting the virtual machine concept.

For each operating system, there is a *supervisor* program which controls the overall function of the system. When a job is run, it resides in the lower-core locations, and takes care of the following operational chores:

1. Scheduling and directing jobs;
2. Allocating time and devices to jobs;
3. Rejecting jobs and printing diagnostic message to the user if errors are detected; and
4. Printing requests to the machine operator.

In each operating system, there is also a collection of the processor programs (compilers and assemblers). We shall now discuss them.

Compilers and Assemblers

The language a programmer uses to communicate with a computer is called the *source language*. There are two classes of source languages in common use: procedure-oriented and assembler languages. Their common aim is to shift some programming burden from humans to computers.

The procedure-oriented languages, or high-level languages, include FORTRAN, COBOL, ALGOL, and PL/I. FORTRAN is probably one of the most widely accepted high-level languages in engineering and science; a typical statement in FORTRAN might look like this:

$$BETA=1.+COS(2.*PI*A/ROOT)$$

COBOL is probably the most popular business-oriented high-level language; a typical COBOL statement is shown below.

```
IF MONTHLY FICA LESS THAN 16.00 GO TO SPECIAL FICA;
ELSE ADD MONTHLY FICA TO ANNUAL FICA.
```

PL/I, first proposed in 1964, has only recently become available for use in some computers. A typical statement in this versatile language is as follows:

```
IF N=1|N=0 THEN RETURN (1)
```

A statement written in a high-level language is akin to our written language. We use a computer to translate this source language into the machine language (object language) by means of a *compiler*—a set of programs that directs the computer to translate a high-level language into machine language.

A single statement in any high-level language is usually translated into a lengthy set of machine language instructions; whereas an instruction written in assembler language is, in general, translated in one machine language instruction. For example, the assembler language intruction for an IBM System/370 or System/360:

```
AR  7,11
```

simply means "add to the contents of register 7 the contents in register 11, and then store the sum in register 7". Its corresponding machine language instruction is shown in Fig. 1.16. We shall discuss this in detail in Chapter 4.

A program written in an assembler language is translated into its machine language instructions by means of an *assembler*. An assembler language is flexible, versatile, and enables complete access to all hardware facilities. A program written in assembler language often saves main storage and produces a much "tighter" object program (thus saving computing time) than a high-level language would.

A good assembler should have not only a rich repertoire of instructions and pseudo operations, but also some more sophisticated features, such as macro instructions and conditional assemblies. This book deals principally with the concepts and instructions needed to write programs in assembler language.

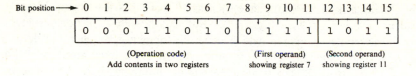

1.6 A SAMPLE PROGRAM IN ASSEMBLER LANGUAGE

The purpose of this section is: First, to present a *complete, tested* program written in assembler language so that the student gets an initial "feel" of the language; second, to point out that the subject of the input and output in assembler language is rather complex and demands more attention and effort than one would normally anticipate.

There are at least three methods of obtaining an output from an assembler language program written for IBM System/370 or System/360. In the order of increasing sophistication, they are: (1) Dump a section of the main memory (or registers) which contains the required answers. (2) Use a main program written in a high-level language (such as FORTRAN, PL/I, or COBOL) to handle primarily the input and output. This main program can also call a subroutine written in assembler language. We apply this approach in Chapters 5 through 12. (3) Handle the input and output through an operating system. We shall discuss this advanced topic in Chapter 14.

To help the student feel the first approach, we list a short program in assembler language in the shaded portion of Fig. 1.17. The program is used to find the sum of ten numbers: $1 + 4 + 9 + 25 + \ldots + 100$.

```
//SAMPLE JOB T361-17,'S S KUO'
//STEP1 EXEC ASMFCLG
//ASM.SYSIN DD *
*     THIS IS A SAMPLE PROGRAM
*        FOR CALCULATING THE SUM OF TEN NUMBERS.
BEGIN    BALR   11,0
         USING  *,11
         LA     9,CZERO LOAD THE ADDRESS OF CZERO IN REGISTER 9
         LA     8,10    LOAD 10 INTO REGISTER 8
         SR     12,12
LOOP     A      12,0(9) ADD A NEW VALUE
         LA     9,4(9)  UPDATE THE ADDRESS OF NEXT VALUE
         BCT    8,LOOP  LOOP FOR CALCULATING SUM
         ST     12,ANS  STORE ANSWER
DUMP     DC     X'82000000'  THIS INSTRUCTION CAUSES A DUMP
ANS      DS     F
CZERO    DC     F'1,4,9,16,25,36,49,64,81,100'
         END
/*
//GO.SYSUDUMP DD SYSOUT=A
//
```

Fig. 1.17 Program list for the sum of ten numbers.

When using a high-level language such as FORTRAN for this problem, we can readily draw a flowchart (see Fig. 1.18). But this flowchart is not designed for a program in assembler language, which generally demands much more detail. For sake of comparison, such flowchart of finding the sum of the ten numbers is shown in Fig. 1.19. Listed in each step is also the section number where the corresponding instructions can be found.

We should point out that the complex, yet important, topic of input/output is put aside temporarily in Fig. 1.17. The output is obtained through a forced dump due to the illegal action of the following intruction:

$$\text{DUMP} \qquad \text{DC} \quad \text{X'82000000'}$$

or by the following legitimate macro instruction:

$$\text{DUMP} \qquad \text{ABEND} \quad \text{0,DUMP}$$

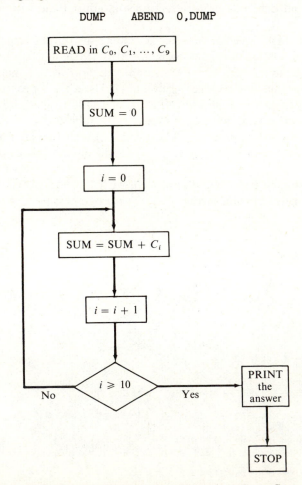

Fig. 1.18   A flowchart for finding the sum of ten numbers: $C_0 + C_1 + \cdots + C_9$ (or the sum $\sum_{i=0}^{9} C_i$), (FORTRAN-oriented).

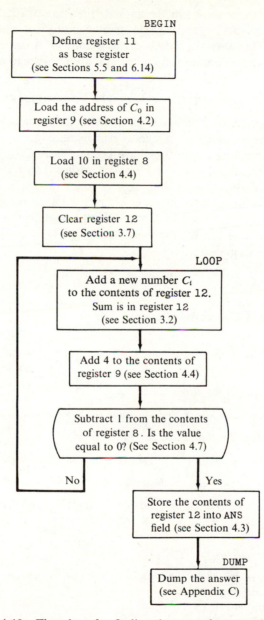

Fig. 1.19 Flowchart for finding the sum of ten numbers.

The *job control* cards shown in the unshaded portion of Fig. 1.17 serve to communicate with a particular operating system used in a given computer installation (see Chapter 13). Therefore the details of these control cards, particularly the first one, are expected to be different from one computation center to another.

1.7 COMMUNICATION WITH A COMPUTATION CENTER

Due to the recent rapid expansion of computation in education, research, and development, the number of computation centers is ever increasing.

As computer operating procedures have become increasingly sophisticated, the knowledge required to use a *computation center*, rather than *computers*, varies from one installation to another, depending on the setup in the individual center. In addition, this knowledge is in many cases either gained by personal trial-and-error procedure or passed on by word of mouth. In this section the readers will find a detailed check list (Table 1.2) for the hardware, software, and operating procedures of their own computation center.

Table 1.2

_____

I. Routine Operation of Computation Center

A. *Type of operation*
   Open shop ☐   Closed shop ☐   Partially closed and
                                                        partially open ☐

B. *Consulting supervisor at the center* _____.

C. *My identification number, if required, for using the computer* _____.

D. *My problem number, if required* _____.

E. *Maximum allowable running time for each program* _____ *min.*

F. *Normal turn-around time* _____ *hours.*

G. *User's manual or new user's packet available*   yes ☐   no ☐

II. Hardware

A. *Digital computer*

1. Type of digital computer to be used   2. Main memory size _____ in bytes ☐
        decimal computer ☐   in bits ☐
        binary computer ☐   in words ☐

3. Internal memory cycle   4. Time to add two numbers
        Less than 2 microseconds (μsec) ☐   Less than 25 μsec ☐
        2–10 μsec   ☐   25–100 μsec   ☐
        Above 10 μsec   ☐   Above 100 μsec   ☐

5. Word length _____ bits

6. Number of general registers ————

7. Number of floating-point registers ————

8. Number of channels: multiplex channels ————
                               selector channels ————

9. Number of control registers ————

10. Interrupt control available   yes ☐   no ☐

B. Peripheral equipment

1. Punched card equipment

    a) Key punch   Type ————
    b) Reproducer   Type ————
    c) Sorter   Type ————
    d) Verifier   Type ————

2. High-speed printer
    ———— lines per min.

3. Additional memory units
    a) Tape transport   yes ☐   no ☐
       Recommended tape density is ———— bytes per in.
       Seven track ☐, or nine track ☐.
    b) Magnetic drum   yes ☐   no ☐
       Additional words ————, or bits ————
    c) Disk drives   yes ☐   no ☐   Model ————
       Additional words ————, or ———— cylinders, or ———— tracks will be
         available to a user.
    d) Data cell   yes ☐   no ☐   Model ————
       Additional words ————, or bytes ————.

4. Readers
    Optical characters   yes ☐   no ☐
    Magnetic characters   yes ☐   no ☐

5. Plotter   yes ☐
           no ☐   Type ————

6. Cathode-ray tube plotting device   yes ☐   no ☐   Model ————
    Output: paper ☐,   35-mm film ☐

7. Oscilloscope display unit   yes ☐
                              no ☐   Type ————

8. Time-sharing terminal   yes ☐
                       no ☐   Type ————.
    Number of terminals available to a user ————.

9. Converters
    a) Card to magnetic tape   yes ☐   no ☐
    b) Card to paper tape   yes ☐   no ☐
    c) Magnetic tape to card   yes ☐   no ☐
    d) Paper tape to card   yes ☐   no ☐

III. Software

A. Compilers and assemblers available

Assembler language   Version G □   Version H □
                                          Other ————————

FORTRAN IV:
   USAS Basic □   IBM Basic FORTRAN IV □   FORTRAN IV G □
   FORTRAN IV H □
COBOL   □   PL/I   □   ALGOL □
WATFOR □   WATFIV □   others   □
BASIC   □   MAD   □

B. Program libraries available

		yes	no
1. FORTRAN built-in functions, such as SIN, COS, SQRT, etc		□	□
2. Routines used to generate plotter tapes		□	□
3. Scientific Subroutine Package (SSP)		□	□
4. General Purpose System Simulator (GPSS)		□	□
5. BioMeDical Statistical Routines (BMD)		□	□
6. PDUMP subroutine		□	□

C. Operating system used

DOS □
OS □
         Primary Control Program (PCP)   □
         Multiprogramming with a fixed number of tasks (MFT)   □
         Multiprogramming with a variable number of tasks (MVT) □
Others ————————
         Release version ————————

D. If OS is used, the following access methods are available:

Queued Access
      QSAM □   QISAM □   QTAM □   others ————————
Basic Access
      BSAM □   BPAM □   BISAM □
      BDAM □   BTAM □   BGAM □   others ————————
Virtual Storage
      VSAM □

E. Simultaneous Peripheral Operation On-line (SPOOL) System used:
      ASP   □   HASP   □   others ————————

F. Virtual memory used   yes □   no □

IV. Conventions Adopted in Your Installation

A. The logical device number used:

	In this book	In your installation
Card reader input	5	_____
On-line printer output	6	_____
Punch output	2	_____

B. The catalogued procedure used to compile, link-edit, and execute an assembler language program has three job steps:

	In this book	In your installation
1. Name of the catalogued procedure (discussed in Section 13.12)	ASMFCLG	_____
2. Name of the first step	ASM	_____
3. Name of the second step	LKED	_____
4. Name of the last step	GO	_____

C. The catalogued procedure used to compile, link-edit, and execute a FORTRAN program has three steps:

	In this book	In your installation
1. Name of the catalogued procedure (discussed in Section 13.13)	FORTGCLG	_____
2. Name of the first step (compile)	FORT	_____
3. Name of the second step (link-edit)	LKED	_____
4. Name of the third step (execute)	GO	_____

D. Names of other FORTRAN catalogued procedures used (discussed in Section 13.13):

	In this book	In your installation
1. Use linkage editor		
a) Compile a FORTRAN program	FORTGC	_____
b) Compile and link-edit	FORTGCL	_____
c) Link-edit object modules	FORTGL	_____
d) Execute	FORTGG	_____
2. Use OS loader Compile, link-and-execute.	FORTGCDG	_____

E. Naming convention of a data set (file) for disk usage

In this book	In your installation
DSNAME=USER.A3141.P5926.NAME1.NAME2	DSNAME=_____
(discussed in Section 13.9)	

F. A list of sample classes used in a JOB *card is shown in Table 13.1 (see page 379). Obtain a copy of list used in your installation.*

G. *A list of sample addresses for input/output devices* (*in three-digit hexadecimal*) *is shown in Table 13.4* (see page 396). Obtain a copy of list specified in your computation center.

V. Job Control Cards

In order to run an assembler program on an IBM System/370 or System/360, a user must submit the following three items:

1. Job control cards
2. Source deck(s) or object deck(s)
3. Data, if any.

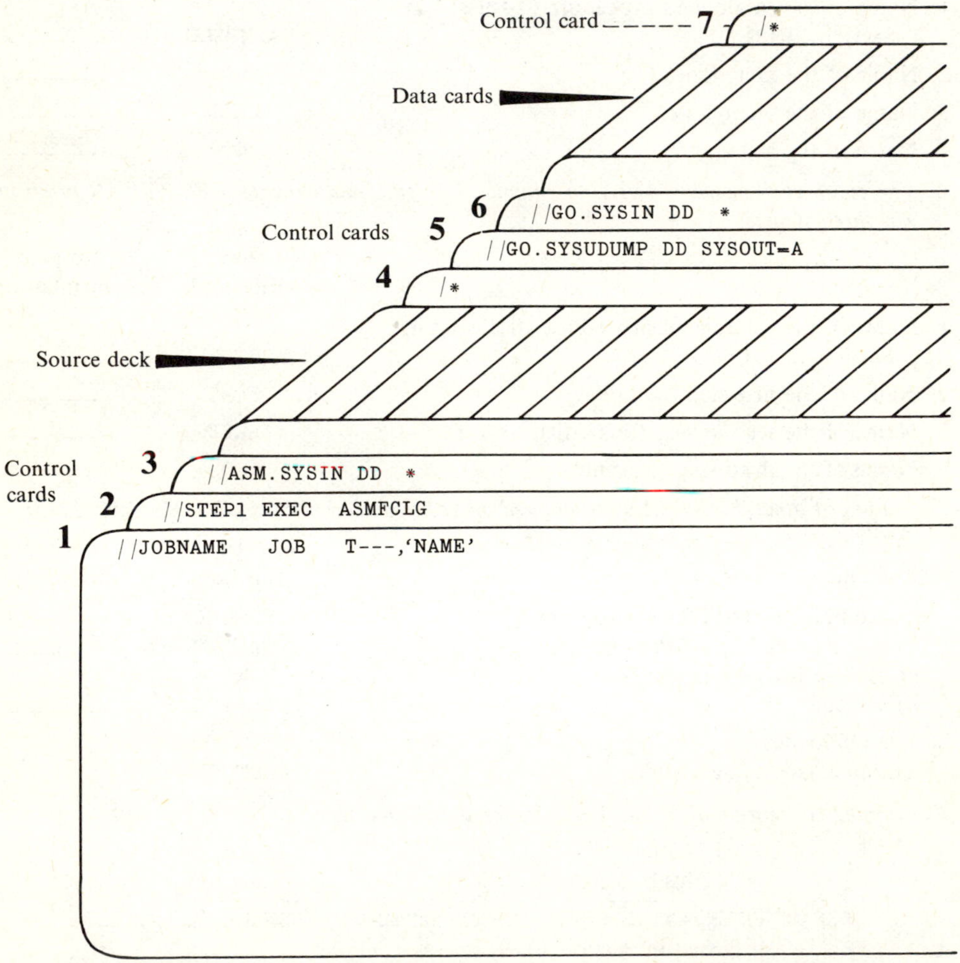

Control card _ _ _ _ _ **7** | *

Data cards

Control cards **5**   **6** | |GO.SYSIN DD *
                                | |GO.SYSUDUMP DD SYSOUT=A

4 | *

Source deck

Control cards **3** | |ASM.SYSIN DD *

2 | |STEP1 EXEC ASMFCLG

1 | |JOBNAME   JOB   T---,'NAME'

Fig. 1.20 A typical run deck. The source program is in assembler language.

Figure 1.20 shows a sample setup at a particular 370 or 360 installation used to obtain final answers for an assembler program. The detailed column description for each job control card is shown in Table 1.3. It is deliberately made far less flexible so that the beginner may find it easier to follow.

Obtain a copy of the standard job setup designed for your installation from your instructor or the programming consultant.

Table 1.3 Column description of the job control cards (as shown in Fig. 1.20) to assemble, link-edit, and execute a source deck in assembler language for System/370 or System/360

Control cards	For 4-character problem number Columns	For 7-character problem number Columns	Description
1	1–2	1–2	//
	3–8	3–8	User must supply job name (no blanks allowed)
	9	9	blank
	10–12	10–12	JOB
	13–16	13–16	blank
	17–20	17–23	User must supply his problem number
	21	24	, (comma)
	22	25	' (Single quote) on 029 (or multi 8,5 punch on 026 keypunch)
	23–42	26–42	User must supply programmer's name
	43	43	' (Single quote)
2		1–7	//STEP1
		8–9	blank
		10–13	EXEC
		14–15	blank
		16–23	ASMFCLG
3		1–12	//ASM.SYSIN
		13–15	blank
		16–19	DD *
4		1–2	/*
5		1–13	//GO.SYSUDUMP
		14–15	blank
		16–17	DD
		18	blank
		19–26	SYSOUT=A
6		1–10	//GO.SYSIN
		11–15	blank
		16–19	DD *
7		1–2	/*

BIBLIOGRAPHY

General

Alt, F. L. (ed.), *Advances in Computers*, Academic Press, New York. Intended to be a continuing publication, the first volume of which appeared in 1960.

Bowden, B. V., *Faster than Thought*, Pitman, London, 1964.

Fano, R. M., and F. J. Corbato, "Time-sharing on computers," *Scient. Am.* **215**, 128–143 (Sept. 1966).

McCarthy, J., "Information," *Scient. Am.* **215**, 64–73 (Sept. 1966).

Rosen, S., "Electronic computers, a historical survey," *Computer Surveys* **1**, 7–36 (1969).

Hardware

Bell, C. G., and A. Newell, *Computer Structures: readings and examples*, McGraw-Hill, New York, 1971.

Chu, Y., *Digital Computer Design Fundamentals*, McGraw-Hill, New York, 1962.

Evans, D. C., "Computer logic and memory," *Scient. Am.* **215**, 74–85 (Sept. 1966).

Heath, F. G., "Large-scale integration in electronics," *Scient. Am.* **222**, 22 (Feb. 1970).

Software

Boehm, B. M., "Software and its impact: A quantitative assessment," *Datamation*, 48–59, (May, 1973).

Denning, P. J., "Virtual Memory," *Computing Surveys* **2**(3), 1970.

Flores, I., *Computer Software*, Prentice-Hall, 1965.

Hartman, Philip H., and David H. Owens, *How to Write Software Specifications*, Proceedings 1967 Fall Joint Computer Conference, pp. 779–790.

Presser, L., and J. R. White, "Linkers and loaders," *Computer Surveys* **4** (3), 149–167, (Sept. 1972).

Wilkes, M. V., *Time-Sharing Computer Systems*, American Elsevier, New York, 1968.

IBM 370/360

Amdahl, G. M., "The Structure of System/360: Part III—Processing Unit Design Consideration," *IBM Systems J.* **3** (2), 1964.

Blaauw, G. A., and F. P. Brooks, "The Structure of System/360, Part I, Outline of the Logical Structure," *IBM Systems J.* **3** (2), 1964.

Conti, C. J., D. H. Gibson, and S. H. Pitowsky, "Structural Aspects of the System/360 Model 85: I General Organization," *IBM Systems J.* **7** (1), 1968.

Liptay, J. S., "Structural Aspects of the System/360 Model 85: II The Cache," *IBM Systems J.* **7** (1), 1968.

Murphey, J. O., and R. M. Wade, "The IBM 360/195," *Datamation* (April, 1970).

IBM System/360: A Programmers' Introduction to the Architecture, Instructions, and Assembler Language, C20–1646, IBM Corp.

IBM System/370 Summary, Form GA22–7001, IBM Corp.

IBM System/370, A Guide to Model 135, Form GC20–1738, IBM Corp.

IBM System/370 Model 145 Functional Characteristics, Form GA24–3557, IBM Corp.

IBM System/370 Guide to Model 155, Form GC20–1729, IBM Corp.

IBM System/370 Model 165 Functional Characteristics, Form GA22–6935, IBM Corp.

CHAPTER 2

Number Systems and Fixed-Point Arithmetic

2.1 INTRODUCTORY REMARKS

An assembler language programmer must know at least three number systems—the decimal, binary, and hexadecimal system.

The most commonly used number system—the decimal system—is based on powers of 10; but systems involving bases† other than 10 are also used. The binary system uses base 2 and the hexadecimal system, base 16. In the binary system only two symbols are used, 1 and 0; whereas the hexadecimal system uses sixteen symbols: 0, 1, 2, 3, 4, 5, 6, 7, 8, 9, A, B, C, D, E, and F.

In this chapter, we shall describe the three number systems and their interrelations, and then discuss the data formats used for a binary integer. A binary integer is often called a *fixed-point number* because (a) the exact position of the binary point is usually stated implicitly at some predetermined position; and (b) the number of binary digits is predetermined for a given computer system. In System/370 and System/360, a fixed-point number occupies either 16 or 32 binary digits. We also refer to arithmetic of two fixed-point numbers as fixed-point arithmetic.

2.2 BINARY SYSTEM

The binary number system, which is at the heart of all modern computers, uses only two digits, 0 and 1. A comparison of the binary and decimal representations of first 14 numbers is shown below.

Decimal system	Binary system	Decimal system	Binary system
0	0000	7	0111
1	0001	8	1000
2	0010	9	1001
3	0011	10	1010
4	0100	11	1011
5	0101	12	1100
6	0110	13	1101

---

† *Base* is synonymous with *radix*.

We can convert binary numbers into decimal form by following the rules set forth in Appendix A. For instance, to represent the binary number 11001 in decimal form, one has to carry out the steps indicated by the example below.

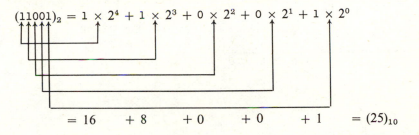

$$(11001)_2 = 1 \times 2^4 + 1 \times 2^3 + 0 \times 2^2 + 0 \times 2^1 + 1 \times 2^0$$

$$= 16 \quad + 8 \quad + 0 \quad + 0 \quad + 1 \quad = (25)_{10}$$

Arithmetic calculations in the binary system have their own rules corresponding to the familiar *carry* and *borrow* associated with the decimal system. These rules, along with simple examples, are given below. The decimal equivalents accompanying each example can be obtained by following the conversion process illustrated previously.

Rules for Binary Calculation

A. *Addition*

1. $(0)_2 + (0)_2 = (0)_2$.
2. $(0)_2 + (1)_2 = (1)_2$.
3. $(1)_2 + (1)_2 = (0)_2$,   carry $(1)_2$ to the left.

Example 1

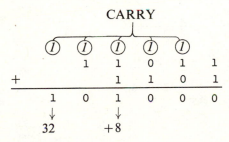

Decimal system   27
equivalent   + 13
               40

B. *Subtraction*

1. $(0)_2 - (0)_2 = (0)_2$.
2. $(1)_2 - (1)_2 = (0)_2$.
3. $(1)_2 - (0)_2 = (1)_2$.
4. $(0)_2 - (1)_2 = (1)_2$,   with $(1)_2$ borrowed from the left.

Example 2

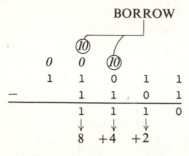

BORROW

		⑩			
0	0	⑩			
	1	1	0	1	1
−		1	1	0	1
	1	1	1	0	
		↓	↓	↓	
		8	+4	+2	

Decimal system	27
equivalent	− 13
	14

C. *Multiplication*

1. $(0)_2 \times (0)_2 = (0)_2$.
2. $(0)_2 \times (1)_2 = (0)_2$.
3. $(1)_2 \times (1)_2 = (1)_2$.

Example 3

$$
\begin{array}{ccccc}
 & 1 & 1 & 0 & 1 & 1 \\
\times & & & & 1 & 1 \\
\hline
\end{array}
$$

① ① ① ① ①

		1	1	0	1	1
	1	1	0	1	1	
1	0	1	0	0	0	1
↓		↓				↓
64		+16				+1

Decimal system	27
equivalent	× 3
	81

D. *Division*

Example 4

$$
\begin{array}{r}
1\ 0\ 0\ 1 \quad (=9) \\
(3=)\quad 11\ \big/\ \overline{1\ 1\ 0\ 1\ 1} \quad (=27) \\
1\ 1 \\
\hline
0\ 1\ 1 \\
1\ 1 \\
\hline
\end{array}
$$

2.3 HEXADECIMAL SYSTEM

As mentioned previously, the hexadecimal system uses ten numerical symbols and six alphabetic symbols. These are, in ascending order, 0, 1, 2, 3, 4, 5, 6, 7, 8, 9, A, B, C, D, E, and F.† All numbers in the hexadecimal system are represented by combinations of these symbols.

---

† This set of symbols is of common choice; it is used in System/370 and System/360.

A comparison of the decimal, binary, and hexadecimal systems is shown below.

Decimal system	Binary system	Hexadecimal system
0	000	0
1	001	1
2	010	2
3	011	3
4	100	4
5	101	5
6	110	6
7	111	7
8	1000	8
9	1001	9
10	1010	A
11	1011	B
12	1100	C
13	1101	D
14	1110	E
15	1111	F
16	10000	10
⋮	⋮	⋮

A piece of binary data is often very long and cumbersome to deal with; it is frequently expressed in its hexadecimal equivalent. The conversion is fairly straight-forward: Separate the given binary number into groups of four beginning at the right. Each group is then represented by its equivalent of a symbol in the hexadecimal system.

Example 1

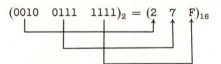

$$(0010 \quad 0111 \quad 1111)_2 = (2 \quad 7 \quad F)_{16}$$

The meaning of a number in hexadecimal system can be best understood by expanding the number in powers of 16. For example,

$$(BA6)_{16} = 11 \times 16^2 + 10 \times 16^1 + 6 \times 16^0 = (2982)_{10}.$$

Likewise, the hexadecimal number 5020 may be converted to a decimal number as follows:

$$5(16)^3 + 0(16)^2 + 2(16)^1 + 0(16)^0 = 20480 + 0 + 32 + 0 = 20512.$$

We can use Table 2.1 to convert a hexadecimal number to its decimal equivalent. Each hexadecimal digit and the decimal equivalent for this digit are first located. These partial equivalents are added to obtain the desired decimal number. Consider

Table 2.1 Hexadecimal and decimal conversion

Hexadecimal number	(1)	(2)	(3)	(4)	(5)	(6)
0	0	0	0	0	0	0
1	1,048,576	65,536	4,096	256	16	1
2	2,097,152	131,072	8,192	512	32	2
3	3,145,728	196,608	12,288	768	48	3
4	4,194,304	262,144	16,384	1,024	64	4
5	5,242,880	327,680	20,480	1,280	80	5
6	6,291,456	393,216	24,576	1,536	96	6
7	7,340,032	458,752	28,672	1,792	112	7
8	8,388,608	524,288	32,768	2,048	128	8
9	9,437,184	589,824	36,864	2,304	144	9
A	10,485,760	655,360	40,960	2,560	160	10
B	11,534,336	720,896	45,056	2,816	176	11
C	12,582,912	786,432	49,152	3,072	192	12
D	13,631,488	851,968	53,248	3,328	208	13
E	14,680,064	917,504	57,344	3,584	224	14
F	15,728,640	983,040	61,440	3,840	240	15

again $(5020)_{16}$. The decimal equivalent of the leftmost digit 5 is 20,480 which is located in column 3 of the table. The final sum 20,512 can readily be obtained as follows:

Hexadecimal digit	From Table 2.1
5	20480
0	0
2	32
0	0 +
	20512

This example also illustrates that a number system is usually *positional*: A given symbol has totally different meaning when placed at a different position.

Like decimal numbers, hexadecimal numbers obey all the rules of arithmetic and can therefore be added, subtracted, multiplied, and divided. In hexadecimal addition, there is no carry until a multiple of $(16)_{10}$ is reached. Some illustrative examples follow.

a) F + 1 = 10.

b) A + E = 18.

c)   75C
+   4B6   here C $= (12)_{10}$,
——————
   C12

$$(12)_{10} + 6 = (18)_{10} = (12)_{16},$$
$$1_{\text{carry}} + 5 + (11)_{10} = (17)_{10} = (11)_{16},$$
$$1_{\text{carry}} + 7 + 4 = (12)_{10} = (C)_{16}.$$

d)   5020   20512
+   8FD   Decimal system equivalent   2301 +
——————   ——————
   591D   22813

As a practical detail, the addition of two hexadecimal numbers can be made by means of Table 2.2. Locate one of the numbers to be added as the heading of a column and the other as the heading of a row. The sum is the intersection of the column and the row.

Table 2.2 Hexadecimal addition and subtraction

	1	2	3	4	5	6	7	8	9	A	B	C	D	E	F	
1	02	03	04	05	06	07	08	09	0A	0B	0C	0D	0E	0F	10	1
2	03	04	05	06	07	08	09	0A	0B	0C	0D	0E	0F	10	11	2
3	04	05	06	07	08	09	0A	0B	0C	0D	0E	0F	10	11	12	3
4	05	06	07	08	09	0A	0B	0C	0D	0E	0F	10	11	12	13	4
5	06	07	08	09	0A	0B	0C	0D	0E	0F	10	11	12	13	14	5
6	07	08	09	0A	0B	0C	0D	0E	0F	10	11	12	13	14	15	6
7	08	09	0A	0B	0C	0D	0E	0F	10	11	12	13	14	15	16	7
8	09	0A	0B	0C	0D	0E	0F	10	11	12	13	14	15	16	17	8
9	0A	0B	0C	0D	0E	0F	10	11	12	13	14	15	16	17	18	9
A	0B	0C	0D	0E	0F	10	11	12	13	14	15	16	17	18	19	A
B	0C	0D	0E	0F	10	11	12	13	14	15	16	17	18	19	1A	B
C	0D	0E	0F	10	11	12	13	14	15	16	17	18	19	1A	1B	C
D	0E	0F	10	11	12	13	14	15	16	17	18	19	1A	1B	1C	D
E	0F	10	11	12	13	14	15	16	17	18	19	1A	1B	1C	1D	E
F	10	11	12	13	14	15	16	17	18	19	1A	1B	1C	1D	1E	F
	1	2	3	4	5	6	7	8	9	A	B	C	D	E	F	

Example 2

      3F4   1012
+   23B   Decimal system equivalent   +   571
——————   ——————
   62F   1583

We can use Table 2.2 also for subtraction. We go down the column with the heading of the subtrahend (the number to be subtracted) until the minuend (the number from which it is subtracted) is located on the right-hand column. The heading of this row is the difference.

Example 3

$$
\begin{array}{r}
3F4 \\
- \quad 23B \\
\hline
1B9
\end{array}
\qquad \text{Decimal system equivalent} \qquad
\begin{array}{r}
1012 \\
- \quad 571 \\
\hline
441
\end{array}
$$

Table 2.3 can likewise be used to perform the multiplication of two hexadecimal numbers. In this table, locate one of the numbers to be multiplied as the heading of a column, and the other as the heading of a row. The product is the number at the intersection of the column and the row.

Table 2.3 Hexadecimal multiplication

1	2	3	4	5	6	7	8	9	A	B	C	D	E	F
2	04	06	08	0A	0C	0E	10	12	14	16	18	1A	1C	1E
3	06	09	0C	0F	12	15	18	1B	1E	21	24	27	2A	2D
4	08	0C	10	14	18	1C	20	24	28	2C	30	34	38	3C
5	0A	0F	14	19	1E	23	28	2D	32	37	3C	41	46	4B
6	0C	12	18	1E	24	2A	30	36	3C	42	48	4E	54	5A
7	0E	15	1C	23	2A	31	38	3F	46	4D	54	5B	62	69
8	10	18	20	28	30	38	40	48	50	58	60	68	70	78
9	12	1B	24	2D	36	3F	48	51	5A	63	6C	75	7E	87
A	14	1E	28	32	3C	46	50	5A	64	6E	78	82	8C	96
B	16	21	2C	37	42	4D	58	63	6E	79	84	8F	9A	A5
C	18	24	30	3C	48	54	60	6C	78	84	90	9C	A8	B4
D	1A	27	34	41	4E	5B	68	75	82	8F	9C	A9	B6	C3
E	1C	2A	38	46	54	62	70	7E	8C	9A	A8	B6	C4	D2
F	1E	2D	3C	4B	5A	69	78	87	96	A5	B4	C3	D2	E1

Example 4

$$
\begin{array}{r}
2F2 \\
\times \quad 3A \\
\hline
1D74 \\
8D6 \\
\hline
AAD4
\end{array}
\qquad \text{Decimal system equivalent} \qquad
\begin{array}{r}
754 \\
\times \quad 58 \\
\hline
6032 \\
3770 \\
\hline
43732
\end{array}
$$

In practice, multiplication or division of two hexadecimal numbers can best be performed in the following way: Convert the hexadecimal numbers to their binary equivalents, and then perform the binary multiplication or division.

2.4 BYTES AND WORDS

A distinguishing characteristic of all elements in a digital computer is their ability to represent two (and only two) distinct states. The magnetic core, located in a main storage, is a typical example. The core can be in either of the two magnetized directions, which can be used to represent two different conditions. For instance, one condition may be interpreted as the digit 0; the other as 1. Similarly, the state of various computer elements can be used to represent yes or no, positive or negative, on or off, etc. Figure 2.1 shows some of the bistate computer elements. The binary digits 0 and 1 are commonly called *bits*; a bit is a contraction of two words: binary and digit.

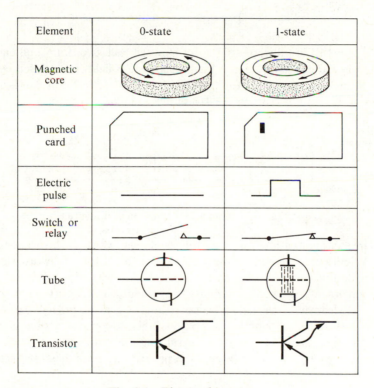

Element	0-state	1-state
Magnetic core		
Punched card		
Electric pulse		
Switch or relay		
Tube		
Transistor		

Fig. 2.1   Bistate element.

In the IBM System/370 or System/360, a sequence of eight contiguous bits is operated on as the basic unit,† known as a *byte*. Each byte has its own 24-bit address. As a result, a *maximum* of $2^{24} = (16,777,216)_{10}$ bytes in main storage is designed to have their own addresses. These addresses are often expressed in six hexadecimal digits, from 000000 to FFFFFF.

A sequence of two adjacent bytes (16 bits) is defined as a *halfword* (see Fig. 2.2). Similarly, a sequence of four adjacent bytes (32 bits) is called a *word*, or a *fullword*. Finally, eight consecutive bytes (64 bits) are defined as a *doubleword*.

---

† Bit manipulation is also possible and will be discussed in Chapter 8.

Byte	Byte	Byte	Byte	Byte	Byte	Byte	Byte	Byte
Halfword		Halfword		Halfword		Halfword		Hal
Fullword				Fullword				
Doubleword								

Fig. 2.2 Byte—the basic addressable unit.

Since a halfword, a fullword, and a doubleword take two, four, and eight bytes, respectively, they are of fixed length. Each fixed-length field is addressed by the leftmost byte of the field. Consider, for example, the fullword in Fig. 2.3. Its address is the address of its leftmost byte, or 000018 in hexadecimal.

Byte address in hexadecimal →	000018	000019	00001A	00001B
Contents in binary →	00011100	11111000	10011110	11110011
in hexadecimal →	1C	F8	9E	F3

Fig. 2.3 Contents and address of a fullword.

There are some restrictions on the addresses of a halfword, a fullword, or a doubleword. For a halfword, the address must be divisible by 2; for a fullword, divisible by 4; and for a doubleword, divisible by 8. They are known, respectively, as halfword boundary alignment, fullword boundary alignment, and doubleword boundary alignment. Collectively, they are referred to as integral boundary alignment. In System/370 and *some* System/360 computers, this severe restriction is removed. However, it is recommended that the integral boundary requirement is observed in writing your programs. We shall discuss the problem in more detail in Section 6.13.

Example

Binary integer data (in hexadecimal)	Length in words	in bytes	Assumed address (in hexadecimal)	Violation of boundary alignment
94E3	Halfword	2	0C041B	Violation
1CF89EF3	Fullword	4	00001C	No violation
4CF1	Halfword	2	00A402	No violation
FFFFFF4C	Fullword	4	00A402	Violation

2.5 COMPLEMENTS AND REPRESENTATION OF NEGATIVE BINARY INTEGERS

In a computer, negative binary integers may be represented either in the sign and magnitude form or in a complement form. The former is similar to the one we normally use with pencil and paper. The latter has the advantage that the sign computation is avoided, and is used in IBM System/370 and System/360.

For simplicity, let us first discuss complements of a decimal number. A decimal number can have two different complement representations: ten's complement and nine's complement. If the decimal number D is L digits long, its ten's complement is equal to $10^L - D$, and its nine's complement, $10^L - D - 1$. For example, the ten's complement of $(653)_{10}$ is $10^3 - 653 = 347$ and the nine's complement of $(653)_{10}$ is $347 - 1 = 346$.

A practical way to find the ten's complement of a decimal number is as follows: Subtract the number from the highest number of that degree; the result is the nine's complement. Then add 1 to this result. For example, the ten's complement of 653 may be calculated as follows.

$$
\begin{array}{rl}
999 & \leftarrow \text{highest number of all three-digit numbers} \\
- \quad 653 & \leftarrow \text{given number} \\
\hline
346 & \leftarrow \text{nine's complement} \\
+ \quad \ \ 1 & \leftarrow \text{add 1} \\
\hline
347 & \leftarrow \text{the required complement (ten's complement)}
\end{array}
$$

This alternative method is clearly equivalent to the first method, since it also performs:

$$(999 + 1) - 653 = 10^3 - 653 = 347.$$

Let us now consider complements in the binary system. A binary number may have one's or two's complements. For a positive binary integer B, N bits long, the two's complement of B is $2^N - B$. Suppose $(+23)_{10}$ is represented in 15-bit configuration ($N = 15$). To find its two's complement, we simply subtract $(23)_{10}$ from 2^{15}, both in binary:

$$
\begin{array}{rl}
2^N = 2^{15} = & 1000\ 0000\ 0000\ 0000 \\
B = (23)_{10} = & \underline{\ 000\ 0000\ 0001\ 0111\ -} \\
2^N - B = & 111\ 1111\ 1110\ 1001
\end{array}
$$

where a group of four bits is separated from its adjacent group by a blank. This blank is used here only for clarity.

As a second example, let us find the two's complement of 31-bit representation of $(+9)_{10}$:

$$
\begin{array}{rl}
2^N = 2^{31} = & 1000\ 0000\ 0000\ 0000\ 0000\ 0000\ 0000\ 0000 \\
B = (9)_{10} = & \underline{\ 000\ 0000\ 0000\ 0000\ 0000\ 0000\ 0000\ 1001\quad -} \\
2^N - B = & 111\ 1111\ 1111\ 1111\ 1111\ 1111\ 1111\ 0111
\end{array}
$$

An alternative way to compute this two's complement is to first form the one's complement and then add 1, as illustrated below.

```
      111 1111 1111 1111 1111 1111 1111 1111  ←  The highest number of all 31-bit
                                                   binary numbers
  −   000 0000 0000 0000 0000 0000 0000 1001  ←  The given binary number
      ───────────────────────────────────────
      111 1111 1111 1111 1111 1111 1111 0110  ←  One's complement
  +                                        1  ←  Add 1
      ───────────────────────────────────────
      111 1111 1111 1111 1111 1111 1111 0111  ←  The required two's complement
```

Note that the result of the above subtraction, the so-called one's complement, can be obtained simply by reversing each binary digit of the given number: every 0 to a 1, and every 1 to a 0.

2.6 REPRESENTATIONS OF A BINARY INTEGER

In the IBM System/360 or System/370, a binary integer is represented in a halfword or in a fullword. A halfword has 16 bits and a fullword, 32 bits. For identification, we number the bit positions 0 through 15 for a halfword, and the bit positions 0 through 31 for a fullword. They are numbered from left to right as shown in Fig. 2.4. The bit position 0—called the sign bit—indicates the sign of the binary integer.

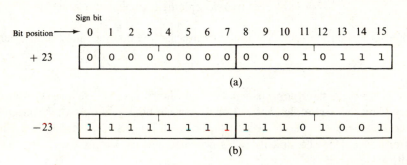

Fig. 2.4 Representation of $+23$ and -23 in a halfword.

Let us first explore the representation of a binary integer *in a halfword.* When the number is positive, the sign bit contains a 0; bit positions 1–15 inclusive contain a string of 0's and 1's, the binary integer itself (see Fig. 2.4a). On the other hand, for a negative number,† the bit positions 0 contains a 1, and bit positions 1–15 contain a quantity representing the negative number in the 2's complement form. For example, the representation of $(-23)_{10}$ in a halfword is shown in Fig. 2.4(b), where the sign bit is 1, indicating a negative number.

A binary integer can also be represented in a fullword. For a positive number, the zero bit position (sign bit) contains a 0, and the remaining 31 bits (bit positions 1

---

† The two's complement notation does not include the representation of a negative zero. Also, the CPU of the System/370 or System/360 cannot represent the complement of the largest negative number, -2^{31}.

through 31) contain a string of 0's and 1's. For a negative number, the sign bit contains a 1, and bit positions 1–31 represent this negative quantity in the 2's complement form. In Fig. 2.5, for example, $+9$ and -9 are, respectively, represented in a fullword.

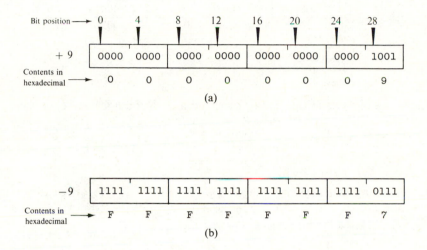

Fig. 2.5 Representation of $+9$ and -9 in a fullword.

In summary, a binary integer occupying a halfword or fullword is often called a fixed-point number. In the leftmost bit position is the sign bit. A 0-sign bit indicates a positive integer while 1 in the sign bit indicates a negative integer. Negative fixed-point numbers are stored in 2's complement notation.

Fixed-point data must satisfy the boundary alignment requirement: The address of a halfword data must be divisible by 2, whereas that of a fullword must be divisible by 4.

2.7 ADDITION AND SUBTRACTION OF TWO FIXED-LENGTH BINARY INTEGERS

In this section we shall examine the addition and subtraction operations of two binary integers. Specifically, we shall consider the case in which each integer is represented in a fullword.† When two signed binary integers are added, there is no need of determining the sign of each number. They are simply added as the following examples illustrate.

---

† This fullword can be in a register or in a location in main storage.

Example 1

Find the sum of $(23)_{10} + (20)_{10}$.

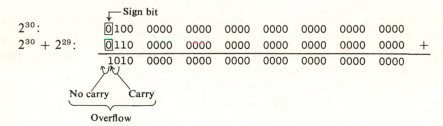

```
                 ┌─ Sign bit
                 ↓
    23:    [0]000 0000 0000 0000 0000 0000 0001 0111
    20:    [0]000 0000 0000 0000 0000 0000 0001 0100  +
    43     [0]000 0000 0000 0000 0000 0000 0010 1011

            No carry    No carry

               No overflow
```

The above binary addition can be carried out in the hexadecimal equivalent. We have

$$00000017$$
$$00000014 \quad +$$
$$\overline{0000002B}$$

It is worth noting that a binary integer is positive if the leftmost digit in the hexadecimal shorthand is 0, 1, ..., or 7. On the other hand, if the leftmost digit is 8, 9, A, B, ..., or F, the given binary integer is negative.

Example 2

Find $I + J$, where $I = 2^{30}$ and $J = 2^{30} + 2^{29}$.

```
                      ┌─ Sign bit
                      ↓
    2^30:       [0]100 0000 0000 0000 0000 0000 0000 0000
    2^30 + 2^29: [0]110 0000 0000 0000 0000 0000 0000 0000  +
                  1010 0000 0000 0000 0000 0000 0000 0000

              No carry    Carry

                 Overflow
```

Since the sum $2^{31} + 2^{29}$ is larger than maximum permissible positive integer $2^{31} - 1$, we say that a fixed-point *overflow* has occurred. Note that the sum in this example is to be considered as a negative number, since a carry 1 appears in the sign bit. Generally speaking, the undesirable occurrence of overflow is signaled by the fact that the sign of the sum is different from the sign of I or J. During addition $I + J$, overflow occurs only when I and J are of the same sign. During subtraction $I - J$, overflow occurs only when I and J are of opposite signs.

This binary addition can be performed in hexadecimal.

$$40000000$$
$$60000000 \quad +$$
$$\overline{A0000000}$$

The answer represents a negative number and is obviously incorrect.

Example 3

Find the sum $(-2^{31}) + (-8)$.

```
                     ┌─── Sign bit
                     ↓
 -2³¹:          [1]000  0000  0000  0000  0000  0000  0000  0000
 -8:            [1]111  1111  1111  1111  1111  1111  1111  1000  +
                ─────────────────────────────────────────────────
                10111  1111  1111  1111  1111  1111  1111  1000
                ↑↗↖↘
        Carry      No carry
        └──────────────┘
            Overflow
```

Since the sum is less than -2^{31}, the smallest permissible number represented in a fullword, a fixed-point overflow has occurred. As the sign bit is 0, it would be incorrect to consider the sum as a positive number. The overflow bit left to the sign bit is lost. We can perform the above addition in hexadecimal.

$$
\begin{array}{r}
80000000 \\
FFFFFFF8 \quad + \\
\hline
1 \quad 7FFFFFF8
\end{array}
$$

Example 4

Find the sum $(-23) + (-9)$.

```
                     ┌─── Sign bit
                     ↓
 -23:          [1]111  1111  1111  1111  1111  1111  1110  1001
 -9 :          [1]111  1111  1111  1111  1111  1111  1111  0111  +
               ──────────────────────────────────────────────────
 -32           ①1111  1111  1111  1111  1111  1111  1110  0000
           ↗       ↑↗↖↘
     Ignored
              Carry  Carry
         └────────────────┘
              No overflow
```

The carry (*out of the sign bit*) is automatically ignored. This binary addition can be written in hexadecimal.

$$
\begin{array}{r}
FFFFFFE9 \\
FFFFFFF7 \quad + \\
\hline
①FFFFFFE0
\end{array}
$$
↗ Ignored

From the four examples above, we see that a fixed-point overflow occurs if
  a) there is a carry *out the bit position 1* but there is not a carry *out the sign bit*; or
  b) there is a carry *out the sign bit* but there is not a carry *out the bit position 1*.
On the other hand, no overflow occurs if
  a) there is a carry *out the bit position 1* and there is also a carry *out the sign bit*; or
  b) there is no carry *out the bit position 1* and there is no carry *out the sign bit*.

Addition is the primary arithmetic process which is carried out in the arithmetic and logic unit (ALU) of a computer system. All other arithmetic operations can be performed by additions, complementations, and shifts.† To find $x - y$, for example, the operation is essentially the same as addition, except that y is complemented first and then added to x. Suppose that x, y, and z have the following 32-bit contents:

$$x: \quad \text{0000A124} \quad (\text{Complement} = \text{FFFF5EDC})$$
$$y: \quad \text{0000050C} \quad (\text{Complement} = \text{FFFFFAF4})$$
$$z: \quad \text{FFFFFFFB} \quad (\text{Complement} = \text{00000005})$$

Then the following additions or subtractions have the results as indicated:

$$x + y = \text{0000A630}$$
$$x + z = \text{0000A11F}$$
$$y + z = \text{00000507}$$
$$x - y = \text{00009C18}$$
$$x - z = \text{0000A129}$$
$$y - z = \text{00000511}$$
$$z - x = \text{FFFF5ED7}$$

We note that no sign computations are needed. The value $z - x$ is the only negative one and is shown in its two's complement form.

2.8 PLACING A HALFWORD DATA IN A FULLWORD

An important operation of data transmission is to place a halfword data in a general register, which contains data only in the form of a fullword. A register is a hardware device that receives data, holds it—usually temporarily—and then releases it as directed by a program. There are 16 general registers in a System/370 or System/360.

In this application, a piece of halfword data is transmitted into a fullword which has 32 bits: a sign bit (bit position 0), and bit positions 1–31. This is done automatically by the machine: Place the original halfword into the bit positions 16–31, and expand to a fullword by setting the bits 0–15 in the fullword to the same binary state (0 or 1) as the sign bit of the halfword. This is sometimes called the *sign extension*. For example, $(23)_{10}$ in a halfword is represented as:

Bit position →	0	1	2	3	4	5	6	7	8	9	10	11	12	13	14	15
	0	0	0	0	0	0	0	0	0	0	0	1	0	1	1	1

When transmitted to a fullword, this piece of data is represented as

0000	0000	0000	0000	0000	0000	0001	0111

---

† Shifts are discussed in Section 7.2.

Consider, as second example, the representation of $(-20)_{10}$ in a halfword:

1	1	1	1	1	1	1	1	1	1	1	0	1	1	0	0

When transmitted into a fullword, the above data automatically become as follows.

1111	1111	1111	1111	1111	1111	1110	1100

To consolidate the concepts introduced so far, let us consider the following representations:

Contents of register 9: 0001A124 (fullword)
A halfword u in main storage: 0017
A halfword v in main storage: FFEC

The following additions or subtractions have the indicated results:

1. To find the sum of contents of register 9 and halfword u.
   Step 1. Make the sign extension for u; we have a fullword 00000017.
   Step 2. Find the sum: 0001A124 + 00000017 = 0001A13B.

2. To find the sum of contents of register 9 and halfword v.
   Step 1. Make the sign extension for v; we have FFFFFFEC.
   Step 2. Find the sum: 0001A124 + FFFFFFEC = 0001A110.

3. To subtract the halfword u from the contents of register 9.
   Step 1. Sign extension for u: 00000017.
   Step 2. Find its complement: FFFFFFD9.
   Step 3. Result: 0001A124 + FFFFFFD9 = 0001A0FD.

2.9 SUMMARY

1. Nearly all computers are internally binary-coded. A piece of binary data, say, 0110111001011101, can conveniently be expressed in its hexadecimal equivalent 6E5D.

2. The basic addressable unit of main storage in System/370 or System/360 is a byte. It is composed of eight bits. Two contiguous bytes make a halfword; four contiguous bytes make a fullword; and eight contiguous bytes make a doubleword.

3. The address of a halfword, a fullword, or a doubleword in the main storage is 24-bit long. It must satisfy the requirement of integral boundary alignment.

4. In System/370 or System/360, a binary integer is represented in a fixed length: a halfword or a fullword. It uses the two's complement notation.

5. Addition is the basic arithmetic process which is carried out in the ALU. All other arithmetic operations are performed by addition, complementation, and shifts.

6. When the sum or difference of two binary integers lies outside of range between -2^{31} and $2^{31} - 1$, there is a fixed-point overflow. During addition, overflow occurs

only when two integers are of the same sign. It is signaled by a change of sign in the sign bit. During subtraction, it occurs only when two integers are of the opposite sign.

7. The IBM System/370 or System/360 has 16 general registers. When a halfword is transmitted from main storage to a register or is added to the contents of a register, it is first expanded into a fullword by propagating its sign bit through the additional 16 bits. The sign extension is automatic and the contents of the halfword do not alter.

BIBLIOGRAPHY

Atkins, D. E., "Higher Radix Division Using Estimates of the Divisor and Partial Remainder," *IEEE Trans. on Computers* 17, 825–934 (1968).

Ehrman, J. R., "Logical Arithmetic on Computers with Two's Complement Binary Arithmetic," *Comm. of Assoc. Computing Machinery* 11, 517–520 (1968).

Freiman, C. V., "Statistical Analysis of Certain Binary Division Algorithms," *Proc. IRE* 49, 91–103 (1961).

Garner, H. L., "Number Systems and Arithmetic," *Advances in Computers* 6, 131–194 (1965).

Krishnamurthy, E. V., and S. K. Nandi, "On the Normalization Requirement of Divisor in Divide-and-Correct Methods," *Comm. of Assoc. Computing Machinery* 10, 809–813 (1967).

Nandi, S. K., and E. V. Krishnamurthy, "A Simple Technique for Digital Division," *Comm. of Assoc. Computing Machinery* 10, 299–301 (1967).

Reitwiesner, G. W., "Binary Arithmetic," *Advances in Computers* 1, 232–308 (1960).

Stein, M. L., "Divide-and-Correct Methods for Multiple Precision Division," *Comm. of Assoc. Computing Machinery* 7, 472–474 (1964).

Tung, C., *Digital Computer Arithmetic*, IBM Research Laboratory Report RJ 669 (San Jose, California), 1970.

Wilson, J. B., and R. S. Ledley, "An Algorithm for Rapid Binary Division," *IRE Trans. Electron. Computers* 10, 662–670 (1961).

PROBLEMS

Section 2.3

2.1. In a computer output, it is printed:

TOTAL MEMORY REQUIREMENTS 00F2A8 BYTES

What are the total memory requirements in bytes as expressed in decimal system?

2.2. The binary number 1111 is frequently used in a branch instruction of System/370 or System/360. What is its decimal equivalent? What is its hexadecimal equivalent?

2.3. Express the following hexadecimal numbers in binary and decimal:

Hexadecimal	00FF	04AC	5020	FFFA
Binary	————	————	————	————
Decimal	————	————	————	————

Section 2.4

2.4. The effective address E of a fullword in main storage is, in some cases, equal to base address B plus displacement D. Find E in hexadecimal if B = 000A1C and D = 1D8. Does this address E satisfy the fullword alignment requirement?

2.5. The following hexadecimal number is used to represent a binary integer.

$$5C20B118$$

a) How many bytes does it take?
b) What is its binary equivalent?
c) If the address of the leftmost byte is 001A0C, what is the address of the rightmost byte?
d) What is the address of this complete data?

2.6. A byte consists of eight bits of information. It *also* has a parity bit for checking the validity of the information bits. The concept of parity check is based on the fact that each piece of data is represented by a string of 1's and 0's. The parity bit is added to the eight information bits in order to make the total number of 1-bits odd. This operation, called an odd-parity check, is used in IBM System/370 and System/360. For example, the parity bit is 1 for the byte contents 10101001, as the total number of 1-bits is 5, an odd number. Find the parity bit for each of the four bytes shown in Fig. 2.3.

Section 2.5

2.7. Show that (a) n bits can represent 2^n different configurations; (b) the addition of one bit to the original n bits will double the capacity for representing numbers.

2.8. a) What is the nine's complement of $(365)_{10}$?
b) What is the ten's complement of $(1458)_{10}$?
c) What is the one's complement of $(001101)_2$?
d) What is the two's complement of $(100101)_2$?

Section 2.6

2.9. Express each of the following decimal numbers as a fullword binary integer:
a) 12,   b) -8,   c) -2^{30}.

2.10. Represent each of the following decimal numbers as a halfword binary integer.
a) -11,   b) 9,   c) 2^{19}.
Which case is not possible?

2.11. Show that (a) the largest positive number in a fullword is $2^{31} - 1$, (b) the largest negative number in a fullword is -2^{31}.

Section 2.7

2.12. Express two decimal numbers in each case as two fullwords. Show their sum and check the overflow.
Case A. 12 and -31.
Case B. 2^{30} and $(2^{30} + 1)$.

2.13. Suppose that the fixed-point data I, J, and K have the following fullword representation:

$$
\begin{aligned}
&\text{I: } 0004C7A2 \\
&\text{J: } FFFF4ACC \\
&\text{K: } 01003B76
\end{aligned}
$$

Express each of the following values in fullword two's complement representation: (a) $I + J$; (b) $I + K$; (c) $J + K$; (d) $I - J$; (e) $I - K$; (f) $J - K$; (g) $K - I$. Write them in hexadecimal.

Section 2.8

2.14. After the division $-7/(-4) = 1\frac{3}{4}$ is performed, the remainder is stored in a register, say, number 9. In System/370 or System/360, this remainder 3 is considered as a negative number, as the sign of a nonzero remainder is always the same as the sign of the dividend. Write out the hexadecimal representation of the contents in register 9 after the division.

2.15. A halfword w in main storage has the two-byte contents: FA1C. Find the sum of this halfword and the contents of register 9 in Problem 2.14.

LABORATORY ASSIGNMENT

1. Keypunch the assembler language shown in Fig. 1.17 in Section 1.6; do it on an IBM 029 keypunch. Submit to your computing center for a *run*. Modify the job control cards; the first card (or the job card), in particular, may have to be modified to suit the requirements of your installation.

2. The output of this assembler language program is a dump—the image of main storage, expressed in hexadecimal, as shown in Fig. C.2 (see Appendix C). This dump is caused by the instruction DC X'82000000'.

   Convert the contents in each of 16 general registers from hexadecimal to decimal values; and to binary values. Save your output and put it in a binder.

CHAPTER 3

Arithmetic Instructions

3.1 INSTRUCTION FORMATS

An instruction for a computer specifies precisely the operation to be performed. In machine language, it consists of a given number of bits; each bit, or a group of contiguous bits, signifies some required action.

For a given computer system, an instruction can have one or several formats. In the IBM System/370 or System/360, for example, there are five types of instruction formats available (see Fig. 3.1).

RR type: register to register operation, 2 bytes long
RX type: register and indexed storage operation, 4 bytes long
RS type: register and storage operation, 4 bytes long
SI type: immediate data and storage operation, 4 bytes long
SS type: storage to storage operation, 6 bytes long

About 67 percent of all instructions use either the RR or the RX format. In this chapter, we shall discuss arithmetic instructions which are typical examples of instructions used for RR and RX formats; the other three formats will be dealt with in Chapter 5.

A word of caution: In the remainder of this book, all addresses, contents of registers, and contents of main storage, except when noted otherwise, are expressed in hexadecimal. The register numbers are generally expressed in decimal.

3.2 RR FORMAT AND ADD REGISTER (AR) INSTRUCTION

As we mentioned before, an instruction for a computer specifies precisely the operation to be performed. For example, this is an instruction: Add two numbers x and y; x is already in register 7; and y, in register 11. This can be expressed in a 16-bit

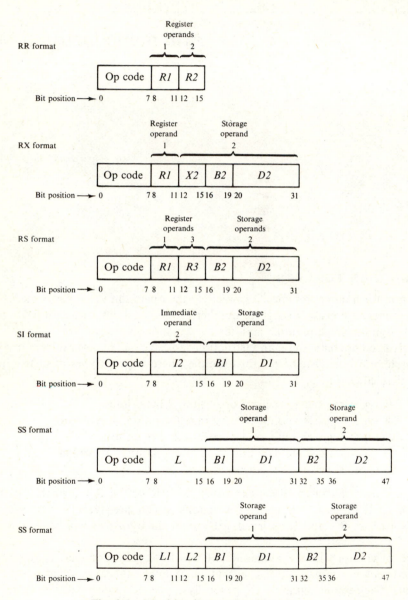

Fig. 3.1 Machine instruction formats.

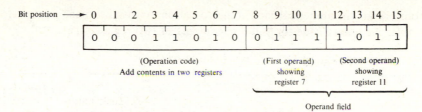

Fig. 3.2   An instruction for adding two numbers.

(halfword) instruction, as shown in Fig. 3.2. The first (or the leftmost) eight bits represent the operation code, or *op code*. The next four bits represent a register number; the contents of this register are the so-called *first operand x*. In Fig. 3.2, for example, register 7 holds this first operand. The bits 12 through 15 indicate another register number; the contents of this second register are *y*, called the *second operand*. In Fig. 3.2, register 11 contains this second operand. The bit positions 8–15 in this instruction are collectively known as the *operand field*.

After the execution of this instruction, the sum $x + y$ is left in register 7. The contents of register 11 remain unchanged. There are 16 general registers, numbered from 0 to 15; each register contains 32 bits (a fullword or 4 bytes). Suppose the initial contents (in hexadecimal) of registers 7 and 11 are as shown below, the sum in register 7 is then as indicated:

Initial contents in register 7	register 11	Final result $x + y$ in register 7
x	y	(register 11 unchanged)
0D00A71C	00000004	0D00A720
0D00A71C	FFFFFFFA	0D00A716
FFFFFFFA	0D00A71C	0D00A716
7FFFFFFF	00000001	overflow
80000000	FFFFFFF1	overflow

The last two cases may need some explanation: When the sum is greater than $2^{31} - 1$, or less than -2^{31}, register 7 is overflowed.

Operation Code

Let us now take a close look at the first eight bits in an instruction, the operation code field as shown in Fig. 3.3. For convenience, bit positions 4–7 are explained first.

Bit position ⟶   0   1   2   3   4   5   6   7

Location of data	Data type	Operation

Fig. 3.3   Operation code.

These four bits are the numerical code of the operation we wish the machine to perform; for example, the binary code for "adding contents of two registers" is 1010.

Table 3.1 Interpretations of first two bits in an instruction

Bit 0	Bit 1	Interpretation	Instruction type	Length of the instruction (in bytes)
0	0	Both operands in general registers	RR	2
1	0 ⎫	One operand in main storage and the	RS or SI	4
0	1 ⎬	other in a general register	RX	4
1	1	Both operands in main storage	SS	6

The bit 0 and bit 1 indicate whether the operands are located in the general registers or in main storage. As listed in Table 3.1, they are also used to indicate total number of bytes in the instruction. If, for example, the bit positions 0 and 1 in an instruction each contains a zero, then this instruction is of RR type (2 byte long), and each of the two operands is contained in a general register.

In connection with bit positions 0 and 1, the bits 2 and 3 indicate the data type: Whether a piece of data is represented in its fixed-length format or in variable-length format. In the former case, the bits 2 and 3 also show whether this piece of data is a halfword or a fullword.

It is important to note that these first eight bits (op code) are common in each of the five types of instruction format.

Operands and Operand Addresses

An *operand* of an instruction is a piece of information which is operated on or operated with by that instruction. An *operand address* specifies where this operand is located; it may be a register number, or an address in main storage. Unfortunately, ambiguity exists about the words *operand* and *operand address* in practice. With minor exceptions,† by *operand field* of an instruction, we mean the portion of the instruction containing operand address or addresses. For example, in the operand field of the Add instruction shown in Fig. 3.2 (bits 8 through 15), two operand addresses are specified— registers 7 and 11. Although the terms *first operand* and *second operand* are used here, they mean the *address* of the first operand and the *address* of the second operand.

In sum, the 16-bit instruction shown in Fig. 3.2 is interpreted as: "Add the contents of register 11 to the contents of register 7, and leave the answer in register 7." To write the instruction in such binary notation is tedious and error-prone. Instead, a programmer can write the instruction in the following symbolic form:

AR 7,11

---

† Immediate operand used in SI format is discussed in Section 5.2.

and the assembler will dutifully translate it into the 2-byte instruction in machine language.

When each of the two operands is contained in a register, the type of instruction is called *register to register*, or *RR* for short. The general format of this type of instructions is shown in Fig. 3.4. A confusion of symbolic notation might occur here: *R1* and *R2* denote, respectively, the actual register numbers containing the first and second operands in the instruction. They do not mean registers no. 1 and no. 2.

Bit position ———▸ 0 1 2 3 4 5 6 7 8 9 10 11 12 13 14 15

| Op code | R1 | R2 |

Fig. 3.4 RR format.

3.3 STORAGE ADDRESSING
USING BASE ADDRESS AND DISPLACEMENT

The RR instruction format treated in the previous section is one of the five types available to the IBM System/370 or System/360. Each of the two operands used in this type of format is in a register. Before we explore the other four types of instructions, we'll have to discuss the base address method which specifies the *address* of an operand located in main storage.

In its elementary form, this method can be expressed in the following equation:

$$E = B + D \tag{3.1}$$

where E = effective address of the operand,

B = base address, or the contents of base register,

  = 0, if register 0 is assigned as base register,

D = displacement ($0 \leq D \leq 4095$), a 12-bit number.

The base address B is contained in one of the 16 available general registers. When a general register is used for this purpose, it is called a *base register*. As we shall see in Section 5.5, a programmer can designate any register as the base register with little effort.

As a special case, when register 0 is assigned as base register, the value B is automatically taken as zero.

The displacement D is a 12-bit binary number. As a result, the maximum possible displacement is

$$(111111111111)_2 = (FFF)_{16} = (4095)_{10}.$$

As mentioned briefly in Section 2.4, the address of an operand in main storage (or the address of an instruction) takes 24 bits, or 3 bytes. After the sum $B + D$ is calculated, only its rightmost 3 bytes are retained and used as the effective address E of a given operand.

Example 1

Compute the effective address of a fullword operand if (1) a programmer designates register 11 as base register; (2) the contents of register 11 (base address) are 0000A03C (in hexadecimal); and (3) the displacement D is 004.

Using Eq. (3.1), we have

Base address	B:	0000A03C
Displacement	D:	004 +
Effective address	E:	00A040
of the operand		

A detailed storage map is shown in Fig. 3.5. Note that the effective address 00A040 is divisible by 4, thus satisfying the fullword alignment requirement. A word of caution: Each of the two vertical arrows shown in Fig. 3.5 points to a particular byte; the exact location of an arrow within the byte is not important.

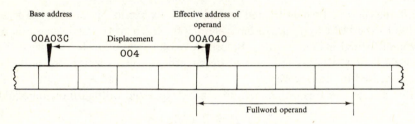

Fig. 3.5   Effective address of an operand in the main storage.

Example 2

Same as Example 1, except that register 11 (appears in two places) is replaced by register 0.

Since the base address B is now zero, the effective address of the operand is simply

$$
\begin{array}{r}
00000000 \\
004 \ + \\
\hline
000004
\end{array}
$$

3.4 STORAGE ADDRESSING USING BASE, INDEX, AND DISPLACEMENT

The base-displacement method discussed in the previous section is primarily used in the instruction of RS, SI, and SS types. For instructions of RX type, the effective address E of the second operand can be computed as follows:

$$E = B + D + X \tag{3.2}$$

where E, B, and D have the same meanings as in Eq. (3.1); the quantity X denotes *index*, the contents of a general register known as the index register, which is usually different from the base register. If register 0 is designated as the index register, then $X = 0$. Index registers provide an efficient means for counting, instruction modification, and loop termination. They will be discussed more fully in Section 4.8.

Example 1

Calculate the effective address of a fullword storage operand. The given conditions are:

1. Register 11 is designated as base register.
2. Register 10 is designated as index register.
3. Contents of register 11 are 000010C4 in hexadecimal.
4. Contents of register 10, or index X, are 00000050.
5. Displacement D is 004.

Using Eq. (3.2), we have

$$
\begin{array}{llr}
\text{Base address} & B: & 000010\text{C}4 \\
\text{Index} & X: & 00000050 \\
\text{Displacement} & D: & 004 \quad + \\
\hline
& E: & 001118
\end{array}
$$

where the leftmost 8 bits are ignored in the result. This base-index-displacement method to compute the effective address of a storage operand is shown in Fig. 3.6. Each of the three vertical arrows shown in Fig. 3.6 points to a particular byte; the exact location of an arrow within a byte is not important. Note that this effective address is divisible by 4, satisfying the fullword alignment requirement.

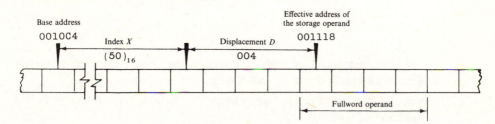

Fig. 3.6   Effective address of a storage operand using the base-index-displacement method.

Example 2

Same as Example 1, except that register 0 is designated as index register. The contents of register 0 are 0000A404.

Using Eq. (3.2), we have

Base address	B:	000010C4	
Index	X:	00000000	(not 0000A404)
Displacement	D:	004 +	
	E:	0010C8	

which is divisible by 4.

The storage addressing method which uses base address, index, and displacement is difficult to learn. By means of this method, however, the total number of bits (in an instruction) needed to address a storage location is reduced from 24 to 20 bits: 4 bits to address the base register, 4 bits to address the index register, and 12 bits for displacement. When index register is not used, such as in Eq. (3.1), the total number of bits needed to address a storage location is further reduced to 16 bits. A second advantage of using the base-index-displacement method is the program relocation. We shall discuss this important topic in Section 6.6.

3.5 RX FORMAT AND ADD (A) INSTRUCTION

All instructions of RX format have one thing in common: The first operand is held in a register, whereas the second, in the main storage. Its general format is shown in Fig. 3.7, where

$R1$ = a register number; this register contains the *first* operand. $R1$ does not mean register number 1.

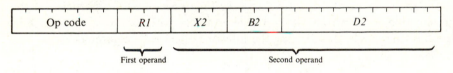

Fig. 3.7   RX format.

$X2$ = a register number; this register contains the index X to compute the effective address E of the *second* operand.

$B2$ = a register number; this register contains the base address B to compute E of the *second* operand.

$D2$ = a 12-bit displacement used to compute E of the *second* operand.

A typical example using this instruction format is an Add (A) instruction shown in Fig. 3.8. The op code takes 8 bits, bits 0 through 7. The first operand address $R1$ is register 9, whereas the second operand is in main storage. The index register 5, base register 8, and 12-bit displacement 1DC = $(476)_{10}$ are specified; they can be used to compute the second operand address. For instance, if index register 5 contains

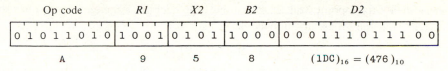

Op code	R1	X2	B2	D2
0 1 0 1 1 0 1 0	1 0 0 1	0 1 0 1	1 0 0 0	0 0 0 1 1 1 0 1 1 1 0 0
A	9	5	8	$(1DC)_{16} = (476)_{10}$

Fig. 3.8　RX format—Add (A) instruction.

00000120 and base register 8 contains 00001000, then the effective address E of the second operand is computed as follows:

$$
\begin{array}{ll}
B: & 00001000 \\
X: & 00000120 \\
D: & \underline{\qquad 1DC \quad +} \\
E: & 0012FC
\end{array}
$$

Thus the effective address of the first byte in the second operand is 0012FC (see Fig. 3.9). Since this Add (A) instruction *demands* implicitly that the second operand contains a fullword, this address must be divisible by 4. This operand occupies four bytes with the following byte addresses: 0012FC, 0012FD, 0012FE, and 0012FF.

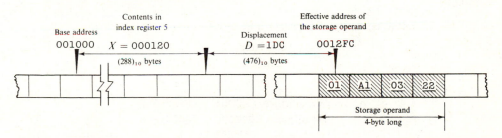

Fig. 3.9　Base-displacement-index method to compute the effective address of an operand.

Let us assume that the contents of register 9 are 0D00A210, and the contents of the second operand are 01A10322 (shaded in Fig. 3.9). The execution of this Add instruction causes the contents of the fullword (effective addresses 0012FC through 0012FF) to be added to the contents of register 9, or

$$
\begin{array}{l}
0D00A210 \\
\underline{01A10322 \quad +} \\
0EA1A532
\end{array}
$$

This sum is left in register 9 and the contents in all four storage bytes (shaded in Fig. 3.9) remain undisturbed.

This Add instruction may be written in symbolic language (better known as assembler language); its general form is

$$
A \quad R1,D2(X2,B2)
$$

where A means fixed-point Add. In particular, the machine language instruction shown in Fig. 3.8 has the following equivalent

$$A \quad 9,476(5,8)$$

where the displacement 476 is expressed in decimal.

Suppose the effective address of the second operand is known symbolically as HERE. We can write the assembler language instruction as

$$A \quad 9,HERE$$

Finally, if the fullword *contents* at the address HERE are 6, we can write

$$A \quad 9,=F'6'$$

where =F'6' is a *literal*. Literals are treated in detail in Section 6.11. However, they are so easy and convenient to use that we shall say a few words about them. Here, the second operand is specified as a fullword; its *contents* represent a decimal 6. Note: The decimal contents are enclosed in a pair of single quotes and preceded by an equal sign and a character F designating a fullword fixed-point number.

Example

Suppose the initial contents of registers and bytes in main storage are:

Register 9:	70A040C4
Register 10:	00000C08
Register 11:	80000000
At symbolic address HERE:	FFFFFF20
At address 000C0C:	00001F12

The result, after the execution of each unrelated A instruction, is as indicated below.

Instruction	Sum is left in register	Answer	Note
A 9,=F'2'	9	70A040C6	
A 9,=F'–2'	9	70A040C2	
A 9,HERE	9	70A03FE4	
A 11,=F'10'	11	8000000A	
A 11,HERE	11	7FFFFF20	→ Overflow. Answer is incorrect.
A 9,4(0,10)	9	70A05FD6	
A 9,4(10,0)	9	70A05FD6	

3.6 ADD HALFWORD (AH) INSTRUCTION

There are three Add instructions for the signed binary (fixed-point) integers: Add Register (AR), Add (A), and Add Halfword (AH). So far, we have studied the first two instructions. AR instruction is of RR format; A instruction, of RX format.

As another example of an instruction using RX format, let us consider Add Halfword (AH) instruction. This instruction is similar to Add (A) instruction we discussed in the previous section, except for one difference: The second operand in an Add (A) instruction is a fullword, whereas that used in an Add Halfword (AH) instruction is a halfword. Consider the Add Halfword instruction shown in Fig. 3.10. It is identical to the Add instruction shown in Fig. 3.8, but in bit position 3, it is 0 that replaces 1.

Op code	R1	X2	B2	D2
0 1 0 0 1 0 1 0	1 0 0 1	0 1 0 1	1 0 0 0	0 0 0 1 1 1 0 1 1 1 0 0
AH	9	5	8	$(476)_{10}$

Fig. 3.10   Add Halfword (AH) instruction in RX format.

In the execution of an Add Halfword (AH) instruction, the following steps are involved:

1. The halfword data (storage operand) are expanded into a fullword by using the sign extension discussed in Section 2.8. Essentially, the sign bit of the halfword operand is copied into the upper half of the fullword. For example, if the original halfword data contain F6E8, the fullword after the sign extension contains FFFFF6E8.

2. This fullword is then added to the register operand. The sum is left in the register, and the original contents of the halfword operand are not disturbed.

For illustration, let us assume that the register contents before execution of the instruction shown in Fig. 3.10 are as follows:

Register number	Register usage	Initial register contents
5	Index register	0000A120
8	Base register	00001000
9	Holding first operand	0100A210

and the displacement D is 1DC. Then, the effective address of the storage operand (the second operand) is 00A120 + 001000 + 1DC = 00B2FC. This address must be divisible by 2 to satisfy the requirement of halfword alignment. The second operand has two-byte contents; their byte addresses are 00B2FC and 00B2FD. During the execution of this instruction, the contents of the halfword storage operand, say, F6E8, are first extended into a fullword FFFFF6E8. They are then added to the contents of register 9.

$$\begin{array}{r} 0100A210 \\ FFFFF6E8 \; + \\ \hline 010098F8 \end{array}$$

The sum is left in register 9, and the contents in the halfword in main storage are not altered.

The corresponding instruction in assembler language for this example is simply

$$\text{AH} \quad 9,476(5,8)$$

where the letter H after A stands for *halfword*, the length of the second operand.

3.7 SUBTRACTION—A REVIEW OF RR AND RX FORMATS

To consolidate the understanding of RR and RX formats discussed so far in this chapter, we shall now explore how one fixed-point number U can be subtracted from another, V.

Case 1. U and V are both contained in registers

The Subtract Register (SR) instruction is designed to perform this subtraction. If U and V are contained in registers 7 and 11, respectively, the instruction

$$\text{SR} \quad 7,11$$

will cause the contents of register 11 to be subtracted from the contents of register 7. The result $U - V$ is left in register 7. The contents of register 11, V, remain unchanged. Suppose the initial contents of register 7 and 11 are given, these contents after the execution of the instruction SR 7,11 are as shown below.

Initial contents		Contents after the execution of SR 7,11	
U	V	$U - V$	V
Register 7	Register 11	Register 7	Register 11
0000A2D8	000000B4	0000A224	000000B4
000000A3	FFFFFFFD	000000A6	FFFFFFFD
FFFFFFFD	000000A3	FFFFFF5A	000000A3
F158A01C	03AC120F	EDAC8E0D	03AC120F
FFFFFFFD	FFE42613	001BD9EA	FFE42613

Case 2. U in a register; fullword V in main storage

The Subtract (S) instruction can best be used in this case. Its general form is

$$\text{S} \quad R1,D2(X2,B2)$$

where register $R1$ contains the binary integer U; and $B2$, $X2$, and $D2$ are used to calculate the effective address of the second operand, a fullword in main storage. The operation is a simple one: The contents of the fullword storage operand are subtracted from the contents of register $R1$. The result is left in this register; and the contents of the storage operand remain unchanged.

Suppose the following items of information are available:

a) Base address B, index X, and displacement D
b) $R1 = 7$
c) Initial contents of register 7
d) Storage map is shown in Fig. 3.11.

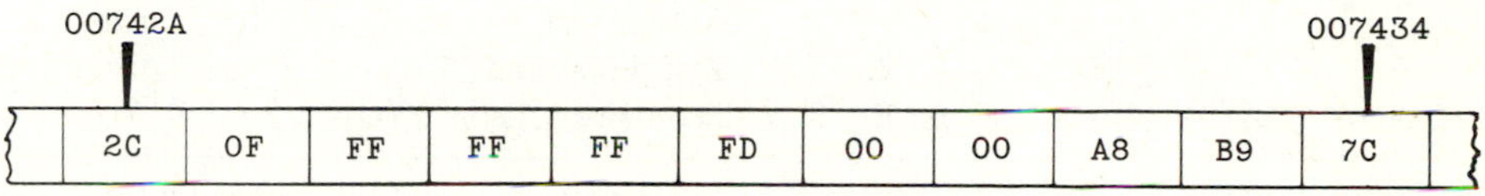

00742A   007434

| 2C | 0F | FF | FF | FF | FD | 00 | 00 | A8 | B9 | 7C |

Fig. 3.11   Storage map.

The contents of register 7 after the execution of the instruction

S $R1,D2(X2,B2)$

are shown below.

B (Given)	X (Given)	D (Given)	E† (From Eq. 3.2)	Contents of second operand (From Fig. 3.11)	Initial contents of $R1$, register 7 (Given)	Contents of register 7 after the execution (Results)
007408	000001	023	00742C	FFFFFFFD	000000A3	000000A6
007404	000008	024	007430	0000A8B9	0A1FBAAC	0A1F11F3

Case 3.   *U in a register; halfword V located in main storage*
The following Subtract Halfword (SH) instruction

SH $R1,D2(X2,B2)$

can be used. It subtracts the halfword data in main storage from the contents of register $R1$. The result is left in the register, and the contents in the halfword remain unchanged. The effective address of the second operand is computed by the base-index-displacement method as expressed in Eq. (3.2).

Before the subtraction is performed, the halfword data are first expanded into a fullword: The sign bit of the halfword is copied into the upper half of the fullword. In subtraction halfword as well as in addition halfword, the whole 32 bits of the register are involved.

---

† The effective address must be divisible by 4.

Suppose the values B, X, D, and initial contents of register 7 are given. The contents of register 7 after the execution of the instruction

$$\text{SH} \quad R1, D2(X2, B2)$$

are shown below.

B (Given)	X (Given)	D (Given)	E (From Eq. 3.2)	Contents of second operand (From Fig. 3.11)	Initial contents of R1, register 7 (Given)	Contents of register 7 after the execution
007408	000001	025	00742E	FFFD	000000A3	000000A6
007404	00000A	024	007432	A8B9	0A1FBAAC	0A2011F3

The student should note that the effective address of each halfword storage operand must be divisible by 2, that is, on a halfword boundary.

3.8 MULTIPLICATION OF TWO NUMBERS

So far we have discussed in detail three Add and three Subtract instructions. AR and SR instructions are of RR type, whereas A, S, AH, and SH instructions are of RX type. There are three Multiply instructions: MR (RR type), M (RX type), and MH (RX type). Although they are of RR and RX types, the Multiply instructions have their own peculiarities and need special treatment.

The fixed-point multiplication is carried out in registers. The multiplicand is always stored in a register, whereas the multiplier can be in a register (for MR instruction) or in a storage location (for M and MH instructions). Generally speaking, when the multiplicand has M bits and the multiplier, N bits, the product will take $M \times N$ bits. As a special case, when contents in two fullwords are multiplied, the length of product is expected to be a doubleword and two registers are needed to house the product. In the IBM System/370 or System/360, these two registers are always an even–odd pair, such as 2 and 3, 4 and 5, and so on. The even-numbered register holds the most significant part of the product. The odd-numered register, initially containing the multiplicand, holds the least significant part of the product.

Multiply Register (MR) Instruction

The MR instruction is as nearly simple as AR or SR instruction, but we must remember that the first operand represents a pair of even–odd numbered registers. For example, the instruction shown in Fig. 3.12, or its equivalent in assembler language:

$$\text{MR} \quad 4, 7$$

multiplies the contents in registers 5 and 7 (not 4 and 7); the product is left in a pair

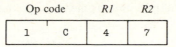

Fig. 3.12   Hexadecimal representation of a Multiply Register (MR) instruction.

of registers 4 and 5. Register 4 holds the most significant 32 bits of the product, whereas register 5, the least significant 32 bits.

Suppose that the initial contents of register 5 and 7 are given, the contents of registers 4 and 5 after the execution of the instruction

$$\text{MR} \quad 4,7$$

are shown below. The contents of register 7 remain unchanged.

Before the execution of MR 4,7		After the execution of MR 4,7	
Contents of register 5	Contents of register 7	Contents of register 4	Contents of register 5
00000008	0000000A	00000000	00000050
00000008	FFFFFFF6	FFFFFFFF	FFFFFFB0
FFFFFFF8	0000000A	FFFFFFFF	FFFFFFB0
FFFFFFF8	FFFFFFF6	00000000	00000050
000F4240	00089540	000000D1	8C2E2800

In each of the first four cases, correct result is contained in register 5. In the fifth case, however, the product extends over into register 4, and there is no automatic warning that the result in register 5 is not a complete product. To move this product into register 5, a programmer must shift† the product to the right for eight bits.

Multiply (M) Instruction

This instruction deals with the multiplication of two signed binary integers. One is in a register; the other is a fullword in main storage. This instruction is of RX type, but it has its own peculiarities: A pair of even–odd registers must be specified to hold the product.

Specifically, let us assume that the multiplicand is stored in register 3, and that the multiplier is a fullword located in the main storage. The effective address‡ of this fullword can be calculated from the following given information:

a) Base address B is stored in register 10.

b) $X = 0$, i.e., no index is used.

c) Displacement $D = (118)_{16}$.

---

† Shift is discussed in Chapter 7. Use the floating-point method in Chapter 12 when product is expected to be greater than 2^{31}.

‡ This address is required to be divisible by 4, since it is for a fullword operand.

We can perform this multiplication by means of the machine language instruction shown in Fig. 3.13.

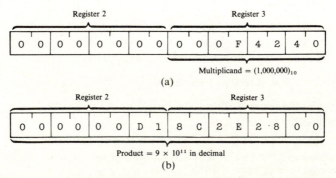

Fig. 3.13   Instruction for multiplication of two numbers.

This instruction can be readily written in hexadecimal form as

$$5C20A118$$

where each hexadecimal digit is conveniently used to represent four bits. Let us now examine each field in this instruction more closely.

5C stands for the operation code for multiplication M.

2 stands for $N - 1$, where N is the register number in which the multiplicand is stored. In other words, the multiplicand in this example is in register 3. *R1* field in Fig. 3.13 must contain an even number.

0 stands for the index register number. From Fig. 3.13, the index $X = 0$.

A stands for the base register number 10.

118 stands for the displacement, or $(280)_{10}$.

During the execution of this instruction, the pair of registers 2 and 3 are first set to zeros before the product is stored as a doubleword. The multiplicand originally held in the odd-numbered register 3 is erased.

Suppose that the multiplicand and the multiplier are $(1,000,000)_{10}$ and $(9,000,000)_{10}$, respectively. The contents in registers 2 and 3 before and after the operation are shown in Fig. 3.14.

Register 2   Register 3

| 0 | 0 | 0 | 0 | 0 | 0 | 0 | 0 | 0 | 0 | 0 | F | 4 | 2 | 4 | 0 |

Multiplicand $= (1,000,000)_{10}$

(a)

Register 2   Register 3

| 0 | 0 | 0 | 0 | 0 | 0 | D | 1 | 8 | C | 2 | E | 2 | 8 | 0 | 0 |

Product $= 9 \times 10^{11}$ in decimal

(b)

Fig. 3.14   Hexadecimal representation of registers 2 and 3 (a) before and (b) after multiplication.

The M instruction shown in Fig. 3.13 has its equivalents in assembler language:

M   2,280(0,10)

or

M   2,RATE

where the symbol RATE is assigned to represent the effective address of the second operand (multiplier, a fullword). If the *contents* of this fullword are, say, 6, we can use the following instruction:

M   2,=F'6'

where the literal is used in the second operand to represent a fullword data having the decimal value 6.

3.9 DIVIDE INSTRUCTIONS: DR AND D

There are two Divide instructions for the binary integers: DR and D. The former uses RR format; the latter, RX format. Both instructions have a common peculiarity: The dividend is initially stored in a pair of even–odd numbered registers; this pair of registers is addressed by the even-numbered register. In each Divide instruction, this even-numbered register is specified as the first operand address *R1*.

In DR instruction, the divisor is held in a third register, whereas in D instruction, it is in a fullword located in main storage. After execution of DR or D instruction, the remainder is left in the even-numbered register; and the quotient, in the odd-numbered register. The signs depend, in part, on whether the quotient or remainder is zero or nonzero. The rules are listed in Table 3.2.

Table 3.2 Signs of a quotient and a remainder

Result	Value of the result		Sign convention
Remainder (left in the even-numbered register)	Zero		(+)
	Nonzero		Same as the sign of the 64-bit dividend
Quotient (left in the odd-numbered register)	Zero		(+)
	Nonzero	Dividend and divisor have the same sign	(+)
		Dividend and divisor are of opposite sign	(−)

For illustration, let us first examine the Divide Register (DR) instruction more closely in connection with the division of two numbers

$$\frac{15}{7} = 2\frac{1}{7}.$$

The dividend (15) is always stored (right adjusted) in *a pair of even–odd numbered registers*, say, registers 4 and 5.   The divisor (7) is stored in a third register, say, register 9 (see Fig. 3.15).

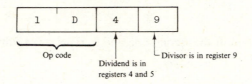

Fig. 3.15   RR format for division of two numbers.

After the division, the result is composed of two parts, the quotient and the remainder.   The quotient, equal to +2 in this specific example, is stored in register 5; and the remainder (+1) is in register 4, as illustrated in Fig. 3.16.

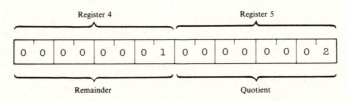

Fig. 3.16   Hexadecimal representation of quotient and remainder in registers 4 and 5.

The instruction in Fig. 3.15 has its equivalent in assembler language:

$$\text{DR}\quad 4,9$$

Note that since a register has only 32 bits, a quotient must have a value λ that satisfies the following condition

$$-2^{31} \le \lambda \le 2^{31} - 1. \tag{3.3}$$

If the relation (3.3) is violated, then no division takes place and the dividend, initially stored in a pair of even–odd registers, is not disturbed.   This is the so-called *fixed-point divide exception*.

As a rule of thumb, we can compare the portion of the dividend *stored in the even register* with the divisor to detect a possible fixed-point divide exception.   If the former is larger than or equal to the value of the latter, then a fixed-point divide exception will occur.

Consider the DR instruction in Fig. 3.15 again. If the contents of register 4 and of register 9 are $(00000044)_{16}$ and $(00000022)_{16}$, respectively, then a fixed-point divide exception takes place, and the contents in registers 4, 5, and 9 are not changed.

Divide (D) Instruction Using RX Format

Generally speaking, an instruction having RX format deals with two operands, one in a register, and the other in a specific fullword in the main memory. But in cases of multiplication and division, a pair of even–odd numbered registers is needed.

Consider again the following division of two numbers:

$$\frac{15}{7} = 2\frac{1}{7}.$$

The dividend (15) is held, not in one register, but in a pair of consecutive even–odd numbered registers, say, registers 4 and 5. The divisor (7) is stored in a fullword in main storage. The effective address of this fullword is given either explicitly (e.g., 00080C) or implicitly. In the latter case, it can be computed, for example, from the contents of the base register 15, the index register 0, and the displacement $(2984)_{10}$. The required instruction is shown in Fig. 3.17 (in hexadecimal). You can write this instruction in assembler language:

$$D\ 4,2984(0,15)$$

and the assembler will dutifully translate it into the four-byte instruction in machine language.

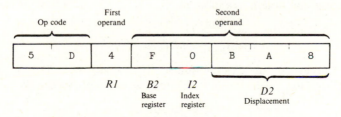

Fig. 3.17   Divide (D) instruction in RX format.

After the execution of this instruction, the remainder and quotient are left in registers 4 and 5, respectively, as shown in Fig. 3.16.

3.10 REMAINDER AND ITS APPLICATIONS

This section presents some practical applications of a remainder.

In prefabrication industries, a product is often cut in a fixed length, say, of 9 feet, known as a *module*. To fit the module, the multiples of 9 should be used as often as possible in design. If, however, a 14-foot piece and a 23-foot piece are specified on a blueprint, the space of 5 feet must be filled in with special handwork in both cases.

The 5 feet come as the remainder in the following two divisions:

$$\frac{14}{9} \quad \text{and} \quad \frac{23}{9}.$$

In both cases the above-mentioned 5-foot handwork can be expressed in mathematics as follows:

$$23 \equiv 14 \,(\text{mod } 9)$$

or "23 is congruent to 14 modulo 9," or "23 and 14 are congruent modulo 9."

Remainder is playing an important role in congruence arithmetic. In particular, the remainder left after division of A by B is often written as

$$A \text{ modulo } B,$$

or as

$$A \text{ mod } B.$$

Thus 5 mod 3 yields 2. Suppose that A is stored in register 4 and B, a fullword in main storage. After execution of the following Divide instruction:

$$D \quad 4,B$$

the remainder A mod B is left in register 4, the first of an even–odd register pair.

Random Number Generator

If X_n is given, we can obtain a random number X_{n+1} by using the following recursion relation:

$$X_{n+1} \equiv MX_n \,(\text{mod } P) \tag{3.4}$$

where M is a multiplier and P, a modulus. If we select $M = 7^5 = 16,807$ and $P = 2^{31} - 1 = 2147483647$, we can use the following two instructions to generate X_{n+1}:

$$M \quad 4,=F'16807'$$
$$D \quad 4,=F'2147483647'$$

Before the execution of M instruction, the given X_n is in register 5. The newly calculated random number X_{n+1}, the remainder from the division, is left in register 4.

If, on the other hand, we take P as 2^{31} for a machine having 32 bits in a fullword, such as the IBM System/370 or System/360, then no division is needed. One simply discards everything in the product of M times X_n that exceeds rightmost 32 bits. Let us use $M = 2^{16} + 3 = 65,539$ and assume that X_n is in register 5. The following single instruction

$$M \quad 4, =F'65539'$$

generates a new random number X_{n+1}, which is held in register 5. The contents in register 4 are discarded.

Hash Function

Hash function determines where a symbol (defined in a user's program) should be placed in a symbol table. It also helps fetch it at later times. Basically, a symbol table is an area in main storage which contains the symbols defined in a user's program and their corresponding numerical values. One such procedure is described below.

1. Convert each character into its eight-bit EBCDIC code (see Appendix B). For example, the symbol ASSEMBLE is converted into C1E2E2C5D4C2D3C5 in hexadecimal.

2. Add two successive four-byte sections together into a register and call the contents S. Thus

$$
\begin{array}{r}
\texttt{C1E2E2C5} \\
+ \quad \texttt{D4C2D3C5} \\
\hline
①\texttt{96A5B68A}
\end{array}
$$

Ignored

3. Find S mod 211. Or, divide S by 211 and obtain the remainder R. If R is a negative integer, add 211 to it. Example:

$$(96A5B68A)_{16} \bmod 211 \qquad \text{yields} \qquad R = 109$$

This means that, among the 211 locations in the symbol table, ASSEMBLE is to be placed in the 109th location. The value R is also known as *hash code*.

4a. If you wish to insert a symbol into the symbol table, and if the location is not previously occupied, simply insert it in the location.

4b. If you wish to insert a symbol into the table, and if the location is already taken by some other symbol, check the next locations sequentially until a free one is found. Insert the symbol into this free location.

4c. If you search for a symbol in the symbol table, you may find it at the location specified by the hash code. If it is not there, search the subsequent locations sequentially until the required symbol is found.

To implement the first three steps described above, let us assume that the contents in registers 5 and 6 are, respectively, C1E2E2C5 and D4C2D3C5 initially. The following program segment can then be used:

```
AR   5,6
M    4,=F'1'
D    4,=F'211'
```

The M instruction is used to propagate the sign bit of register 5 into register 4. As a result, the contents of register 4 are now either all 0's or all 1's depending on whether the sum (in register 5) is positive or negative. This is necessary before a Divide instruction is written. Otherwise, the contents in register 4 (used as the most significant part of the dividend) may be a piece of garbage. After the division, the remainder is in register 4. If the remainder is a positive value, it is then the required hash code. If this is a negative number, add 211 to it for the hash code.

3.11 EVALUATION OF A SIMPLE EXPRESSION

In this chapter, a total of 11 instructions dealing with arithmetic operations has been introduced so far. We are now in a position to write some simple instruction sequences.
Consider first the evaluation of the following expression:

$$ANS = ((A + B - C) \times E)/F.$$

We assume that the values of A, B, C, and F are already loaded† into registers 5, 7, 8, and 9, respectively, and that the value of E takes a fullword in main storage. At the risk of causing some confusion, let us call the address of this fullword also E. This symbolic address may be calculated from Eq. (3.2).
The following instructions carry out the necessary evaluation:

After the operation

AR	5,7	$(A + B)$ in reg. 5
SR	5,8	$(A + B - C)$ in reg. 5
M	4,E	$(A + B - C) \times E$ in reg. 4 and 5
DR	4,9	ANS in reg. 5 and the remainder in reg. 4

The corresponding instructions in machine language, as represented in hexadecimal, are as follows:

1A57

1B58

5C403078

1D49

In the third instruction, we assumed that a) register 3 is used as the base register; b) no index is involved; and c) displacement = $(078)_{16}$.
As second example, suppose that the register contents in hexadecimal are as follows:

Register 9:	0000005E
Register 11:	000001C2
Register 12:	0000002D
Register 14:	00000004
Register 15:	FFFFFFF6

---

† How to load a number into a register will be discussed in Section 4.2.

and partial program is given:

$$
\begin{array}{ll}
\text{AR} & 9,11 \\
\text{SR} & 9,12 \\
\text{M} & 8,200(0,14) \\
\text{DR} & 8,15
\end{array}
$$

The partial storage map is

0203	0204	0205	0206	0207	0208	0209	0210	◀—— Address in
A6	02	00	00	00	02	FF	F2	*decimal*

It is required to find the contents of each register used in the program after the execution of the DR instruction.

Solution

After the execution of the AR 9,11 instruction, the following result is accomplished:

$$
\begin{array}{rl}
& \text{0000005E} \\
+ \ & \text{000001C2} \qquad \text{Remains in register 11} \\
\hline
& \text{00000220} \qquad \text{Stored in register 9}
\end{array}
$$

After the execution of SR 9,12 instruction, we obtain

$$
\begin{array}{rl}
& \text{00000220} \\
- \ & \text{0000002D} \qquad \text{In register 12} \\
\hline
& \text{000001F3} \qquad \text{In register 9}
\end{array}
$$

In the instruction M 8,200(0,14) the multiplicand is in register 9; and the effective address of the fullword in main storage is as follows:

$$
\begin{array}{r}
\text{00000004} \\
\text{00000000} \\
\text{0C8} \quad + \\
\hline
\text{0000CC}
\end{array}
$$

or $(204)_{10}$. The product is stored in both registers 8 and 9 as follows:

$$
\begin{array}{rl}
& \text{000001F3} \\
& \text{02000000} \quad \times \\
\hline
\text{00000003} \quad & \text{E6000000} \\
\text{Register 8} \quad & \text{Register 9}
\end{array}
$$

The instruction DR 8,15 divides the contents in both registers 8 and 9 by FFFFFFF6, the contents of register 15. This divisor is a negative number $(-10)_{10}$ as can be seen from taking its complement.

$$
\begin{array}{r}
\text{FFFFFFFF} \\
- \quad \text{FFFFFFF6} \\
\hline
00000009 \\
+ \qquad 1 \\
\hline
-A = (-10)_{10}
\end{array}
$$

Disregarding this negative sign temporarily, the quotient can be found as follows:

```
                    63CCCCCC
               A⟌3E6000000
                    3C
                   ─────
                    26
                    1E
                   ─────
                     80
                     78
                    ────
                     80
                     78
                    ────
                      80
                      78
                     ────
                      80
                      78
                     ────
                       80
                       78
                      ────
                       80
                       78
                      ────
                        8 = Remainder
```

The complement of 63CCCCCC is 9C333334, which is stored in register 9. The remainder 8 is stored in register 8.

In summary, after the execution of the DR instruction, each register used in the program has the following contents:

Register 8:	00000008
Register 9:	9C333334
Register 11:	000001C2
Register 12:	0000002D
Register 14:	00000004
Register 15:	FFFFFFF6

We conclude this chapter by a short comment on main storage address for an instruction of RX format. As mentioned before, the basic form of this address is $D2(X2,B2)$. An example is 4(10,11) in the following Add instruction:

$$A \quad 7,4(10,11)$$

This explicit address form is sometimes not used. Rather, an implicit form is written such as RATE(10) in the following instruction:

$$A \quad 7,RATE(10)$$

where RATE represents symbolically the base address B plus the displacement D.

If register 0 is used as the index register $X2$ (meaning that the index $X = 0$), one can replace the main storage address $D2(0,B2)$ simply with $D2(,B2)$. An example is 4(,11) in the instruction:

$$A \ 7,4(,11)$$

This instruction can also be written as

$$A \quad 7,RATE1$$

where RATE1 stands for displacement (4) plus the contents in base register 11.

Generally speaking, the explicit forms of main storage address in instructions of RX type have corresponding implicit forms as follows:

Explicit form	Implicit form
$D2(X2,B2)$	$S2(X2)$
$D2(0,B2)$ same as $D2(,B2)$	$S2$

Examples

Instruction using explicit form for the second operand		Corresponding instruction using implict form for the second operand
A 9,476(5,8)		A 9,VALUE(5)
	or	A 9,PLACE+4(5)
	or	A 9,HERE
M 2,280(0,11)		
or M 2,280(,11)		M 2,RATE2
M 8,200(0,14)		
or M 8,200(,14)		M 8,LOC1

Note that (1) PLACE+4 has the same value as VALUE; (2) HERE represents the same address as VALUE plus the contents of register 5; (3) RATE2 is equal to 280 plus the base address in register 11; and (4) LOC1 = 200 plus the contents in register 14.

3.12 SUMMARY

1. In the IBM System/370 or System/360 machine instructions use five different formats: RR, RX, RS, SI, and SS. All arithmetic instructions dealing with binary integers are of RR and RX formats.

2. RR denotes a register to register operation. A typical example is an Add Register (AR) instruction which adds the second operand to the first operand, both in registers, or

$$R1 \leftarrow C(R1) + C(R2),$$

and the contents in *R2* are not disturbed.

3. RX denotes a register and an indexed storage operation. A typical example is an Add (A) instruction which adds the second operand (a fullword in main storage) to the first operand (in a register).

$$R1 = C(R1) + C(S2).$$

4. The effective address *E* of the second operand in instructions of RX type is computed from

$$E = B + D + X$$

where *B* is base address, *X* is index, and *D* is displacement. *B* and *X* are contained in registers. This 24-bit effective address for a fullword must be exactly divisible by 4. For a halfword, it must be divisible by 2.

5. The advantages of the base-index-displacement method to calculate the effective address of a storage operand are: (a) It uses only 20 bits in RX-type instructions to represent a 24-bit address. (b) Program relocation.

6. The Multiply Register (MR) instruction is of RR type, but it has its own peculiarities: (a) An even–odd pair of registers is always used to hold the 64-bit product. The 32-bit multiplicand is originally in the odd-numbered register. (b) A third register is used to contain the 32-bit multiplier. (c) The even-numbered register holds the most significant part of the product; the odd-numbered register holds the least significant part.

$$[R1, R1 + 1] \leftarrow C(R1 + 1) \times C(R2), \qquad R1 = \text{an even integer.}$$

7. The Multiply (M) instruction is of RX type. The 32-bit multiplicand is originally contained in an odd-numbered (*R1* + 1) register. The product is stored in an even–odd pair of registers *R1* and *R1* + 1. The 32-bit multiplier is originally in main storage; its address can be calculated by means of base-index-displacement method.

$$[R1, R1 + 1] \leftarrow C(R1 + 1) \times C(S2).$$

8. The 64-bit dividend using D or DR instruction is in even–odd register pair (register numbers *R1* and *R1* + 1), which is addressed by *R1*, an even number. The remainder is left in register *R1*, and the quotient in register *R1* + 1. The signs of remainder and quotient follow the rules in Table 3.2.

9. Remainder plays an important role in the congruence arithmetic.

BIBLIOGRAPHY

IBM System/370 Principles of Operations, Form GA22–7000, IBM Corp.

IBM System/360 Principles of Operations, Form GA22–6821, IBM Corp.

Winograd, S., "How Fast Can Computers Add?" *Scient. Am.* **219**, 93–100 (Oct. 1968).

Winograd, S., "On the Time Required to Perform Multiplication," *J. of Assoc. Computing Machinery* **14**, 793–802 (1967).

Random Number Generator

Knuth, D. F., *Seminumerical Algorithms*, Vol. 2, Chapter 3, Addison-Wesley, Reading, Mass., 1969.

Kuo, S. S., *Computer Applications of Numerical Methods*, Chapter 14, Addison-Wesley, Reading, Mass., 1972.

P. A. W. Lewis, A. S. Goodman, and J. M. Miller, "A Pseudo-Random Number Generator for the System/360," *IBM Systems J.* **8** (2), 136–146 (1969).

G. Marsaglia, "Random Numbers Fall Mainly in the Planes," *Proceedings of the National Academy of Sciences* **61** (2), 25–28 (1968).

J. R. B. Whittlesey, "A Comparison of the Correlational Behavior of Random Number Generators for the IBM System/360," *Communications of the ACM* **11** (9), 641–644 (1968).

Hashing

Heising, W. P., "Note on Random Addressing Techniques," *IBM Systems J.* **2**, 112–116 (June 1963).

Maurer, W. D., "An Improved Hash Code for Scatter Storage," *CACM* **11** (1), 35–38, (Jan. 1968).

Morris, Robert, "Scatter Storage Techniques," *CACM* **11** (1), 38–44 (Jan. 1968).

Peterson, W. W., "Addressing for Random Access Storage," *IBM J. of Research and Development* **1** (2), 130–146 (April 1957).

PROBLEMS

Section 3.2

3.1. The numbers stored in registers 7 and 13 are to be added and the result is to be stored in register 13. Write the binary, its hexadecimal, and the symbolic representations of this instruction.

3.2. a) How many bits are there in the operation code?
   b) Explain the significance when the bit positions 0 and 1 in an instruction contain 1 and 0, respectively.

3.3. Translate the following machine-language instructions to assembler-language instructions (in symbolic form).
   a) 0001101011001010 in binary
   b) 1A29 in hexadecimal.

Section 3.4

3.4. Find the effective address E (in hexadecimal) of a fullword in main storage if the displacement $D = (256)_{10}$, the base register 6 contains the base address $B = (4096)_{10}$, and the index register number is zero. Does this effective address satisfy the requirement of fullword boundary alignment?

3.5. If the effective address of a halfword is $E = $ 001A0C, index $X = $ 00000004, and the displacement $D = $ 2BC, what are the rightmost 24-bit contents in the base register expressed in hexadecimal?

Section 3.5

3.6. Given: Contents in register 5 = 0000021A
Partial memory map:

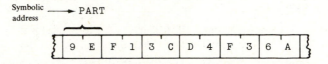

Find: Contents in register 5 after the execution of the instruction A 5,PART.

Section 3.6

3.7. Translate each of the following instructions in symbolic form (assembler language) to its machine language representation in hexadecimal:

$$AH \quad 7,256(0,6)$$
$$AR \quad 9,6$$
$$A \quad 9,256(4,7)$$

3.8. Translate each of the following machine language instructions to its assembler language instruction:

a) 0100010101010010100100100000010010 in binary

b) 4A100064 in hexadecimal.

3.9. The initial contents of registers and storage locations are as follows:

Register 4:   0000001C
Register 5:   00000002
Register 7:   FFFFFFF6
Register 10:   0000000A
Register 11:   0000A02D
Storage location I: 03A041BF
Storage location J: 003002AC

Fill out the blanks below:

Instruction	Sum is left in register	Sum
AR 7,4	7	00000012
AR 4,7	_____	_____
A 4,=F'64'	_____	_____

```
A    7,=F'256'        _____    _____
A    11,I             _____    _____
A    7,J              _____    _____
AH   11,I             _____    _____
AH   4,I+2                 4                  000041DB
AH   4,J+2            _____    _____
```
(*Note:* I+2 means the address of I plus 2 bytes.)

Section 3.7

3.10. The initial contents of registers and storage locations are the same as in Problem 3.9. Fill out the blanks below.

Instruction	Difference is left in register	Difference
SR 7,4	_____	_____
SR 4,7	_____	_____
SH 10,I+2	_____	_____
SH 4,J	_____	_____
S 4,J	_____	_____
S 7,=F'80'	_____	_____
S 10,=F'4096'	_____	_____

Section 3.8

3.11. The initial contents of registers and storage locations are same as in Problem 3.9. Fill out the blanks below.

Instruction	Product in registers	Products
MR 4,11	4,5	00000000 0001405A
MR 10,5	_____	_____
M 4,=F'3'	_____	_____
M 6,=F'-2'	_____	_____

3.12. The Multiply Halfword (MH) instruction is of RX type. It is used to multiply the first operand (fullword) in register *R1* by a halfword in main storage. Generally speaking, the product has 48 bits. But only the rightmost 32 bits of the product are left in the register *R1*. Suppose that the contents of register 4 are 0000003A, and these at location W are 0002 (a halfword). Write out the contents of register 4 after the execution of following instruction:

$$\text{MH} \quad 4,W$$

Section 3.9

3.13. Translate the following instructions from assembler language to machine language. Express them in hexadecimal.

```
M    6,916(0,12)
DR   6,9
D    6,916(0,12)
```

3.14. Given: Contents in registers:

$$\begin{array}{lll}
\text{Register} & 6: & \texttt{00000000} \\
\text{Register} & 7: & \texttt{000F9C10} \\
\text{Register} & 9: & \texttt{00000002} \\
\text{Register} & 12: & \texttt{00000010}
\end{array}$$

Partial storage map:

FF	FF	A2	A3	3C	BA	A6	1C

Address in *decimal*:   929   930   936

Required: The hexadecimal representation of contents in registers 6 and 7 after the execution of each instruction in Problem 3.13.

Section 3.10

3.15. Find the hash code for the symbol ROTATION. Use the procedure proposed in Section 3.10.

3.16. A popular error-detection method of input errors is the use of *check digits*, especially suitable for account or part numbers. A simple algorithm is as follows: Take a weighted sum of the individual digits and divide it by an integer. The remainder is the check digit. For example, a modulo 11 check digit, with weights 3, 2, and 5 for a 3-digit number, may be used for the part number 716:

$$3 \times 7 + 2 \times 1 + 5 \times 6 = 53,$$

$$\frac{53}{11} = 4\frac{9}{11}.$$

Thus the remainder 9 is obtained, and the part number as used would be 7169. Write a program segment to obtain the check digit for a three-digit number

$$X \cdot 10^2 + Y \cdot 10 + Z.$$

Use the symbols WX, WY, and WZ for the weights, M as modulus, and X, Y, and Z for original values.

Section 3.11

3.17. The sum $x = \sum_{i=1}^{4} c_i y^i$ can be obtained by the following algorithm using a minimal number of operations:

$$x = y\{c_1 + y[c_2 + y(c_3 + yc_4)]\}.$$

The computation is carried out from the inside out, or from yc_4. Write a program segment to calculate x. Assume that c_1, c_2, c_3, and c_4 are at the storage location C1, C1 + 4, C1 + 8, and C1 + 12, respectively, and that y is in register 6. State clearly where x-value is held.

LABORATORY ASSIGNMENT

1. Draw a detailed flowchart for the program shown in the assembly listing (Fig. 3.18).
   Keypunch the program and the required job control cards; submit to your installation
   for a run. (Don't keypunch the statements 23 through 29; 33 and 34.)

```
LOC    OBJECT CODE    ADDR1 ADDR2  STMT    SOURCE STATEMENT

000000 05B0                          1 BEGIN    BALR  11,0          DEFINE BASE REGISTER
000002                               2          USING *,11
                                     3 *
                                     4 * THE FOLLOWING INSTRUCTION COPIES THE FIRST
                                     5 *  HALF OF ASSEMBLE INTO REGISTER 5
                                     6 *
000002 5850 802A          0002C      7          L     5,WORD
                                     8 *
                                     9 * THE FOLLOWING INSTRUCTION ADDS THE SECOND PART
                                    10 *  OF ASSEMBLE TO ITS FIRST PART
                                    11 *
000006 5A50 802E          00030     12          A     5,WORD+4
                                    13 *
                                    14 * THE FOLLOWING INSTRUCTION EXTENDS THE SIGN BIT
                                    15 *
00000A 5C40 8036          00038     16          M     4,=F'1'
00000E 5D40 803A          0003C     17          D     4,=F'211'     DIVIDE SUM BY 211
                                    18 *
                                    19 * THE FOLLOWING INSTRUCTION PUTS REMAINDER IN ANS
                                    20 *
000012 5040 B026          00028     21          ST    4,ANS
                                    22          ABEND 777,DUMP          DUMP
000016                             23+          DS    0H
000016 0700                        24+          CNOP  0,4
000018 47F0 B01E          00020    25+          B     *+8 BRANCH AROUND CONSTANT
00001C 80                          26+          DC    AL1(128) DUMP/STEP CODE
00001D 000309                      27+          DC    AL3(777) COMPLETION CODE
000020 5810 B01A          0001C    28+          L     1,*-4 LOAD CODES INTO REG 1
000024 0A0D                        29+          SVC   13 LINK TO ABEND ROUTINE
000028                             30 ANS       DS    F
00002C C1E2E2C5404C2D3C5           31 WORD      DC    CL8'ASSEMBLE'
000000                             32          END BEGIN
000038 00000001                    33          =F'1'
00003C 000000D3                    34          =F'211'
```

Fig. 3.18   An assembly listing.

2. After the execution of the program, find out the contents in register 5, in register 11,
   and in the fullword ANS. What are these contents if you replace the statement 12 by the
   following instruction

$$AL \quad 5,WORD+4 ?$$

CHAPTER 4

Five Most Common Instructions

4.1 INTRODUCTION

In the previous chapter, we learned various Add, Subtract, Multiply, and Divide instructions for binary integers; they are of RR and RX formats. In this chapter, we shall explore the assembler instructions of most frequent occurrence. To determine which instructions enjoy extensive usage is not as easy as it seems. First, the instruction distribution depends heavily on the job classifications—whether it is scientific, mixed, commercial, or a compiler. Second, although these results come from some typical examples, they are not necessarily representative of all possible applications in each job category.

In this chapter, we shall explore the usage of the following five instructions which are most often used:

> L: Load a register from a fullword in main storage.
> ST: Store the contents of a register in a fullword in main storage.
> LA: Load Address, or load a register with a given number.
> C: Compare.
> BC: Branch on Condition.

They are selected because they are widely applied in all job classifications. It is interesting to note that these five instructions are all of RX format. The Program Status Word (PSW) is closely related to some of them and is used to control the path along which the program is to be executed. The PSW is a special doubleword register. The information in bit positions 34 and 35, and in bit positions 40 through 63 will be explained in Section 4.5.

4.2 LOAD A REGISTER FROM A FULLWORD IN MAIN STORAGE—L

The load instruction (L)—probably the most common instruction used in all types of jobs—copies the contents of a fullword (four bytes) from the main storage into a register. It is of RX format: The first operand is positioned in a register number $R1$, and the second operand, in main storage, whose effective address can be calculated by the base-index-displacement method as expressed in Eq. (3.2). Consider, for example, the instruction in Fig. 4.1. After the execution of this instruction, the contents of a fullword are loaded in register 3. If the base address B is assumed as 00908C, the effective address E of this fullword can be readily computed as follows:

$$
\begin{array}{rll}
B \text{ in register } 9: & \text{00908C} & \text{in hexadecimal} \\
X: & 0 & \\
D: & \text{074} & \text{in hexadecimal} \\
\hline
\text{Effective address } E: & \text{009100} &
\end{array}
$$

For an IBM System/360, this effective address must be on a fullword boundary, that is, it must be divisible by 4.

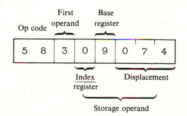

Fig. 4.1   RX format for a Load (L) instruction. [*Note:* $(074)_{16} = (116)_{10}$]

We can write the instruction shown in Fig. 4.1 in assembler language as follows:

L   3,116(0,9)

or simply

L   3,116(,9)

Two variants of this instruction are of practical importance. First, if the effective address of the second operand (the fullword in main storage) is represented by a symbol, say, SALE, then the assembler language instruction can be written as

L   3,SALE

Second, the *contents* of the second operand, say, $(21)_{10}$ may be directly written in the L instruction by using a literal:

L   3,=F'21'

The prefix F stands for a fullword binary integer constant, whose value (in decimal)

is enclosed in apostrophes. The effective address of this fullword constant, in the base-index-displacement form, is automatically coded as the second operand in the machine language equivalent. After the execution of this L instruction using a literal, the 32-bit contents of register 3 become

$$00000000 \quad 00000000 \quad 00000000 \quad 00010101$$

4.3 STORE REGISTER CONTENTS
INTO A FULLWORD IN MAIN STORAGE—ST

In the previous section, we discussed how to transfer the contents of a fullword in the main storage to a given register by using a Load (L) instruction. We shall now deal with this transfer problem from the opposite direction. Specifically, we shall consider what instruction one can use to transfer this fullword from register 3 to a given symbolic address, say, SALE in the main storage. This can be done by the following STore (ST) instruction:

$$\text{ST} \quad 3,\text{SALE}$$

After the execution of this instruction, the contents of register 3 are moved to the four consecutive bytes in main storage; the symbolic address of the first byte is SALE.

In its basic form, the effective address of the second operand is expressed in terms of B, D, and X, as discussed in Section 3.4. For example, the following instruction

$$\text{ST} \quad 13,276(10,4)$$

moves the contents of register 13 (a fullword) to a fullword in main storage whose effective address E can be computed as follows:

B (contents in base register 4)	0000684C	(assumed)
X (contents in index register 10)	00000004	(assumed)
D (displacement)	114	
E (effective address of second operand)	006964	

where $(114)_{16} = (276)_{10}$.

As a review, the arithmetic statements in FORTRAN or PL/I and the corresponding sequences in assembler language are listed in Table 4.1.

The comparison between a statement in high-level language and its corresponding instructions in assembler language shows some striking differences.

a) It takes several assembler language instructions for one simple FORTRAN or PL/I statement.

b) For a programmer using high-level language, the difference between the contents of a variable and the address of this variable is not significant. Thus in the FORTRAN statement

$$I = I + 1$$

Table 4.1 Corresponding arithmetic statements in FORTRAN (or PL/I) and in assembler language

FORTRAN or PL/I	Assembler language
I = I + J	L 3,I A 3,J ST 3,I
K = I + J	L 6,AI A 6,BJ ST 6,CK
K = I − J	L 7,I S 7,J ST 7,K
N = (I+J) * 4	L 7,I A 7,J M 6,=F'4' ST 7,N LOW−ORDER 32−BIT ANSWER ONLY
I = J/4	**** J ASSUMED (+) L 7,JPLUS L 6,=F'0' D 6,=F'4' ST 7,ZI **** J ASSUMED (−) L 11,JMINUS L 7,=F'4' L 10,=F'−1' DR 10,7 ST 11,I **** J PLUS OR MINUS L 5,J M 4,=F'1' PROPAGATE SIGN D 4,=F'4' ST 5,I **** J PLUS OR MINUS L 4,J SRDA 4,32(4) DISCUSSED IN D 4,=F'4' SECTION 7.2. ST 5,I
K(I+1) = K(I) + 5	L 9,K A 9,=F'5' ST 9,K+4

I is often interpreted by a beginner as the contents of the variable I. However, for a programmer using assembler language, the difference between the contents of I, or C(I) and the address of I is too important to be ignored. Thus in the instruction

A   4,I

I stands for the symbolic address of the fullword operand in main storage.

c) In FORTRAN, the names of variables which take on fixed-point values must start with I, J, K, L, M, or N, unless otherwise specified. In assembler language, there is no such restriction.

d) In FORTRAN, each variable takes a fullword, unless double precision is declared. In assembler language, the length of an operand is implicitly defined in the instruction format.

e) The memory unit used in a FORTRAN statement is in words. For example, K(I+1) is one word away from K(I). In assembler language, the memory unit is in bytes. Thus, the symbolic address K+4 is 4 bytes away from the symbolic address K.

4.4 LOAD AN ADDRESS INTO A REGISTER—LA

The Load Address (LA) instruction is a powerful one to move a piece of data into a register. Its general format is shown in Fig. 4.2. Despite the fact that it is of RX format, it does *not* retrieve any data from main storage. Rather, it loads the 24-bit address of the second operand into the rightmost 24 bits of the register number $R1$; bit positions 0 through 8 in the register $R1$ are automatically set to zeros.

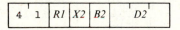

Fig. 4.2   LA instruction of RX format: LA $R1, D2(X2, B2)$.

The applications of LA instructions are numerous. We shall list some important ones below together with illustrative examples.

1. To zero a register

Each of the following two instructions clears register 7:

LA   7,0(0,0)

or

LA   7,0

2. To initialize a variable

The following LA instruction loads $(10)_{10}$ into register 9, perhaps used as a counter:

LA   9,10

The number must be between 0 and $(2^{12} - 1) = (4095)_{10}$. The actual machine language instruction as constructed by the assembler is

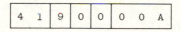

4	1	9	0	0	0	0	A

3. To increment a register

The contents of a register (1, 2, ..., 15) can be incremented by the displacement specified in an LA instruction. For example, each of the following instructions

$$\text{LA} \quad 5,4(5) \qquad \text{B2=0}$$

or

$$\text{LA} \quad 5,4(5,0) \qquad \text{B2=0}$$

or

$$\text{LA} \quad 5,4(0,5) \qquad \text{X2=0}$$

increments the contents of registers 5 by 4. If the initial contents of register 5 represent the symbolic address FIRST, then the new contents will be FIRST+4 (probably the address of the next fullword).

Secondly, we can use the following LA instructions to set I=0, and then update I=1:

```
LA   9,0        SET I=0
LA   9,1(9)     ADD 1 TO I
```

Thirdly, when we wish to evaluate the expression I = (I+2)*J, where I and J are two positive, small integers, we write the following four instructions to carry out this operation:

```
L    7,I
LA   7,2(7)
M    6,J
ST   7,I
```

In order to be able to distinguish clearly between the LA and L instructions, let us compare the following two instructions, assuming the base register 5 contains 00000F1A:

```
LA   13,446(0,5)
L    13,446(0,5)
```

After the execution of the first instruction, the value $(0010D8)_{16} = (000F1A+1BE)$ is loaded into register 13. Note that $(446)_{10} = (1BE)_{16}$. But the second instruction loads the contents of the fullword into register 13. The address of the fullword is 0010D8.

Before we turn to the next section, let us examine the usage of many instructions discussed so far by considering an array K whose dimension is $M \times N$. A special case of a 4×3 array is shown in Fig. 4.3(b). In most FORTRAN compilers, this array is translated as a linear list shown in Fig. 4.3(a). A program segment has to be written to store the address of the element K(IROW,ICOL) of the M × N array K into register 8, and the contents of the same element in register 11. Assume that

a) Each element takes four bytes.

b) The symbolic address of element K(1,1) is called HERE.

c) Total number of rows M is held in register 10.

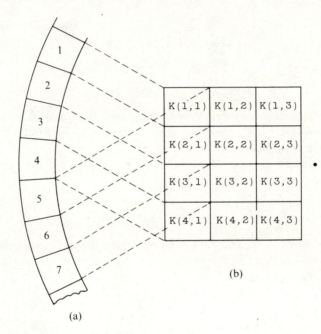

Fig. 4.3 Array K. (a) Order as a linear list. (b) 4 × 3 array.

A possible program segment is shown below.

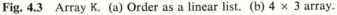

```
L    7,ICOL
A    7,=F'-1'          GET ICOL-1
MR   6,10              (ICOL-1)*M
A    7,IROW
S    7,=F'1'           GET IROW-1
M    6,=F'4'           4 BYTES PER ELEMENT
LA   8,HERE(7)         ADDRESS OF K(IROW,ICOL) IN REGISTER 8
L    11,0(8)           CONTENTS OF K(IROW,ICOL) IN REGISTER 11
```

Note that the total number of column N is not involved in these instructions.

4.5 PROGRAM STATUS WORD, CONDITION CODE, AND COMPARE INSTRUCTIONS

This and next section deal with the implementation—in assembler language—of a decision box used in a flowchart. Such box as shown in Fig. 4.4 can be expressed in the following words: Compare the value of $I - J$ with zero. If it is greater or equal to zero, go to α; otherwise, go to β.

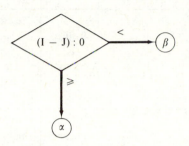

Fig. 4.4 A decision box.

Before we start discussing the instructions needed to implement this decision box, we have to introduce the concept of the program status word (PSW). The PSW is a special doubleword register, which indicates the status of the "current" program being run.

For our discussion, let us consider only the information in bit positions 34 and 35, and in bit positions 40 through 63, as shaded in Fig. 4.5. The bit positions 34 and 35 are used jointly as the condition code (CC), while the positions 40 through 63 form the 24-bit *instruction address* field, in which the address of the next instruction to be executed is stored.

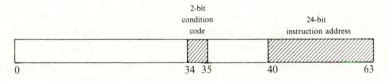

Fig. 4.5 PSW is a special doubleword register.

Condition Code

The sole purpose of the condition code is to decide whether or not a conditional branch will take place. Since condition code field comprises two bits, it has only four possible binary configurations: 00, 01, 10, and 11. The condition code is automatically set as a result of one of the many instructions. A programmer can also set the condition code by writing one of the many Compare instructions.

After the execution of each of a number of instructions, particularly of the arithmetic ones, the condition code is automatically set. Its value depends on the result

Table 4.2 Condition code settings resulting from the execution of instructions discussed in Chapters 3 and 4

Instruction		Condition code setting			
	Binary	00	01	10	11
	Decimal	0	1	2	3
Add A Add Halfword AH Add Register AR Subtract S Subtract Halfword SH Subtract Register SR		Result is zero	Result is less than zero	Result is greater than zero	Overflow
Compare C Compare Halfword CH Compare Register CR		First operand is equal to second operand	First operand is less than second operand (First operand is low)	First operand is greater than second operand (First operand is high)	—
Load Positive Register LPR		Result is zero	—	Result is greater than zero	Overflow

of the operation. For example, when two positive numbers are added by using an AR, A, or AH instruction, the condition code is automatically set to 10. Table 4.2 shows four possible condition code settings after the execution of instructions covered in Chapters 3 and 4. In general, if the result of such an instruction is positive (excluding zero), the CC is automatically set to 10. If the result is negative, the CC is set to 01. If the result is zero, the CC is set to 00. Finally, if the result is in an overflow condition—greater than $2^{31} - 1$ or less than -2^{31}—then the condition code is set to 11; the overflow bit is lost.

Forced Setting of CC by Using Compare Instructions

A programmer can set a condition code (CC) by writing any one of the following Compare instructions:

CR	*R1,R2*	RR format
C	*R1,D2(X2,B2)*	RX format
CH	*R1,D2(X2,B2)*	RX format

The contents in register $R1$ are compared with the second operand. In CR instruction this second operand is in register $R2$. In both C and CH instructions, the second operand is in the main storage: fullword for C instruction and halfword for CH instruction. For example, the instruction

C   3,ZERO

compares the contents of register 3 with the contents at symbolic address ZERO (a fullword), and sets the condition code in accordance with Table 4.2. Suppose the contents in register 3 and these in the storage operand, respectively, are 00000027 (decimal 39) and FFFFFFB6 (decimal -74), then the first operand is greater than the second one. As a result, the value of CC is set to 10. Note that the condition code setting (as a result of a Compare instruction) reflects the status of the first operand.

During the execution of a Compare Halfword (CH) instruction, the contents of a register (the first operand) are compared with the contents of a fullword. This fullword is the result of sign extension of the given halfword in main storage. The sign extension was discussed in Section 2.8.

We should point out that there is a large number of instructions which do not set the condition code. After the execution of such an instruction the CC remains unchanged. In Table 4.3, such instructions, as discussed in Chapters 3 and 4, are listed. Note that they include most common instructions, such as Multiply, Divide, Load, and STore instructions.

Table 4.3 Instructions (discussed in Chapters 3 and 4) which do not set condition code

	Instruction	Chapter and section reference
BC	Branch on Condition	4.6
BCR	Branch on Condition to Register	4.6
BCT	Branch on Count	4.7
D	Divide	3.9
DR	Divide Register	3.9
L	Load	4.2
LA	Load Address	4.4
LH	Load Halfword	4.2 (Problem 4.5)
LR	Load Register	4.2 (Problem 4.4)
M	Multiply	3.8
MH	Multiply Halfword	3.8 (Problem 3.12)
MR	Multiply Register	3.8
ST	STore	4.3
STH	STore Halfword	4.3 (Problem 4.7)

4.6 BRANCH ON CONDITION—BC

In the previous section, we have learned how the value of condition code is set. First, it is automatically set as a result of one of the many arithmetic instructions listed in Table 4.2. Then it may be set by means of a Compare instruction: CR, C, or CH. Once the setting of CC is accomplished, a programmer usually writes a Branch on Condition (BC) instruction; this completes the assembler language implementation of the decision box in Fig. 4.4.

Basically, the Branch on Condition (BC) instruction examines the condition code (CC) in the PSW and compares it with a coded number specified in the *mask field* (bit positions 8 through 11) of the BC instruction. (See Fig. 4.6.) If the CC setting and the mask agree, a branch takes place to a branch-to address specified in the BC instruction. On the other hand, if they do not agree, next sequential instruction is executed.

M1 X2 B2   D2

4	7	4	0	8	1	0	0

Branch on   mask   "Branch-to" address
condition   field

Fig. 4.6 RX format for Branch on Condition instruction: BC 4,256(0,8).

Although the BC instruction is of RX format, it has at least two peculiarities: First, the first operand address is *not* a register number $R1$. Rather, it becomes the mask field $M1$. Second, the second operand address becomes the branch-to address. It must be the address of *another instruction* and cannot be the address of a piece of data.

Let us examine closely the BC instruction in Fig. 4.6. The execution of this instruction consists of the following steps.

1. Test the value in the mask field against the CC in the PSW. The test is rather simple, basically using the matching table as shown in Table 4.4. For instance, if the current CC is 01 and the mask field contains a 1 in bit position 9, then a match is made. Note that the mask field in Fig. 4.6 contains 4 in hexadecimal, or 0100 in binary.

Table 4.4 Relationship between mask field in an instruction and the condition code

Mask field				Condition code (CC)
Bit position 8	9	10	11	
1	0	0	0	00
0	1	0	0	01
0	0	1	0	10
0	0	0	1	11

2. If a match is made, (a) the branch-to address specified in this BC instruction replaces the 24-bit instruction address field, bits 40–63, in PSW (see Fig. 4.5). Assum-

ing the contents in base register 8 are 0000A200, then the branch-to address in Fig. 4.6 is 00A300. (b) The branch takes place.

3. If a match is not made, (a) the address of the next sequential instruction replaces the 24-bit instruction address field in PSW. This address is computed as follows:

The address of the BC instruction: 000A08 (say)
Length of the BC instruction: 4 bytes
The address of the next instruction: 000A0C

(b) Go to the next instruction.

In the mask field, any one of the four-bit positions may have 1. For example, if the mask field has the following bit configuration:

1   0   1   1

then a branch will occur when CC has *any* one of the following three-bit patterns:

00, 10, or 11

This is known as multiple checking of condition codes.

As a second example for the multiple checking of CC, let us assume the mask field has all 1's in its four bits, or

1   1   1   1

Here, a branch occurs regardless of the condition code. It is, in fact, an unconditional branch.

Mask and CC Expressed in Decimal

In Table 4.4, the relationship between the mask field $M1$ and the values of CC is expressed in binary. In practice, the contents in $M1$ field and the value of CC are often written in decimal. The matching table now becomes

Condition code   0   1   2   3
Mask field   8   4   2   1

For example, the instruction

BC   4,HERE

causes a branch to the *instruction* whose symbolic address is HERE if the condition code is 1 (meaning 01 in binary). The branch will not be taken if CC is 0, 2, or 3 (meaning 00, 10, or 11 in binary).

When multiple checking of CC is needed, the contents in mask field are often written in decimal. For instance, if we wish to check whether the value of CC is 1 *or* 2.

Table 4.5 Matching table for mask, condition codes, and results

(1) Machine instruction	(2) Mask in branch instruction — Decimal	(2) Binary	(3) Condition Codes (in decimal) causing branch	(4) After Compare instruction ($A:B$)	(5) After arithmetic instruction (A = first operand; B = second operand)	(6) Instruction	(6) Meaning
BC 15, $D2(X2,B2)$	15	1111	0,1,2,3	All	All	B $D2(X2,B2)$	Unconditional branch
BCR 15, $R2$	15	1111	0,1,2,3	All	All	BR $R2$	Unconditional branch
BC 0, $D2(X2,B2)$	0	0000	None	None	None	NOP $D2(X2,B2)$	No operation
BCR 0, $R2$	0	0000	None	None	None	NOPR $R2$	No operation
BC 2, $S2$	2	0010	2	$A > B$	$A > B$	BH $S2$	Branch on A high
BC 4, $S2$	4	0100	1	$A < B$	$A < B$	BL $S2$	Branch on A low
BC 6, $S2$	6	0110	1,2	$A \neq B$	$A \neq B$	—	—
BC 8, $S2$	8	1000	0	$A = B$	$A = B$	BE $S2$	Branch on A equal B
BC 10, $S2$	10	1010	0,2	$A \geq B$	$A \geq B$	—	—
BC 12, $S2$	12	1100	0,1	$A \leq B$	$A \leq B$ *(No overflow and)*	—	—
BC 14, $S2$	14	1110	0,1,2	All	(No overflow only)	—	—
BC 1, $S2$	1	0001	3	None	(Overflow only)	—	—
BC 3, $S2$	3	0011	2,3	$A > B$	$A > B$	—	—
BC 5, $S2$	5	0101	1,3	$A < B$	$A < B$	—	—
BC 7, $S2$	7	0111	1,2,3	$A \neq B$	$A \neq B$ *(Overflow or)*	BNE $S2$	Branch on $A \neq B$
BC 9, $S2$	9	1001	0,3	$A = B$	$A = B$	—	—
BC 11, $S2$	11	1011	0,2,3	$A \geq B$	$A \geq B$	BNL $S2$	Branch on A not low
BC 13, $S2$	13	1101	0,1,3	$A \leq B$	$A \leq B$	BNH $S2$	Branch on A not high

The following BC instructions can be used consecutively:

$$\text{BC} \quad 2, \text{BRANCH}$$
$$\text{BC} \quad 4, \text{BRANCH}$$

where BRANCH is the symbolic branch-to address. On the other hand, one instruction is all that is needed:

$$\text{BC} \quad 6, \text{BRANCH}$$

where the decimal mask value 6 represents the bit configuration 0110 in the mask field.

Table 4.5 (columns 2 and 3) shows a complete matching relationship between the mask field and CC setting. For example,

$$\text{BC} \quad 15, \text{GOTO}$$

represents an unconditional branch to the symbolic address GOTO, whereas after the execution of the instruction

$$\text{BC} \quad 0, \text{NOOP}$$

no branch will take place, and the next sequential instruction will be executed.

Let us now explore how to use the Compare and Branch on Condition instructions as a pair. Figure 4.7 shows a portion of flowchart and its corresponding program segment. Corresponding to the decision box number 1, there is a pair of instructions C and BC. For example, if the contents of register 7 are 3—and as a result of Compare (C) instruction—the condition code will be set to 0. Since the mask value 8 is specified in the BC instruction, a branch will take place.

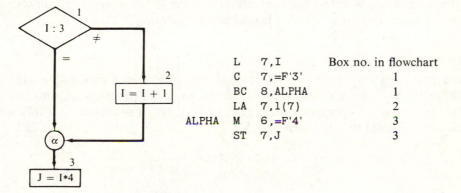

		Box no. in flowchart
L	7,I	
C	7,=F'3'	1
BC	8,ALPHA	1
LA	7,1(7)	2
ALPHA M	6,=F'4'	3
ST	7,J	3

Fig. 4.7   A decision box.

Similarly, two decision boxes are shown in Fig. 4.8. The Load Positive from Register (LPR) instruction

$$\text{LPR} \quad R1, R2$$

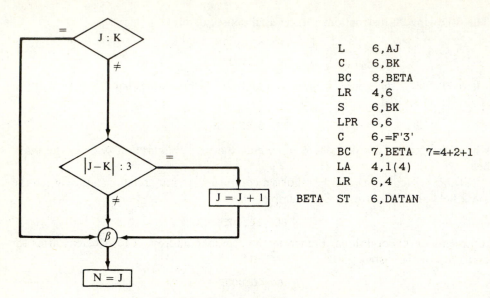

```
                           L    6,AJ
                           C    6,BK
                           BC   8,BETA
                           LR   4,6
                           S    6,BK
                           LPR  6,6
                           C    6,=F'3'
                           BC   7,BETA    7=4+2+1
                           LA   4,1(4)
                           LR   6,4
                      BETA ST   6,DATAN
```

Fig. 4.8 Two decision boxes.

loads the register *R1* with the *absolute* value of the contents of the register *R2*. Thus, the instruction

$$\text{LPR}\quad 6,6$$

has the following effect: If the contents of register 6 represent a positive number, it is untouched; if, however, the contents of register 6 are a negative number, its complement (a positive number) is loaded into register 6.

Extended Mnemonics

As a convenience to programmers, the mask field of a Branch on Condition (BC or BCR) instruction can often be omitted. In this case, the programmer must use an extended mnemonic operation code in place of BC or BCR. For example, the following two unconditional Branch instructions

$$\text{BC}\quad 15,\text{LOOP}$$
$$\text{B}\quad \text{LOOP}$$

have the same meaning. The extended mnemonics B in the second instruction is not a part of the set of the machine instructions for the IBM System/370 or System/360, but is translated by the assembler into the correct operation code and mask. Similarly, the instruction

$$\text{BC}\quad 4,256(0,8)$$

can be written simply as a Branch on Low instruction

$$BL \quad 256(0,8)$$

and its machine language version is the same as shown in Fig. 4.6, or 47408100. Table 4.5 shows various extended mnemonic codes (see column 6) together with their equivalents in machine instructions (see column 1). Some examples of extended mnemonics follow below.

BL	HERE	is same as	BC	4,HERE
BH	BRANCH	is same as	BC	2,BRANCH
B	GOTO	is same as	BC	15,GOTO
NOP	NOOP	is same as	BC	0,NOOP
BE	NEXT	is same as	BC	8,NEXT
BNE	4(2,3)	is same as	BC	7,4(2,3)

4.7 LOOPING—A PROGRAMMING TECHNIQUE

The purpose of this and following sections is to consolidate the usage of L, LA, ST, C, and BC instructions. They are illustrated in the light of two important programming techniques: looping and indexing.

Looping is a repetition of a group of instructions in a program. It is very rare that a program does not contain one or more loops. In structure, a loop normally consists of four separately identifiable parts: initialization, body, updating the count, and test for conclusion of the loop.

For simplicity, let us consider a flowchart to find the sum of 10 numbers, or to evaluate the following sum

$$S = \sum_{i=0}^{9} C_i \tag{4.1}$$

The four parts of a loop are marked in Fig. 4.9.

We set $S = 0$ and $i = 0$ before executing the loop. This step, called initialization, is necessary to take, as we shall now examine closely. In block 5, for example, each i is determined by the one preceding it. However, in the first pass through the loop, we need an initial value of i to work with. Thus, the value i must be defined (initialized) *before* the loop is entered, and Eq. (4.1) demands that the first value of i be zero. The reasoning here is similar to that used in summations. The expressions

$$\sum_{i=0}^{m} y_i^2 \quad \text{and} \quad \sum_{i=1}^{m} y_i^2$$

have therefore different meanings, and the initial value of i must be defined. Similarly, the initial value of S must be defined as in block 2. One has to bear in mind that these two initialization steps must precede the entry of the loop.

The body of the loop is the basic part of instructions which is repeated a specified

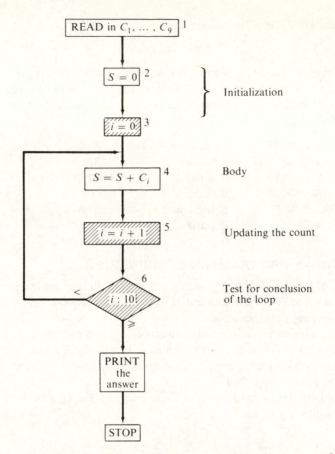

Fig. 4.9 Flowchart for computing the sum of ten numbers $S = \sum_{i=0}^{9} C_i$.

number of times. In Fig. 4.9, it contains only one step, but, in general, it can comprise instructions such as computations, input/output, branches, tests, and so on.

We may consider updating as reinitialization for the next pass. Basically, this operation can be accomplished by incrementing a counter, which records the number of passes through the loop. Updating can also be performed by adjusting the value of a certain variable used in the loop. More discussion on this point will follow in the next section.

Finally, a test is necessary to determine whether the loop should be terminated at the end of this pass. In its simplest form, a counter containing, say, a given number of passes N is tested. The exit occurs if the value N is reached. The ultimate goal of the initialization, updating, and testing in a loop structure is to make sure that the body itself has gone through a correct number of passes.

Referring again to Fig. 4.9, the three shaded boxes associated with updating, testing, and initialization of the value i can be implemented with a single statement in each high-level language.

FORTRAN: DO 127 I = 1, 10, 1

     or

             DO 127 I = 1, 10

PL/I: DO I = 1 BY 1 TO 10;

COBOL: PERFORM L1 THRU L2 VARYING I FROM 1 BY 1
                UNTIL I EXCEEDS 10

However, in assembler language programming, each part of a loop is usually implemented with one or several instructions. Two such program segments, shown in Fig. 4.10, are based on the following assumptions:

Loop structure	Block number in Fig. 4.9	Instructions	Instructions
Initialization	3 3 — —	LA 11,0 S=0 LA 10,0 I=0 LA 9,CZERO *	LA 11,0 * LA 9,CZERO LA 8,10
Body	4	LOOP A 11,0(9)	LOOP A 11,0(9)
Updating	5 —	LA 10,1(10) I=I+1 LA 9,4(9)	* LA 9,4(9)
Testing	6 6	C 10,=F'10' BL LOOP	BCT 8,LOOP
		(a)	(b)

Fig. 4.10 Two program segments each for sum of ten values. Note four parts in each loop. Number of passes (10) is explicitly given.
  (a) Two instructions used in the testing step.
  (b) Only one instruction used in the testing step.

1. The values $C_0, C_1, \ldots, C_9$ are already read into ten consecutive fullwords in the main storage. The symbolic *address* of C_0 is CZERO; that of C_1 is CZERO+4; and finally, that of C_9 is CZERO+36.

2. Register 11 contains the value S.

3. Register 10 contains the value i.

4. Register 9 initially contains the address CZERO.

The following two instructions appearing in Fig. 4.10(a):

               LA 9,CZERO
               LA 9,4(9)

are not covered in Fig. 4.9, depicting a flowchart oriented toward high-level languages. Here, register 9 holds the current address of a C-value. Thus, the first LA instruction is used to initialize register 9 with the address of C_0, called CZERO. In the updating step, we need to modify the contents of register 9 from CZERO to CZERO+4. This is accomplished by the instruction

$$\text{LA} \quad 9,4(9)$$

using a displacement 4. In writing a program in a high-level language, there is no need to initialize or update the address of C_i, but this must be done in an assembler language program. Furthermore, the number of bytes for each C_i must be explicitly or implicitly known.

Modified Version—Number of Loops Explicitly Given

The program segment in Fig. 4.10(a) uses register 10 to hold the i-value. We shall now attempt to improve this segment by eliminating the usage of register 10. Let us first study a new instruction.

The Branch on Count (BCT) instruction is of RX type having the following general form:

$$\text{BCT} \quad R1, D2(X2, B2)$$

The contents in register $R1$ are algebraically reduced by one and then a test is automatically made to examine whether the result is zero. If it is not, a branch is taken and the branch-to address is in the second operand. If it is zero, the control goes to the next sequential instruction.

Suppose that the contents of register 8 are *initially* 10. After the execution of the instruction

$$\text{BCT} \quad 8,\text{LOOP}$$

a) The contents of register 8 are reduced by one, or $10 - 1 = 9$;

b) Since $9 \neq 0$, a branch is taken to LOOP.

Thus, we can use this BCT instruction to replace the two instructions in the testing step shown in Fig. 4.10(a):

```
C    10,=F'10'
BL   LOOP
```

and two more instructions involving register 10 can also be removed from Fig. 4.10(a):

```
LA   10,0        BOX NO. 3 IN FLOWCHART
```

and

```
LA   10,1(10)    BOX NO. 5 IN FLOWCHART
```

However, in consequence of this reduction register 8 has to be initialized with a value 10. This is accomplished by placing the instruction:

```
LA   8,10
```

in the initialization step. The modified version is shown in Fig. 4.10(b). Note that there are only three instructions *inside* the loop, as compared with five instructions in Fig. 4.10(a).

4.8 INDEXING—A PROGRAMMING TECHNIQUE

In the flowchart shown in Fig. 4.9 and its associated assembler language instructions in Fig. 4.10(a), the loop is terminated when $i \geq 10$. As the value i changes, so does the address of C_i. This relationship is listed in Fig. 4.11. It is clear that the loop is terminated when the address of C_i goes higher than CZERO+36. In this section we shall explore how this idea can be implemented with assembler language instructions.

i	0	1	2	3	...	8	9
Address of C_i	CZERO	CZERO+4	CZERO+8	CZERO+12	...	CZERO+32	CZERO+36

Fig. 4.11   Value of i versus address of C_i.

As we learned in Section 3.4, the effective address can be calculated from the following important equation:

$$E = B + X + D. \tag{3.2}$$

If we wish to modify the address E such as increasing it by 4, we can use any one of the three techniques of address modification, collectively known as *indexing*: (1) increase index register contents X by 4; (2) increase the base register contents B by 4; or (3) increase the displacement D by 4. The first approach is easy to implement and is probably the most common one used in practice. We shall now discuss it in detail.

Increment the Index Register Contents X by 4

Let us examine the flowchart in Fig. 4.12. Register 10 is initially cleared (block 3). During each pass in the loop, its contents are increased by 4 (block 5); the loop is terminated when the contents in register 10 are equal to or greater than 40 (block 6).

The body of the loop is shown in block 4. The new sum S_{new} is equal to the old sum S_{old} plus a new C_i. The address of this new C_i is the sum of the contents in registers 11 and 10. The contents in register 11 are always equal to CZERO, whereas the contents of the index register 10 increase by 4 in each pass. The sum S at the end of each pass is shown below.

At the end of first phase: $S_1 = 0 + C(\text{CZERO}+0) = C(\text{CZERO}) = C_0$
At the end of second pass: $S_2 = S_1 + C(\text{CZERO}+4) = C_0 + C_1$

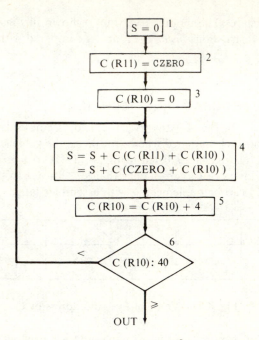

Fig. 4.12   Flowchart for sum of ten numbers $S = \sum_{i=0}^{9} C_i$ by using index register 10. CZERO is the symbolic address of C_0. [*Note:* R11 denotes register 11; C(R10) denotes the contents in register 10.]

At the end of third pass: $S_3 = S_2 + \text{C}(\text{CZERO}+8) = C_0 + C_1 + C_2$

$\vdots$

At the end of tenth pass: $S_{10} = S_9 + \text{C}(\text{CZERO}+36) = C_0 + C_1 + C_2 + C_3 + \dots$
$$+ C_9$$

where C(CZERO) means the *contents* of the fullword whose symbolic address is CZERO; C(CZERO+4) means the *contents* of the fullword whose symbolic address is CZERO+4; and so on.

The program segment corresponding to this flowchart is shown in Fig. 4.13(a). A comparison with the segment in Fig. 4.10(a) in the previous section indicates that one instruction is saved in the updating step.

In the previous discussion, register 11 always contained the address CZERO. We shall now consider a variation of the above procedure. In the segment in Fig. 4.13(a), let us delete the following instruction

```
LA   11,CZERO
```

in the initialization step (see block 2 in Fig. 4.12) and replace the only instruction in the body part

```
LOOP   A  9,0(10,11)
```

Loop structure	Block no. in Fig. 4.12	Instruction
Initialization	1	LA 9,0 S=0
	2	LA 11,CZERO
	3	LR 10,9
Body	4	LOOP A 9,0 (10,11)
Updating	5	LA 10,4 (10)
Testing	6	C 10,=F'40'
	6	BL LOOP

(a) A segment of instructions.

Block no. in Fig. 4.12	Instruction
1	LA 9,0
	***REG. 11 NOT USED**
3	LR 10,9
4	LOOP A 9,CZERO (10)
5	LA 10,4(10)
6	C 10,=F'40'
6	BL LOOP

(b) Modified version.

Instruction
LA   9,0
*
LR 10,9
LA   8,10
LOOP A   9,0(10,11)
LA 10,4(10)
BCT 8,LOOP

(c) Same as (a) except that BCT instruction is used.

Instruction
LA   9,0
LA 11,CZERO
LR 10,9
LA   8,10
LOOP A   9,CZERO(10)
LA 10,4(10)
BCT 8,LOOP

(d) Same as (b) except that BCT instruction is used.

Fig. 4.13   Indexing used in the program segment to add ten numbers.

with the following

LOOP A 9,CZERO(10)

The modified version is shown in Fig. 4.13(b). Note that the logical steps are not changed and the end result should be the same.

In the testing step of both Fig. 4.13(a) and (b), a pair of C and BL instructions is used:

C 10,=F'40'
BL LOOP

As mentioned in the last section, it can be replaced by a single Branch on Count

(BCT) instruction

$$\text{BCT}\quad 8,\text{LOOP}$$

When this change and the necessary initialization of register 8 are made, program segments shown in Fig. 4.13(a) and (b) become, respectively, those in Fig. 4.13(c) and (d).

As another example of index register usage, let us take a look at the flowchart (shown in Fig. 4.14) for the sum of ten numbers. Here, register 11 is used as the index register. Its contents are initially set as CZERO (the address of C_0), and are increased by 4 in each pass. When the contents of register 11 reach CZERO+40, the loop is terminated.

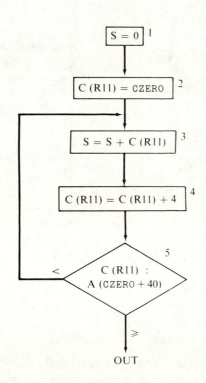

Fig. 4.14   Flowchart for $S = \sum_{i=0}^{9} C_i$ using register 11.

The corresponding program segment is shown in Fig. 4.15. Two remarks are in order here. First, both instructions used in the body and updating steps are of RX format. As discussed in Section 3.11, their second operands are both written in

Step	Block no. in Fig. 4.14	Instruction
Initialization	1	`LA  9,0      S=0`
	2	`LA 11,CZERO LOAD CZERO IN`
Body	3	`LOOP A   9,0(11) REGISTER 11`
Updating	4	`LA 11,4(11)`
Testing	5	`C  11,=A(CZERO+40)`
	5	`BL LOOP`

Fig. 4.15   Find the sum of ten numbers $S = \sum_{i=0}^{9} C_i$, a program segment.

the implicit form. At the risk of repetition, we note this form and its explicit version for both instructions are as follows:

Explicit form	Implicit form used in Fig. 4.15
`LOOP A   9,0(11,0)`	`LOOP A   9,0(11)`
`     LA 11,4(11,0)`	`     LA 11,4(11)`

General format

Op code $R1,D2(X2,0)$	Op code $R1,D2(X2)$
Op code $R1,D2(0,B2)$	Op code $R1,S2$
Op code $R1,D2(X2,B2)$	Op code $R1,S2(X2)$

Second, the second operand of the Compare (C) instruction, `=A(CZERO+40)`, is a literal. It represents the address CZERO+40. Note that this address, a constant, is preceded by an equal sign. The value of the constant is enclosed in parentheses, with the prefix A.

BIBLIOGRAPHY

Connors, W. D., Mercer, V. S., and Sorlini, T. A., *System/360 Instruction Usage Distribution*, Report TR 00.2025, IBM Systems Development Division, Poughkeepsie, N. Y., 1970.

Kuo, S. S., *Frequency Distribution of Instruction Usage in Compilers*, Report 6804, Computation Center, University of New Hampshire, 1968.

Falkoff, A. D., K. E. Iverson, and E. H. Sussenguth, *A Formal Description of System/360*, IBM Systems J. **3**, 198–261 (1964).

IBM System/370 Principles of Operation, Form GA22-7000, IBM Corp.

IBM System/360 Principles of Operation, Form GA22-6821, IBM Corp.

Ruggiero, J. F., and D. A. Coryell, "An Auxiliary Processing System for Array Calculation," *IBM Systems J.* **8** (2), 118–135 (1969).

PROBLEMS

Section 4.3

4.1. Given: a) The initial contents of register 8 = 00000A14.
    b) A program segment:

```
L   13,0(8)
M   12,4(8)
D   12,8(8)
ST  13,12(8)
```

   c) Initial storage contents:

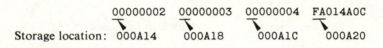

	00000002	00000003	00000004	FA014A0C
Storage location:	000A14	000A18	000A1C	000A20

Required: Contents in registers 12 and 13 after the execution of the program segment. Write the answers in hexadecimal.

4.2. Write a program segment to compute

$$J = [M/(K + 2)] + N/7.$$

Assume that N is a negative number; M and K are positive.

4.3. Write a program segment to perform the following: Load register 5 with a fullword at location DIVIDEND. Multiply this number by 1 so that its sign can be extended into all bit positions in register 4. Divide this product by the fullword at location DIVISOR. Store the remainder at location REM and the quotient at location QUO.

4.4. The Load from Register (LR) instruction loads register *R1* with the contents of register *R2*. Thus, the instruction LR 7,11 loads register 7 from register 11; the contents of register 11 remain unchanged. If the initial contents of register 3 are 00000004, write the contents of register 3, 4, and 5 after the execution of the following two instructions:

```
LR  5,3
LR  4,5
```

4.5. The Load Halfword (LH) instruction is of RX format:

```
LH   R1,D2(X2,B2)
```

Its second operand is a halfword in the main storage. During the execution of this instruction, the halfword is first extended into a fullword—the sign extension, and the resulting fullword is then loaded in register $R1$. If the initial storage map is same as in Problem 4.1(c), write the contents of register 6 after the execution of the instruction LH 6,16(0,8) where the contents of register 8 are 00000A14.

4.6. (a) If the contents of registers 8 and 12 are 0000020C and 000000A4, respectively, write the contents of register 3 after the execution of the following instruction:

$$\text{LA } 3,8(8,12)$$

(b) Write an LA instruction that will add 4 to the existing contents of register 7.

4.7. The STore Halfword (STH) instruction is of RX format:

$$\text{STH } R1,D2(X2,B2)$$

It stores the rightmost 16 bits of register $R1$ in the halfword addressed by $B2$, $X2$, and $D2$. The second operand address must satisfy the halfword boundary alignment requirement. Suppose that the initial contents are same as shown in Problem 3.14. What does the instruction

$$\text{STH } 7,916(12)$$

accomplish?

4.8. Given: The contents in register 4 = 0000021C and a partial memory map:

Address:	00036A	36B	36C	36D	36E	36F	370
	A 6	F 0	0 0	0 0	2 1	3 6	4 E

Find: The contents in register 8 after the execution of each of the following four unrelated instructions:

$$\text{LA } 8,336(,4)$$
$$\text{L } 8,336(,4)$$
$$\text{L } 8,336(4)$$
$$\text{LA } 8,336(4)$$

Section 4.5

4.9. The initial contents of registers and storage locations are taken as

Register	8:	00264FF7
Register	10:	FFFFFFFD
Register	11:	00AC16E9
Location	N:	0A1024DB
Location	K:	FF467A3C

Write the condition code setting in decimal for each of the following unrelated instructions:

Condition code
_____

C 8,N   _____

CR 10,8   _____

```
SR   8,8            _____
 A  11,K            _____
AH  10,K+2          _____
 S  10,K            _____
 S  10,=F'21'       _____
AR  10,11           _____
 C  10,K            _____
```

Section 4.6

4.10. a) Write an unconditional Branch instruction to branch to an instruction whose address is not known, but this address can be computed with the following information: Registers 2 and 3 are used as the base and index registers, respectively, and the displacement is equal to 400 in decimal. Write this Branch instruction both in hexadecimal and in assembler language.

b) Which of following mask fields would be used by a BC instruction to check only for a condition code of 2:

$$\text{a)} \quad 1000 \qquad \text{b)} \quad 0010 \qquad \text{c)} \quad 0011 \qquad \text{d)} \quad 1100.$$

4.11. The following Branch instruction is used after *each* of the nine unrelated instructions in Problem 4.9:

$$\text{BC} \quad 5,\text{LOOP}$$

Which of the nine instructions will result in a branch to LOOP?

4.12. The Branch on Register (BCR) instruction is of RR format, but its first operand contains a mask field, whose relationship with condition code (CC) is listed in Table 4.5. (a) Write in extended mnemonic for the following instruction:

$$\text{BCR} \quad 15,7$$

(b) Does the mask field 3 in the following BCR instruction (used after the Compare instruction) make sense?

$$\text{C} \quad \text{A,B}$$
$$\text{BCR} \quad 3,7$$

4.13. In IBM System/370 Scientific Subroutine Package written in FORTRAN, M is taken as $2^{16} + 3 = 65539$ and P as $2^{31} = 2,147,483,648$ in the following equation to generate random numbers:

$$x_{n+1} \equiv M \cdot x_n \bmod P.$$

Translate the associated flowchart (Fig. 4.16) into a program segment.

LABORATORY ASSIGNMENT

1. Keypunch the assembler language program in Fig. 4.17. Modify the job control cards to suit the requirements of your computation center. The associated flowchart is shown in Fig. 4.18. What does this program do and where do you locate your answer in the output?

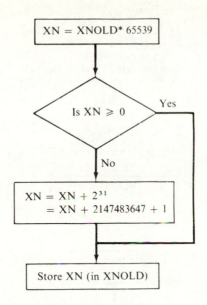

$$XN = XNOLD * 65539$$

Is $XN \geqslant 0$ — Yes

No

$$XN = XN + 2^{31}$$
$$= XN + 2147483647 + 1$$

Store XN (in XNOLD)

Fig. 4.16 Flowchart for generation of random numbers.

```
//SAMPLE JOB T361-13.'SS KUO'
//STEP1 EXEC ASMFCLG
//ASM.SYSIN DD *
* THIS IS A SAMPLE PROGRAM
* FOR CALCULATING N FACTORIAL
BEGIN      BALR   11,0       THIS AND NEXT INSTRUCTIONS ARE
           USING  *,11          USED TO DEFINE THE BASE REGISTER
           L      4,N         LOAD N VALUE IN REGISTER 4
           LA     3,1         LOAD 1 INTO REGISTER 3
           SR     5,5         ZERO REGISTER 5
           CLR    4,5
           BC     4,DUMP      TERMINATE THE PROGRAM WHEN N
           BC     8,ANSWER       IS LESS THAN OR EQUAL TO ZERO
LOOP       MR     2,4
           BCT    4,LOOP      LOOP FOR CALCULATING N FACTORIAL
ANSWER     ST     3,PRODUCT   STORE THE PRODUCT IN REGISTER 3
DUMP       DC     X'820000005 THIS CAUSES DUMP.
N          DC     F'5'        DEFINE N=5
PRODUCT    DS     F           RESERVE A FULLWORD FOR PRODUCT
           END BEGIN
/*
//GO.SYSUDUMP DD SYSOUT=A
//
```

Fig. 4.17 A sample program in assembler language to compute N factorial.

107

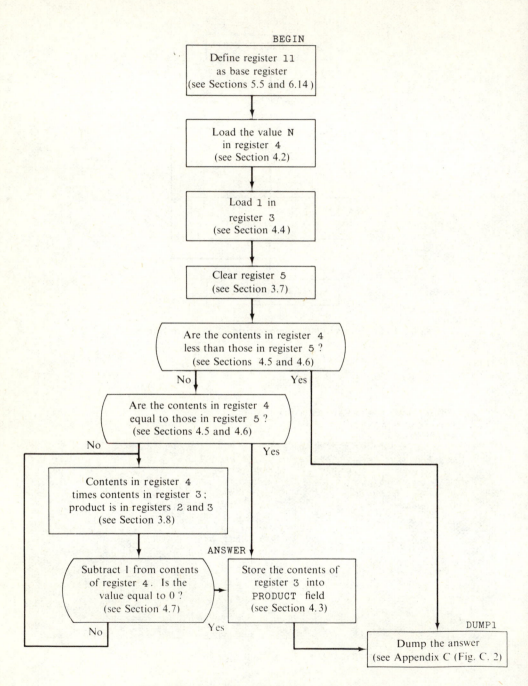

Fig. 4.18 Flowchart for finding *N* factorial.

CHAPTER 5

Most Common Instructions of SS, SI, and RS Formats

5.1 PRELIMINARY REMARKS

All the instructions presented so far in the previous two chapters use two instruction formats: Register-to-Register (RR) format and Register-to-Indexed-Storage (RX) format. There are in total five instruction formats available for the IBM System/370 and System/360. The RR or RX formats are used in about 67 percent of all instructions. The remaining instruction formats are listed below.

Storage and *Immediate-operand* (*SI*) *format* deals with information between main storage and the immediate field in the instruction.

Storage-to-Storage (*SS*) *format* deals with information between main storage and main storage.

Register-to-Storage (*RS*) *format* deals with information between a register and main storage.

The most frequently encountered instruction(s) in each of these three formats seems to be as follows:

Instruction name	Mnemonic	Operand	Format
MoVe Immediate	MVI	$D1(B1),I2$	SI
MoVe Character	MVC	$D1(L,B1),D2(B2)$	SS
Load Multiple	LM $\}$	$R1,R3,D2(B2)$	RS
Store Multiple	STM		

In this chapter, we shall explore these four instructions in some detail. Other common instructions of SS, SI, and RS formats will be also introduced.

As an important application of the instructions discussed in this and the previous chapters, we shall illustrate how assembler language subroutines can be written independently of a main program. We shall also show how a main program can be written in a high-level language, used primarily to handle the input/output. As a result, one can write complete programs and test on a computer much sooner than it is possible otherwise.

5.2 SI FORMAT AND MOVE IMMEDIATE (MVI) INSTRUCTION

In Chapters 3 and 4, we studied the instructions of RR format mainly dealing with a transfer of data between two registers and those of RX format involving data between a register and the main storage. By contrast, the instructions of SI format deal with a transfer of data from a field *in the instruction* to a byte location in the main storage.

The structure of SI format (see Fig. 5.1) is quite similar to that of RX format. The operation code takes the first eight bits; the *B1* and *D1* fields, taken as the base register and displacement, respectively, are used to calculate the effective address in main storage. The index register *X* is not used. The bit positions 8–15, or *I2* field, contain a byte of "immediate" data to be used by this instruction. The usage of this field varies with the instructions. For example, Move Immediate (MVI) instruction can move a *one-byte* constant to a byte location in the main storage and this constant is specified in the *I2* field.

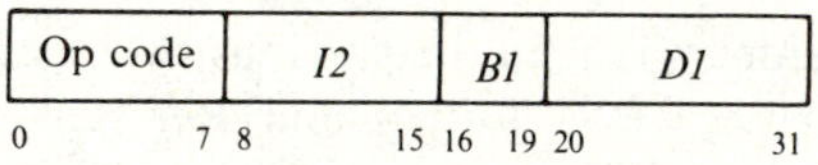

Op code	*I2*	*B1*	*D1*

0   7 8   15 16 19 20   31

Fig. 5.1   Storage-Immediate (SI) format.

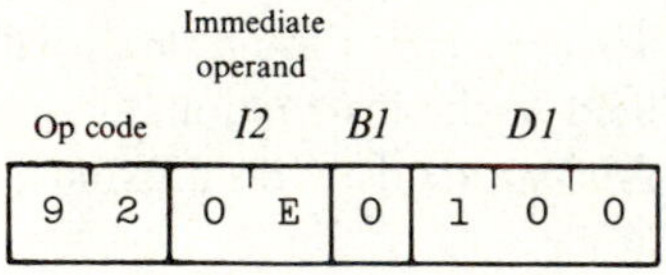

Immediate
operand

Op code   *I2*   *B1*   *D1*

9	2	0	E	0	1	0	0

Fig. 5.2   Move the byte contents 0E to address 000100.

Let us consider a specific MVI instruction (see Fig. 5.2). This instruction moves the decimal constant 14 or $(0E)_{16}$, specified in the immediate operand (a byte long), to a location in the main storage:

$$\text{Effective address } E = B + D$$
$$= 00000000 + (100)_{16}$$
$$= 000100 = (256)_{10}.$$

The corresponding instruction in assembler language is

    MVI   256(0),14

or

    MVI   256(0),X'0E'

where X'0E' stands for a self-defining term whose value is 0E in hexadecimal. We shall discuss this type of term in more detail in the next chapter, but it is important to mention now that a hexadecimal self-defining term must be enclosed between single quotes (e.g., X'0E') and preceded by the letter X, whereas a decimal self-defining term is simply written as a sequence of decimal digits (e.g., 14). The displacement is usually written in decimal in an assembler language instruction.

Assuming the contents in the address 000100 are C6 before the execution of the instruction, the byte contents at that address after the execution will become 0E.

The above example illustrates how to move a decimal or a hexadecimal number into a byte in the main storage. Similarly, a character such as a blank or a '7' can also be moved into a byte location. For example, if one wishes to move a blank to a byte in the main storage, whose address is OUTREA, the following instruction can be used:

```
              MVI   OUTREA,C' '
```

where C stands for a character represented by the eight-bit code (see Appendix B). This type of character self-defining term will also be discussed in more detail in Section 6.3.

Suppose that the initial contents are as follows:

```
        Register  4:      000050AC
        Register 13:      00009084
        Location 0050B0 through 0050B3:    FB1F2C4A
```

After the execution of the following isolated MVI instructions, the new contents are shown below.

| | New byte contents | Location where new byte |
Instructions	(hexadecimal)	contents are stored
MVI 4(4),8	08	0050B0
MVI 6(4),8	08	0050B2
MVI 6(4),X'5A'	5A	0050B2
MVI OUTAREA,C'*'	5C	OUTAREA
MVI 12(13),X'FF'	FF	009090
MVI 0(4),X'00'	00	0050AC

We notice that, in each MVI instruction, the implied length of data to be moved is one byte. Also, the immediate operand is written as the second operand in the assembler language instruction.

5.3 SS FORMAT AND MOVE CHARACTER (MVC) INSTRUCTION

In this section, we shall explore the fourth and the longest instruction format, the storage-to-storgae (SS) format, which uses three halfwords (Fig. 5.3). For the sake of discussion, we shall illustrate this format with a specific instruction—Move Character (MVC) instruction.

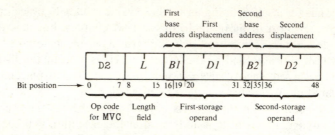

Fig. 5.3   SS format.

Let us take a look at Fig. 5.4. The MVC instruction is used to move the contents of five consecutive bytes from locations 000F00 through 000F04 to new locations 000800 through 000804. The actual number of bytes to be moved *minus one* is stored

Fig. 5.4   MVC instruction to move five bytes from address 000F00 to 000800.

in the length (*L*) field (bit positions 8 through 15). In this example, $L = 5 - 1 = 4$ is specified in the machine language instruction.

The move-from address can be easily calculated from the second storage operand (bits 32 through 47):

$$C(B2) + D2 = 0 + (F00)_{16} = (3840)_{10}.$$

The move-to address is specified in the first storage operand (bits 16 through 31):

$$C(B1) + D1 = 0 + (800)_{16} = (2048)_{10}.$$

Here are some important details to be pointed out. First, the movement of these bytes is accomplished *one byte at a time*, starting from the low-numbered byte address to the high-numbered one specified in the second operand. Second, the contents of the second operand remain unchanged. Finally, the total number of bytes to be moved can be 1, 2, ..., up to 256 bytes.

During execution of the MVC instruction (Fig. 5.4), the byte contents at location 000F00 are first moved into location 000800; these at location 000F01 into 000801; and so on. Suppose that the contents of these bytes before moving are shown in Fig. 5.5(a). After the execution of the instruction, the contents are shown in Fig. 5.5(b).

The instruction shown in Fig. 5.4 can be expressed in the following assembler language:

MVC   2048(5,0),3840(0)

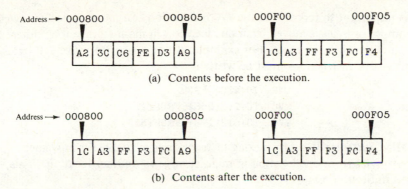

(a) Contents before the execution.

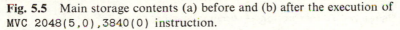

(b) Contents after the execution.

Fig. 5.5 Main storage contents (a) before and (b) after the execution of
MVC 2048(5,0),3840(0) instruction.

It is important to note that, in this instruction, the *actual* number of bytes to be moved,
not the actual number minus one, is specified.

In assembler language instruction, the length field may be specified either explicitly (as we have done above) or implicitly as we shall show in the following
examples.

Suppose that FIELD1 and FIELD2 each contain five bytes and the initial contents
are

$$\begin{array}{ll} \text{FIELD1:} & \text{F976C1AE9B} \\ \text{FIELD2:} & \text{46F17AB6EC} \end{array}$$

The final contents after the execution of each MVC instruction are shown as below.

	Instruction	Number of bytes moved	Explicit (*E*) or implicit (*I*) length field	Final result FIELD1	FIELD2
MVC	FIELD1(5),FIELD2	5	*E*	46F17AB6EC	46F17AB6EC
MVC	FIELD1,FIELD2	5	*I*	46F17AB6EC	46F17AB6EC
MVC	FIELD2,FIELD1	5	*I*	F976C1AE9B	F976C1AE9B
MVC	FIELD1(2),FIELD2	2	*E*	46F1C1AE9B	46F17AB6EC
MVC	FIELD2(1),FIELD1	1	*E*	F976C1AE9B	F9F17AB6EC
MVC	FIELD1(3),FIELD2+2	3	*E*	7AB6ECAE9B	46F17AB6EC
MVC	FIELD1,FIELD2+1	5	*I*	F17AB6EC??	46F17AB6EC

Each item of new information is underlined. The '??' in the last example stands for
the original byte contents in location FIELD2+5 which are not given. The number of
bytes to be moved in this case is given only implicitly as 5, the length of FIELD1.

It is important to repeat that the MVC instruction can move up to 256 bytes. If a large number of bytes is moved from one location in main storage to another, several MVC instructions must be used. For example, if one wishes to move 710 bytes, three consecutive MVC instructions must be written:

```
MVC   TO(256),FROM
MVC   TO+256(256),FROM+256
MVC   TO+512(198),FROM+512
```

In IBM System/370, a Move Long instruction is available for movement of up to 16 million bytes from one location in main storage to another location. This will be discussed in Section 5.11.

Special Usage of MVC Instruction—Propagation of a Byte

It is something desirable to copy a character throughout a given number of contiguous bytes. Specifically, we wish to copy the byte contents 00 (hexadecimal representation of eight-bit contents 00000000) in address 000800 into the next *seven* bytes: 000801 through 000807. First, we set the contents of location 000800 to 00 by using the following instruction:

$$MVI   2048(0),X'00'$$

where $(2048)_{10} = (800)_{16}$. Next, we can use the MVC instruction shown in Fig. 5.6 which can be expressed in the following assembler language:

$$MVC   2049(7,0),2048(0)$$

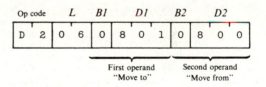

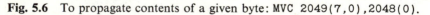

Fig. 5.6 To propagate contents of a given byte: MVC 2049(7,0),2048(0).

This instruction carries out the following operations:

Step 1. Move contents 00 in location 000800 into location 000801.
Step 2. Move contents 00 in location 000801 into location 000802.
⋮
Step 7 (the final step). Move contents 00 in location 000806 into location 000807.

In this instruction, the address of the first operand is only one higher than that of the second operand. On the other hand, the *L*-field has a value 6, implying that the contents of seven bytes will be moved. This apparent inconsistency is used to move

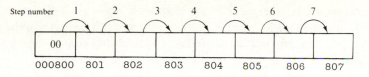

Fig. 5.7 Propagation of character 00 (seven times).

one byte at a time from the byte address 000800 to 000801; from 000801 to 000802; and, finally, from 000806 to 000807. This is depicted in Fig. 5.7.

Suppose the initial contents at locations 000800 through 000808 are as shown in Fig. 5.8(a). As the first step in execution, 00 is placed in byte address 000801 (Fig. 5.8b). After the next successive six steps, the contents 00 are placed in each byte at a time. The final result after execution of the MVC instruction is shown in Fig. 5.8(c).

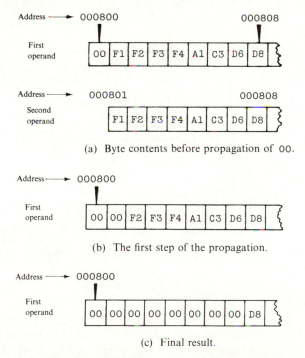

(a) Byte contents before propagation of 00.

(b) The first step of the propagation.

(c) Final result.

Fig. 5.8 Propagation of a given byte 00.

As a second example for the propagation of a given byte, we wish to zero out 80 bytes; the address of the first byte is held in register 2. The following two sequential instructions can be used:

```
MVI   0(2),X'00'
MVC   1(79,2),0(2)
```

If the contents of base register 2 are 00001000, the first instruction will move $(00000000)_2$ into the byte at location 001000. The MVC instruction will then propagate $(00000000)_2$ into locations 001001, 001002, ..., and 00104F (for 79 times).

The general format of MVC instruction is assembler language is

$$MVC \quad D1(L1,B1),D2(B2)$$

where *L1* is the *actual* number of bytes to be moved to the first operand address.

Before we turn to the next section, it is worthwhile to mention that MVI and MVC are two popular instructions used for byte movement (Fig. 5.9). In MVC instruction, the contents of a given number of contiguous bytes are moved from one part of main storage to another, thus the name Storage-to-Storage (SS) format. By contrast, the MVI instruction moves one byte of *immediate* data to its first operand address. The other two popular instructions dealing with byte movement—Insert Character (IC) and Store Character (STC) instructions—are left as Problems 5.11 and 5.12. Both are of RX format.

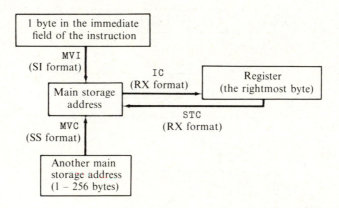

Fig. 5.9   Four instructions for byte movement.

5.4 RS FORMAT

Let us explore the fifth and last instruction format—Register-Storage (RS) format. This format is very similar in structure to the RX format discussed in Section 3.5. Like RX format, the RS format is four bytes long (see Fig. 5.10); the first eight bits

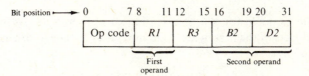

Fig. 5.10   RS format.

contain the operation code, and the next four bits (bit positions 8–11) contain the first operand address—a register number. The *B2* and *D2* fields are used in the same way as in RX format: The *B2* field (bits 16–19) specifies the base register number, and the *D2* field (bits 20–31), the displacement. The principal difference between RS and RX formats lies in bits 12–15. In RX format, these four bits represent an index register number, whereas there is no index register involved in the RS format. The usage of this *R3* field in RS format differs in various instructions. In some instructions, this field is simply ignored; in others, these four bits specify a register number used as a *third operand*.

Load Multiple (LM) Instruction

To be specific, we shall illustrate the RS format with the Load Multiple (LM) instruction.

For example, if we wish to load registers 5, 6, and 7 from three contiguous full-words in main storage at locations I, I+4, and I+8, respectively, we can use the following instructions:

$$\text{L} \quad 5,\text{I}$$
$$\text{L} \quad 6,\text{I}+4$$
$$\text{L} \quad 7,\text{I}+8$$

or, alternatively, the Load Multiple (LM) instruction

$$\text{LM} \quad 5,7,\text{I}$$

whose machine language equivalent is shown in Fig. 5.11.

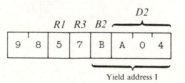

Fig. 5.11   Load Multiple instruction: LM 5,7,I [*Note:* The general format is LM *R1*,*R3*,*D2*(*B2*)].

In one operation, this LM instruction moves the contents of three consecutive fullwords in main storage into three contiguous registers. The address of the first fullword is specified in the *B2* and *D2* fields; or, I = C(*B2*) + *D2* = 000000 + A04 = 000A04. This first fullword is moved into register *R1* or register 5; the next fullword into register *R1*+1 or register 6; the third and last fullword into register *R3* or register 7. It is important to note that *R1* and *R3* are written first and second (not first and third) in an LM instruction.

The Load Multiple (LM) instruction is sometimes used to load a pair of even–odd registers in preparation for a division. If the data at the location DIVIDEND consist of two consecutive fullwords, then the following instructions perform the necessary division:

```
LM   8,9,DIVIDEND
D    8,DIVISOR
ST   9,QUO
```

and the quotient is stored at location QUO in main storage.

In the LM instructions illustrated so far, *R3* is greater than *R1* (for example, 5 < 7 in Fig. 5.11). If, on the other hand, *R3* < *R1*, then the registers are considered as in the form of a continuous loop (Fig. 5.12). Thus, register 0 is the successor of register 15, often known as *wrap-around*. Consider, for example, the following instruction

```
LM   14,12,12(13)
```

which changes the contents in 15 registers: registers 14, 15, 0, 1, ..., 11, and 12. Register 14 is loaded with the first fullword in main storage, whose address is equal to the contents of register 13 plus 12 bytes; register 15 with the second fullword; register 0 with the third; register 1 with the fourth; and finally, register 12 is loaded with the fifteenth fullword in main storage.

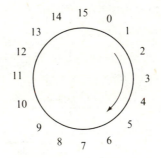

Fig. 5.12   Wrap-around of 16 general registers.

Store Multiple (STM) Instruction

The Store Multiple (STM) instruction

$$STM \quad R1, R3, D2(B2)$$

is exactly the converse of the LM instruction. For example, the following instruction

```
STM  14,15,12(13)
```

stores the contents of registers 14 and 15 into two contiguous fullwords in main storage. We obtain the address of the first fullword by adding 12 bytes to the contents of register

13. Similarly, the following instruction

$$\text{STM } 14,12,12(13)$$

stores the contents of 15 consecutive registers $(14, 15, 0, 1, 2, \ldots, 12)$ into 15 contiguous fullwords in main storage. The address of the first fullword is $C(R13) + 12$, or the contents of register 13 plus 12 bytes.

As another example, let us write a program segment to compute the following expression:

$$K = I*21$$

This segment can consist of the following three instructions:

$$
\begin{array}{ll}
\text{L} & \text{9,=F'21'} \\
\text{M} & \text{8,I} \\
\text{STM} & \text{8,9,PROD}
\end{array}
$$

where PROD is the address of the two consecutive fullwords in the main storage containing the product.

5.5 SUBROUTINE LINKAGE—A PROGRAMMING TECHNIQUE

In this section, we shall discuss a standard subroutine linkage using the instructions treated in the previous sections. We assume that the reader has some basic knowledge of FORTRAN, COBOL, or PL/I languages, and is familiar with the concept of a subroutine.†

Basically, it is often necessary to repeat a group of statements many times in writing a computer program. To avoid the undesirable repetition, we often use a subroutine subprogram, sometimes called simply a subroutine (Fig. 5.13). A subroutine is a collection of statements, or "package statement," which we apply to achieve some specific objectives, such as finding the inverse of a given matrix. Frequently, a subroutine has already been written and tested by one programmer, and can be obtained and called with a main program written by another.

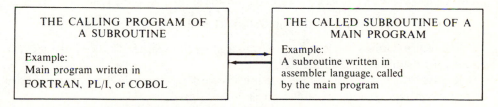

THE CALLING PROGRAM OF A SUBROUTINE	THE CALLED SUBROUTINE OF A MAIN PROGRAM
Example: Main program written in FORTRAN, PL/I, or COBOL	Example: A subroutine written in assembler language, called by the main program

Fig. 5.13   Calling program and called subroutine.

† See, e.g., Shan S. Kuo, *Computer Applications of Numerical Methods*, Addison-Wesley, Reading, Mass., 1972, page 64.

The language used in a calling program may be different from the one used in a called subroutine. For example, it is possible to write a main program in FORTRAN, COBOL, or PL/I, whereas its subroutine is written in assembler language. This flexible feature enables one to write the required input/output as a part of the main program in a high-level language.† However, a small price has to be paid for this convenience: One must know the linkage conventions between a main program and its assembler language subroutine.

It is convenient to consider the following two cases: (1) the subroutine is a lowest-level one, meaning that it does not call another subroutine. This case is discussed later in this chapter. (2) The subroutine *does* call another subroutine, a more involved case which will be studied in Chapter 8.

Basic Conventions Used in Subroutine Linkage

There are 16 general registers in the IBM System/370 or System/360.‡ Since they are used in both the main program and its subroutine, steps have to be taken to avoid a possible conflict. A plan is adopted under OS/360: Right after a subroutine takes control, all register contents (except register 13) used in the main program are saved in the main storage area, known as a *save area*. These registers are then available to the called subroutine. As a reverse process, the register contents must be restored just before the return to the main program.

A number of conventions has been established. First, the main program (the calling program) has the responsibility of reserving a 18-word save area, in which the register contents in the main program are saved. It is important to note that the actual saving of these contents is not carried out in the main program. Rather, it is performed in the called subroutine.

Second, registers 0, 1, 13, 14, and 15, called *linkage registers*, have special assignments.

Register 1 contains the *address* of the argument list. For example, in a FORTRAN or PL/I main program, such argument list can contain the five items written within the parentheses:

> CALL MATINV (A, N, B, M, DET)

and a typical example in COBOL can contain the following three items:

> CALL 'ARITH' USING ARG1, ARG2, ARG3

The return address to the main program is stored in register 14; the entry address to the called subroutine is in register 15.

Register 13 contains the address of the 18-word save area, in which the contents of many registers used in the calling program are stored.

The fifth linkage register is register 0. It has a rather peculiar assignment to hold an integer result of a FORTRAN function subprogram. This result is then fetched from

---

† A discussion of input/output in assembler language is presented in Chapter 14.

‡ In the larger models.

register 0 by the calling program. Because of this uncommon function, register 0 is less frequently used than the other four linkage registers.

Third, the main program (the calling program) is responsible for putting the argument list into contiguous fullwords in the main storage. (By the second convention, the *address* of this list is placed in register 1.) This convention will be illustrated with an example in the next section.

Implementation of Saving and Linkage in Assembler Language

Immediately after obtaining control, the lowest-level subroutine is expected to take the following three steps:

1. Name the subroutine.
2. Store all register contents used in the main program in a save area SAVEMAIN (except register 13). This 18-word save area has been reserved by the main program.
3. Define an implied base register.

Before returning to the main program, the answers must be stored in the locations specified in the argument list. In the rare cases when the subroutine is a function subprogram, the single-word result is stored in register 0. From the standpoint of linkage, the subroutine should also:

4. Restore the register contents, a reverse process of step 2.
5. Erect a signpost indicating that the execution of the subroutine is just completed (optional).
6. Branch to main program.

We are now in a position to present a sample package of instructions used to link a main program (written in FORTRAN, COBOL, or PL/I) to its subroutine. We reiterate that this subroutine, arbitrarily named SUBR1, does not call another subroutine. As shown in Fig. 5.14, this package is divided into two parts: The first implements the items 1 through 3, and the second, the items 4 through 6 in the above discussion. The user's source statements, or the core of the subroutine, is sandwiched between them.

In this housekeeping package, the BC, STM, LM, MVI, and BCR instructions have already been discussed, but START, DC, USING, END, and BALR have not been mentioned yet.

At this point, it is worth noting that there are two types of assembler language instructions—machine instructions and assembler instructions. The former are translated into machine language coding; the latter type does not generate any coding for operation. Typical examples of the assembler instructions include START, DC, USING, and END. They are viewed as special notes from the programmer and often known as pseudo-operation instructions.

In the following paragraphs, we shall review the instructions already discussed, and make only brief comments on the new instructions as they will be discussed in more detail in the next chapter.

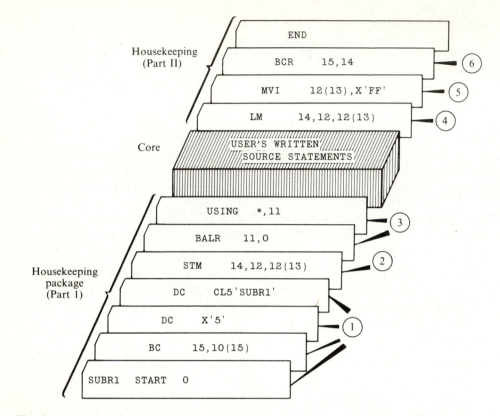

Fig. 5.14 Sample housekeeping package for linkage in a subroutine. Part I performs items 1 through 3, and Part II carries out items 4 through 6. The BC and two DC instructions in ① are optional. The MVI instruction in ⑤ is also optional.

SUBR1 START 0

This assembler instruction defines the subroutine name as SUBR1. It also sets the initial value of the location counter to zero. The location counter may be considered as an area where the addresses of all assembler language instructions in a program are recorded.

BC 15,10(15)

This is an unconditional branch instruction; the branch-to address is

> 10 + the contents in register 15
> = 10 + the entry-point address of this subroutine
> = 10 + SUBR1
> = SUBR1+10.

The net effect is a branch to the STM statement. This instruction itself is four bytes long, and the next two instructions take a total of six bytes. The general format of this instruction is

$$BC \quad 15, M(15)$$

where $M = N + 5$, and N (preferably 1, 3, or 5) is defined below.

DC X'5'

This assembler instruction defines a hexadecimal constant 5 (the number of characters in SUBR1) in one byte (see Fig. 5.15). In general, this instruction is DC X'N'.

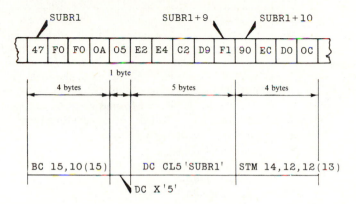

Fig. 5.15 Instructions are sequentially stored in main memory.

DC   CL5'SUBR1'

This instruction defines the 5-character symbol SUBR1 in five bytes, as each character takes one byte (Fig. 5.15). The general form of this instruction is

$$DC \quad CLN'namesub'$$

where length value N must not be greater than 6 and is preferably an odd number. In other words, select a symbol which consists of only one, three, or five characters.

The machine language equivalents of the above-mentioned three instructions, sequentially stored in the main storage, are depicted in Fig. 5.15. *These three instructions are optional and may be taken out as a group.*

STM   14,12,12(13)

Before the registers can be released for usage in the subroutine SUBR1, the contents in each register (except register 13) used in the main program must be stored in a save area. The address of this save area (called SAVEMAIN in our discussion) is stored in register 13.

This instruction stores the contents of register 14 into the fullword at SAVEMAIN + 12 bytes, or SAVEMAIN + 3 words; the contents of register 15 into SAVEMAIN + 4 words; the contents of register 0 into SAVEMAIN + 5 words; . . . ; and finally, the contents of register 12 into SAVEMAIN + 17 words (see Fig. 5.16). Since register 13 contains the address of SAVEMAIN, it should not be disturbed. Alternatively, the subroutine SUBR1 may store the contents of register 13 in a temporary location outside the SAVEMAIN area.

	Save area SAVEMAIN		
	Word	Address	Remarks
Contents in register	1	SAVEMAIN	
	2	SAVEMAIN+4	The usage of the first three words will be
	3	SAVEMAIN+8	discussed in Section 8.2 (Table 8.1)
14	4	SAVEMAIN+12	Return address of the main program
15	5	SAVEMAIN+16	Entry-point address of the subroutine
0	6	SAVEMAIN+20	Result from a function subprogram
1	7	SAVEMAIN+24	Address of the argument list
2	8	SAVEMAIN+28	
3	9	SAVEMAIN+32	
4	10	SAVEMAIN+36	
5	11	SAVEMAIN+40	
6	12	SAVEMAIN+44	
7	13	SAVEMAIN+48	
8	14	SAVEMAIN+52	
9	15	SAVEMAIN+56	
10	16	SAVEMAIN+60	
11	17	SAVEMAIN+64	
12	18	SAVEMAIN+68	

Fig. 5.16 Save area SAVEMAIN to store register contents used in main program.

```
BALR  11,0
USING *,11
```

These two instructions are usually used as a pair. They provide information on the base register number and the base address. These two items of information are extremely important and must be supplied near the beginning of a program. Here, register 11 is assigned as the base register, and the base address at the object time is given as the address of the next machine instruction. From Fig. 5.14, we can see that this base address is equal to the address of the first executable machine instruction in the user's own source instructions.

There are two basic usages of the Branch and Link instruction (BALR). One is to load an address into the base register; the other, to branch out from a main program and later return to it.

We shall now discuss only the first usage, leaving the second usage of this instruction for discussion in Section 8.3.

The BALR instruction has the register-to-register (RR) format. When used to load a base register, the second operand is always set to zero. For example, the following instruction

BALR   5,0

loads register 5 with the address of the next *machine* instruction. When its second operand is zero, no branch is involved.

When a USING *,11 instruction immediately follows the BALR 11,0 instruction, it promises the assembler that base register 11 contains the address of the next machine instruction. In other words, the base address is expected to be equal to the address of the next machine instruction.

LM 14,12,12(13)

This is the first housekeeping instruction after the user's written source statements. It aims at restoring the register contents previously used in the main program, which is a reverse process of the STM instruction already discussed. As shown in Fig. 5.16, this instruction will load 15 fullwords in SAVEMAIN, each into a register. For example, a fullword is loaded into register 14; the address of this word is: contents of register 13 plus 12 bytes = SAVEMAIN+12. Likewise, the fullword at SAVEMAIN+16 is loaded into register 15, etc.

In writing this LM instruction, we assume that register 0 does not contain any output of the subroutine. If this assumption is not valid, that is, if the register 0 contains a single-word result to be retrieved by the main program, then the following two LM instructions should be used instead:

LM   14,15,12(13)
LM   1,12,24(13)

Finally, if registers N through 12 ($2 \leq N \leq 12$) are not used in the user's part of subroutine, we can use the following LM instruction

LM   2,N,28(13)

to replace the instruction LM 14,12,12(13). In this case, the instruction STM 14,12,12(13) can also be replaced by

STM   14,N,12(13)

MVI 12(13),X'FF'

Just before returning to the main program, we consider as useful to erect a signpost to indicate that a successful incursion into the subroutine is to be completed. This is done by inserting FF into the first byte in the fourth word of the save area SAVEMAIN, or SAVEMAIN+12 in Fig. 5.16. This instruction is optional and may be omitted.

BCR   15,14

Unconditional branch to the main program. The register 14 contains the return address. The mask field 15 signifies an *unconditional* branch.

END

A subroutine always has an END statement as its final statement. It signifies the end to the assembler. When no operand is specified, the control is passed back to the first byte of the program, after the program is loaded in the main storage.

5.6   AN EXAMPLE OF LINKAGE—ARITHMETIC OPERATIONS

In the previous section, we learned the linkage convention between a main program and its assembler language subroutine. We shall now illustrate this type of linkage with an example.

Two variables n_1 and n_2 are read in from a main program (written in a high-level language) which calls subroutine in assembler language to add, subtract, multiply, and divide two variables. The answers are labeled as SUM, DIFF, PROD, and QUOT, respectively.

In Figs. 5.17 through 5.19 are shown a FORTRAN, COBOL, and PL/I main program, respectively. Each main program is not only an instrument for input/output, but it also calls a subroutine ARITH (see Fig. 5.20), which has an argument list N1, N2, SUM, DIFF, PROD, and QUOT.

```
      READ(5,5) N1,N2
    5 FORMAT(2I5)
      CALL ARITH(N1,N2,SUM,DIFF,PROD,QUOT)
      WRITE(6,10) N1,N2,SUM,DIFF,PROD,QUOT
   10 FORMAT(1H1,'FIRST VARIABLE = ',1X,I5/' SECOND VARIABLE = ',I5//
     1' SUM IS ',8X,I6/' DIFFERENCE IS ',1X,I6/' PRODUCT IS ',I10/
     2' QUOTIENT IS ',4X,I5)
      CALL EXIT
      END
```

Fig. 5.17   FORTRAN main program.

In Fig. 5.20 the housekeeping package for linkage is shaded; the instructions in the unshaded portion have to be written by a programmer. The first four Load (L) instructions often puzzle beginners and need some explanations.

In the previous section, we learned that the address of the argument list is stored in register 1. For illustration, we assume this address is 001A60 (Fig. 5.21). At this location, we find six contiguous fullwords, each containing an address for an argument specified in the argument list. From these six addresses or pointers, the *value* of each argument can be readily found. As illustrated in Fig. 5.21, the value of n_1 can be found at the address 003CB4. To implement this concept, the following two instructions are used.

```
IDENTIFICATION DIVISION.
PROGRAM-ID. 'COBOL1'.
ENVIRONMENT DIVISION.
CONFIGURATION SECTION.
SOURCE-COMPUTER. IBM-360-50.
OBJECT-COMPUTER. IBM-360-50.
INPUT-OUTPUT SECTION.
FILE-CONTROL.
      SELECT OUTFILE ASSIGN TO 'PRINT' UNIT-RECORD 1403 UNIT.
      SELECT INFILE ASSIGN TO 'READER' UTILITY.
DATA DIVISION.
FILE SECTION.
FD   INFILE LABEL RECORDS ARE OMITTED DATA
     RECORD IS NPUT RECORDING MODE IS F.
01   NPUT.
     02 NPUT1 PICTURE 9(5).
     02 NPUT2 PICTURE 9(5).
     02 FILLER PICTURE X(70).
FD   OUTFILE, LABEL RECORDS ARE OMITTED DATA RECORD IS UTPUT.
01   UTPUT PICTURE X(133).
WORKING-STORAGE SECTION.
77   ARG1 PICTURE IS S9(5) COMPUTATIONAL.
77   ARG2 PICTURE IS S9(5) COMPUTATIONAL.
77   ARG3 PICTURE IS S9(6) COMPUTATIONAL.
77   ARG4 PICTURE IS S9(6) COMPUTATIONAL.
77   ARG5 PICTURE IS S9(9) COMPUTATIONAL.
77   ARG6 PICTURE IS S9(5) COMPUTATIONAL.
01   UTPUT21.
     02 FILLER PICTURE X(18) VALUE ' FIRST VARIABLE = '.
     02 UTPUT11 PICTURE 9(5).
     02 FILLER PICTURE X(110) VALUE SPACES.
01   UTPUT22.
     02 FILLER PICTURE X(19) VALUE ' SECOND VARIABLE = '.
     02 UTPUT12 PICTURE 9(5).
     02 FILLER PICTURE X(109) VALUE SPACES.
01   UTPUT23.
     02 FILLER PICTURE X(8) VALUE ' SUM IS '.
     02 UTPUT13 PICTURE 9(6).
     02 FILLER PICTURE X(119) VALUE SPACES.
01   UTPUT24.
     02 FILLER PICTURE X(15) VALUE ' DIFFERENCE IS '.
     02 UTPUT14 PICTURE 9(6).
     02 FILLER PICTURE X(112) VALUE SPACES.
01   UTPUT25.
     02 FILLER PICTURE X(12) VALUE ' PRODUCT IS '.
     02 UTPUT15 PICTURE 9(10).
     02 FILLER PICTURE X(111) VALUE SPACES.
01   UTPUT26.
     02 FILLER PICTURE X(13) VALUE ' QUOTIENT IS '.
     02 UTPUT16 PICTURE 9(5).
     02 FILLER PICTURE X(115) VALUE SPACES.
PROCEDURE DIVISION.
     OPEN INPUT INFILE OUTPUT OUTFILE.
     READ INFILE AT END GO TO EOJ
     EXHIBIT NAMED NPUT1, NPUT2.
     MOVE NPUT1 TO ARG1.
     MOVE NPUT2 TO ARG2.
     EXHIBIT NAMED ARG1, ARG2.
     EXHIBIT NAMED ARG1, ARG2, ARG3, ARG4, ARG5, ARG6. (continued)
```

Fig. 5.18   COBOL main program to call subroutine ARITH.

```
            ENTER LINKAGE.
            CALL 'ARITH' USING ARG1, ARG2, ARG3, ARG4, ARG5, ARG6.
            ENTER COBOL.
            EXHIBIT NAMED ARG1, ARG2, ARG3, ARG4, ARG5, ARG6.
            MOVE ARG1 TO UTPUT11.
            MOVE ARG2 TO UTPUT12.
            MOVE ARG3 TO UTPUT13.
            MOVE ARG4 TO UTPUT14.
            MOVE ARG5 TO UTPUT15.
            MOVE ARG6 TO UTPUT16.
            EXHIBIT NAMED UTPUT11, UTPUT12, UTPUT13, UTPUT14, UTPUT15,
            UTPUT16.
            WRITE UTPUT   FROM UTPUT21 AFTER ADVANCING 2 LINES.
            WRITE UTPUT   FROM UTPUT22 AFTER ADVANCING 2 LINES.
            WRITE UTPUT   FROM UTPUT23 AFTER ADVANCING 2 LINES.
            WRITE UTPUT   FROM UTPUT24 AFTER ADVANCING 2 LINES.
            WRITE UTPUT   FROM UTPUT25 AFTER ADVANCING 2 LINES.
            WRITE UTPUT   FROM UTPUT26 AFTER ADVANCING 2 LINES.
     EOJ. CLOSE INFILE, OUTFILE, STOP RUN.
```

Fig. 5.18 (*concl.*)

```
    MATH:   PROCEDURE OPTIONS(MAIN);
            /*DECLARE ALL VARIABLES FIXED BINARY IN ORDER TO TRANSFER*/
            /* CONTROL TO THE ASSEMBLER LANGUAGE SUBROUTINE */
            DECLARE(A,B,QUOT,SUM,DIFF,PROD)FIXED BINARY;
            GET LIST(A,B);
            CALL ARITH(A,B,SUM,DIFF,PROD,QUOT);
            /* PRINT OUT RESULTS*/
            PUT SKIP LIST('FIRST VARIABLE = ',A);
            PUT SKIP LIST('SECOND VARIABLE = ',B);
            PUT SKIP(2) LIST('SUM IS ',SUM);
            PUT SKIP LIST('DIFFERENCE IS ',DIFF);
            PUT SKIP LIST('PRODUCT IS ',PROD);
            PUT SKIP LIST('QUOTIENT IS ',QUOT);
    END MATH;
```

Fig. 5.19   PL/I main program.

L 2,0(1)

The address of the fullword containing the address N1 is loaded in register 2.

L 3,0(2)

The value of n_1 is stored in register 3.

The reader should have no difficulty in following the remainder of the subroutine which deals with the four arithmetic computations.   The output is shown in Fig. 5.22.

5.7 AN EXAMPLE OF LINKAGE—SUM OF TEN NUMBERS

To be able to compute the sum of ten numbers, we have discussed seven different program segments, which are shown in Figs. 4.10(a), 4.10(b), 4.13(a) through (d), and 4.15. Let us consider only four segments in Figs. 4.10(b), 4.13(b), 4.13(c), and 4.15.

```
ARITH     START  0
          BC     15,10(15)      BRANCH AROUND NAME LIST
          DC     X'5'           NUMBER OF CHARACTERS IN NAME
          DC     CL5'ARITH'     NAME OF SUBPROGRAM
          STM    14,12,12(13)   SAVE REGS IN SAVEAREA OF CALLING PROG
          BALR   11,0           ESTABLISH BASE REGISTER
          USING  *,11
          L      2,0(1)         PUT FIRST ARG PTR IN GR2
          L      3,0(2)         PUT FIRST ARG INTO GR3
          L      2,4(1)         PUT SECOND ARG PTR INTO GR2
          L      4,0(2)         PUT SECOND ARG INTO GR4
          LR     6,3            PUT FIRST ARG INTO GR6
          AR     6,4            ADD 1ST&2ND ARG, PUT RESULT IN GR6
          L      2,8(1)         PUT THIRD ARG PTR INTO GR2
          ST     6,0(2)         STOREC(GR6) IN 3RD ARG
          LR     6,3            LOAD 1ST ARG INTO GR6
          SR     6,4            1ST ARG - 2ND ARG, RESULT IN GR6
          L      2,12(1)        PUT 4TH ARG PTR INTO GR2
          ST     6,0(2)         STORE DIFF IN GR6 IN 4TH ARG
          LR     7,3            PUT FIRST ARG  INTO GR7
          MR     6,4            MULT 1ST&2ND ARG, RESULT IN GR6
          L      2,16(1)        PUT 5TH ARG PTR IN GR2
          ST     7,0(2)         STORE PRODUCT IN 5TH ARG
          SR     6,6            ZERO GR6
          LR     7,3            PUT FIRST ARG I TO GR7
          DR     6,4            DIVIDE 1ST ARG BY 2ND ARG, RESULT IN GR7
          L      2,20(1)        PUT 6TH ARG PTR INTO GR2
          ST     7,0(2)         STORE QUOTIENT IN 6TH ARG ADD
          LM     2,12,28(13)      RESTORE REGISTERS
          MVI    12(13),X'FF'   INDICATE RETURN OF CONTROL TO MAIN
          BCR    15,14          BRANCH BACK TO CALLING PROG
          END    ARITH
```

Fig. 5.20 Subroutine ARITH.

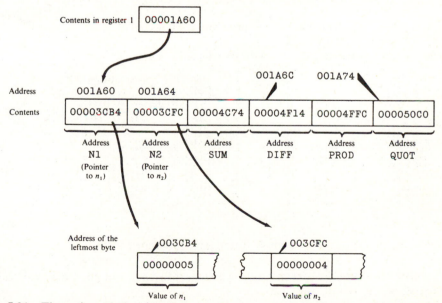

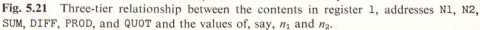

Fig. 5.21 Three-tier relationship between the contents in register 1, addresses N1, N2, SUM, DIFF, PROD, and QUOT and the values of, say, n_1 and n_2.

129

```
FIRST VARIABLE =      5
SECOND VARIABLE =      4

SUM IS             9
DIFFERENCE IS      1
PRODUCT IS        20
QUOTIENT IS        1
```

Fig. 5.22 Output for the ARITH problem.

```
      INTEGER SQRS(10),SUM
      DO 2 I=1,10
    2 SQRS(I)=I*I
C SQRS NOW CONTAINS FIRST TEN SQUARES
      SUM=0
      CALL S410B(SQRS,SUM)
      WRITE(6,3) SUM
    3 FORMAT(////,T15,'ACCORDING TO S410B, SUM IS ',I10,//)
      SUM=0
      CALL S413B(SQRS,SUM)
      WRITE(6,4) SUM
    4 FORMAT(T15,'ACCORDING TO S413B, SUM IS ',I10,//)
      SUM=0
      CALL S413C(SQRS,SUM)
      WRITE(6,5) SUM
    5 FORMAT(T15,'ACCORDING TO S413C, SUM IS ',I10,//)
      SUM=0
      CALL S415(SQRS,SUM)
      WRITE(6,6) SUM
    6 FORMAT(T15,'ACCORDING TO S415, SUM IS ',I10)
      STOP
```

Fig. 5.23 Main program in FORTRAN.

```
LOC    OBJECT CODE    ADDR1 ADDR2  STMT     SOURCE STATEMENT

000000                             1 S410B    START  0
000000 47F0 F00A       0000A       2          B      10(0,15)    BRANCH AROUND ID
000004 05                          3          DC     AL1(5)
000005 E2F4F1F0C2                  4          DC     CL5'S410B'   IDENTIFIER
00000A 90EC D00C       0000C       5          STM    14,12,12(13) SAVE REGISTERS
00000E 05C0                        6          BALR   12,0         SET REGISTER 12
000010                             7          USING  *,12            AS BASE REGISTER
000010 5831 0000       00000       8          L      3,0(1)       LOAD ADDRESS OF SQR IN R3
000014 5030 C030       00040       9          ST     3,CZERO         AND STORE IT IN CZERO
000018 5841 0004       00044      10          L      4,4(1)       LOAD ADDRESS OF SUM IN R4
00001C 41B0 0000       00000      11          LA     11,0         ZERO R11
000020 5890 C030       00040      12          L      9,CZERO      LOAD ADDRESS OF SQR IN R9
000024 4180 000A       0000A      13          LA     8,10         PUT 10 IN R8
000028 5AB9 0000       00000      14 LOOP      A      11,0(9)      ADD SQR(I) TO C(R11). PUT SUM IN R11
00002C 4199 0004       00004      15          LA     9,4(9)       INCREMENT R9 BY 4
000030 4680 C018       00028      16          BCT    8,LOOP       EXIT IF HAVE LOOPED 10 TIMES
000034 50B4 0000       00000      17          ST     11,0(4)      STORE SUM IN ITS ADDRESS
000038 98EC D00C       0000C      18          LM     14,12,12(13) RESTORE THE REGISTERS
00003C 07FE                       19          BR     14           RETURN
000040                            20 CZERO     DS     F
                                  21          END
```

Fig. 5.24 Assembly listing for Subroutine S410B.

1. Transform each of the four program segments into a subroutine. Let us call them, say, S410B, S413B, S413C, and S415.

2. Assuming the ten given numbers are 1, 4, 9, 16, 25, ..., 100, write one main program in a high-level language to call these four subroutines. It is suggested (a) to generate the ten numbers, (b) to echo-print the input, (c) to call a subroutine, and

```
 LOC   OBJECT CODE     ADDR1 ADDR2   STMT    SOURCE STATEMENT

000000                                  1 S413B    START 0
000000 47F0 F00A         0000A          2           B     10(0,15)      BRANCH AROUND ID
000004 05                               3           DC    AL1(5)
000005 E2F4F1F3C2                       4           DC    CL5'S413B'     IDENTIFIER
00000A 90EC D00C         0000C          5           STM   14,12,12(13)  SAVE REGISTERS
00000E 05C0                             6           BALR  12,0          SET REGISTER 12
000010                                  7           USING *,12           AS BASE REGISTER
000010 5831 0000         00000          8           L     3,0(1)        LOAD POINTER TO ARG LIST (ADDRESS OF SQR)
000014 5030 C02C         0003C          9           ST    3,CZERO        IN R3 AND STORE IT IN CZERO
000018 5841 0004         00004         10           L     4,4(1)         LOAD ADDRESS OF SUM IN R4
00001C 4190 0000         00000         11           LA    9,0            ZERO R9
000020 18A9                            12           LR    10,9           ZERO R10
000022 5A93 A000         00000         13 LOOP      A     9,0(3,10)      LOOP TO FIND SUM OF SQR'S
000026 41AA 0004         00004         14           LA    10,4(10)       INCREMENT R10 BY 4
00002A 59A0 C030         00040         15           C     10,=F'40'      CHECK IF ADDED 10 NUMBERS
00002E 4740 C012         00022         16           BL    LOOP           IF NOT, LOOP. IF SO, EXIT LOOP
000032 5094 0000         00000         17           ST    9,0(4)         STORE SUM IN ITS ADDRESS
000036 98EC D00C         0000C         18           LM    14,12,12(13)   RESTORE THE REGISTERS
00003A 07FE                            19           BR    14             RETURN
00003C                                 20 CZERO     DS    F
                                       21           END
000040 00000028                        22                 =F'40'
```

Fig. 5.25   Assembly listing for Subroutine S413B.

```
 LOC   OBJECT CODE     ADDR1 ADDR2   STMT    SOURCE STATEMENT

000000                                  1 S413C    START 0
000000 47F0 F00A         0000A          2           B     10(0,15)      BRANCH AROUND ID
000004 05                               3           DC    AL1(5)
000005 E2F4F1F3C3                       4           DC    CL5'S413C'     IDENTIFIER
00000A 90EC D00C         0000C          5           STM   14,12,12(13)  SAVE REGISTERS
00000E 05C0                             6           BALR  12,0          SET REGISTER 12
000010                                  7           USING *,12           AS BASE REGISTER
000010 5831 0000         00000          8           L     3,0(1)        LOAD POINTER TO ARG LIST IN R3
000014 5030 C030         00040          9           ST    3,CZERO        AND STORE IT IN CZERO
000018 5841 0004         00004         10           L     4,4(1)         LOAD ADDRESS OF SUM IN R4
00001C 4190 0000         00000         11           LA    9,0            ZERO R9
000020 5880 C030         00040         12           L     8,CZERO        LOAD ADDRESS OF SQR IN R11
000024 18A9                            13           LR    10,9           ZERO R10
000026 4180 000A         0000A         14           LA    8,10           PUT 10 IN R8
00002A 5A9A B000         00000         15 LOOP      A     9,0(10,11)     ACCUMULATE SUM OF SQR'S IN R9
00002E 41AA 0004         00004         16           LA    10,4(10)       INCREMENT R10 BY 4
000032 4680 C01A         0002A         17           BCT   8,LOOP         IF HAVE DONE 10 PASSES, EXIT LOOP
000036 5094 0000         00000         18           ST    9,0(4)         STORE THE SUM IN ITS ADDRESS
00003A 98EC D00C         0000C         19           LM    14,12,12(13)   RESTORE THE REGISTERS
00003E 07FE                            20           BR    14 RETURN
000040                                 21 CZERO     DS    F
                                       22           END
```

Fig. 5.26   Assembly listing for Subroutine S413C.

```
 LOC   OBJECT CODE     ADDR1 ADDR2   STMT    SOURCE STATEMENT

000000                                  1 S415     START 0
000000 47F0 F00A         0000A          2           B     10(0,15)      BRANCH AROUND ID
000004 05                               3           DC    AL1(5)
000005 E2F4F1F540                       4           DC    CL5'S415 '     IDENTIFIER
00000A 90EC D00C         0000C          5           STM   14,12,12(13)  SAVE REGISTERS
00000E 05C0                             6           BALR  12,0          SET REGISTER 12
000010                                  7           USING *,12           AS BASE REGISTER
000010 5831 0000         00000          8           L     3,0(1)        LOAD POINTER TO ARG LIST IN R3
000014 D227 C030 3000  00040 00000      9           MVC   CZERO(40),0(3) MOVE YTES AT SQR THRU SQR+40 TO CZERO
00001A 5841 0004         00004         10           L     4,4(1)         LOAD ADDRESS OF SUM IN R4
00001E 4190 0000         00000         11           LA    9,0            ZERO R9
000022 41B0 C030         00040         12           LA    11,CZERO       LOAD CZERO IN R11
000026 5A9B 0000         00000         13 LOOP      A     9,0(11)        ACCUMULATE SUM OF SQR'S IN R9
00002A 41BB 0004         00004         14           LA    11,4(11)       INCREMENT R11 BY 4
00002E 5980 C058         00068         15           C     11,=A(CZERO+40) SET CONDITION CODE
000032 4740 C016         00026         16           BL    LOOP           IF HAVE ADDED 10 NUMBERS, EXIT LOOP
000036 5094 0000         00000         17           ST    9,0(4)         STORE ANSWER IN ADDRESS OF SUM
00003A 98EC D00C         0000C         18           LM    14,12,12(13)   RESTORE THE REGISTERS
00003E 07FE                            19           BR    14 RETURN
000040                                 20 CZERO     DS    10F
                                       21           END
000068 00000068                        22                 =A(CZERO+40)
```

Fig. 5.27   Assembly listing for Subroutine S415.

(d) to print the answer for each subroutine right after each return to the main program and give an identification for each answer. Repeat steps (c) and (d) three more times.

A possible main program written in FORTRAN is shown in Fig. 5.23. Four subroutines (S410B, S413B, S413C, and S415) are shown in Figs. 5.24 through 5.27;

```
ACCORDING TO S410B, SUM IS          385

ACCORDING TO S413B, SUM IS          385

ACCORDING TO S413C, SUM IS          385

ACCORDING TO S415, SUM IS           385
```

Fig. 5.28 Output.

the output is shown in Fig. 5.28. Note that, in each of the four subroutines, the following instruction

```
DC  AL1'5'
```

is used. It has the same effect as the following DC instruction

```
DC  X'5'
```

shown earlier in Fig. 5.14.

5.8 AN EXAMPLE OF LINKAGE— COUNTING FIXED-POINT AND FLOATING-POINT SYMBOLS

The purpose of this example is twofold. First, to illustrate the linkage between a main program and its called subroutine; and second, to demonstrate how the first character in a variable name can be tested.

Write a FORTRAN main problem to do the following: Read in one data card which contains a number of FORTRAN variable names with blank(s) between each variable; then branch to an assembler language subprogram which totals up the number of fixed-point variables and the number of floating-point variables on the data card. This assembler language subprogram returns to the FORTRAN main program which prints out these totals. A sample data card and its printout are shown in Figs. 5.29 and 5.30, respectively.

A possible main program written in FORTRAN is shown in Fig. 5.31, which

Fig. 5.29 A sample data card.

```
CARD ANALYZED      XY  II  KKK  APLE            Z  JQ                    Y

TOTAL FIXED POINT = 3

TOTAL FLOATING POINT = 4
```

Fig. 5.30 Sample printout.

```
      DIMENSION CARD(20)
      READ(5,6)N
    6 FORMAT(I2)
      DO 10 I=1,N
      NUMI=0
      NUMX=0
      READ(5,1)CARD
    1 FORMAT(20A4)
      CALL FLOFIX(CARD,NUMI,NUMX)
      WRITE(6,2)CARD,NUMI,NUMX
    2 FORMAT(1H1,' THE LETTERS ON THE CARD ARE '//1X,20A4,//' TOTAL FIXE
     1D POINT = ',I2,//1X,' TOTAL FLOATING POINT = ',I2)
   10 CONTINUE
      STOP
      END
```

Fig. 5.31   A FORTRAN main program to call to subroutine FLOFIX.

calls the subroutine FLOFIX written in assembler language (Fig. 5.32). A corresponding flowchart for the subroutine FLOFIX is shown in Fig. 5.33.

The Compare Logical Immediate (CLI) instruction used in Fig. 5.32 is of SI format. It has the following general format:

$$\text{CLI} \quad D1(B1),I2$$

The comparison is between first operand, which is one byte in the main storage, and the second operand, which is a byte in the immediate field of the instruction. The condition code is set accordingly.

	Condition code (decimal)
First operand = second operand	0
First operand < second operand	1
First operand > second operand	2

The comparison is made on a logical basis; that is, they are compared as two unsigned integers. The *logical* comparison is carried out from left to right one bit at a time. For example,

$$\text{CLI} \quad 0(2048),\text{X'AF'}$$

compares the byte contents at location $(800)_{16} = (2048)_{10}$, with the second operand, the immediate field contents $(AF)_{16}$. Similarly, the following instruction

$$\text{CLI} \quad \text{LOC1},\text{C'*'}$$

compares the byte contents in the main storage at the location LOC1 with the character *. This character is represented by an eight-bit code (EBCDIC) as 01011100, or 5C in hexadecimal (see Appendix B).

```
LCC    OBJECT CODE     ADDR1 ADDR2   STMT     SOURCE STATEMENT

000000                                  1  FLOFIX    START  0
000000  47FF 000C             000C      2            BC     15,12(15)
000004  07                               3            DC     X'7'
000005  C6D3D6C6C9E740                   4            DC     CL7'FLOFIX '
00000C  90EC 000C             000C      5            STM    14,12,12(13)
000010  05B0                             6            BALR   11,0
000012                                   7            USING  *,11
000012  5851 0000             00000      8  APROG     L      5,0(1)
000016  5871 0004             00004      9            L      7,4(1)
00001A  1897                             10           LR     9,7
00001C  5881 0008             00008     11            L      8,8(1)
000020  18A8                             12           LR     10,8
000022  5877 0000             00000     13            L      7,0(7)
000026  5888 0000             00000     14            L      8,0(8)
00002A  4120 0001             00001     15            LA     2,1
00002E  47F0 B030             00042     16            B      CPARE
000032  5920 B09E             000B0     17  ADDX      C      2,=F'80'
000036  47A0 B090             000A2     18            BC     10,RETRN
00003A  4122 0001             00001     19            LA     2,1(2)
00003E  4155 0001             00001     20  ADINX     LA     5,1(5)
000042  9540 5000             00000     21  CPARE     CLI    0(5),C' '
000046  4780 B020             00032     22            BE     ADDX
00004A  95C9 5000             00000     23            CLI    0(5),C'I'
00004E  4780 B068             0007A     24            BE     NEXT
000052  95D1 5000             00000     25            CLI    0(5),C'J'
000056  4780 B068             0007A     26            BE     NEXT
00005A  95D2 5000             00000     27            CLI    0(5),C'K'
00005E  4780 B068             0007A     28            BE     NEXT
000062  95D3 5000             00000     29            CLI    0(5),C'L'
000066  4780 B068             0007A     30            BE     NEXT
00006A  95D4 5000             00000     31            CLI    0(5),C'M'
00006E  4780 B068             0007A     32            BE     NEXT
000072  95D5 5000             00000     33            CLI    0(5),C'N'
000076  4770 B070             00082     34            BNE    FLT
00007A  4177 0001             00001     35  NEXT      LA     7,1(7)
00007E  47F0 B074             00086     36            B      COMP
000082  4188 0001             00001     37  FLT       LA     8,1(8)
000086  5920 B09E             000B0     38  COMP      C      2,=F'80'
00008A  47A0 B090             000A2     39            BC     10,RETRN
00008E  4122 0001             00001     40            LA     2,1(2)
000092  4155 0001             00001     41            LA     5,1(5)
000096  9540 5000             00000     42            CLI    0(5),C' '
00009A  4770 B074             00086     43            BNE    COMP
00009E  4780 B020             00032     44            BE     ADDX
0000A2  5079 0000             00000     45  RETRN     ST     7,0(9)
0000A6  508A 0000             00000     46            ST     8,0(10)
0000AA  98EC 000C             000C      47            LM     14,12,12(13)
0000AE  07FE                             48            BR     14
                                         49            END
0000B0  00000050                        50            =F'80'
```

Fig. 5.32 Assembly listing for FLOFIX.

134

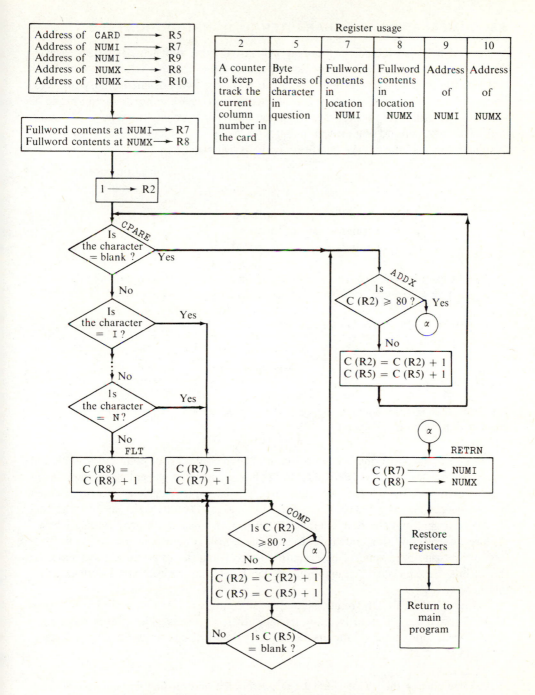

Fig. 5.33 Flowchart for Subroutine FLOFIX.

135

5.9 COMPARE LOGICAL CHARACTER (CLC) INSTRUCTION†

In Section 5.2, we studied the popular MVC instruction, which used the SS format. As another example of SS format, let us explore the Compare Logical Character (CLC) instruction, which is primarily used to compare two unsigned binary integers. The word *logical*, as used earlier in the CLI instruction, is not concerned with mode of reasoning. Rather, it indicates that the given binary integer is treated as an unsigned one. This instruction compares two character string (e.g., JOHN versus LUKE) as two unsigned integers, and set the condition code as follows:

	Condition code (decimal)
First operand = second operand	0
First operand < second operand	1
First operand > second operand	2

Let us examine the CLC instruction shown in Fig. 5.34. It compares the four-byte string starting at location 000800 with another four-byte string at 000F00.

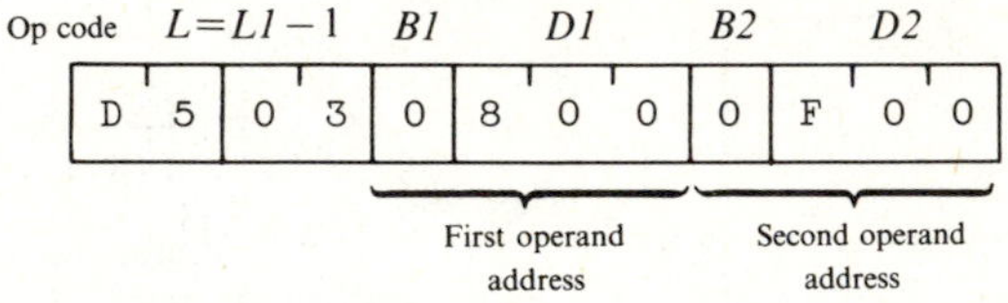

Fig. 5.34 CLC instruction to compare two unsigned binary integers. *L1* is the actual number of bytes to be compared.

Suppose that locations 000800 through 000803 contain four characters JOHN, and locations 000F00 through 000F03, LUKE. Each character is represented by an eight-bit code known as EBCDIC (see Appendix B). For example, character J is represented by 11010001, and L by 11010011. Since 11010001 < 11010011, the second operand (LUKE) is larger than the first operand (JOHN) on an unsigned binary (logical) basis. As a result, the condition code is set to 01. The *logical* comparison is carried out from left to right one bit a time. The execution stops when (a) an inequality is found, or (b) all bits are checked. A maximum of 256 bytes may be compared with one CLC instruction.

Although the EBCDIC (eight-bit code) will be discussed in more detail in Chapter 10, it is convenient to note its basic design. In *logical* sense, the special characters rank lowest, alphabetic characters next, and numerical characters highest. This is shown in Fig. 5.35.

---

† The remainder of this chapter may be skipped in the first reading without loss of continuity.

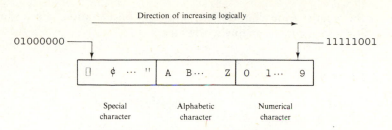

Fig. 5.35   Sequence of eight-bit EBCDIC.

The machine language instruction in Fig. 5.34 can be written in assembler language:

CLC   2048(4,0),3840(0)

or

CLC   HERE(4),THERE

where HERE and THERE are two symbolic addresses. In general, the Compare Logical Character (CLC) instruction has the following form:

CLC   *D1(L1,B1),D2(B2)*

where *L1* is the number of *bytes* to be compared.

Suppose that the character string at each location is as follows:

	In characters	In hexadecimal
At location HERE:	BROWN	C2D9D6E6D5
THERE:	SMITH	E2D4C9E3C8
PART:	B306	C2F3F0F6

After the execution of each of the unrelated CLC instructions, the condition code is set as shown below.

Instruction	Explicit length	Condition code setting
CLC HERE(5),THERE	5	1
CLC THERE(5),HERE	5	2
CLC HERE(3),THERE	3	1
CLC HERE(3),PART	3	1
CLC HERE(1),PART	1	0

The number of characters (bytes) to be compared is explicitly written in each of the above five instructions. This is not necessary if the length of a character string (a field) is defined elsewhere in the program. In this case, the length field is *implicitly*

assumed as the length of the character string under consideration. For example, the
first instruction above may be simply written as

```
                        CLC     HERE,THERE
                          ⋮
        HERE    DC      CL5'BROWN'
        THERE   DC      CL5'SMITH'
```

5.10 A SYSTEM/370
INSTRUCTION—COMPARE LOGICAL LONG (CLCL)

The Compare Logical Character (CLC) instruction discussed in the last section has a
severe constraint: 256-byte limit on character comparison. In IBM System/370 (not
available in IBM System/360), the Compare Logical Long (CLCL) instruction is available to compare two fields up to $2^{24} = 16,777,216$ bytes in length. The sole purpose
of this instruction is to set the condition code.

CC = 0   if two operands are equal, or if both fields have zero length

CC = 1   if the first operand < the second operand

CC = 2   if the first operand > the second operand

CC = 3   not possible.

Although the CLCL instruction is of RR format (see Fig. 5.36), it compares two
operands in main storage, not in the registers. Also, this instruction of RR format has
its peculiarities. The *R1* and *R2* fields each represent a pair of even–odd registers.

OF	R1	R2
0 7	8 11	12 15

Fig. 5.36 Compare Logical Long instruction: CLCL *R1,R2*.

Therefore, there are four registers involved. As listed in Table 5.1, the address of
the leftmost byte of each operand is contained in an even-numered register, while the
number of bytes for each operand is contained in an odd-numbered register of the
even–odd pair of registers. In case that the operands compared are not equal in
number of bytes, the right end of the shorter operand is automatically extended by
using the padding characters specified by a programmer (see the last column in
Table 5.1).

Let us assume that the contents in registers are as follows:

```
                Register  4     000BD720
                Register  5     40000005
                Register 10     000889A0
                Register 11     40000004

        Location  0889A0–0889A7     C0A018F3 05EF187F
        Location  0BD720–0BD727     D3C3E3D9 D30090EC
```

Table 5.1　Four registers involved in a CLCL instruction

Bit positions in each register	Two registers used (in connection with the first operand in storage)		Two registers used (in connection with the second operand in storage)	
	R1 (even)	*R1*+1 (odd)	*R2* (even)	*R2*+1 (odd)
0–7	Not used	Not used	Not used	Padding characters
8–31	Address of the leftmost byte of the first operand	Number of bytes in the first operand†	Address of the leftmost byte of the second operand	Number of bytes in the second operand†

† If zero byte is specified in both *R1*+1 and *R2*+1 registers, then the operands are considered to be equal.

After execution of each CLCL instruction, the pertinent information is shown below.

Instruction	First operand		Second operand		CC setting	Remarks
	Addresses	Contents	Addresses	Contents		
CLCL 4,10	0BD720– 0BD724	D3C3E3D9D3	0889A0– 0889A3	C0A018F340	2	40 is padded
CLCL 10,4	0889A0– 0889A3	C0A018F340	0BD720– 0BD724	D3C3E3D9D3	1	40 is padded
CLCL 5,10					—	Illegal instruction

There is an added feature of a CLCL instruction: After an unequal comparison, the two bytes that caused inequality are identified. We shall now see how it is carried out. During the execution of a CLCL instruction, the comparison is made from left to right. The contents of all four registers are constantly updating. The contents in each of the two even-numbered registers are increasing as the address of each operand is going up. After the execution of a CLCL instruction, the contents of these registers signify the last addresses compared. On the other hand, the contents in each of the two odd-numbered registers (for byte length) are decreasing toward zero. After the execution of a CLCL instruction, the contents of these two registers indicate the numbers of bytes still uncompared.

5.11 MOVE LONG (MVCL) INSTRUCTION—AN EXTENSION TO MVC

The MVC instruction discussed in Section 5.3 has a severe drawback: It only permits up to 256 bytes per move. To alleviate this limitation, a new Move Long (MVCL) instruction is included in IBM System/370 standard set of instructions. It can move up to $2^{24} = 16,777,216$ bytes from one storage location to another.

The MVCL instruction is of RR format (Fig. 5.37), but it has many peculiarities. The *R1* and *R2* fields, each representing a pair of even–odd registers, deal with, respectively, move-to and move-from fields. Thus, there are four registers involved in an MVCL instruction. The detailed uses of four registers as shown in Table 5.2 are similar to those listed in Table 5.1. Note that this instruction of RR format copies data from one place in main storage to another place in main storage. It does not copy from or to the registers.

OE	*R1*	*R2*
0 7	8 11	12 15

Fig. 5.37 Move Long instruction: MVCL *R1,R2*.

The length of the move-from field (second operand count) need not agree with that of the move-to field (first operand count). If the second operand is shorter than the first operand, the rightmost bytes of the first operand are padded with the padding characters (specified in bits positions 0–7 in register *R2* + 1). On the other hand, if the second operand is longer than the first operand, the rightmost bytes of the second operand are truncated. The important point: The copying is accomplished one byte at a time

Table 5.2 Four registers used in a Move Long (MVCL) instruction

Bit positions in each register	Two registers used in connection with the first operand (move-to) in main storage		Two registers used in connection with the second operand (move-from) in main storage	
	R1 (even)	*R1*+1 (odd)	*R2* (even)	*R2*+1 (odd)
0–7	Not used	Not used	Not used	Padding characters
8–31	The address of leftmost byte of the first operand	The number of bytes in the first operand (count field); if 0, no movement	The address of leftmost byte of the second operand	The number of bytes in the second operand (count field)

from left to right (starting from the low-numbered byte address to the high-numbered one).

In the action of this instruction, the condition code is set.

CC = 0   if the first operand count = the second operand count.

CC = 1   if the first operand count < the second operand count (truncation took place).

CC = 2   if the first operand count > the second operand count (padding was used).

CC = 3   if destructive overlap occurs and no movement is performed.

The destructive overlap of the operands occurs when the part of contents in the first operand is used as a source after a piece of data has already been moved into it. An example of destructive overlap is shown in Fig. 5.38, as the movement starts at the high-order end of two operands and proceeds to the right.

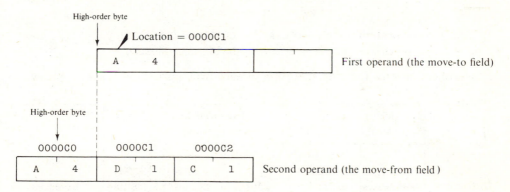

Fig. 5.38 Occurrence of destructive overlap (contents and location of various bytes are shown for illustration only).

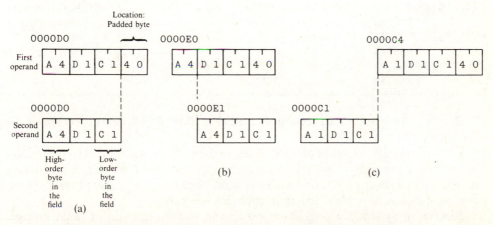

Fig. 5.39 Three possible cases for movement in MVCL instruction.

By contrast, three examples of possible movement are shown in Fig. 5.39. In Fig. 5.39(a), the high-order byte of the move-to field (first operand) coincides with the high-order byte of the move-from field (second operand). In Fig. 5.39(b), the high-order byte of the move-to field is positioned to the left of high-order byte of the move-from field. Finally, in Fig. 5.39(c), the high-order byte of the move-to field is to the right of the rightmost byte in the move-from field.

For example, if the contents in registers are as follows:

Register 4	000BD720
Register 5	40000005
Register 6	000BD720
Register 7	00000000
Register 8	000BD720
Register 9	40000004
Register 10	000889A0
Register 11	40000004

Location	0889A0–0889A7	C0A018F3 05EF187F
Location	0BD720–0BD727	D3C3E3D9 D30090EC

the pertinent information after execution of each `MVCL` instruction is shown below.

Instruction	Move-from field (second operand)		Move-to field (first operand)		CC setting	Remarks
	Addresses	Contents after execution	Addresses	Contents after execution		
`MVCL 4,10`	0889A0–0889A3	C0A018F3	0BD720–0BD724	C0A018F340	2	
`MVCL 10,4`	0BD720–0BD724	D3C3E3D9D3	0889A0–0889A3	D3C3E3D9	1	No movement because the count field in the first operand = 0
`MVCL 6,10`	0889A0–0889A3	C0A018F3	—	—	1	
`MVCL 8,10`	0889A0–0889A3	C0A018F3	0BD720–0BD723	C0A018F3	0	

Before we turn to the next section, two other aspects of `MVCL` instruction are worth mentioning.

First, during the execution of an `MVCL` instruction, the contents of all four registers are constantly changing. Two even-numbered registers (see Table 5.2) are counting up, byte by byte, as the addresses increase, while the two odd-numbered registers are counting down to zero as the length in each field decreases.

Second, in System/370 or System/360 having 16,777,216 bytes of main storage, storage addresses *wrap around* from the maximum byte address $2^{32} - 1 = 16,777,215$

to address 0. When the move-from field specified in an MVCL instruction wraps around, care must be taken so that the overlapping of the operand locations does not affect the final contents of the move-to field.

5.12 AN IBM SYSTEM/370 INSTRUCTION—COMPARE LOGICAL CHARACTER UNDER MASK (CLM) INSTRUCTION

The Compare Logical Character under Mask (CLM) instruction is used primarily by a system programmer. It compares a piece of data (not necessarily a fullword long nor on a fullword boundary) with data in a register.

It is of RS format (see Fig. 5.40). The second operand is compared logically with the first operand under control of a mask. The sole purpose of this instruction is to set the condition code. The four bits in positions 12–15, known as the mask, are

BD	R1	M3	B2	D2

Bit position ⟶ 0   7 8   11 12 15 16 19 20   31

Fig. 5.40   CLM instruction is of RS format: CLM $R1, M3, D2(B2)$.

designed to correspond with the four bytes of the register $R1$. The comparison is performed in the following manner: The byte positions (in the register $R1$) corresponding to ones in the masks are collected together as a contiguous field. It is then compared with the second operand. The starting address of the second operand is $D2 + C(B2)$; its length is equal to the number of 1-bits in the mask, and is always equal to the length of the first operand. Thus, no more than four bytes can be compared in the action of this instruction.

The condition code setting is as follows:
CC = 0   if the selected bytes are identical, or if the mask field contains four bits: 0000.
CC = 1   if the selected bytes in the first operand < those in the second operand.
CC = 2   if the selected bytes in the first operand > those in the second operand.
CC = 3   not used.

For example, if the contents of registers and that of storage are

Register 4:	D1C1C3D2	(JACK)
Register 9:	D1D0D3D3	(JILL)
Storage location HERE:	D1D6C8D5	(JOHN)
Storage location NOW:	D0D3D34B	(ILL)

after the execution of each of the following instructions, the condition code is set as indicated:

Instruction	Contents compared (in hexadecimal) First operand : Second operand	Condition code setting
CLM 4,15,HERE	D1C1C3D2 : D1D6C8D5	1
CLM 4,0,HERE	no bytes compared	0
CLM 4,3,HERE	C3D2 : D1D6	1
CLM 9,7,NOW	D0D3D3 : D0D3D3	0
CLM 4,1,HERE	D2 : D1	2

Note that, in a CLM instruction, the second operand is actually written last. Its general format in assembler language is

$$CLM \quad R1, M3, D2(B2)$$

BIBLIOGRAPHY

IBM Operating System/360 COBOL (F) Programmer's Guide, Form GC28-6380, IBM Corp.

IBM Operating System/360 Concepts and Facilities, Form C28-6535, IBM Corp.

IBM System/360 Operating System Fortran IV (G) Programmer's Guide, Form GC28-6639, IBM Corp.

IBM System/360 Operating System PL/I (F) Programmer's Guide, Form GC28-6594, IBM Corp.

IBM System/360 Principles of Operation, Form GA22-6821, IBM Corp.

IBM System/370 Principles of Operation, Form GA22-7000, IBM Corp.

IBM System/360 Programming with Base Registers and the USING *Instruction*, Form C20-1614, IBM Corp.

PROBLEMS

1. A given byte is required to set to A3 in hexadecimal. The effective address of this byte is not given, but its displacement is known as $(1500)_{10}$ and register 9 is used as the base register. Write the instruction in hexadecimal form as well as in assembler language.

2. A special character # is to be moved to the first byte of a fullword whose address is NUMBER. Write the instruction in assembler language.

3. Given:
The instruction in hexadecimal: 92FA0100

The main storage before the execution (from address 00009E through 000106) contains 00 in each byte.

Required: Byte contents in hexadecimal from address 00009E through 000106 after the execution of the instruction.

4. If the contents of register 1 are 00001A64, what will be the contents in register 6 after the execution of each of the following two instructions in sequence:

$$L \quad 6,0(1)$$
$$L \quad 6,0(6)$$

Refer to the middle and lowest tier in Fig. 5.21 when solving this problem.

5. a) Write an assembler language instruction that would compare the byte of immediate data $(79)_{10}$ with the byte of data at the main storage address $(6678)_{10}$. Register 3 is used as the base register; the base address is $(4444)_{10}$.

b) Write the instruction in part (a) in machine language using hexadecimal notation.

6. What is the condition code setting after each of the comparisons below, where the immediate data A are logically compared to the contents in byte B.

a) A: 11001100
B: 11001110

b) A: 00000001
B: 00000001

7. The following pair of instructions

$$L \quad 3,A$$
$$ST \quad 3,B$$

is not as efficient as a single MVC instruction:

$$MVC \quad B,A$$

Under what condition(s) do they produce the same result?

8. It is desired to move the symbol ∗ into an area whose first byte address is STAR. The following two instructions can be effectively used.

$$MVI \quad STAR,C'*'$$
$$MVC \quad STAR+1(131),STAR$$

After the execution of these two instructions, how many bytes will there be having contents ∗? Give their symbolic addresses.

9. a) Write instructions in assembler language to move a total of 80 blank characters into an area, the first byte having the address OUTPUT.

b) Given:

The instruction: D20708000F00

Main storage area

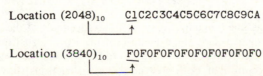

Location $(2048)_{10}$ C1C2C3C4C5C6C7C8C9CA

Location $(3840)_{10}$ F0F0F0F0F0F0F0F0F0F0

Show the contents of the storage agea after the MVC instruction is executed.

10. The area `INAREA` in the main storage contains the detailed information of a student. It is desirable to move each item into the area `OUTAREA` in the main storage. Fill out each blank with an `MVC` instruction and use explicit length.

	INAREA	OUTAREA	MVC instruction
Student number	0–6 (7 bytes)	10–16	MVC OUTAREA+10(7),INAREA
Name	8–27 (20 bytes)	21–40	_____
University address	30–49 (20 bytes)	55–75	_____
Home address	60–109 (50 bytes)	101–150	_____
Street	60–79 (20 bytes)	161–180	_____
City	80–100 (21 bytes)	190–210	_____
State	101–104 (4 bytes)	5–9	_____
Zip code	105–109 (5 bytes)	0–4	_____
Sex	110 (1 byte)	17	_____
Department	120–129 (10 bytes)	211–220	_____

11. The Insert Character (`IC`) instruction is of RX type and has the general format:

$$IC \quad R1, D2(X2, B2)$$

After the execution, the single byte at the second operand location is placed into bits 24–31 of the register $R1$ and the bits 0–23 in the register $R1$ are unchanged. For example, if `INBYTE` contains A4 in hexadecimal and the initial contents of register 7 are FFFFFFF8, the contents of register 7 will be changed to FFFFFFA4 after the execution of the instruction

```
IC   7,INBYTE
```

The Store Character (`STC`) instruction is the converse of `IC` instruction.

Write the machine language version (in hexadecimal) of the `MVI` instruction in the following segment both before and after the execution of the `STC` instruction

```
         LA   5,0
         STC  5,HERE+1
          ⋮
HERE     MVI  10(7),X'FF'
```

12. Given: The following program segment

```
         IC   5,X'FF'
         STC  5,HERE+1
          ⋮
HERE     MVC  10(3,7),16(10)
```

a) Write the machine language version (in hexadecimal) of the `MVC` instruction in the program segment before the execution of the `STC` instruction,

b) same as (a), except that after execution of the `STC` instruction,

c) after the execution of both `STC` and `MVC` instructions, how many bytes will be moved?

13. Translate the following instructions into their hexadecimal form.

$$\text{LM} \quad 14,12,12(13)$$
$$\text{STM} \quad 14,6,12(13)$$

14. A "dump" is a snapshot of the storage contents in a specified area. Below are two lines from a dump, each representing 8 instructions. The first instruction has the address 006300. The program was executed on an IBM System/360.

```
006300  5840B400  4150B3FC  5A50B404  59450000  074AD20B  5000B03E  07FE0000  00000008
006320  00000010  00000001  00000000  00000000  00000000  00000000  00000000  00000000
```

   a) Translate all the instructions into assembler language.
   b) What caused the program to dump? (That is, what instruction during execution failed to work and why?)
   c) What register is being used as the base register?
   Note: Contents of register 11 = 00005F20

15. It is decided that the subroutine SUBR1 in Fig. 5.14 is to be called subroutine SUB. Modify the housekeeping package to conform with this change.

16. The package shown in Fig. 5.14 (Part I) has the following three instructions which can be taken out without causing trouble: BC, DC, DC. What purpose(s) do they serve?

LABORATORY ASSIGNMENT

Do one of the following problems and run it on a computer. In Appendix D is shown several sample sets of control cards for the main program written in a high-level language, and subroutine in assembler language. Be sure to check with your own installation before you use them.

1. Convert the program in Fig. 1.17 into a subroutine in assembler language. Write a main program in a high-level language to handle the required output.

2. The purpose of this problem is to count the number of commas in a given card. In order to do so, write a subroutine COMMA in assembler language. The main program in high-level language is used (a) to call the subroutine COMMA, (b) to read a card in 20A4 format, and (c) to print out the number of commas in I2 format.

3. a) Write a subroutine CALCU to calculate the following expression:

$$E = \frac{C}{D}$$

   where $C = A^2 + B^2$ and $D = A^2 - B^2$.
   The integers A and B are known from a main program. The values C, D, and E must be stored to be printed by a main program.
   b) Write a main program in FORTRAN, COBOL, or PL/I to read in A, B, then call subroutine CALCU; and print out A, B, C, D, and E.

4. Write a complete subprogram COMP in assembler language to compute the following expression:

$$\text{ANS} = ((A + B - C) \times D)/E \qquad \text{if} \quad B \le C$$
$$\text{ANS} = ((A - B + C) \times D)/E \qquad \text{if} \quad B > C$$

This subprogram is to be called by a main program written in a high-level language. All variables are fixed-point numbers.

5. Modify the subroutine ARITH (see Fig. 5.20) so that the value of the remainder after the division will be retained in a register. Also modify a main program (Figs. 5.17 through 5.19) to include the remainder as a part of the output.

CHAPTER 6

An Introduction to Assembler Language

6.1 PRELIMINARY REMARKS

In the previous three chapters, we discussed many instructions of common occurrence. For example, the following 16-bit instruction in machine language

0001	1010	0111	1011

or its hexadecimal equivalent

1	A	7	B

has the following interpretation: "Add the contents of register 11 to the contents of register 7, and keep the answer in register 7." We have also briefly mentioned its equivalent in symbolic (assembler) language:

AR 7,11

Similarly, many other assembler language instructions have been thus introduced. These examples should help provide motives for exploring more details of assembler language—the principal objective of this chapter.

A typical assembler language instruction consists of four fields: *name, operation, operands,* and *comments,* which are discussed in the next section. The operand field may contain one or more operands. The components used in an operand are subject to many restrictions; they are discussed in Sections 6.3 through 6.8.

There are two types of assembler language instructions—machine instructions and assembler instructions. A machine instruction, such as L, LA, ST, etc., tells the assembler to generate a machine language instruction, whereas the assembler instruction does not. The latter serves as a special note to the assembler. For example, the character * in column 1 of an assembler instruction card signifies that this is a comment card,† and no translation to machine language is required. This and many other pseudo-operation instructions will be discussed in Sections 6.9 through 6.14.

Assembler

Let us begin with a brief discussion on an assembler—its functions and, specifically, how can it help a programmer.

Each type of computer accepts only one particular language for computation—its machine language. The current practice is to code in a language (source language) akin to our written language, and then utilize the computer to translate this language into the machine's language (object language). This machine language program is called the *object program* or *object module*; this step is known as *assembly* or *compilation*. The object module, combined with any subroutines that may be needed, creates a *load module*; this step is known as *linking* or *linkage editing*. At this point the computer loads and executes the instructions in the load module and dutifully performs the necessary computations. The student should note in this connection that computers are used for three purposes: translation, linking, and computation (see Fig. 6.1).

Computer manufacturers and users of computers have devoted much effort in a search for ways to shift the burden of programming from humans to computers. Their work has led to the development of compilers (for source languages written in the high-level languages such as FORTRAN, PL/I, or COBOL) and assemblers for source programs written in assembler languages.

Clerical Functions for an Assembler

An assembler is a program which translates a user's program written in assembler language‡ into machine language (see Fig. 6.1). There are a number of clerical functions which, tedious and error-prone to humans, can be performed well by an assembler.

a) An assembler can translate, say, ST to its numeric operation code 50 by referring to a table. In assembler language programming, a programmer can use mnemonics such as ST for STore, A for Add, or M for Multiply. The word mnemonics is derived from a Greek word meaning *aid to memory*.

b) In an assembler language program, constants can be written in decimal (e.g., 67), in hexadecimal (e.g., 5A3), in binary (e.g., 01011010), etc. An assembler can dutifully translate them into the correct representations in the machine language.

---

† Same as a comment card in a FORTRAN program, indicated by the "C" punched in the first column.

‡ Also known as "assembly language"; there is, unfortunately, not standard terminology for this type of language.

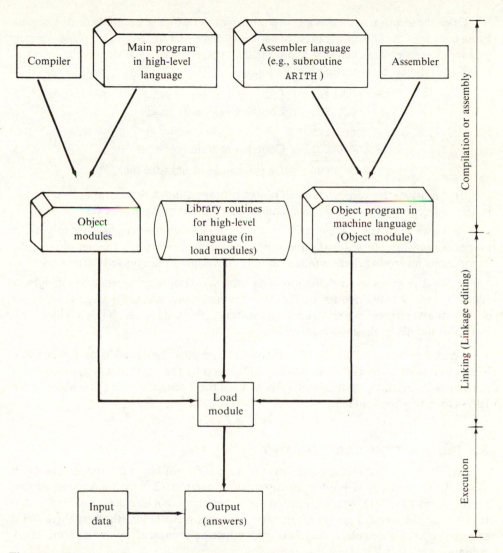

Fig. 6.1 Typical processing for a main program in high-level language and subroutine in assembler language.

   c) It assigns storage locations for each instruction, constant, or data area; and makes sure they are available. A programmer can then refer to these locations with symbols. For example, the symbolic address SALE in the following assembler language instruction

ST   6,SALE

indicates the location of a fullword in main storage.

Once the location of SALE is known, the assembler can also compute displacement. For example, if the effective address of SALE is 000F60, and the contents of base register and index register are 00000F40 and 00000000, respectively, then the displacement is readily computed by the assembler as follows:

	00000F60	Effective address of SALE
−	00000F40	Contents in base register
	00000020	
−	00000000	Contents in index register
	020	Displacement in hexadecimal

d) An assembler can produce an object program, indicate clerical errors, if any, in the source program, and make a listing (see Fig. C.3 in Appendix C).

e) As we shall see in Chapter 9, an assembler allows the programmer to write a *macro instruction*. It will make the necessary macro expansion; the net effect is to expand one macro instruction into a number of assembler language instructions.

f) Small changes in the definition of a problem do not require extensive changes in the program. This is due to the fact that the assembler automatically reassigns all addresses and references to instructions, constants, and data areas. Thus, it eliminates potential pitfalls in the modification of a program.

There are several assemblers available for the IBM System/370 or System/360. The selection of an assembler is strongly influenced by the operating system used in a particular installation. In this book we shall limit the discussion to the assembler under IBM Operating System/360.

6.2 INSTRUCTION CARD FORMAT

The symbolic instructions are punched one to a card similar to the format shown in Fig. 6.2. Columns 1–71 are for the instruction, column 72 indicates a continuation, and columns 73–80 are for identification and sequencing. An instruction is divided into four fields: the name, operation, operand, and comment fields; the first three fields are used by the assembler. Any two fields must be separated by at least one blank column.

The name field is optional, but it should have a symbol if the instruction is referred to elsewhere in the program. This name field must begin in column 1; it may not have any embedded blanks in the symbol (e.g., DIVIDE in Fig. 6.2, not DI VIDE). If column 1 is blank, the assembler will assume that the name field is not used. We shall describe the symbols in greater detail in Section 6.5.

The operation field usually begins with column 10, although it may begin with the first nonblank after the name field. This field is mandatory. It contains either the mnemonic operation code for an assembler language instruction (e.g., DR in Fig. 6.2), or the name of a previously defined macro, which will be discussed in Chapter 9.

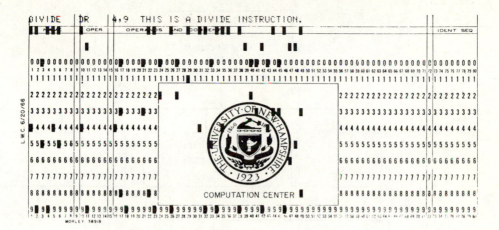

Fig. 6.2 A source card in the assembler language.

There should not be any embedded blanks within the operation field. A rather complete list of operation codes is shown in Appendix F.

The operand field usually begins with column 16, although it may begin with the first nonblank after the operation field. A comma must be used to separate two operands (e.g., 4,9 in Fig. 6.2). No blanks are permitted between an operand and its adjacent comma. Hence the following instruction is illegal:

$$DR \quad 4, 9$$

We shall discuss the possible components of an operand in more detail in the next six sections.

Finally, comments may begin in any column as long as they are separated from the last operand by at least one blank. In other words, the comment field may begin with the column following the blank column that terminates the operand field. It cannot go further than column 71 because the restriction is that column 72 must be left blank. A whole card can be used for a comment if an asterisk is placed in column 1 and column 72 is left blank. The assembler does not translate this card, but the comments are printed in the listing.

If an instruction has to be continued on another card, a nonblank character, such as X, must be punched in column 72, and the remaining instruction must start in column 16 of the next card. If there is no continuation, column 72 is left blank. Use of the identification and sequencing field is optional; anything punched there will appear in the assembler listing.

6.3 A BASIC BUILDING BLOCK OF AN OPERAND—TERM

The operand field in an assembler language instruction consists of one, two, or three operands. An *operand* of a given instruction is a piece of data which is operated on

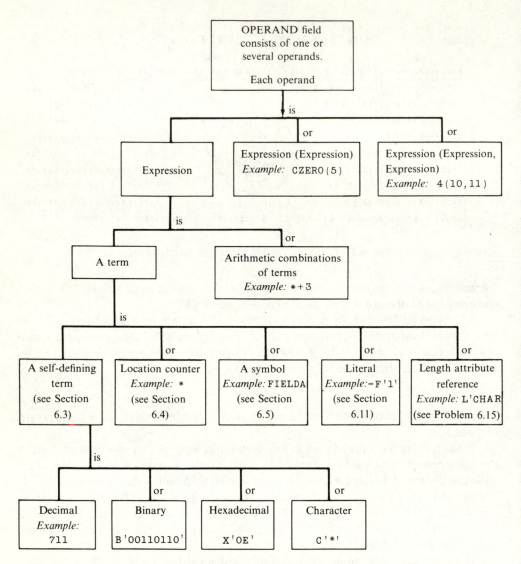

Fig. 6.3   Terms and expressions.

or with by that instruction. On the other hand, an *operand address* means the address of an operand of an instruction. Ambiguity often exists about these two different words; context must be relied on for the meaning.

Basically, an operand comprises one or more expressions (see Fig. 6.3, particularly for examples). In turn, an expression may consist of a single term or some arithmetic combinations of terms.

A term is representation of a value. Five classes of terms are recognized by the assembler. As shown in Fig. 6.3, they are self-defining terms, symbols, location counter references, literals, and length attribute references. Now we shall discuss the simplest one—a self-defining term. The location counter references and symbols will be discussed in the next two sections. The literals, closely related to DC instruction in appearance, will be dealt with in Section 6.11, while the length attribute references will be taken up in Problem 6.15 and in Chapter 9.

Self-Defining Item

A self-defining term is one whose value is inherently defined in the term. It is usually used to specify

    a) A register number such as both 4 and 9 in Fig. 6.2.

    b) A displacement to compute the storage address such as 280 in the following instruction (see Fig. 3.13):

$$M \quad 2,280(0,10)$$

    c) A mask such as 4 in the following instruction (see Fig. 4.6):

$$BC \quad 4,256(0,8)$$

    d) Storage-area length such as five bytes moved in the following instruction (see Fig. 5.4):

$$MVC \quad 2048(5,0),3840(0)$$

    e) An immediate field such as 14 in the following instruction (see Fig. 5.2):

$$MVI \quad 256(0),14$$

All the self-defining terms shown in items (a) through (e) are expressed in decimal. Each decimal term may consist of up to eight digits, forming an unsigned decimal number 0 through 16,777,215, or $(2^{24} - 1)$. A decimal term is assembled in its binary equivalent.

Aside from its decimal representation, a self-defining term can also be expressed in hexadecimal, binary, or character form; they are described in detail below.

Hexadecimal representation

A self-defining term using the hexadecimal representation consists of up to six hexadecimal digits enclosed in apostrophes and preceded by the letter X. Hence, the maximum value of a hexadecimal term is X'FFFFFF'. A typical example is the immediate operand using two hexadecimal digits in the following instruction (see Fig. 5.2):

$$MVI \quad 256(0),X'0E'$$

Character representation

A character is represented in one byte using the eight-bit code, known as EBCDIC (see Appendix B). Of the 256 possible combinations, only 62 are printable:

Letters   A, B, C, . . . , Z
Digits   0, 1, 2, . . . , 9
Special characters   #, @, $, ?, ¢, <, >, |, !, ;, ¬, %, :, '',
                      +, −, *, ,, /, =, ', (,), ., &, and blank.

The character representation of a self-defining term consists of up to three characters. The second operand of the following instruction presents a typical example

       MVI   OUTAREA,C'#'

where the single character # is enclosed in apostrophes and preceded by the letter C.
A word of caution: When an apostrophe (') or an ampersand (&) is used in a character self-defining term, *two* are required. Thus, the character string M&H must be written as C'M&&H'.

Binary representation

A self-defining term using the binary representation consists of up to 24 bits enclosed in apostrophes and preceded by the letter B. The assembler translates this information into the bit pattern with leftmost zeros added when necessary. For example, the mask field in the following instruction

       BC   B'0100',LOOP

is a binary self-defining term. It causes a branch to LOOP if condition code is 1. This binary representation can be replaced by its decimal equivalent 4; and a programmer has the complete freedom to choose one of the four representations: decimal, binary, hexadecimal, or character.

6.4 LOCATION COUNTER

As mentioned in Section 6.1, an assembler not only translates a symbolic language instruction into its machine language equivalent, but also takes care of many tedious chores. For example, it can assign an address each to a set of sequential instructions.
This is carried out by means of the location counter. This counter increments after each machine instruction; the amount of increment is equal to the byte number used in the instruction. Consider, for example, a set of instructions shown in Fig. 6.4.

Location counter setting	Instruction			Length of instruction in bytes
00000E	ATHREE	L	3,FIELDA	4
000012		A	3,FIELDB	4
000016	CLEAR	SR	4,4	2
000018	A5	L	5,FIELDA	4
00001C		D	4,FIELDB	4
000020				

Fig. 6.4 Portion of program to illustrate the location counter.

Let us assume that the location counter setting is 00000E for the first instruction. Since the first instruction (L) is four-byte long, the location counter is updated to $(00000E)_{16} + 4 = (000012)_{16}$ for the second instruction. Likewise, the second instruction is four-byte long, and the location counter is incremented by 4 again. Or, $000012 + 4 = 000016$. The third instruction SR is only two-byte long, and the location counter setting for the next instruction is then $000016 + 2 = 000018$. The remaining two instructions are each four-byte long. As a result, the location counter settings are 00001C and 000020, respectively.

Initial Setting of Location Counter

A programmer can dictate the initial value of the location counter by simply writing as assembler instruction START as the first instruction in the program. Actually, a START card can serve two purposes: to designate a symbolic name to the present program and to assign the initial value to the location counter. Consider, for example, the following instruction:

BETA   START   300

After assembly, the program name is assigned as BETA; and the initial value of the location counter is set at decimal 300. However, if the operand field in START is left blank, or if the START instruction is not written, then the initial value in the location counter will be set at zero.

Location Counter Reference

During the processing of an instruction, the location counter setting represents the address of the instruction. A programmer may refer to this address by using the asterisk (∗). For example, the asterisk in the second operand of the following instruction

Location counter
——————————

000034   MVC AREA(6),∗

represents the *current* location counter setting, or $(000034)_{16}$. As such, the asterisk (∗) is known as *location counter reference*. The net effect of this instruction is to move this very instruction MVC into the six-byte area AREA, which must be defined in a name field somewhere in the program.

6.5 SYMBOLS AND SYMBOL TABLE

We are now in the position to discuss the third common type of terms—symbols. At the point, the reader should refer to Fig. 6.3 in Section 6.3 for the relationships between a symbol and an operand.

As far as a programmer is concerned, the symbol he or she selects in an operand must be *defined*, which means that it also appears in the name field somewhere in the program, once and only once.

A symbol must be 1–8 alphanumeric characters in length. The first character must be an alphabetic character and it may be one of the special letters #, @, or $. However, one should avoid to use these special letters as *some* assemblers will reject them if used as the first character.

Examples

Valid	Invalid	Reason
FIELDA	FIELD A	Embedded blank
BUS1	1BUS	First character not alphabetic
DOLLAR	DOLL*	Special character
STUDENNO	STUDENTNO	Nine characters

Symbol Table

The assembly in Fig. 6.1 is a two-pass process; each pass is the processing of the complete source program once. During the first pass, each instruction is processed individually and the assembler updates the location counter. All the symbols used in the name field are entered into a storage area known as the *symbol table*. One such symbol table is constructed (see Fig. 6.5) for the instruction sequence illustrated in Fig. 6.4.

Symbol in character (8 bytes)	Location counter setting in hexadecimal (3 bytes)	Length of instruction or constant in hexadecimal (1 byte)	Absolute (*A*) or relocatable (*R*) (1 byte)
ATHREE␣␣	00000E	04	*R*
CLEAR␣␣␣	000012	02	*R*
A5␣␣␣␣␣␣	000016	04	*R*
FIELDA␣␣	00006C	04	*R*
FIELDB␣␣	000070	04	*R*

Fig. 6.5   A typical symbol table, 13 bytes per entry.

In the second pass the instructions are assembled. For each symbol used in the operand field (say, FIELDA), a search is made through the symbol table. When a correct match is made, its location counter setting (say, 00006C) is fetched from the symbol table and inserted in the assembled instruction in machine language.

From the preceding discussion we can see: (1) A symbol, used in an operand of an instruction, but not defined in a name field somewhere in the program, will not be retrieved from the symbol table in the second pass. (2) A confusion will occur if a given symbol is used in two different name fields. The last column in Fig. 6.5 indicates that the symbol is absolute or relocatable. We shall now explore this topic in the next section.

6.6 PROGRAM RELOCATION AND ITS EFFECTS ON TERMS

The location counter setting of an instruction discussed in Section 6.4 is *not* the actual address in the main storage, often known as *core address*. The difference between the core address and its corresponding location counter setting is called the *relocation quantity*. For the sake of discussion, let us assume that the relocation quantity for a main program is $(5020)_{16}$. During execution time, instructions are loaded into their locations in main storage. Figure 6.6 shows the difference between core address and location counter setting for each of the five instructions studied in Fig. 6.4. The technique of adjusting a program so that it may be placed in an arbitrary area in main storage is commonly known as *program relocation*.

Location counter setting	Instruction			Core address
00000E	ATHREE	L	3,FIELDA	00000E + 5020 = 00502E
000012		A	3,FIELDB	000012 + 5020 = 005032
000016	CLEAR	SR	4,4	000016 + 5020 = 005036
000018	A5	L	5,FIELDA	000018 + 5020 = 005038
00001C		D	4,FIELDB	00001C + 5020 = 00503C

Fig. 6.6   Core addresses.

The relocation technique also permits the movement of a main program and its associated subroutines at the loading time. It is worth noting that the object program of a main program (or that of a subroutine), as produced by an assembler, is relocatable and, during loading, can be placed anywhere in main storage. Usually, a main program and its subroutines, each independently assembled, are automatically linked together and loaded in a nonoverlapping storage area without empty space between them. For example, the main program and four subroutines S410B, S413B, S413C, and S415 considered in Section 5.7, may have the core addresses as shown below.

	Location counter setting	Core address
Main program	000000–000327	005020–005347
Subroutine S410B	000000–000043	005348–00538F
Subroutine S413B	000000–000043	005390–0053D7
Subroutine S413C	000000–000043	0053D8–00541F
Subroutine S415	000000–00006B	005420–00548B

Absolute and Relocatable Terms

We shall now examine the effect of a program relocation on each of the three types of terms we have studied; they are self-defining terms, location counter references, and symbols. A term can be either relocatable or absolute. An absolute term is one whose value is not affected by a program relocation. A self-defining term (e.g., X'09') is clearly an absolute term. As another example, in the following Equate (EQU) instruction

                    REGNØ   EQU   11

the symbol REGNØ is defined as equal to 11. It is an absolute term; EQU is an assembler instruction.

In contrast with an absolute term, a relocatable term is one whose value changes with a program relocation. For example, all symbols used in Figs. 6.5 and 6.6 are relocatable terms. Similarly, a location counter reference, written as an asterisk (∗) is relocatable term. As a result, the base address is affected by a program relocation. Consider, for example, the following instruction (see subroutine S410B in Fig. 5.24)

                 Location counter
                    setting
                 ─────────────
                    000010   USING   ∗,12

which defines the base address. Since this subroutine is "moved" up by the following amount

              Relocation quantity (say)   005020
              Length of main program   000328   +
                                          ─────────
                                           005348

the current base address in core is promised to be 005348 + 000010 = 005358.

6.7 ABSOLUTE AND RELOCATABLE EXPRESSIONS

So far we have discussed three types of terms commonly used in assembler language programming. They are self-defining terms, symbols, and location counter references. A term is the basic building block for an operand; it represents a value.

As shown in Fig. 6.3, an expression may comprise only one term. It may also have two or more terms connected by an arithmetic operator: +, −, ∗, or /. Thus we have the following valid expressions:

                    FIELD+8
                    ∗−16
                    X'A1'+AREA

The arithmetic operations are performed in much the same way as in FORTRAN: They are carried out from left to right, with + and – after * and /. Parentheses can be used to alter the order of evaluation. A student is warned that a division yields only an integer quotient, with no rounding. Also, division by 0 yields 0 as the result. In the following two examples, the actual value of each term is used:

a) $(1 / 5) * 6 = 0 * 6 = 0$.

b) $7 / 0 = 0$.

An expression must not begin with an arithmetic operator such as *ONE–TWO; nor contain two successive terms such as ONE TWO; nor include two successive arithmetic operators such as ONE+–TWO.

Since an expression comprises one or more terms connected by arithmetic operators, it can be either absolute or relocatable. The value of an *absolute expression* is not affected by a program relocation, whereas that of a *relocatable expression* is.

Absolute Expressions

An absolute expression, in the simplest case, can comprise an absolute term or any combination of absolute terms, such as X'4A9'+1.

Next, an absolute expression may comprise only relocatable terms; it may also include arithmetic combination of both relocatable and absolute terms. These constructions are subject to the following restrictions:

1. The relocatable terms must be paired (in even numbers); such paired terms need not be contiguous.

2. Each pair of relocatable terms must have opposite sign so that the effect of program relocation is canceled out.

3. In an absolute expression, one of the relocatable terms may be multiplied or divided by an absolute term 1; the result is treated as relocatable. However, if this relocatable term enters into a Multiply or Divide operation with any other absolute terms, the result is considered as absolute and an error is indicated.

Let A stand for any absolute term, and R for any relocatable term; the list below gives some examples of absolute expressions with their counterparts in assembler language:

	Absolute expression in assembler language
$A+A$	X'76'+1
$A*A$	4*X'A0'
$A+A-A$	X'76'+1–X'A'
$R+A-R$	*+8–AREA
$R-R+A$	FIELD–AREA+3
$(R-R)*A$	(AREA–FIELD)*2

where FIELD and AREA are taken as relocatable terms.

Relocatable Expressions

A relocatable expression, in the simplest case, can be one relocatable term or any combination of relocatable terms. It can also comprise several relocatable terms in combination with absolute terms. The restrictions are as follows:

1. A relocatable expression must have an odd number of relocatable terms. Or, all but one of them must be paired, but a minus sign must not precede the unpaired relocatable term. Thus, ∗+AREA−FIELD is not permitted.

2. Each pair of relocatable terms must have opposite signs. They do not have to be adjacent to each other.

   Each of the following arithmetical operations produces a relocatable expression: (a) multiplication and division of a relocatable term by an absolute term 1, or (b) multiplication and division of 1 by a relocatable term. The following examples are valid relocatable expressions:

	Relocatable expression in assembler language
R	FIELD
$R+A$ or $A+R$	∗+8
$R-R+A+R$	FIELD−AREA+8+∗

6.8 TWO PRACTICAL EXAMPLES OF ABSOLUTE AND RELOCATABLE EXPRESSIONS

The objective of this section is to illustrate the absolute and relocatable expressions with two important examples—relative addressing technique and main-storage operand address.

Relative Addressing

When a programmer needs to refer to storage locations only a few bytes away from a location previously defined by a symbol, he should use the relative addressing technique. The chief advantage of this technique is that it reduces the number of symbols in a program. As a result, both storage space and assembly time are saved. This technique can be applied to a data area as well as a machine instruction.

Example 1

This example illustrates the application of the relative addressing technque to a data area. Consider the following instructions:

```
        L  2,FIELD
        A  2,FIELD+8
```

After the execution of the first instruction, the contents of the fullword whose first byte has the address FIELD (see Fig. 6.7) are loaded into register 2. The Add instruction would then add the contents of the fullword (whose first byte has the address FIELD+8 to the contents in register 2. The sum 03A1B27F + 001AF3CA = 03BCA649 is stored in register 2. In this example, the relocatable expression FIELD+8 is used as a *relative address*.

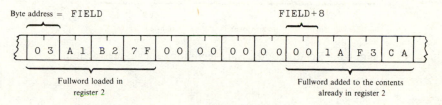

Byte address = FIELD   FIELD+8

```
03  A1  B2  7F  00  00  00  00  00  1A  F3  CA
```

Fullword loaded in   Fullword added to the contents
register 2   already in register 2

Fig. 6.7   Relationship between FIELD and FIELD + 8.

Example 2

In this example, we shall show a rather simple way to refer to an address by its relative position to the "current" instruction. Specifically, we wish to translate the following words into an instruction: Branch unconditionally to the instruction eight bytes beyond the first byte of this instruction.

Since the location counter setting of this branch instruction can be written as an asterisk (*), this branch instruction can be written as

$$\text{BC} \quad 15,*+8$$

where the asterisk (*) is the location counter reference; a programmer is not really interested in its value.

For clarity, let us assume that the location counter setting of this BC instruction is 0000A0, and that the BC instruction is followed in sequence by several instructions as shown below.

Location counter setting			
0000A0		BC	15,*+8
0000A4	SKIP	A	6,FIELD
0000A8		MVC	TO,FROM

The branch-to address is *+8 = 0000A0 + 8 = 0000A8; this is the address of the MVC instruction (Fig. 6.8). The net effect: the Add (A) instruction is skipped. Note that, in this case, the instruction

$$\text{BC} \quad 15,*+8$$

can be replaced by another Branch on Condition instruction:

$$\text{BC} \quad 15,\text{SKIP+4}$$

because the address of the MVC instruction can also be written as SKIP+4.

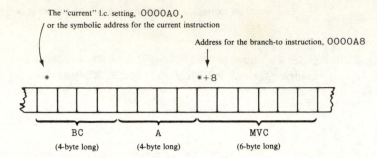

Fig. 6.8 Relative addressing technique for an instruction.

Table 6.1 Main-storage addresses in operands

Instruction format	Explicit address			Implicit address	
	Operand form	Example		General form	Example
RX (second operand)	$D2(X2,B2)$	A 7,4(2,11)		$S2(X2)$	S 5,CZERO(3)
	$D2(,B2)$ If $X2=0$	L 1,8(,1)		$S2$	L 11,*+X'12'
RS (second operand)	$D2(B2)$	LM 14,12,12(13)		$S2$	STM 14,12,SAVE+12
SI (first operand)	$D1(B1)$	MVI 8(12),X'E4'		SI	CLI LOOP,C'*'
SS (both operands)	First operand $D1(L1,B1)$	MVC 30(5,8),156(8)		$S1(L1)$	MVC FIELD1(5),FIELD2
	$D1(L,B1)$			$S1(L)$	
	Second operand $D2(L2,B2)$			$S2(L2)$	
	$D2(B2)$			$S2$	

164

A word of caution: Relative addressing is always counted in bytes. It should not be counted in bits, halfwords, or fullwords.

Main-Storage Operand Address

As further illustrations of absolute and relocatable expressions, we now present various forms of a main-storage operand address. Table 6.1 lists various possible forms for each instruction format. Let us examine them more closely. First, for instructions of RX format, two forms are possible, depending on whether the index register is used or not. When it is not used ($X2 = 0$) no indexing is involved. Second, each operand address can be written in the explicit or implicit form. Finally, displacement $D1$, $D2$; index $X2$; base registers $B1$, $B2$; lengths L, $L1$, $L2$ are absolute expressions, whereas $S1$ and $S2$ are relocatable expressions.

6.9 PSEUDO-OPERATIONS—LIST CONTROL

As mentioned before, there are two types of assembler language instructions—machine instructions and assembler instructions. A machine instruction tells the assembler to generate a machine language coding; typical examples are L, LA, ST, A, S, M, D, MVI, and MVC. On the other hand, the assembler instructions do not generate any coding. Often called pseudo-operation instructions, they are viewed by the assembler as special notes from the programmer. Their principal functions are as follows:

1. Control the listing.
2. Generate a constant.
3. Reserve storage locations.
4. Control the assembly process.
5. Tell the computer to use a symbol defined in another program.

An important example of the list control pseudo-operation is a comment statement by writing an asterisk in column 1. Arbitrary comments can then start anywhere in this statement. This assembler instruction is basically used to echo-print the comments on the assembly listing, and has no effects on the assembled program.

A second example of list control pseudo-operation is the EJECT instruction. This instruction, which has no operand, causes the next line of listing to appear at the top of the next page.

A third example is the TITLE instruction. For instance, the following instruction

```
TITLE  'THIRD EDITION'
```

provides a heading THIRD EDITION on each page in the listing right after this instruction is used. This heading will be changed if another TITLE statement is encountered.

We shall discuss several other types of pseudo-operations later in this chapter. A rather complete list of assembler instructions is given in Appendix E.

6.10 PSEUDO-OPERATION—DEFINE CONSTANT (DC)

The Define Constant pseudo-operation instruction introduces constants into a program. Consider, for example, a decimal integer constant. It may be generated in two different lengths: a fullword or a halfword. Specifically, a fullword constant A = 17 can be defined in the following instruction:

A   DC   F'17'

where the decimal number 17 is placed within two simple quotation marks, and F denotes a fullword. The hexadecimal representation of the generated fullword contents is 00000011. Similarly, a halfword constant B = 10 can be defined in the following DC instruction:

B   DC   H'10'

where H denotes a halfword and the hexadecimal representation of this generated halfword is 000A. Each of the above two defined constants is written as a decimal number. We can also define a one-byte hexadecimal number 6F as follows:

C   DC   X'6F'

where X denotes the hexadecimal digits, and C, the address of the field. If the hexadecimal digits 6F are stored in the rightmost position of the four-byte D field, we can write the instruction as

D   DC   XL4'6F'

where X denotes the hexadecimal digits and L4, the length of data in bytes. Since the designated length value (explicit length) 4 is greater than that of the data to be stored (or 1 byte), the assembler will pad the leftmost three bytes with zeros as shown in Fig. 6.9. Here the explicit length 4 overrules the implied length 1.

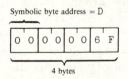

Fig. 6.9   Padding with zeros.

It is often required to store the same digits several times and consecutively in main storage. In this case, a duplication factor can be used in the DC instruction. For example, if the digits $(08)_{10}$ are stored in a halfword successively for 3 times (see Fig. 6.10), the following DC instruction may be used:

E   DC   3H'8'

where the duplication factor 3 indicates the number of times to store the data.

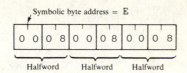

Fig. 6.10   Duplication factor 3.

The DC instruction can be also used to define alphanumeric data (character string). Consider, for example, the seven characters FILE #3 which are to be placed in a seven-byte field FG. We can use the following instruction

FG   DC   CL7'FILE #3'

where C denotes characters and L7, the length value 7 (six characters plus one blank within the simple quotation marks). This instruction can also be written as

FG   DC   C'FILE #3'

Here the length value is not explicitly given and the assembler would automatically use the implied length by counting the number of characters within the simple quotation marks. If, however, a count error does occur as in the following instruction

G   DC   CL3'FILE #3'

where the length value is smaller than the number of characters within the simple quotation marks, only the leftmost three characters (FIL) are defined; and the four characters E #3 are ignored, or truncated. Conversely, if the length value in a DC instruction is larger than the number of characters within the simple quotation marks, then the rightmost bytes are padded with blanks. Consider, for example, the following instruction:

H   DC   CL7'FILE'

As shown in Fig. 6.11, the rightmost three bytes are each padded with a blank, or a 40 code. The codes for all characters are listed in Appendix B and will be discussed later in Section 10.3.

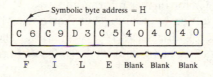

Fig. 6.11   Padding for character constants.

In general, a DC instruction, used to establish a constant, has one of the following two formats:

ADDR   DC dtLm'C'

or

ADDR   DC dtLm(C)

where d = duplication factor (it can be omitted if $d = 1$),

  t = type of constant (see Table 6.2),

 Lm = length value (can be left out),

 'C' = data constant, enclosed within single quotes,

 (C) = address constant, enclosed with parentheses (for types A, S, V, and Y), and

ADDR = a name appearing in the symbolic location field.

The two formats above can be written as

$$[\text{ADDR}] \quad \text{DC} \quad [d]t\,[\text{L}m] \begin{Bmatrix} 'C' \\ (C) \end{Bmatrix}$$

where brackets [ ] contain an operand subfield (or a name field) that may be omitted and braces { } contain options, one of which must be selected.

 Table 6.2 gives a summary of characteristics of various types of constants. The beginner should first concentrate on the four common types of constants in the table. Then he is advised to refer to this table for other types of constants. The boundary alignment as listed in column 5 will be discussed in Section 6.13. However, it is useful to mention here that the use of an explicit length field suppresses the automatic boundary alignment action of the assembler.

 Except for B, C, or X type, two or more constants can be written in one DC statement. For example, the following DC instruction

      DC F'0,1,4'

is equivalent to the following three instructions:

      DC F'0'
      DC F'1'
      DC F'4'

 An explicit length can also be written in bits. In addition, for DC constants of D, E, F, or H type, it is possible to have a scale modifier and an exponent modifier. We shall not go into details here. The interested reader is referred to the manuals listed at the end of this chapter for further information.

 We conclude this section by pointing out that Load Multiple (LM) instruction is often used in connection with a set of DC instructions. The instruction sequence in Fig. 6.12 clears registers 3, 4, and 5, and loads 00000001 in register 6 and 000000FF in register 7.

        LM   3,7,VALUES

            .

            .

            .

    VALUES DC   3F'0'
         DC   F'1'
         DC   XL4'FF'
         END

Fig. 6.12 Joint usage of LM and DC instructions.

Table 6.2 Characteristics of DC and DS instructions

Columns	1	2	3			4	5	6		7
	Type	Constant specification	Length in bytes			Padding or truncation	Boundary alignment (when *Lm* is not given)	Typical examples		Chapter section reference
(*t*)	Meaning		Implied	Explicit (*Lm*) min.	max.			Assembler instructions	Assembled constants (in hexadecimal except noted)	
C	Character	Characters	directly from the constant	1	256 (DC) 65,535 (DS)	From right	Byte	DC C'CENSUS680' DC 2CL3'CENSUS680'	CENSUS680 (in character) CENCEN (in character)	5.5 and 6.10
F	Fullword	Decimal digits	4	1	8	From left	Fullword	DC F'26'	0000001A	6.10
H	Halfword	Decimal digits	2	1	8	From left	Halfword	DC H'26'	001A	6.10
X	Hexadecimal	Hexadecimal digits	directly from the constant	1	256 (DC) 65,535 (DS)	From left	Byte	DC XL3'FFF' DC X'1A76D'	000FFF 01A76D	1.6, 5.5 and 6.10
A	Fullword	A relocatable expression	4	3	4		Fullword	DC A(ABC) DC AL3(ABC)	000005A6 0005A6 (if ABC has address 0005A6)	8.5
A	Address	An absolute expression	4	1	4	From left	Fullword	DC 2AL1(X'516'+1)	1717	5.7
B	Binary	Binary digits	directly from the constant	1	256	From left	Byte	DC B'10101' DC 3L2'10101'	15 (8 bits) 0015	—
D	Long floating point	Decimal number	8	1	8	From right	Doubleword	DC D'47.123' DC D'47123E-3'	$(47.123)_{10}$ as a positive doubleword floating-point constant	12.3
E	Short floating point	Decimal number	4	1	8	From right	Fullword	DC E'47.123' DC E'+471.23E-1'	$(47.123)_{10}$ as a positive fullword floating-point constant	12.3
P	Packed decimal	Decimal number	directly from the constant	1	16	From left	Byte	DC P'+867' DC PL3'-128'	867C 00128D	10.5 and 11.1
S	Base register and disp. address	One or two expressions	2	2	2	None	Halfword	DC S(125(3)) DC S(SYM)	307D	—
V	Address for external symbol	A relocatable symbol	4	3	4	From left	Fullword	DC V(ABC)	00000000	8.5
Y	Halfword address	An expression	2	1	2	From left	Halfword	DC 2YL1(7) DC Y(ABC)	0707 05A6 (if ABC has address 0005A6)	Chapter 8 Lab. Assign. 2.
Z	Zoned decimal	Decimal number	directly from the constant	1	16	From left	Byte	DC ZL5'4236' DC 2ZL3'4236'	F0F4F2F3F6 F2F3F6F2F3F6	10.5

Commonly used: C, F, H, X, A

Less common: B, D, E, P, S, V, Y, Z

169

6.11 A DIGRESSION ON LITERALS

We now digress to study literals. A literal in a machine instruction represents a value, and as such belongs to a class of terms. To refresh his or her memory the reader should now refer to Fig. 6.3 in Section 6.3 for the relationship between literals and terms.

To write a literal in a machine instruction one has to follow closely the rules that govern the operand in a DC instruction. For example, the second operand in the instruction

$$L \quad 8,=F'258'$$

is a literal. The net effect of this instruction is to load a fullword 258 into register 8.

Table 6.3 Differences between a DC operand and a literal

Item	DC operand(s) (with correct examples)	Literal (with correct examples)
Equal sign preceding the constant	No equal sign. DC F'1'	Must have equal sign. L 4,=F'1'
Number of operands permitted	One or more than one. DC F'7',C'AB',2X'F6'	One only. MVC OUTAREA(12),=3CL4'WHAT'
A zero duplication factor	Permitted to perform boundary alignment in some cases. DC 0F'12'	Not permitted. L 6,=F'12'
Contents in the assembled machine code	The constant itself. DC C'SUMb=bb' is assembled as E2E4D4407E4040 (where b stands for a blank)	The second operand (the literal) is assembled as the base-and-displacement address for the constant. D 4,=F'3' may be assembled as 5D40B1D4.
The duplication factor or length modifier written as a positive absolute expression	Permitted, but must be enclosed in parentheses. DC (X'A')F'11'	No. Only a signed decimal integer of single digit is permitted. MVC AA(12),=3F'2'
S-type and Q-type (see Table 6.1)	Permitted.	Not permitted.

Note that the literal is written as a constant, in the same way as it is used in a DC instruction, but preceded by an equal sign (=).

A literal is always used as a main-storage operand in the machine instructions. Its *address*, not its contents, is assembled in the instruction. Consider, for example, the instruction

M   4,=F'80'

which uses a literal. A possible assembled machine code is shown in Fig. 6.13. As a storage operand, a literal is assembled in the base-and-displacement form; hence, a literal is a relocatable term. The literal constant itself is automatically placed in a specific area of the main storage, called the *literal pool*.

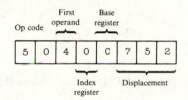

Fig. 6.13   A literal is compiled in base and displacement form.

Although literals are similar in form to the operands specified in DC instructions, they have the following minor differences.

=X'1'   As mentioned before, an equal sign (=) is required for a literal, but must not be used in the operand field of a DC instruction.

=X'2'   The duplication factor is permitted in a literal. If used, it must be an unsigned nonzero decimal integer. Thus, (X'A')H'24' or 0H'24' are valid operands for DC statements, but the corresponding literals =(X'A')H'24' and =0H'24' are not permitted.

=X'3'   A literal term is a loner; it cannot be combined with any other terms. Only one literal may appear in each machine instruction; assembler instructions such as DC cannot contain literals.

These and other differences are summarized in Table 6.3.

6.12 PSEUDO-OPERATION—STORAGE ALLOCATION INSTRUCTION (DS)

We shall now discuss the problem how to reserve a block of the main storage for an array of numbers† used in a user's program. Its form is similar to that of a DC instruction:

$$[\text{Symbol}] \quad \text{DS} \quad [d]\, t\, [\text{L}m] \left[\left\{ \begin{array}{c} 'C' \\ (C) \end{array} \right\} \right]$$

---

† This requirement is similar to that of DIMENSION statement in FORTRAN with one difference. The DIMENSION statement is generally used to reserve a block of words, while the requirement for DS instruction is to reserve a block of bytes.

where, as before, brackets [ ] contain an operand subfield (or the name field) that may be omitted and braces {} contain options, one of which must be selected. We note that the fourth subfield $'C'$ or (C) may be and *is usually* omitted completely; but it is required in a DC statement.

For example, the following instruction

```
AREA   DS   CL120
```

reserves a 120-byte AREA field; any assembled machine instructions or other data are not permitted in this reserved area.

Two things are accomplished during the assembly. First, the address of the reserved field is assigned as the location counter setting. Consider, for example, the following DS instructions:

```
AREA1   DS   CL16
AREA2   DS   CL120
```

If the location counter setting for AREA1 is $(2000)_{16}$, then that for AREA2 can be readily computed as follows:

$$(2000)_{16} + (16)_{10} = (2000)_{16} + (10)_{16} = (2010)_{16}.$$

Second, the number of bytes in the storage area is reserved according to the following rules:

1. If the constant subfield $'C'$ or (C) is not used, the number of bytes to be reserved is dictated by
   a) the implied length as shown in column 3 of Table 6.2, or
   b) the length value Lm in the instruction. The maximum lengths for character (C) and hexadecimal (X) data types are 65,535 bytes in a DS instruction.
2. If the constant subfield is specified, the number of bytes reserved follow the same rule as in a DC instruction.

It should be pointed out that a DS instruction only reserves a block of bytes, but does not clear them. It does not assemble any constant, even when the constant subfield is stated by the programmer.

A DS statement with the zero duplication factor is frequently written to indicate a subdivision of a data storage area. When a duplication factor is set to zero, no reservation of storage area is made and the location counter is not stepped. Its net effect is to define a symbol. For example, the following four DS instructions reserve a total of eight consecutive bytes:

```
DATE    DS   0CL8
YEAR    DS   CL4
MONTH   DS   CL2
DAY     DS   CL2
```

The zero duplication factor in the first instruction is used to define the symbol DATE. If, for instance, its location counter setting is $(1000)_{16}$, then the location counter setting for the second instruction is also $(1000)_{16}$, since no stepping has taken place. The location counter settings for the third and fourth instructions are $(1004)_{16}$ and $(1006)_{16}$, respectively (see Fig. 6.14).

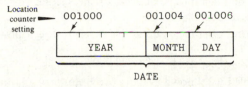

Fig. 6.14 Subdivision of a data storage area.

To give another example of using a zero duplication factor to indicate a subdivision of data storage area, let us examine the five fields shown in Fig. 6.15. The UNIV field (120 bytes) is subdivided into two fields: COLLEGE (80 bytes) and SCHOOL (40 bytes); the COLLEGE field, in turn, is subdivided into DEPT1 and DEPT2 fields, with 60 and 20 bytes, respectively. To define these five fields, the five DS instructions may be used:

```
UNIV        DS      0CL120
COLLEGE     DS      0CL80
DEPT1       DS      CL60
DEPT2       DS      CL20
SCHOOL      DS      CL40
```

Another important application of zero duplication factor is the forcing alignment, which we shall discuss in the next section.

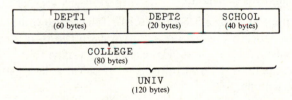

Fig. 6.15 Subdivision of a data storage area.

6.13 BOUNDARY ALIGNMENT AND FORCING ALIGNMENT

Perhaps one of the most common pitfalls in writing assembler language programs lies in the area of boundary alignment. In System/360, a piece of fixed-length data (such as halfword, fullword, or doubleword data) must be located in main storage on an *integral boundary*. For example, the second operand address FULLWORD in the following instruction

```
L   9,FULLWORD
```

must be a multiple of the number 4, known as fullword boundary alignment. As a second example, consider the following Load instruction:

$$L \quad 3,114(0,9)$$

This instruction would not be valid if the contents in base register 9 were assumed as 0000F0, or $(240)_{10}$. The reason: The address of the second operand becomes $114 + 240 = 354$, which is not divisible by 4.

Similarly, the second operand address HALFWORD in the following instruction

$$LH \quad 8,HALFWORD$$

must be exactly divisible by 2, known as halfword boundary alignment. In System/370 and *some* System/360 computers, this severe restriction of boundary alignment for operands—a hardship for beginners—is removed. The operand is thus *byte-oriented*. However, it is recommended that the integral boundary requirement is observed in writing programs, because (a) A program using byte-oriented operand does not run on most System/360 machines, (b) Operands of privileged instructions (see Section 15.5) for System/370 must satisfy the boundary alignment, and (c) The byte-operand feature does not apply to machine instructions and CCW's (see Section 15.3).

Now we shall study the alignment for (a) all machine instructions, and (b) constants defined by DC and DS instructions.

Alignment for All Machine Instructions

During assembly process, the assembler automatically aligns all machine instructions on halfword boundary. In other words, the first byte address of a machine instruction is always divisible by 2.

Automatic Alignment for Constants

As shown in column 5 of Table 6.2 (Section 6.10), if the length value Lm is not specified, a constant is automatically aligned on a halfword, fullword, or any byte depending on what type of constant is involved. For example, a F-type constant is automatically aligned to the beginning of the next fullword. Specifically, let us study the following sequential DC instructions:

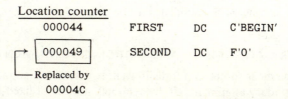

```
          Location counter
             000044          FIRST     DC     C'BEGIN'

          ┌→ │ 000049 │      SECOND    DC     F'0'
          │
          └─ Replaced by
             00004C
```

We assume that the first DC instruction starts at the address 000044. Since the FIRST field takes five bytes, this will bring the SECOND field up to 000049 which is not divisible by 4, a violation of fullword boundary alignment required by an F-type constant. The assembler will now *automatically* update this address to 00004C, which is the nearest fullword boundary. The three bytes 000049, 00004A, and 00004B are, of course, not counted as part of the SECOND field; these three bytes serve no particular purpose.

When the length value Lm is explicitly given, the automatic alignment by assembler is suppressed, and the constant is assembled at the first available byte in the main storage.

Forcing Alignment

A constant of the type C, P, or X is assembled at the first available byte in the main storage (see column 7 in Table 6.2). There is no automatic alignment on halfword or fullword. If a programmer desires to align a constant of such type on, say, fullword boundary, he can use a DS statement with a zero duplication factor ($d = 0$). Specifically, if he wants to make sure that the constant X'8B04A' (defined as FORCE) is aligned on a fullword boundary, the following two instructions can be used:

```
          DS    0F
FORCE     DC    X'8B04A'
```

CNOP Instruction for Boundary Alignment

The Conditional NO-OP (CNOP) assembler instruction aligns the location counter on a fullword or doubleword boundary. For example, the following instruction aligns on a fullword boundary

```
          CNOP  0,4
```

where the first operand 0 denotes that the alignment begins at the beginning of a word; and 4, fullword boundary. For further illustration, let us consider the following four sequential instructions:

Location counter		
000178	DC	F'0'
00017C	DC	A(1)
000180	CNOP	0,4
000180	BAL	1,*+8

where the location counter setting of the CNOP instruction is 000180. Since this value is exactly divisible by 4, the BAL instruction is already on a fullword boundary. In this example, the CNOP instruction is redundant and actually nonoperational.

As a counterexample, consider the following four instructions:

Location counter
```
0011B8          BALR        14,15
0011BA          CNOP        0,4
0011BC          BAL         1,*+8
0011C0          DC          AL1(128)
```

where the location counter setting of the CNOP instruction is now 0011BA, which is not exactly divisible by 4. As a result, the CNOP instruction advances the location counter setting to 0011BC, exactly divisible by 4; and the BAL instruction now aligns on a fullword boundary.

The boundary alignment is not limited to a fullword. In Table 6.4 are shown the six possible operands and their associated alignments. For example, the following instruction

```
            CNOP  2,4
```

demands to align the boundary at the middle of a fullword.

Table 6.4. Boundary alignment in a CNOP instruction

Operands	Boundary alignment
0,4	Beginning of a fullword
2,4	Middle of a fullword
0,8	Beginning of a doubleword
2,8	Second halfword of doubleword
4,8	Middle of a doubleword
6,8	Fourth halfword of doubleword

6.14 ORGANIZATIONAL PSEUDO-OPERATIONS

The list control, define constant, and storage allocating pseudo-operation instructions discussed in the previous sections each pertain to a single instruction, not to the entire program. There is also a class of pseudo-operation instructions related to the entire program, which signifies the outstanding characteristics of the program to the assembler. Two notable examples in this class of pseudo-operation instructions are START and USING. The START instruction was introduced earlier in Sections 5.5 and 6.4 in connection with the initial setting of location counter. In this section we shall explore the assembler instruction USING.

The USING instruction is an answer to the following two important questions: Which general register is used in this program as the base register; and what is the *promised* value in this base register *at the execution time* of the object program.

Example 1

USING X'10',11

This instruction states that register 11 is being assigned as the base register (known as the implied base register), and the base address is promised to be $(10)_{16}$ *at the execution time*.

Example 2

USING *,11

This instruction also states that register 11 is the implied base register; the base address at the object time is the location counter setting of this USING instruction. As discussed in Section 6.4, when an asterisk is used as an operand, it always takes the value of the current setting of the location counter. The asterisk is known as the location counter reference. It cannot be overemphasized that the USING instruction only *promises* that the base address will be in the base register during execution time. The programmer must load this address himself, normally by using a BALR instruction (see Section 5.7).

Figure 6.16 shows a typical set of first three statements in an assembler language program. Here, the Branch and Link (BALR) instruction loads the address of the next instruction (e.g., 000102) into register 11. This address then becomes the base address. When the second operand in a BALR instruction is 0, there is no branch, and the next sequential instruction will then be executed. It is important to note that, in Fig. 6.16, the base address (000102) is not the same as the starting address (000100).

Location counter	Name	Op code	Operand
000100	BEGIN	START	X'100'
000100		BALR	11,0
000102		USING	*,11

Fig. 6.16 Typical first three statements in an assembler program.

A relocatable symbol is sometimes used as the first operand of a USING instruction. Consider, for example, the first five instructions of a rather typical program (see Fig. 6.17). From the USING instruction, we know that (a) the implied base register is register 11, and (b) the promised base address is a symbol BEGIN—the entry-point address of this program. To actually load this address into register 11, the LR instruction is used. Note that register 15, by convention discussed in Section 5.5, contains the entry-point address. In Fig. 6.17, the starting address is also used as the base address.

In summary, the BALR and USING instructions are usually used as a pair. The USING instruction promises that base address will be loaded in the base register during execution time, but BALR or LR instruction actually loads this address in the base register.

```
BEGIN     START
          DS        0H
          STM       14,12,12(13)
          LR        11,15
          USING     BEGIN,11
            .
            .
            .
```

Fig. 6.17 Typical first five statements in an assembler program.

Conversion From Symbolic Address to Base-Displacement Form

After the information on the implied base register and base address are provided by the USING instruction, the assembler is in the position to translate a symbolic address into an address in the form of base register and displacement. Consider, for example, the instructions and location counter setting in Fig. 6.18. Specifically, we wish to show how the assembler translates the operand address CZERO in the L instruction into its base-displacement form. As discussed above, the implied base register is register 11 and the *promised* base address is $B = 000102$. Second, the assembler automatically takes $X = 0$. Now the displacement D is readily obtained (by the assembler) as follows: $D = E - B - X = 000240 - 000102 - 0 = 13E$. The assembled Load instruction is shown in Fig. 6.19.

Location counter setting	Object code			
		⋮		
000102			USING	*,11
000102				
		⋮		
000220	5890B13E		L	9,CZERO
		⋮		
000240		CZERO	DS	F

Fig. 6.18 Conversion from a symbolic address CZERO to its base-displacement form.

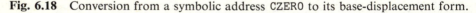
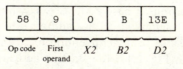

58	9	0	B	13E
Op code	First operand	X2	B2	D2

Fig. 6.19 Assembled instruction.

The base-displacement form has its unique advantages. First, the operand address is reduced from 24 bits to 20 bits for RX format, and to 16 bits for RS, SI, or SS format. Second, the base-displacement address system is independent of the relocation quantity, thus making the program relocatable.

6.15 COMMON ERRORS IN ASSEMBLER LANGUAGE

This section presents some common errors along with examples of incorrect assembler language programming. They are taken from a large number of actual runs. It must be emphasized that logical errors are not discussed here. These consist principally of incorrect original equations or an incorrect sequence of instructions. Furthermore, errors in key punching are rather commonplace. In particular, the letter O is often mistaken for zero (0); or an I for a number one (1).

In this section, we shall consider only the most frequent beginner's errors which occur in the following general areas:

   A. Errors associated with all instructions.

   B. Errors associated with instructions for arithmetic and information moves.

   C. Errors associated with instructions for branching, conversion, and comparison.

   D. Errors associated with linkage conventions.

A. Rules to follow for all instructions

1. There must be at least one blank between the last operand and the comments.

Examples

```
AR   3,7SUM IS IN R3
AR   3,7 SUM IS IN R3
```
                                Incorrect
                                Correct

2. No blanks are allowed between operands.

Examples

```
AR   3, 7
AR   3,7
```
                                Incorrect
                                Correct

3. A byte is the basic unit in storage.

Examples

If HERE is the symbolic address of a fullword, the address of next fullword is

```
HERE+1
HERE+4
```
                                Incorrect
                                Correct

4. A symbol must be defined.

Examples

```
ST   3,HERE
     ⋮
(no HERE in the name field)
```
                                } Incorrect

```
ST   3,HERE
     ⋮
HERE DS  F
```
                                } Correct

5. The address of a fullword is not same as its contents.

Example

If the contents of HERE are 00ABCDEC, after execution of the following instruction

$$\text{L} \quad 4,\text{HERE}$$

the contents in register 4 are 00ABCDEC (not HERE).

6. The base register must not be used for any other purposes.

Examples

```
BALR   8,0
USING  *,8
       .
       .
LA     8,10
```
} Incorrect

```
BALR   8,0
USING  *,8
       .
       .
LA     11,10
```
} Correct

7. DC or DS instructions should be placed near the end of program. If they are not, they should be branched around by a BC instruction.

Examples

```
FLOFIX  START
        DC    X'7'
        DC    CL7'FLOFIX '
        STM   12,14,12(13)
              .
              .
```
} Incorrect

```
FLOFIX  START
        BC    15,12(15)
        DC    X'7'
        DC    CL7'FLOFIX '
        STM   12,14,12(13)
              .
              .
```
} Correct

B. Rules to follow with instructions for arithmetic and information moves

1. An equal sign must be written in a literal.

Examples

```
A  3,F'10'                        Incorrect
A  3,=F'10'                       Correct
```

2. The first operand in a Multiply or Divide instruction must be an even register.

M 3,=F'10'	Incorrect
M 2,=F'10'	Correct

3. If the dividend (in an odd-numbered register) is a small number (less than $2^{31} - 1$), then its sign bit must be propagated across the even register before division is carried out.

```
SR   5,5
AR   5,=F'10'        ⎫  Incorrect
D    4,=F'3'         ⎭
```

```
SR   5,5
AR   5,=F'10'        ⎫
M    4,=F'1'         ⎬  Correct
D    4,=F'3'         ⎭
```

4. L and LA instructions are *not* identical.

5. The length field of MVC instruction (in machine language) is not the actual number of bytes to be moved.

C. **Rules to follow with instructions for branching, conversion, and comparison**

1. No extended mnemonic corresponds to BC 10 instruction. (BNH is not correct, if used.)

2. The Compare instruction is used to set a condition code (CC). CC = 1 if the first operand is *less* than the *second* operand. (*Not* the first operand is greater than the second.)

3. In execution of BCT or BCTR the first step is that the contents of *R1* are decremented by 1 before comparison. (*Not* compare first, then decrease by 1.)

D. **Rules to follow for linkage conventions**

1. Keep straight the following:
   a) Pointer to the argument list
   b) Pointer to the value
   c) The value itself.

Examples

Assume that the calling sequence in main program is CALL ADD(SQRS,SUM)

```
L    3,0(1)
ST   3,TEMP               ⎫
LA   9,TEMP (SHOULD BE L)  ⎬  Incorrect
     ⋮                    
TEMP   DS   10F            ⎭
```

The sum would be incorrect because TEMP is the pointer to the value to be added, not the value itself.

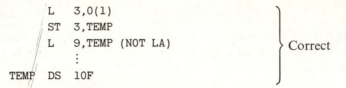

```
    L    3,0(1)
    ST   3,TEMP
    L    9,TEMP (NOT LA)          } Correct
         ⋮
TEMP  DS  10F
```

2. Answers must be stored in a proper place before passing back to the main program.
3. Use BR instruction to return control to the main program.

```
    B    14                      Incorrect
    BR   14                      Correct
```

BIBLIOGRAPHY

A Programmer's Introduction to the IBM System/360 Architecture, Instructions, and Assembler Language, Form C20-1646, IBM Corp.

Barron, D. W., *Assemblers and Loaders*, American Elsevier, New York, 1972.

Batson, Alan, "The Organization of Symbol Tables," *Comm. Assoc. Comp. Mach.* **8** (2), 111–112 (February 1965).

Corbato, F. J., J. W. Poduska, and J. H. Saltzer, *Advanced Computer Programming*, MIT Press, Cambridge, Mass., 1963.

Falkoff, A. D., K. E. Iverson, and E. H. Sussenguth, "A Formal Description of System/360," *IBM Systems J.* **3**, 198–261 (1964).

IBM System/360 Operating System Assembler Language, Form C28-6514, IBM Corp.

IBM System/360 Operating System Linkage Editor and Loader, Form GC28-6538, IBM Corp.

McGee, W. C., "On Dynamic Program Relocation," *IBM Systems J.* **4** (3), 184–199 (1965).

Compiler Construction

Gries, D., *Compiler Construction*, Wiley, New York, 1971.

Hopgood, F. R. A., *Compiler Techniques*, American Elsevier, New York, 1969.

Lee, J. A. N., *The Anatomy of a Compiler*, Reinhold, New York, 1967.

McKeeman, W. M., J. J. Horning, and D. B. Wortman, *A Compiler Generator Implemented for the IBM System/360*, Prentice-Hall, Englewood Cliffs, N.J., 1970.

PROBLEMS

1. Debug the following unrelated instructions:

Incorrect	Correct
DR4, 9	_____
AR 7,5ADD	_____

```
     ZERO  S 6,6              _____
           M 3, 2(0,9)        _____
           A 11, 4(12)        _____
           MVI X'F9',256(0)   _____
           M 6, =F'4'         _____
```

2. Point out the difference, if any, in the following instructions

```
      *  LA  8,4
      A  LA  8,4
```

where both * and A are punched in column 1.

3. Fill out the location counter setting for the following instructions:

```
0011AC  LA    1,CHAROUT
_____  LA    0,OUTAREA
_____  L     15,48(0,1)
0011B8  BALR  14,15
_____  CNOP  0,4
0011BC  BAL   1,*+8
```

4. Fill out the location counter settings in the assembler listing shown in Fig. 6.20.

LOC	OBJECT CODE	ADDR1	ADDR2	STMT		SOURCE STATEMENT	
001000				1	SUB1	START	X'1000'
				2		ENTRY	LENGTH
001000				3		USING	*,15
_____	9837 F01C		0101C	4	LENGTH	LM	3,7,PARAM
_____	5890 1000		00000	5		L	9,0(0,1)
_____	4180 0004		00004	6		LA	8,4
_____	1B22			7		SR	2,2
_____	4352 9003		00003	8	IC	IC	5,3(2,9)
_____	1A36			9		AR	3,6
_____	1A28			10		AR	2,8
_____	8674 F00E		0100E	11		BXH	7,4,IC
_____	07FE			12		BCR	15,14
_____	000000000000000			13	PARAM	DC	3F'0'
_____	00000001			14		DC	F'1'
_____	000000FF			15		DC	XL4'FF'
				16		END	

Fig. 6.20. An assembly listing.

5. Assume that the relocation quantity is $(005020)_{16}$. (a) Calculate the absolute (core) address for each of six instructions used in Problem 3. (b) What is the core address for the second operand used in the last instruction (BAL)?

6. Draw the byte configuration in hexadecimal for the storage area defined by each of the following DC instructions:

```
A1  DC  H'425'
A2  DC  F'2106'
A3  DC  X'7FA3'
A4  DC  CL7'369'
A5  DC  5CL3'AOK'
A6  DC  5CL3'AOKS'
A7  DC  6CL4'AOK'
A8  DC  3CL2'*'
A9  DC  2H'7'
```

7. Write the assembler storage instructions which would define an area of 24 bytes called TIME, which is divided equally into three sections labeled HOURS, MINS, and SECS.

8. a) The instruction DC XL4'1776' generates a constant in hexadecimal
      (i) 1776, (ii) 01776, (iii) 001776, (iv) 0001776, (v) 00001776.
   b) The instruction DS 0D set the location counter to an address which is a _____ word boundary.
   c) The instruction DS 4CL80 sets up storage:
      i) An area of 400 bytes long
      ii) 4 areas, each 80 bytes long
      iii) 80 areas, each 4 bytes long.

9. The contents of registers are

   Register 14:   00264CF7
   Register 15:   0000FFF6
   Register 0:   000FFC6A
   Register 1:   FF46C6B4

   What are the contents in AREA1, AREA2, AREA3, respectively, after the execution of the following program segment?

   ```
           STM   15,1,AREA1
   AREA1   DS    F
   AREA2   DS    F
   AREA3   DS    F
   ```

10. What are the contents of registers 3 through 7 (in hexadecimal) after the execution of the LM instruction shown in Fig. 6.20?

11. Explain the meaning of the asterisk (*) used in each of the following four lines:

   ```
   *   L     3,AN ABSOLUTE EXPRESSION
       L     3,B+4*N
   *   MVC   LENGTH=12,B2=1
       MVC   *+8(12),4(1)
   ```

12. Fill out the location counter setting and the number of bytes reserved or used (length attribute) for each of the following sequential instructions:

Location counter				Length attribute
000030		DS	0F ON FULLWORD BOUNDARY	_____
_____	HALF	DC	H'0'	2
_____	CHAR	DC	C'PRTR'	_____
_____	BINARY	DC	2BL1'00000010'	_____
_____	FULL	DC	F'0' WATCH BOUNDARY ALIGNMENT	_____
_____	HEX	DC	X'FFFF0A'	3
_____	DOUBLE	DS	D WATCH ALIGNMENT	_____
_____	BLANK	DC	132C'66'	_____
_____	STAR	DC	CL132'*'	_____

13. Given: The first three instructions in a program:

$$\begin{array}{ll} \text{START} & \\ \text{BALR} & 7,0 \\ \text{USING} & *,7 \end{array}$$

What are the contents in the base register?

14. a) Write an assembler instruction to reduce the location counter by 400.

b) Write an assembler instruction to assign the name REG11 to decimal number 11.

15. The length attribute of a named constant CHAR (see Problem 12) is written L'CHAR. Its value is an integer, which is obtained by one of the two ways:

a) Explicit length in a length modifier, or

b) Implied length,

and is kept in the symbol table. The initial contents of CHAR and BLANK fields are given in Problem 12. After the execution of following instruction

$$\text{MVC} \quad \text{BLANK(L'CHAR-1),CHAR}$$

what are the contents in CHAR and BLANK fields?

LABORATORY ASSIGNMENT

The purpose of this assignment is to select the numerical code of a given mnemonic operation code for a mini-computer which has only five instructions as listed below.

Mnemonic code	Numerical code (in hexadecimal)
A	5A
D	5D
L	58
LA	41
ST	50

A suggested procedure: A main program in a high-level language is written to perform the following steps:

1. Read the above information from cards into main storage.

2. Read a card containing only the mnemonic code of an instruction, starting from column 10.

3. Call a subroutine SEARCH in assembler language to translate the mnemonic code into its numeric equivalent.

4. Print out the mnemonic code and its numerical code. If the mnemonic code is illegal, print a message.

5. Go to step 2 till the card contains a stopper.

CHAPTER 7

Bit Manipulation

7.1 INTRODUCTORY REMARKS

In Chapter 5, we have introduced several instructions that enable a programmer to move bytes around in storage. The MVI instruction in Section 5.2 moves a single byte from one location to another in the main storage, whereas the MVC instruction in Section 5.3 moves the contents of several consecutive bytes to a new storage area. Also, we can use the CLI instruction (Section 5.8) to compare the immediate character in the instruction with a given byte in the main storage, and then set the condition code in the PSW. These three instructions are typical examples of a class of instructions called *logical operations*—operations on unsigned bytes or bits.

In this chapter, we shall introduce other logical instructions of most frequent occurrence, with particular emphasis on the manipulation of a bit, rather than a whole byte. We shall begin our discussion by examining in detail the Shift operations— to shift bits from left to right or right to left in a register. Then, we shall study other most common logical instructions such as AND, OR, Exclusive OR, and Test under Mask.

7.2 REORDER OF INPUT DATA—SHIFT INSTRUCTIONS

If the contents of a register are shifted one place to the left, the net result is that the original positive number is doubled. Consider, for example, the 32-bit contents of register 11 before and after such a shift (see Fig. 7.1). After the shift, the number is doubled. To implement on a System/370 or System/360, we can apply the following Shift Left single Algebraic instruction:

```
SLA   11,1
```

where register 11 is used, and 1 denotes the number of places to be shifted to the left.

During the action of this shifting instruction, the sign bit in Fig. 7.1 remains un-disturbed. The bit from the position 1 is dropped and the vacated bit position 31 is filled in with zero.

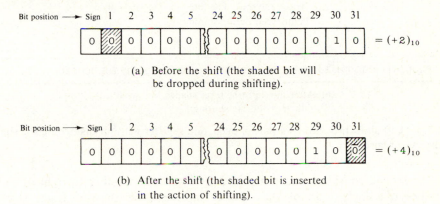

(a) Before the shift (the shaded bit will be dropped during shifting).

(b) After the shift (the shaded bit is inserted in the action of shifting).

Fig. 7.1   Left-shift one bit in a register without disturbing the sign bit.

Before shifting a piece of data, we have to ask ourselves the following questions:

a) Is the length of the data 32 bits or 64 bits?

b) Is this piece of data shifted to the left, or to the right?

c) Is the leftmost bit (the sign bit) involved in the shifting operation?

We shall now consider these three important questions. First, all shift instructions move data only within registers. If the shift is within one register only, it is called a *single shift*. The shift can also be made within a pair of even–odd registers, which are considered as a single, continuous, 64-bit unit. This two-word shift is referred to as *double shift*.

Example

The contents of registers 8 and 9 are to be shifted as a unit to the left three places. The sign bit of register 8 remains undisturbed. This requirement can be fulfilled by the following Shift Left Double Algebraic instruction:

$$\text{SLDA} \quad 8,3$$

where 8 indicates that the registers 8 and 9 function as an even–odd pair; 3 is the number of places to be shifted to the left. Figures 7.2(a) and 7.2(b) show, respectively, the contents in registers 8 and 9 before and after the execution of the SLDA instruction. After the execution of this instruction, the sign bit of register 8 remains undisturbed. The contents in bit positions 1 through 63 shift three places to the left while those in positions 1 through 3 are dropped; the vacated bit positions 61, 62, and 63 are filled in with zeros.

Register 8					Register 9			
0110 0010	01010111	00110101	10001110	01101110	11110101	11000011	00101111

(a) Before the shift (The three shaded bits will
be dropped during shifting).

00010010	10111001	10101100	01110011	01110111	10101110	000110010111 1000

(b) After the shift (the three shaded bits are filled
with zeros during shifting).

Fig. 7.2 Left-shift three bits in a pair of even–odd register without disturbing the sign bit of the even register.

The second consideration in a shift is its direction: whether to right or to left, regardless of a single or double shift. For example, consider the Shift Right Algebraic instruction below

$$\text{SRA} \quad 7,4$$

It makes a *right* shift of four positions in register 7 without disturbing its sign bit, thus accomplishing a single-register shift. The contents in register 7 before and after the shift are shown in Fig. 7.3(a) and 7.3(b), respectively. The sign bit remains undisturbed, but the bits supplied in the vacated positions 1 through 4 have the *same binary* configuration as the sign bit. The bits in positions 28 through 31 are pushed out and cannot be recovered.

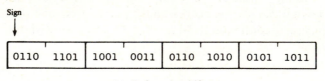

Sign

0110 1101	1001 0011	0110 1010	0101 1011

(a) Before the shift.

0000 0110	1101 1001	0011 0110	1010 0101

(b) After the shift (the four shaded bits
are supplied in the action of shift).

Fig. 7.3 Register contents before and after the instruction SRA 7,4.

The third and last question about a shift: Is it a logical or an algebraic shift? In a logical shift, the leftmost bit (either in one-register or in double-register unit) is involved in the shifting operation. On the other hand, the leftmost bit is ignored in an algebraic shift. Thus the sign bit is preserved, as shown in Fig. 7.1 through 7.3.

To sum up, it is necessary to check the correct answer for each of the three questions for a shift operation: a right or a left shift? single or double registers? and, finally, logical or arithmetic shifts? As a result eight different shiftings are possible and their corresponding instructions are as follows:

SRA	Shift Right Single Algebraic
SLA	Shift Left Single Algebraic
SRDA	Shift Right Double Algebraic
SLDA	Shift Left Double Algebraic
SRL	Shift Right Single Logical
SLL	Shift Left Single Logical
SRDL	Shift Right Double Logical
SLDL	Shift Left Double Logical

The mnemonic S signifies a Shift instruction. Letters R, L signify a right or a left shift. Single shift is normally assumed unless the letter D is used to signify a double shift. Ending letters of A and L signify the algebraic (or arithmetic) and logical shifts, respectively. All eight shift instructions are of RS format; and the *R3* field of the instruction is ignored.

As an example illustrating a logical shift, consider the contents in double register 4 and 5, as shown in Fig. 7.4(a).

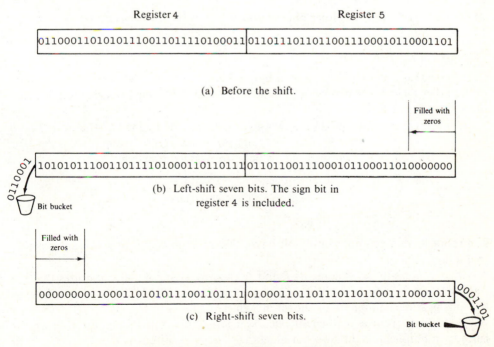

Register 4   Register 5

011000110101011001101111010001 1 011011101101100111000101100011 01

(a) Before the shift.

Filled with zeros

1010101110011011110100011011011 1 011011001110001011000110100000 00

(b) Left-shift seven bits. The sign bit in
register 4 is included.

Bit bucket

Filled with
zeros

0000000011000110101011001101111 01000110110111011011001110001011

(c) Right-shift seven bits.

Bit bucket

Fig. 7.4 Logical shift for double-register.

After the execution of the instruction

```
SLDL   4,7   SHIFT CONTENTS OF 4&5 LEFT 7 PLACES
```

the contents of both registers are shown in Fig. 7.4(b). Here, the sign bit in register 4 is disturbed. In fact, the leftmost 7 bits in register 4 are pushed out of register 4 and lost. The rightmost 7 bits in register 5 are vacated, and filled in with zeros.

Assuming that the original register contents are given as shown in Fig. 7.4(a), during the action of the logical shift instruction

```
SRDL   4,7   SHIFT CONTENTS OF 4&5 RIGHT 7 PLACES
```

the rightmost 7 bits in register 5 are pushed out (see Fig. 7.4c). The leftmost 7 bits, including the sign bit, in register 4 are vacated, and filled in with zeros.

Before we turn to the next section, we note that a SRDA instruction is often used to perform a binary integer division operation. Consider, for example, the division $K/3$. If the value K is initially stored in the main storage, then the following program segment can be used:

```
L      4,K
SRDA   4,32
D      4,=F'3'
ST     5,QUO
```

where the value K may be either plus or minus (see Table 4.1 in Section 4.3).

7.3 AND INSTRUCTIONS

In the previous section, we have seen how a Shift instruction is used. We turn now to the other logical instructions which include AND, OR, and Exclusive OR instructions.

The logical operator AND for two given bits may be defined as follows: *If both bits are* 1, *the resulting bit is equal to* 1; *otherwise, the result is zero.* Consider, for example, the following two operands which are ANDed together:

```
First operand     10101100
Second operand    11001001
                  ────────
Result            10001000
```

The result is obtained on a bit-by-bit basis. There is no carry from one bit position to another.

If we represent two statements P and Q each by a bit. A 1-bit indicates that the statement is true; and an 0-bit, it is false. The statement P AND Q is true or false as the four possible combinations shown in Table 7.1.

Note that, from a mathematician's viewpoint, the AND operator follows the rules of multiplication in Boolean algebra. They are listed in the last column of Table 7.1.

Table 7.1 AND operator

P	Q	P and Q	$(P \times Q)$
True (1)	True (1)	True	$(1 \times 1 = 1)$
True (1)	False (0)	False	$(1 \times 0 = 0)$
False (0)	True (1)	False	$(0 \times 1 = 0)$
False (0)	False (0)	False	$(0 \times 0 = 0)$

The basic purpose of the AND operation is to change the bit configuration from 1 to 0. If we wish to change the rightmost bit in the following byte from 1 to 0:

```
01101101
```

a new byte, called a mask, must be first selected in such way that all bit configurations are 1 except in the rightmost bit:

```
11111110
```

When these two bytes are ANDed, the rightmost bit of the first byte is changed from 1 to 0; and the contents of the remaining bits are undisturbed.

```
Given byte     0110 1101
               1111 1110
Changed to     0110 1100
```

It is convenient to consider such a rightmost bit as a *program switch*. This switch is initially on; it is then turned off after an AND operation. In System/370 or System/360, there are four instructions available to turn off a program switch. As shown in Table 7.2, all AND instructions use the mnemonic N. They are, respectively, of the RX, RR, SI, and SS instruction formats with the ending letters R, I, and C in the mnemonic.

Table 7.2 Four AND instructions

Mnemonic	Format
N	RX
NR	RR
NI	SI
NC	SS

Example

The contents (expressed in hexadecimal) of registers 2 and 5 are shown in Fig. 7.5. It is desirable to find the contents in these two registers after the execution of an AND instruction NR 2,5.

Register 2   Register 5

F7A8 E2A3   B762 C5B2

Fig. 7.5   Contents in two registers.

After the execution of the instruction, the contents of register 2 can be readily obtained as follows:

```
1111  0111  1010  1000  1110  0010  1010  0011
1011  0111  0110  0010  1100  0101  1011  0010
─────────────────────────────────────────────
1011  0111  0010  0000  1100  0000  1010  0010
```

or, B720C0A2 in hexadecimal. The contents of register 5 are not disturbed during the execution.

There are two possible condition code settings associated with an AND instruction: 00 and 01. When the result is not zero, the condition code is set to 01; otherwise, it is set to 00. The Branch on Condition (BC) instruction can then be used after an AND instruction to examine if all bits are set to zero.

7.4 OR INSTRUCTIONS

In the last section, we learned that the principal usage of the AND instructions is to change a 1-bit to an 0-bit. If one wishes to change a bit configuration from 0 to 1, a group of OR instructions may be used. The logical operator OR has the following definition: *If either or both bits are* 1, *the resulting bit is equal to* 1; *otherwise, it is equal to* 0. Consider, for example, the following two operands to be ORed together:

First operand   0110110**0**
Second operand   11001001
Result   1110110**1**

After the operation, both the rightmost and the leftmost bits are changed from 0 to 1. If we view these two bits as a pair of switches, both are now turned on.

If bit configuration is used to indicate the truth or falsity of a statement P (or Q), then the statement that P OR Q is true or false can be determined as shown in the first three columns of Table 7.3. The last column serves to point out that the OR operator follows the rules of addition in Boolean algebra.

Turning now to the assembler language instructions, we shall discuss a group of

Table 7.3 OR operator

P	Q	P or Q	(P + Q)
True (1)	True (1)	True	(1 + 1 = 1)
True (1)	False (0)	True	(1 + 0 = 1)
False (0)	True (1)	True	(0 + 1 = 1)
False (0)	False (0)	False	(0 + 0 = 0)

four OR instructions which can be used to turn on a switch. Similar to AND instructions, all four OR instructions (shown in Table 7.4) use the menmonic O, but each has its own instruction format.

Table 7.4 Four OR instructions

Mnemonic	Format
O	RX
OR	RR
OI	SI
OC	SS

We shall now illustrate the usage of the OR instruction with an example. In Fig. 7.6 are shown the contents in registers 6 and 7 before the execution of the following instruction:

$$\text{OR} \quad 7,6$$

What are the register contents after the execution?

Register 6

0000 0000	0000 0000	0000 0000	0101 1101

Register 7

1001 0011	0110 1011	1010 1101	0000 0000

Fig. 7.6 Register contents before the instruction OR 7,6

Solution

As the first step, the contents in both registers 7 and 6 are ORed together.

```
1001   0011   0110   1011   1010   1101   0000   0000
0000   0000   0000   0000   0000   0000   0101   1101
1001   0011   0110   1011   1010   1101   0101   1101
```

The result is then stored in register 7, or the first operand; the contents in register 6 are unchanged (see Fig. 7.7). It is interesting to note the net effect of this OR instruction: The rightmost eight bits in register 6 are transferred to the rightmost eight bits in register 7.

Register 6	0000 0000	0000 0000	0000 0000	0101 1101

Register 7	1001 0011	0110 1011	1010 1101	0101 1101

Fig. 7.7   Register contents after the instruction OR 7,6

Like the AND instructions, the condition code is set by OR instructions. It is set to 00 if every bit in the result is 0; and to 01 if at least one bit of the result is 1. In the above example, the condition code is set to 01.

7.5 EXCLUSIVE OR INSTRUCTIONS

In the previous two sections, we learned that the AND and OR instructions can be used to turn off and turn on respectively the program switches. The AND instructions change a bit configuration from 1 to 0; and OR instructions, from 0 to 1. In this section, the Exclusive OR instructions will be discussed. We define an Exclusive OR operation as follows: *If one and only one of the two bits is 1, the result is 1; otherwise, the result is 0.* Like AND and OR instruction, the Exclusive OR operation is carried out on each corresponding bit position in two operands. There are no carries or other interactions with the adjacent bit positions. For example, consider the following Exclusive OR operation:

First operand	01101100
Second operand	11111111
Result	10010011

This result clearly shows that the state of program switches in the first operand is completely changed after the operation.

If we wish to change one particular program switch in the first operand, such as the one shown in the box below, without disturbing the remaining bits, a suitable mask must be first selected as the second operand.

```
                              ┌──────Only bit to be changed
                              ↓
First operand      01 1 01100
Second operand     00 1 00000
Result             01 0 01100
```

This mask should contain all zeros except the bit corresponding to the bit shown in the box. After the Exclusive OR operation, the desired result is obtained.

We shall now discuss the assembler language instructions associated with the Exclusive OR operation. In System/370 or System/360, four instructions are available, each using the letter X in the mnemonic. Like the AND and OR instructions, the group of Exclusive OR instructions uses four instruction formats (see Table 7.5). The condition code settings after the execution of each Exclusive OR instruction follow

Table 7.5 Four exclusive OR instructions

Mnemonic	Format
X	RX
XR	RR
XI	SI
XC	SS

the same rule as for the AND and OR instructions. Each Exclusive OR instruction will set the condition code to 00 for an all-zero result; and to 01 for a non-zero result.

As a practical matter, the XR instruction can be used to zero out a register. For example, after executing the instruction

$$XR \quad 7,7$$

the contents in register 7 will be all zeros.

In many practical applications, XR instructions are often used to swap two registers without the help of a third. This is readily accomplished by using three consecutive Exclusive OR instructions. Consider, for example, the swapping of two registers 7 and 11. This can be performed by the following instructions:

$$XR \quad 7,11$$
$$XR \quad 11,7$$
$$XR \quad 7,11$$

Likewise, three consecutive XC instructions are often used to swap two areas of storage without using a third.

7.6 TEST UNDER MASK (TM) INSTRUCTION

We shall now discuss the Test under Mask (TM) instruction. It is of SI format and we use it to test some selected bits of a given byte in the main storage—sometimes called the qualification byte. The sole result of this instruction is to set the condition code. For example, the following instruction

$$TM \quad 100(10),X'D9'$$

or

$$TM \quad 100(10),B'11011001'$$

tests five bits in a qualification byte, whose effective address is obtained as the base address in register 10 plus 100. The five bits are selected because they correspond to the five 1's in the immediate field 11011001 (see Fig. 7.8).

(a) Eight bits of the qualification byte in the main storage. Bits selected for testing are shaded.

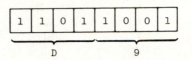

(b) The immediate field in the TM instruction.

Fig. 7.8   Selected bits in a byte and the immediate field.

This test can have three possible results: All selected bits are 1's; all bits tested are 0's; or some bits are 1's, while others are 0's. Table 7.6 lists the condition code settings for these results. Note that a condition code setting 10 is impossible after the execution of a TM instruction. Since some shaded bits are 0's and others are 1's in Fig. 7.8(a), the condition code is set to 01. At this point, you would probably write a Branch on Condition (BC) instruction.

Table 7.6   Relationship between the test result and CC setting

Result of the test for selected bits	CC setting
All 0's	00
All 1's	11
Some 0's and some 1's	01

As a practical application, let us see how a TM instruction can be used to determine whether an applicant meets the given minimum requirements for admission to a college. First, the given minimum requirements in binary (see Fig. 7.9) are used as the immediate field—or mask field—in the instruction. Second, the qualification of an applicant, John Doe, is stored in the qualification byte. In order to meet the minimum requirements, the shaded bits in the qualification byte (Fig. 7.10) must be all 1's. This is indeed the case. As a result, the condition code is set to 11 after the

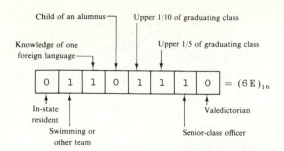

Fig. 7.9   Minimum requirements for the applicant specified in the immediate field.

execution of the following TM instruction:

$$\text{TM} \quad 2304(0),B'01101110'$$

where the address of the qualification byte is assumed to be $(2304)_{10}$.

Fig. 7.10   Qualification byte for John Doe stored in main storage.

7.7   EXAMPLE—ROTATION OF CONTENTS IN A REGISTER

The purpose of this section is to further illustrate the usage of two typical logical instructions SLDL and OR by a specific example. A subroutine SHUFFL in assembler language is to be written to rotate N bits in a given word. The given word and the value N are supplied by a main program. For example, if the contents (in hexadecimal) of the input word is 5D936BAD (see Fig. 7.11a) and if the value of N is 8, the result of the rotation will then be 936BAD5D (see Fig. 7.11b).

Figure 7.12 presents the main program in FORTRAN. It is used to perform the input/output and to call the subroutine SHUFFL. The N-value is in I format, while the

5 D	9 3	6 B	A D
0101 1101	1001 0011	0110 1011	1010 1101

(a)   Input word – the shaded bits are to be rotated.

9 3	6 B	A D	5 D
1001 0011	0110 1011	1010 1101	0101 1101

(b)   The result after rotation of eight bits.

Fig. 7.11   Rotation of contents in a word.

```
10 READ (5,1,END=26) HEX,N
 1 FORMAT( Z8,I4 )
   WRITE(6,3) HEX,N
 3 FORMAT(1H0,Z8,I4)
   CALL SHUFFL(HEX,N)
   WRITE(6,4) HEX
 4 FORMAT(1H0,Z8)
   GO TO 10
26 CALL EXIT
   END
```

Fig. 7.12 FORTRAN main program to call SHUFFL.

input word is in Z or hexadecimal format. A typical input card is shown in Fig. 7.13 which corresponds to the input word shown in Fig. 7.11(a). The final result after rotation is also printed in hexadecimal format, not in binary.

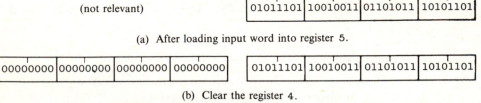

Fig. 7.13 Input card for FORTRAN main program.

The algorithm used in the assembler language subroutine SHUFFL can be described as follows: First, load the input word into register 5 (see Fig. 7.14a); clear register 4 (Fig. 7.14b); then double shift the contents in both registers 4 and 5 as a unit to the left N-places (Fig. 7.14c); and finally, OR back by using the following instruction:

$$\text{OR}\quad 5,4$$

Register 4	Register 5
(not relevant)	`01011101` `10010011` `01101011` `10101101`

(a) After loading input word into register 5.

| `00000000` `00000000` `00000000` `00000000` | `01011101` `10010011` `01101011` `10101101` |

(b) Clear the register 4.

| `00000000` `00000000` `00000000` `01011101` | `10010011` `01101011` `10101101` `00000000` |

(c) Double shifts left (logical) N places. Take $N = 8$.

| `00000000` `00000000` `00000000` `01011101` | `10010011` `01101011` `10101101` `01011101` |

(d) OR back.

Fig. 7.14 Contents of two registers in the course of rotation of a binary number.

```
SHUFFL    START 0
*                             HOUSEKEEPING PACKAGE PART 1
          BC    15,12(15)     R15 HAS ENTRY ADDRESS
          DC    X'6'
          DC    CL6'SHUFFL'
          STM   14,12,12(13)  R13 HAS POINTER ADDRESS
          BALR  9,0
          USING *,9
          L     2,0(1)        R2=ADDRESS OF HEX. INPUT NO.
          L     5,0(2)        R5=VALUE OF HEX. NUMBER
*                             GENERATE LENGTH AND INSERT INTO SRDL INST
          L     6,4(1)        R6=ADDRESS OF N
          L     7,0(6)        R7 CONTAINS THE NUMBER OF BITS TO SHIFT
          SR    4,4           CLEAR REG 4
          SLDL  4,0(7)
          OR    5,4           OR BACK
          ST    5,0(2)        R5 HAS SHIFTED BITS
*                             HOUSEKEEPING PART 2
          LM    2,12,28(13)
          MVI   12(13),X'FF'
          BCR   15,14
          END
```

Fig. 7.15 Subroutine SHUFFL to rotate bits.

The final result is in register 5 as illustrated in Fig. 7.14(d). The corresponding subroutine SHUFFL is shown in Fig. 7.15 where the shaded portion indicates the linkage package discussed in Chapter 5. The printer output from the main program is presented in Fig. 7.16.

```
5D936BAD    8
936BAD5D
```

Fig. 7.16 Printer output.

BIBLIOGRAPHY

IBM System/360 Principles of Operation, Form GA22-6821, IBM Corp.

McCluskey, E. J., Jr., and T. C. Bartee (eds.), *A Survey of Switching Circuit Theory*, McGraw-Hill, New York, 1962.

Application of Bit Manipulation

Botvinnik, M. M., *Computers Chess and Long-Range Planning*, Springer-Verlag, New York (1969).

Kuo, S. S., and W. K. Young, "Computer Studies of the Traveling Salesman Problem," *Q. Bull., Can. Inf. Process. Soc.* **8** (5), 31–36 (1968).

Kuo, S. S., *Evaluation of Identification Factors*, PB-174 009, U. S. Department of Commerce, National Technical Information Service, Springfield, Va., (1968).

Samuel, A. L., *Programming Computers to Play Games, in Advances in Computers*, Vol. 1 (edited by Franz Alt), Academic Press, New York, 1960, pages 165–192.

Scott, J. J., A chess playing program. *Machine Intelligence IV*, American Elsevier, New York (1969).

PROBLEMS

1. The contents in register 7 are $(-8)_{10}$. (a) Express this quantity in binary as stored in the register; (b) Shift this quantity one place to the left. Is the answer $(-16)_{10}$?

2. The Shift instruction

$$SRL \quad 5,0(7)$$

makes the contents in register 5 shift to right, with the shift amount defined in register 7. Fill out the register contents after the execution of the instruction.

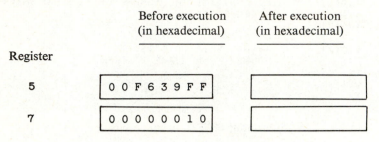

	Before execution (in hexadecimal)	After execution (in hexadecimal)
Register		
5	0 0 F 6 3 9 F F	
7	0 0 0 0 0 0 1 0	

3. After the execution of the following instruction

$$SRDL \quad 6,8$$

what are the contents in registers 6 and 7?
The original contents are

B A 1 2 3 C 5 6	F F A B 7 D E F
Register 6	Register 7

4. The following Logical Compare instruction of RX format

$$CL \quad 0,MASK$$

causes the contents of register 0 to compare with the MASK field. The condition code settings are shown in the explanatory note 4 (Appendix F). If the next instruction in the sequence is

$$BC \quad 2,HERE$$

what does this instruction do?
Note: In a CL instruction, the comparisons are made by taking both operands as unsigned 32-bit integers.

5. If the first operand is 10010101 and the second one is 00110111, find the result for the AND operation.

6. An automobile insurance policy byte has the following codes: The first bit is 1 if a property damage liability policy is carried; the second bit is 1 if a bodily injury liability policy is carried; the third bit is 1 if a collision policy is carried, and so on.

Thus, the following byte represents a collision policy and a bodily injury is carried.

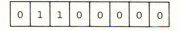

Set up a mask such that, when ANDed with the byte from any record, the result will be zero in all but the third position from the left. In other words, if the record has a collision policy, the result should be 00100000; otherwise, the result shall be all zeros.

7. What are the contents of register 4 (in hexadecimal) after the execution of the following AND instruction:

$$\text{NR} \quad 4,4$$

The contents in register 4 are originally FFFFFFFF.

8. Which of the following instructions would clear register 6?
   a) XR 6,6
   b) SR 6,6
   c) LA 6,0
   d) All of the above.

9. The Exclusive OR operation is often used to determine the sign of a product or a quotient in floating-point operations. The sign bit of each of the two operands are Exclusive ORed, and the result is the required sign bit. Find the sign bit for the result, if

	Sign bit	
	First operand	Second operand
Case *a*	1	0
Case *b*	1	1
Case *c*	0	1

10. Obtain the answer for each of the following Exclusive OR operations:

01	0110	01001100
11	1010	00001000

11. Given the following two bytes, show the result after they are (a) ANDed together; (b) ORed, (c) Exclusive ORed:

First operand	11010110
Second operand	10010101

12. What is the condition code after the execution of the instruction

$$\text{TM} \quad 100(10), \text{X'D9'}$$

if the qualification byte is shown as follows:
a) 00000000   b) 11111111
c) 11001001   d) 11111001

13. The mask field in a TM instruction is X'49', and the qualification byte, or the data tested, is 10011101. What will the condition code setting after the execution of the TM instruction be?

14. Given:
a) The initial storage contents (in hexadecimal):

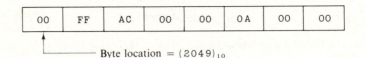

Byte location $= (2049)_{10}$

b) Instruction in hexadecimal:

| 91 | F8 | 0 | 804 |

Required:
a) After the execution, the condition code is set to _____.
b) The bit configuration in the mask field is _____.
c) The bit configuration in the main storage to be tested is _____.

LABORATORY ASSIGNMENT

Try to solve the following problems.

1. Write a subroutine in assembler language to decode the contents in register 3 in the following manner. In the first and third bytes, the even bits contain the valid information and the odd bits contain the "garbage". In the second and fourth bytes, the odd bits contain information, and the even bits contain the garbage.

   Also, a main program is to be written in FORTRAN or any other high-level language to read in a random assortment of bits into register 3 and to take care of output. For a test case, use the input word shown in Fig. 7.11(a).

2. Figure 7.17 illustrates a subroutine to implement the algorithm of the following equation to compute pseudo random numbers:

$$x_{i+1} \equiv A x_i (\text{mod } p)$$

```
RANDCM    START
          USING  *,15                  INITIAL LINKAGE
          STM    2,5,28(13)
          LM     2,3,0(1)              LOAD ADDRESSES OF VARIABLES PASSED
          L      5,A                   COMPUTE NEXT INTEGER
          M      4,0(2)                RANDOM NUMBER WITH X(I+1)=AX(I) (MOD P)
          D      4,P
          ST     4,0(2)
          SRL    4,7                   COMPUTE NEXT REAL RANDOM NUMBER
          A      4,CHAR
          ST     4,0(3)
          LM     2,5,28(13)            TERMINAL LINKAGE
          BR     14
CHAR      DC     F'1073741824'  CONSTANTS. CHAR FIRST
A         DC     F'16807'       SO A IS ON DOUBLE WORD
P         DC     F'2147483647'  BOUNDARY. MAKES LM
          END                   INSTRUCTION FASTER
```

Fig. 7.17 Subroutine RANDOM, a pseudo random number generator.

This subroutine may be called by a FORTRAN statement in a main program as follows:

$$\text{CALL RANDOM(INT,REAL)}$$

where INT is any fullword integer variable and REAL is any fullword real, single precision variable. The value INT should be given an initial value before calling the subroutine RANDOM. The subroutine returns an integer random number in INT and a real random number between 0 and 1 in REAL.

a) Draw a detailed flowchart for this subroutine.
b) Write a main program in FORTRAN or other high-level language to calculate first 1,000 real random numbers. Run your program on a computer.

3. The FORTRAN calling sequence for a NOT subroutine is

$$\text{CALL NOT(I,K)}$$

where I is the INTEGER*4 variable to be negated, and K is an INTEGER*4 variable set equal to the 1's complement of I.

Write a NOT subroutine in assembler language. Treat the first argument I as an unsigned 32-bit integer and return the result K as an unsigned 32-bit integer.

Example

Let

$$I = (F0F0F0F0)_{16} = 1111\ 0000\ 1111\ 0000\ 1111\ 0000\ 1111\ 0000$$

then

$$K = (0F0F0F0F)_{16} = 0000\ 1111\ 0000\ 1111\ 0000\ 1111\ 0000\ 1111$$

Note that the result K has a 1-bit everywhere the first argument I has 0, and a 0 bit everywhere the first argument has 1. For a given bit a, (NOT a) can be expressed as (a Exclusive OR 1).

CHAPTER 8

Subroutine Linkage and Control Sections

8.1 PROGRAMS, MODULES, AND CONTROL SECTIONS

In Section 5.5, we discussed how a main program written in a high-level language may be linked to an assembler language subroutine; and that subroutine is a lowest-level one, meaning that it does not call another subroutine. In this chapter, we shall extend our discussion to a linkage package for a subroutine which *does* call another sub-routine.

Two facts which relate to the subroutine linkage are not commonly recognized:

1. Assembler does not recognize a main program or a subroutine, it only accepts an assembly (or a compilation). Physically speaking, the last statement of each assembly is an END statement.

2. An assembly or a compilation, sometimes called a *module,* is made of one or more than one *control sections.* A control section is a group of machine instructions and assembler instructions, whose position relative to each other is fixed. For example, a typical short main program, written in a high-level language to handle input/output, consists of about ten control sections. In another example, the subroutine ARITH (see Fig. 5.20 on page 129), which is assembled independently, is the sole control section in the module.

Despite the fact that assembler does not recognize such a thing as a program, the concept of main program and subroutine is still very useful to a programmer. For this reason, we shall view a subroutine or a main program as an independently assembled module.

In Sections 8.2 through 8.7, we shall assume that a subroutine has only one control section. The basic purpose of these six sections is to study the linkage between the control sections. However, it is generally a good practice to write a long program (or a subroutine) as a sequence of many control sections. In Section 8.8, we shall see how this may be accomplished. The application of a dummy section (DSECT) for transferring variables is discussed in Section 8.9. Finally, the advanced usage of USING instruction for a long control section (longer than 4096 bytes) is presented in Section 8.10.

Before we turn to the next section, let us examine how to identify a control section. The answer to this problem is: Use the assembler instruction CSECT as the first instruction in the control section. Its general format is

[*symbol*]   CSECT

The operand field must be left blank. For example, the following instruction

SHUFFL   CSECT

defines a control section with the name SHUFFL.

If this control section is the *first* one or the *only* one in a module, you can identify it in three possible ways.

1. Placing a START instruction as its first instruction. The symbol in its name field, if used, becomes the name of this control section. Only a self-defining term is permitted in the operand field: If specified, it indicates the initial location counter-setting for this control section. If not used, the location counter-setting is taken as zero. As mentioned before, the group of instructions shown in Fig. 5.20 constitutes a control section. The first instruction

ARITH   START   0

defines the name of this control section as ARITH. Its initial location counter setting is zero.

2. Writing a CSECT instruction such as

ARITH   CSECT

as its first instruction.

3. Using neither START nor CSECT.

If the name field in a CSECT or START instruction is left blank, *or* if neither CSECT nor START instruction is specified at the beginning, then this control section is known as *unnamed* to the assembler. As an illustration, consider the group of instructions listed in Fig. 1.17. To a programmer, this group of instructions may constitute a program; but to the assembler, it represents an *unnamed* control section, a unique identification.

8.2 EXTERNAL LINKAGE PACKAGE

By external linkage we mean the linkage between two modules. In this and the next five sections, we shall consider a special case, in which each module consists of only one control section. Such separately assembled control sections are then joined together to form a load module by the linkage editor (see Fig. 6.1). Alternatively, they may be

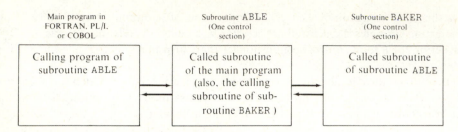

Fig. 8.1 The called and calling subroutines. Each box represents an independently assembled module.

linked together and loaded into main memory by a direct linking loader (OS loader). For simplicity, let us consider two separately assembled control sections (subroutines), ABLE and BAKER. Subroutine ABLE calls BAKER, as shown in Fig. 8.1, and BAKER is the lowest-level one which does not call another subroutine.

A typical external linkage package used in ABLE is presented in Fig. 8.2. Note that the first instruction, which specifies the beginning of a control section,

        ABLE   CSECT

has the identical meaning as

        ABLE   START 0

where ABLE is written in the name field. For the purpose of our discussion, this subroutine (the sole control section) is divided into six parts. Part 3 and 5 are user's written source instructions. The remaining four parts in Fig. 8.2 consist of the required instructions for the external linkage; they are discussed in this and next two sections.

Part 1: ENTRY and EXTRN

Before the linkage editor (or direct linking loader) can join together two separately assembled control sections, it needs specific information. First, what symbols are defined in ABLE, but used in BAKER. To provide this information, a programmer can write an ENTRY assembler instruction in control section ABLE. Its general format is

        ENTRY   *symbol*[,*symbol*, . . . ,*symbol*]

where *symbol* in the operand field stands for a relocatable symbol. Each symbol and its assigned value are included in the external symbol dictionary, a part of output in the linkage editing step.

It is important to note that the name of the control section ABLE, already specified in a CSECT or a START instruction, need not be included in the operand field of an ENTRY instruction, since the names of all control sections are automatically placed in the external symbol dictionary.

Second, the linkage editor has to know what *external* symbols, used in control

```
ABLE        CSECT
*
*** PART 1        EXTRN AND ENTRY ***
*
            EXTRN ...
            ENTRY ...
*
*** PART 2        SAVE ROUTINE ***
*
            BC      15,10(15)
            DC      X'5'
            DC      CL5'ABLE '
            STM     14,12,12(13)
REGNO       EQU     11
            BALR    REGNO,0
            USING   *,REGNO
            LR      12,13    LOAD POINTER TO SAVEMAIN INTO R12
            LA      13,SAVEABLE
            ST      13,8(12)
            ST      12,4(13)
            BC      15,HERE
SAVEABLE    DS      18F
*
*** PART 3        USER'S WRITTEN SOURCE INST.
*
HERE        .
            .
            .
*
*** PART 4(A)     CALLING SEQUENCE
*
            LA      1,ARGADRES    THIS STATEMENT IS NEEDED
*                                 ONLY IF THE PROGRAMMER WANTS
*                                 TO PASS THE ARGUMENT LIST HIMSELF.
            L       15,VCONST
            BALR    14,15         GO TO BAKER
*
*** PART 5        MORE USER'S SOURCE INSTR.
*
            .
            .
            .
*
*** PART 6        RESTORE REGISTERS AND RETURN
*
            L       13,SAVEABLE+4
            LM      2,12,28(13)
            L       14,12(13)
            MVI     12(13),X'FF'
            BCR     15,14
*
*** PART 4(B)     ADDRESS CONSTANTS
*
VCONST      DC      V(BAKER)      THE FOLLOWING DC INSTRUCTIONS
*                                 NEEDED ONLY IF THE PROGRAMMER
*                                 WISHES TO PASS THE ARGUMENTS HIMSELF.
ARGADRES    DC      AL4(ARGUMENT 1)
            DC      AL4(ARGUMENT 2)
            .
            .
            .
            DC      AL4(LAST ARGUMENT)
            END
```

Fig. 8.2 External linkage package.

section ABLE, were defined in BAKER. This information is supplied through an instruction in control section ABLE. Its format is

$$\text{EXTRN} \qquad symbol[,symbol,\dots,symbol]$$

where *symbol* in the operand field stands for an external symbol (a relocatable symbol). There is no need to include the control section name BAKER in the operand field of this EXTRN statement.

Part 2: SAVE Routine

As mentioned in Section 5.5, a calling subroutine, by convention, must set up a 18-word area to save *its* register contents; the actual saving, however, is performed in the called subroutine. For the purpose of our discussion, we shall use the following symbols for the two "save areas" involved:

SAVEMAIN—the save area set up in the main program to save the register contents used in main program; the actual saving is performed in ABLE.

SAVEABLE—the save area set up in the subroutine ABLE to save its register contents. The actual saving is done in BAKER.

Two points should be stressed here. (1) Since we have assumed that BAKER is the lowest-level subroutine, there is no need to save its register contents. (2) As mentioned in Section 5.5, the general registers 0, 1, 13, 14, and 15 are linkage registers; they should not be used by a called subroutine until their contents are transferred and stored in a save area.

If we compare Part 2 in Fig. 8.2 and the first part in Fig. 5.5, we see that the former contains four more instructions to save two addresses.

```
LR   12,13    LOAD POINTER TO SAVEMAIN INTO R12
LA   13,SAVEABLE
ST   13,8(12)
ST   12,4(13)
```

First, the address of SAVEABLE is stored in the third word of SAVEMAIN; second, the address of SAVEMAIN is stored in the second word in SAVEABLE. Just after the execution of this save routine, the contents of the 18-word area SAVEMAIN are summarized in Table 8.1.

8.3 SECOND USAGE OF BALR INSTRUCTION

Each time a calling subroutine sends control to a called subroutine, the former is expected to (1) know the entry-point address of the called subroutine; (2) supply to the called subroutine the return address; and, as an option, (3) pass to the called subroutine an argument list. These items of information constitute Part 4 of the external linkage package shown in Fig. 8.2. We shall discuss items 1 and 2 in this section, leaving item 3 for the next.

In Sections 5.5 and 6.14, we mentioned that the Branch and Link instruction has

Table 8.1. Contents of 18-word area SAVEMAIN just after the execution of the save routine in ABLE (as listed in Part 2 in Fig. 8.2).

Fullword number in SAVEMAIN	Address of the fullword	Contents saved		
		Register (or a pointer) used in main program	Function of the register used in main program (or function of the pointer)	Instructions used to save the contents
1	SAVEMAIN	—	A part of standard linkage convention by operating system. (For assembler language program, this word can be used for any purpose).	—
2	SAVEMAIN+4	Pointer	Address of save area for the program (supervisor in OS) which calls the main program.	Save routine in MAIN: LR 12,13 LA 13,SAVEMAIN ST 12,4(13)
3	SAVEMAIN+8	Register 13	Address of SAVEABLE, the save area ABLE of the called subroutine.	Save routine in ABLE: LR 12,13 LA 13,SAVEABLE ST 13,8(12)
4	SAVEMAIN+12	Register 14	Return address of the calling program (the main program).	
5	SAVEMAIN+16	Register 15	Entry point address to the called subroutine (ABLE)	
6	SAVEMAIN+20	Register 0	Result from the function subprogram only	STM 14,12,12(13) in ABLE
7	SAVEMAIN+24	Register 1	Address of argument list	
8	SAVEMAIN+28	Register 2		
9	SAVEMAIN+32	Register 3	Registers used in main program.	
⋮		⋮		
18	SAVEMAIN+68	Register 12		

two basic usages. The first one, discussed in Section 5.5 and characterized by its zero second operand, serves primarily to load a base register. For example, the first instruction in the following pair

```
BALR   11,0
USING  *,11
```

loads register 11 with the location counter setting of the next instruction. It does not branch, since its second operand contains a zero.

A BALR instruction can also be used to branch out from a calling subroutine and later return to it. Let us again consider the case: ABLE calls BAKER. The instruction

```
BALR   14,15
```

in ABLE results in:

1. Loading the address of the instruction next to the BALR (i.e., the first instruction in Part 5 of Fig. 8.2) into register 14. Consequently, register 14 now contains the *return address*.

2. Branching to the entry point in BAKER. The entry-point address is loaded into register 15 by the instruction

```
L   15,VCONST
```

where VCONST, an external address constant, specifies the entry-point address. This and other types of address constants will be dealt with in more detail in Section 8.5.

In sum, the instruction

```
BALR   14,15
```

loads the address of the next instruction (the return address) into register 14, and then branches to the entry-point of the called subroutine. The actual address of the subroutine entry-point is in register 15.

8.4 ARGUMENT LIST

Apart from the return address, a called subroutine sometimes expects information on the argument list, which contains the address of each argument. As a convention, the calling subroutine has responsibility to (1) put the argument list into *consecutive fullwords* in the main storage; and (2) put the address of its first word into register 1. For simplicity, let us consider the argument list for four arguments A, B, C, and ANSWER. As shaded in Fig. 8.3, this list takes four consecutive words. If the main program is written in a high-level language, the address of the list, or the address of the first fullword, say, 00F200, is automatically loaded into register 1. From this address list, the contents of each argument can be readily found by following the arrows shown in Fig. 8.3.

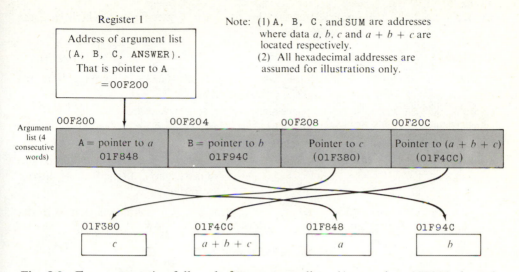

Fig. 8.3   Four consecutive fullwords for argument list. (Assumed as 00F200 through 00F20F.)

In assembler language programming, the address of the argument list is loaded into register 1 by the instruction

$$\text{LA} \quad 1, \text{ARGADRES}$$

which is shown in Part 4(a) in Fig. 8.2.

8.5 ADDRESS CONSTANTS

In the previous sections, we examined Parts 1, 2, and 4(a) of a typical external linkage package (see Fig. 8.2). We shall now discuss Part 4(b) in Fig. 8.2, which involves A-type and V-type DC assembler instructions.

A-type Address Constant

The general format of an A-type address constant is as follows:

$$symbol \quad \text{DC} \quad \text{A}(expression, \ldots, expression)$$

A typical example is

$$\text{ADCON1} \quad \text{DC} \quad \text{A}(\text{ADD})$$

where the address of the symbol ADD is stored in a fullword ADCON1. If the address of symbol ADD is assumed to be 00A1A8, then ADCON1 establishes a fullword constant 0000A1A8.

Note that the operand field in this instruction is an A followed by one or several expressions enclosed in parentheses, not single quotations. The expression may be either absolute or relocatable. Each A-type constant is generated in a fullword, aligned on fullword boundary, unless a length code is specified, in which case the boundary alignment is not performed.

Examples

ADCON2   DC   AL3(ADD)   generates 3-byte constant 00A1A8. (Assume that the address ADD is 00A1A8).

ADCON3   DC   2AL1(X'BA4'+1)   generates 2-byte constant A5A5.

ADCON4   DC   A(*+20)   generates 4-byte constant containing the current location counter setting +20.

ADCON5   DC   A(BASE,BASE+4096,BASE+8192)   generates 3-fullword address constants, each aligned on fullword boundary.

In a typical A-type DC instruction, a relocatable symbol is usually specified in the operand field. For simplicity, let us study the following instruction

ADCON   DC   A(ARGUMENT)

where ARGUMENT is taken as a relocatable symbol. Two possible cases are considered below.

Case 1. ARGUMENT is defined in an independently assembled control section, say, ABLE, and the A-type DC instruction is written in the same control section.

This is a very simple case. The above instruction establishes, at location ADCON, a constant which contains the address of the relocatable symbol ARGUMENT. The actual assembled constant is a fullword, say, 000000B0, which is the location counter setting of ARGUMENT. The symbol considered in this case is commonly called an *internal* symbol, and the process of adjusting the address constant of an internal symbol is known as *relocation*.

Case 2. The relocatable symbol ARGUMENT is defined in one independently assembled control section, say, BAKER; but its associated A-type DC instruction is written in another independently assembled control section, say, ABLE. In this case, ARGUMENT is considered as an external symbol to ABLE and, as a result, the following instruction

EXTRN   ARGUMENT

should be placed in ABLE and

ENTRY   ARGUMENT

in BAKER. The following instruction

ADCON   DC   A(ARGUMENT)

can then be written in ABLE to refer *data* in BAKER. This process of supplying information of the address constant for an external symbol is known as *linking*.

As a practical example, let us implement, in assembler language programming, the passing of an argument list to the called subroutine. In particular, we wish (1) to pass four parameters A, B, C, and SUM from control section ABLE to BAKER, and (2) to

```
              LA    1,ARGADRES
                       ⋮
  ARGADRES    DC    AL4(A)
              DC    AL4(B)
              DC    AL4(C)
              DC    AL4(SUM)
```

Fig. 8.4 Instructions for passing the argument list to a called subroutine.

load the address of this argument list into register 1. To achieve this we can use the sequence of instructions shown in Fig. 8.4. Each A-type DC instruction defines an address constant. For example, the DC instruction,

```
       ARGADRES    DC    AL4(A)
```

defines ARGADRES as the address of A. L4 indicates that the established constant is four-byte long. Note that the instruction

```
           LA    1,ARGADRES
```

loads the pointer of argument list into register 1, and can be replaced by the following instruction using a literal:

```
       LA    1,=A(A,B,C,SUM)
```

V-type Address Constant

The A-type constant in the above discussion is usually employed to refer data defined either in the same control section or in another independently assembled control section. There is also a V-type constant, whose sole purpose is to define an entry-point address.

Its format is quite similar to that of A-type constant:

symbol   DC   V(*external symbol*, . . . , *external symbol*)

Specifically, let us consider a branch to the control section BAKER from ABLE. It may be accomplished in the following three steps:

1. Define a V-type address constant in ABLE.

```
           VCONST    DC    V(BAKER)
```

2. Load this constant into register 15.

```
           L    15,VCONST
```

3. Branch to the entry-point address of BAKER.

```
           BALR    14,15
```

As mentioned before, it is not necessary to specify the external symbol BAKER in an EXTRN instruction used in the control section ABLE.

During the assembly of control section ABLE, the V-type DC instructon (see Step 1) generates the following four-byte constant: 00000000, and the assembler puts VCONST as an external symbol in the external symbol dictionary. The actual address of BAKER is later inserted by the linkage editor or OS loader into the location VCONST in control section ABLE, a process called *linking*. As with A-type constants, the implied length of a V-type constant is four bytes; it is aligned on a fullword boundary.

In retrospect, each time a calling subroutine sends control to the called subroutine, the former is expected to pass the required return address and argument list to the latter. This can be accomplished by a sequence of instructions, shown in Fig. 8.5, which is commonly known as the *calling sequence*. Two special cases are worth noting.

```
                LA      1,ARGADRES
                L       15,VCONST
                BALR    14,15
                  ⋮
VCONST          DC      V(BAKER)
ARGADRES        DC      AL4(A)
                DC      AL4(B)
                DC      AL4(C)
                DC      AL4(ANSWER)
```

Fig. 8.5   Calling sequence.

1. The passing of argument list is handled through a CALL statement in main program written in a high-level language.

2. Only one input argument and one output argument are to be transmitted to the called subroutine.

In either case, the passing of argument list from subroutine ABLE to BAKER becomes unnecessary. As a result, the calling sequence becomes

```
                L       15,VCONST
                BALR    14,15
                  ⋮
VCONST   DC     V(BAKER)
```

8.6 AN EXAMPLE—MAIN PROGRAM IN HIGH-LEVEL LANGUAGE AND TWO SUBROUTINES IN ASSEMBLER LANGUAGE

In the previous four sections, we have discussed the housekeeping package for a subroutine which calls another subroutine. In this section, we shall present an example.

Basically, this is an extension of the example discussed in Section 5.6. Two variables n_1 and n_2 are read in from a high-level language main program. The main program calls a subroutine ARITH1 in assembler language to multiply and divide the two variables. The answers are stored in PROD and QUOT, respectively. In addition, subroutine ARITH1 calls another subroutine ADD (see Fig. 8.6), which adds and subtracts the two variables. The answers are stored in SUM and DIFF, respectively. The subroutine ADD then adds the (algebraically) larger of two results in locations SUM and DIFF to n_1. This new sum is called NEWSUM.

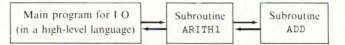

Fig. 8.6   Two subroutines in assembler language. The argument list is passed from main program.

Figure 8.7 presents the subroutine ARITH1 which is divided into six parts. Since the argument list is passed from a high-level language main program, the pointer to this list is automatically in register 1. After the execution of the following instruction, the first instruction in Part 3

$$\text{L} \quad 2,0(1)$$

the pointer to the variable n_1 is loaded in register 2. Then, after the execution of the next instruction

$$\text{L} \quad 3,0(2)$$

the data n_1 itself is loaded in register 3.

Note that the entry-point to the subroutine ADD (Fig. 8.8) is the address of its sixth instruction. As far as subroutine ARITH1 is concerned, the symbol ADD is defined externally. As a result, the following external card

$$\text{EXTRN} \quad \text{ADD}$$

must be placed in Part 1 of subroutine ARITH1. The A-type DC instruction in Part 4(b) is assembled as fullword 00000000. In other words, the assembler does not know this address; it will be filled in later by the linkage editor or OS loader.

Before branching to subroutine ADD, the subroutine ARITH1 loads register 15 with the entry-point address of ADD. As a result, there is no need for the subroutine ADD to actually load a base register. In other words, no BALR 15,0 instruction is needed at the beginning of subroutine ADD.

The main program used for input output should be essentially same as those shown in Figs. 5.17 through 5.19. Two minor changes are necessary for each main program. First, a new variable NEWSUM should be included in the argument list. For example, the CALL statement in FORTRAN (see Fig. 5.17) should be changed from

$$\text{CALL} \quad \text{ARITH(N1,N2,SUM,DIFF,PROD,QUOT)}$$

to

$$\text{CALL} \quad \text{ARITH1(N1,N2,SUM,DIFF,PROD,QUOT,NEWSUM)}$$

```
DECK2      START  O
*
*   PART   1   ENTRY AND EXTRN
*
           ENTRY ARITH1
           EXTRN ADD
*
*   PART   2      SAVE ROUTINE
*
           B      14(15)
           DC     X'7'
           DC     CL7'ARITH1 '    IDENTIFIER
ARITH1     STM    14,12,12(13)    SAVE REGISTERS
           BALR   11,0            R(11) USED AS BASE REGISTER
           USING  *,11
           LR     12,13           R(13) CONTAINS ADDRESS OF MAIN
           LA     13,AREA
           ST     13,8(0,12)      ADDRESS OF AREA GOES TO SAVEAREA +8
           ST     12,4(0,13)      ADDRESS OF SAVEAREA GOES TO AREA+4
           BC     15,SUB2         BRANCH AROUND SAVEAREA
AREA       DS     18F
*
*   PART   3      USER'S WRITTEN SOURCE INSTRUCTIONS
*
SUB2       L      2,0(1)          LOAD FIRST ARG PTR IN R(2)
           L      3,0(2)          LOAD FIRST ARG IN R(3)
           L      2,4(1)          LOAD SECOND ARG PTR INTO R(2)
           L      4,0(2)          LOAD SECOND ARG IN R(4)
*
*   PART   4(A)      ENTRY POINT ADRESS AND RETURN ADDRESS
*
           L      15,ADCON
           BALR   14,15
*
*   PART   5      USER'S WRITTEN INSTRUCTIONS
*
           LR     7,3             LOAD FIRST ARG IN R(7)
           MR     6,4             MULT FIRST ARG WITH SECOND ARG
           L      2,16(1)         LOAD FIFTH ARG PTR IN R(2)
           ST     7,0(2)          STORE PROD IN FIFTH ARG
           SR     6,6             CLEAR R(6)
           LR     7,3             LOAD FIRST ARG IN R(7)
           DR     6,4             DIVIDE 1ST ARG BY 2ND ARG
           L      2,20(1)         LOAD SIXTH ARG PTR IN R(2)
           ST     7,0(2)          STORE QUOTIENT IN SIXTH ARG
*
*   PART   6      RETURN TO MAIN PROGRAM
*
           L      13,AREA+4       RESTORE REGISTERS
           LM     14,12,12(13)
           BR     14              RETURN TO MAIN
*
*   PART   4(B)      ADDRESS CONSTANTS
*
ADCON      DC     A(ADD)
           END
```

Fig. 8.7 Subroutine ARITH1. Note its six parts.

```
DECK3     START  0
          ENTRY  ADD
          DC     CL3'ADD'         NAME OF SUBROUTINE
          DC     X'3'             NUMBER OF CHARACTERS IN NAME
          USING  *,15
ADD       STM    14,12,12(13)     SAVE REGISTERS IN SAVEAREA
          LR     6,3              LOAD FIRST ARG IN R(6)
          AR     6,4              ADD 2ND ARG WITH 1ST ARG
          L      2,8(1)           LOAD 3RD ARG PTR INR(2)
          ST     6,0(2)           STORE SUM IN 3RD ARG
          LR     7,6              LOAD SUM INTO R(7)
          LR     6,3              LOAD 1ST ARG IN R(6)
          SR     6,4              SUBTRACT 2ND ARG FROM 1ST
          L      2,12(1)          LOAD 4TH ARG PTR IN R(2)
          ST     6,0(2)           STORE DIFFERENCE IN 4TH ARG
          LR     8,6              LOAD DIFFERENCE OF THE TWO NUMBERS IN R(8)
          L      2,24(1)          LOAD 5TH ARG PTR IN R(2)
          CR     7,8              COMPARE R(7) AND R(8)
          BH     SUM              IF R(7) IS HIGHER THAN R(8) GO TO SUM
          AR     8,3              ADD THE DIFFERENCE AND ARG 1
          ST     8,0(2)           STORE SUM IN R(2)
          BC     15,CONT          GO TO CONT
SUM       AR     7,3              ADD 'SUM' AND ARG 1
          ST     7,0(2)           STORE SUM INR(2)
CONT      LM     2,12,28(13)      RESTORE REGISTERS
          MVI    12(13),X'FF'
          BR     14               RETURN TO MAIN
          END
```

Fig. 8.8 Subroutine ADD, the lowest-level subroutine.

Second, in the WRITE statement and statement 10, this variable NEWSUM should also be added.

8.7 AN EXAMPLE—APPLICATION OF NONNUMERICAL PROBLEM

It is required to read 40 characters, each in its hexadecimal representation, e.g., E9, and print each character until a character FF has been detected; in other words, print the complete record ending with FF. A sample output is shown in Fig. 8.9, in which the first line is the echo print of the input, and the second line is the required result.

```
A1C21463A125C7E921537586A10AA53BC2239462541DD53683FF1148765450577CC65CDA45E35F6B
A1C21463A125C7E921537586A10AA53BC2239462541DD53683FF
```

Fig. 8.9 Sample output.

The input/output are handled by a main program written in FORTRAN, as shown in Fig. 8.10. The statement number 1 in the main program perhaps needs some explanation. This is one of the advanced FORMAT statement in FORTRAN, used to transmit data in hexadecimal form. Z8 means eight hexadecimal digits, or four bytes;

10Z8 means ten hexadecimal numbers, each having eight digits. Hence, the data are read into the computer in a group of ten hexadecimal numbers, each having eight digits.

```
      DIMENSION INPUT(20),OUTPUT(20)
      READ(1,1)(INPUT(I),I=1,10)
      WRITE(3,3)(INPUT(I),I=1,10)
    1 FORMAT(10Z8)
    3 FORMAT(1H0,10Z8)
      CALL RECORD(INPUT,OUTPUT)
      WRITE (3,3)(OUTPUT(I),I=1,10)
      CALL EXIT
      END
```

Fig. 8.10   FORTRAN main program for input/output.

When the Z format is used, only the hexadecimal digits 0, 1, 2, ..., 9, A, B, ..., and F may appear in the input field.

The FORTRAN main program calls the subroutine RECORD, which has two parameters INPUT and OUTPUT. The pointer to the argument list (or known as the parameter list) is stored in register 1 (see Fig. 8.11). The addresses of INPUT and OUTPUT are automatically placed in two consecutive fullwords in the main storage.

Once the record is read in, it is processed by the assembler language subroutine RECORD, shown in Fig. 8.12. The basic objectives of this subroutine are: (1) to call the subroutine LENGTH; and (2) to move the proper number of characters from the input to the output area.

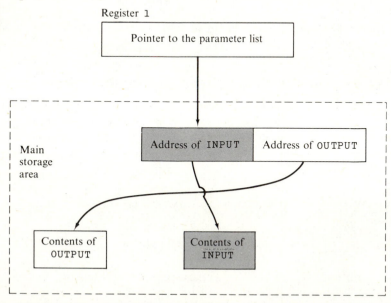

Fig. 8.11   The three-tier relationship: the parameter list, address of parameters, and the contents of each parameter.

```
RECORD    CSECT
*
*    PART  1   NOT NEEDED
*
*    PART  2
*
          B       12(15)
          DC      AL1(7)
          DC      CL7'RECORD '          IDENTIFIER
          STM     14,12,12(13)          SAVE RGISTERS
          BALR    11,0                  R11 USED AS BASE REGISTER
          USING   *,11
          LR      12,13                 SAVE POINTS
          LA      13,AREA
          ST      13,8(12)
          ST      12,4(13)
          BC      15,SUB2               BRANCH AROUND SAVE AREA
AREA      DS      18F
*
*    PART  3   NOT NEEDED
*
*    PART  4(A)
*
*        GO TO SUBROUTINE LENGTH
*
SUB2      L       15,ADCON      ADDRESS OF SUBROUTINE LENGTH
          BALR    14,15         BRANCH TO LENGTH
*
*        THIS IS WHERE THE PROGRAM RETURNS TO AFTER COMPLETION OF
*        SUBROUTINE LENGTH
*    PART  5
*
          L       8,0(1)        R(8) = ADDRESS OF INPUT BLOCK
          L       2,4(1)        R(2) = ADDRESS OF OUTPUT BLOCK
          MVI     0(2),C' '     CLEAR OUTPUT AREA
          MVC     1(79,2),0(2)  MOVE BLANK INTO OUTPUT AREA
          BCTR    3,0           CONTENTS OF R(3)=CONTENTS OF R(3)-1
          STC     3,*+5         STORE STRING LENGTH IN BITS 8-15 OF MVC
          MVC     0(1,2),0(8)   MOVE CHARACTERS FROM INPUT TO OUTPUT
*
*    PART  6
*
          L       13,AREA+4     RESTORE REGISTERS
          LM      14,12,12(13)  RESTORE REGISTERS
          BR      14            RETURN TO MAIN PROGRAM
*
*    PART  4(B)
*
ADCON     DC      V(LENGTH)
          END
```

Fig. 8.12 Subroutine RECORD which calls for the subroutine LENGTH.

```
LENGTH     CSECT
           USING  *,15
           LM     3,7,VALUES      SET R(3),(4),(5)=0,R(6)=1.R(7)=000000FF
           L      9,0(1)          LOAD ADDRESS OF R(1) INTO R(9)
IC         IC     5,0(3,9)        INSERT CHARACTER INTO R(5)
           AR     3,6             R(3)=R(3)+1
           CR     7,5             COMPARE R(7) WITH R(5)
           BC     2,IC            BRANCH TO IC IF R(7) IS GREATER THAN R(5)
           BCR    15,14           IF R(5)=FF RETURN TO RECORD
VALUES     DC     3F'0'
           DC     F'1'
           DC     XL4'FF'
           END
```

Fig. 8.13   Subroutine LENGTH, the lowest subroutine.

Right after the execution of its save routine, the subroutine RECORD calls the assembler language subroutine LENGTH (see Fig. 8.13), the lowest-level subroutine which examines each byte for FF. We shall first discuss several instructions which are used in the lowest-level subroutine LENGTH:

USING *,15

The instruction L 15,ADCON in subroutine RECORD (Fig. 8.12) loads register 15 with the beginning address of subroutine LENGTH. As a result, there is no need for subroutine LENGTH to load a base register (no BALR instruction is needed). Thus, only a USING *,15 instruction is needed.

LM   3,7,VALUES

The net effect is to load registers 3 through 7 with the following values:

Register number	Values loaded	Purpose of the register
3	00000000	Index
4	00000000	Always zero (used in Problem 8.13 only)
5	00000000	Temporary home for a byte
6	00000001	Increment
7	000000FF	Always FF

```
   L    9,0(1)
IC IC   5,0(3,9)
```

It is important to know that register 1 contains the pointer to the argument list. After the execution of this Insert Character instruction for the first time, a byte is taken at this address and placed in the rightmost byte position in register 5; the remaining contents of register 5 are unaltered.

AR 3,6

After the execution of this instruction for the first time, the contents of register 3 are increased from 0 to 1.

On finishing the subroutine LENGTH, the control is returned to Part 5 of the subroutine RECORD. We shall take a look at the instructions in Part 5 (see Fig. 8.12).

```
L  8,0(1)
L  2,4(1)
```

These two Load instructions load two pointers. The pointer to the input block is loaded in register 8; that to the output block, in register 2.

```
MVI  0(2),C' '
MVC  1(79,2),0(2)
```

These two instructions clear the output area.

```
BCTR  3,0
```

This instruction has same effect as S 3,=F'1'.

```
STC  3,*+5
MVC  0(1,2),0(8)
```

The STC instruction stores the rightmost eight bits of register 3 into the length field of the MVC instruction (see Fig. 8.14). After the execution of the modified MVC instruction, a proper number of characters is moved from the input block to the output one. In Fig. 8.9, for example, 25 characters are moved.

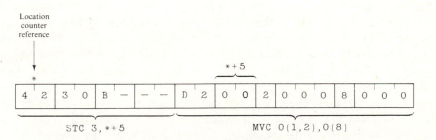

Fig. 8.14 Replacement of the length field in MVC instruction.

8.8 TWO OR MORE CONTROL SECTIONS IN ONE ASSEMBLY

In Section 5.7, the sum of ten numbers was obtained by using four different subroutines—S410B, S413B, S413C, and S415 (see Figs. 5.24 through 5.27). Each subroutine was assembled individually; in other words, each subroutine is the sole control section of an assembly. Alternatively, they can be assembled as four control sections within one module. As shown in Fig. 8.15, this is readily accomplished by (a) removing each END instruction in subroutines S410B, S413B, and S413C; (b) writing a CSECT instruction at the beginning of each control section with appropriate name in the name field; and (c) stacking together the control sections S410B, S413B, S413C, and S415. For the sake of convenience, we used also the following macro instruction

$$\text{SAVE} \quad (14,12),,*$$

four times in Fig. 8.15. Although the SAVE macro instruction will be discussed in detail in the next chapter, it is worth mentioning here that each SAVE macro instruction automatically generates four instructions; each is marked with a plus sign near its statement number.

We shall now discuss some important practical details of multisections in an assembly.

First, if literals are used in any one of the control sections, they are collected and placed in the literal pool at the end of *all* control sections. To ensure that literals are placed right after a particular control section, the programmer must write the LTORG instruction at the end of that control section. In Fig. 8.15, for example, such instruction is required at the end of control section S413B as well as at the end of S415.

Second, as a convenience to a programmer, several control sections in a module can be intermixed. As shown in Fig. 8.16, each group of instructions beginning with the instruction, say,

$$\text{S413B} \quad \text{CSECT}$$

identifies the beginning or the continuation of control section S413B. The assembler (a) recognizes the various groups of a given control section; (b) assigns them to the contiguous locations; and (c) assembles them as one control section.

The location of the *first* control section is set to zero if a CSECT instruction is used. It may also be specified by a self-defining term in the operand field of the START instruction. On the other hand, the location counter of the second section is automatically set by the assembler at the next available byte position, aligned to the doubleword boundary. Similarly, the location counter of the third control section is set at the next available byte position after the second control section.

Finally, the *first* control section need not have a name. If the name field in the CSECT or START instruction is blank, the control section is recognized as the *unnamed* control section. It can also be intermixed with other named control sections.

Internal Linkage

The control sections S410B, S413B, S413C, and S415, assembled in one module, are each called by FORTRAN main program such as shown in Fig. 5.23. Although they coexist in one module, there is really no communication among them. But this is not always the case. We shall now explore the possibility of intercommunication between two control sections *in one module* by giving a specific example.

In the previous section, the subroutines RECORD and LENGTH are assembled individually. (Note that the last statement of each section is an END. See Figs. 8.12 and 8.13). Alternatively, both control sections can be assembled as one single module. This can be readily accomplished by removing the END statement in Fig. 8.12 and stack

```
LOC    OBJECT CODE      ADDR1 ADDR2  STMT    SOURCE STATEMENT

000000                                 1 S410B    CSECT
                                       2          SAVE  (14,12),,*
000000 47F0 F00A          0000A        3+         B     10(0,15) BRANCH AROUND ID
000004 05                              4+         DC    AL1(5)
000005 E2F4F1F0C2                      5+         DC    CL5'S410B' IDENTIFIER
00000A 90EC D00C          0000C        6+         STM   14,12,12(13) SAVE REGISTERS
00000E 05C0                            7          BALR  12,0
000010                                 8          USING *,12
000010 5831 0000          00000        9          L     3,0(1)
000014 5841 0004          00004       10          L     4,4(1)
000018 41B0 0000          00000       11          LA    11,0
00001C 1893                           12          LR    9,3
00001E 4180 000A          0000A       13          LA    8,10
000022 5AB9 0000          00000       14 LOOP     A     11,0(9)
000026 4199 0004          00004       15          LA    9,4(9)
00002A 4680 C012          00022       16          BCT   8,LOOP
00002E 5084 0000          00000       17          ST    11,0(4)
                                      18          RETURN (14,12)
000032 98EC D00C          0000C       19+         LM    14,12,12(13) RESTORE THE REGISTERS
000036 07FE                           20+         BR    14 RETURN
000038                                21 S413B    CSECT
                                      22          SAVE  (14,12),,*
000038 47F0 F00A          0000A       23+         B     10(0,15) BRANCH AROUND ID
00003C 05                             24+         DC    AL1(5)
00003D E2F4F1F3C2                     25+         DC    CL5'S413B' IDENTIFIER
000042 90EC D00C          0000C       26+         STM   14,12,12(13) SAVE REGISTERS
000046 05C0                           27          BALR  12,0
000048                                28          USING *,12
000048 5831 0000          00000       29          L     3,0(1)
00004C 5841 0004          00004       30          L     4,4(1)
000050 4190 0000          00000       31          LA    9,0
000054 18A9                           32          LR    10,9
000056 5A93 A000          00000       33 LOOP1    A     9,0(3,10)
00005A 41AA 0004          00004       34          LA    10,4(10)
00005E 59A0 C028          00070       35          C     10,=F'40'
000062 4740 C00E          00056       36          BL    LOOP1
000066 5094 0000          00000       37          ST    9,0(4)
                                      38          RETURN (14,12)
00006A 98EC D00C          0000C       39+         LM    14,12,12(13) RESTORE THE REGISTERS
00006E 07FE                           40+         BR    14 RETURN
000070                                41          LTORG
000070 00000028                       42                =F'40'
000078                                43 S413C    CSECT
                                      44          SAVE  (14,12),,*
000078 47F0 F00A          0000A       45+         B     10(0,15) BRANCH AROUND ID
00007C 05                             46+         DC    AL1(5)
00007D E2F4F1F3C3                     47+         DC    CL5'S413C' IDENTIFIER
000082 90EC D00C          0000C       48+         STM   14,12,12(13) SAVE REGISTERS
000086 05C0                           49          BALR  12,0
000088                                50          USING *,12
000088 5831 0000          00000       51          L     3,0(1)
00008C 5841 0004          00004       52          L     4,4(1)
000090 4190 0000          00000       53          LA    9,0
000094 18B3                           54          LR    11,3
000096 18A9                           55          LR    10,9
000098 4180 000A          0000A       56          LA    8,10
00009C 5A9A B000          00000       57 LOOP2    A     9,0(10,11)
0000A0 41AA 0004          00004       58          LA    10,4(10)
0000A4 4680 C014          0009C       59          BCT   8,LOOP2
0000A8 5094 0000          00000       60          ST    9,0(4)
                                      61          RETURN (14,12)
0000AC 98EC D00C          0000C       62+         LM    14,12,12(13) RESTORE THE REGISTERS
0000B0 07FE                           63+         BR    14 RETURN
0000B8                                64 S415     CSECT
                                      65          SAVE  (14,12),,*
0000B8 47F0 F00A          0000A       66+         B     10(0,15) BRANCH AROUND ID
0000BC 04                             67+         DC    AL1(4)
0000BD E2F4F1F5                       68+         DC    CL4'S415' IDENTIFIER
0000C1 00
0000C2 90EC D00C          0000C       69+         STM   14,12,12(13) SAVE REGISTERS
0000C6 05C0                           70          BALR  12,0
0000C8                                71          USING *,12
0000C8 5831 0000          00000       72          L     3,0(1)
0000CC D227 C030 3000 000F8 00000     73          MVC   CZERO(40),0(3)
0000D2 5841 0004          00004       74          L     4,4(1)
0000D6 4190 0000          00000       75          LA    9,0
0000DA 41B0 C030          000F8       76          LA    11,CZERO
0000DE 5A9B 0000          00000       77 LOOP3    A     9,0(11)
0000E2 41BB 0004          00004       78          LA    11,4(11)
0000E6 59B0 C058          00120       79          C     11,=A(CZERO+40)
0000EA 4740 C016          000DE       80          BL    LOOP3
0000EE 5094 0000          00000       81          ST    9,0(4)
                                      82          RETURN (14,12)
0000F2 98EC D00C          0000C       83+         LM    14,12,12(13) RESTORE THE REGISTERS
0000F6 07FE                           84+         BR    14 RETURN
0000F8                                85 CZERO    DS    10F
000120                                86          LTORG
000120 00000120                       87                =A(CZERO+40)
                                      88          END
```

Fig. 8.15 Assembly listing showing multi-control sections in one assembly.

```
     LOC   OBJECT CODE      ADDR1 ADDR2   STMT    SOURCE STATEMENT

    000000                                    1 S410B    CSECT
                                              2          SAVE    (14,12),,*      SAVE REGISTERS
    000000 47F0 F00A             0000A         3+         B       10(0,15) BRANCH AROUND ID
    000004 C5                                  4+         DC      AL1(5)
    000005 E2F4F1F0C2                          5+         DC      CL5'S410B' IDENTIFIER
    00000A 90EC D00C             0000C         6+         STM     14,12,12(13) SAVE REGISTERS
    00000E C560                                7          BALR    6,0             BASE REGISTER
    000010                                     8          USING   *,6
    000010 5831 0000            00000          9          L       3,0(1)          LOAD 1ST ARQU. PTR. INTO R(3)
    000014 5841 0004            00004         10          L       4,4(1)          LOAD 2ND ARQU. PTR. INTO R(4)
    000038                                    11 S413B    CSECT
                                              12          SAVE    (14,12),,*      SAVE REGISTERS
    000038 47F0 F00A             0000A        13+         B       10(0,15) BRANCH AROUND ID
    00003C C5                                 14+         DC      AL1(5)
    00003D E2F4F1F3C2                         15+         DC      CL5'S413B' IDENTIFIER
    000042 90EC D00C             0000C        16+         STM     14,12,12(13) SAVE REGISTERS
    000046 0570                               17          BALR    7,0             BASE REGISTER
    000048                                    18          USING   *,7
    000048 5831 0000            00000         19          L       3,0(1)          LOAD 1ST ARQU. PTR. INTO R(3)
    00004C 5841 0004            00004         20          L       4,4(1)          LOAD 2ND ARQU. PTR. INTO R(4)
    000078                                    21 S413C    CSECT
                                              22          SAVE    (14,12),,*      SAVE REGISTERS
    000078 47F0 F00A             0000A        23+         B       10(0,15) BRANCH AROUND ID
    00007C C5                                 24+         DC      AL1(5)
    00007D E2F4F1F3C3                         25+         DC      CL5'S413C' IDENTIFIER
    000082 90EC D00C             0000C        26+         STM     14,12,12(13) SAVE REGISTERS
    000086 0550                               27          BALR    5,0             BASE REGISTER
    000088                                    28          USING   *,5
    000088 5831 0000            00000         29          L       3,0(1)          LOAD 1ST ARQU. PTR. INTO R(3)
    00008C 5841 0004            00004         30          L       4,4(1)          LOAD 2ND ARQU. PTR. INTO R(4)
    00000C                                    31 S410B    CSECT
    000018 41B0 000C            00000         32          LA      11,0            LOAD 0 INTO R(11)
    00001C 1893                               33          LR      9,3             LOAD CONTENTS R(3) INTO R(9)
    00001E 4180 000A            0000A         34          LA      8,10            LOAD 10 INTO R(8)
    000022 5A69 0000            00000         35 LOOP     A       11,0(9)         ADD R(9) AND R(11)
    000026 4199 0004            00004         36          LA      9,4(9)          UPDATE ADDRESS OF R(9)
    00002A 4680 6012            03022         37          BCT     8,LOOP          R(8)-1  AND BRANCH TO LOOP
    00002E 50B4 0000            00000         38          ST      11,0(4)         LOAD SUM INTO ADDRESS OF SUM
                                              39          RETURN  (14,12)         RETURN TO MAIN
    000032 98EC D00C             0000C        40+         LM      14,12,12(13) RESTORE THE REGISTERS
    000036 07FE                               41+         BR      14 RETURN
    000038                                    42          LTORG                   LITERAL POOL OF CONTROL SECTIONS
    000038                                    43 S413B    CSECT
    000050 4190 0000            00000         44          LA      9,0             LOAD 0 INTO R(9)
    000054 18A9                               45          LR      10,9            LOAD 0 INTO R(10)
    000056 5A93 A000            00000         46 LOOP1    A       9,0(3,10)       (CONTENTSR(10)+R(3))+CONTENTSR(9)
    00005A 41AA 0004            00004         47          LA      10,4(10)        UPDATE ADDRESS OF R(10)
    00005E 59A0 7028            03070         48          C       10,=F'40'       CHECKING NUMBER OF TIMES GONE THROUGH
    000062 4740 700E            03056         49          BC      4,LOOP1         GO BACK TO ADDING NUMBERS
    000066 5094 0000            00000         50          ST      9,0(4)          STORE SUM INTO ADDRESS OF SUM
                                              51          RETURN  (14,12)         RETURN TO MAIN
    00006A 98EC D00C             0000C        52+         LM      14,12,12(13) RESTORE THE REGISTERS
    00006E C7FE                               53+         BR      14 RETURN
    000070                                    54          LTORG                   LITERAL POOL OF CONTROL SECTION
    000070 00000028                           55          =F'40'
    000078                                    56 S413C    CSECT
    00009C 4190 0000            00000         57          LA      9,0             LOAD 0 INTO R(9)
    000094 18B3                               58          LR      11,3            LOAD R(3) INTO R(11)
    000096 18A9                               59          LR      10,9            LOAD R(9) INTO R(10)
    000098 4180 000A            0000A         60          LA      8,10            LOAD  10 INTO R(8)
    00009C 5A9A B000            03000         61 LOOP2    A       9,0(10,11)      (CONTENTS R(11)+R(10))+CONTENTS R(9)
    0000A0 41AA 0004            00004         62          LA      10,4(10)        UPDATE ADDRESS OF R(10)
    0000A4 4680 5014            0009C         63          BCT     8,LOOP2         R(8)-1  AND BRANCH TO LOOP2
    0000A8 5094 0000            00000         64          ST      9,0(4)          STORE SUM INTO ADDRESS OF SUM
                                              65          RETURN  (14,12)         RETURN TO MAIN
    0000AC 98EC D00C             0000C        66+         LM      14,12,12(13) RESTORE THE REGISTERS
    0000B0 C7FF                               67+         BR      14 RETURN
    0000B8                                    68          LTORG                   LITERAL POOL OF CONTROL SECTIONS
                                              69          END
```

Fig. 8.16 Assembly listing showing intermix of three control sections in one assembly.

224

```
RECORD    CSECT
*
*   PART 1   NOT NEEDED
*
*   PART 2
*
          B      12(15)
          DC     AL1(7)
          DC     CL7'RECORD '          IDENTIFIER
          STM    14,12,12(13)          SAVE REGISTERS
          BALR   11,0                  R11 USED AS BASE REGISTER
          USING  *,11
          LR     12,13                 SAVE POINTS
          LA     13,AREA
          ST     13,8(12)
          ST     12,4(13)
          BC     15,SUB2               BRANCH AROUND SAVE AREA
AREA      DS     18F
*
*   PART 3   NOT NEEDED
*
*   PART 4(A)
*
*      GO TO SUBROUTINE LENGTH
*
SUB2      L      15,ADCON              ADDRESS OF SUBROUTINE LENGTH
          BALR   14,15                 BRANCH TO LENGTH
*
*      THIS IS WHERE THE PROGRAM RETURNS TO AFTER COMPLETION OF
*      SUBROUTINE LENGTH
*   PART 5
*
          L      8,0(1)                R(8) = ADDRESS OF INPUT BLOCK
          L      2,4(1)                R(2) = ADDRESS OF OUTPUT BLOCK
          MVI    0(2),C' '             CLEAR OUTPUT AREA
          MVC    1(79,2),0(2)          MOVE BLANK INTO OUTPUT AREA
          BCTR   3,0                   CONTENTS OF R(3)=CONTENTS OF R(3)-1
          STC    3,*+5                 STORE STRING LENGTH IN BITS 8-15 OF MVC
          MVC    0(1,2),0(8)           MOVE CHARACTERS FROM INPUT TO OUTPUT
*
*   PART 6
*
          L      13,AREA+4             RESTORE REGISTERS
          LM     14,12,12(13)          RESTORE REGISTERS
          BR     14                    RETURN TO MAIN PROGRAM
*
*   PART 4(B)
*
ADCON     DC     A(LENGTH)
LENGTH    CSECT
          USING  *,15
          LM     3,7,VALUES            SET R(3),(4),(5)=0,R(6)=1,R(7)=000000FF
          L      9,0(1)                LOAD ADDRESS OF R(1) INTO R(9)
IC        IC     5,0(3,9)              INSERT CHARACTER INTO R(5)
          AR     3,6                   R(3)=R(3)+1
          AR     7,4                   SET R(7)=R(7)+R(4)
          CR     7,5                   COMPARE R(7) WITH R(5)
          BC     2,IC                  BRANCH TO IC IF R(7) IS GREATER THAN R(5)
          BCR    15,14                 IF R(5)=FF RETURN TO RECORD
VALUES    DC     3F'0'
          DC     F'1'
          DC     XL4'FF'
          END
```

Fig. 8.17   Internal linkage.

the remaining instructions on these shown in Fig. 8.13. The resulting module is shown in Fig. 8.17. Note that the linkage routine must be written in control section RECORD, as discussed in Sections 8.2 through 8.5. Some minor differences are listed below.

1. All ENTRY and ENTRN instructions are eliminated, since two control sections are not external to each other.

2. All V-type DC instructions are changed to A-type instructions.

The linkage between two such control sections is called *internal linkage*.

8.9 IMPLICIT METHOD OF
TRANSFERRING VARIABLES—DUMMY SECTIONS

A symbol defined in a main program or in a subroutine is only *local* to that segment. For illustration, let us consider once again the problem of finding the sum of ten numbers. The symbol CZERO defined in the CALL statement of a main program (see Fig. 5.23)

```
CALL   S410B(CZERO,SUM)
```

is not comprehensible by its subroutine S410B. To pass the values of the symbol CZERO to subroutine, we have so far used the mechanism of an argument list. As discussed in Sections 5.5 and 8.4, the pointer to this argument list is, by convention, automatically loaded in register 1 by FORTRAN main program. The instructions

```
L    3,0(1)
ST   3,CZERO
```

in subroutine S410B (Fig. 5.24) then load the first value of CZERO. At this point the symbol CZERO in subroutine S410B is made equivalent to the symbol CZERO(1) in FORTRAN main program. This method is known as an *explicit* transfer of variables between a main program and a subroutine.

The *implicit* transfer of variables, described in this section does not use the argument list written in the CALL statement in FORTRAN main program; a COMMON statement is used instead. In addition, since there is no argument list to work with, there is no need to employ its mechanism in the subroutine. Instead, a dummy section is defined by means of a DSECT instruction.

Let us first review the labeled COMMON statement in FORTRAN IV language. The following statements, for instance,

```
INTEGER   CZERO(10),SUM
COMMON    /AREA1/CZERO,SUM
```

would set up a common area called AREA1 containing eleven integers: CZERO(1), CZERO(2), ..., CZERO(10), and SUM. A complete main program is shown in Fig. 8.18, which presents a reprogramming of Fig. 5.23. This main program calls a subroutine

```
C
C                    THIS PROGRAM IS TO GENERATE THE 1ST TEN SQUARES,
C              TRANSFER THESE TEN VALUES TO SUBROUTINE S410B AND TAKE
C              THEIR SUM.  THE OUTPUT PRINTER 1ST LISTS THE 10 VALUES AND
C              THEN THE SUM FROM THE SUBROUTINE.
C
               INTEGER CZERO(10),SUM
               COMMON /AREA1/CZERO,SUM
               DO 10K=1,10
     10        CZERO(K)=K*K
               WRITE(6,30)
     30        FORMAT(//' THE GENERATED VALUES ARE ')
               WRITE(6,50)(K,CZERO(K),K=1,10)
     50        FORMAT(/10(/2X,I3,2X,I3))
               SUM=0
               CALL S410B
               WRITE(6,40)SUM
     40        FORMAT(//' THE ANSWER FROM S410B IS ',I5)
               STOP
               END
```

Fig. 8.18   Main program using a labeled COMMON statement.

S410B, which may be written either in a high-level language (such as FORTRAN) or in assembler language.

If the subroutine is written in FORTRAN, a COMMON statement must be used. We write the identical name AREA1 in the COMMON statement to put the eleven variables in the same labeled common area. Thus the following single statement can be placed in a FORTRAN subroutine

```
               COMMON/AREA1/INPUT(10),ISUM
```

as shown in Fig. 8.19.

```
               SUBROUTINE S410B
               COMMON/AREA1/INPUT(10),ISUM
               DO 20 K=1,10
     20        ISUM=ISUM+INPUT(K)
               RETURN
               END
```

Fig. 8.19   Subroutine in FORTRAN using a labeled COMMON statement.

It is also possible to establish a common area in assembler language programming by means of a dummy section (DSECT). In Fig. 8.20, for example, the name of such a section is COMAREA, which contains eleven fullwords: ten for CZERO and one for SUM. Note that the external address of the common area AREA1 (defined in FORTRAN main program) is loaded into register 5:

```
               L  5,=V(AREA1)
```

In addition, register 5 is promised to contain base address COMAREA:

```
               USING  COMAREA,5
```

```
S410B      CSECT
BEGIN      B       10(15)
           DC      AL1(5)
           DC      CL5'BEGIN' IDENTIGIER
           STM     14,12,12(13)    SAVE REGISTERS
           BALR    7,0
           USING   *,7
*
*          LOAD THE EXTERNAL ADDRESS OF THE COMMON AREA INTO R(5)
*
           L       5,=V(ARFA1)
*
*          ASSEMBLER IS TO USE R(5) AS BASE REGISTER WHEN DEALING WITH
*          VARIABLES IN THE COMMON AREA
*
           USING   COMAREA,5
           LA      11,0
           LA      9,CZERO
           LA      8,10
LOOP       A       11,0(9)
           LA      9,4(9)
           BCT     8,LOOP
           ST      11,SUM          STORE ANSWER INTO SUM
           LM      14,12,12(13)    RESTORE REGISTERS
           BR      14   RETURN
*
*          ADVISE ASSEMBLER TO DEFINE LITERALS BEFORE GOING ON
*
           LTORG
COMAREA    DSECT
CZERO      DS      10F
SUM        DS      F
           END     BEGIN
```

Fig. 8.20   Control section S410B using DSECT.

In other words, this USING instruction promises that register 5 is the base register when dealing with the variables CZERO and SUM in the dummy section.

8.10 CONTROL SECTION LONGER THAN 4096 BYTES

If a control section is more than 4096 bytes in length, more than one base register is needed. As shown in Fig. 8.21, a second USING instruction is used at the beginning of the control section, and its base address is loaded by the second LA instruction. The two USING instructions in Fig. 8.21 can be replaced by the following single statement

$$\text{USING   } *,11,12$$

where the third operand indicates that the register 12, the second base register, is *promised* to contain the value *+4096.

In general, the USING instruction may have multiple operands (as many as 17). The general format is

USING $v,r1[,r2,r3,\ldots,r16]$

In this general form, $r1$, $r2$, ... are the register numbers; v stands for an absolute or relocatable expression. The basic aim of v is to inform the assembler about the promised base address. However, it also tacitly specifies a range in which the assembler

Location counter Setting	Name	Op code	Operand
	ADVUSING	CSECT	
000000		BALR	11,0
000002		USING	*,11
000002		USING	*+X'1000',12
000002		LA	12,X'800'
000006		LA	12,X'800'(11,12)

Fig. 8.21 Two USING statements are needed for a control section containing more than 4096 bytes.

can translate a symbolic operand address into the base-displacement form. The lower limit of the range is the value v; the upper limit is automatically set at $v + 4096$. For example, in the instruction

USING *,11,12,9,10,5

registers 11, 12, 9, 10, and 5 are promised to contain the values *, *+4096, *+2*4096, *+3*4096, and *+4*4096, respectively.

The upper limit of a previous USING ($v_1 + 4095$) may be overruled by the lower limit of another USING instruction, v_2, if $v_2 < v_1 + 4095$. For illustration, consider the two sequential USING instructions:

USING 1000,10
USING 5000,11

A value of $(1000)_{10}$ is assumed to be stored in base register 10. The first USING instruction implicitly specifies a range of 3999 bytes, beginning at byte 1000 and ending at 4999. Note that the upper limit of the range is not equal to $1000 + 4095 = 5095$, as it is overruled and replaced by the specification $v_2 = 5000$ in the second USING instruction.

BIBLIOGRAPHY

IBM System/360 Operating System Assembler Language, C28-6514, IBM Corp.

PROBLEMS

1. Replace each of the following START instructions with a CSECT instruction:

START instruction			Used in	May be replaced by
SUBR1	START	0	Fig. 5.14	SUBR1 CSECT
ARITH	START	0	Fig. 5.20	_____
S410B	START	0	Fig. 5.24	_____
S410B	START		—	_____
FLOFIX	START	100	Fig. 5.32	_____
	START		—	_____
	START	0	—	_____

2. Assume that the initial contents of register 13 are 00A03B0C and the address of SAVEBLK is 09A00C. After the execution of the following instructions

```
LR   12,13
LA   13,SAVEBLK
ST   13,8(,12)
```

   a) What are the fullword contents starting at location 00A03B14?
   b) According to the standard linking conventions, what do the contents obtained from (a) represent?
   c) What do the contents 00A03B0C represent?

3. Assume that the contents of register 13 are 00014C00 and the address of SAVE is 05806C. After the execution of the following instructions

```
LR   12,13
LA   13,SAVE
ST   12,4(13)
```

   a) What are contents in register 12?
   b) What are the fullword contents starting at location 00058010?
   c) What are the fullword contents starting at SAVE+4?
   (d) According to OS/360 linkage convention, what do the contents in (c) represent?

4. Subroutine SUB1 calls another subroutine SUB2. If the entry-point address of SUB2 is 00A03C and the return address in SUB1 is 0C4E0C, and if the following instruction is written in SUB1

```
BALR   14,15
```

   then after the execution of this instruction

   a) What are the contents in register 14?
   b) What are the contents in register 15?

   Use OS/360 linkage convention.

5. In Fig. 8.3, C in the argument list (A, B, C, ANSWER) has only one element. Modify Fig. 8.3 if C is a linear list containing three elements. In other words, there is a DIMENSION statement C(3) when FORTRAN main program is used.

6. Assuming that the address TEXT is equal to 00AC1C, generate the following constants as a result of assembly:

```
            DC   A(TEXT)
            DC   AL4(TEXT)
            DC   2AL1(X'314'+1)
            DC   V(TEXT)
   ADSR1    DC   A(TEXT+24)
```

7. In control section LENGTH (Fig. 8.13), no BALR 15,0 instruction is used to load base register. Why is it not needed?

8. Part 6 of Fig. 8.2 serves to restore register contents and return. The following instructions are used:

```
        LM   14,12,12(13)
        BR   14
```

If the contents of register 13 are 00A1C020 and the fullword contents starting at location 00A1C02C are 004A16D0

a) What are the contents of register 14 after the LM instruction is executed?
b) What is the return address?

9. The following instruction segment may be used to designate two base registers:

Location counter

		START	X'1600'
001600		BALR	11,0
001602		USING	*,11
001602	ALPHA	L	12,ADBETA
001606		USING	BETA,12
001606		.	
:		:	
001800	ADBETA	DC	A(BETA)
001804	BETA	DS	CL10

They are registers 11 and 12.

a) What is the base address in register 11?
b) What is the base address in register 12?

10. Subroutine RECORD (Fig. 8.12) calls the subroutine LENGTH (Fig. 8.13). The save area AREA is reserved in RECORD for future storage of register contents used in the subroutine RECORD. This will free the registers so that subroutine LENGTH may use them. Write the register numbers used in each subroutine; and state clearly the functions of each register.

11. The subroutine names in Fig. 8.12 are to be changed from RECORD to REC and from LENGTH to LEN. Modify Fig. 8.12 to take care of the changes.

12. In a computing center newsletter from an eastern university, an item reads: "Previously, the CMS loader would not correctly load multiple control sections that occur within the same text deck. Example:

```
LDRBUG      START
            USING   *,15
            L       1,=V(ALPHA)
ALPHA       CSECT
            DC      F'1'
            BR      14
            END
```

The standard CMS loader (LDR) has been modified to remove this restriction."

a) How many control sections are there in this module (text deck)?
b) The literal used in the L instruction is =V(ALPHA). Can this be replaced by =A(ALPHA)?

13. The Branch on Index High (BXH) instruction is a very powerful one used in indexed looping. Its general form is

$$\text{BXH} \quad \mathscr{R}, R, D(B)$$

where $\mathscr{R}$ is a register number containing the starting value, which will be incremented and tested; the second operand $D(B)$ is the branch-to address in the form of displacement and base register; and the third operand R represents an even–odd pair of registers, if R is an even number. The contents of register R depend on whether R is an even or odd number.

Case 1. R is an even number. Its contents are the increment to be added to Register $\mathscr{R}$; the contents in register $R + 1$ are the terminating value used to stop the looping.

Case 2. R is an odd number. Its contents are used as both the increment and the terminating value for the looping.

The initial contents in the three registers $\mathscr{R}$, R, $R + 1$ are summarized in Table 8.2.

Table 8.2. Initial contents in three registers for instruction BXH $\mathscr{R}, R, D(B)$

Register	Even or odd	Contents	Comments
$\mathscr{R}$	Either	Starting value	First operand
R	Even	Increment	This is the third operand, not the second operand
	Odd	Increment and terminating value	
$R + 1$	Odd	Terminating value	R is an even number

The mechanics of execution of a single BXH instruction is rather complex. The details of execution of the instruction

$$\text{BXH} \quad \mathscr{R}, R, D(B)$$

can best be shown in a flowchart form as in Fig. 8.22. First, the contents in register $\mathscr{R}$ are replaced by its original contents plus the contents in register R. Second, examine if R is an even number. If it is, a comparison is then made: $C(\mathscr{R}) > C(R + 1)$. If true, it branches to the address $D(B)$. If $C(\mathscr{R}) \leq C(R + 1)$, it gets out of the loop and takes the next instruction.

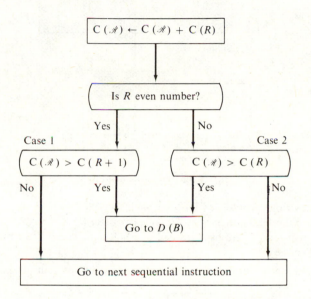

Fig. 8.22 Mechanics of the execution of instruction BXH $\mathscr{R}, R, D(B)$.

In the event that R is an odd number, a comparision is made: $C(\mathscr{R}) > C(R)$. If true, it branches to $D(B)$; if not, goes to the next instruction.

Replace the CR and BC instructions on subroutine LENGTH (Fig. 8.13) with the BXH instruction. Make any other changes necessary to make subroutine LENGTH bug-free.

14. Replace the BCT instruction in Fig. 1.17 with the BXH instruction and make other necessary changes.

15. The Branch on Index Low or Equal (BXLE) instruction is similar to the BXH instruction in that two register operands and a main storage operand are used. This instruction has the following format

BXLE $\mathscr{R}, R, D(B)$

The mechanics of the execution of a BXLE instruction is shown in Fig. 8.22, but each of the two "greater than" signs (>) must be replaced with a "less than or equal to" sign ($\leq$). Suppose that the initial register contents are shown in Problem 3.9 (page 76).
(a) Find the contents of register 10 after the execution of the instruction BXLE 10,4,0(7).
(b) Is there a branch? to where?

16. The flowchart shown in Fig. 8.23 illustrates how to count by two.

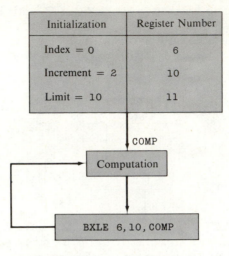

Fig. 8.23   Counting by two.

a) How may times would this loop go back to COMP?
b) What are the final contents in the index register 6?
c) If BXH instruction were used instead of BXLE one, what would the answers to parts (a) and (b) be?

17. The flowchart shown in Fig. 8.24 can be used to count by four.

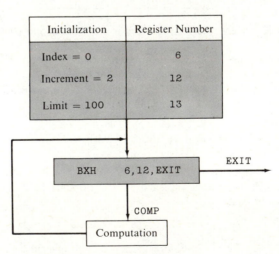

Fig. 8.24   Counting by four.

a) How many times would the loop go through COMP?
b) What would the value in the index register 6 be when the branch to EXIT is taken?
c) If the limit were 99 instead of 100, what would the answers to the above be?

18. What do the following instructions do?

```
INITIA    SR  9,9      INDEX
          LA 11,1      INCREMENT AND LIMIT
          ⋮
          BC 10,COUNT
          ⋮
COUNT     BXLE 9,11,*+4
```

LABORATORY ASSIGNMENT

1. Write a main program in a high-level language to print the sum:

$$\sum_{i=1}^{20} \sum_{j=1}^{40} (i + j).$$

The main program calls a subroutine LOOP to keep track of the loop within a loop. The subroutine LOOP calls subroutine ADD whose sole function is to calculate the simple sum of $i + j$.

2. Figure 8.25 presents a FORTRAN main program and two subroutines. One subroutine is in FORTRAN; the other, in assembler language. The purpose of SUB1 is to pass the addresses of the functions SIN, COS, TAN, and others into the array IARRAY. Debug and run the program shown in Fig. 8.25 and interpret the results in detail.

```
          DIMENSION IARRAY(10)
          CALL SUB1(IARRAY)
          WRITE(6,55) IARRAY
      55  FORMAT(' ',10Z8)
          CALL EXIT
          END
          SUBROUTINE SUB2(IARRAY)
          DIMENSION IARRAY(10)
          RETURN
          END
SUB1      CSECT
          EXTRN SIN
          EXTRN COS
          EXTRN TAN
          EXTRN SUB2
          SAVE  (14,12),,*
          BALR  11,0
          USING *,11
          L     7,0(1)
          L     7,0(7)
          MVC   0(LAST-FIRST,7),FIRST
          BR    14
FIRST     DC    V(SIN)
          DC    V(COS)
          DC    VL3(TAN)
          DC    VL4(SUB2)
          DC    A(SIN)
          DC    AL3(COS)
          DC    AL3(SIN+COS-TAN)
          DC    Y(SUB1+4)
          DC    Y(SIN)
LAST      EQU   *
          END
```

Fig. 8.25 Program to pass the addresses of several functions.

CHAPTER 9

Macro Programming and Conditional Assembly

9.1 MACRO

In the previous chapters, we have seen that *one* symbolic language instruction is translated into *one* machine language instruction. However, there is an exception to this rule: When a macro† instruction is used, it is translated into a set of sequential instructions—machine instructions, assembly instructions, or a combination of these two.

Consider, for example, the macro instruction

RETURN (14,12)

which is automatically translated by the assembler into two assembler language instructions (Fig. 9.1). The two substituted instructions are marked by the plus sign (+) in the left margin of the listing; this operation is known as *text substitution*. This RETURN macro instruction (or simply macro), which was previously defined, is included in a system macro library and used much the same way as FORTRAN Scientific Subroutine Package (SSP). In IBM OS/360, these "system" macros are formally called Data Management and Supervisor Services Macros.

As another example of system macros, consider the following popular SAVE macro instructions:

BEGIN1   SAVE   (14,12)
BEGIN2   SAVE   (4,8),T
BEGIN   SAVE   (14,12),,*

During assembly time, each generates an instruction sequence in assembler language as listed in Figs. 9.2 through 9.4.

---

† Macro is of Greek origin, meaning enlarged or excessively developed.

```
                RETURN (14,12)
    +           LM      14,12,12(13) RESTORE THE REGISTERS
    +           BR      14 RETURN
```

Fig. 9.1   Assembly listing for RETURN macro.

Before we explain the SAVE macros, we shall have the basic understanding of the standard linkage convention, as shown in Table 8.1 on page 209. Essentially, the contents of registers used in a calling program must be saved first before these registers can be used by a called subroutine. In this linkage convention, the contents of registers 14, 15, 0, 1, 2, ..., 11, and 12 are stored in word 4 through word 18 of a save area; and the pointer to this save area is in register 13. Let us now discuss the details of the three SAVE macros.

```
    BEGIN1      SAVE    (14,12)
    +BEGIN1     DS      0H
    +           STM     14,12,12(13)  SAVE REGISTERS
```

Fig. 9.2   Assembly listing for a SAVE macro.

The first macro has its own name BEGIN1 (see Fig. 9.2). The parameter (14,12) signifies that the registers to be saved are 14, 15, 0, 1, ..., 11, and 12; the only one not to be saved is register 13.

The second macro has its own name BEGIN2 (see Fig. 9.3). The second parameter T demands that the contents in registers 14 and 15 must be saved. In addition, the contents of registers 4, 5, 6, 7, and 8 are also saved as required by the first parameter (4,8).

```
    BEGIN2      SAVE    (4,8),T
    +BEGIN2     DS      0H
    +           STM     14,15,12(13)  SAVE REGISTERS
    +           STM     4,8,36(13)    SAVE REGISTERS
```

Fig. 9.3   Listing for a second SAVE macro.

The third macro (Fig. 9.4) has its own name BEGIN. Note that the second parameter T is omitted in this macro because the contents of registers 14 and 15 are already saved by the first parameter (14,12). The third parameter is an asterisk (*), which requires that a *count byte* is formed. It contains the number of characters in the identifier name BEGIN. In the second generated instruction in Fig. 9.4, this number is shown as 5. The third generated instruction forms the character string BEGIN.

These examples of SAVE macros demonstrate clearly that, depending on whether certain parameters are specified or not, the generated instruction sequences are different; this is known as *text parameterization*.

The SAVE and RETURN are two typical system macros; any user can use them in his program since their original definitions are stored in a macro library. Alternatively,

```
      BEGIN     SAVE    (14,12),,*
     .+BEGIN    B       10(0,15) BRANCH AROUND ID
     .+         DC      AL1(5)
     .+         DC      CL5'BEGIN' IDENTIFIER
     .+         STM     14,12,12(13) SAVE REGISTERS
```

Fig. 9.4   Listing for a third SAVE macro.

you can define your own macro(s). This aspect of macroprogramming is covered in the next three sections.

Another very important aspect of macroprogramming is conditional assembly. By using IF–THEN type statements, only selected instructions are actually *assembled*. These statements belong to a class of special languages—the so-called conditional assembly language, which is radically different from the assembler language we have studied so far. It has its own arithmetic statements, one-dimensional arrays and subscripted variables, branch and looping statements, and parameter-passing techniques. We shall explore these elements in Sections 9.5 through 9.11.

9.2 USER'S OWN MACRO DEFINITIONS

In the previous section, two important macro instructions were introduced. Basically, each macro instruction generates many assembler language instructions. In this and next two sections, we shall study several basic elements in a *macro definition*. Once a macro definition is made, it may be called any number of times in a source program in assembler language. To call a macro definition, a user writes macro instructions (macro calls) intermixed with one-for-one assembler language instructions in his or her program.

There are four parts to a macro definition: the header statement, the prototype statement, the main body of the macro, and the trailer statement. A typical example is given in Fig. 9.5.

The header statement indicates that the instructions following it constitute a macro definition. This single statement has the word MACRO usually punched in

```
              MACRO                               —Header statement
&LABEL        ENTER   &AREA,&REG                  —Prototype statement
.*
.*            &AREA   ADDRESS OF THE SAVEAREA.  ⎫
.*                    18 WORDS LONG, STARTING   ⎬
.*                    ON A FULLWORD BOUNDARY.   ⎬ —Comments
.*            &REG    BASE REGISTER             ⎭
&LABEL        SAVE    (14,12),,*                ⎫
              BALR    &REG,0                    ⎬
              USING   *,&REG                    ⎬ —Main body
              ST      13,&AREA.+4               ⎬
              LA      13,&AREA                  ⎭
              MEND                                —Trailer statement
```

Fig. 9.5   Macro definition for macro ENTER.

columns 10–14. The trailer statement is the last card in the macro definition. Like the header statement, it has only one word MEND, which is usually punched in columns 10–13.

The prototype statement will be discussed in more detail in the next two sections. However, it is worth mentioning here that it serves dual purposes: (1) It assigns the name to the macro definition now in consideration; and (2) specifies the arguments. For example, consider the prototype statement shown in Fig. 9.5. The name of the macro is ENTER and two arguments &AREA and &REG are specified. Each argument must have an ampersand (&) as its leftmost character; the number of arguments may be from zero to 200. The label &LABEL may be omitted if no looping back to this macro from other parts of the program is involved. If a label is used in the prototype statement, the first letter must be an ampersand.

Two types of comment cards can be placed in a macro definition (after the header statement). The first type requires punching .* in columns 1 and 2, respectively, as shown in Fig. 9.5. The comment cards thus punched will not be generated in the program. Alternatively, comments can be placed on the same card behind an instruction in the main body, leaving at least one blank space between the comment and the instruction.

The main body contains a sequence of *model instructions* which will be copied, with or without modifications during the macro expansion—a macro is expanded into the full sequence of assembler language instructions.

Once a macro definition is completed, you can call it in your source program. For example, you can place the following macro instruction—or the so-called macro call—in your program:

```
FIRST   ENTER   SAVEAREA,REGIS
```

Many instructions will then be generated from this ENTER macro (see the bottom block in Fig. 9.6), which are the result of the *macro expansion*. Writing this macro call is simple: Macro name (ENTER) is written in the op-code field followed by argument names. These names must be in correct order and are separated by commas. A blank indicates that the argument list is terminated. For this reason, no blanks are allowed before or after a comma.

In connection with Fig. 9.6, let us make the following observations: First, the SAVE macro is written inside the main body of ENTER macro; these two macro instructions are called an *inner macro call* and an *outer macro call*, respectively. During macro expansion, the text substitution or text modification of the outer macro call is interrupted until that of an inner macro call has been completed.

Second, the number of macro definitions associated with the user's program is not restricted. They must be placed physically at the beginning of the program† in which macro call(s) is (are) issued. The first card has to be a header card, not a comment card.

---

† In the Disk Operating System (DOS), a macro must be stored in the macro library before it can be called.

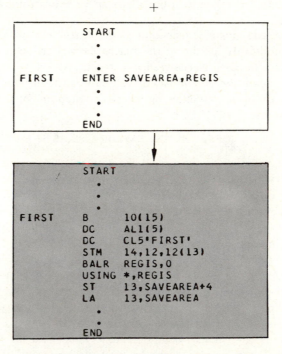

```
          MACRO
&LABEL    ENTER  &AREA,&REG
          SAVE   (14,12),,*
          BALR   &REG,0
          USING  *,&REG
          ST     13,&AREA.+4
          LA     13,&AREA
          MEND
```

+

```
          MACRO
          SAVE
.*   THIS IS DEFINED AND CATELOGUED
.*     IN THE MACRO LIBRARY.
          •
          •
          •
          MEND
```

+

```
          START
          •
          •
          •
FIRST     ENTER SAVEAREA,REGIS
          •
          •
          •
          END
```

```
          START
          •
          •
FIRST     B      10(15)
          DC     AL1(5)
          DC     CL5'FIRST'
          STM    14,12,12(13)
          BALR   REGIS,0
          USING  *,REGIS
          ST     13,SAVEAREA+4
          LA     13,SAVEAREA
          •
          •
          END
```

Fig. 9.6 Instructions (shown in the bottom block) generated from the macro definition ENTER.

240

9.3 PROTOTYPE STATEMENTS—POSITIONAL TYPE

In the previous section, we learned that the macro definition is divided into four parts—the header, the prototype, the main body, and the trailer. The header and the trailer are the first and last statements, respectively, in a macro definition. The main body of a macro definition contains a set of model instructions which will be copied (with possible variations) to form the macro expansion. Finally, the prototype statement is simply a model for a macro call. We shall now explore some details of this statement.

The prototype statement has two basic types: positional and keyword. The positional type, in turn, can be either with fixed or with variable expansion. The most widely used one is probably the positional type with fixed expansion, which has the following general format:

$$\&label \qquad name \qquad \&arg1,\&arg2,\&arg3,\ldots$$

An ordinary symbol headed by an ampersand (&) is called a *symbolic parameter*. Each symbolic parameter is (a) a constant throughout a macro defintion; and (b) is to be substituted by the argument in the corresponding position specified in a macro call. Thus in Fig. 9.6, the following substitutions are made:

Symbolic parameter in macro definition ENTER		Symbol in macro expansion
&LABEL	becomes	FIRST
&AREA	becomes	SAVEAREA
&REG	becomes	REGIS
&AREA.+4	becomes	SAVEAREA+4

The period (.) in &AREA.+4 indicates the end of the name of a symbolic parameter. It is also called the *vanishing delimiter*, since it disappears in the expansion. For example, the expression SAVEAREA+4 in the macro expansion (see the bottom block in Fig. 9.6) does not contain a period.

The period placed after a symbolic parameter is basically a *concatenation operator*; its fundamental function is to link together a character string and a symbolic parameter. The general rule is: A period must be placed right after the symbolic parameter, if you wish to concatenate a symbol parameter with (a) an alphanumeric character (i.e., a letter or a digit), (b) a left parenthesis, or (c) another period. On the other hand, this period *may* be omitted if the symbolic parameter is concatenated with (a) another symbolic parameter, or (b) a special character other than a left parenthesis or another period. Let us amplify this rule with the following cases.

Case 1. Symbolic parameter is placed before a character string.

In the main body of a macro definition, a period must appear after the symbolic parameter if the character string begins with one of the following characters:

                                                          Example

1. An alphanumeric character (a letter or a digit)   &AREA.K4

    2. A left parenthesis   &FROM.(256)
    3. A period   &TO..A

A word of caution: If the above rule is violated, a blank field is generated.

Example 1 (incorrect)

    Statement in the definition: ST   13,&AREAK4
    Generated statement: ST   13,

The statement in the definition is incorrect because there is no period between the symbolic parameter &AREA and the character string K4. (We assume here that &AREAK4 is *not* a defined symbolic parameter.)

    If this character string begins with a special character (such as +, but excluding the left parenthesis and the period), it is then *optional* to place a period between the symbolic parameter and the character string.

Example 2 (correct)

    Statement in the definition: ST   13,&AREA.+4
    Generated statement: ST   13,SAVEAREA+4

Case 2. A symbolic parameter is placed behind a character string.

When a symbolic parameter is placed immediately behind a character string (the rightmost character in the string is not a comma), the character string is expanded to include the corresponding argument in the generated statement. Figure 9.7 shows an example. The SECT&ID in statement 3 of macro definition SECTION is assembled as SECTA in statement 10 (in the first expansion), and as SECTB in statement 16 (in the second expansion).

```
  LCC   OBJECT CODE    ADDR1 ADDR2   STMT    SOURCE STATEMENT

                                      1                MACRO
                                      2                SECTION &ID,&BASENO
                                      3 SECT&ID        CSECT
                                      4 .*  CONCATENATE---LINK TOGETHER
                                      5 &ID.BASE  EQU     &BASENO
                                      6                BALR   &ID.BASE,0
                                      7                USING *,&ID.BASE
                                      8                MEND
                                      9                SECTION A,11
 000000                              10+SECTA        CSECT
 00000B                              11+ABASE        EQU    11
 000000 05B0                         12+             BALR   ABASE,0
 000002                              13+             USING *,ABASE
                                     14 *
                                     15                SECTION B,12
 000008                              16+SECTB        CSECT
 00000C                              17+BBASE        EQU    12
 000008 05C0                         18+             BALR   BBASE,0
 00000A                              19+             USING *,BBASE
                                     20                END
```

                    Fig. 9.7 Macro SECTION.

Case 3. One symbolic parameter is followed by another.

When two symbolic parameters are placed together, such as &NAME1&NAME2, they are generated as a single symbol without embedded blanks. This is shown in statements 2, 3, 9, and 10 in Fig. 9.8. The period between the two symbolic parameters is optional.

```
 LOC   OBJECT CODE    ADDR1 ADDR2   STMT    SOURCE STATEMENT

                                      1                MACRO
                                      2                CONTROL  &BASE,&NAME1,&NAME2
                                      3    &NAME1&NAME2 CSECT
                                      4    .*   CONCATENATE---LINK TOGETHER
                                      5    &NAME1.REG        EQU     &BASE
                                      6                      BALR    &NAME1.REG,0
                                      7                      USING   *,&NAME1.REG
                                      8                      MEND
                                      9                CONTROL    11,SECT,B
000000                               10+SECTB    CSECT
00000B                               11+SECTREG  EQU    11
000C00  05B0                         12+         BALR   SECTREG,0
000002                               13+         USING  *,SECTREG
                                     14                CONTROL    9,,D
000008                               15+D    CSECT
000009                               16+REG  EQU   9
000008  0590                         17+     BALR  REG,0
000C0A                               18+     USING *,REG
                                     19                END
```

Fig. 9.8   Macro CONTROL.

We see now that the mechanics of substituting the arguments (of a macro call) into a positional phototype statement (of a macro definition) resembles that of substituting function values in a function definition. However, a beginner must be aware of the following special situations:

First, blanks or commas may be contained in an argument specified in a macro call. However, they must be placed between quotes.

Second, an argument may be omitted in a macro call. Consider, for example, the second macro call in Fig. 9.8 (the statement 14). Its second argument is omitted— an indication that it has an empty string. This affects each of the generated statements (statements 15 through 18).

In a practical application, an empty string (an omitted argument) in a macro call often modifies an op-code of a model statement in the macro definition. In Fig. 9.9, the macro call in statement 10 has its third argument omitted. As a result, L&TAIL is substituted by an L instruction and an empty string, as shown in statement 11. Similarly, the last argument is omitted in macro call SELECT (statement 15). The branch instruction B&LOCK is generated as B instruction in statement 18.

We shall conclude this section by presenting a complete example to further demonstrate the usage of the prototype statements of positional type. In this example, it is desirable to find the square of a given quantity N. The input/output is handled by a main program written in a high-level language. Its FORTRAN, PL/I, and COBOL

```
LOC   OBJECT CODE    ADDR1 ADDR2  STMT   SOURCE STATEMENT
                                    1            MACRO
                                    2  &NAME     SELECT  &REG,&DISP,&LTAIL,&FIELD,&POINT,&LOCK
                                    3            L&LTAIL  &REG,&DISP.(&REG)
                                    4            A        &REG,&FIELD
                                    5            B&LOCK   &POINT
                                    6            MEND
000000                              7  BEGIN     CSECT
000000 18AF                         8            LR       10,15
000000                              9            USING BEGIN,10
                                   10            SELECT  1,0,,B,HERE,P
000002 5811 0000            00000  11+           L        1,0(1)
000006 5A10 A01C            0001C  12+           A        1,B
00000A 4720 A020            00020  13+           BP       HERE
                                   14 *
                                   15            SELECT  5,AREA+4,A,C,THERE
00000E 4155 A02C            0002C  16+           LA       5,AREA+4(5)
000012 5A50 A02C            0002C  17+           A        5,C
000016 47F0 A024            00024  18+           B        THERE
00001C                             19 B          DS       F
000020                             20 HERE       DS       F
000024                             21 THERE      DS       F
000028                             22 AREA       DS       F
00002C                             23 C          DS       F
                                   24            END
```

Fig. 9.9   Omitted arguments.

```
      READ(5,5) N
    5 FORMAT(I3)
      CALL SQBAL(N,N2)
      WRITE(6,10) N,N2
   10 FORMAT(1H1,'VARIABLE IS ',I3,5X,'VARIABLE SQUARED IS ',I9)
      CALL EXIT
      END
```

Fig. 9.10   Main program to call subroutine SQBAL.

```
SQTEST:   PROC OPTIONS (MAIN);
DCL (N,N2) BIN FIXED(31,0);
DCL SQBAL ENTRY(BIN FIXED(31,0), BIN FIXED (31,0));
DCL IHEDUMP ENTRY(BIN FIXED(31,0)); ON ERROR CALL IHEDUMP(27);
GET LIST (N);
CALL SQBAL(N,N2);
PUT PAGE LIST('VARIABLE IS ',N,' VARIABLE SQUARED IS ',N2);
END;
```

Fig. 9.11   PL/I main program to call subroutine SQBAL.

versions are respectively shown in Figs. 9.10, 9.11, and 9.12. Each main program calls the subroutine SQBAL (Fig. 9.13) which uses two macro instructions ENTER and SQR. The macro definition ENTER, which we discussed in Section 9.2, is shown in Fig. 9.5; the macro definition SQR comprises three simple instructions to perform the square operation. Figure 9.13 illustrates that these two macro definitions are placed in front of the user's program.

Also, all source statements with the + sign near the statement number (Fig. 9.13) are the generated statements. The printer output is shown below.

```
      VARIABLE IS   3     VARIABLE SQUARED IS        9
```

```
IDENTIFICATION DIVISION.
PROGRAM-ID.
    'MAINSQ'. PROGRAM NAME.
AUTHOR.
    S. S. KUO.
REMARKS.
    THIS IS A MAIN PROGRAM TO CALL SQBAL.
ENVIRONMENT DIVISION.
CONFIGURATION SECTION.
SOURCE-COMPUTER.
    IBM-360 G50.
OBJECT-COMPUTER.
    IBM-360 G50.
INPUT-OUTPUT SECTION.
FILE-CONTROL.
    SELECT CARD-FILE ASSIGN TO 'CARDIN' UNIT-RECORD.
    SELECT PRINT-FILE ASSIGN TO 'PRINTER' UTILITY.
DATA DIVISION.
FILE SECTION.
FD  CARD-FILE
    RECORDING MODE IS F
    LABEL RECORDS ARE OMITTED
    DATA RECORDS ARE CARD-REC.
01  CARD-REC                     PICTURE X(80).
FD  PRINT-FILE
    RECORDING MODE IS F
    LABEL RECORDS ARE OMITTED
    DATA RECORDS ARE PRT-LINE.
01  PRT-LINE                     PICTURE X(133).
WORKING-STORAGE SECTION.
77  N-X      PICTURE S9(6) COMPUTATIONAL.
77  N2-X     PICTURE S9(6) COMPUTATIONAL.
01  CARD-REC-1.
    02  N                        PICTURE 9999.
    02  FILLER                   PICTURE X(76).
01  PRT-LINE-1.
    02  TITLE-1                  PICTURE X(13) VALUE
                                 ' VARIABLE IS '.
    02  N-AGAIN                  PICTURE ZZZ9.
    02  FILLER                   PICTURE X(4) VALUE SPACES.
    02  TITLE-2                  PICTURE X(23) VALUE
                                 'VARIABLE SQUARED IS '.
    02  N2                       PICTURE ZZZ9.
    02  FILLER                   PICTURE X(29) VALUE SPACES.
PROCEDURE DIVISION.
OPEN-FILES.
    OPEN INPUT CARD-FILE OUTPUT PRINT-FILE.
    READ CARD-FILE INTO CARD-REC-1, AT END GO TO PRINTING.
    MOVE N TO N-AGAIN.
    MOVE N TO N-X.
    ENTER LINKAGE.
    CALL 'SQBAL' USING N-X N2-X.
    ENTER COBOL.
PRINTING.
    MOVE N2-X TO N2.
    WRITE PRT-LINE FROM PRT-LINE-1 AFTER ADVANCING 0 LINES.
CLOSING.
    CLOSE CARD-FILE PRINT-FILE.
    STOP RUN.
```

Fig. 9.12 COBOL main program to call subroutine SQBAL.

245

```
 LOC   OBJECT CODE    ADDR1 ADDR2   STMT    SOURCE STATEMENT

                                      1            MACRO
                                      2 &HERE      SQR     &ARG1,&ARG2
                                      3 .*    THIS MACRO INSTRUCTION WILL SQUARE
                                      4 .*    ANY NUMBER SPECIFIED BY &ARG1 AND
                                      5 .*    PLACE THE RESULT IN &ARG2.
                                      6 &HERE      L       3,&ARG1
                                      7            MR      2,3
                                      8            ST      3,&ARG2
                                      9            MEND
                                     10            MACRO
                                     11            ENTER   &AREA,&REG
                                     12 .*
                                     13 .*         &AREA ADDRESS OF THE SAVEAREA.
                                     14 .*               18 WORDS LONG, STARTING
                                     15 .*               ON A FULLWORD BOUNDARY.
                                     16 .*         &REG  BASE REGISTER
                                     17            SAVE    (14,12),,*
                                     18            BALR    &REG,0
                                     19            USING   *,&REG
                                     20            ST      13,&AREA.+4
                                     21            LA      13,&AREA
                                     22            MEND
000000                               23 SQBAL      CSECT
                                     24            ENTER   SAVEAREA,11
000000 47F0 F00A        0000A        25+           B       10(0,15) BRANCH AROUND ID
000004 05                            26+           DC      AL1(5)
000005 E2D8C2C1D3                    27+           DC      CL5'SQBAL' IDENTIFIER
00000A 90EC D00C        0000C        28+           STM     14,12,12(13) SAVE REGISTERS
00000E 05B0                          29+           BALR    11,0
000010                               30+           USING   *,11
000010 50D0 B038        00048        31+           ST      13,SAVEAREA+4
000014 41D0 B034        00044        32+           LA      13,SAVEAREA
000018 5861 0000        00000        33            L       6,0(1)
00001C 5876 0000        00000        34            L       7,0(6)
000020 5070 B07C        0008C        35            ST      7,NUM1
                                     36            SQR     NUM1,NUM2
000024 5830 B07C        0008C        37+           L       3,NUM1
000028 1C23                          38+           MR      2,3
00002A 5030 B080        00090        39+           ST      3,NUM2
00002E 5870 B080        00090        40            L       7,NUM2
000032 5821 0004        00004        41            L       2,4(1)
000036 5072 0000        00000        42            ST      7,0(2)
00003A 58D0 B038        00048        43            L       13,SAVEAREA+4
                                     44            RETURN  (14,12)
00003E 98EC D00C        0000C        45+           LM      14,12,12(13)
000042 07FE                          46+           BR      14 RETURN
000044                               47 SAVEAREA   DS      18F
00008C                               48 NUM1       DS      F
000090                               49 NUM2       DS      F
                                     50            END
```

Fig. 9.13   Subroutine SQRAL using two macros SQR and ENTER.

9.4 PROTOTYPE STATEMENTS—KEYWORD TYPE

In the previous section, we learned that the arguments specified in a macro call must be in the same order as those defined in a positional prototype statement. The mechanics involved resemble very closely that of subroutine call written in FORTRAN and other high-level languages. Alternatively, the so-called *keyword prototype statement* is often used.

Consider, for example, a typical keyword prototype statement in the macro

```
              MACRO
&HERE         EQUAT &A=N1,&B=N2,&C=N3,&D=,&E=
.* THIS MACRO-INSTRUCTION WILL TAKE ANY INTEGER SPECIFIED BY A
.* AND MULTIPLY IT BY B, SUBTRACT C FROM THE PRODUCT AND THEN
.* ADD D TO THAT DIFFERENCE. THE ANSWER WILL BE GIVEN BY E.
.* THE STANDARD VALUES OF A,B, AND C ARE 2,6, AND 5 RESPECTIVELY.
.* IF OTHER VALUES ARE DESIRED, THEY MAY BE SPEICIFIED BY THE
.* ARGUMENTS IN THE CORRESPONDING MACRO-INSTRUCTION.
.* THE VALUES FOR D AND E MUST BE GIVEN IN THE MACRO-INSTRUCTION.
* MACRO-GENERATED INSTRUCTIONS BEGIN HERE
&HERE         SR       2,2             ZERO OUT GR2
              L        3,&A            GR3 = A
              L        4,&B            GR4 = B
              MR       2,4             GR3 = A*B
              L        4,&C            GR4 = C
              SR       3,4             GR3 = (A*B)-C
              L        4,&D            GR4 = D
              AR       3,4             GR3 = D+((A*B)-C)
              ST       3,&E            E = GR3
              LA       10,N3           GR10 = ADDRESS OF N3
              BC       15,4(10)        BRANCH AROUND CONSTANT DEFINITIONS
N1            DC       F'2'
N2            DC       F'6'
N3            DC       F'5'
* MACRO-GENERATED INSTRUCTIONS END HERE
              MEND
```

(a) Original macro EQUAT.

```
+* MACRO-GENERATED INSTRUCTIONS BEGIN HERE
+             SR       2,2 ZERO OUT GR2
+             L        3,N1 GR3 = A
+             L        4,N2 GR4 = B
+             MR       2,4 GR3 = A*B
+             L        4,NC GR4 = C
+             SR       3,4 GR3 = (A*B)-C
+             L        4,NUMD GR4 = D
+             AR       3,4 GR3 = D+((A*B)-C)
+             ST       3,LEAV E = GR3
+             LA       10,N3 GR10 = ADDRESS OF N3
+             BC       15,4(10) BRANCH AROUND CONSTANT DEFINITIONS
+N1           DC       F'2'
+N2           DC       F'6'
+N3           DC       F'5'
+* MACRO-GENERATED INSTRUCTIONS END HERE
```

(b) Generated instructions from the macro call

EQUAT   D=NUMD,E=LEAV,C=NC.

Fig. 9.14   Keyword macro.

definition EQUAT (the second statement in Fig. 9.14a)

&HERE   EQUAT   &A=N1,&B=N2,&C=N3,&D=,&E=

where each symbolic parameter is followed by an equal sign (=). An outstanding advantage of using a keyword prototype statement is that the arguments used in a macro call may be written in any order. And secondly, the *standard* value or default value of each argument may be declared in the original macro definition. An argument can be omitted from a macro call if its standard value is to be used. In addition, a programmer can override a standard value by simply writing a new value in a macro call.

Let us look at the macro definition EQUAT (Fig. 9.14a) and its macro expansion (Fig. 9.14b), This macro definition evaluates the following expression:

$$E = D + (A \cdot B - C)$$

where A, B, C, and D are integers, and the *standard values* of A, B, and C are, respectively, N1=2, N2=6, and N3=5. In the keyword prototype statement, the values of the first three symbolic parameters &A=N1, &B=N2, and &C=N3 are explicitly declared. The last two variable symbols &D= and &E= are each terminated only with an equal sign. As a result, their values must be supplied later in a macro call.

The generated statements due to the macro call

EQUAT   D=NUMD,E=LEAV,C=NC

are shown in Fig. 9.14(b). Here we shall make several important observations. First, the arguments A and B are ignored in the macro call, and as a result, the original values N1 and N2, specified in the keyword prototype statement, are used. Second, the order of the arguments specified in a macro call is immaterial. Finally, a user may override the values A, B, or C which were originally specified in the keyword statement. For example, the value for C is now NC, replacing the original value N3 which was specified in the macro EQUAT in Fig. 9.14(a).

```
* YOU MUST PUT MACRO EQUAT(SHOWN IN FIG.9.14A) HERE.
KEYMC     CSECT
          SAVE   (14,12),,*
          BALR   11,0
          USING  *,11
          L      5,0(1)
          L      6,0(5)
          ST     6,NUMD
          L      7,16(1)
          L      8,0(7)
          ST     8,NC
          EQUAT  D=NUMD,E=LEAV,C=NC
          L      7,LEAV
          L      8,4(1)
          ST     7,0(8)
          L      7,N1
          L      8,8(1)
          ST     7,0(8)
          L      7,N2
          L      8,12(1)
          ST     7,0(8)
          RETURN (14,12)
NC        DS     F
NUMD      DS     F
LEAV      DS     F
          END
```

Fig. 9.15 Subroutine KEYMC using key macro EQUAT.

```
  READ(5,1) NUMD,NC
1 FORMAT(2I3)
  CALL KEYMC(NUMD,NANS,NA,NB,NC)
  WRITE(6,5)
5 FORMAT(//////5X,'EQUATION IS ANS=D+( A*B-C)'/)
  WRITE(6,7) NA,NB,NC,NUMD,NANS
7 FORMAT(5X,'VALUES ARE'/5X,'A=',I3/5X,'B=',I3/5X,'C=',I3/5X,'D=',I3
 1//5X,'ANS=',I5)
  CALL EXIT
  END
```

Fig. 9.16 FORTRAN main program to call subroutine KEYMC.

```
KEYTST: PROC OPTIONS (MAIN);
DCL (A,B,D,C,ANS) FIXED BINARY(31);
GET LIST (D,C);
CALL KEYMC(D,ANS,A,B,C);
PUT EDIT('EQUATION IS ANS=D+(A*B-C)')(X(5),A);
PUT DATA(A,B,C,D,ANS);
END;
```

Fig. 9.17 PL/I main program to call subroutine KEYMC.

```
IDENTIFICATION DIVISION.
PROGRAM-ID.
    'MAINK'. PROGRAM NAME
AUTHOR.
    S. S. KUO.
REMARKS.
    THIS IS A PROGRAM TO CALL KEYMC.
ENVIRONMENT DIVISION.
CONFIGURATION SECTION.
SOURCE-COMPUTER.
    IBM-360 G50.
OBJECT-COMPUTER.
    IBM-360 G50.
INPUT-OUTPUT SECTION.
FILE-CONTROL.
    SELECT CARD-FILE ASSIGN TO 'CARDIN' UNIT-RECORD.
    SELECT PRINT-FILE ASSIGN TO 'PRINTED' UTILITY.
DATA DIVISION.
FILE SECTION.
FD  CARD-FILE
    RECORDING MODE IS F
    LABEL RECORDS ARE OMITTED
    DATA RECORDS ARE CARD-REC.
01  CARD-REC                    PICTURE X(80).
FD  PRINT-FILE
    RECORDING MODE IS F
    LABEL RECORDS ARE OMITTED
    DATA RECORDS ARE PRT-FILE.
01  PRT-FILE                    PICTURE X(133).
WORKING-STORAGE SECTION.
77  NUMD-X  PICTURE S9(6) COMPUTATIONAL.
77  NANS-X  PICTURE S9(6) COMPUTATIONAL.
77  NA-X    PICTURE S9(6) COMPUTATIONAL.
77  NB-X    PICTURE S9(6) COMPUTATIONAL.
77  NC-X    PICTURE S9(6) COMPUTATIONAL.
01  CARD-RECORD.
    02  NUMD                    PICTURE 9999.
```

Fig. 9.18 COBOL main program to call subroutine KEYMC.

```
        02   NC                              PICTURE 9999.
        02   FILLER                          PICTURE X(72).
    01  HEADER-LINE.
        02   FILLER                          PICTURE X(5) VALUE SPACES.
        02   HEAD-1                          PICTURE X(26) VALUE
                                             'EQUATION IS ANS=D+(A*B)-C'.
    01  TITLE-LINE.
        02   FILLER                          PICTURE X(5) VALUE SPACES.
        02   TITLE-1                         PICTURE X(10) VALUE 'VALUES ARE'.
        02   FILLER                          PICTURE X(118) VALUE SPACES.
    01  DETAIL-1.
        02   FILLER                          PICTURE X(6) VALUE SPACES.
        02   TITLE-2                         PICTURE XX VALUE 'A='.
        02   NA                              PICTURE ZZZ9.
        02   FILLER                          PICTURE X(121) VALUE SPACES.
    01  DETAIL-2.
        02   FILLER                          PICTURE X(6) VALUE SPACES.
        02   TITLE-3                         PICTURE XX VALUE 'B='.
        02   NB                              PICTURE ZZZ9.
        02   FILLER                          PICTURE X(121) VALUE SPACES.
    01  DETAIL-3.
        02   FILLER                          PICTURE X(5) VALUE SPACES.
        02   TITLE-4                         PICTURE XX VALUE 'C='.
        02   NC-1                            PICTURE ZZZ9.
        02   FILLER                          PICTURE X(122) VALUE SPACES.
    01  DETAIL-4.
        02   FILLER                          PICTURE X(5) VALUE SPACES.
        02   TITLE-5                         PICTURE XX VALUE 'D='.
        02   NUMD-1                          PICTURE ZZZ9.
        02   FILLER                          PICTURE X(122) VALUE SPACES.
    01  DETAIL-5.
        02   FILLER                          PICTURE X(4) VALUE SPACES.
        02   TITLE-6                         PICTURE X(4) VALUE 'ANS='.
        02   NANS                            PICTURE ZZZ9.
        02   FILLER                          PICTURE X(121) VALUE SPACES.
    01  BLANK-LINE.
        02   FILLER                          PICTURE X(133) VALUE SPACES.
PROCEDURE DIVISION.
OPENING.
    OPEN INPUT CARD-FILE OUTPUT PRINT-FILE.
    READ CARD-FILE INTO CARD-RECORD, AT END GO TO PRINT-RESULT.
    MOVE NUMD TO NUMD-X.  MOVE NC TO NC-X.
    ENTER LINKAGE.
    CALL 'KEYMC' USING NUMD-X NANS-X NA-X NB-X NC-X.
    ENTER COBOL.
PRINT-RESULT.
    MOVE NUMD-X TO NUMD-1.  MOVE NC-X TO NC-1.
    MOVE NANS-X TO NANS.  MOVE NA-X TO NA.  MOVE NB-X TO NB.
    WRITE PRT-FILE FROM BLANK-LINE AFTER ADVANCING 3 LINES.
    WRITE PRT-FILE FROM HEADER-LINE AFTER ADVANCING 3 LINES.
    WRITE PRT-FILE FROM TITLE-LINE AFTER ADVANCING 1 LINES.
    WRITE PRT-FILE FROM DETAIL-1 AFTER ADVANCING 1 LINES.
    WRITE PRT-FILE FROM DETAIL-2 AFTER ADVANCING 1 LINES.
    WRITE PRT-FILE FROM DETAIL-3 AFTER ADVANCING 1 LINES.
    WRITE PRT-FILE FROM DETAIL-4 AFTER ADVANCING 1 LINES.
    WRITE PRT-FILE FROM DETAIL-5 AFTER ADVANCING 2 LINES.
CLOSE-FILES.
    CLOSE CARD-FILE PRINT-FILE.
    STOP RUN.
```

Fig. 9.18   (*continued*)

```
EQUATION IS ANS=D+( A*B-C)

VALUES ARE
A=   2
B=   6
C=   6
D=  10

ANS=    16
```

Fig. 9.19 Output.

A macro definition must be placed in front of its associated assembler language, regardless of the kind of prototype statement used in the definition. Thus, in this example, the macro EQUAT has to be positioned ahead of the subroutine KEYMC, as shown in Fig. 9.15. For the purpose of input and output, this subroutine is called by a main program written in a high-level language; its FORTRAN, PL/I and COBOL versions are respectively presented in Figs. 9.16, 9.17, and 9.18. The output is shown in Fig. 9.19.

9.5 CONDITIONAL BRANCH AT ASSEMBLY TIME

This section will illustrate how to skip certain instructions in a macro definition so that they will not be *assembled* in the macro expansion.

It is required to write a macro definition for evaluating the following three expressions:

$$((A + B - C) \times E)/F,$$

then

$$(A + X - C) \times E,$$

and finally

$$(A + Y - C).$$

We quickly rule out the following scheme: Writing a long definition to compute three expressions one by one, because there is a better way. Figure 9.20(a) shows a macro definition EVAL together with three expansions; its associated flowchart is shown in Fig. 9.20(b).

In Fig. 9.20(a), the AIF instruction

```
            AIF   (&INDEX EQ 1).OUT
```

is a conditional branch instruction of a class of language—conditional assembly language. It resembles IF statement in a high-level language. The logical expression &INDEX EQ 1 between the parentheses has the following meaning: If &INDEX is equal to 1, then go to .OUT. (In other words, do not assemble the statements 8 through 13.) Otherwise, go to the next instruction. The symbol .OUT is used as a branch-to name.

```
STMT    SOURCE STATEMENT

   1             MACRO
   2  &NAME      EVAL    &INDEX,&A,&B,&C,&E,&F,&SUM,&PRODUCT,&QUOTIEN
   3             L       5,&A
   4             A       5,&B
   5             S       5,&C
   6             ST      5,&SUM
   7             AIF     (&INDEX EQ 1).OUT   IF INDEX=1,OUT
   8             M       4,&E                PRODUCT IN REG.5
   9             ST      5,&PRODUCT
  10             AIF     (&INDEX EQ 2).OUT   IF INDEX=2,OUT
  11             L       5,&PRODUCT
  12             D       4,&F
  13             ST      5,&QUOTIEN
  14  .OUT       MEND
  15             CSECT
  16             STM     14,12,12(13)
  17             BALR    11,0
  18             USING   *,11
  19  FIRST      EVAL    3,A,B,C,E1,F1,SUM,PROD,QUO
  20+            L       5,A
  21+            A       5,B
  22+            S       5,C
  23+            ST      5,SUM
  24+            M       4,E1 PRODUCT IN REG.5
  25+            ST      5,PROD
  26+            L       5,PROD
  27+            D       4,F1
  28+            ST      5,QUO
  29  SECOND     EVAL    2,A,X,C,E1,F1,SUM,PROD
  30+            L       5,A
  31+            A       5,X
  32+            S       5,C
  33+            ST      5,SUM
  34+            M       4,E1 PRODUCT IN REG.5
  35+            ST      5,PROD
  36  THIRD      EVAL    1,A,Y,C,,,SUM
  37+            L       5,A
  38+            A       5,Y
  39+            S       5,C
  40+            ST      5,SUM

  41  A          DC      F'100'
  42  B          DC      F'25'
  43  X          DC      F'25'
  44  Y          DC      F'25'
  45  C          DC      F'5'
  46  E1         DC      F'4'
  47  F1         DC      F'2'
  48  SUM        DS      F
  49  PROD       DS      F
  50  QUO        DS      F
  51             END
```

(a) Macro EVAL and its generated instructions.

Fig. 9.20 Conditional assembly.

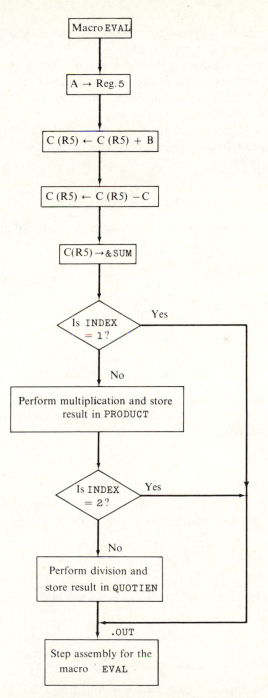

Fig. 9.20 (*continued*) (b) Flowchart to show the conditional branch at assembly time.

All symbols headed by a period are *sequence symbols*. A sequence symbol is valid only locally—valid only in a macro definition.

The expansions corresponding to three macro calls are also shown in Fig. 9.20(a). Note that the AIF instructions disappear in all expansions. They have only one function: Skip certain instructions in macro definition only if the value of the symbolic parameter &INDEX satisfies certain conditions.

Let us conclude this section by exploring in more detail the logical expressions. It is a powerful means to test a given set of conditions. The value of a logical expression is either true or false.

True: represented by 1,
False: represented by 0.

A logical expression, in its simplest form, involves relational operators.

GT   Greater than
GE   Greater than or equal to
EQ   Equal to
NE   Not equal to
LE   Less than or equal to
LT   Less than

Example 1

```
AIF   (&TO GE &LENGTH).FINISH
```

means: If the value of &TO is greater than or equal to that of &LENGTH, then go to .FINISH. (In this case, the logical expression is true and its value is 1.) Otherwise, go to the next instruction.

Example 2

```
AIF   (&LOOP EQ N'&B).OUT
```

means: If the value of &LOOP is equal to the number of the sublist &B, then go to .OUT. Otherwise, go to the next instruction. Sublist will be discussed in the next section.

Example 3

```
AIF   (&ID).HERE
```

means: If the value of &ID is 1 (true), then go to .HERE. Otherwise, go to the next instruction.

Example 4

```
AIF   ('&RESULT' EQ ' ').FINI
```

means: If the character string &RESULT is a null string, then go to .FINI. Otherwise, go to the next instruction. The character strings will be further discussed in Section 9.9.

A logical expression may also involve AND, OR, and NOT operating on various logical relations.†

Example 5

                    AIF   ('&DO' EQ 'A' OR '&DO' EQ 'S').LOC1

means: If a character string '&DO' is equal to either 'A' or 'S', then go to .LOC1. Otherwise, go to the next instruction.

Two additional examples using more involved logical expressions are as follows:

            AIF   (&ID GT &TERM OR '&DISP'(&ID+1) EQ 'C').LOOP
            AIF   (&D AND '&C'(&ID,1) EQ 'C').THERE

9.6 THREE FACETS OF A PIECE OF DATA

In the previous section, we learned that, during assembly time, instructions might be skipped (not assembled) by using a conditional branch instruction AIF. This instruction is perhaps most common in the conditional assembly language. Its repertoire of instructions is quite impressive and includes instructions such as conditional branches (AIF), unconditional branches (ANOP), and GO TO (AGO). Table 9.1 lists some common instructions. In addition, it has its own data types, makeshift I/O, and many other features.

Table 9.1   Common instructions in conditional assembly

Instruction	Example	Meaning
AIF	AIF (&I EQ 1).HERE	If &I is equal to 1, go to .HERE; otherwise, go to the next instruction
AGO	AGO .THERE	Unconditionally go to .THERE
ANOP	.LOCI ANOP	No operation
ACTR	ACTR 88	Limit the executed AIF and AGO instructions to only 88.
MEXIT	.LOC2 MEXIT	The sequence symbol is optional. The current macro expansion is terminated, and assembly process continues with the instruction following the macro call.
MNOTE	.BAD MNOTE 'ERROR DUE TO ...'	The message is printed in the assembly listing following the last instruction generated.

† Note its striking resemblance to the logical expressions used in FORTRAN IV.

In conditional assembly language, a piece of data differs from another one in three different ways. First, there are single-valued data and one-dimensional arrays. Second, there are local and global data. Local data are temporary, valid only in a particular macro definition, whereas global data are valid in various macro definitions. Third, there are three data types: (1) integers; (2) true (represented by 1) or false (represented by 0); and (3) character strings. They are conveniently called A (for arithmetic) type, B (for Boolean) type, and C (character) type. These three facets of a piece of data are shown in the three-dimensional diagram (see Fig. 9.21).

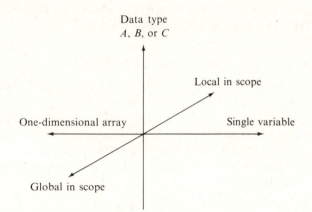

Fig. 9.21 Characteristics of a piece of data in conditional assembly language.

Let us now examine the first facet: single-value data versus one-dimensional array. In conditional assembly language, a piece of data may consist of either one element or many elements as one-dimensional array. Two or three-dimensional arrays are not permitted. For example, consider the following *macro call*

```
LOOP1   A,(B,X,Y),C,E1,F1,SUM,PROD,QUO
```

where the second argument is a one-dimensional array of three elements B, X, and Y (between the parentheses). An argument of this form is known as argument sublist, or operand sublist.

We shall now illustrate the practical application of argument sublist with an example of loop control at assembly time.

In the previous section, a macro definition EVAL was written to evaluate the following three expressions one by one:

$$((A + B - C) \times E)/F,$$

then

$$(A + X - C) \times E,$$

```
STMT    SOURCE STATEMENT

   1              MACRO
   2  &NAME       LOOP1  &A,&B,&C,&E,&F,&SUM,&PROD,&QUOT
   3              LCLA   &LOOP
   4  &LOOP       SETA   1
   5  .START      L      5,&A
   6              A      5,&B(&LOOP)
   7              S      5,&C
   8              ST     5,&SUM
   9              AIF    (&LOOP EQ N'&B).OUT
  10              M      4,&E
  11              ST     5,&PROD
  12              AIF    (&LOOP EQ N'&B-1).HERE
  13              D      4,&F
  14              ST     5,&QUOT
  15  .HERE       ANOP
  16  &LOOP       SETA   &LOOP+1
  17              AGO    .START
  18  .OUT        MEND
  19  BEGIN       CSECT
  20  *
  21  *           DEFINE BASE REGISTER
  22  *
  23              LR     11,15
  24              USING BEGIN,11
  25  *
  26  *           CALL MACRO
  27  *
  28  RUN         LOOP1  A,(B,X,Y),C,E1,F1,SUM,PROD,QUO
  29+             L      5,A
  30+             A      5,B
  31+             S      5,C
  32+             ST     5,SUM
  33+             M      4,E1
  34+             ST     5,PROD
  35+             D      4,F1
  36+             ST     5,QUO
  37+             L      5,A
  38+             A      5,X
  39+             S      5,C
  40+             ST     5,SUM
  41+             M      4,E1
  42+             ST     5,PROD
  43+             L      5,A
  44+             A      5,Y
  45+             S      5,C
  46+             ST     5,SUM
  47  *
  48  *           DEFINE CONSTANTS
  49  *
  50  A           DC     F'100'
  51  B           DC     F'25'
  52  X           DC     F'25'
  53  Y           CC     F'25'
  54  C           DC     F'5'
```

```
STMT    SOURCE STATEMENT

  55  E1          DC     F'5'
  56  F1          DC     F'2'
  57  SUM         DS     F
  58  PROD        DS     F
  59  QUO         DS     F
  60              END
```

Fig. 9.22 Macro definition LOOP1 to show the usage of an argument sublist.

and, finally,

$$(A + Y - C).$$

Three macro calls were issued in the user's program (Fig. 9.20). We wish now to improve this macro definition so that *one* macro call will do the same job. A macro definition LOOP1, which uses loop control instructions, is shown in Fig. 9.22. In designing this definition, it was anticipated that the second parameter, the symbol variable &B, will have three different values in the macro call. In other words, the argument &B is a list of three elements. Thus, the number attribute N'&B = 3.

Although the following two instructions (see the statements 3 and 4 in Fig. 9.22)

```
          LCLA    &LOOP
&LOOP     SETA    1
```

will be discussed more fully in the next section, it is worthwhile to briefly introduce them now. The LCLA instruction indicates that the symbolic parameter &LOOP is *local* to this macro LOOP1; it is temporary and its value is not accessible to other macros, if any. The SETA instruction sets the value of &LOOP as 1, an integer. (This replaces the initial value of a local variable which was automatically set to zero.) SETA instructions are generally used as loop counters.

Before we turn to the next section, it is worth mentioning that an argument in a macro call can be referred by its numeric position in the argument list. Thus the second argument in the macro call

```
     SELECT  1,0,,B,HERE,P
```

may be referred to in the macro definition as &SYSLIST(2), where &SYSLIST is a standard name for the argument list provided by OS/360. The contents enclosed in parentheses are not limited to a number; it may be an expression containing certain variables. For example, a practical application of &SYSLIST(K) is shown in Fig. 9.23.

```
STMT    SOURCE STATEMENT

   1                MACRO
   2                STORAREA
   3                LCLA    &IDS
   4    .HERE       AIF     (&IDS EQ N'&SYSLIST).FINISH
   5    &IDS        SETA    &IDS+1
   6    DS&SYSLIST(&IDS)   DS   CL&SYSLIST(&IDS)
   7                AGO     .HERE
   8    .FINISH     MEND
   9    BEGIN       CSECT
  10                LR      11,15
  11                USING   BEGIN,11
  12                STORAREA  60,20,40,32
  13+DS60           DS      CL60
  14+DS20           DS      CL20
  15+DS40           DS      CL40
  16+DS32           DS      CL32
  17                END
```

Fig. 9.23 Practical application of &SYSLIST(K).

Table 9.2 Variable symbols

Variable symbol	Example	Defined by	Initial value (or the value is set to)	Value Constant throughout definition	Value Variable changed by	Reference section
Symbolic parameter	&AREA	Prototype statement	Corresponding operand value in a macro instruction	Yes	—	Section 9.3
&SYSLIST(K)	DS&SYSLIST(&IDS)	Automatically by assembler	Corresponding operand value in a macro instruction	Yes	—	Section 9.6
&SYSLIST	N'&SYSLIST	Automatically by assembler	—	—	—	—
&SYSNDX	PATN&SYSNDX.(5)	Automatically by assembler	Macro instruction index	Yes	—	Problem 9.8
&SYSECT	BACK&SYSECT	Automatically by assembler	Control section in which the macro instruction appears	Yes	—	Problem 9.9
SETA	LCLA &VALUE	LCLA or GBLA instruction	0	—	SETA instruction	Section 9.7
SETB	LCLB &WEO	LCLB or GBLB instruction	0	—	SETB instruction	Section 9.8
SETC	LCLC &TYPE	LCLC or GBLC instruction	'' (Null character string)	—	SETC instruction	Section 9.9

A net result: Four DS instructions are generated. This technique can be applied equally well to generate a sequence of DC instructions.

The &SYSLIST(K) and symbolic parameters (discussed in Section 9.3) are two important examples of *variable symbols*. Other variable symbols are tabulated in Table 9.2.

9.7 FIRST TYPE OF DATA—ARITHMETIC (*A*)

We turn now to the data type—the key facet of a piece of data used in conditional assembly language. There are three types of data: integers used in arithmetic (*A*), Boolean (*B*), and character strings (*C*).

We have already introduced *A*-type data in the previous section. They are used primarily as loop counters or subscripts in a list. For example, the following three instructions deal with *A*-type data &I and &J:

```
        LCLA    &I,&J
&I      SETA    1
&J      SETA    &J+2
```

The two variables in the first instruction above serve to declare that the values of &I and &J are valid only locally (only in this macro definition).

Each language has some idiosyncrasies, and the conditional assembly language is of no exception. Perhaps the most apparent one is its dual demand:

1. You must declare whether a variable is local or global by using, say, LCLA or GCLA instructions.

2. You must then assign an integer value to this variable by using, say, a SETA instruction.

The operand field of a SETA instruction must be an expression—an arithmetic combination of terms. In Fig. 6.3 on page 154, we see that terms permitted in assembler language are (1) self-defining terms; (2) location counter references; (3) symbols; (4) literals; and (5) length attribute references. In contrast, the terms permitted in conditional assembly language are (1) self-defining terms; (2) variable symbols, and (3) six attribute references, including the length attribute references. The connectors are addition, subtraction, multiplication, and division. Thus a SETA instruction may be as simple as

```
&J      SETA    1
```

or

```
&I      SETA    &I+1
```

and as complex as

```
&A      SETA    &A+1+(B'1001'-X'FF'+C'XYZ')+N'&A
```

Example 1

In Section 5.3, we saw that the Move (MVC) instruction could move a maximum of 256 bytes. We want now to write a complete macro definition† to move any number of bytes (up to $2^{24} = 16,777,216$ bytes). Figure 9.24 suggests a possibility. We note that the variable symbols &COUNT and &RESIDUE are declared first as local in the LCLA instruction, before the value of each symbol is assigned by means of a SETA instruction. The value of a symbol can be reassigned by another SETA instruction.

```
 1   ****************************************************************************
 2   *           THIS PROGRAM IS TO MOVE ANY NUMBER OF BYTES BY USING          *
 3   *           A MACRO DEFINITION.  THE VARIABLE SYMBOLS &COUNT,             *
 4   *           &RESIDUE ARE DECLARED AS LOCAL.                               *
 5   ****************************************************************************
 6            MACRO
 7  &NAME     MOVEBYTE  &ORIGIN,&MOVETO,&LENGTH
 8            LCLA      &COUNT,&RESIDUE
 9  .PATH1    AIF       (&LENGTH LE &COUNT+256).PATH2
10            MVC       &MOVETO+&COUNT.(256),&ORIGIN+&COUNT
11  &COUNT    SETA      &COUNT+256
12            AGO       .PATH1
13  .PATH2    ANOP
14  &RESIDUE  SETA      &LENGTH-&COUNT
15            MVC       &MOVETO+&COUNT.(&RESIDUE),&ORIGIN+&COUNT
16            MEND
17  BEGIN     CSECT
18  *
19            LR        10,15           DEFINE BASE REGISTER
20            USING     BEGIN,10
21            MOVEBYTE  FROM,TO,710
22+           MVC       TO+0(256),FROM+0
23+           MVC       TO+256(256),FROM+256
24+           MVC       TO+512(198),FROM+512
25  TO        DS        F
26  FROM      DS        F
27            END
```

Fig. 9.24 Usage of SETA.

Example 2

Fibonacci numbers are obtained by starting 1 and 1. The sum of the last two numbers is used as the next: 1, 1, 2, 3, 5, 8, 13, ... We wish to write macro definition FIBO to generate this set of numbers. A possible FIBO is shown in Fig. 9.25 and its associated flowchart in Fig. 9.26.

We note that, in the generated statements 69 and 77, some Fibonacci numbers are already obtained in the assembly process; they are: $F(5) = 8$ and $F(10) = 89$.

---

† Assume that the Move Long (MVCL) instruction is not available in this installation.

```
  1              MACRO
  2 &NAME      FIBO  &I,&ANSWER
  3 .*
  4 .*    ANSWER IS IN REGISTER 8 AND ALSO IN &ANSWER
  5 .*
  6              LCLA  &II,&RESULT,&TEMP1,&TEMP2,&COUNTER
  7 .*    LOCAL DEFINITON OF &II,&RESULT,&TEMP1,&TEMP2,&COUNTER
  8 &II        SETA  &I              SET &II TO THE VALUE OF &I
  9              AIF   (&II GT 1).HERE  IF &II IS GREATER THAN 1  GO TO .HERE
 10 .*
 11 .*    FIBONACCI NUMBER =1 FOR I=0,I=1
 12 .*
 13 &RESULT   SETA  1               SET &RESULT = TO 1
 14              AGO   .THERE          GO TO .THERE
 15 .HERE      ANOP
 16 .*
 17 .*    INITIALIZATION OF VALUES
 18 .*
 19 &TEMP1    SETA  1
 20 &TEMP2    SETA  1
 21 &COUNTER  SETA  2
 22 .*
 23 .*    FIND  F(I)=F(I-1)+F(I-2)   START WITH I=2
 24 .*
 25 .LOOP      ANOP
 26 &RESULT   SETA  &TEMP1+&TEMP2  SET &RESULT =&TEMP1+&TEMP2
 27 &TEMP1    SETA  &TEMP2         SET &TEMP1 = &TEMP2
 28 &TEMP2    SETA  &RESULT        SET &TEMP2 = &RESULT
 29 &COUNTER  SETA  &COUNTER+1     SET &COUNTER =&COUNTER+1
 30              AIF   (&COUNTER LE &II).LOOP
 31 .*
 32 .*    STORE ANSWER
 33 .*
 34 .THERE     LA    8,&RESULT       LOAD &RESULT INTO R(8)
 35 .*
 36 .*    IF SECOND ARGUMENT IS OMITTED, SKIP STORE INSTRUCTION
 37 .*
 38              AIF   (T'&ANSWER EQ 'O').FINISH
 39              ST    8,&ANSWER       LOAD &RESULT INTO &ANSWER
 40 .FINISH    MEND
 41 FIBNAR     CSECT
 42              SAVE  (14,12),,*
 43+             B     12(0,15) BRANCH AROUND ID
 44+             DC    AL1(6)
 45+             DC    CL6'FIBNAR' IDENTIFIER

 46+             STM   14,12,12(13) SAVE REGISTERS
 47              BALR  11,0
 48              USING *,11
 49 *
 50 *     TEST FOR OMISSION OF 2ND ARGUMENT
 51 *
 52              FIBO  0
 53+             LA    8,1 LOAD &RESULT INTO R(8)
 54              LR    5,8             LOAD CONTENTS OF R(8) INTO R(5)
 55              L     6,0(1)          LOAD 1ST ARGU. PTR. INTO R(6)
 56              ST    5,0(6)          STORE &RESULT INTO ARGU. LIST
```

Fig. 9.25 Macro FIBO and its generated statements.

```
57  *
58  *        TEST THAT F(2) STOPS WHEN &COUNTER=3
59  *
60           FIBO   2
61+          LA     8,2 LOAD &RESULT INTO R(8)
62           LR     7,8           LOAD CONTENTS OF R(8) INTO R(7)
63           L      9,4(1)        LOAD 2ND ARGU. PTR. INTO R(9)
64           ST     7,0(9)        STORE &RESULT INTO 2ND ARGU. LIST
65  *
66  *        TEST FOR F(5)=8
67  *
68           FIBO   5
69+          LA     8,8 LOAD &RESULT INTO R(8)
70           LR     10,8          LOAD CONTENTS OF R(8) INTO R(10)
71           L      11,8(1)       LOAD 3RD ARGU. PTR. INTO R(11)
72           ST     10,0(11)      STORE &RESULT INTO 2ND ARGU. LIST
73  *
74  *        TEST FOR F(10)=89
75  *
76           FIBO   10,ANS
77+          LA     8,89 LOAD &RESULT INTO R(8)
78+          ST     8,ANS LOAD &RESULT INTO &ANSWER
79           L      2,ANS         LOAD &RESULT INTO R(2)
80           L      3,12(1)       LOAD 4TH ARGU. PTR. INTO R(3)
81           ST     2,0(3)        STORE ANS INTO ARGU. LIST
82           RETURN (14,12)
83+          LM     14,12,12(13) RESTORE THE REGISTERS
84+          BR     14 RETURN
85  ANS      DS     F
86           END
```

Fig. 9.25 (*continued*)

9.8 SECOND TYPE OF DATA—BOOLEAN (*B*)

So far we have studied the arithmetic data type, denoted by the letter *A*. We saw *A*-type data has its own declarations (e.g., LCLA) and its own assignment statement (e.g., &K SETA 3). The operand field in SETA instruction is an arithmetic expression.

The second type of data is Boolean, also called logical. This type uses basically two numbers: 1 for true, and 0 for false. The statements corresponding to *B* data type are as follows:

1. Declaration statement to indicate the range of validity. For example: LCLB means that the piece of Boolean data is local, valid only in this macro definition.

2. Assignment statement such as

$$\text{\&A SETB (\&B GE 6)}$$

Here, if the value of &B is greater than 6 (i.e., true), then &A = 1. Otherwise, &A = 0. The operand field in a SETB instruction must be a binary digit (1 or 0), or a logical (Boolean) expression which was discussed in Section 9.5.

Figure 9.27 shows a simple macro definition BOOLE using LCLB and SETB instructions. Note that the variable symbol &TEST is first declared *local*, before its value is set to either 1 or 0. The MEXIT instruction indicates that the macro generation

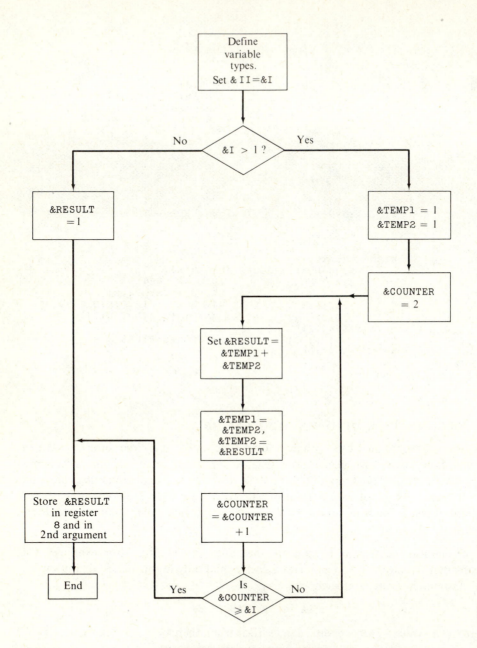

Fig. 9.26 Flowchart for FIBO.

264

```
 LOC   OBJECT CODE    ADDR1 ADDR2  STMT    SOURCE STATEMENT

                                    1               MACRO
                                    2               BOOLE  &REAR1,&REAR2,&TAIL,&BINARY
                                    3               LCLB   &TEST
                                    4  &TEST        SETB   (&BINARY EQ 1)
                                    5               AIF    (&TEST).HERE
                                    6               B&TAIL     LOC&REAR1
                                    7               MEXIT
                                    8  .HERE        ANOP
                                    9               B&TAIL     LOC&REAR2
                                   10               MEND
000000                             11  BEGIN        CSECT
000000  18BF                       12               LR     11,15
000000                             13               USING  BEGIN,11
                                   14               BOOLE  ONE,TWO,NH,0
000002  47D0 B00C        0000C     15+              BNH    LOCONE
                                   16  *
                                   17               BOOLE  ONE,TWO,NH,1
000006  47D0 B010        00010     18+              BNH    LOCTWO
00000C                             19  LOCONE       DS     F
000010                             20  LOCTWO       DS     F
                                   21               END
```

Fig. 9.27   Boolean data type.

is to be terminated. Note that MEXIT is different from MEND. MEND must be physically the last instruction of every macro definition which may contain no, one, or several MEXIT instructions.

9.9 THIRD TYPE OF DATA—CHARACTER (*C*)

The third and final type of data used in conditional assembly language is the character (*C*) type of data. The statements corresponding to this type are as follows:

1. Declaration statement to indicate the domain. For example, the instruction

$$\text{LCLC} \quad \text{\&STRING}$$

declares that the variable symbol &STRING is a character string, valid only in this macro definition.

2. Assignment statement such as

$$\text{\&A} \quad \text{SETC} \quad \text{'\&A.WAY'}$$

where the operand field is a character expression between the quotes.

The two basic operations of a character expression are described below.

The first operation which links one term to another, is called *concatenation*. By the term as used here we mean either a variable symbol or a character string. For example, at the end of the following SETC instructions

```
&A    SETC    'ON'
&B    SETC    'TRO'
&A    SETC    'C&A&B.L'
```

the value of &A is the character string CONTROL, since (a) &A and &B are substituted, respectively, by ON and TRO; and (b) the period, the vanishing delimiter, automatically disappears. Thus the character expression 'C&A&B.L' is set as

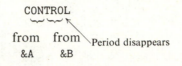

The general rule (discussed in Section 9.3) to concatenate a symbolic parameter with other characters apply equally well to the following case: Concatenation of any variable symbol with a character string.

Table 9.3 shows the detailed requirement of the vanishing delimiter in various concatenation operations.

Table 9.3 Vanishing delimiter (a period in concatenation operation)

Concatenation	Example	Is period required?
Variable symbol–variable symbol	&A&B	No
Variable symbol–character string	&B.L	Yes
Character string–variable symbol	L&B	No
Character string–character string	LV	No

The second basic operation of a character string, which brings out certain characters (substring) from a given character string, is called *substring extraction*. For example, the value of &A in the following SETC instruction

```
&A   SETC   'PHILLIPS'(2,4)
```

is the substring HILL. The substring operator (2,4) is placed after the given string and outside the right quote. The first number, 2, indicates the starting position of the substring, or the character H; the second number, 4, indicates the length of the substring. Thus, the substring is HILL.

As second example, we wish to find the value of &AA at the end of the following four consecutive SETC instructions:

```
&A    SETC   'ON'
&B    SETC   'TRO'
&A    SETC   'C&A&B.L'
&AA   SETC   '&A'(2,2).'&A'(5,1)
```

From the above discussion, we see that the final value of &A is CONTROL. Thus the value of &AA is ONR.

The operations of concatenation and substring extraction may coexist in a character expression. For example, the value of &AAA in the instruction

```
&AAA   SETC   '('.'HILL'(2,3).')'
```

is assigned as (ILL), where two periods have disappeared.

Figure 9.28 shows a macro TRUTH and its expansion (with machine language listing) to illustrate the usage of SETC and LCLC.

```
 LOC    OBJECT CODE    ADDR1 ADDR2   STMT     SOURCE STATEMENT

                                      1                MACRO
                                      2                TRUTH  &WHAT1,&WHAT2
                                      3                LCLC   &T,&I,&B,&S,&T1
                                      4   &T           SETC   'THEREFOR'
                                      5   &T1          SETC   'E '
                                      6   &I           SETC   'I '
                                      7   &B           SETC   ' '
                                      8   ONE          DC     C'&I&WHAT1&B&T&T1&I&WHAT2.'
                                      9   &S           SETC   '&T'(6,3).'&B'
                                     10   &T           SETC   '&T'(1,5).'&B'
                                     11   TWO          DC     C'&S&T&I&WHAT1&B&I&WHAT2.'
                                     12                MEND
000000                               13   CART         CSECT
000000  05F0                         14                BALR   15,0
000002                               15                USING  *,15
                                     16                TRUTH  THINK,AM
000002  C940E3C8C9D5D240             17+ONE           DC     C'I THINK THEREFORE I AM'
000018  C6D6D940E3C8C5D9             18+TWO           DC     C'FOR THERE I THINK I AM'
                                     19                END
```

Fig. 9.28   Usage of SETC and LCLC.

9.10 SIX ATTRIBUTES

In assembler language programming, the number of bytes occupied by a constant is called its length attribute (see Problem 6.15). In conditional assembly language, there are six attributes of a symbol variable (Table 9.4) which supply additional information on the variable. In this section, we shall examine how this information can be used in conditional assembly programming.

We have already seen that the number of elements in the sublist in a macro call can be referenced as, say, N'&B. For example, the number of elements for the second argument in the macro call in Fig. 9.22

```
LOOP1   A,(B,X,Y),C,E1,F1,SUM,PROD,QUO
```

is 3. Or, N'&B = 3.

The type of a piece of data (T') is perhaps another popular attribute used in conditional assembly programming. For instance, if a variable symbol &FULHALF is associated with a piece of fullword (F) data, then the *type attribute* can be used in a conditional branch instruction

```
AIF   (T'&FULHALF EQ 'F').HERE
```

Table 9.4 Six attributes of a symbol variable

Attribute	Examples	Main limitations

Length
L'
	`&D    SETC 'DISP'`
	`&DD   SETC 'L'''`
	`      MVC  &D.(&DD&D),FROM`
	
	Generated as
	`      MVC  DISP(L'DISP),FROM`
	where `L'DISP` is the number of bytes in symbol `DISP`
		1. Reference to the length attribute of a variable symbol is not permitted except for symbolic parameters in SETA, SETB, and AIF instructions.
		
		2. Reference to the length attributes of symbols or operands in a macro call is illegal if the symbols or operands have type attributes of M, N, O, T, or V.

Number
N'
	`&A` is a sublist in a macro call:
	`      (I,J,K)` `N'&A=3`
	`&B` is a sublist:
	`      (I,,J,K)` `N'&B=4`
	`&C` is a sublist:
	`      (I,J,K,,)` `N'&C=5`
	`&D` is *not* a sublist:
	`                         N'&D=1`
	`&E` is omitted in a macro call
	`                         N'&E=0`
		You may refer to this attribute of operands in a macro call only.

Count
K'
	In the following macro call:
	`MOVEME   A=IJK,B=(1,2,3)`
	`K'A=3`
	`K'B=7` (including two parentheses and two commas)
	`K'C=0` if C is an omitted operand
		You may refer to this attribute of operands in a macro call only.

Type T'	`T'NAME` refers to the type attribute of the symbol NAME (e.g., F)	`T'NAME` is a letter. It has restrictions when used with symbols.
Scaling S'	*For a fixed-point or floating-point number* `ABC`: `S'ABC` = scale modifier *For a decimal number* `DEF`: `S'DEF` = number of decimal digits to the right of the decimal point.	Type attributes must be H, F, G, D, E, K, P, or Z.
Integer I'	*For a fixed-point or floating-point number* `ABC`: `I'ABC` is a function of the scale and `L'ABC`. *For a decimal number* `DEF`: `I'DEF` = number of decimal digits to the left of the assumed decimal point.	Type attributes must be H, F, G, D, E, K, O, or Z.

which means: If the variable symbol &FULHALF is a fullword fixed-point integer, then go to .HERE. Otherwise, go to the next instruction. Its application is shown in Fig. 9.29.

Table 9.5 gives a complete list of the type attributes.

```
LOC   OBJECT CODE     ADDR1 ADDR2  STMT    SOURCE STATEMENT

                                   1              MACRO
                                   2              TYPE    &FULHALF,&REG
                                   3              LCLC    &TAIL
                                   4              AIF     (T'&FULHALF EQ 'F').HERE
                                   5 &TAIL        SETC    'H'
                                   6 .HERE        L&TAIL  &REG,&FULHALF
                                   7              A&TAIL  &REG,&FULHALF
                                   8              ST&TAIL &REG,&FULHALF
                                   9              MEND
000000                             10 BEGIN       CSECT
000000 18BF                        11             LR      11,15
000002                             12             USING   *,11
                                   13             TYPE    HALF,8
000002 4880 B018             0001A 14+            LH      8,HALF
000006 4A80 B018             0001A 15+            AH      8,HALF
00000A 4080 B018             0001A 16+            STH     8,HALF
                                   17             TYPE    FULL,5
00000E 5850 B01A             0001C 18+            L       5,FULL
000012 5A50 B01A             0001C 19+            A       5,FULL
000016 5050 B01A             0001C 20+            ST      5,FULL
00001A 0014                        21 HALF        DC      H'20'
00001C 0000002E                    22 FULL        DC      F'46'
                                   23             END
```

Fig. 9.29   Type attribute.

Table 9.5   Type attribute

Argument		Meaning
	A	A-type address constant
	B	Binary constant
	C	Character constant
	D	Floating-point constant (long)
	E	Floating-point constant (short)
	F	Fullword integer
	H	Halfword integer
A	I	Machine instruction
symbol	J	Control section name
	M	Macro instruction
	P	Packed decimal constant
	S	S-type address constant
	V	V-type address constant
	X	Hexadecimal constant
	Z	Zoned decimal constant
Not a	N	Self-defining term
symbol	O	Argument is omitted

Apart from the number, length, and type attributes, there are three more attributes available in conditional assembly language: integer, count, and scaling attributes. For example, the first argument HALF in macro call TYPE (see the statement 13 in Fig. 9.29) has four characters and its count attribute is equal to 4 (written as K'&FULHALF = 4).

9.11 LOCAL VARIABLES VERSUS GLOBAL VARIABLES

So far we have seen how a variable may be declared local by using LCLA, LCLB, or LCLC instructions. The value of a local variable declared in macro definition A is *not* valid in macro definition B. It is *not* valid even if macro definition B is called by macro A. In either case, the value of a local variable is discarded at the exit of macro definition A. By contrast, the value of a global† variable is shared in many macro definitions, provided that the variable is declared as global in each macro definition. It will not be wiped out between different calls on a given macro definition.

Consider, for example, the three macro definitions in Fig. 9.30. They represent three different levels in that LEVEL1 calls LEVEL2, which in turn calls LEVEL3. Note that &REGA is common in LEVEL1 and LEVEL2, but not in LEVEL3. Similarly, &REGB is common in LEVEL1 and LEVEL3, but not in LEVEL2. Thus, a variable in some macro definitions can be declared as local, whereas in the other ones it can be established as global.

Up to this point, the global declaration instruction such as GBLB and assignment instructions (e.g., SETB) have only been used in the main body of a macro definition. Actually, there is no such restriction, since they can be written in a user's program, as shown in Fig. 9.31. (See the statement numbers 17, 18, 22, and 23.)

To sum up, it is necessary to check the correct answer to each of the three questions for a piece of data used in conditional assembly language. First, is it a single variable or a one-dimensional array (list)? Second, is it local (temporary), or global (throughout the macro definition and the program)? Finally, is it type A, B, or C? As a result, the following twelve declaration instructions are possible:

LCLA	&*name*
LCLB	&*name*
LCLC	&*name*
GCLA	&*name*
GCLB	&*name*
GCLC	&*name*
LCLA	&*name*(n)
LCLB	&*name*(n)
LCLC	&*name*(n)
GCLA	&*name*(n)
GCLB	&*name*(n)
GCLC	&*name*(n)

---

† Like COMMON statement in FORTRAN language.

```
STMT    SOURCE STATEMENT

   1   ****************************************************************************
   2   *                                                                         *
   3   *          IN THIS PROGRAM WE HAVE 3 MACRO DEFINITIONS.  LEVEL1           *
   4   *     CALLS LEVEL2, WHICH IN TURN CALLS LEVEL3.  &REGA IS                 *
   5   *     COMMON IN LEVEL1 AND LEVEL2, BUT IS NOT IN LEVEL3.                  *
   6   *     &REGB IS COMMON IN LEVEL1 AND LEVEL3, BUT NOT IN                    *
   7   *     LEVEL2.  THE VARIABLES WILL BE DECLARED IN SOME MACRO               *
   8   *     DEFINITIONS AS LOCAL AND AS GLOBAL SO THAT THE VALUES               *
   9   *     MAY CHANGE THROUGHOUT THE PROGRAM.                                  *
  10   ****************************************************************************
  11           MACRO
  12   &NAME   LEVEL1
  13   .*      1ST MACRO DEFINITION
  14           GBLA    &REGA,&REGB    TO BE DEFINED THROUGHTOUT PROGRAM
  15   &REGA   SETA    8
  16   &REGB   SETA    3
  17           LR      &REGA,&REGB
  18           LEVEL2                 CALL LEVEL2
  19           MEND
  20           MACRO
  21   &NAME   LEVEL2
  22   .*      2ND MACRO DEFINITION
  23           GBLA    &REGA          &REGA MAINTAINS OLD VALUE
  24           LCLA    &REGB          NEW VALUE IS GIVEN TO &REGB
  25   &REGB   SETA    4
  26           SR      &REGA,&REGB
  27           LEVEL3                 CALL LEVEL3
  28           MEND
  29           MACRO
  30   &NAME   LEVEL3
  31   .*      3RD MACRO DEFINITION
  32           GBLA    &REGB          &REGB MAINTAINS OLD VALUE
  33           LCLA    &REGA          NEW VALUE IS GIVEN TO &REGA
  34   &REGA   SETA    6
  35           AR      &REGA,&REGB
  36           MEND
  37   BEGIN   CSECT
  38           LR      10,15
  39           USING   BEGIN,10
  40           LEVEL1
  41+          LR      8,3
  42+          SR      8,4
  43+          AR      6,3
  44   *   CALL 1ST MACRO DEFINITION WHICH INTURN CALLS THE 2ND,
  45   *   WHICH CALLS THE 3RD MACRO DEFINITION.
  46           END
```

Fig. 9.30   Three macro definitions.

where n denotes the number of elements in a list. For instance, if a variable symbol &K (a) is a single element (not a one-dimensional array); (b) is valid only in the macro definition; and (c) represents an integer, then we obtain the following declaration instruction:

$$\text{LCLA} \qquad \text{\&K}$$

According to the third assumption above it is not only necessary to write the LCLA (not LCLB or LCLC) instruction, but an assignment instruction such as

$$\text{\&K} \quad \text{SETA} \quad 2$$

```
STMT    SOURCE STATEMENT

  1              MACRO
  2  &NAME       PICKONE &TAIL1,&TAIL2,&REG
  3              GBLB   &BINARY         TO BE DEFINED THROUGHOUT PROGRAM
  4              GBLC   &HEAD           TO BE DEFINED THROUGHTOUT PROGRAM
  5              AIF    (&REG EQ 6).AGE    IF &REG=6   GO TO .AGE
  6              A&TAIL1 &REG,A
  7              B&TAIL2 &HEAD.AGE     ADD 'AGE' TO THE CHARACTER STRING &HEAD
  8              MEXIT                 GO OUT OF THE MACRO DEFINITION
  9  .AGE        S&TAIL1 &REG,S
 10              B&TAIL2 &HEAD&TAIL2 PUT THE TWO CHARACTER STRINGS TOGETHER
 11              MEND
 12              GBLB   &BINARY
 13              GBLC   &HEAD
 14  BEGIN       CSECT
 15              LR     10,15
 16              USING BEGIN,10
 17  &BINARY     SETB   1               SET &BINARY EQUAL TO 1
 18  &HEAD       SETC   'LINK'          &HEAD =THE CHARACTER STRING 'LINK'
 19              PICKONE H,Z,4
 20+             AH     4,A
 21+             BZ     LINKAGE ADD 'AGE' TO THE CHARACTER STRING &HEAD
 22  &BINARY     SETB   0
 23  &HEAD       SETC   'PACK'          &HEAD = THE CHARACTER STRING 'PACK'
 24              PICKONE H,P,6
 25+             SH     6,S
 26+             BP     PACKP PUT THE TWO CHARACTER STRINGS TOGETHER
 27  A           DC     X'5'

 28  S           DC     H'2'
 29  LINKAGE     DS     F
 30  PACKP       DS     F
 31              END
```

Fig. 9.31   Global variables in a user's program.

is also required to assign the value of &K to 2. The syntax of an assignment instruction is

&*name*   SETA   *an arithmetic expression*

or

&*name*   SETB   (*a logical expression*)

or

&*name*   SETC   '*a character expression*'

BIBLIOGRAPHY

Barron, D. W., *Recursive Techniques in Programming*, American Elsevier, New York, 1968.

Brown, P. J., "A Survey of Macro Processors," *Annual Review in Automatic Programming*, Vol. 6, Pergamon Press, Oxford and New York, pages 37–88.

Farber, D. J., R. E. Griswold, and I. P. Polonsky, "SNOBOL: A String Manipulation Language," *J. of the ACM* 11 (2), 21–30 (1964).

Freeman, D. N., "Macro Language Design for System/360," *IBM Systems J.* 5, 62–77 (1966).

Graham, M. L., and P. Z. Ingerman, "A Universal Assembly Mapping Language," *Proceedings, ACM 20th National Conference*, 1965, pages 409–421.

Greenwald, I. D., "A Technique for Handling Macro Instructions," *CACM* **2** (11), 21–22 (1959).

IBM System/360 Supervisor and Data Management Macro Instructions, Form GC28-6647, IBM Corp.

IBM System/360 Operating System Assembler Language, Form C28-6514, IBM Corp.

Kent, William, "Assembler-Language Macroprogramming," *Computing Surveys* **1**, (4) 183–196 (1969).

Maurer, Ward Douglas, "The Compiled Macro Assembler," *Proceedings, AFIPS*, 1969 SJCC, pages 89–93.

McIlroy, M. D., "Macro Instruction Extensions of Compiler Language," *CACM* **3** (4), 214–220 (1960).

Strachey, C., "A General Purpose Macrogenerator," *Computer J.* **8** (3), 225–241 (1965).

Wegner, P. *Programming Languages, Information Structure and Machine Organization*, McGraw Hill, New York, 1968.

PROBLEMS

1. The operand RC=(15) in the macro

```
        RETURN   (2,12),RC=(15)
```

indicates that a return code is already contained in register 15, and that its contents must not be altered. After the execution of the following instruction segment, what are the contents of register 15?

```
                SR       15,15          ZERO R15.
                IC       15,STATUSBY    LOAD RETURN CODE.
                SLA      15,2           SET RETURN CODE TO
                RETURN   (2,12),RC=15      MULTIPLE OF 4.
                ⋮
    STATUSBY    DC       X'FF'
```

2. A programmer *A* has made the following definition:

```
                MACRO
    &BEGIN      ADD      &QUID,&PRO,&QUO
    &BEGIN      ST       2,TEMP
                L        2,&QUID
                A        2,&PRO
                ST       2,&QUO
                L        2,TEMP
                MEND
```

What is the macro expansion if a programmer *B* uses this macro and writes in his program the following macro instruction:

```
PB   ADD   BETA,GAMMA,DELTA
```

3. The system macro

```
DUMP1   ABEND   0,DUMP
```

generates the following seven instructions:

```
DUMP1   DS    0H
        CNOP  0,4
        B     *+8           BRANCH AROUND CONSTANT
        DC    AL1(128)      DUMP/STEP CODE
        DC    AL3(0)        COMPLETION CODE
        L     1,*-4         LOAD CODES INTO REG 1
        SVC   13            LINK TO ABEND CODE
```

Explain the purpose of each instruction.

4. The macro definition SECTION is given in Fig. 9.7. Write the generated instructions if the macro call is as follows:

```
SECTION  C,9
```

5. The macro definition CONTROL is shown in Fig. 9.8. Write the generated instructions if the macro call is

a) CONTROL   12,A
b) CONTROL   12,PART,A

6. The macro definition PROB6 is shown below.

```
MACRO
PROB6   &SUB,&REG=R11
L       &REG,=A(&SUB)
BALR    R6,&REG
MEND
```

In this *mixed format macro*, the operand field contains both the positional and the keyword parameters. The positional ones are written first and are followed by the keyword parameters.

Write the generated instruction if the macro call is:

a) PROB6   SUB1
b) PROB6   SUB2,REG=R12

7. The following macro definition is given.

```
        MACRO
        HALF
        LCLA   &K
.HERE   AIF    (&K EQ N'&SYSLIST).FINISH
&K      SETA   &K+1
```

```
H&SYSLIST(&K)      DC       H'&SYSLIST(&K)'
                   AGO    .HERE
.FINISH            MEND
```

Write the generated instruction for the following macro call:

```
HALF  12,9,146
```

8. In System 370/360 assembler, a system parameter &SYSNDX is available. It has an initial value of 0001 and is incremented by 1 for each macro expansion. It is often concatenated with other symbols so that unique names may be formed. For example, the A&SYSNDX in the following definition would generate the names A0001, A0002, and so on.

```
            MACRO
            LINKAGE   &SUBNAME
            L         15,A&SYSNDX
            BALR      14,15
            B         A&SYSNDX+4
A&SYSNDX    DC        V(&SUBNAME)
            MEND
```

Write the macro expansion for the macro call

```
LINKAGE    BAKER
```

a) if the macro LINKAGE is called for the first time, and
b) if the macro LINKAGE is called for the 67th time.

9. A system parameter &SYSECT is available in System 370/360 assembler. It will be substituted by the name of control section in which the macro call is made. For example, if the following definition is given:

```
            MACRO
            HERE
BAKER       CSECT
            DC        A(&SYSECT)
            MEND
```

and if a macro call HERE is made in control section ABLE, then the following two instructions will be generated:

```
BAKER       CSECT
            DC        A(ABLE)
```

Write the generated instruction if a macro call HERE is made in control section PROB9.

LABORATORY ASSIGNMENT

1. Given the following two macros:

```
          MACRO
          GOGET   &REG,&THING
          GBLC    &RREG(15)
          LCLA    &I
          AIF     ('&RREG(&REG)' NE '&THING').PATH1
          MEXIT
.PATH1    AIF     (&I EQ 15).PATH2
&I        SETA    &I+1
          AIF     ('&RREG(&I)' NE '&THING').PATH1
          LR      &REG,&I
          AGO     .PATH3
.PATH2    L       &REG,&THING
.PATH3    ANOP
&RREG(&REG) SETC '&THING'
          MEND
          MACRO
          SUM     &QUID,&PRO,&QUO
          GBLC    &RREG(15)
          GOGET   2,&QUID
          A       2,&PRO
          ST      2,&QUO
&RREG(1)  SETC    '&QUO'
          MEND
```

write a program to obtain the generated instructions for the following three consecutive macro calls:

```
          GOGET   1,BASE
          SUM     BASE,A,B
          SUM     B,C,D
```

Run your program on a computer. Is it necessary to execute your program, or can you just compile?

PART II

DECIMAL AND FLOATING-POINT PROGRAMMING

In System/370 or System/360, there are four different data formats: fixed-point, floating-point, and two versions of decimal formats. Fixed-point programming was discussed throughout Part I. Part II concentrates on the programming techniques using decimal and floating-point data formats. The two types of decimal formats are described in Chapter 10; and the most common set of decimal instructions is presented in Chapter 11. Chapter 12 deals with the floating-point programming, which is designed primarily for scientific programmers.

Many instructions which we discussed in Part I—such as the logical instructions in Chapter 7—may also be applied to decimal or floating-point programming. Another common area is the macro programming introduced in Chapter 9. Macro facility and its associated conditional assembly language are basically used to extend the assembler language. We can employ them in fixed-point, floating-point, as well as decimal programming.

CHAPTER 10

Decimal Data

10.1 DATA FORMATS

Arithmetic in the System/370 or System/360 may be performed on binary integers, decimal numbers, or floating-point numbers. In Chapter 2, we discussed two types of binary integer data formats associated with fixed-point instructions; they appear either in halfwords (two bytes) or in fullwords (four bytes), as shown in Fig. 10.1. The bit position 0 contains the sign of the binary integer. If the sign bit is a 0, the number is positive; if a 1, the number is negative. The 16-bit or 32-bit numbers are strings of 1's and 0's. A binary integer is represented in the 2's complement notation.

In this chapter, we shall study two types of decimal data formats. One is the character representation of a decimal digit, better known as *unpacked decimal* or *zoned decimal* (Section 10.5); the other is *packed decimal*, or two decimal digits packed into one byte (Section 10.6). This chapter will mainly explore how a piece of fixed-point binary data can be converted to or from the decimal data. This is of

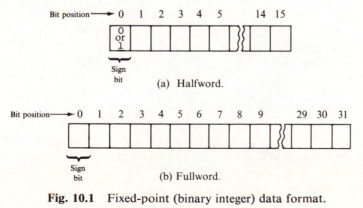

(a) Halfword.

(b) Fullword.

Fig. 10.1 Fixed-point (binary integer) data format.

practical importance, since it is easier to read a decimal answer than a binary result or its hexadecimal equivalent.

10.2 BINARY CODED DECIMAL REPRESENTATION

The individual decimal digits 0–9, alphabetic characters (A–Z), and other special characters (such as $, @, *, etc.) can be represented by a group of binary digits according to some given rules. For example, the alphabetic character E is represented as 010101 in the so-called Standard Binary Coded Decimal (BCD) Code.

In this convention each character is represented by six bits: four numerical bits and two zone bits. In Fig. 10.2, the alphabetic character E is explained in detail in this Standard BCD Code.

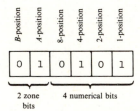

Fig. 10.2   BCD representation of the letter E.

Here, the two zone bits, consisting of the so-called B and A positions, are combined with four numerical bits (called 8-position, 4-position, 2-position, and 1-position, respectively) to represent a numeric, alphabetic, or special character.

The two leftmost bits are called *zone bits* because they correspond to the zone portion of a standard Hollerith coded punched card. The four rightmost numerical bits represent the numerical portion of the punched card. The zone portion of a punched card consists of the uppermost three rows, while the numerical portion consists of rows 0 through 9 (see Fig. 10.3).

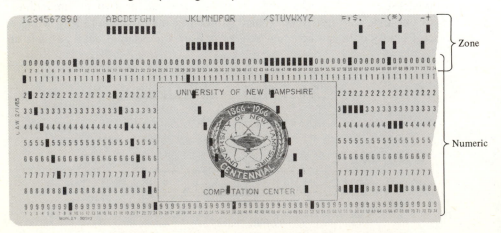

Fig. 10.3   A standard Hollerith coded punched card.

Table 10.1 Standard BCD code

Zone bits				Numerical bits
00	01	10	11	
0	&	—	Blank	0000
1	A	J	/	0001
2	B	K	S	0010
3	C	L	T	0011
4	D	M	U	0100
5	E	N	V	0101
6	F	O	W	0110
7	G	P	X	0111
8	H	Q	Y	1000
9	I	R	Z	1001
	+ or 0	$\bar{0}$	$\ddagger$	1010
= or #	.	$	,	1011
@	◇ or)	*	(or %	1100

Example: K = 100010

A complete Standard BCD Code is shown in Table 10.1. Note that each representation is made of two parts: two zone bits and four numerical bits. When trying to find the BCD representation of a character, say K, the user finds its zone bits first at the top of the column; it is 10. Then he locates its numerical bits at the right of the same row, that is, 0010. Therefore the BCD representation of the alphanumeric character K is 100010.

The BCD representations of 0 through 9, A through R, and S through Z follow logically from the punched card, whereas the special symbols are represented somewhat arbitrarily. Moreover, certain pairs of special characters are represented by the same standard code; for example, both "(" and "%" are presented in BCD as 111100. The printed output for these symbols depends on the typebar used on the printer.

10.3 EXTENDED BCD INTERCHANGE CODE

The standard BCD code discussed in the last section does not differentiate between the upper-case and lower-case alphabetic characters. To overcome this difficulty, the IBM System/370 or System/360 uses the Extended BCD Interchange Code (EBCDIC).

In this code, eight bits are required to represent a character. For example, the upper-case character A and lower case a are represented as shown in Table 10.2.

Let us label the eight bits 0 through 7 from left to right (see Fig. 10.4). The bit positions 0 through 3 are zone bits, and the 4 through 7 bits are numerical bits. Note that there are four possible binary representations in bit positions 0 and 1: 01, 10, 11, and 00. Their meanings are shown in Fig. 10.4.

Similarly, there are four possible binary representations in bit positions 2 and 3,

Table 10.2. Representation of Characters A and a

Character	EBCDIC	Standard BCD
A	11 00 0001	01 0001
a	10 00 0001	Not possible

where 00 indicates A through I; 01, J through R; 10, S through Z; and 11 indicates numerical digits.

The numerical bits (bit positions 4 through 7 in Fig. 10.4) are used in the same way as the ones appearing in the Standard BCD Code. Also, the bit positions 2 and 3 of the Extended BCD Interchange Code are applied in the same manner as the A and B bits in the BCD code, but some differences occur as illustrated in Table 10.3.

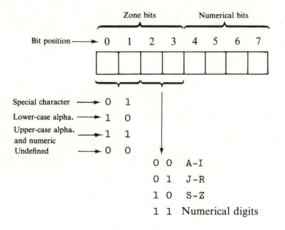

Fig. 10.4 Eight bits for the EBCDIC.

Table 10.3 Bits 2 and 3 in the Extended BCD Interchange Code

Characters to be represented	Bits 2 and 3 in EBCDIC		Positions A and B in BCD	
	2	3	B	A
A–I	0	0	0	1
J–R	0	1	1	0
S–Z	1	0	1	1
Numeric	1	1	0	0

Examples

Character	EBCDIC representation	Hexadecimal equivalent
B	1100 0010	C2
Y	1110 1000	E8
0	1111 0000	F0
2	1111 0010	F2
(blank)	0100 0000	40
d	1000 0100	84

A fairly complete table of character representation in EBCDIC is given in Appendix B.

10.4 AN EXAMPLE—CHARACTER CONVERSION

The purpose of this example is twofold: First, it illustrates the so-called standardization problem in computer industry. For example, a card cannot be listed correctly unless the lister is compatible with the keypunch. Second, to remedy this situation we can write a subroutine, using the important MVI instruction rather extensively.

The IBM 407 lister, bought by XYZ University before the 029 keypunch appeared on the market, lists cards correctly if punched on the 026 keypunch. However, it does not list correctly a number of characters punched on the 029 keypunch so that, for example, ")" punched with it will be listed as "*". As far as simple FORTRAN statements are concerned, the following three characters are affected:

Character as punched on 029 keypunch	(	)	+
Character as listed on 407 lister	)	*	.

a) Write a subroutine CONVER in assembler language to convert a given FORTRAN statement card punched on 029 punch into its equivalents:

	Character punched on 029 punch	(	)	+	Any other characters
Given	Hexadecimal equivalent	4D	5D	4E	
Converted to	Character	%	<	&	No change
	Hexdecimal equivalent	6C	4C	50	

b) Write a main program in a high-level language to read five or more FORTRAN statements punched on 029 punch, and obtain a converted deck of five or more

FORTRAN statements. This deck should list correctly on the 407 lister. List them. A subroutine CONVER is shown in Fig. 10.5. Its logic is fairly straightforward:

```
 LOC   OBJECT CODE    ADDR1 ADDR2  STMT   SOURCE STATEMENT

000000                                1  CONVER  CSECT
                                      2          SAVE  (14,12),,*
000000 47F0 F00C          0000C       3+         B     12(0,15) BRANCH AROUND ID
000004 06                             4+         DC    AL1(6)
000005 C3D6D5E5C5D9                   5+         DC    CL6'CONVER' IDENTIFIER
00000B 00
00000C 90EC D00C          0000C       6+          STM  14,12,12(13) SAVE REGISTERS
                                      7 *  THE ABOVE GENERATED INSTRUCTION ALIGNS ON HALFWORD BOUNDARY.
000010 05C0                           8          BALR  12,0
000012                                9          USING *,12
000012 5841 0000          00000      10          L     4,0(1)             ADDRESS OF CARD INTO REGISTER 4
000016 58A0 C046          00058      11          L     10,=F'80'          INITIALIZE BYTE COUNTER
                                     12 *  EXAMINE THE CARD CHARACTERS
00001A 954D 4000    00000           13  LOOP     CLI   0(4),X'4D'
00001E 4780 C024          00036     14           BE    SUB1
000022 955D 4000    00000           15           CLI   0(4),X'5D'
000026 4780 C02C          0003E     16           BE    SUB2
00002A 954E 4000    00000           17           CLI   0(4),X'4E'
00002E 4780 C034          00046     18           BE    SUB3
000032 47F0 C038          0004A     19           B     COUNTER
                                    20 *  MAKE SUBSTITUTIONS
000036 926C 4000    00000           21  SUB1     MVI   0(4),X'6C'
00003A 47F0 C038          0004A     22           B     COUNTER
00003E 924C 4000    00000           23  SUB2     MVI   0(4),X'4C'
000042 47F0 C038          0004A     24           B     COUNTER
000046 9250 4000    00000           25  SUB3     MVI   0(4),X'50'
00004A 4144 0001          00001     26  COUNTER  LA    4,1(4)             INCREMENT BYTE ADDRESS
00004E 46A0 C008          0001A     27           BCT   10,LOOP            RETURN AFTER 80 COLUMNS
                                    28           RETURN (14,12)
000052 98EC D00C          0000C     29+          LM    14,12,12(13) RESTORE THE REGISTERS
000056 07FE                         30+          BR    14 RETURN
                                    31           END
000058 00000050                     32           =F'80'
```

Fig. 10.5   Assembly listing of subroutine CONVER.

```
C   THE LEFT AND RIGHT PARENTHESES AND THE ASTERISK PUNCHED ON THE 029
C   KEY PUNCH ARE NOT LISTED CORRECTLY BY THE 407 ACCOUNTING MACHINE.
C   THIS PROGRAM EMPLOYS AN ASSEMBLER LANGUAGE SUBROUTINE TO TRANSLATE
C   A FORTRAN LANGUAGE DECK SO THAT IT WILL LIST CORRECTLY ON THE 407.
      DIMENSION CARD(20),CARDS(100,20)
      READ(5,100)N
      WRITE(6,110)N
      DO 40 L=1,N
      READ(5,130)CARD
      WRITE(6,140)CARD
      CALL CONVER(CARD)
      WRITE(7,130)CARD
      DO 40 LL=1,20
      CARDS(L,LL)=CARD(LL)
   40 CONTINUE
      WRITE(6,150)
      WRITE(6,140)((CARDS(I,J),J=1,20),I=1,N)
      STOP
  100 FORMAT(I3)
  110 FORMAT('1THE INPUT DECK CONSISTS OF',I4,' CARDS. THE STATEMENTS AR
     1E AS FOLLOWS.'/)
  130 FORMAT(20A4)
  140 FORMAT(' ',20A4)
  150 FORMAT('1THE CONVERTED STATEMENTS READ AS FOLLOWS IN EBCDIC.'/)
      END
```

Fig. 10.6   FORTRAN main program to call subroutine CONVER.

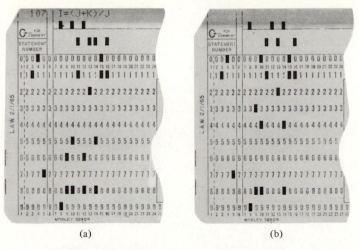

Fig. 10.7   Original and converted cards.

Check input character one at a time to see if it should be replaced. Note that MVI instruction (Section 5.2) has been used exclusively to move a character. The equivalent instructions are presented below.

Instructions used in Fig. 10.5	Their equivalents
MVI 0(4),X'6C'	MVI 0(4),C'%'
MVI 0(4),X'4C'	MVI 0(4),C'<'
MVI 0(4),X'50'	MVI 0(4),C'&'

A main program written in FORTRAN to handle input/output is displayed in Fig. 10.6. After execution, a FORTRAN statement card punched on 029 keypunch (Fig. 10.7a) will be converted into the one shown in Fig. 10.7(b), which should be listed correctly on an IBM 407 lister.

```
 1              MACRO
 2  &NAME       REPL    &OLD,&NEW
 3  .*
 4  .*          THE VALUES FOR OLD AND NEW ARE STANDARD VALUES EACH HAVING
 5  .*          THREE VALUES TO BE CALLED UPON AT VARIOUS TIMES.
 6  .*
 7              LCLA    &LOOP              &LOOP IS DEFINED LOCALLY
 8  &LOOP       SETA    1                  SET &LOOP EQUAL TO 1
 9  .AGAIN      CLI     0(4),X'&OLD(&LOOP)'  TEST FOR &OLD
10              BNE     A&LOOP             IF NOT EQUAL GO TO A&LOOP
11              MVI     0(4),X'&NEW(&LOOP)'  IF &OLD,REPLACE BY &NEW
12              B       NEXT               WHEN CHANGED CHARACTER BRANCH TO NEXT
13  A&LOOP      BCR     0,0                GO TO NEXT STATEMENT
14  &LOOP       SETA    &LOOP+1            &LOOP=&LOOP+1
15              AIF     (&LOOP LE N'&OLD).AGAIN
16  .*
17  .OUT        MEND
```

Fig. 10.8   Macro REPL.

```
18  *
19  *        BEGINNING OF SUBROUTINE
20  *
21  CHGST     CSECT
22            SAVE    (14,12),,*      SAVE REGISTERS
23+           B       10(0,15) BRANCH AROUND ID
24+           DC      AL1(5)
25+           DC      CL5'CHGST' IDENTIFIER
26+           STM     14,12,12(13) SAVE REGISTERS
27            BALR    11,0            BASE REGISTER
28            USING   *,11
29            L       4,0(1)          LOAD 1ST ARGU. PTR. TO STRING INTO R(4)
30            LA      6,79(4)         LOAD ADDRESS OF STRING +79 INTO R(4)
31  *
32  *        CALL MACRO TO TEST CHARACTERS
33  *
34  BEGIN     BCR     0,0             GO TO NEXT STATEMENT
35            REPL    (4D,5D,4E),(6C,4C,50)
36+           CLI     0(4),X'4D' TEST FOR &OLD
37+           BNE     A1 IF NOT EQUAL GO TO A&LOOP
38+           MVI     0(4),X'6C' IF &OLD,REPLACE BY &NEW
39+           B       NEXT WHEN CHANGED CHARACTER BRANCH TO NEXT
40+A1         BCR     0,0 GO TO NEXT STATEMENT
41+           CLI     0(4),X'5D' TEST FOR &OLD
42+           BNE     A2 IF NOT EQUAL GO TO A&LOOP
43+           MVI     0(4),X'4C' IF &OLD,REPLACE BY &NEW
44+           B       NEXT WHEN CHANGED CHARACTER BRANCH TO NEXT
45+A2         BCR     0,0 GO TO NEXT STATEMENT
46+           CLI     0(4),X'4E' TEST FOR &OLD
47+           BNE     A3 IF NOT EQUAL GO TO A&LOOP
48+           MVI     0(4),X'50' IF &OLD,REPLACE BY &NEW
49+           B       NEXT WHEN CHANGED CHARACTER BRANCH TO NEXT
50+A3         BCR     0,0 GO TO NEXT STATEMENT
51  *
52  *        UPDATE IN ORDER TO CHECK NEXT CHARACTER IN STRING
53  *
54  NEXT      LA      4,1(4)          UPDATE ADDRESS OF R(4)
55            CR      6,4             COMPARE R(4) WITH R(6)
56            BNL     BEGIN           IF R(4) IS NOT LESS THAN R(6) GO TO BEGIN
57            RETURN  (14,12)         RETURN TO MAIN
58+           LM      14,12,12(13) RESTORE THE REGISTERS
59+           BR      14 RETURN
60            END
```

Fig. 10.9 Subroutine CHGST calling the macro REPL.

Before concluding this section, we shall examine the subroutine CONVER (Fig. 10.5), in which a certain instruction sequence has been repeated several times. As such, this subroutine is a good candidate for macro calls which we discussed in the last chapter. A macro definition REPL is shown in Fig. 10.8 and the new subroutine CHGST, using the macro calls, is listed in Fig. 10.9.

10.5 DECIMAL DATA—UNPACKED AND PACKED FORMATS

A decimal number can be stored in a System/370 or System/360 in one of two formats: *unpacked* or *packed*. In either case, a piece of decimal data can be from 1 to 16 bytes long; these are the so-called variable-length data.

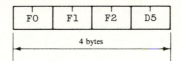

Fig. 10.10　Unpacked format for a negative decimal number -0125.

Let us first consider the unpacked format of a negative decimal number -0125 (see Fig. 10.10). This representation takes four bytes. The leftmost byte containing $(F0)_{16} = (11110000)_2$, representing the numerical digit 0 in the Extended BCD Interchange Code (see Appendix B), which we discussed in Section 10.3. Likewise, the second byte from the left, F1, represents the decimal digit 1. The rightmost byte is a little involved and needs explanation. By convention, this byte is made of two parts: The first four bits indicate the sign of this decimal number, and the rightmost four bits indicate the decimal value of the last digit. In this example, it is $(D5)_{16} = (11010101)_2$, representing $(-5)_{10}$. The four-bit sign code $(\mathcal{S})$ is shown in Table 10.4.

Table 10.4　Four-bit sign code $(\mathcal{S})$ in the unpacked format

First four bits in the rightmost byte		Positive or negative value for the decimal number
Binary	Hexadecimal	
1010	A	$+$
1011	B	$-$
1100	C	$+$
1101	D	$-$
1110	E	$+$
1111	F	$+$

In general, a decimal number, as represented in its unpacked format, is represented in Fig. 10.11, where F represents the four *zone bits* 1111; $\mathcal{D}$ represents the four *numerical bits* in EBCDIC for the decimal digits 0, 1, ., ., ., 9; $\mathcal{S}$ represents the

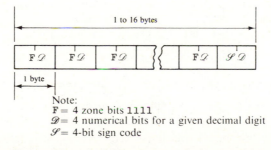

Note:
F = 4 zone bits 1111
$\mathcal{D}$ = 4 numerical bits for a given decimal digit
$\mathcal{S}$ = 4-bit sign code

Fig. 10.11　Unpacked format for a decimal number.

four-bit *sign code*. Because of the presence of the zone bits in each byte except in the rightmost one, the unpacked format is sometimes referred to as *zoned format*.

In order to save on storage space, the System/370 or System/360 uses *packed* format for decimal arithmetic operations. In this format, the first four bits of each byte are not used as zone bits. Instead, two digits are "packed" in each byte. The sign is put in the four rightmost bits. Consider the decimal number -0125 again. Its unpacked format is reproduced in Fig. 10.12(a), while its packed format is shown in Fig. 10.12(b).

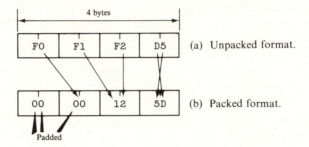

Fig. 10.12   Packed and unpacked representations for a decimal number 0125.

In the packed format, two things stand out. First, the sign bit, namely, D in this example, is located in the rightmost position in the representation. Second, all decimal digits are packed together, two in a byte. Note also that the leftmost three bits in Fig. 10.12(b) are padded with zeros.

In its general form, the packed format can be represented as in Fig. 10.13, where $\mathscr{D}$ represents 0, 1, 2, ..., 9 in numerical bits of EBCDIC; $\mathscr{S}$ the sign code as shown in Table 10.4.

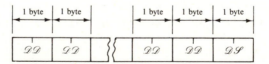

Fig. 10.13   Packed or unzoned format.

10.6 DATA CONVERSION—BINARY TO DECIMAL FOR OUTPUT

We have so far used I-format in FORTRAN, or its equivalent in COBOL and PL/I, to print or punch a binary integer in a main program. Alternatively, we may first convert this binary integer into its unpacked decimal (EBCDIC) equivalent (in an assembler language subroutine). We then print or punch this unpacked piece of data

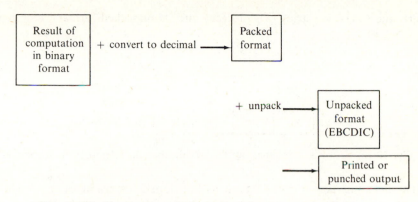

Fig. 10.14   Conversion of binary data into decimal format.

by using, say, an A-format in FORTRAN main program. The conversion is fairly simple and readily accomplished in the following two steps (Fig. 10.14):

1. Convert a binary integer into its decimal equivalent (in packed format). Use the Convert to Decimal (CVD) instruction.
2. Unpack this decimal number. In other words, transform it from the packed format to the unpacked (EBCDIC) format by using the Unpack (UNPK) instruction.

The Convert to Decimal instruction

$$\text{CVD} \quad R1, D2(X2, B2)$$

converts a fullword binary integer in register $R1$ into its packed decimal equivalent. After conversion, the result is stored in a packed field (the second operand), which must be a doubleword and requires doubleword boundary alignment. For example, the instruction

$$\text{CVD} \quad 5, \text{DIGIT}$$

converts the assumed contents in register 5, $(0012D687)_{16}$, into its equivalent packed decimal in the field DIGIT:

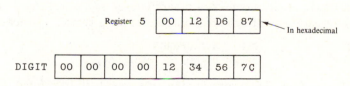

where $(12D687)_{16} = (1234567)_{10}$.

The Unpack (UNPK) instruction transforms a decimal number from the packed format into its unpacked one. For example, the instruction

$$\text{UNPK} \quad \text{GOTO}(4), \text{SOURCE}(3)$$

converts the three-byte string (Fig. 10.15a) into its unpacked format which has four bytes (Fig. 10.15b).

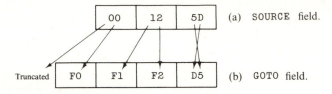

(a) SOURCE field.

(b) GOTO field.

Fig. 10.15   Unpack a decimal number. Note that the leftmost 0 is truncated.

The UNPK instruction is of SS type, as both operands are in main storage. Each operand contains the address and the length (1 to 16 bytes) of the field. Note that some instructions of SS type include *two* length subfields. The UNPK instruction is a notable example, in which the length fields for two operands may be different. Truncation occurs if the length specified in the unpacked field (the second operand) cannot accommodate the expansion. Thus, in Fig. 10.15(a), the leftmost 0 is truncated as length in Fig. 10.15(b) is only four. On the other hand, padding occurs during the execution of the instruction

UNPK TO(4),FROM(2)

as shown in Fig. 10.16. The leftmost byte in TO field is padded with F0.

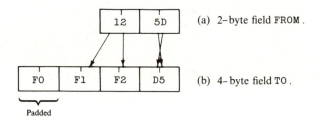

(a) 2–byte field FROM .

(b) 4–byte field TO .

Fig. 10.16   Padding with F0.

To sum up: In order to convert a binary integer, say, in register 5 into EBCDIC (unpacked) format for print or punch output, we use a typical instruction sequence

CVD   5,TWOWORDS
UNPK   FIELDA(9),TWOWORDS(8)

where FIELDA, nine-byte long, contains the results ready to be printed or punched.

10.7 EXAMPLE—BINARY TO DECIMAL FOR OUTPUT

In this section, we shall illustrate the conversion of a binary number to its decimal equivalent by presenting an example of the so-called Indian or Island problem:

Manhattan island was sold by Indians 338 years ago for the amount of $24. We want to write an assembler-language subroutine to determine the total amount today, if a three-percent yearly interest rate is paid.

A main program is used to perform the input/output, and to call the subroutine ISLAND. Figures 10.17, 10.18, and 10.19, respectively, present the main program in FORTRAN, COBOL, and PL/I versions. The necessary computation and conversion is depicted in the flowchart in Fig. 10.20, in which the shaded portion indicates the important conversion from binary integer to decimal. To implement this flowchart

```
C            MANHATTAN ISLAND WAS SOLD 338 YEARS AGO BY THE INDIANS FOR
C                $24. WE WISH TO FIND THE TOTAL AMOUNT TODAY, IF A 3%
C                YEARLY INTEREST RATE IS PAID.
C
             DIMENSION ANS(3)
             WRITE(6,1)
      1      FORMAT (1H1,T64,'OUTPUT'///)
C
C      CALL SUBROUTINE WITH FIXED POINT INSTRUCTUINS
C
             CALL ISLAND(ANS)
             WRITE(6,2) (ANS(I),I=1,3)
      2      FORMAT(10X,'THE FINAL ANSWER IS',3A4)
             CALL EXIT
             END
```

Fig. 10.17   FORTRAN main program to call the subroutine ISLAND.

in assembler language, subroutine ISLAND is written as shown in Fig. 10.21. The computation in the subroutine is performed in fixed-point binary and the result is then converted to decimal.

We shall conclude this section by studying some arithmetic and conversion instructions, used in subroutine ISLAND. To be able to do this we need the contents of some registers. Figure 10.22 shows these contents just before the execution of the following Multiply (M) instruction for the first time.

M   2,RATE   Stored in Register 3†

    (SAVE) × (RATE)
    2400 × 103 | 247200 |

AH   3,ROUND   Stored in Register 3

      247200
  +   50 | 247250 |
    ——————
      247250

† We assume that, after the execution of this Multiply instruction, no carry is going from register 3 to register 2. Register contents are shown in decimal.

```
IDENTIFICATION DIVISION.
PROGRAM-ID.
    'MAIN9'. PROGRAM-NAME.
AUTHOR.
    S. S. KUO.
REMARKS.
    THIS IS A MAIN PROGRAM TO CALL ISLAND.
ENVIRONMENT DIVISION.
CONFIGURATION SECTION.
SOURCE-COMPUTER.
    IBM-360 G50.
OBJECT-COMPUTER.
    IBM-360 G50.
INPUT-OUTPUT SECTION.
FILE-CONTROL.
    SELECT PRINT-FILE ASSIGN TO 'PRINTER' UTILITY.
DATA DIVISION.
FILE SECTION.
FD  PRINT-FILE
    RECORDING MODE IS F
    LABEL RECORDS ARE OMITTED
    DATA RECORDS ARE PRT-LINE.
01  PRT-LINE                    PICTURE X(133).
WORKING-STORAGE SECTION.
01  PRT-LINE-1.
    02  FILLER                  PICTURE X(63) VALUE SPACES.
    02  OUT-PRT                 PICTURE X(6) VALUE 'OUTPUT'.
    02  FILLER                  PICTURE X(64) VALUE SPACES.
01  PRT-LINE-2.
    02  FILLER                  PICTURE X(10) VALUE SPACES.
    02  ANS-PRT                 PICTURE X(20) VALUE
                                'THE FINAL ANSWER IS '.
    02  ANS-1                   PICTURE X(4).
    02  ANS-2                   PICTURE X(4).
    02  ANS-3                   PICTURE X(4).
    02  FILLER                  PICTURE X(91) VALUE SPACES.
01  ANSWER-TABLE.
    02  ANS-ENTRY OCCURS 3 TIMES.
        03  ANS                 PICTURE X(4).
01  SUB                         PICTURE 9 VALUE ZEROS.
PROCEDURE DIVISION.
OPEN-FILES.
    OPEN OUTPUT PRINT-FILE.
    ENTER LINKAGE.
    CALL 'ISLAND' USING ANS (1).
    ENTER COBOL.
MOVING-ROUTINE.
    ADD 1 TO SUB. MOVE ANS (SUB) TO ANS-1.
    ADD 1 TO SUB. MOVE ANS (SUB) TO ANS-2.
    ADD 1 TO SUB. MOVE ANS (SUB) TO ANS-3.
PRINTING.
    WRITE PRT-LINE FROM PRT-LINE-1 AFTER ADVANCING 0 LINES.
    WRITE PRT-LINE FROM PRT-LINE-2 AFTER ADVANCING 0 LINES.
CLOSING.
    CLOSE PRINT-FILE.
    STOP RUN.
```

Fig. 10.18   COBOL main program to call subroutine ISLAND.

```
MANHAT:   PROC OPTIONS(MAIN);
/* PL/I MAIN TO CALL SUBROUTINE ISLAND IN ASSEMBLER LANGUAGE */
DCL ISLAND ENTRY(BIN FIXED(31,0));
DCL AN(3) BIN FIXED(31);
DCL CHARSTR CHAR(12) DEFINED AN;
/* SET UP TITLE FOR OUTPUT PAGE */
PUT PAGE EDIT('OUTPUT')(COLUMN(64),A);
CALL ISLAND(AN(1));
PUT SKIP(4) EDIT('THE FINAL ANSWER IS ',CHARSTR)
                (COL(11),A(20),A(12));
END;
```

Fig. 10.19   PL/I main program to call subroutine ISLAND.

DR   2,9

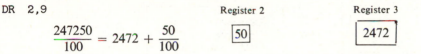

$$\frac{247250}{100} = 2472 + \frac{50}{100}$$

Register 2   Register 3

50   2472

BCT   10,HERE

After the execution of this instruction, the contents of register 10 are first reduced by 1, and then the branch is made to HERE. This branch occurs each time until the contents of register 10 become zero; then the program proceeds to the next sequential instruction.

After 338 loops, the final answer $(52399822)_{10}$ is stored in register 3 as a binary integer. The following instruction converts it from binary to the packed decimal format.

CVD   3,RESULT

Here the answer—computed in binary format and stored in register 3—is converted to packed decimal and placed in an area called RESULT.

When using this instruction, the programmer must make sure that
a) The binary data to be converted are in a register.
b) The area receiving the converted data is a doubleword. (See eight-byte RESULT field in Fig. 10.23a).

UNPK   2(9,6),RESULT+3(5)

This unpack instruction converts the five-byte packed decimal data starting at the location RESULT+3 (see Fig. 10.23a) to the unpacked format. The unpacked data take nine bytes; their starting address equals 2 plus the contents of register 6. This piece of converted data is shown in Fig. 10.23(b). The contents of register 6 are called symbolically ANS.

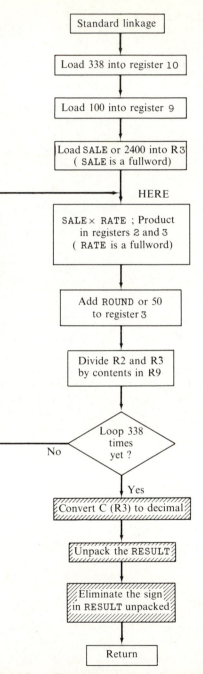

Fig. 10.20 Flowchart for the subroutine ISLAND. Shaded portion indicates the conversion from binary to decimal number.

```
ISLAND      CSECT
            SAVE    (14,12),,*
+           B       12(0,15) BRANCH AROUND ID
+           DC      AL1(6)
+           DC      CL6'ISLAND' IDENTIFIER

+           STM     14,12,12(13) SAVE REGISTERS
            BALR    11,0
            USING   *,11
            L       6,0(1)          LOAD 1ST ARGU. POINTER INTO R(1)
            LA      10,338          SET UP COUNTER
            LA      9,100           LOAD ADDRESS OF 100 INTO R(9)
            L       3,SALE          LOAD AMOUNT OF SALE INTO R(3)
HERE        M       2,RATE          MULT  PERCENT AND AMOUNT OF SALE
            AH      3,ROUND         ADD 50 TO NEW AMOUNT OF SALE
            DR      2,9             ROUNDING OFF NUMBER
            BCT     10,HERE         R(1) -1 IF NOT=0 BRANCH TO HERE
            CVD     3,RESULT        PACKED ANSWER IS PUT INTO RESULT
            UNPK    2(9,6),RESULT+3(5)      UNPACK RESULT
            MVZ     10(1,6),9(6)    REMOVE THE 4 SIGN BITS
            MVC     11(1,6),10(6)   MOVE CHARACTER TO THE RIGHT
            MVC     10(1,6),9(6)    MOVE CHARACTER TO THE RIGHT
            MVI     9(6),C'.'       PLACE A . IN ANSWER
            MVI     0(6),C' '       PLACE A BLANK IN FRONT OF ANSWER
            MVI     1(6),C'$'       PLACE A $ IN ANSWER
            RETURN  (14,12)
+           LM      14,12,12(13) RESTORE THE REGISTERS
+           BR      14 RETURN

SALE        DC      F'2400'
RATE        DC      F'103'
ROUND       DC      H'50'
RESULT      DS      D
            END
```

Fig. 10.21 Subroutine ISLAND.

MVZ 10(1,6),9(6)

This Move Zones instruction eliminates the four sign bits in Fig. 10.23(b). These four bits, represented by $(C)_{16}$, have to be replaced by $(F)_{16}$, four zone-bits. After the execution of this instruction, the four zone-bits are moved from address ANS+9 to the address ANS+10, as shown in Fig. 10.24.

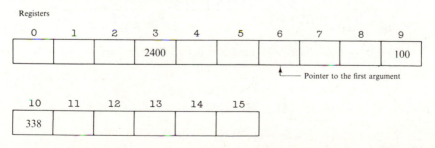

Registers

0	1	2	3	4	5	6	7	8	9
			2400						100

— Pointer to the first argument

10	11	12	13	14	15
338					

Fig. 10.22 Initial contents of registers (in decimal).

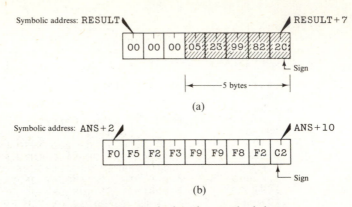

(a)

(b)

Fig. 10.23 Packed and unpacked data.
(a) Packed data in five bytes.
(b) Unpacked data take nine bytes.

The net effect: We now have a string of decimal digits with no sign involved, ready to be printed out as an unsigned decimal number. In general, the MVZ instruction moves the leftmost four bits of *each* byte in the second operand to the corresponding byte in the first operand. It is of SS format with single length (1 to 256 bytes).

A blank, a dollar ($) sign, and a decimal point(.) are then inserted† in the ANS field by using three MVI instructions (see Fig. 10.21). The configuration of this field just before the printing is shown in Fig. 10.25. Figure 10.26 presents the actual output.

Fig. 10.24 Elimination of sign bits.

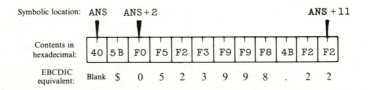

Fig. 10.25 ANS field just before the printing.

OUTPUT

THE FINAL ANSWER IS $0523998.22

Fig. 10.26 Output.

---

† A far easier way to accomplish these insertions will be discussed in Sections 11.4 through 11.7.

10.8 AN INSTRUCTION FOR SYSTEM/370—SHIFT AND ROUND DECIMAL (SRP)

The Shift and Round Decimal (SRP) instruction can shift (right or left) a piece of packed decimal data. It is of SS format (see Fig. 10.27), but has some peculiar features.

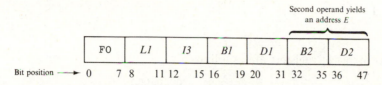

Second operand yields an address E

| FO | L1 | I3 | B1 | D1 | B2 | D2 |

Bit position ⟶ 0   7 8   11 12   15 16   19 20   31 32   35 36   47

Fig. 10.27   Shift and Round decimal instruction. SS format: SRP $D1(L1,B1), D2(B2), I3$

The second operand yields an address $E = D2 + C(B2)$. The rightmost six bits of E are treated as a signed binary integer (see Fig. 10.28). The S-bit indicates the direction of a shift:

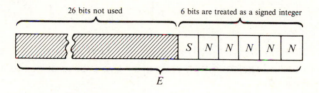

26 bits not used   6 bits are treated as a signed integer

| | S | N | N | N | N | N |

E

Fig. 10.28   Contents of $E = D2 + C(B2)$.

Case 1. $S = 0$ means left shift.
NNNNN (a true binary number) represents the number of digit positions to be shifted. Thus the range of shift is from 0 for no shift, to $+31$ for a maximum left shift.

Case 2. $S = 1$ means right shift.
NNNNN (a binary number in two's complement notation) represents the number of digit positions to be shifted. Thus the range of shift is from 0 for no shift, to -31 for a minimum right shift.

Using this information, the first operand (in the packed decimal form) is shifted. Note that only digit portion (packed-decimal numbers) is shifted, but not its sign. The vacated digit positions are padded with zeros. During the execution of this instruction, the condition code is set as follows:

$$CC = 0 \qquad \text{Result} = 0$$
$$CC = 1 \qquad \text{Result} < 0$$
$$CC = 2 \qquad \text{Result} > 0$$
$$CC = 3 \qquad \text{Overflow to the left only}$$

During the left shift, it is possible to have a significant digit shifted out of the high-order digit position. In this case, a decimal-overflow exception will be issued and the condition code set to 3. However, an overflow to the right does not set the condition code and the numerical characters are lost.

The *I3* field (see Fig. 10.27) is significant only during the right shift. It is a rounding factor; the sum of this factor and the last digit shifted out rounds the shifted operand. Any carry is propagated to the left. Although no rounding is involved in a left shift, a rounding factor must be specified in the third operand.

Example 1

Assume that

1. The contents of registers are as follows:

Register 9   0000A000
Register 8   00000002

2. Packed decimal contents in locations 0000A002 and on are

OOA002

1	3	1	4	1	5	9	2	6	5	3	C

3. The instruction SRP 2(6,9),1(8),0 is given. It is required to find the contents of the first operand and the condition code after the execution of the SRP instruction. We first calculate

$$E = 00000002 + 1 = 3 = (000011)_2$$

Sign bit

Now the sign bit $S = 0$ indicates a left shift. Thus the first operand is required to shift left three digits. After execution of this instruction, the first operand becomes 41592653000C in packed decimal format. (The leftmost three digits 131 are lost.)

The condition code is set to 3 and no rounding is involved.

Example 2

Assume that

a) Contents of registers are as follows:

Register 6   00000002
Register 4   0000B000

b) Packed decimal contents in locations 0000B008 and on are 421529276C.
c) Instruction SPR 8(5,4),60(6),5 is given.

It is required to find the contents of the first operand and the condition code after the execution of the SRP instruction.

Step 1. Calculate E:

$$E = 00000002 + 60 = (62)_{10} = (3E)_{16} = (111110)_2$$

$$\underset{\text{Sign bit}}{\underline{\hspace{1cm}}\uparrow}$$

Thus a right shift of the first operand is required.

Step 2. Find the two's complement of $11110 = (00010)_2 = (2)_{10}$. Thus a right shift of two digits is required. In practice, you can combine steps 1 and 2 by simply looking up Table 10.5. Thus, a decimal value 62 in the second operand of a SRP instruction means a right shift of two places.

Table 10.5 Values of the second operand in a SRP instruction and the places of right shift

Decimal value in the second operand of SRP instruction	Number of places of right shift
63	1
62	2
61	3
60	4
59	5
58	6
57	7
⋮	⋮
50	14
49	15
⋮	⋮
33	31

Step 3. Rounding:

$$
\begin{array}{r}
0042152927 \\
+ \qquad 5 \\
\hline
0042152932
\end{array}
$$

After the execution of this instruction, the first operand becomes 004215293C in packed decimal; the condition code is set to 2.

BIBLIOGRAPHY

IBM System/360 Principles of Operation, Form GA22-6821, IBM Corp.

PROBLEMS

1. Represent 5, 6, Y, S, and @ in the standard BCD code.

2. Which one of the above codes can be used to represent two different characters?

3. Give the EBCDIC representation of the blank character. Mark the zone bits and numerical bits.

4. a) In EBCDIC, the numerical portion of a character uses bits _____ through _____ of a byte; the zone portion uses bits _____ through _____ of a byte.
   b) For the character 7, the EBCDIC is _____.

5. A card has blanks in all columns except

Column	Punched
10	3
11	1
12	4
13	1
14	6 and 12

If the entire card record has been read into main storage, starting at location $(3052)_{10}$, columns 10 through 14 will be in locations _____ through _____.

6. On a logical basis, the character A is less than the character Z, as $1100000 < 11101001$. Compare A and # on logical basis. Which character is greater?

7. a) What are the contents in the doubleword DOUBLE after the execution of the instruction

   CVD   7,DOUBLE

   if the contents in register 7 are 0000D687?
   b) Same as Part (a), except that the contents in register 7 are FFFFFF72.

8. What is the CC setting after the execution of the CLC instruction below?

   D5   07 0 800 0 F00

   Also, the byte locations 2048 through 2055 (in decimal) contain JOHNSTON and the byte locations 3840 through 3847 (in decimal) contain JOHNSON.

9. State the difference, if any, between the zoned format and the unpacked format.

10. If the incoming data are in EBCDIC, a PACK instruction will create a packed decimal data. For example, the following EBCDIC data in ABLE field:

F 1	F 2	F 4	F 6	F 8	$\mathscr{S}$ 3

will be packed and appear in BETA field

2 4	6 8	3 $\mathscr{S}$

by using the following instruction:

```
        PACK   BETA(3),ABLE(6)
```

Both operands are processed from right to left. If the first operand (the packed result) is exhausted before the second operand (the incoming unpacked data), the remaining leftmost digits in the second operand are ignored (as shown above). On the other hand, if the second operand is exhausted before the first, zeros are filled into the remaining leftmost positions in the second operand. What will be stored in the BETA area after the execution of the instruction if the ABLE field is now as follows:

F 6	F 7	F 1	F 3	F 5	C 5

11. The contents of the three-byte field FIELDP are 34627C. After the execution of the instruction

```
        UNPK   ZONED,FIELDP
```

the six-byte field ZONED looks like this:

a) F0F3F4F6F2C7
b) F3F4F6F2F7C0
c) F0F3F4F6F2D7
d) F3F4F6F2F7D0

   Note: Circle the correct expression.

12. a) What are the contents in register 9 after the execution of the instruction

```
        CVB   9,EIGHTBY
```

   if the contents in the eight-byte field EIGHTBY are 000000000061449C in hexadecimal?

   b) Same as (a), except that the contents in EIGHTBY are 000000000061449D.

   Note: The CVB (ConVert to Binary) instruction is the converse of the CVD instruction.

LABORATORY ASSIGNMENT

1. Write a main program in a high-level language to read one card, echo print the card, and call a subroutine in assembler language to convert all apostrophes to minus signs. Return to the main program to print the converted message.

2. In the subroutine ISLAND (Fig. 10.21), we assumed that, after the execution of M instruction, no carry is going from register 3 to register 2. Modify the subroutine to remove this assumption. Run your program with an eight-percent yearly interest rate.

CHAPTER 11

Decimal Programming

11.1 DECIMAL ADDITIONS

In Chapter 10, we discussed the packed and unpacked decimal representations of a number. The packed representation expresses a number from 1 up to 31 digits in such a way that two digits are packed in one byte, except in the last byte where the sign occupies the last digit (see three typical packed numbers in Fig. 11.1). In this chapter, after a short discussion of decimal additions, we shall introduce six important decimal

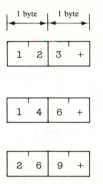

Fig. 11.1 Decimal addition +123 plus +146. (*Note:* The plus sign in the rightmost digit is often represented by the character C.)

arithmetic instructions, all of SS format. We shall then examine two editing instructions which are used primarily by business programmers to make printed output easy to read.

In adding two packed decimal numbers, their signs are first examined. If they agree, the sign is retained and two numbers are added. Consider, for example,

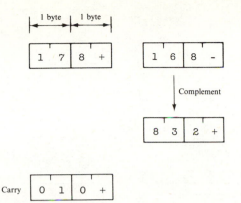

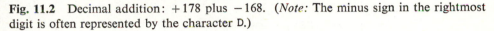

Fig. 11.2 Decimal addition: +178 plus −168. (*Note:* The minus sign in the rightmost digit is often represented by the character D.)

+123 plus +146. As shown in Fig. 11.1, both numbers are expressed in the packed format. They are simply added and the sum is equal to 269+. If, however, the signs are different, the two numbers must be complement added. In other words, the negative number is first complemented and then added to the positive number. Consider, for instance, +178 plus −168. The complement addition is shown in Fig. 11.2. There is a carry from the leftmost digit of the result 010+. As a result, this is the true answer.

By contrast, if there is no carry in the result, then it is not the true answer, but a complement answer. Consider, for example, +125 plus −261 (see Fig. 11.3). The answer 864 is only a complement answer. In order to produce the true answer −136, it must be recomplemented and its sign changed.

Note that the result of a decimal addition replaces the contents of the first operand.

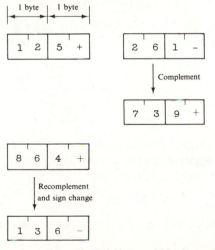

Fig. 11.3 Decimal addition: +125 plus −261.

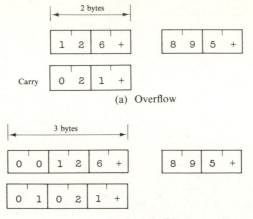

(a) Overflow

(b) No overflow

Fig. 11.4   Decimal addition: + 126 plus + 895.

If the number of bytes required by the result is greater than that provided by the first operand, the leftmost digits are lost, thus causing a decimal overflow. Consider, for example, the decimal addition +126 plus +895, as shown in Fig. 11.4(a). Since the result requires more than two bytes, an overflow occurs. To correct this situation, we have to provide three bytes in the first operand to obtain the result, as shown in Fig. 11.4(b), thus the undesirable overflow is prevented.

Before turning to the decimal arithmetic instructions in the next section, we shall discuss how a DC assembler instruction can define a packed decimal number. The DC instruction

CONST1   DC   PL6'1206'

defines a packed decimal number, six bytes long (see Fig. 11.5). A sign zone C is first stored in the rightmost four bits. The data are then defined, four bits at a time,

| 0 | 0 | 0 | 0 | 0 | 0 | 0 | 1 | 2 | 0 | 6 | C |

Fig. 11.5   Six-byte field for a packed decimal.

from right to left. The packed zeros are used to fill in the remaining bytes until the resulting area has the required length, or six bytes in total. As another example, let us consider the following DC instruction:

CONST2   DC   PL3'−316'

which defines a three-byte field (see Fig. 11.6), in which the last digit D indicates a minus sign.

Each of the above two DC instructions uses an explicit length (six and three bytes,

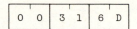

Fig. 11.6　Three-byte field for a negative packed number.

respectively). As mentioned in Section 6.10, the assembler picks up the implied length attribute of a symbol unless it is overruled by an explicit indication.

11.2 DECIMAL ARITHMETIC INSTRUCTIONS

There are eight basic instructions used in the decimal programming: six arithmetic and two editing instructions. In this section, we shall discuss the following six arithmetic instructions of SS format:†

ZAP	Zero and Add Packed
AP	Add Packed
SP	Subtract Packed
CP	Compare Packed
MP	Multiply Packed
DP	Divide Packed

In each instruction, two operands are used and each contains a packed number. Also, each of the two operands used in the first four instructions is from one to sixteen bytes in length. Consider, for example, the Add Packed (AP) instruction

$$AP\quad 200(4,7),800(3,7)$$

where the length fields for the two operands are four and three, respectively. If register 7 contains a base address $(1000)_{10}$, then this instruction adds a three-byte packed decimal field at decimal address 1800 to a four-byte packed field at a byte address $(1200)_{10}$. The sum is stored in the four-byte field, as shown in Fig. 11.7. The above instruction may also be written as

$$AP\quad DATA4,DATA3$$

where DATA4 and DATA3 are two defined symbols to represent the four-byte and the three-byte fields, respectively. If we wish to add only two rightmost bytes in the DATA3 field to the entire DATA4 field, we can use the following instruction:

$$AP\quad DATA4,DATA3+1(2)$$

where 2 denotes the length of the second operand.

The subtract Packed (SP) instruction is used in the same way as the AP instruction. Assume that DATA4 and DATA3 represent the two data fields shown on the top two lines in Fig. 11.7. The following instruction

$$SP\quad DATA4,DATA3+1(2)$$

---

† No arithmetic instructions involving *unpacked* decimal numbers are available.

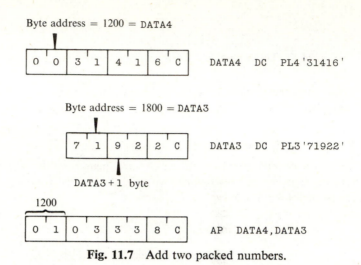

Fig. 11.7 Add two packed numbers.

first computes the difference $31416 - 922 = 30494$, and stores it in the DATA4 field. The final configuration in DATA4 field is 0030494C in packed decimal format.

The Zero and Add Packed (ZAP) instruction moves a packed decimal number from a field of 1 to 16 bytes into another field of 1 to 16 bytes; the lengths of the two fields may be different. Consider, for instance, two fields, F3 and F2, as shown in Fig. 11.8(a).

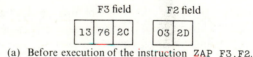

(a) Before execution of the instruction ZAP F3,F2.

(b) After execution.

Fig. 11.8 Contents in two fields F3 and F2.

Figure 11.8(b) presents the contents in these two fields after the execution of the instruction

ZAP F3,F2

The substantial effect of this instruction is that all bytes in F3 field are first cleared; the contents of the F2 field, or 032D, are then moved to the F3 field. As a common practice, this instruction is often used to establish a longer field, so that any possible overflow can be avoided.

We often apply the ZAP instruction jointly with a Multiply Packed (MP) instruction, which we shall now discuss.

As with the five other decimal arithmetic instructions, the MP instruction uses the SS format:

$$\text{MP} \quad D1(L1,B1), D2(L2,B2)$$

In a typical example such as

    MP   SALE,RATE

the first and second operands contain respectively the multiplicand SALE and the multiplier RATE. As a rule, the second operand cannot contain more than eight bytes, but the first operand can. Since the product is to be stored in the first operand, the length of the first operand must be carefully planned so that some zero digits are placed in its leftmost positions. The number of such zero digits must be at least equal to that of decimal and sign digits in the multiplier. For simplicity, the required length of the first operand may be obtained by adding the length of the multiplicand (SALE) and that of the multiplier (RATE).

A practical way to avoid the possible overflow is to first set up a product field, and then use the ZAP and MP instructions jointly. A possible sequence of instructions to compute the product of ALPHA × BETA is shown in Fig. 11.9. We note that a

```
        ZAP     PROD,ALPHA
        MP      PROD,BETA
        ZAP     GAMMA,PROD
                 .
                 .
                 .
ALPHA   DC      PL6'1206'       0 0  0 0  0 0  0 1  2 0  6 C
BETA    DC      PL3'074'                         0 0  0 7  4 C
GAMMA   DC      PL9'0'
PROD    DC      PL9'0'
```

Fig. 11.9   Joint usage of ZAP and MP instructions.

product area PROD is first established; then the multiplicand ALPHA is moved in the PROD field. After the execution of the MP instruction, the product remains in the PROD field, which is then stored in the GAMMA field.

We shall now discuss the Divide Packed (DP) instruction:

$$\text{DP} \quad \underbrace{D1(L1,B1)}_{\text{Dividend}}, \underbrace{D2(L2,B2)}_{\text{Divisor}}$$

The first operand is the dividend and the second, the divisor. The divisor cannot be longer than eight bytes (15 hexadecimal digits and a sign);† no such restriction is imposed on the dividend. After the execution of the DP instruction, the answers (quotient and remainder) replace the dividend in the first operand. Their signs and

---

† Another restriction: The length of the divisor cannot be greater than or equal to that of the dividend. If violated, it causes a specification exception and the program is interrupted.

Table 11.1 Signs and lengths of the quotient and the remainder

	Quotient	Remainder
Resulting length	Length of dividend − length of divisor	Same as that of divisor
Sign	Follow rule of algebra from the signs of the dividend and divisor.	Same as dividend (even when remainder = 0)
Remarks	If alloted length is not sufficient, decimal divide exception will occur.	Length cannot be greater than 8 bytes.

lengths are listed in Table 11.1. The quotient is placed leftmost; and the remainder, rightmost in the first operand.

In practice, an area for the quotient and the remainder (QR) is first established; its length is equal to the sum of the length of the dividend and that of the divisor. Figure 11.10 shows a typical example, in which the length of the dividend and that of divisor are assumed to be four and three respectively.

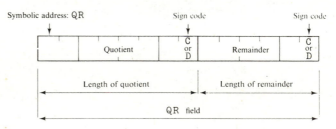

Fig. 11.10   Establishment of a QR field.

A ZAP instruction is used to move the four-byte dividend into the rightmost bytes of the QR field (see Fig. 11.11). After the execution of the DP instruction, the quotient and the remainder are stored in the QR field.

We shall conclude this section by discussing the CP instruction, which is used to compare two packed decimal data *algebraically*. As with the Add Packed or Subtract Packed instruction, the maximum field length for either operand is 16 bytes. If two data fields are of different lengths, the shorter field is internally padded with high-order zeros just for comparison.

The basic function of a CP instruction is to set the condition code according to the outcome of the comparison, as shown in Table 11.2. Consider, for example, the ALPHA and BETA fields as shown in Fig. 11.9. After the execution of the instruction

        CP   ALPHA,BETA

the condition code is set to 10 in binary.

```
        ZAP     QR,UP
        DP      QR,DOWN
                  .
                  .
                  .
UP      DC      PL4'40'     UP IS DIVIDEND
DOWN    DC      PL3'12'     DOWN IS DIVISOR
QR      DC      PL7'0'      QR IS AREA FOR QUOTIENT AND REMAINDER
```

Fig. 11.11 Joint usage of ZAP and DP instructions.

Table 11.2 Condition code setting for a CP instruction

CP A,B	CC setting (in binary)
A = B†	00
A < B	01
A > B	10

† (+0) compares equal to a (−0).

11.3 EXAMPLE—DECIMAL PROGRAMMING

In Section 10.7, the so-called Indian or Island problem was programmed in fixed-point binary instructions; the binary answer was then converted to an unpacked decimal answer. The subroutine to perform this computation was shown in Fig. 10.21. For comparison, we shall now solve this problem using the decimal programming, making the binary–decimal conversion unnecessary. Figures 11.12 and 11.13 show, respectively, a possible subroutine in decimal programming and its answer. Any one of the three main programs in Figs. 10.17 through 10.19 on pages 291–293 can be used to call the subroutine ISLAND in its new version of decimal programming (see Fig. 11.12). In this subroutine, we introduce a new MoVe Numerics (MVN) instruction:

$$\text{MVN   RESULT+5(1),RESULT+6}$$

which needs some explanation. The principal purpose of an MVN instruction is to move the sign of a packed decimal number. It moves the rightmost four bits of each byte in the second operand to the corresponding positions in the first operand, leaving the leftmost four bits unchanged. For example, consider the original contents of the seven-byte RESULT field, as shown in Fig. 11.14(a). After the execution of this MVN instruction, the contents of the RESULT field are changed (see Fig. 11.14b).

There is also another important Move instruction often used in connection with decimal operation: the MoVe with Offset (MVO) instruction of SS format which moves a piece of packed data. It takes every half-byte in the second operand and places it in the first operand *offset to the left* by a half-byte. As a result, the sign of the first operand is not disturbed. If the first operand is longer than the second operand, then the leftmost digits in the first operand are filled with zeros. Consider, for example,

```
ISLAND    CSECT
          SAVE    (14,12),,*      MACRO TO SAVE REGISTERS
+         B       12(0,15) BRANCH AROUND ID
+         DC      AL1(6)
+         DC      CL6'ISLAND' IDENTIFIER

+         STM     14,12,12(13) SAVE REGISTERS
          BALR    11,0            BASE REGISTERS
          USING   *,11
          L       5,0(1)          LOAD 1ST ARGU. LIST INTO R(5)
          MVC     COUNTER,C338    SET UP COUNTER TO EQUAL 338
          ZAP     RESULT,SALE     LOAD AMOUNT OF SALE
LOOP      MP      RESULT,RATE     MULT. RATE AND AMOUNT OF SALE
          AP      RESULT,ROUND    ROUND OFF NUMBER
          MVN     RESULT+5(1),RESULT+5    MOVE THE SIGN OF PACKED DECIMAL
          ZAP     RESULT,RESULT(6)        ADD ZEROS ON LEFT
          SP      COUNTER,ONE     SUBT. ONE FROM COUNTER
          BP      LOOP            BRANCH TO LOOP
          UNPK    2(9,5),RESULT   UNPACK THE RESULT    IN 5 BYTES
          MVZ     10(1,5),9(5)    ELIMINATE THE SIGN
          MVC     11(1,5),10(5)   MOVE CHARACTER TO THE RIGHT
          MVC     10(1,5),9(5)    MOVE CHARACTER TO THE RIGHT
          MVI     9(5),C'.'       PUT A . IN THE ANSWER
          MVI     0(5),C' '       PUT A SPACE IN FRONT OF NUMBER
          MVI     1(5),C'$'       PUT A $ IN THE ANSWER
          RETURN  (14,12)         RETURN TO MAIN PROGRAM
+         LM      14,12,12(13) RESTORE THE REGISTERS
+         BR      14 RETURN
COUNTER   DS      PL2
C338      DC      PL2'338'
RESULT    DS      PL7
SALE      DC      PL3'2400'
RATE      DC      PL2'103'
ROUND     DC      PL2'50'
ONE       DC      PL1'1'
          END
```

Fig. 11.12 Subroutine ISLAND (version 2) using decimal programming. Version 1 was shown in Fig. 10.21 using fixed-point programming.


```
                THE FINAL ANSWER IS $0523998.22
```

Fig. 11.13 Output from the subroutine ISLAND, as shown in Fig. 11.12, and its main program.

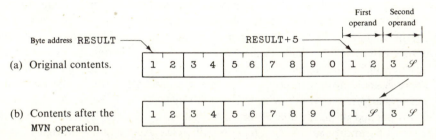

Fig. 11.14 Contents of the RESULT field before and after the execution of the instruction MVN RESULT+5(1),RESULT+6.

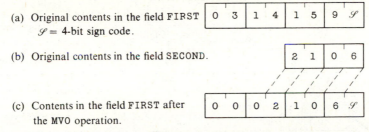

(a) Original contents in the field FIRST
$\mathscr{S}$ = 4-bit sign code.

(b) Original contents in the field SECOND.

(c) Contents in the field FIRST after
the MVO operation.

Fig. 11.15 Contents in the fields FIRST and SECOND before and after the instruction
MVO   FIRST,SECOND.

the FIRST and SECOND fields shown in Figs. 11.15(a) and 11.15(b), respectively. After
execution of the instruction

                    MVO   FIRST,SECOND

the contents in the field FIRST are changed as shown in Fig. 11.15(c), while the
contents in the field SECOND remain unchanged.

11.4 EDIT FEATURES IN DECIMAL PROGRAMMING†

In the preceding sections, we studied six decimal arithmetic instructions. We shall
now discuss two additional ones—the EDit (ED) and the EDit and MarK (EDMK)
instruction. Their principal purposes are (1) to insert proper punctuations such as
commas, decimals, or $ signs in a decimal field, and (2) to suppress leading zeros.
For example, after inserting a $ sign in the front, and two commas and a decimal point
in their proper places, a decimal field 124907107 is edited as $1,249,071.07.

In an Editing operation, two fields in the main storage area are involved: the
source field and the pattern field (see Fig. 11.16). The former field contains the packed
data to be edited, while the latter, *designed by a programmer*, is used to prescribe the
editing requirements. A typical EDit instruction is as follows:

                    ED   PATTRN,SOURCE

Each digit in the SOURCE field is fetched and examined, and the edited result is stored
in the PATTRN field.

Let us first examine the pattern field. Each digit in the pattern field (Fig. 11.16c)
may contain any character in EBCDIC; but there are four special control characters
which are frequently used to dictate the editing details.

1. Fill character, either a blank or an "*" is most commonly used.

2. Digit selector character, "d", or X'20'.

3. Significance start character, "(", or X'21'.‡

4. Field separator character, ")", or X'22'.

---

† Sections 11.4 through 11.9 may be skipped in the first reading.

‡ Note that the significant start character and field separator character are represented by
special characters. They are not parentheses in EBCDIC.

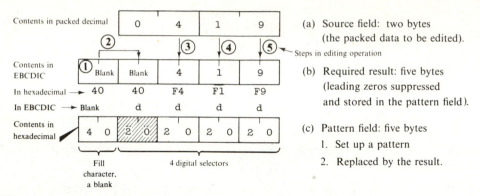

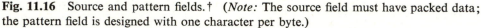

(a) Source field: two bytes
(the packed data to be edited).

Steps in editing operation

(b) Required result: five bytes
(leading zeros suppressed
and stored in the pattern field).

(c) Pattern field: five bytes
1. Set up a pattern
2. Replaced by the result.

Fill character, a blank

4 digital selectors

Fig. 11.16 Source and pattern fields.† (*Note:* The source field must have packed data; the pattern field is designed with one character per byte.)

All EBCDIC characters, excluding the last three control characters mentioned above, are called the *message characters*; the most commonly used ones are ",", ".", C, and R. Note that the fill character is a message character.

In the remaining part of this section, we shall discuss the fill character and the digit selector character, leaving the discussion of the other two special control characters for the next two sections.

In a pattern field, the leftmost byte, commonly represented by an X'40' (a blank in EBCDIC), is automatically taken as the *fill character*. The *digit selector character* can appear anywhere in the pattern field except in the leftmost byte. It is represented by a X'20', or "d" in EBCDIC. Note that the pattern field is designed by a programmer to suit a particular output need. Once designed, it is kept in the main storage as an constant. For example, the pattern field designed in Fig. 11.16(c) can be readily defined by the following DC instruction:

PATTRN   DC   X'4020202020'

In an editing operation, the pattern field is scanned from left to right. As the first step, the leftmost byte in the pattern field is automatically taken as the fill character. The editing continues by checking the character just to the right of the fill character in the pattern field. If a digit selector character (d or X'20') is encountered, go to the source field and fetch a source digit (from left to right) and observe the following general rule:

1. *If the source digit encountered is a zero, the fill character replaces the digit selector character* d.

2. *If the source digit examined is not a zero, then it replaces the digit selector character.*

---

† Figures 11.16, 11.18 through 11.23, and 11.25 are aligned to make reading easier. As a result, the following fact may not have been reflected: The source field is in packed decimal, while the pattern field is designed with one character per byte.

The editing operation then continues by checking the next character in the pattern field, and by following the same rule.

Example 1

Given: The source field and the pattern field are shown, respectively, in Figs. 11.16(a) and 11.16(c).

Required: Step-by-step description to get the edited result (see Fig. 11.16b), which replaces the original contents in the pattern field designed by a programmer.

Solution

Step 1. The leftmost character in the pattern field (a blank or X'40') is taken as the fill character. (*Note*: Each step number is shown in a circle in Fig. 11.16.)

Step 2. a) The second character (from the left) in the pattern field is examined. It is a digit selector character (d or X'20').
   b) Fetch and examine the leftmost digit in the source field; it is a zero digit.
   c) As a result of the rule described above, the second character (from the left) in the pattern field (the shaded digit in Fig. 11.16c) is replaced by the fill character, a blank.

Step 3. a) The third character in the pattern field is examined; it is d.
   b) Fetch and examine the second digit (from the left) in the source field; it is 4 in packed decimal.
   c) Following the rule, the third character (from the left) in the pattern field is replaced by 4 (automatically in unpacked decimal).

Step 4. a) The fourth character (from the left) in the pattern is examined; it is d.
   b) Fetch and examine the third digit in the source field; it is 1.
   c) The fourth character in the pattern is replaced by 1.

Step 5. a) The rightmost character in the pattern is examined; it is d.
   b) Fetch and examine the rightmost digit in the source field; it is 9.
   c) The rightmost character in the pattern is replaced by 9.

At this point, the editing operation stops as there is no more character left in the pattern field. The net effect of this editing: The leading zero in the source field is suppressed.

Note that the source field must be given in the packed decimal format. Whenever a source digit is replacing the associated digit selector character in the pattern field, it is unpacked into a zoned decimal byte by attaching a zone $(1111)_2$ or $(F)_{16}$. This is shown in Fig. 11.17. For example, if a source digit 4 is fetched to replace a digit selector character, the edited result in the pattern field is F4 in hexadecimal. The last digit in the source field shown in Fig. 11.17 is a sign digit. The editing of a sign digit will be discussed in Section 11.6.

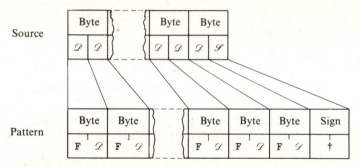

† In the edited result, the sign code specified in the source field usually
becomes either blank (for +) or characters CR (for −).

Fig. 11.17   Packed data are changed to zoned decimal as the edited result.

Example 2

Given: The seven-byte pattern field X'40202020202020'.

(Given) Three-byte source field (six digits)	Edited result in the pattern field	
	in hexadecimal	in EBCDIC
324759	40F3F2F4F7F5F9	⬜324759
003247	404040F3F2F4F7	⬜⬜⬜3247
000032	4040404040F3F2	⬜⬜⬜⬜⬜32
000000	40404040404040	⬜⬜⬜⬜⬜⬜⬜

We see from this example that all leading zeros in each source field are eliminated.

Example 3

Given: The five-byte pattern field X'5C20202020'.

(Given) Two-byte source field (four digits)	Edited result in the pattern field	
	in hexadecimal	in EBCDIC
3247	5CF3F2F4F7	*3247
0324	5C5CF3F2F4	**324
0003	5C5C5C5CF3	****3
0000	5C5C5C5C5C	*****

Note that the fill character used in this example is X'5C', or *.

11.5 SIGNIFICANCE TRIGGER

Having discussed the fill character and the digit selector character in the preceding section, we shall now study a "memory" device in the system, the so-called significance trigger or simply the S-trigger, which plays an important rôle in carrying out an Edit operation. The S-trigger can be set to one of two states: 0 or 1. At the beginning of any edit operation, the S-trigger is automatically set to 0. *As long as the S-trigger is 0, each digit selector character in the pattern field is replaced with the fill character.* On the other hand, *if the S-trigger contains 1, the digit selector character in the pattern field is replaced with the source digit fetched.*

The S-trigger is automatically set to 1 right after either of the following two conditions is met:

1. A nonzero digit—a significant digit—is fetched from the source field.
2. A significant start character—X'21' or "(" in EBCDIC—appears in the pattern field.

The first condition is illustrated in Fig. 11.18. The nonzero digit in the source field appears for the first time in the third digit from the left. The S-trigger is set to 1 (or turned on) right after this nonzero digit is detected, and remains as 1 (see Fig. 11.18c).

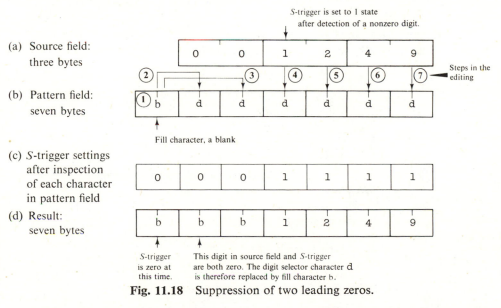

Fig. 11.18 Suppression of two leading zeros.

When the S-trigger is turned on (1-state), a zero digit fetched from the source field will not be suppressed. Rather, it will be expanded into a packed decimal character (X'F0') to replace the digit selector character (d or X'20') in the pattern field. The following example shows that any zero digit to the right of first significant digit in the source field will not be suppressed.

Example 1

Given: a) Source field: 001049 (three bytes)
   b) Pattern field: ⌷dddddd in EBCDIC, or XL7'40202020202020' in hexadecimal (seven bytes)

Required:

   a) The S-trigger setting after scanning each character in the pattern field.
   b) The edited result to replace the pattern field.

Solution

   a) The S-trigger setting right after each character in pattern field is inspected:

$$0001111$$

   b) The edited result is as follows:

In EBCDIC	In hexadecimal
⌷⌷⌷1049	404040F1F0F4F9
(not ⌷⌷⌷1⌷49)	(not 404040F140F4F9)

Before we illustrate the second condition stated in the preceding page, it is important to know that the significance start character ("(" or X'21' used in a pattern field) is a glorified digital selector character d. It acts in every way like a digital selector character, but it also turns on the S-trigger.

Let us now illustrate the application of the second condition by focusing the third character (from the left) in the pattern field shown in Fig. 11.19(b). It is detected

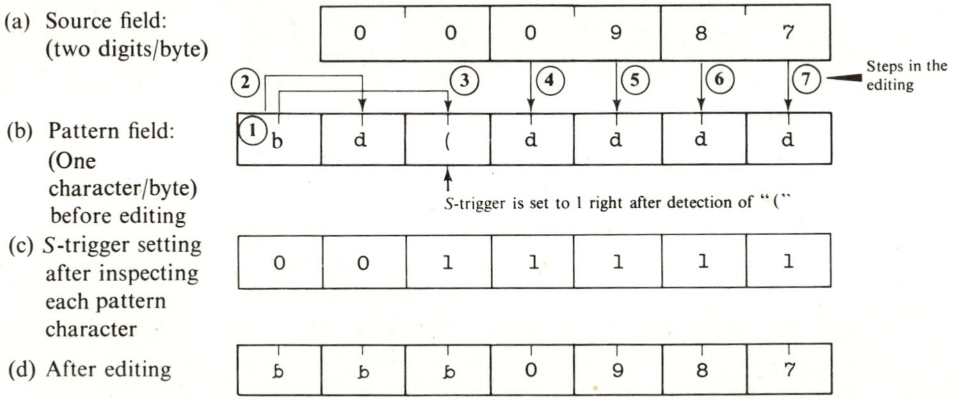

Fig. 11.19   Application of a significant start character (.

as "(", a significant start character. Since it functions basically as a "d", this character is replaced by the fill character (see Fig. 11.19d). Also, the detection of the character "(" turns on the S-trigger; this is shown in Fig. 11.19(c).

The editing continues by scanning the fourth character (from the left) in the pattern field. As shown in Fig. 11.19(b), it is a digit selector character. Note that the

S-trigger is in 1-state and, as a result, the zero digit (the third digit from the left) now fetched from the source field (see Fig. 11.19a) is not suppressed. Rather, a zero character is stored in the pattern field as shown in Fig. 11.19(d).

We see now that a zero digit in the source field is not suppressed if the *S*-trigger is turned on. In addition, whenever the *S*-trigger is turned on, any message character, including a comma ("," or X'6B') or a period ("." or X'4B'), designed in the pattern field remains undisturbed. On the other hand, if *S*-trigger is turned off (0-state), any message character in the pattern field will be replaced by the fill character.

We also see that the total number of the digital selector characters "d" plus that of the significance start characters "(" specified in the pattern field must be equal to the number of digits used in the source field. In Fig. 11.19, for example, we have

Number of "d" designed in pattern field: 5
Number of "(" designed in pattern field: 1 +
—————
Number of digits specified in source field: 6

If the number of digits in the source field is, say, eight, then the last two digits are lost (not fetched).

Example 2

Given: The pattern field contains XL11'402020206B2020204B2020' or the 11-character field ⌷ddd,ddd.dd in EBCDIC.

Required: (1) The edited result and (2) the state of *S*-trigger *after* the detection of each pattern character, for each of the four source fields indicated.

(Given) Source field	Edited result (in EBCDIC) stored in the pattern field: ⌷ddd,ddd.dd	*S*-trigger configuration after the inspection of a character in the pattern: ⌷ddd,ddd.dd
03140592	⌷⌷31,405.92	00111111111
00140592	⌷⌷⌷1,405.92	00011111111
00040592	⌷⌷⌷⌷⌷405.92	00000111111
00000092	⌷⌷⌷⌷⌷ ⌷⌷⌷⌷92	00000000011

11.6 EDITING A SIGN DIGIT

In the previous two sections, we discussed three special control characters used in a pattern field: the fill character commonly represented by a blank or a "*", the digit selector character "d", and the significance start character "(". We have also learned that an *S*-trigger controls the rightmost limit of zero and punctuation suppression.

Note that all source fields illustrated so far in the various examples do not involve a sign digit. This has been deliberately done for the sake of simplicity. In practice, the

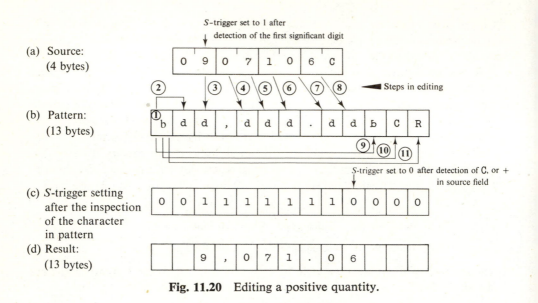

Fig. 11.20 Editing a positive quantity.

rightmost digit in a source field often contains a sign digit as, for example, shown in Fig. 11.20(a). During editing, we would like to eliminate a plus sign digit (A, C, E, or F). On the other hand, if a minus sign digit (B or D) is detected, it is customary to insert the characters CR. We shall now explore this phase of editing.

As we mentioned in the previous two sections, if a digit selector character "d" is detected in the pattern field, a source digit is fetched. This source digit may be either the left one or the right one of a byte in the source field. If this digit is a left one, the following check is automatically made: Is the right digit of the same byte a sign digit (e.g., C or D) or not.

Case 1. The right digit is not a sign digit.

This is the case we discussed so far in the previous two sections. The net results are:

a) The right digit in this source byte is the next one to be fetched.
b) *S*-trigger remains undisturbed.

Case 2. The right digit contains a plus sign (e.g., C).

a) The *S*-trigger is set to 0 (turned off).
b) The next digit to be fetched from the source field is the left digit of the next byte (if any).

Case 3. The right digit contains a minus sign (e.g., D).

a) The *S*-trigger stays undisturbed.
b) The next digit to be fetched from the source field is the left digit from the next byte (if any). *Note:* A minus sign code has no effect on the *S*-trigger.

Example 1

Given: The source field, containing a positive quantity, is shown in Fig. 11.20(a). The pattern field, designed by a programmer, is shown in Fig. 11.20(b). To improve the readability of the output, two possible types of editing are suggested: (a) to insert a comma and a decimal point; and (b) to eliminate the leading and trailing zeros as well as the plus sign (see Fig. 11.20d).

Required: The edited result and the S-trigger settings after the examination of each character in the pattern field.

Solution

Let us focus our attention on the rightmost byte of the source field. As the rightmost digit selector character "d" (the tenth character from the left) is scanned in the pattern field, the left digit of the rightmost source byte (a digit 6) is fetched. At the same time, the right digit in the same source byte is searched for a sign digit. It does contain a sign digit C. As a result, the S-trigger is automatically set from 1 to 0 (see Fig. 11.20c). Any message character (including C and R) encountered in the remainder of the pattern field will be replaced by the fill character. The edited result is shown in Fig. 11.20(d).

Example 2

Same as Example 1, except that the source field contains a negative quantity, $-9,071.06$. The source field is shown in Fig. 11.21(a), which contains a sign digit D. The pattern field is identical to the one shown in Fig. 11.20(b).

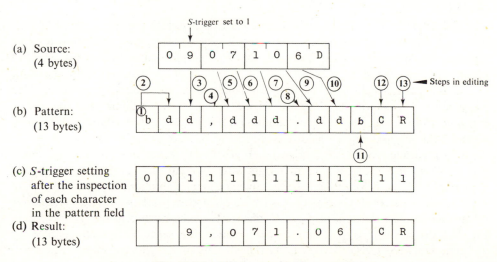

Fig. 11.21   Editing a negative quantity.

Solution

Let us again concentrate on the rightmost byte of the source byte. As the last digit selector character "d" is inspected in the pattern field, the left digit of the last source byte (a digit 6) is fetched. Also, the right digit in the same byte is checked to see if it is a sign digit. It is a D which has no effect on the S-trigger. As a result, all message characters, including the characters C and R are not disturbed and are retained in the edited result (see Fig. 11.21d).

In summary, the S-trigger plays an important role in editing a sign digit. Assuming that

a) the S-trigger is 1, and
b) the sign digit is detected,

we then have the following two cases:

Case 1. The sign digit is positive: The fill character is propagated through the remainder of the pattern field.

Case 2. The sign digit is negative: The remainder of the pattern field remain undisturbed.

11.7 FIELD SEPARATOR CHARACTER

As mentioned before, the EBCDIC characters used in a pattern field may be divided into two groups. The first group consists of the three special control characters: digit selector character "d", significant start character "(", and the field separator character ")". The second group is formed by the remaining EBCDIC characters, known as the message characters. In this section we shall discuss the field separator character: ")" or X'22'.

Basically, the field separator character is used to reset the S-trigger to 0; it is then replaced by a fill character. As a result, the whole editing operation may be repeated for an adjacent field. Consider, for example, the source field in Fig. 11.22(a) which contains two adjacent fields. On the detection of the field separator character ")" in the pattern field (Fig. 11.22b), the S-trigger is automatically set to 0. The character ")" is then replaced by the original fill character, a blank, and the editing continues for the next field whose contents are 0000107D. The edited result which replaced the original pattern field is given in Fig. 11.22(d).

In this editing process, the S-trigger changes its state three times. In the beginning, it is set to 0. It is then changed to 1 right after the detection of the first significant digit in the source field. When the significance start character "(" (byte 00C807 in Fig. 11.22b) is detected, the S-trigger is already in 1-state, and as a result, no action is taken. Right after the detection of ")" character in the pattern field (byte 00C80D in Fig. 11.22b), the S-trigger is changed to 0. Finally, it is set to 1 after detection of the "(" character in byte 00C813 in the pattern field. The state of S-trigger *after* the inspection of each digit in the pattern field is shown in Fig. 11.22(c).

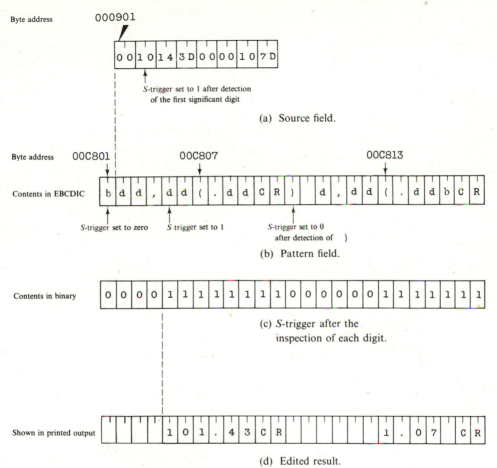

Fig. 11.22   Edit a multiple adjacent field.

We see now that *S*-trigger plays an important role in an editing operation. It controls the following four editing details:

1. Suppression of leading zeros.
2. Indication of a sign.
3. Suppression of some punctuation characters designed in the pattern.
4. Recognition of a multifield.

For convenience, we summarize the two states of the *S*-trigger in Fig. 11.23. The *S*-trigger is set to 0 at the beginning of an editing operation. The ways how to change its state and other important details a beginner should know are also listed on the next page.

State	Each condition will reset *to* this state (if not already so)	Important actions to know for this state	
		Actions	Reference example
0, off, or	1. At the beginning of an editing operation. 2. When fetching the left digit in a source byte, a plus digit is detected as the right digit. 3. After a field separator character ")" is found in the pattern field.	a) If a zero digit is fetched from the source field (on the demand of a digit selector character), the digit selector character will be replaced by the fill character.	Fig. 11.18
		b) A nonzero digit (1 through 9) from source field, if fetched, will be stored in the pattern field as an unpacked decimal to replace the digit selector character.	Fig. 11.18
		c) Each message character in pattern field will be replaced by the fill character. (In particular, if a comma is to the left of the first significant digit, it will be replaced by the fill character.)	Fig. 11.22(b)
		d) A significant start character "(" behaves like a digit selector character "d", except that it turns *on* the *S*-trigger.	Fig. 11.19
1, on, or	1. After the leftmost significant (nonzero) digit is fetched from the source field. 2. After a significance start character "(" is found in the pattern.	a) A numerical digit (0 through 9) from source field, if fetched, will be stored in the pattern field as an unpacked decimal (e.g., F0, F1, etc.). In particular, any zero digit to the right of the first significant digit will not be suppressed.	Fig. 11.19
		b) Each message character in the pattern field remains undisturbed.	Fig. 11.20
		c) Any punctuation character to the right of the significance start character "(" is not suppressed.	Fig. 11.22(b)

Fig. 11.23   A summary of *S*-trigger.

11.8 EXAMPLES OF EDITING

In the preceding three sections, the details of an editing operation were described. Although the mechanics seems complex, the actual programming is not. For example, a portion of the program concerning the editing as shown in Fig. 11.24 demonstrates how to edit the source field in Fig. 11.21(a). The pattern field is established by a DC instruction; its contents are then moved into a work area (before the editing operation) by means of the first MVC instruction. As a result, the pattern field may be used again to edit another field.

We shall now present a simple example to illustrate the usage of these instructions.

```
          MVC    WKAREA,PATTRN
          ED     WKAREA,SOURCE
          MVC    OUTAREA,WKAREA
                 •
                 •
                 •
PATTRN    DC     X'4020206B2020204B202040C3D9'
SOURCE    DC     X'0907106D'
WKAREA    DC     XL13'0'
```

Fig. 11.24   Instructions relative to editing.

We want to write a subroutine EDIT in assembler language to eliminate the leading zeros in the number 00123456. In addition, a comma and a decimal point are required to be inserted in the number; thus, the edited result should read 1,234.56.

Figures 11.25(a) and (b) show, respectively, the given source field, and a pattern field designed to yield the required result. In assembler language, each field may be defined in a DC statement as shown in Fig. 11.26, which is the listing of the subroutine EDIT. The main program which calls the subroutine EDIT is primarily used for output only. The three versions in FORTRAN, PL/I, and COBOL are presented in Figs. 11.27, 11.28, and 11.29, respectively.

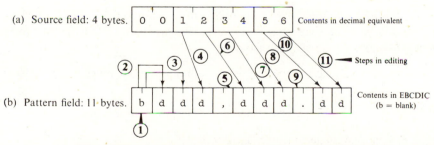

Fig. 11.25   A given source field and its pattern field.

```
EDIT     START   0
         SAVE    (14,12),,*
         BALR    11,0
         USING   *,11
         MVC     WKAREA,PATTRN
         ED      WKAREA,SOURCE
         MVC     OUTAREA,WKAREA
         L       6,0(1)          GR6=ADDRESS OF FIRST WORD IN RES
         MVI     0(6),X'40'          BLANK RESULT AREA
         MVC     1(15,6),0(6)
         MVC     0(11,6),OUTAREA    PUT OUTAREA IN RES AREA
         RETURN  (14,12)
PATTRN   DC      X'402020206B2020204B2020'
WKAREA   DC      XL11'0'
SOURCE   DC      X'00123456'
OUTAREA  DC      XL11'0'
         END
```

Fig. 11.26 Subroutine EDIT.

```
C        SET UP OUTPUT PAGE
         DIMENSION RES(4)
         WRITE(6,1)
       1 FORMAT(1H1,T64,'OUTPUT'/)
         CALL EDIT(RES)
         WRITE(6,2) (RES(I),I=1,4)
       2 FORMAT(10X,'EDITED RESULT',1X,4A4)
         CALL EXIT
         END
```

Fig. 11.27 FORTRAN main program to call subroutine EDIT.

```
EDITER:  PROC OPTIONS (MAIN);
DCL EDIT ENTRY(BIN FIXED(31,0));
DECLARE RES(4) BINARY FIXED (31);
DCL CHARSTR CHAR(16) DEFINED RES;
CALL EDIT(RES(1));
PUT EDIT('OUTPUT','EDITED RESULT',CHARSTR)
    (COL(57),A,SKIP(2),COL(45),A,SKIP,COL(45),A(16));
END;
```

Fig. 11.28 PL/I main program to call subroutine EDIT.

Note that the sign digit was not specified in the source field in Fig. 11.25(a). To take care of a possible sign digit, the SOURCE field written in the assembler language EDIT (Fig. 11.26) may be changed from

SOURCE   X'00123456'   containing four bytes

to

SOURCE   X'000123456C'   containing five bytes,

and the originally designed 11-byte pattern field

PATTRN   X'402020206B2020204B2020'

changed to the following 15-byte field

PATTRN   X'40202020206B2020204B202040C3D9'

As another example of editing, let us reexamine the subroutine ISLAND using the decimal instructions discussed in Section 11.3. As shown in Fig. 11.13, the output from the subroutine ISLAND (see Fig. 11.12) contains a leading zero. The $ sign and decimal point are made possible through the use of several MVI instructions. We shall now use an EDit (ED) instruction to (a) eliminate the leading zeros, and (b) insert the decimal point, but we shall not be concerned with the $ sign in this example.

Figure 11.30 shows the third version of subroutine ISLAND, using the EDit (ED) instruction and the associated pattern field, work area, and output area. If we link this subroutine with any one of the three main programs shown in Figs. 10.17 through 10.19, the resulting output is given in Fig. 11.31.

Note here that the Edit (ED) instruction makes no provision for loading a floating currency symbol (such as $) as part of the editing process. For this purpose we can use the EDit and MarK (EDMK) instruction which will be described in the next section.

The third example of using the ED instruction involves the subroutine CLOCK (see Fig. 11.32) whose basic purpose is to tell the time of day during the execution of a program. In this subroutine, the system macro TIME used has three formats, as shown in Table 11.3. The time of day is returned in register 0.

After the macro instruction TIME DEC is executed, the time of day is returned as packed decimal digits in the form **HHMMSShh** whose meanings are shown in Table 11.3. The ED instruction in Fig. 11.32 serves to insert three periods: from **HHMMSShh** to **HH.MM.SS.hh**.

The calling sequence in a FORTRAN main program to call the subroutine CLOCK is

CALL CLOCK(KLOCKA,KLOCKB)

Table 11.3 System Macro TIME

Macro instruction used	Time of day returned as	Remarks
TIME BIN	Unsigned 32-bit binary number in 1/100th of a sec.	
TIME DEC or TIME	Packed decimal digits in the form **HHMMSShh**.	**HH** = hours of the time of day **MM** = minutes of the time of day **SS** = seconds of the time of day **hh** = hundredths of second of the time of day
TIME TU	Unsigned 32-bit binary number in timer units.	1 timer unit = 26.04 microsec

```
IDENTIFICATION DIVISION.
PROGRAM-ID.
    'MAINAV'. PROGRAM NAME
AUTHOR.
    S. S. KUO.
ENVIRONMENT DIVISION.
CONFIGURATION SECTION.
SOURCE-COMPUTER.
    IBM-360 G50.
OBJECT-COMPUTER.
    IBM-360 G50.
INPUT-OUTPUT SECTION.
FILE-CONTROL.
    SELECT PRINT-FILE ASSIGN TO 'PRINTER' UTILITY.
DATA DIVISION.
FILE SECTION.
FD  PRINT-FILE
    RECORDING MODE IS F
    LABEL RECORDS ARE OMITTED
    DATA RECORDS ARE PRT-LINE.
01  PRT-LINE                     PICTURE X(133).
WORKING-STORAGE SECTION.
01  PRT-LINE-1.
    02  FILLER                   PICTURE X(63) VALUE SPACES.
    02  PRT-OUTPUT               PICTURE X(6) VALUE 'OUTPUT'.
    02  FILLER                   PICTURE X(64) VALUE SPACES.
01  PRT-LINE-2.
    02  FILLER                   PICTURE X(10) VALUE SPACES.
    02  PRT-TITLE                PICTURE X(14) VALUE
                                 'EDITED RESULT '.
    02  FILLER                   PICTURE X VALUE SPACES.
    02  RES-1                    PICTURE X(4).
    02  RES-2                    PICTURE X(4).
    02  RES-3                    PICTURE X(4).
    02  RES-4                    PICTURE X(4).
    02  FILLER                   PICTURE X(96) VALUE SPACES.
01  ANSWER-TABLE.
    02  ANSWER-ENTRY OCCURS 4 TIMES.
        03  RES                  PICTURE X(4).
01  SUBSCRIPT                    PICTURE 9 VALUE 1.
PROCEDURE DIVISION.
OPEN-FILES.
    OPEN OUTPUT PRINT-FILE.
    ENTER LINKAGE.
    CALL 'EDIT' USING RES (1).
    ENTER COBOL.
PRINT-DETAIL.
    MOVE RES (SUBSCRIPT) TO RES-1. ADD 1 TO SUBSCRIPT.
    MOVE RES (SUBSCRIPT) TO RES-2. ADD 1 TO SUBSCRIPT.
    MOVE RES (SUBSCRIPT) TO RES-3. ADD 1 TO SUBSCRIPT.
    MOVE RES (SUBSCRIPT) TO RES-4.
    WRITE PRT-LINE FROM PRT-LINE-1 AFTER ADVANCING 0 LINES.
    WRITE PRT-LINE FROM PRT-LINE-2 AFTER ADVANCING 0 LINES.
CLOSE-FILES.
    CLOSE PRINT-FILE.
    STOP RUN.
```

Fig. 11.29 COBOL main program to call subroutine EDIT.

where KLOCKA contains the time of day in the form of **HH.MM.SS.hh** (see Table 11.3) and KLOCKB contains the same in 1/100th seconds.

KLOCKA is an array, it must appear in a DIMENSION statement

DIMENSION KLOCKA(3)

and can only be printed using an A format. KLOCKB is returned to the user as an unsigned 32-bit binary number. A sample main program in FORTRAN is presented in Fig. 11.33, and its output, in Fig. 11.34.

```
ISLAND    CSECT
          SAVE   (14,12),,*      MACRO TO SAVE REGISTERS
+         B      12(0,15) BRANCH AROUND ID
+         DC     AL1(6)
+         DC     CL6'ISLAND' IDENTIFIER

+         STM    14,12,12(13) SAVE REGISTERS
          BALR   11,0          BASE REGISTERS
          USING  *,11
          MVC    COUNTER,C338    SET UP COUNTER TO EQUAL 338
          ZAP    RESULT,SALE     LOAD AMOUNT OF SALE
LOOP      MP     RESULT,RATE     MULT. RATE AND AMOUNT OF SALE
          AP     RESULT,ROUND    ROUND OFF NUMBER
          MVN    RESULT+5(1),RESULT+6    MOVE THE SIGN OF PACKED DECIMAL
          ZAP    RESULT,RESULT(6) DROP LAST RIGHTMOST BYTE
          SP     COUNTER,ONE     SUBT. 1 FROM COUNTER
          BP     LOOP            BRANCH TO LOOP
          ZAP    RESULTA(5),RESULT  DELETE ZEROS ON THE LEFT
          MVC    WKAREA,PATTRN MOVE PATTRN INTO WKAREA
          ED     WKAREA,RESULTA EDITING DONE IN WKAREA
          MVC    OUTAREA,WKAREA  MOVE EDITED RESULT INTO OUTAREA
          L      5,0(1)          LOAD 1ST ARGU. LIST INTO R(5)
          MVI    0(5),X'40'      BLANK OUT RESULT AREA
          MVC    0(12,5),OUTAREA    MOVE EDITED RESULT INTO R(5)
          RETURN (14,12)          RESTORE THE REGISTERS
+         LM     14,12,12(13) RESTORE THE REGISTERS
+         BR     14 RETURN
COUNTER   DS     PL2
C338      DC     PL2'338'
SALE      DC     PL3'2400'
RESULT    DS     PL7
RATE      DC     PL2'103'
ROUND     DC     PL2'50'
ONE       DC     PL1'1'
PATTRN    DC     X'402020202068202020484B2020'
WKAREA    DC     XL12'0'
RESULTA   DS     PL5
OUTAREA   DC     XL12'0'
          END
```

Fig. 11.30 Subroutine ISLAND (version 3). Using decimal programming and EDIT instruction.

THE FINAL ANSWER IS 523,998.22

Fig. 11.31 Output.

```
CLOCK     CSECT
          SAVE    (14,12),,*              SAVE 15 REGISTERS
  +       B       10(0,15) BRANCH AROUND ID
  +       DC      AL1(5)
  +       DC      CL5'CLOCK' IDENTIFIER
  +       STM     14,12,12(13) SAVE REGISTERS
          BALR    11,0                    BASE REGISTER DESIGNATION
          USING   *,11

          L       7,0(1)                  R7 CONTAINS POINTER TO KLOCKA
          L       8,4(1)                  R8 CONTAINS POINTER TO KLOCKB
          TIME    DEC                     GET TIME IN HHMMSSHH FORMAT
  +       LA      1,2(0,0) LOAD 1 TO SPECIFY UNIT
  +       SVC     11 ISSUE TIME SVC
          ST      0,SOURCE                STORE IT IN SOURCE FIELD
          MVO     WKAREA,SOURCE
          ED      PATTERN,WKAREA          EDIT--PUT 3 PERIODS IN
          MVC     0(12,7),PATTERN+1 MOVE RESULT TO
          TIME    BIN                     GET TIME IN 1/100TH SECONDS
  +       LA      1,1(0,0) LOAD 1 TO SPECIFY UNIT
  +       SVC     11 ISSUE TIME SVC
          ST      0,0(8)                  STORE IT IN KLOCKB
          RETURN  (14,12)
  +       LM      14,12,12(13) RESTORE THE REGISTERS
  +       BR      14 RETURN
SOURCE    DS      F                       SOURCE HAS PACKED DATA
WKAREA    DS      PL5'0'                  PATTERN DESIGNED WITH UNPACKED
PATTERN   DC      XL13'4021202048202048202048202048202048202020'
          END
```

Fig. 11.32   Subroutine CLOCK.

```
  DIMENSION KLOCKA(3)
  CALL CLOCK(KLOCKA,KLOCKB)
  WRITE(6,11) KLOCKA,KLOCKB
11 FORMAT('1TIME OF THE DAY WHEN PROGRAM WAS EXECUTED',/' IN HRS,MINS
 1,SECS, AND HUNDREDTHS OF SECONDS = ',3A4/' THE TIME IN HUNDREDTHS
 2OF SECONDS IS ',I9)
  CALL EXIT
  END
```

Fig. 11.33   FORTRAN main program for the time of day.

```
  TIME OF THE DAY WHEN PROGRAM WAS EXECUTED
  IN HRS,MINS,SECS, AND HUNDREDTHS OF SECONDS =  09.59.38.63
  THE TIME IN HUNDREDTHS OF SECONDS IS    3597863
```

Fig. 11.34   Output for the time of day.

11.9 EDIT AND MARK INSTRUCTION

The EDit and MarK (EDMK) instruction is identical to the EDit (ED) instruction except that it also places in register 1† the address of the first significant digit of the result.

---

† Only in bit positions 8 through 31 of register 1, leaving bit positions 0 through 7 undisturbed. The address is not loaded into register 1 if the S-trigger is turned on by a significant start character "(".

```
MVC    WKAREA,PATTRN
EDMK   WKAREA,SOURCE
BCTR   1,0      SUBTRACT 1 FROM GR1
MVI    0(1),X'5B'     INSERT $
```

Fig. 11.35 Typical sequence of instructions to insert a dollar sign.

A programmer can obtain a new address by reducing the value in register 1 by one, and load a dollar sign or minus sign into this new address. Since register 1 is used exclusively for this purpose, it should not be disturbed. A typical sequence of instructions to reduce the address of one and insert a dollar sign is shown in Fig. 11.35. The Branch on Count to Register (BCTR) instruction reduces the contents of register 1 by one; it does not branch because the second operand contains a zero.

```
ISLAND    CSECT
          SAVE   (14,12),,*     MACRO TO SAVE REGISTERS
+         B      12(0,15) BRANCH AROUND ID
+         DC     AL1(6)
+         DC     CL6'ISLAND' IDENTIFIER

+         STM    14,12,12(13) SAVE REGISTERS
          BALR   11,0           BASE REGISTERS
          USING  *,11
          L      5,0(1)         LOAD 1ST ARGU. LIST INTO R(5)
          MVI    0(5),X'40'     BLANK OUT RESULT AREA
          MVC    COUNTER,C338 SET UP COUNTER TO EQUAL 338
          ZAP    RESULT,SALE    LOAD AMOUNT OF SALE
LOOP      MP     RESULT,RATE    MULT. RATE AND AMOUNT OF SALE
          AP     RESULT,ROUND   ROUND OFF NUMBER
          MVN    RESULT+5(1),RESULT+6     MOVE THE SIGN OF PACKED DECIMAL
          ZAP    RESULT,RESULT(6)  DROP LAST RIGHTMOST BYTE
          SP     COUNTER,ONE    SUBTRACT 1 FROM COUNTER
          BP     LOOP           BRANCH TO LOOP
          ZAP    RESULTA(5),RESULT   DELETE ZEROS ON LEFT
          MVC    WKAREA,PATTRN      MOVE PATTRN INTO WKAREA
          EDMK   WKAREA,RESULTA   EDITING DONE IN WKAREA
          BCTR   1,0            REDUCE CONTENTS OF R(1) BY 1
          MVI    0(1),X'5B'     INSERT $ TO RESULT
          MVC    OUTAREA,WKAREA    MOVE EDITED RESULT TO OUTAREA
          MVC    0(12,5),OUTAREA   MOVE EDITED RESULT INTO R(5)
          RETURN (14,12)        RESTORE THE REGISTERS
+         LM     14,12,12(13) RESTORE THE REGISTERS
+         BR     14 RETURN
COUNTER   DS     PL2
C338      DC     PL2'338'
SALE      DC     PL3'2400'
RESULT    DS     PL7
RATE      DC     PL2'103'
ROUND     DC     PL2'50'
ONE       DC     PL1'1'
PATTRN    DC     X'402020202068202020204B2020'
WKAREA    DC     XL12'0'
RESULTA   DS     PL5
OUTAREA   DC     XL12'0'
          END
```

Fig. 11.36 Subroutine ISLAND (version 4) using EDMK instruction.

We shall now illustrate the usage of the EDMK instruction with a concrete example.

Example

Use the EDMK instruction to modify the subroutine ISLAND (version 3) in Fig. 11.30. We wish to (a) insert a dollar sign just before the leftmost significant digit; (b) permit no leading zeros; and (c) print a comma and a decimal point.

THE FINAL ANSWER IS $523,998.22

Fig. 11.37 Output.

A possible subroutine ISLAND (version 4) is shown in Fig. 11.36. If we use this subroutine in conjunction with any one of three main programs in Figs. 10.17 through 10.19, the output in Fig. 11.37 is obtained.

BIBLIOGRAPHY

IBM System/370 Principles of Operation, Form GA22-7000, IBM Corp. Intended for the shift and round decimal instruction.

IBM System/360 Edit, Translate, and Execute Instructions, Form C20-1624, IBM Corp.

PROBLEMS

Section 11.1

11.1 Represent $(+126)_{10}$ in two and then in three bytes in packed decimal format.

11.2 Perform the decimal addition: +211 plus (−156) (refer to Fig. 11.2). Each number is represented in a two-byte (packed decimal) field.

11.3 Perform the decimal addition +156 plus (−261) (refer to Fig. 11.3). Each number is represented in a two-byte (packed decimal) field.

11.4 Does the decimal overflow occur in each of the following additions?

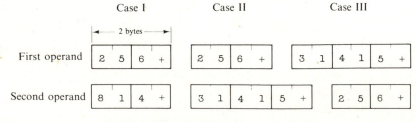

11.5 How many bytes does the following DC instruction take?

ABLE   DC   PL4'−17'

Express the contents of these bytes in *binary*.

11.6 Use a DC instruction to set up a packed decimal field of two bytes containing −1.

11.7 The assembler version of the following instruction is $\boxed{00\ |\ 00\ |\ 4C}$

$$\text{ALPHA}\quad\text{DC}\quad\text{PL3'.04'}$$

where the decimal point is ingored. Set up a four-byte field name BETA, containing .007.

11.8 Write an instruction to reserve 21 adjacent packed decimal fields of four bytes each, beginning at ROW.

Section 11.2

11.9 Given: Instructions

$$
\begin{array}{lll}
 & \text{AP} & \text{A,B} \\
\text{A} & \text{DC} & \text{X'0081565C'} \\
\text{B} & \text{DC} & \text{X'69213D'}
\end{array}
$$

What are the contents in field A after execution of the AP instruction?

a) 0150776C, b) 0012352C, c) 0012353D.

11.10 Given: Instructions

$$
\begin{array}{lll}
 & \text{MP} & \text{A(3),A+3(1)} \\
\text{A} & \text{DC} & \text{X'01137D'} \\
\text{B} & \text{DC} & \text{X'3C'}
\end{array}
$$

What are the contents in bytes A through A+3 after the execution of the MP instruction?

a) 03 41 1D 3C,   b) 00 03 41 1D,
c) 03 41 1D 00,   d) 00 03 41 1C.

11.11 What are the contents in ANS field after the execution of the following instruction:

$$\text{SP}\quad\text{ANS,ANS}$$

11.12 The instruction

$$\text{ZAP}\quad\text{ZERO,=PL4'0'}$$

moves a four-byte constant into the ZERO area. The constant has the following configuration:

$$\boxed{00\ \ |\ \ 00\ \ |\ \ 00\ \ |\ \ 0C}$$

Write a ZAP instruction which will move a three-byte constant of

into the DELTA area.

11.13 The condition code setting after a ZAP instruction follows the rule after an AH instruction as shown in Table 4.2. What is the CC setting after the execution of the following instruction:

$$\text{ZAP}\quad\text{TWO,=PL3'2'}$$

11.14 After the execution of the DP instruction in the following program segment, show the result in the QR field. Draw a sketch similar to that shown in Fig. 11.10.

```
            ZAP   QR,UP
            DP    QR,DOWN
                  ⋮
    UP      DC    PL6'123'
    DOWN    DC    PL3'5'
    QR      DC    PL9'0'
```

11.15 Check the decimal overflow after the execution of an AP instruction for the following cases:

	First operand	Second operand	Decimal overflow (yes or no)
a)	39 6C	46 1C	
b)	39 6C	00 46 1C	
c)	39 6C	02 46 1C	

Section 11.3

11.16 The contents of the four-byte QUAN field are

00	36	41	2C

What are its contents after the execution of the following instruction:

```
MVN   QUAN+2(1),QUAN+3
```

11.17 The MVO instruction may be used for decimal shift of an odd number of places. If the SOURCE field is originally given as

1	2	3	4	5	6	7	8	9	D

what are its contents after the execution of the instruction below?

```
MVO   SOURCE(5),SOURCE(3)
```

11.18 Assume that the three-byte PAY field in packed decimal is

a	b	c	d	e	$\mathscr{S}$

where the decimal point is between b and c, and $\mathscr{S}$ can be positive (C) or minus (D). The purpose of this exercise is to round the PAY field to the nearest cent, or

0	a	b	c	d	$\mathscr{S}$

Essentially, the following two steps may be taken:

Step 1. If $\mathscr{S}$ is positive, add 5 to the PAY field; if negative, subtract 5.

a) Set up a constant field containing one byte (a 5 digit and a sign digit)

$$\text{FIVE} \quad \text{DC} \quad \text{P'5'}$$

b) Move sign from PAY field to FIVE field:

$$\text{MVN} \quad \text{FIVE,PAY+2(1)}$$

c) Add the modified FIVE to PAY:

$$\text{AP} \quad \text{PAY(3),FIVE}$$

Step 2. Shift the answer one place to the right, thus dropping *e*:

$$\text{MVO} \quad \text{PAY(3),PAY(2)}$$

Assume that the PAY field is -31.416, and trace through these two steps in detail.

Section 11.4

11.19 Assume that the source field contains

0	1	2	8

(two-byte long and no sign digit involved), and that the pattern field contains

*	d	d	d	d

(five-byte long). Write out the edited result.

11.20 Same as Problem 11.19, except that the pattern field is five-byte long, containing

b	d	d	d	d

or X'4020202020'. Write out the edited result.

11.21 Assume that the source field contains

0	0	1	2	3	4

(three-byte long and no sign digit involved), and that the pattern field contains

b	d	d	d	d	d	d

(seven-byte long). Write out the edited result.

Section 11.5

11.22 Is the *S*-trigger set at 0 or 1 at the beginning of each EDit (ED) operation?

11.23 During an editing operation, a digit selector character is found in the pattern field, and its associated digit in the source field is zero; what is the edited result for this digit if (a) *S*-trigger is 0; and (b) *S*-trigger is 1. The fill character is a blank.

11.24 The character to be stored in the pattern field during an editing operation depends on three items. What are they?

11.25 Is the fill character always a blank?

11.26 Given:

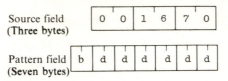

Source field
(Three bytes): 0 0 1 6 7 0

Pattern field
(Seven bytes): b d d d d d d

Fill out the blank spaces in the following two fields:

Pattern field (after editing): [ ][ ][ ][ ][ ][ ][ ]

S-trigger (starts at zero)
after each character operation: 0 [ ][ ][ ][ ][ ][ ]

Section 11.7

11.27 The *S*-trigger is set to zero in three conditions: One occurs at the beginning of the execution of an EDit instruction; the second is the detection of a plus sign digit in the source field. What is the third?

11.28 Given:

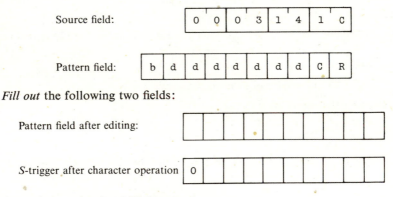

Source field: 0 0 0 3 1 4 1 C

Pattern field: b d d d d d d d C R

Fill out the following two fields:

Pattern field after editing: [ ][ ][ ][ ][ ][ ][ ][ ][ ][ ]

S-trigger after character operation 0 [ ][ ][ ][ ][ ][ ][ ][ ][ ]

11.29 The ED instruction is of SS format:

$$ED \quad D1(L,B1),D2(B2)$$

where *L* = the length field, usually the length of the required output field plus 1, to allow a position for a fill character specification. As a result, the value *L* is the number of bytes in the pattern field;

D = displacement; and

B = contents in base register.

The first operand specifies the address of the pattern field; and the second operand, the source field.

Find the edited result after the execution of the following instruction:

$$ED \quad 234(13,7),201(7)$$

if the contents of register 7 are 2000 in decimal, and the source field is

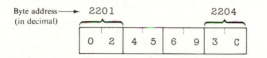

and the pattern field contains:

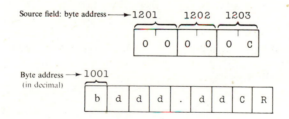

11.30 The purpose of the following ED instruction is to blank a zero field:

$$ED \quad 1(9,6),1(5)$$

where the contents of registers 5 and 6 are 1200 and 1000, respectively, in decimal. The contents of two required fields are shown below:

(a) Find the edited result and *S*-trigger after each character operation. (b) Same as part (a), except that the source field contains 00000D.

Section 11.9

11.31 The EDMK instruction

$$EDMK \qquad D1(L,B1),D2(B2)$$

is identical to the ED instruction except that the byte address of the first significant result is recorded in register 1. In a program, the following sequence of three instructions is used:

```
EDMK   101(12,7),1(7)
BCTR   1,0
MVC    0(1),X'5B'
```

Fill out the following table.

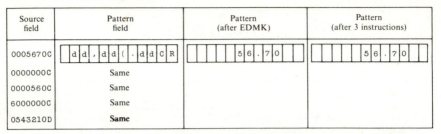

Source field	Pattern field	Pattern (after EDMK)	Pattern (after 3 instructions)
0005670C	dd,dd(.ddCR	56.70	56.70
0000000C	Same		
0000560C	Same		
6000000C	Same		
0543210D	**Same**		

11.32 The Z type operand in a DC instruction is identical to the P type one except that the constant is assembled as a zoned decimal. The maximum length for Z type constant is 16 bytes. Write the assembled result in hexadecimal for the instruction:

DC   Z'−2,78,1206'

LABORATORY ASSIGNMENT

1. We are to write a subroutine using decimal instructions to compute the sum, the difference, and the product of two numbers A and B. In addition, the quotient Q is also to be computed:

$$Q = B/A \quad \text{if} \quad A > B$$
$$Q = A/B \quad \text{if} \quad A \leq B$$

Write a main program in a high-level language to print out your answers by means of the A-format.
Consider the following cases:

Case 1 $A = 3.1$, $B = 2.6$
Case 2 $A = 3.1$, $B = 5.6$

2. A source field contains 0314159D; and the desirable result to be left in the pattern field is

Write a subroutine in assembler language to perform the editing, and a main program in one of the high-level languages.

3. The Translate and Replace (TR) instruction for code conversion

TR $D1(L,B1),D2(B2)$

is of SS format. During the execution of this instruction, the following three steps are taken:

Step 1. Fetch a byte from the first operand location.

Step 2. The byte contents, treated as a binary number, are added to the second operand *address*. A new byte address is thus obtained.

Step 3. Fetch the byte contents from this new address, and place them in the byte location discussed in Step 1.

Steps 1 through 3 are repeated until the first operand is exhausted. Modify Subroutine CONVER shown in Fig. 10.5 (by using the TR instruction). Use a main program to make a run.

Suggestion: Set up a 256-byte table containing bytes 00, 01, 02,..., FF. In this table, 4D must then be replaced by 6C, 5D by 4C, and 4E by 50. If this modified table starts at the location TABLE and the card image in main storage starts at the location INPUT, then the following instruction may be used:

```
TR  INPUT(80),TABLE
```

Note that the maximum length field (*L*) is 256. The second operand is often considered as a table of *function values* of one byte each, while the first operand as a string of *arguments* to the function. Each argument is one-byte long.

4. The TRanslate and Test (TRT) instruction is quite similar to TR instruction with the following differences: (a) the first operand (the string containing the argument bytes) is not changed; (b) the operation stops either when a nonzero function byte (in the second operand) is found or the first operand field is exhausted; and (c) condition code is set as shown in Appendix F. The TRT instruction *searches for the first argument byte whose corresponding function byte is nonzero.*

The address of this argument byte, if found, is placed in the rightmost 24 bits in register 1, and the corresponding nonzero function byte in the rightmost eight bits in register 2. The bit positions 0–7 of register 1 and bit positions 0–23 of register 2 remain unchanged.

For example, if the contents of the two given fields are as follows:

	ARGUMENT field (three bytes)		FUNCTION field (eleven bytes)	
	Address	Contents	Address	Contents
First byte	ARGUMENT	02	FUNCTION	25
Second byte	ARGUMENT + 1	03	FUNCTION + 1	00
Third byte	ARGUMENT + 2	0A	FUNCTION + 2	00
Fourth byte			FUNCTION + 3	01
			$\vdots$	
Eleventh byte			FUNCTION + X'A'	00

then during the execution of the TRT ARGUMENT(3),FUNCTION instruction, the following steps are taken: (1) The first byte contents of the ARGUMENT field are fetched (i.e., 02), which are added to the address FUNCTION, obtaining FUNCTION + 2. (2) The byte contents in FUNCTION + 2 are zeros. Thus, the second byte contents in the ARGUMENT field are fetched. (3) They are 03, which are then added to the address FUNCTION, yielding FUNCTION + 3. (4) The byte contents in FUNCTION + 3 are nonzero (it is 01). Thus the address ARGUMENT + 1 is inserted in the rightmost 24 bits of register 1. The function byte 01 is inserted in the rightmost eight bits of register 2. The condition code is set to 1.

The TRT instruction is used to locate special or invalid characters, and is very powerful in compiler construction. Write a subroutine to find the length of the *first* symbol in a data card (e.g., the one shown in Fig. 5.29.)

CHAPTER 12

Floating Point Data and Programming

12.1 FLOATING-POINT DATA FORMATS

In Part I, a binary integer was represented in the fixed-point format. In this representation, a fictitious binary point is inserted at a fixed location:

a) To the right of the rightmost bit (always representing an integer) or
b) To the left of the leftmost bit (always representing a fraction).

This method of number representation, the so-called fixed-point representation, has a severe drawback: The range is limited. To overcome this difficulty, a second method—the floating-point representation—is widely used in scientific and engineering applications.

A floating-point number has two parts: an exponent and a fraction. Although a misnomer, the fraction is often referred to as *mantissa*. Consider, for example, the floating-point number:

$$E = 0.3 \times 10^8$$

Here the exponent is 8 and the fractional part is .3.

In general, a floating-point number A has the following form:

$$A = M \cdot \beta^k,$$

where β = radix
$\quad$ = 16 for a hexadecimal machine, such as System/370 or System/360,
$\quad$ = 2 for binary computers,
$\quad$ = 10 for decimal computers,
$\quad k$ = the exponent, an integer, and
$\quad M$ = a signed fraction, $-1 < M < 1$.

We shall illustrate the restriction on M with the following example.

338

Example

Given: A decimal number $A = -.000000192$ and its floating-point representation -19.2×10^{-8}.

Find: Does the given format for A meet the requirements of a floating-point number?

Solution

The given format does not meet the requirement because the fraction part, -19.2, is smaller than -1. Now let us rewrite the entire number as $A = -0.192 \times 10^{-6}$. The exponent is equal to -6, an integer; and the fraction $-.192$ lies between $+1$ and -1. Thus it meets the requirements of a floating-point number.

The purpose of this chapter is (a) to present three types of the floating-point data format used in System 370/360; and (b) to explore floating-point instructions of most frequent occurrence.

The three types of formats are *short* format (single precision), *long* format (double precision), and *extended precision*. The short format (Fig. 12.1a) takes 32 bits: a sign bit (the bit position 0), 7 bits (bit position 1–7) for the characteristic, and 24 bits (bit positions 8–31) for the fraction. The long format (Fig. 12.1b) contains 64 bits: a

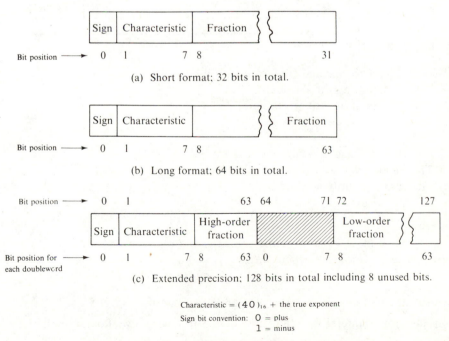

(a) Short format; 32 bits in total.

(b) Long format; 64 bits in total.

(c) Extended precision; 128 bits in total including 8 unused bits.

Characteristic $= (40)_{16} +$ the true exponent

Sign bit convention: $0 =$ plus
                             $1 =$ minus

Fig. 12.1   Three floating-point data formats.

sign bit (the 0-bit position), next 7 bits for the characteristic (bit positions 1–7), and 56 rightmost bits (bit positions 8–63) for the fraction. Finally, the extended precision format† (Fig. 12.1c) contains two doublewords. The bit position 0 contains a sign bit, and bit positions 1–7 contain the characteristic. The fraction of the low-order part is treated as an extension to the fraction of the high-order part. Thus, the bit positions 8–63 and 72–127 are considered as the fraction. An extended precision floating-point number carries accuracy of approximately 34 decimal places.

Note that in Fig. 12.1 no sign bit for the exponent is available. In order to take care of a negative exponent, we arbitrarily add $(64)_{10} = (40)_{16}$ to the exponent; this adjusted exponent is often referred to as the *characteristic*. This representation is called *excess sixty-four*.

It is important to note that the two's complement notation discussed in Part I is not used in the floating-point programming for System/370 or System/360. Instead, each *four-bit* (a hexadecimal digit) forms a basic unit. As a result, the magnitude of a floating-point number is the fraction times a power of 16. The true exponent (i.e., characteristic − 64) indicates this power.

Example

Given: The short format representation:

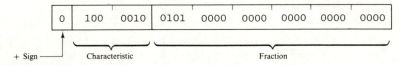

Find: a) Characteristic and true exponent in hexadecimal
      b) Fraction part in decimal
      c) The total quantity in decimal.

Solution

  a) The characteristic is $(42)_{16}$; the true exponent is $(42)_{16} - (40)_{16} = 2$.
  b) The fraction is $(.0101)_2 = 2^{-2} + 2^{-4}$; or $(.5)_{16} = 5 \times 16^{-1}$.
  c) The entire quantity is equal to:

$$16^2 \times (2^{-2} + 2^{-4}) = 80; \quad \text{or} \quad 16^2 \times (5 \times 16^{-1}) = 80.$$

As shown in this example, the characteristic represents a power of 16, *as each shift is done in increments of four bits.*

Normalization of a Floating-Point Number

Consider, for example, the difference of the following two floating-point numbers

---

† Special feature for some models of the System/370 and System/360.

in the decimal system:

$$.27143247 \times 10^7$$
$$- \quad .27072236 \times 10^7$$
$$\overline{.00071011 \times 10^7}$$

Here the floating-point result has three leading zeros. These zeros can be removed if we shift the fractional part of the result three places to the left, yielding $.71011 \times 10^4$. This process is called *normalization*. In decimal system, a floating-point number without leading zero digits is called normalized; otherwise, unnormalized.

We mentioned before that the fraction part of a floating-point number must lie between -1 and $+1$, or $-1 < M < 1$. If the value of fraction M also satisfies the following condition:

$$\frac{1}{\beta} \le |M| < 1$$

we then say that $A = M \cdot \beta^k$ is a *normalized* floating-point number.

The System/370 or System/360 can be considered as a hexadecimal machine. A normalized floating-point number may contain a zero in each of the first three high-order bits (bit positions 8, 9, and 10) in the fraction part. Consider, for example, the two representations of a given normalized floating-point number shown in Fig. 12.2(a) and (b), respectively, for a short and long form. In either representation, both bit positions 8 and 9 contain zeros, yet this floating-point number is a *normalized* one.

Here the true exponent is $(3D)_{16} - (40)_{16} = (-3)_{16}$; and the total quantity in decimal can be computed as follows:

$$16^{-3} \times (2 \times 16^{-1} + 15 \times 16^{-3} + 1 \times 16^{-4} + \cdots)$$
$$= 2 \times 16^{-4} + 15 \times 16^{-6} + 16^{-7} + \cdots$$
$$= 2 \times 2^{-16} + 15 \times 2^{-24} + 2^{-28} + \cdots$$
$$= 0.000031416.$$

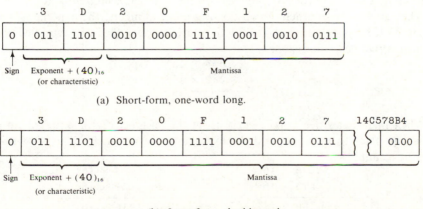

(a) Short-form, one-word long.

(b) Long-form, doubleword.

Fig. 12.2   Floating-point notation for 0.000031416.

Before turning to the next section, let us explore some details of the three floating-point representations:

1. Since the characteristic uses seven bits, its range is from 0 to 127. As a result, the true exponent has a range from -64 to $+63$ (in decimal) as can be seen below:

$$0 - 64 = -64$$

and

$$127 - 64 = 63.$$

This is true for the short, long, and the extended precision formats.

2. The largest number, which may be represented in short form, is $.FFFFFF \times 16^{63}$ (or approximately $.7237005 \times 10^{76}$). The smallest one is $.1 \times 16^{-64}$ (or approximately $.5397605 \times 10^{-78}$).

3. The largest number, which may be represented in long form, is $.FFFFFFFFFFFFFF \times 16^{63}$. The smallest one is $.1 \times 16^{-64}$.

4. The largest number, which may be represented in the extended precision, is $.FFFFFFFFFFFFFFFFFFFFFFFFFFFFF \times 16^{63}$. The smallest one is $.1 \times 16^{-64}$.

5. An attempt to represent a floating-point number (in short form) with magnitude greater than $.FFFFFF \times 16^{63}$ or smaller than $.1 \times 16^{-64}$ results in an *exponent overflow* or *exponent underflow*, respectively. They are considered as program errors; similar errors may occur for a floating-point number in long form and for that in the extended precision.

6. If two floating-point numbers have equal exponents and fractions, their difference is defined as zero.

12.2   FLOATING-POINT ADDITION

In the preceding section, we learned that the floating-point is a form of number representation in which quantities are represented by a fraction and an exponent (or a characteristic). We shall now discuss arithmetic operations involving two floating-point numbers with a particular emphasis on the numbers using radix 16.

When adding or subtracting two floating-point numbers, the exponents are first compared. If they are identical, the fractions are simply added or subtracted and the exponent is retained. For example:

$$
\begin{array}{r}
.563 \times 16^2 \\
+ \quad .389 \times 16^2 \\
\hline
.8EC \times 16^2
\end{array}
$$

When there is an overflow (a carry from the leftmost digit), both fractions are moved one place to the right, and the exponent is increased by 1, as shown in the following example:

$$
\begin{array}{r}
.C48 \times 16^2 \\
+ \quad .573 \times 16^2 \\
\hline
(1).1BB \times 16^2
\end{array}
\qquad
\begin{array}{r}
.0C4 \times 16^3 \\
+ \quad .057 \times 16^3 \\
\hline
.11B \times 16^3
\end{array}
$$

During the shift, the rightmost digit B is lost.

When the exponents are not equal, the larger exponent is retained, and the smaller one is converted. For example:

$$
\begin{array}{r}
.587 \times 16^4 \\
+ \quad .743 \times 16^3 \\
\hline
\end{array}
\qquad
\begin{array}{r}
.587 \times 16^4 \\
+ \quad .074 \times 16^4 \\
\hline
.5FB \times 16^4
\end{array}
$$

During the shift, the rightmost digit 3 is lost.

If a leading zero appears in the answer, the number can be normalized. For example:

$$
\begin{array}{r}
.538 \times 16^3 \\
- \quad .526 \times 16^3 \\
\hline
.012 \times 16^3
\end{array}
$$

$$\text{Normalized result} \quad = \quad .120 \times 16^2$$

In the System/370 or System/360, there are four floating-point registers (Fig. 12.3). The registers are doubleword (64 bits) in length and are numbered 0, 2, 4, and 6. They are not a part of the 16 general registers.

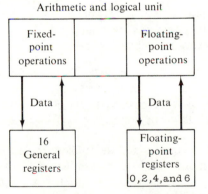

Fig. 12.3   Floating-point registers.

When an arithmetic operation deals with two long-form or short-form floating-point numbers, it is performed in the following way: The operation code in a given instruction dictates whether only the data in the left half of a floating-point register are to be used (the so-called short-form operation); or whether the data in the entire register are used (the long-form operation). Each operand is then moved to a special *nonadressable* working register. Each working register has an extra four-bit unit, known as a guard digit, which is inserted after the fraction part. Thus, in a short-form operation, the fraction part has 7 hexadecimal digits (6 plus 1 guard digit); in a long-form operation, 15 hexadecimal digits (14 plus 1 guard digit). A guard digit is basically used to increase accuracy, and its contributions will be further illustrated in Section 12.6.

Some models of the System/370 and System/360 use the extended-precision numbers (see Fig. 12.1c). The contents of each extended-precision number are stored in *two* adjacent floating-point registers: either in registers 0 and 2 (as a unit) or in registers 4 and 6 (as the other possible unit).

12.3 DEFINE FLOATING-POINT CONSTANTS AND STORAGE INSTRUCTIONS

In Section 12.1, we learned that a floating-point number could be represented in three different data formats—short, long, and extended precision. Corresponding to each of the first two formats, there is a Define Constant (DC) assembler instruction. A short floating-point constant is represented with an E in a DC instruction, while a long constant with a D. For example, $(31415926)_{10}$ can be defined by one of the following instructions:

```
DC   E'+31415926'     (Short form)
DC   E'31415926'      (Short form)
DC   D'+31415926'     (Long form)
DC   D'31415926'      (Long form)
```

where the plus sign is optional (see also Table 6.2 in Section 6.10).

To define a constant containing a decimal point such as -0.00003141592, we can use any one of the following assembler instructions:

```
DC   E'-.00003141592'     (Short form)
DC   D'-.00003141592'     (Long form)
DC   E'-.3141592E-4'      (Short form)
DC   D'-.3141592E-4'      (Long form)
```

The prefix E outside the quotes and the suffix E inside the quotes have completely different meanings and should not be confused with each other. The prefix E outside the quotes indicates that the floating-point number is in *short* format, whereas the E inside the quotes represents the exponent.† Here the exponent is –4 and the number is $-.3141592 \times 10^{-4}$.

To define an extended-precision constant, two successive DC instructions are commonly used. For example, the constant 1.0 in extended-precision may be defined in the field DJ as follows:

```
DJ   DS   0D
     DC   X'4110000000000000'
     DC   X'0000000000000000'
```

where the DS instruction is used to align the field DJ on a doubleword boundary. In

---

† Same as FORTRAN floating-point format.

order to place this constant in a pair of floating-point registers, two successive floating-point Load instructions are required. These instructions will be discussed in Section 12.9.

If we wish to reserve a block of storage for floating-point data, the Define Storage (DS) instruction can be applied. For example, if 50 fullwords are to be reserved, we can use:

$$\text{X} \quad \text{DS} \quad \text{50F}$$

Likewise, the following instruction reserves 16 doublewords:

$$\text{DOUBLE} \quad \text{DS} \quad \text{16D}$$

As a matter of interest, note that the last doubleword in this reserved block can be referred to as DOUBLE+15*8.

12.4 FLOATING-POINT ADD AND SUBTRACT INSTRUCTIONS

We have examined the three floating-point data formats. We have also learnt how DC instructions can be used to define these data. We shall now discuss some important floating-point arithmetic instructions, starting with the floating-point Add instruction. In general, *a floating-point instruction uses either the RR or the RX format*. If the RX format is followed, the storage address of the second operand must be divisible exactly by four for short operands, and by eight for long operands. (The op code of a floating-point instruction also specifies the length of data involved.) There are five floating-point Add Normalized instructions:

AER	*R1, R2*	(RR, short operands)
ADR	*R1, R2*	(RR, long operands)
AXR	*R1, R2*	(RR, extended-precision operands)
AE	*R1, D2(X2, B2)*	(RX, short operands)
AD	*R1, D2(X2, B2)*	(RX, long operands)

After the execution of each instruction, the contents in the second operand are added to those in the first operand, and the sum is normalized before being placed in the first operand. Note that the AXR instruction is the only Add instruction available for extended-precision operands.

Consider, for example, the following Add Normalized instruction for the short operands:

$$\text{AER} \quad 4,6$$

The left-half contents in floating-point registers 4 and 6 are shown in Fig. 12.4.

After the execution of this floating-point Add instruction, the contents of the left-half of floating-point register 6 are added to the left-half in floating-point register 4 in four stages listed below.

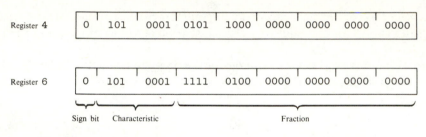

Fig. 12.4   Contents in two floating-point registers (left half only).

1. The characteristics of the two operands are compared. If they are the same as in this example, they are left undisturbed. If they do not agree, the fraction associated with the smaller characteristic is right-shifted *four bits* each time. Each shift increases the value of its characteristic by 1; the shift stops when the two characteristics agree.

2. The fraction portions are added algebraically. The intermediate sum is computed as follows:

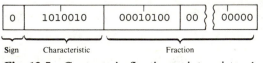

3. There is a carry in step 2 and, as a result, the intermediate sum is required to shift right four bits. The characteristic is now increased by 1 as illustrated in Fig. 12.5. Note that this answer is already postnormalized, in spite of the fact that it has three leading zeros in the fraction.

| 0 | 1010010 | 00010100 | 00 { | 00000 |

Fig. 12.5   Contents in floating-point register 4.

4. The sign bit is determined as zero.

In the above example, which illustrates one of the five Add *Normalized* instructions, the result was automatically normalized. However, there is also a set of four Add *Unnormalized* instructions:

AUR	*R1, R2*	(RR, short operands)
AWR	*R1, R2*	(RR, long operands)
AU	*R1, D2(X2, B2)*	(RX, short operands)
AW	*R1, D2(X2, B2)*	(RX, long operands)

During the execution of each instruction, the second operand is added to the first operand, and the *unnormalized* sum is placed in the location of the first one. The fraction part of the result is then truncated to the proper length.

Corresponding to the nine Add instructions already discussed, there are nine floating-point Subtract instructions as shown in Table 12.1. During the execution of

Table 12.1 Floating-point Subtract instructions

Subtract normalized		Unnormalized		Remarks
SER	$R1, R2$	SUR	$R1, R2$	RR, short operands
SDR	$R1, R2$	SWR	$R1, R2$	RR, long operands
SXR	$R1, R2$	—		RR, extended-precision operands
SE	$R1, D2(X2, B2)$	SU	$R1, D2(X2, B2)$	RR, short operands
SD	$R1, D2(X2, B2)$	SW	$R1, D2(X2, B2)$	RX, long operands

each instruction, the second operand is subtracted from the first operand and the result, normalized or unnormalized depending on the instruction, is placed in the first operand.

For example, consider the instruction

$$\text{SER} \quad 4,6$$

The contents in the floating-point registers 4 and 6 are shown in Fig. 12.4.

First, the characteristics of the two operands are compared and found to be the same, so they are left undisturbed. Second, the fraction portions are then subtracted algebraically as shown below:

```
     0101 1000 0000 0000 0000 0000  0000 ——— Fraction in first operand
  −  1111 0100 0000 0000 0000 0000  0000 ——— Fraction in second operand
  −  1001 1100 0000 0000 0000 0000  0000
```
Guard digit

Since there is neither carry nor leading zero, the fraction is already in normalized form. Finally, the sign bit is determined. Since the result is a negative quantity, the sign bit is changed to 1. The contents in register 4 after the execution are shown in Fig. 12.6.

1101	0001	1001	1100	0000	0000	0000	0000

Fig. 12.6 Contents in floating-point register 4 after the execution of instruction SER 4,6 (left half only).

During the execution of each floating-point Add or Substract instruction, the condition code is set according to the rules below.

Condition code	Result
0	if fraction = 0
1	if result < 0
2	if result > 0
3	not used

12.5 FLOATING-POINT MULTIPLY INSTRUCTIONS

In the last section we mentioned that a floating-point instruction uses either the RR or RX format. Also, the length of an operand can be a short, a long, or an extended precision one. These possibilities are also reflected in the seven Multiply instructions shown in Table 12.2.

Table 12.2 Seven floating-point Multiply instructions

Instruction	Format	Length of each of two operands	Product (always normalized)	Example
MER $R1,R2$	RR	Short	The fraction has full 14 hexadecimal digits, and the rightmost two digits are always 00.	MER 2,4 The product is placed in floating-point register 2.
ME $R1,D2(X2,B2)$	RX			
MDR $R1,R2$	RR	Long	The fraction part is truncated to 15 hexadecimal digits before left shifting (or normalization) if any.	MDR 4,6 The product is placed in floating-point register 4.
MD $R1,D2(X2,B2)$	RX			
MXDR $R1,R2$	RR	Long	The product is in extended precision. The fraction part is truncated to 28 hexadecimal digits.	MXDR 4,0 The product is placed in floating-point registers 4 and 6 as a unit.
MXD $R1,D2(X2,B2)$	RX			
MXR $R1,R2$	RR	Extended precision	The product is in extended precision and is placed in the first operand register and the next higher-addressed register.	MXR 0,4 The product is placed in floating-point registers 0 and 2 as a unit.

The second operand in each instruction represents the multiplier and the first operand, the multiplicand. After the execution of each instruction, the *normalized* product replaces the multiplicand. The condition code is *not* set.

For example, the following instruction involves two long operands:

$$\text{MDR} \quad 2,4$$

and the register contents (in hexadecimal) are assumed as follows:

	Characteristics	Fraction
Floating-point register 2	41	111111111111111
Floating-point register 4	42	111111111111111

The intermediate product consists of two parts: the characteristic and the fraction. The characteristic is the sum of the two characteristics minus $(40)_{16}$, or $41 + 42 - 40 = (43)_{16}$.

The fractions in both registers are first prenormalized and then multiplied. The fraction part of the intermediate product, in hexadecimal, is then equal to

$$\text{0123456789ABCDEDCBA987654321}$$

which is truncated to 15 hexadecimal digits:

$$\text{0123456789ABCDE}$$

and the rightmost digit E is pushed into the guard digit. Finally, the quantity in fractional part is *postnormalized* and stored in the floating-point register 2:

$$\text{123456789ABCDE}$$

As shown above, the multiplication of two floating-point numbers is obtained in two steps: a characteristic addition and a fraction multiplication. The sum of the two characteristics is subtracted by $(40)_{16}$. In addition, as a rule, the *sign* of the product can be determined by performing an Exclusive OR operation on the sign bits of the two operands. In this example, the sign is 0 (EXCLUSIVE OR) 0 = 0.

12.6 CONTRIBUTION OF A GUARD DIGIT

In the old System/360, when a double precision floating-point Multiply instruction is executed, only the first 56 bits of a product develop—the bit positions 8–63 in Fig. 12.1(b). When more than three leading binary zeros are generated, the result is shifted left or normalized, and the binary zeros are inserted on the right, thus causing unusual loss of accuracy in the product. In half the cases, by multiplying a random double-precision operand by unity, one does not obtain the original value of the operand. For example, if the contents of the floating-point registers 4 and 6 are a random number and 1, respectively, as shown in Fig. 12.7, the result after the execution of the instruction

$$\text{MDR} \quad 4,6$$

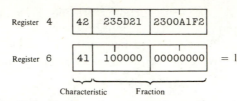

Register 4 | 42 | 235D21 | 2300A1F2 |

Register 6 | 41 | 100000 | 00000000 | = 1

Characteristic   Fraction

Fig. 12.7   Contents in two floating-point registers.

is expected to be the same as the first operand. But we find that this is not so, as shown below.

1. Prenormalization: not necessary
2. Fraction multiplication: 235D21 2300A1F2 × 100000 00000000

    or

    0235D2 12300A1F 20000000 000000

   where blanks are placed for clarity.
3. Characteristic of quotient: 42 + 41 − 40 = $(43)_{16}$
4. Sign: 0
5. Intermediate result: 43 0235D2 12300A1F
6. Postnormalization: 42 235D21 2300A1F0

This illustrates that the first operand times unity does not necessarily yield its original value.

In all floating-point arithmetic operations (long or short), each operand is first moved to a special nonaddressable working register. To obtain a more accurate intermediate result, an engineering change in System/360 hardware was made by inserting a four-bit guard digit at the right end of each of the special nonaddressable working registers. Thus in a short arithmetic operation, the fraction part has 7 hexadecimal digits; and in a long operation, 15 hexadecimal digits. In step 5, discussed above, the intermediate result has one additional digit as shaded in Fig. 12.8. After the postnormalization, the original value is restored.

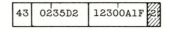

| 43 | 0235D2 | 12300A1F 2 |

Fig. 12.8   Guard digit inserted at the right end of fraction.

We shall further illustrate the contribution of the guard digit in the short addition operation. The two operands are shown in Fig. 12.9. The first operand is a positive number, while the second, a negative one.

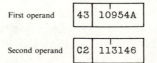

First operand | 43 | 10954A |

Second operand | C2 | 113146 |

Fig. 12.9   Contribution of guard digits.

The result at the end of each step with and without a guard digit is listed below:

	With a guard digit	Without a guard digit
1. Characteristic adjustment:	43 10954A⟦0⟧	43 10954A
	C3 011314⟦6⟧	C3 011314
2. Intermediate sum:	43 0F8235⟦A⟧	43 0F8235
3. Normalization:	42 F8235A⟦0⟧	42 F82350

The result 42 F8235A represents an improvement over the less accurate result 42 F82350 when no guard digit is inserted.

12.7 FLOATING-POINT DIVIDE INSTRUCTIONS

We shall now turn our attention to the four available floating-point Divide instructions, which are listed in Table 12.3. During the execution of each instruction, two steps are involved: a characteristic subtraction and a fraction divide. If both dividend and divisor are the normalized floating-point numbers, the characteristic of the quotient is obtained by subtracting the characteristic of the divisor from that of dividend, plus $(40)_{16}$. This result should not exceed 127, otherwise an exponent overflow would occur. The divide operation does not set a condition code. The remainder is not preserved.

Example 1

Given: The original register contents in hexadecimal are as shown in Fig. 12.10.

Find: The quotient after the execution of the following floating-point Divide (Short) instruction

$$\text{DER} \quad 4,0$$

which uses the RR format and the short operands.

Table 12.3 Floating-point Divide instructions

Instructions†	Remarks
DDR *R1 , R2*	RR format; long operands
DER *R1 , R2*	RR format; short operands
DD *R1 , D2(X2 , B2)*	RX format; long operands
DE *R1 , D2(X2 , B2)*	RX format; short operands

† No extended-precision Divide instruction is available. However, a DXR *macro*, which parallels the MXR instruction, is available in the system macro library of many computer installations.

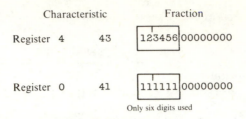

Fig. 12.10   Contents in floating-point registers 4 and 0.

Because the operands specified in this instruction are in short form, the rightmost eight hexadecimal digits of both floating-point registers are not disturbed during the execution of instruction (see Fig. 12.10). The characteristic part of the intermediate quotient is $43 - 41 + 40 = (42)_{16}$; its fraction is 1.111110. This result is post-normalized and the quotient, stored in the floating-point register 4, is shown in Fig. 12.11. As a rule, the *sign* of the quotient can be determined by performing an

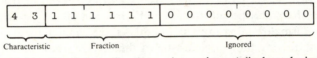

Fig. 12.11   Quotient in floating-point register 4 (in hexadecimal).

Exclusive OR operation on the sign bits of the two operands. Thus we have 0 (EXCLUSIVE OR) 0 = 0.

Example 2

Given: The original contents in the floating-point register 4 and those in the double-word field SIX (see Fig. 12.12).

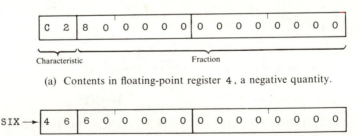

(a) Contents in floating-point register 4, a negative quantity.

(b) Contents in doubleword SIX.

Fig. 12.12   Contents in two operands.

Find: The step-by-step details of the execution of the instruction

DD   4,SIX

During the execution of the DD instruction the following four steps are taken:

1. Prenormalization: not necessary
2. Characteristic of quotient: $42 - 46 + 40 = (3C)_{16}$
3. Fraction division:

$$80000000000000/60000000000000$$
$$= \boxed{1}555555\ 55555555$$
$$\underset{\text{Carry}}{\overset{}{\uparrow}}$$

4. Sign of the quotient: 0 (Exclusive OR) $1 = 1$

The intermediate result is BC$\boxed{1}$555555 55555555 where the leading digit $\boxed{1}$ in the fraction is in a carry position. After a right shift of one position, the final result in the floating-point 4 becomes BD155555 55555555. No condition code is set during the entire operation, and no remainder preserved.

Let us now consider two special conditions of the floating-point division: (1) zero fraction in the divisor; and (2) zero fraction in the dividend.

First, the execution of a floating-point Divide instruction will be suppressed if the fraction part of the divisor contains all zeros. In this case, the dividend remains unchanged, and a program interruption for floating-point divide is issued (see Table C.1 in Appendix C).

Second, if the fraction part of a dividend is zero, the sign bit and characteristic of the quotient are both set to zero, yielding a true zero result.

Before concluding this section, we shall consider the following Halve instructions which we may use to halve a number:

HDR	*R1, R2*	Long operands
HER	*R1, R2*	Short operands

They are not related to the four floating-point Divide instructions. After the execution of each Halve instruction, the second operand is halved, and the quotient is placed in the first operand. The Halve operation basically shifts the fraction part of a floating-point number one bit to the right. Both sign bit and characteristic are not disturbed. Neither normalization nor the test for zero fraction is made.

12.8 FLOATING-POINT COMPARE AND STORE INSTRUCTIONS

In the previous sections, we described in detail four basic groups of floating-point arithmetic instructions. There are three more groups of important instructions which are available to a programmer—Compare, Store, and Load instructions.

Briefly speaking the only purpose of all Compare instructions is to set the condition code. The floating-point Store instructions, like the corresponding instructions in fixed-point programming, store the contents of a floating-point register in the main-storage area. Finally, the floating-point Load instructions load a floating-point register. The user should note that some floating-point Load instructions set the condition code, others do not. In addition, there is a class of floating-point Load instructions which performs various operations on the sign bit of the result. We shall discuss these three groups of instructions in this and next section.

As mentioned before, the floating-point Compare instructions only serve to set the condition code. In each of the four available Compare instructions (Table 12.4)

Table 12.4 Floating-point Compare instructions

Instructions		Remarks
CDR	$R1,R2$	RR format; long operands
CER	$R1,R2$	RR format; short operands
CD	$R1,D2(X2,B2)$	RX format; long operands
CE	$R1,D2(X2,B2)$	RX format; short operands

the first operand is compared with the second operand and the condition code is set according to the convention listed in Table 4.2, or as follows:

CC = 0, if the first operand is equal to the second operand;
   = 1, if the first operand is less than the second operand;
   = 2, if the first operand is greater than the second operand.

The comparison takes into account the sign, the characteristic, and the fraction of each operand. However, if the fraction is zero, then the associated sign and characteristic are disregarded. Note that the CD and CE instructions (see Table 12.4) are of RX format. Each storage address in a CD instruction must be aligned on a doubleword boundary, whereas that in a CE instruction, on a fullword boundary. For example, when the contents of floating-point register 2 and those in main-storage area before the execution of the instruction:

                    CD   2,RANDOM

are as shown in Fig. 12.13, then the condition code will be set to 2.

Floating-point
Register 2 | 41 | 200000 | 00000000 |

RANDOM | 3F | 46AF1B | 243F701E |

Fig. 12.13 Contents used in CD instruction (hexadecimal).

Let us now examine the two available floating-point Store instructions of RX format as shown below.

        STE $R1,D2(X2,B2)$
        STD $R1,D2(X2,B2)$

They are used to store either a short or long floating-point number from a floating-point register to main storage. The STE instruction requires the second operand on a fullword boundary; the STD instruction, on a doubleword boundary. After the execution of either Store instruction, the first operand is stored at the location of the second operand and condition code is not affected. For example, after the execution of the following instructions:

$$\text{STD} \quad 6, \text{RANDOM}$$

the contents of the floating-point register 6 are stored in the doubleword RANDOM (see Fig. 12.13). The address RANDOM must be exactly divisible by 8.

12.9 FLOATING-POINT LOAD INSTRUCTIONS

There are five sets of Load instructions available for loading a short or long floating-point number: Load, Load and Test, Load Positive, Load Negative, and Load Complement. A set of Load Register Rounded instructions is also available on some models of System/370 and System/360 to round off the extended-precision answers to the long or short format.

Load Instructions and Load and Test Instructions

These two sets serve the same basic purpose, but differ in that the Load and Test instructions set the condition code, whereas the Load instructions do not; both sets are shown in Table 12.5.

Table 12.5 Floating-point Load instructions, and Load and Test instructions

Instructions			Format	Operands	Condition code setting
Load	LDR	$R1, R2$	RR	Long	No
	LER	$R1, R2$	RR	Short	No
	LD	$R1, D2(X2, B2)$	RX	Long	No
	LE	$R1, D2(X2, B2)$	RX	Short	No
Load and Test	LTDR	$R1, R2$	RR	Long	Yes
	LTER	$R1, R2$	RR	Short	Yes

After the execution of each instruction, the first operand is replaced by the second operand; and the latter is not changed. When short operands are used such as in LER, LE, and LTER instructions, the right half of the result register remains unchanged. Finally, the integral boundary requirements must be observed for the main-storage address used in LD and LE instructions. If the initial contents in floating-point registers and main storage area are as shown in Fig. 12.14, the contents of the answer registers after executing various instructions are indicated in Table 12.6.

As mentioned before, the Load and Test (LTDR and LTER) instructions differ from

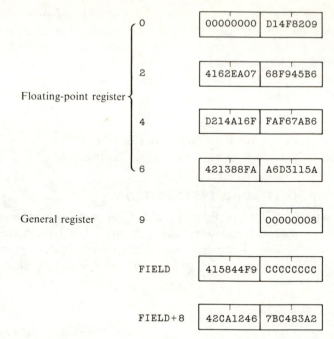

Fig. 12.14 Contents in registers and storage area FIELD which is on doubleword boundary.

Table 12.6 Register contents after the execution of various floating-point Load instructions

	Instruction	New contents in the first operand	Condition code setting
LDR	4,6	421388FA A6D3115A	No
LER	4,6	421388FA FAF67AB6	No
LD	2,FIELD	415844F9 CCCCCCCC	No
LE	2,FIELD	415844F9 68F945B6	No
LD	2,FIELD(9)	42CA1246 7BC483A2	No
LE	4,FIELD+4	CCCCCCCC FAF67AB6	No
LTDR	4,6	421388FA A6D3115A	Yes; CC = 2
LTER	4,6	421388FA FAF67AB6	Yes; CC = 2
LTER	4,0	00000000 FAF67AB6	Yes; CC = 0

Load (LDR and LER) instructions in only one point: The former instructions set the condition code. This is carried out in the following way: After the first operand is loaded with its new contents, test is made on its sign as well as the fraction part. Depending on the outcome, the condition code is automatically set as shown in

Table 12.7. Note that in LTER instruction which deals with short-form data, the rightmost 32 bits of result are not tested (they are not even changed). The condition code 3 is not used.

Table 12.7 Condition code setting for LTER, LTDR, LPDR, LPER, LNDR, LNER, LCDR, and LCER instructions

Results in the first operand after Load instruction			Condition code (in decimal)
Sign bit	Fraction	Value	
1	= 0	0	0
0	= 0	0	0
1	≠ 0	< 0	1
0	≠ 0	> 0	2

Two practical details to remember: First, since the Load and Test instructions set the condition code, they may be used to test the value of a floating-point register. Specifically, the sequence of instructions in Fig. 12.15 may be used for testing if the doubleword value of floating-point register 2 is zero, plus or minus.

```
        LTDR    2,2
        BC      8,ZERO
        BC      4,PLUS
MINUS ........
```

Fig. 12.15 Instructions used to test the contents in floating-point register 2.

Second, if you wish to load a short operand into a floating-point register and perform a long operation with it, you must zero the entire 64 bits of the register before loading the short operand.

Load Positive, Load Negative, and Load Complement Instructions

If a programmer wishes to ensure that the floating-point result is positive after a Load operation, he or she may use one of the Load Positive instructions shown in Table 12.8. After the execution of either instruction, the second operand is placed in the first operand location with a plus sign, that is, the sign bit of the copied number is changed to zero before it is placed in the first operand. The contents of the second operand are not disturbed.

Similarly, after the execution of a Load Negative instruction (Table 12.8), the second operand is placed in the first operand location with a minus sign. The sign bit of the copied number is changed to 1, even when the fraction is zero.

The two available Load Complement instructions (Table 12.8) are used to change

Table 12.8 Load Positive, Load Negative, and Load Complement instructions

Instructions			Format	Operands	Condition code setting
Load Positive	LPDR	*R1, R2*	RR	Long	Yes
	LPER	*R1, R2*	RR	Short	Yes
Load Negative	LNDR	*R1, R2*	RR	Long	Yes
	LNER	*R1, R2*	RR	Short	Yes
Load Complement	LCDR	*R1, R2*	RR	Long	Yes
	LCER	*R1, R2*	RR	Short	Yes

the sign of a floating-point number by switching 1 to 0 and 0 to 1 in the sign bit. If the initial contents of floating-point registers are

$$\text{Floating-point register 2:} \quad \text{4162EA07 68F945B6}$$
$$4: \quad \text{D214A16F FAF67AB6}$$
$$6: \quad \text{00000000 00000000}$$

the contents of the answer registers after executing various instructions are presented in Table 12.9. The rules of condition code setting are shown in Table 12.7.

Table 12.9 Register contents after the execution of some Load instructions

Instruction	New contents in the first operand		Condition code
LPDR 4,4	5214A16F	FAF67AB6	2
LPER 2,4	5214A16F	68F945B6	2
LPDR 2,4	5214A16F	FAF67A86	2
LNER 2,2	C162EA07	68F945B6	1
LNER 2,4	D214A16E	68F945B6	1
LNDR 2,4	D214A16F	FAF67AB6	1
LCER 2,4	5214A16F	68F945B6	2
LCDR 2,4	5214A16F	FAF67A86	2
LCER 4,6	80000000	FAF67A86	0

Load Register Rounded Instructions

As an optional feature, two instructions are available to round off the extended-precision results to the short or long format: Load Register Short Rounded (LRER) and Load Register Long Rounded (LRDR). Both instructions use RR format:

$$\text{LRER} \quad \textit{R1, R2}$$
$$\text{LRDR} \quad \textit{R1, R2}$$

After the execution of each instruction, the second operand is rounded off (without normalization) and the result is placed in the first-operand location.

The process of rounding depends on the instruction.

1. *During the execution of an* LRER *instruction*

   It consists of adding 1 (in absolute value) to the bit content in bit position 32 of the floating-point register *R2*. The carry, if any, is propagated to the left.

2. *During the execution of an* LRDR *instruction*

   The following three steps are taken:

   a) Inspect the bit position 8 of the floating-point register *R2 + 2*. For example, during the execution of the following instruction

   $$\text{LRDR} \quad 0,4$$

   the bit position 8 of the floating-point register 6 is inspected.
   b) If this bit is 0, no action is taken, and the contents in bit positions 0 through 63 are placed in the floating-point register *R1*.
   c) If this bit is 1, add an absolute 1 to the contents of the bit position 63 in floating-point *R2*.

   If the rounding process causes a carry out of the leftmost four-bit position of the fraction, the fraction is shifted right a four-bit position and the characteristic is increased by one.

12.10 EXAMPLE—FLOATING-POINT ARITHMETIC

In the previous sections, we discussed floating-point instructions one by one, making no attempt to tie them together. To obtain an overall view, we shall present two complete examples: the first deals with the floating-point arithmetic operations; and the second illustrates how an existing library subroutine, such as a square root routine, can be readily called by a user's program written in assembler language.

In the first example, let *A* and *B* be two double-precision numbers. A subroutine is to be written in assembler language to compute the sum, the difference, the product of these two numbers. In addition, the quotient *Q* is also to be computed as follows:

$$Q = B/A \quad \text{if} \quad A > B$$
$$Q = A/B \quad \text{if} \quad A \leq B$$

The main program written in a high-level language is used to read in two numbers *A* and *B*; to call the subroutine ILOAT; and to print out all the answers in double precision. Three main programs are offered: FORTRAN, COBOL, and PL/I versions are shown in Figs. 12.16, 12.17 and 12.18, respectively.

The reliance of high-level language main program makes life easier for a programmer. An assembler-language programmer using floating-point arithmetic has to convert numbers from binary integer to floating-point and back, which is not an easy

```
   DOUBLE PRECISION A,B,SUM,DIFF,PROD,QUOT
   WRITE(6,4)
 4 FORMAT(1H1,T10,'A',T30,'B',T49,'SUM',T68,'DIFF',T87,
 1'PROD',T106,'QUOT')
   DO 2 I=1,5
   READ(5,1) A,B
 1 FORMAT(2F5.2)
   CALL ILOAT(A,B,SUM,DIFF,PROD,QUOT)
   WRITE(6,5) A,B,SUM,DIFF,PROD,QUOT
 5 FORMAT(2X,F16.12,5(4X,F16.12))
 2 CONTINUE
   CALL EXIT
   END
```

Fig. 12.16   FORTRAN main program to call subroutine ILOAT.

```
      IDENTIFICATION DIVISION.
      PROGRAM-ID.
          'MAINFL'. PROGRAM NAME
      AUTHOR.
          S. S. KUO.
      REMARKS.
          THIS IS A MAIN PROGRAM TO CALL ILOAT.
      ENVIRONMENT DIVISION.
      CONFIGURATION SECTION.
      SOURCE-COMPUTER.
          IBM-360 G50.
      OBJECT-COMPUTER.
          IBM-360 G50.
      INPUT-OUTPUT SECTION.
      FILE-CONTROL.
          SELECT CARD-FILE ASSIGN TO 'CARDIN' UNIT-RECORD.
          SELECT PRINT-FILE ASSIGN TO 'PRINTER' UTILITY.
      DATA DIVISION.
      FILE SECTION.
      FD  CARD-FILE
          RECORDING MODE IS F
          LABEL RECORDS ARE OMITTED
          DATA RECORDS ARE CARD-REC.
      01  CARD-REC                  PICTURE X(80).
      FD  PRINT-FILE
          RECORDING MODE IS F
          LABEL RECORDS ARE OMITTED
          DATA RECORDS ARE PRT-LINE.
      01  PRT-LINE                  PICTURE X(133).
      WORKING-STORAGE SECTION.
      77  C-A                       COMPUTATIONAL-2.
      77  C-B                       COMPUTATIONAL-2.
      77  SUMS                      COMPUTATIONAL-2.
      77  DIFF                      COMPUTATIONAL-2.
      77  PROD                      COMPUTATIONAL-2.
      77  QUOT                      COMPUTATIONAL-2.
      77  LOOP-CNT                  COMPUTATIONAL VALUE ZERO
                                    PICTURE S999.
      01  CARD-RECORD.
          02  A                      PICTURE S9999V99.
          02  B                     PICTURE S9999V99.
          02  FILLER                PICTURE X(66).
```

Fig. 12.17   COBOL main program to call subroutine ILOAT.

(continued)
```
        01   PRT-LINE-1.
             02   FILLER                    PICTURE X(9) VALUE SPACES.
             02   HEAD-A                    PICTURE X VALUE 'A'.
             02   FILLER                    PICTURE X(19) VALUE SPACES.
             02   HEAD-B                    PICTURE X VALUE 'B'.
             02   FILLER                    PICTURE X(18) VALUE SPACES.
             02   HEAD-SUM                  PICTURE XXX VALUE 'SUM'.
             02   FILLER                    PICTURE X(16) VALUE SPACES.
             02   HEAD-DIFF                 PICTURE X(4) VALUE 'DIFF'.
             02   FILLER                    PICTURE X(15) VALUE SPACES.
             02   HEAD-PROD                 PICTURE X(4) VALUE 'PROD'.
             02   FILLER                    PICTURE X(15) VALUE SPACES.
             02   HEAD-QUOT                 PICTURE X(4) VALUE 'QUOT'.
             02   FILLER                    PICTURE X(24) VALUE SPACES.
        01   DETAIL-LINE.
             02   FILLER                    PICTURE XX VALUE SPACES.
             02   A-1                       PICTURE ZZZ9.99.
             02   FILLER                    PICTURE X(13) VALUE SPACES.
             02   B-1                       PICTURE ZZZ9.99.
             02   FILLER                    PICTURE X(13) VALUE SPACES.
             02   SUM-1                     PICTURE ZZZ9.99.
             02   FILLER                    PICTURE X(13) VALUE SPACES.
             02   DIFF-1                    PICTURE ZZZ9.99.
             02   FILLER                    PICTURE X(13) VALUE SPACES.
             02   PROD-1                    PICTURE ZZZ9.99.
             02   FILLER                    PICTURE X(13) VALUE SPACES.
             02   QUOT-1                    PICTURE ZZZ9.99.
             02   FILLER                    PICTURE X(14) VALUE SPACES.
    PROCEDURE DIVISION.
    OPEN-FILES.
         OPEN INPUT CARD-FILE OUTPUT PRINT-FILE.
         WRITE PRT-LINE FROM PRT-LINE-1 AFTER ADVANCING 0 LINES.
    READ-CARD.
         READ CARD-FILE INTO CARD-RECORD AT END GO TO EOJ.
         MOVE A TO C-A. MOVE B TO C-B.
         ENTER LINKAGE.
         CALL 'ILOAT' USING C-A C-B SUMS DIFF PROD QUOT.
         ENTER COBOL.
         MOVE C-A TO A-1. MOVE C-B TO B-1.
         MOVE SUMS TO SUM-1. MOVE DIFF TO DIFF-1.
         MOVE PROD TO PROD-1. MOVE QUOT TO QUOT-1.
         WRITE PRT-LINE FROM DETAIL-LINE AFTER ADVANCING 1 LINES.
         ADD 1 TO LOOP-CNT.
         IF LOOP-CNT IS EQUAL TO 5 GO TO EOJ ELSE GO TO READ-CARD.
    EOJ.
         CLOSE CARD-FILE PRINT-FILE.
         STOP RUN.
```

Fig. 12.17   COBOL main program to call subroutine ILOAT.*(continued)*

```
FLOATER:  PROCEDURE OPTIONS (MAIN);
DECLARE (A,B,SUM,DIFF,PROD,QUOT)FLOAT BINARY(53);
PUT FILE (SYSPRINT)EDIT('A','B','SUM','DIFF','PROD','QUOT')
                      (A(11),(5)A(20));
ON ENDFILE (SYSIN) GO TO ENDIT;
GET FILE (SYSIN) LIST(A,B);
CALL ILOAT(A,B,SUM,DIFF,PROD,QUOT);
PUT FILE(SYSPRINT) EDIT(A,B,SUM,DIFF,PROD,QUOT)(SKIP,(6)F(20,12));
ENDIT: END;
```

Fig. 12.18   PL/I main program to call subroutine ILOAT.

```
LOC     OBJECT CODE       ADDR1  ADDR2   STMT   SOURCE STATEMENT

                                            1   * THIS IS A SUBROUTINE WHICH TAKES THE SUM, DIFF., PRODUCT
                                            2   * AND QUOTIENT OF TWO NUMBER A AND B IN DOUBLE PRECISION
000000                                      3   ILOAT CSECT
000000  47F0 F00A                0000A      4         SAVE  (14,12),,*
000004  05                                  5+        B     10(0,15)      BRANCH AROUND ID
000005  C9D3D6C1E3                          6+        DC    AL1(5)
00000A  90EC D00C                0000C      7+        DC    CL5'ILOAT'    IDENTIFIER
00000E  05B0                                8+        STM   14,12,12(13)  SAVE REGISTERS
000010                                      9         BALR  11,0
                                           10         USING *,11
000010  58C1 0000                00000     11         L     12,0(1)       LOAD ADDRESS OF A INTO GR12
000014  682C 0000                00000     12         LD    2,0(12)       LOAD VALUE OF A IN FPR=2
000018  5891 0004                00004     13         L     9,4(1)        LOAD ADDRESS OF B INTO GR9
00001C  6A29 0000                00000     14         AD    2,0(9)        A+B
000020  5881 0008                00008     15         L     8,8(1)        LOAD ADDRESS OF SUM INTO GR8
000024  6028 0000                00000     16         STD   2,0(8)
000028  682C 0000                00000     17         LD    2,0(12)
00002C  6B29 0000                00000     18         SD    2,0(9)        A-B
000030  5871 000C                0000C     19         L     7,12(1)       LOAD ADDRESS OF DIFF. IN GR7
000034  6027 0000                00000     20         STD   2,0(7)
000038  682C 0000                00000     21         LD    2,0(12)
00003C  6C29 0000                00000     22         MD    2,0(9)        AXB
000040  5861 0010                00010     23         L     6,16(1)       LOAD ADDRESS OF PROD. INTO GR6
000044  6026 0000                00000     24         STD   2,0(6)
000048  682C 0000                00000     25         LD    2,0(12)
00004C  6929 0000                00000     26         CD    2,0(9)
000050  4720 B04C                0005C     27         BC    2,AGTB        BRANCH IF A IS GREATER THAN B
000054  6D29 0000                00000     28         DD    2,0(9)
000058  47F0 B054                00064     29         BC    15,OUT
00005C  6829 0000                00000     30   AGTB  LD    2,0(9)
000060  6D2C 0000                00000     31         DD    2,0(12)       B/A
000064  5851 0014                00014     32   OUT   L     5,20(1)
000068  6025 0000                00000     33         STD   2,0(5)
                                           34         RETURN (14,12)
00006C  98EC D00C                0000C     35+        LM    14,12,12(13)  RESTORE THE REGISTERS
000070  07FE                               36+        BR    14            RETURN
                                           37         END
```

Fig. 12.19 Subroutine ILOAT.

362

task. An advantage of high-level language main program is that it does the job with much less work on the part of the programmer.

The subroutine ILOAT is used basically to perform the four floating-point calculations (see Fig. 12.19). Let us now focus our attention on the first four instructions in the calculations:

L   12,0(1)

After executing the instruction, the address of the double precision number A is loaded in the general register 12.

LD   2,0(12)

This is a double-precision floating-point load instruction. The value of A is loaded in the floating-point register 2.

L   9,4(1)

The address of B is loaded in the general register 9.

AD   2,0(9)

$A + B$ and the sum is stored in the floating-point register 2.

At this point, the reader is advised to trace through the remaining part of the subroutine ILOAT. After returning to the main program, the output is made (see Fig. 12.20).

A	B	SUM
9.111000000000	0.237000000000	9.348000000000
3.199000000000	2.981000000000	6.180000000000
6.296000000000	2.107000000000	8.403000000000
5.122000000000	4.122000000000	9.244000000000

DIFF	PROD	QUOT
8.874000000000	2.159307000000	0.026012512348
0.218000000000	9.536219000000	0.931853704283
4.189000000000	13.265672000000	0.334656925032
1.000000000000	21.112884000000	0.804763764155

Fig. 12.20   Output from subroutine ILOAT and its main program.

12.11 EXAMPLE—CALL A BUILT-IN FUNCTION IN FORTRAN

A high-level language compiler (e.g., FORTRAN compiler) normally contains many built-in functions such as SIN, COS, EXP, and SQRT. This section will illustrate how to link a user's assembler language subroutine to one of these built-in functions. It is

```
C       MAIN PROGRAM TO CALL SUBROUTINE SQAB
        WRITE(3,1)
    1 FORMAT('1')
        READ(1,10) A,B
   10 FORMAT(2F10.4)
        CALL SQAB(A,B,RESULT)
    )   WRITE (3,15) A,B,RESULT
   15 FORMAT('0THE RESULT WITH A= 'F10.4,', B= 'F10.4,
    1 ' IS 'F10.4)
        CALL EXIT
        END
```

Fig. 12.21 FORTRAN main program to call subroutine SQAB.

important to note that many such functions are written in the floating-point programming; they are compatible with the user's subroutine only when the latter is also written in the floating-point. We shall conclude this chapter by illustrating the linkage convention with a specific example.

Write a subroutine SQAB in assembler language to compute the following expression:

$$Y = \sqrt{B(A + B)}$$

All floating-point calculations are performed with single-precision, and the square root operation is executed by the function SQRT.

The main program, primarily used for input/output, is written in a high-level language. Figures 12.21, 12.22, and 12.23, respectively, show its FORTRAN, COBOL, and PL/I versions. Note that the arguments used in the call statement are in the order of A, B, and RESULT.

We present a block diagram of the three-level linkage in Fig. 12.24. In the linkage between the subroutine SQAB and the built-in function SQRT, the address of this external routine SQRT is not known. However, we may use the following DC statement in the subroutine SQAB (see Fig. 12.25):

SQR   DC   V(SQRT)

This statement demands that a fullword in the main storage is reserved for the address of the exterior symbol SQRT; it is filled in during linking. In addition, the linkage between the function SQRT and the subroutine SQAB (including the automatic return to SQAB) is readily accomplished by the following instructions:

L   15,SQR
BALR   14,15

As discussed in Chapter 8, the Load (L) instruction loads the address of the function SQRT in the general register 15; and BALR instruction branches to the function SQRT and, on completion, returns to the instruction next to this BALR instruction.

We shall conclude this section with the following three remarks. First, as a convention, a FORTRAN built-in function returns its value either to floating-point

```
IDENTIFICATION DIVISION.
PROGRAM-ID.
    'MAINSQ'. PROGRAM NAME
AUTHOR.
    S. S. KUO.
REMARKS.
    THIS IS A MAIN PROGRAM TO CALL SQAB.
ENVIRONMENT DIVISION.
CONFIGURATION SECTION.
SOURCE-COMPUTER.
    IBM-360 G50.
OBJECT-COMPUTER.
    IBM-360 G50.
INPUT-OUTPUT SECTION.
FILE-CONTROL.
    SELECT CARD-FILE ASSIGN TO 'CARDIN' UNIT-RECORD.
    SELECT PRINT-FILE ASSIGN TO 'PRINTER' UTILITY.
DATA DIVISION.
FILE SECTION.
FD  CARD-FILE
    RECORDING MODE IS F
    LABEL RECORDS ARE OMITTED
    DATA RECORDS ARE CARD-REC.
01  CARD-REC                     PICTURE X(80).
FD  PRINT-FILE
    RECORDING MODE IS F
    LABEL RECORDS ARE OMITTED
    DATA RECORDS ARE PRT-LINE.
01  PRT-LINE                     PICTURE X(133).
WORKING-STORAGE SECTION.
77  A-X                          COMPUTATIONAL-1.
77  B-X                          COMPUTATIONAL-1.
77  RESULT-X                     COMPUTATIONAL-1.
01  CARD-IN.
    02  A                        PICTURE 99999V9999.
    02  B                        PICTURE 99999V9999.
    02  FILLER                   PICTURE X(60).
01  SPACE-LINE.
    02  FILLER                   PICTURE X(133) VALUE SPACES.
01  PRT-LINE-1.
    02  FILLER                   PICTURE X VALUE SPACES.
    02  TITLE-1                  PICTURE X(19) VALUE
                                 'THE RESULT WITH A= '.
    02  A-1                      PICTURE ZZZZ9.9999.
    02  TITLE-2                  PICTURE X(5) VALUE ', B= '.
    02  B-1                      PICTURE ZZZZ9.9999.
    02  TITLE-3                  PICTURE X(4) VALUE ' IS '.
    02  RESULT                   PICTURE ZZZZ9.9999.
    02  FILLER                   PICTURE X(74) VALUE SPACES.
PROCEDURE DIVISION.
OPEN-FILES.
    OPEN INPUT CARD-FILE OUTPUT PRINT-FILE.
    READ CARD-FILE INTO CARD-IN, AT END GO TO CLOSE-FILES.
    MOVE A TO A-X.  MOVE B TO B-X.
    ENTER LINKAGE.
    CALL 'SQAB' USING A-X B-X RESULT-X.
    ENTER COBOL.
PRINT-ROUTINE.
    MOVE A TO A-1. MOVE B TO B-1.
    MOVE RESULT-X TO RESULT.
    WRITE PRT-LINE FROM SPACE-LINE AFTER ADVANCING 0 LINES.
    WRITE PRT-LINE FROM PRT-LINE-1 AFTER ADVANCING 2 LINES.
CLOSE-FILES.
    CLOSE CARD-FILE PRINT-FILE.
    STOP RUN.
```

Fig. 12.22 COBOL main program to call subroutine SQAB.

```
SQABT:  PROC OPTIONS(MAIN);
PUT PAGE;
DECLARE (A,B,RESULT)FLOAT BINARY;
GET LIST (A,B);
CALL SQAB(A,B,RESULT);
PUT EDIT('THE RESULT WITH A=',A,' B= ',B,' IS ',RESULT)(A,F(10,4));
END;
```

Fig. 12.23   PL/I main program to call subroutine SQAB.

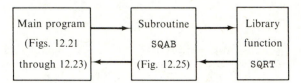

Fig. 12.24   Block diagram showing program in three levels.

```
*   THIS SUBROUTINE SOLVES FOR RESULT = SQRT(B(A+B))
*
SQAB       START 0
           SAVE  (14,12),,*
           BALR  11,0
           USING *,11
           LR    12,13
           LA    13,SAVEAREA
           ST    12,SAVEAREA+4
           ST    13,8(12)
           L     2,0(1)         GR2=ADDRESS OF A.
           L     3,4(1)         GR3=ADDRESS OF B.
           LE    0,0(2)         F.P.R0=A
           LE    2,0(3)         F.P.R2=B.
           AER   0,2            F.P.R0=A+B
           MER   2,0            F.P.R2=B(A+B)
           STE   2,PROD         STORE THE PRODUCT IN PROD.
           ST    1,TEMP         PUT FORTRAN ARGUMENT
*                              LIST POINTER IN TEMP.
           LA    1,APROD        GR1=ARG.LIST POINTER FOR SQRT
           L     15,SQR         GR15=ADDRESS FOR SQRT
           BALR  14,15          BRANCH TO SQRT ROUTINE
           L     1,TEMP         RESTORE FORT. ARG. LIST POINTER
           L     2,8(1)         GR2=ADDRESS OF RESULT
           STE   0,0(2)         STORE RESULT
           L     13,SAVEAREA+4
           RETURN (14,12)
PROD       DS    E
SAVEAREA   DS    18F
TEMP       DS    F
APROD      DC    A(PROD)
SQR        DC    V(SQRT)
           END   SQAB
```

Fig. 12.25   Subroutine SQAB to call library routine SQRT.

register 0 or to general register 0, depending on whether the function is written in the floating-point or in fixed-point arithmetic. Since the FORTRAN function SQRT is written in the floating-point arithmetic, it returns its result to *floating-point* register 0 (see STE instruction in Fig. 12.25). Second, PL/I does not adhere to this convention, but requires an argument where the result is placed. Third, a system macro, which is almost identical to the FORTRAN call statement, may be available in your installation.

BIBLIOGRAPHY

Anderson, S. F., J. G. Earle, R. E. Goldschmidt, and D. M. Powers, "The IBM System/360 Model 91; Floating-Point Execution Unit," *IBM J. of Res. and Development* **11**, 34–53 (1967).

Ashenhurst, R. L., and N. Metropolis, "Unnormalized Floating-Point Arithmetic," *J. Assoc. Computing Machinery* **6**, 415–429 (1959).

Gray, H. L., and C. Harrison, Jr., "Normalized Floating-Point Arithmetic with an Index of Significance," *Proc. 1959 Eastern Joint Computer Conference* (Dec. 1–3, 1959, Boston), pages 244–248.

IBM System/370 Principles of Operation, Form GA22-7000, IBM Corp.

IBM System/360 Principles of Operation, Form GA22-6821, IBM Corp.

Sweeney, D. W., "An Analysis of Floating-Point Addition," *IBM Systems J.* **4**, 31–42 (1965).

Wadey, W. G., "Floating-Point Arithmetics," *J. of Assoc. Computing Machinery* **7**, 129–139 (1960).

PROBLEMS

Section 12.1

12.1. The radius of an object is 0.625 cm. Express this quantity in both short and long forms for System/360 and System/370 (normalized), (a) in binary; and (b) in hexadecimal.

12.2. Same as the above problem except that the quantity is negative.

12.3. a) When the short form is used, how many hexadecimal digits represent the fraction? How many decimal digits does it represent?
   b) Same as (a), except that the long form is used.

12.4. Which of the floating point numbers below is normalized?
   a) 4E2EF247
   b) 3F0A37E6
   c) 3A1F627A87B6954E
   d) 5A061B6426A7BF14

12.5. Express the contents in floating-point register 4 (see Fig. 12.4) in its decimal equivalent.

Section 12.2

12.6. a) How many bits are there in a general register?
b) How many bits are there in a floating-point register?
c) How many general registers are there in a System/360 or System/370?
d) And how many floating-point registers?

12.7. Is there floating-point register 3 in a System/360 or System/370?

12.8. Perform the following floating-point additions:

$$
\begin{array}{lll}
.265 \times 16^3 & .DA6 \times 16^2 & .DA6 \times 16^3 \\
+ \quad .1EA \times 16^3 & + \quad .5B5 \times 16^2 & + \quad .5B5 \times 16^2 \\
\hline
\end{array}
$$

Section 12.3

12.9. Translate each of the following DC instructions in its floating-point expression. State whether it is in a short or a long form.

```
a)          SUN   DC   E'1495E+10'
b)          PI    DC   D'3.14159265358'
c)          RAD   DC   E'.281784E-12'
```

12.10. How many bytes are reserved by each of the following instructions?

```
a)          MATRIX   DS   20D
b)          VEC      DS   15F
```

Section 12.4

12.11. The following instruction is invalid. Why?

```
                AER   0,5
```

12.12. The contents of floating-point register 2 are $(14)_{16}$, and those in four-byte VEC field are $(6)_{16}$; write the contents of the result register after the execution of the following instruction:

```
                AE   2,VEC
```

Section 12.5

12.13. Compute the result after the execution of the following instruction:

```
                MER   2,4
```

The contents in registers are in hexadecimal:

	Characteristic	Fraction
Floating-point register 2	41	111111 00000000
Floating-point register 4	42	111111 00000001

12.14. If floating-point register 6 contains 41200000 00000000 and ALPHA contains 42241232 30000012, what is the result in product register after the execution of the instruction

```
                ME   6,ALPHA
```

Is the prenormalization necessary? Is the postnormalization necessary?

12.15. Same as Problem 12.14, except that the instruction is MD   6,ALPHA.

12.16. Same as Problem 12.13, except that the instruction is MDR   2,4.

Section 12.6

Show the results of the following operations (a) with guard digit, and (b) without it. The initial contents are

Floating-point register 0:	42112217 046389C1
2:	42200000 00000000
4:	C110778A 10FF5724
6:	413146A1 4BE392A2
Doubleword field NH:	43335421 23001632
Fullword field S19:	C221A176

12.17. The given instruction is AER 0,4.

12.18. The given instruction is ME 2,NH.

12.19. The given instruction is AE 6,S19.

Section 12.7

12.20. Is the remainder preserved after a floating-point Divide operation? After a fixed-point Divide operation?

12.21. If the contents of the floating-point register 2 are

| 41400000 | 00000000 |

and eight-byte DENOM field contains

| 41600000 | 00000000 |

find the quotient in hexadecimal after the execution of the following instruction:

DE   2,DENOM

12.22. If the contents of the floating-point register 2 are

| 41400000 | 00000000 |

and the floating-point register 0 contains

| C4300000 | 00000000 |

what is the quotient, in hexadecimal, after executing the instruction below?

DDR   2,0

Where is the quotient located?

Section 12.8

12.23. The basic purpose of a floating-point Compare instruction is to set the condition code. Where is the exact location of this condition code?

12.24. In reference to Fig. 12.10, after the execution of the instruction

$$\text{CDR}\quad 4,0$$

what is the condition-code setting?

12.25. In reference to Fig. 12.12, after the execution of the instruction

$$\text{CE}\quad 4,\text{SIX}$$

what is the condition-code setting?

12.26. If the address RANDOM in Fig. 12.13 is $(009093)_{16}$, will the instruction

$$\text{CD}\quad 2,\text{RANDOM}$$

work?

LABORATORY ASSIGNMENT

1. Given: the coordinates of two points (x_1, y_1) and (x_2, y_2). Write a subroutine using floating-point instructions to find (1) the distance S between the two points:

$$S = \sqrt{(x_2 - x_1)^2 + (y_2 - y_1)^2}$$

and (2) the angle of inclination θ of the line passing through the two points:

$$\theta = \tan^{-1}\left[\frac{y_2 - y_1}{x_2 - x_1}\right]$$

It is desirable to convert θ from radians to degrees. Write a main program in a high-level language which handles the input and output.

2. Rewrite the subroutine ISLAND (see Fig. 11.12 in Section 11.3) in floating-point programming. Modify the main program (Figs. 10.16 through 10.18) if necessary to perform output.

3. The subroutine RANDA in Fig. 12.26 generates random numbers using a similar algorithm as discussed in Problem 4.13 and Fig. 4.16. Since the subroutine is used repetitively, it is highly important that we have a "tight" program. For example, at the beginning of this subroutine, only registers 14, 15, 0, 1, ..., 5 are saved. Near the exit of the subroutine, only registers 2 through 5 are used in the LM instruction. Debug and further optimize the coding used in Fig. 12.26. Write a main program to call the subroutine RANDA and to print out the first 100 random numbers.

```
RANDA  CSECT
************************************************************
*                                                        *
*     SUBROUTINE TO COMPUTE RANDOM NUMBERS BY THE SAME    *
*     ALGORITHM SHOWN IN FIG. 4.16.  SINCE THIS PROGRAM   *
*     WOULD BE USED MANY TIMES, IT HAS BEEN WRITTEN       *
*     TO CONSERVE TIME BY ONLY SAVING THOSE REGISTERS     *
*     WHICH THE SYSTEM REQUIRES AND ONLY RESTORING        *
*     THOSE WHICH WERE USED.                              *
*                                                        *
************************************************************
           USING  *,15
           BC     15,COMP
           DC     AL1(5)
           DC     C'RANDA'
COMP       STM    14,5,12(13)
           LM     2,3,0(1)
           SR     4,4
           L      5,0(2)
           M      4,MAGIC
           N      5,MASK
           ST     5,0(2)
           IC     4,CHAR
           SLDL   4,24
           STM    4,5,HOLD
           LD     0,HOLD
           MD     0,ITEM
           STE    0,0(3)
           LM     2,5,28(13)
           BCR    15,14
HOLD       DS     D
ITEM       DC     D'.465661287524579E-9'
MAGIC      DC     F'65539'
MASK       DC     X'7FFFFFFF'
CHAR       DC     X'48'
           END
```

Fig. 12.26 Control section RANDA.

4. The EXecute (EX) instruction, of RX format, is essentially a glorified CALL statement to a one-instruction subroutine, known as the *subject instruction*. The address of the subject instruction is the second operand address in the EXecute instruction

$$\text{EX} \quad \underbrace{R1}, \underbrace{D2(X2, S2)}$$

$$\begin{array}{cc} \text{Modifier} & \text{Address of the} \\ \text{register} & \text{subject instruction} \end{array}$$

and the subject instruction is usually modified before execution.

The modification is accomplished as follows: The bit positions 8 through 15 of the subject instruction are ORed with the bit positions 24 through 31 of the modifier register. The modification takes place in the CPU after the subject instruction is fetched from its main storage location. Neither the subject instruction nor the modifier register is physically changed. If *R1* is 0, no modification occurs at all.

The modified or unmodified instruction is then executed. After that, the control is passed back to the instruction immediately following the EXecute instruction.

For example, the EX instruction in the following instruction sequence is used to modify the general register numbers:

```
        IC   7,=X'C4'
        EX   7,SUBJECT
        :
SUBJECT SR   1,8  SUBJECT INSTRUCTION
```

The SR instruction as executed by the EX instruction is

```
        SR   13,12
```

and the subject instruction itself is not changed.

The EX instruction can also be used to modify the length field, mask field, immediate data, or index. In particular, it is powerful to use EX instruction in connection with the TRT instruction (see page 337). Using this combination, write a subroutine to count the number of symbols on an input card. The first symbol starts on the second column, and each of the remaining symbols is separated by a blank from the preceding symbol.

PART III

JOB CONTROL LANGUAGE AND INPUT/OUTPUT

In a typical computer installation using an operating system, a programmer cannot expect his programs to get processed unless he has some knowledge in communicating with the operating system. Chapter 13 provides basic information on job control statements used in OS/360. Chapter 14 deals with input/output using system macros, which eliminate the dependence on the main program written in FORTRAN or other high-level language. Chapter 15 is concerned with the program status word, interrupts, masking, and protection. Only important principles are set forth in detail; many options and details are presented only in an abridged form and some are not even mentioned. The materials should enable the reader to cope with the approximately one-foot thickness of extensively cross-referenced manuals, which are supplied by the vendors.

CHAPTER 13

Elements of Job Control Language

13.1 FIVE COMPONENTS OF AN OPERATING SYSTEM

An operating system is a collection of service programs usually supplied by a vendor. It aims at maximizing the productivity of the computer installation by cutting down operator intervention and idle time between jobs; by efficiently allocating computer facilities; and by providing the best possible schedule for jobs.

Most operating systems are designed to assist in carrying out five major tasks: *program processing and utilities, job control, data control, task control, and recovery control* (see Fig. 13.1). The processing program accepts a user's program written in a source language; then directs an appropriate compiler to translate its statements into machine language instructions. This unexecutable output, the so-called *object module*, can be on disk, tape, or in cards. Several object modules, including canned routines, can be linked together to make a *load module*. This module is a set of executable instructions in machine language, ready to be executed.

The job control routines consist of two major parts—the *job scheduler* and *master scheduler*. The *reader/interpreter*, a component of job scheduler (Fig. 13.1), has an important function: reading and interpreting a set of job control cards. These cards, punched in Job Control Language (JCL), serve to communicate between a programmer and the operating system. Figure 13.2 represents a typical OS/360 job control card. Based on its coded information, the *initiator/terminator*, another component of the job scheduler (Fig. 13.1), checks the availability of input/output devices and, if these are satisfactory, initiates the job under consideration. The job scheduler is also responsible for "getting to" a program and its associated data. It brings a job to its successful termination, or forces a *dump* (see Appendix C). The second part of job control routines—the master scheduler—is primarily used to initiate and terminate the job scheduler.

Third, the data control aspect of an operating system is intended to provide a

PROCESSING PROGRAM
AND UTILITIES

CONTROL PROGRAMS

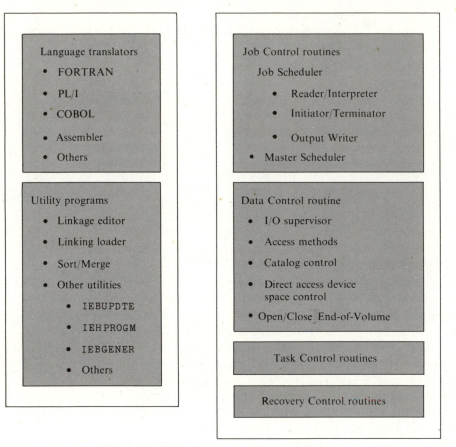

Fig. 13.1   Overview of an operating system.

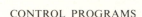

Fig. 13.2   A typical job control card showing the requested program IEUASM.

programmer with the standard forms of data organization and the access method
(see Chapter 14). The data control routines are used to move information between
main storage and auxiliary storage (e.g., a disk drive).

Fourth, the task control is concerned mainly with the allocation of CPU and other
computer resources (except input/output devices) to problem programs, executing them

in the order of their priority. A task may be thought as a program which has been brought into main storage, ready for execution.

Finally, the recovery control routines are basically used to collect and record computer and program data immediately after a machine check or an error occurred in an input/output channel.

13.2 THREE CONFIGURATIONS OF THE CONTROL PROGRAM

In the previous section, we learned that a typical operating system is designed to perform five major tasks: job control, data control, task control, recovery control, and program processing (see Fig. 13.1). The routines dealing with these tasks are collectively called a control program. A basic portion of this large program is stored in the main-storage area, known as the *resident portion* or the *nucleus*.† Its remaining portion, the *nonresident portion*, is not needed all the time and is usually placed in a disk-storage area. A typical main storage is shown in Fig. 13.3.

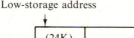

Low-storage address

(24K)	(104K)
Nucleus of control program	Problem programs including users' programs, compilers, and linkage editor

128K bytes

Fig. 13.3 A typical main storage.

There are three different configurations of the control program: Primary Control Program (PCP), multiprogramming with a fixed number of tasks (MFT), and multiprogramming with a variable number of tasks (MVT).

The PCP version‡ applies to a very simple situation with only one problem program existing in the main storage until it is terminated. In this version, a common area in the main storage (having low-storage addresses) is used to store the reader/interpreter, initiator, and a program (e.g., a compiler) at three different points in time, respectively. This is shown in Fig. 13.4. As mentioned before, the reader/interpreter, a part of job control, determines what devices should be available; and

---

† In a typical computer installation, the main-storage area is normally cleared each morning. By pushing LOAD button on a 370 or 360 computer console, the nucleus portion is transferred from a disk area to the main storage. This is known as *Initial Program Loading* (*IPLing*).

‡ On certain models of System/370 and System/360, PCP is not supported.

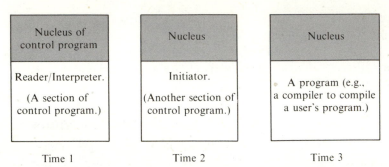

Fig. 13.4   Common usage of a main storage area by reader/interpreter, initiator, and a program.

the initiator, another part of the job control, makes sure that they will be available. The reader/interpreter reads the coded input/output requirement and the name of problem program; it then interprets them and passes them on to the initiator.   For example, a program name IEUASM is coded in Fig. 13.2.   This is written in the so-called Job Control Language, which we shall discuss more fully later in this chapter.

At the request of the reader/interpreter, the initiator is loaded into the main memory; it checks the availability of the input/output devices required by the program such as a compiler.   If each device is available, the nucleus begins to load the program; otherwise, an error message is printed.

In the PCP environment, only one task is residing in the main storage, ready to be executed, whereas in multiprogramming environment, a number of tasks can be residing in the main storage.   There are two basic versions: multiprogramming with a fixed number of tasks (MFT), and multiprogramming with a variable number of tasks (MVT).   In either version, main storage may be considered as having two areas: nucleus and dynamic areas.   It is in this dynamic area (as shaded in Fig. 13.5), the tasks to be executed, the reader/interpreter, the initiator/terminator,† and the *output writers* come and go.

In MFT environment (Fig. 13.5), the tasks are residing in *partitions* whose number is specified by the individual computer installation, but it must be no greater than 15. The number of bytes allocated to each partition is generally not the same.   The initiator determines which task is put in what partition, but a programmer must declare how many storage bytes and other things his program needs by specifying a *class*.   Each class has a one-letter code (A through 0).   A sample classification code used in a particular installation is shown in Table 13.1.   For example, if the program needs 128 K bytes and no tape units is needed, the program may be classified as Class G.

---

† Initiator/terminator and reader/interpreter are collectively called *job scheduler*.   Terminator will be discussed in Section 13.5.

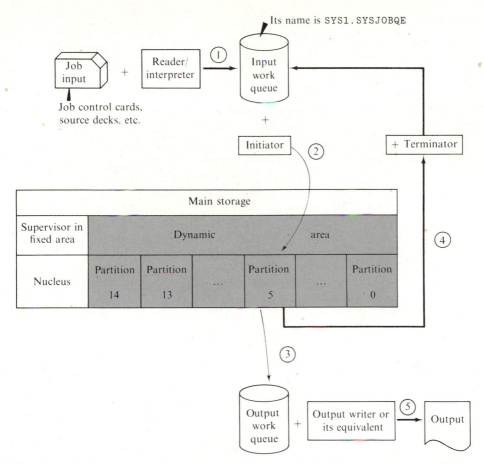

Fig. 13.5   Basic operations in multiprogramming with fixed number of tasks (MFT).

Table 13.1   Sample classification code

Class	CPU time	Tape drives	Size	Type
A	Under 15 min	Any number	256 K	Normal
B	Under 15 min	None	256 K	Normal
C	Over 15 min	Any number	256 K	Special
D	Under 15 min	three or more	128 K	Normal
E	Under 15 min	two 9-track drive	128 K	Normal
F	Under 15 min	one 9-track or two 7-track	128 K	Normal
G	Under 15 min	None	128 K	Normal

13.3 JOB STEP, JOB, AND JOB STREAM

A typical example of a job step is to assemble a source deck in assembler language. Each job step may have a name. One or more related job steps are called a job (see Fig. 13.6). Whether job steps are related to one another is defined by a programmer, not by the system. For example, a programmer may wish to compile a FORTRAN source program as the first job step, and then assemble a totally unrelated assembler-language source program as the second job step. These two job steps form a job; they are called STEP1 and STEP2, repectively, in Fig. 13.6. The second job shown in Fig. 13.6 has only one job step—to compile a PL/I source deck.

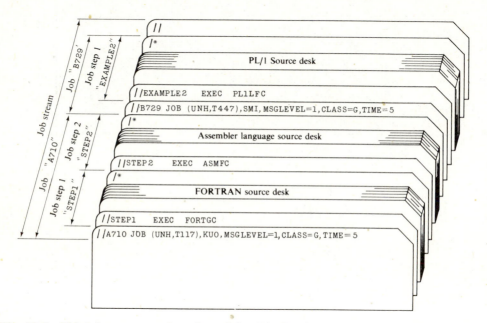

Fig. 13.6   This job stream consists of two jobs. The first job has two job steps; the second job has only one job step.

As another example, the following three job steps may be defined as a job:

1. Compilation of source deck written in assembler language; its output is not executable; (*Note: Compilation* is often considered as synonymous with *assembly.*)
2. Link editing the compiled output;
3. Execution of the executable output from the second job step.

Similarly, the following two job steps form another job:

1. Compilation of source deck written in assembler language.
2. Use OS loader to do the linking and then execute.

Many jobs make a job stream.

In the previous section, we learned that a programmer had to supply two items of information to the reader/interpreter in the control program: *the name of the requested program; and a list of the required input/output devices.* A programmer describes these information data in the job control language (JCL), which are then punched on standard 80-column cards, known as job control cards. A programmer can make use of four types of control cards: JOB, EXEC, DD, and /*. In terms of job control cards, a job step consists of one EXEC card, and none, one or more DD cards. Each job is separated by a JOB card. A card containing // in columns 1 and 2, and all blanks in columns 3 through 80 marks the end of a job stream; it may be also placed at the end of each job. A delimiter card (/*) indicates that the end of input "data" has been reached. The "data" may be numerical data, source deck, or object deck.

Now let us discuss the JOB and EXEC statements.

The syntax for JOB or EXEC statement has the following requirement:

$$//[name] \;\overset{\text{(b)}}{\downarrow} \left\{ {JOB \atop EXEC} \right\} \overset{\text{(b)}}{\downarrow} \; \begin{matrix} operands\ separated \\ by\ commas \end{matrix} \; \overset{\text{(b)}}{\downarrow} \; [remarks]$$

where   // are punched on the first two card columns,

name is one through eight alphameric characters, the first one being alphabetic, and

(b) indicates that at least one blank is required.

Generally speaking, symbols used in a syntax have the following meanings:

1. Any capitalized word in a syntax must be used.

   Example

JOB1	(incorrect)
JOB	(correct)

2. Any lower-case word shall be replaced by a word selected by the programmer.

   Example: name in the above syntax may be replaced by

   A1701   or   STEP1.

3. The contents in a square bracket [ ] are optional to the statement and may be ignored completely.

4. The programmer has to choose one and only one of the options staked in the{ }.

   Example

   $$\left\{ {JOB \atop EXEC} \right\} \quad means \quad JOB \; or \; EXEC$$

There are many possible operands for the JOB and EXEC statements. The first two operands in a JOB statement deal with the accounting information and the programmer's name, respectively; their requirements are generally prescribed by a particular computer center as shown in the following three typical examples of JOB statement:

```
//J91353 JOB (N6460,30,15,5000,500,SRI=DEFER),'S.S.KUO',MSGLEVEL=1 ASSIGN
//AVERG JOB T376,'S.S.KUO'
//A0054707 JOB (UNH,T577-23),KUO,MSGLEVEL=1,CLASS=G,TIME=01
```

The necessary information should be available from the programming consultant or the instructor. The programmer's name, a positional parameter‡ is usually enclosed in apostrophes(') if it contains any special characters. If the name includes an apostrophe, such as O'CONNOR, the apostrophe should be punched as two consecutive apostrophes such as 'O''CONNOR'.

Other operands in a JOB statement include keyword parameters‡ such as MSGLEVEL, CLASS, COND, TYPRUN, PRTY, REGION, and MSGCLASS, (see Table 13.2). Not every operand

Table 13.2 Some operands used in JOB statement

Operand	Meaning	Example	Reference
CLASS	Classification of job	CLASS=G	Section 13.3
COND	Conditions under which the job is to be ended (other than normal end)	COND=((40,GE),(50,LT))	Section 13.4
MSGCLASS	Output unit on which messages are displayed	MSGCLASS=A	†
MSGLEVEL	Print Job Control Language (JCL) and diagnostic, or just diagnostic messages?	MSGLEVEL=1	Section 13.3
PRTY	Priority of the job (high of 12 to a low of 0)	PRTY=12	†
REGION	Amount of main storage used in MVT environment	REGION=100K	†
TYPRUN	Type of this run	TYPRUN=HOLD	†

† See *IBM System/360 Operating System Job Control Language Reference*, Form GC28–6539, IBM Corp.

---

‡ Positional and keyword parameters used in the operand field in a job control card resemble very closely those specified in a prototype statement for a macro definition discussed in Chapter 9.   Essentially, a positional parameter must be placed in a particular place on the job control card in relation to other entries on the card, while a keyword parameter includes an equal sign, followed by the variable value which is specified by the programmer. The order of keyword parameters is not important.

is meaningful for a system used in a particular computer installation. Now we shall limit our discussion to two most common keyword parameters: MSGLEVEL and CLASS.

MSGLEVEL

The parameter MSGLEVEL specifies what information a programmer wants as part of the output: He or she can specify (a) echo print of all job control statements as well as diagnostics, or (b) just diagnostics, no echo print of job control statements. This keyword parameter has the following format:

MSGLEVEL=(*statement* , *message*)

The first subparameter, or "*statement*", has the following meaning:
  0 = only the JOB statement is to be printed.
  1 = all input job-control statements, catalogued procedure statements,† and the internal representation of statements after symbolic substitution are to be printed.
  2 = only the input job control statements are to be printed, but not the catalogued procedure statements.

The second subparameter, or *message*, has the following meaning:
  1 = all device allocation/termination messages are to be printed.
  0 = no allocation/termination messages are to be printed, unless the job terminates abnormally.

The second subparameter is often omitted in practice. If so, the parentheses need not be coded such as MSGLEVEL=1. On the other hand, if the first subparameter is omitted, a comma must be coded such as MSGLEVEL=(,1). In addition, each computer installation normally prescribes its own default options for the operand MSGLEVEL. For a beginner, MSGLEVEL=1 is recommended because a complete control statement listing helps track down errors.

CLASS

This operand is used to specify the classification code of a job in multiprogramming environment (see Table 13.1 in the previous section). Its purpose is to make sure that a given job is placed in a proper partition. For example, if a job is classified as class G, then the following operand should be written in a JOB statement:

CLASS=G

as illustrated in Fig. D.1(b) on page 540. This operand must be given in MFT or MVT environment.

Before turning to the next section to discuss the details of EXEC statements, we

---

† Catalogued procedure is discussed in the next section.

note that information on any job control card cannot be punched in columns 72 through 80. If the information has more than 71 characters, the job control card may be continued by placing additional operands on a continuation card in the following manner:

   a) punching a comma after the last operand on the control card;
   b) punching // in columns 1 and 2 in a new card to start the continuation; and
   c) punching the remaining operands on this continuation card, starting any column between columns 4 and 16.

The information in columns 73 through 80 contains identification or sequencing data, and is not recognized by reader/interpreter. All job control cards must be punched on an 029 card punch, not an 026 punch.

13.4 EXEC STATEMENT

Let us begin by explaining what is a *procedure*. A large number of job control cards is often required in a typical job step. If this job step is used many times a day (e.g., in compilation of a FORTRAN program), it would demand keypunching of many sets of these same job control cards, which is an error-prone and time-consuming operation. To cut down the clerical work, we may store these JCL cards as card images in a specific disk area SYS1.PROCLIB. This collection of a particular set of job control cards is called a *procedure*. Each procedure must have a name (e.g., FORTGCLG). To use any set of images now on the disk, one needs to write only the name of the procedure in an EXEC card.

The syntax of an EXEC statement is:

$$//[\text{stepname}] \xrightarrow{\text{(b)}} \text{EXEC} \xrightarrow{\text{(b)}} \left\{ \begin{array}{l} \text{PROC=}\textit{procname} \\ \textit{procname} \\ \text{PGM=}\textit{progname} \end{array} \right\} [,\textit{other parameters}] \xrightarrow{\text{(b)}} [\textit{comment}]$$

Since each job step requires an EXEC card, the *stepname* is often replaced by STEP1, STEPA, or other similar names.

The first operand takes one of the following two basic forms:

        PROC=*procname*   (or simply *procname*)
        PGM=*progname*

where PROC designates the procedure, and PGM, the program to be executed.

Note that the first operand in an EXEC statement is a positional parameter and must be explicitly given.

Example 1

```
//STEP1  EXEC   PGM=IEBGENER
```

This statement requests the execution of the program IEBGENER which is already stored in a program library. (This popular IBM utility program is often used to copy the information on cards as card image in the reserved disk space.)

Example 2

```
//STEPA  EXEC   PROC=FORTGCDG
```

This statement requests the execution of the procedure FORTGCDG (FORTRAN compile, OS-loader link and execute). This statement can also be written as follows:

```
//STEPA  EXEC   FORTGCDG
```

There are many other parameters available in an EXEC statement, including PARM, ACCT, COND, TIME, REGION, ROLL, and RD. Two most common ones seem to be PARM and COND. We shall discuss them below.

PARM

When you rent or buy a computer system, the vendor usually supplies you with various programs, such as FORTRAN compilers and assemblers. These programs are written for everybody and many options are built in to suit different needs. For example, to assemble an assembler language program we often use an IBM-supplied assembler; its name is IEUASM. One programmer may wish to put the result of compilation in a specific disk area so that it may later be used in the linking step, whereas another programmer may not want to do so. The first programmer can then use the PARM operand in the following EXEC statement:

```
//STEP1  EXEC   PGM=IEUASM,PARM='LOAD'
```

On the other hand, the second programmer does not have to write any keyword PARM, since the program IEUASM assumes that no result is to be written in a disk area unless PARM='LOAD' is specified.

As a second example, we often use an IBM-supplied compiler to compile a FORTRAN program. The official name of this compiler (actually a program) is IEYFORT which, like many other compilers, has many built-in options, three of which are given below.

a) A listing of names, which appear in the object module, is required (MAP).
b) A listing in assembler language (LIST) is required.
c) An object deck (DECK) is requested.

If these options are needed, the following EXEC statement can be used

```
//STEP1  EXEC   IEYFORT,PARM=(MAP,LIST,DECK)
```

Finally, let us consider the linkage editor, a program used to make a load module ready to be executed, which is called IEWL. In the following EXEC statement:

```
//LKED  EXEC  PGM=IEWL,PARM=(XREF,LET,LIST,NCAL)
```

the parameter LIST demands that the linkage editor lists the control cards it has processed on the diagnostic output; the XREF requests that the linkage editor produces a cross-reference table of symbols as part of listing. The parameters LET and NCAL pass the information to the linkage editor. When the LET option is specified, the load module will *not* be marked as nonexecutable even if some error conditions have been detected; the NCAL option asks *not* to search the subroutine libraries.

Condition

When your program has bugs and fails to get compiled, it would be pointless to go through the next step. This idea may be implemented in two parts:

a) The designer of the FORTRAN compiler IEYFORT agrees to place a value v in register 15. If the compilation fails, $v < 4$. Otherwise, or when compilation is successful, $v \geq 4$. This compilation step has a *stepname*; let us call it FORT.

b) The programmer places the keyword parameter COND=(4,LT,FORT) in the EXEC card used in the linkage-editing step:

```
//LKED  EXEC  PGM=IEWL,PARM=(XREF,LET,LIST,NCAL),COND=(4,LT,FORT)
```

The keyword COND demands the following action: If the contents (v) in register 15 are less than 4, the linkage editing step will be bypassed. Otherwise, go through the linkage editing and obtain a load module.

13.5 DATA SETS

In the last two sections, we have discussed the JOB and EXEC statements. Before we present the syntax for DD statements, it is necessary to explain some important concepts and terminologies.

Data Sets

The word *set*, as used in mathematics, means a collection or an aggregate of things. The things which make up a set are called its elements. If the elements of a set consist of data or other information, then this set is a *data set*. A data set† usually has its own name. Examples of data set are given below.

1. Daily information of drivers licensed in a state; a valid name is U.DRIVER.79214. Naming convention is discussed in the next section.
2. The collection of FORTRAN subroutines; its official name is SYS1.FORTLIB.
3. An object deck; its name may be &LOADSET.

---

† Data set is often called *file* in data processing field.

Data sets are often stored in secondary storage units, such as tapes, disks, and cells. Figure 13.7 shows a typical layout of three disk-pack areas used in a medium-size computer installation. The contents in areas SYS1.SSPLIB, SYS1.PROCLIB, and SYS1.LINKLIB are further examples of a data set. They are respectively the scientific subroutine package, procedure library, and the library containing a large number of compiler and assembler programs, the linkage editor program, sorting program, and so on.

A data set may be organized in secondary storage in one of the several standard forms, called data set organizations: *sequential, partitioned, indexed sequential, random*, and *telecommunication* data sets. The first two are more often used than the others. A notable example of sequential data set is the one stored on a reel of magnetic tape. Its data bytes are stored in physically contiguous locations. To reach a subset of a sequential data set, one must start at the beginning of this data set. A data set of this organization may be residing on a magnetic tape or a direct access device.

An example of a partitioned data set is SYS1.SSPLIB, the scientific subroutine package. The package is made of many subroutines, each having its own name. Each named subroutine is called a member in the partitioned data set SYS1.SSPLIB. A partitioned data set, only possible on direct access devices, has a *directory* that lists the names and addresses of all members. Once its name is given, a member can be located directly without searching through the disk sequentially from the beginning.

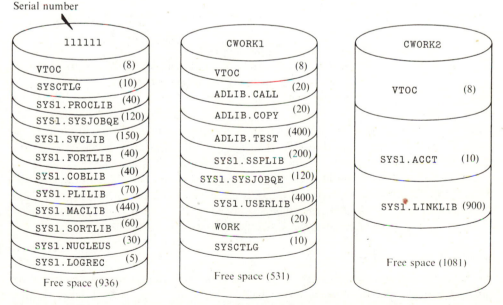

Fig. 13.7 Layout of three disk areas in a typical computer installation (number in tracks).

Volume

In Fig. 13.7, the serial numbers are used to distinguish one disk pack from the other. Each consists of up to six alphameric characters such as 111111, CWORK1, or CWORK2. These serial numbers should not only be written on the label pasted on each disk pack, but also be magnetically recorded on the first track of a disk pack.

A disk pack and a tape reel are examples of a *volume*, as each may be physically carried around. On each of the three volumes in Fig. 13.7, many data sets are magnetically recorded. In order to facilitate the control program or the user's program

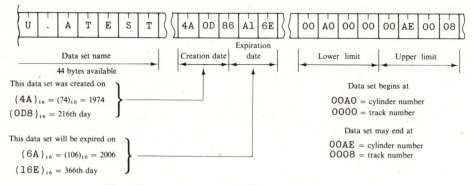

Fig. 13.8   An entry in VTOC (schematic drawing).

in locating a data set it needs, a directory of all data sets in the pack (volume) is compiled, the so-called *volume table of contents* (VTOC) (see Fig. 13.7). Every direct-access volume (a disk pack or data cell) has a VTOC.

The space on a direct-access volume for a data set cannot be reserved unless an entry for the data set is already created in VTOC. The information for such entry (see Fig. 13.8) includes the data set name, the amount of space requested, and the location of the space on the volume. These items of information are taken from a DD card, which is a job control card punched by the user. (Detailed information on DD cards is given in the next section.) At the time the job containing the DD card is run, the VTOC entry is recorded and the space is automatically allocated.

Another important detail to note: VTOC may be located anywhere in the volume. The information on track address of the beginning of VTOC and the length of VTOC are contained in the volume's *label*, which is always positioned at the beginning of the volume. A typical volume label for a disk pack is shown in Fig. 13.9.

Disposition of a Data Set

At the beginning of each job step, the age status of all data sets must be reported to the initiator, which determines and ensures the availability of the input/output devices requested by a problem program. The age status of a data set may be OLD or NEW among others. A data set is OLD if already existed before the execution of the step

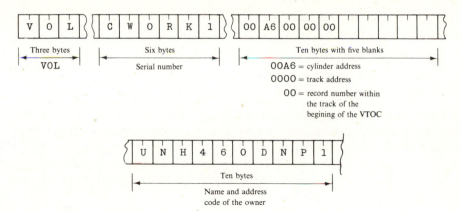

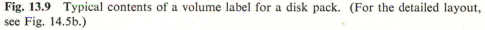

Fig. 13.9   Typical contents of a volume label for a disk pack. (For the detailed layout, see Fig. 14.5b.)

as, for example, the input data set in a link-editing step, since it was already in existence in the compilation step. A data set is NEW if it is to be created in the job step by the program. New data sets necessarily also need space if they are placed on direct access devices.

When a step terminates, the input/output devices originally allocated by the initiator must be unallocated; this is the function of another nonresident portion of the control program—the *terminator*. At the end of each job step, the terminator must be informed about what to do with this particular data set: Should its name be kept in or deleted from the active file? (In case that a data set resides in a disk pack, this active name file is the VTOC). If the name is deleted, then the track space, originally used by this data set, will be restored to the inventory. In addition to the KEEP and DELETE status, a PASS status is also possible in a multistep job. The concept of passing a data set is rather straightforward: The data set, created during one job step, is to be used during the next job step of the same job and then abandoned. For example, the input data set for the link-editing step is actually *passed* from the compilation step.

In summary, the initiator must be informed of whether the data set in consideration is, say, NEW or OLD; the terminator must be informed as to what is to be done with a data set. All this information is essential for the final disposition of a data set. The following operand in a DD statement (fully discussed in the next section):

$$DISP=(OLD,KEEP)$$

provides information about the disposition of a data set for the initiator: It is an OLD data set, already in existence and named; and for the terminator: KEEP this data set at the end of this job step.

Allocation of Space

Information cannot be stored in a disk or data cell unless space is reserved for the data set. To allocate space, an entry for the data set in VTOC (Fig. 13.8) on the device must be first created. A programmer accomplishes this by preparing a DD card containing the required items for a VTOC entry. Some typical items are as follows:

1. Name of the data set,
2. Amount of space to be allocated,
3. Serial number of the volume.

As soon as the job-control card setup containing this DD card is run, the entry for the data set in VTOC is automatically created and the required space reserved. The data set can then be stored in the allocated space.

Let us examine now how the initiator retrieves this data set for the processing task. To pinpoint this data set, a programmer has to submit the following three items of information to the initiator:

a) Name of data set.
b) The serial number of the volume on which the data set is stored.
c) The device required by this volume.

These items are punched on a DD card. Note that the items (b) and (c) together act as the pointer to the volume label which, in turn, is the pointer to VTOC. In the VTOC, the initiator will find the needed information: This data set starts at, say, track 0 of cylinder 160, and may be 14 cylinders long, as shown in Fig. 13.8.

Cataloguing and Uncataloguing a Data Set

If a data set is referenced over and over again, it is convenient to place the items (a), (b), and (c) in the system catalog (SYSCTLG in Fig. 13.7). Once a data set is catalogued, there is no need to punch the items (b) and (c) on a DD card. When only the data set name is punched, the initiator makes the following assumption: Items (b) and (c) are stored in the system catalog SYSCTLG. For example, if only data set name SYS1.FORTLIB is given in a DD card, the initiator will take the following steps:

1. Search the system catalog SYSCTLG for the name SYS1.FORTLIB.
2. Find the associated volume serial number, say, 111111, and the device type, say, 2311.
3. Using 111111 and 2311 jointly as a pointer, locate the volume label.
4. Using the information in the volume label, locate the VTOC in the volume.
5. Find the entry in VTOC for the data set SYS1.FORTLIB and get its detailed information (see Fig. 13.8).

To uncatalogue a data set is the reversed process of cataloguing it. By using a DD card, the reference to the volume serial number and device type of a data set may also be removed from the system catalog. The terminator carries out this operation—uncataloguing a data set—at the end of a job step. However, the data set itself is not erased.

To instruct the initiator to create a new data set and catalogue it, you simply write the following disposition operand in a DD statement:

$$DISP=(NEW,CATLG)$$

Similarly, the following operand

$$DISP=(OLD,UNCATLG)$$

instructs the initiator not to create this data set, as it is already in existence; and instructs the terminator to uncatalogue it at the end of this job step.

13.6 SYNTAX OF DD STATEMENT

The initiator must have information on each data set before it can initiate a task. The information may include:

a) The name of the data set.
b) Is this data set to be created (the so-called NEW data set) or is it already in existence (OLD)?
c) For a NEW data set, the required disk space (in cylinders and tracks) or the required number of reels of tape.
d) Serial number of the volume on which the data set is recorded.
e) Output device required, if any (e.g., printer or punch).

A programmer provides these and other items of information through a DD card. DD stands for *data definition* or *device description*. Its basic purpose is to define the data media such as cards, tapes, or disks. Sometimes, it may also help describe the physical form of each data set to the data control routines discussed in Chapter 14.

The DD statement is perhaps the most difficult one to learn in Job Control Language, mainly because it involves many possible operands, each in turn having many different forms. In addition, the framework of understanding of the operands must be learned well. We shall subdivide this topic into four sections.

In this section, we shall present its syntax and deal with a special case when only one operand is specified. The next three sections deal with the case with more than one operand involved: In Section 13.7, the most common operands—DSNAME and UNIT—are discussed; Section 13.8 examines VOLUME, SPACE, and DISP operands; and finally, in Section 13.9 some less common operands are described.

As with the JOB and EXEC statement, the syntax for a DD statement is as follows:

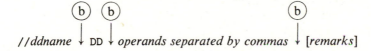

$//ddname$ ↓ DD ↓ *operands separated by commas* ↓ [*remarks*]

where (b) indicates at least a blank, and *ddname* is up to eight characters starting with an alphabetic character.

The operand field of a DD statement contains either one operand or a combination of several operands. When only one operand is specified, it is usually one of the following special forms:

1. //*ddname* DD SYSOUT=A
   indicates that this data set is to be printed (see, for example, the job control card No. 5 in Fig. 1.20 on page 26).

2. //*ddname* DD SYSOUT=B
   indicates that this data set is to be punched.

3. //*ddname* DD *
   indicates that the input to this job step follows on *cards* immediately (see, for example, the job control card No. 3 or No. 6 in Fig. 1.20). The input cards may not contain job control cards.

4. //*ddname* DD DATA
   The DD DATA statement is same as the DD * statement with one difference: the input cards may now contain any job control cards except a delimiter card with /* in columns 1 and 2, and blanks in other columns.

5. //*ddname* DD DUMMY
   offers the facility for bypassing input/output operations. When a READ operation is requested on this data set, an end-of-file is signaled. No action is taken when a WRITE operation is given.

6. //*ddnam1* DD DDNAME=*ddnam2*
   indicates that all information concerning this DD statement will be supplied from the following DD card. For example, in the following DD statements:

   ```
   //FT13F001  DD  DDNAME=DISK
   //DISK      DD  UNIT=2311,DCB=...
   ```

   by execution time, only one name, FT13F001, is associated with this data set.

13.7 DSNAME AND UNIT OPERANDS

In the previous section, we discussed a special case of only one operand being specified in a DD statement. In many cases, there are several operands specified in the operand field, including:

```
DSNAME=dsname or DSN=dsname
UNIT=identification
VOLUME=REF=dsname
VOLUME=SER=serial number
DISP=disposition
SPACE=(unit,(quantity,increment))
SEP=channel separation
LABEL=(file number,type)
DCB=(parameters, except DSORG, MACRF, and DDNAME)
```

It is worth noting that: (a) not all operands are required in all cases; (b) they must be separated by commas; and (c) no spaces can be included in or between operands. Now we shall discuss the most common operands: DSNAME and UNIT.

DSNAME

The data set name (DSNAME) operand† specifies the name of a data set. Its basic form is

$$\text{DSNAME}=dsname$$

where *dsname* can be up to 44 characters in length, including the embedded periods.

Case 1. The name has one through eight alphameric characters, the first of which must be alphabetic.

   Example: DSNAME=BETA2

Case 2. dsname is a fully qualified name. Let us see what does this mean. All data sets may be divided into two categories: (a) those which are part of operating system—system data sets; and (b) those which are used in applications—user's data sets. If a system data set and a user data set have the same name, then there will be a collision. In order to prevent it, OS/360 permits the names to be qualified. Thus, system data sets are usually qualified with SYS1 (such as SYS1.SSPLIB, SYS1.PROCLIB, or SYS1.LINKLIB shown in Fig. 13.7). The user's data sets can be qualified with, say, USERFILE. For example, a data set containing 1980 census information may be named as

$$\text{DSNAME}=\text{USERFILE.STATE42.TOWN961.CENSUS80}$$

Note that for each eight alphameric character or less, there must be a period. The similar information for 1990 census may have the *dsname* as

$$\text{DSNAME}=\text{USERFILE.STATE42.TOWN961.CENSUS90}$$

Also note that the above data set name is *fully qualified* (but TOWN961.CENSUS90 is not). The USERFILE is said to have the highest index level, whereas the CENSUS90 has the lowest one. This is depicted in Fig. 13.10.

There are five other possible formats of the DSNAME operand:

1. For a member in a partitioned data set whose name is *dsname*, the general format is DSNAME=*dsname*(*member name*). For example, DSNAME=PDS(GO) is a valid reference to the member GO of the partitioned data set PDS.

2. A data set is *temporary* if it is created in a job step and used only in the remaining steps of a job as, for example, is the result of compilation. This data set, often called LOADSET, forms a load module in the subsequent linking step, but after that, it becomes useless.

---

† This operand is required in a DD statement except in the case of unlabeled tapes or of certain data sets such as work areas for SORT/MERGE.

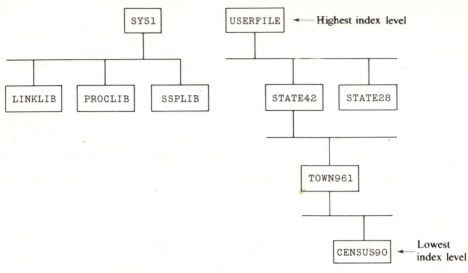

Fig. 13.10 Levels of index for a qualified data set name.

For a temporary data set, the format is:

DSNAME=&&*dsname*

where *dsname* is an arbitrary name, with one through eight alphameric characters, the first of which must be alphabetic. For example, the following operand

DSNAME=&&LOADSET

indicates the data set &&LOADSET is temporary, its longevity being limited to the life either a step or the remaining job. Under some restrictions, the *dsname* of a temporary data set may be preceded by only one ampersand, such as DSNAME=&LOADSET.

3. A newly created, but temporary data set, to be used in a later step in the same job, need not have a name. Instead, it can be identified by the *ddname* and the *stepname* when the data set was created. The general format is DSNAME=*.*stepname*.*ddname*. For example, the following operand:

DSNAME=*.LKED.SYSLMOD

refers to the data set which was created in the LKED step of the current job, and was associated with the *ddname* SYSLMOD. The symbol * demands to look back at a previous DD card in this job, known as the *backward reference*.

4. This is an extension of the above format. For a data set newly created in a job step in which a catalogued procedure is requested, a *dsname* is not necessary. Instead, it may be identified by the *ddname*, name of the procedure step and the *stepname* with the format DSNAME=*.*stepname*.*procstepname*.*ddname* . For example, the following operand:

DSNAME=*.STEP1.STEPC.FILE2

indicates that a temporary data set is created in STEP1 of the current job. In this step, a catalogued procedure is requested; and a DD statement whose name has FILE2 occurred in STEPC of the procedure. This passed data set is defined in the DD statement whose *ddname* is FILE2.

5. For a newly created, but temporary data set in a given step, a name is not necessary. Instead, it can be linked to the *ddname* with the format DSNAME=∗.*ddname* . For example, the following operand:

$$\text{DSNAME}=∗.\text{DD1}$$

refers to a data set which is associated the *ddname* DD1 in the current step.

The formats 3, 4, and 5 are collectively called the *backward reference form*. They are used to obtain the name of a data set from an *ddname* in an earlier DD statement specified in the same job. In this method, a *stepname* is not necessary if the same job step is involved. Similarly, a *procstepname* is omitted if no catalogued procedure is being used.

UNIT

The UNIT operand specifies a single or a class of input/output unit where the data set will be found. There are three types of unit parameter:

$$\text{UNIT}=group$$
$$\text{UNIT}=model\ number$$
$$\text{UNIT}=address$$

The first type, the group parameter, is an alphabetic representation of a class of input/output units. Table 13.3 presents some UNIT operands with a group parameter frequently used in a DD statement. For example, the operand UNIT=SYSDA requests a direct access unit, but does not specify any particular one. Note that all group names are installation defined.

The second type is a model number of the input/output device (Table 13.3). For example, the operand UNIT=2311 specifies that the data set is to be created on any of the model 2311 disk drives.

Finally, the address parameter in a UNIT operand expresses the address of an input/output device. Each address must be a three-digit hexadecimal number. Table 13.4 shows some input/output devices and their addresses used in a typical computer installation. The details of a device address will be discussed in Section 15.2.

Among the three types of UNIT parameter, the group parameter is most flexible in application; and should be used whenever possible.

For multiple-volume data sets on tape, the following unit operand is used:

$$\text{UNIT}=(a,n)$$

where *a* is a four to six character alphameric word discussed above; *n* specifies the number of volumes. For example, UNIT=(TAPE7,4) requests four seven-track tape drives. The operator will then be instructed to mount tapes on each drive.

The UNIT operand must be specified except (a) when the data set is catalogued; or (b) when the VOLUME operand takes the form of VOLUME=REF=, which will be discussed in the next section.

Table 13.3 Common UNIT operands used in a DD statement

	Operand	Comments
Group	UNIT=SYSDA	Any direct access unit
	UNIT=SYSSQ	Any sequential unit
	UNIT=TAPE	Any tape drive
	UNIT=TAPE9 or UNIT=24009	Any 9-channel tape drive
	UNIT=TAPE7 or UNIT=24007	Any 7-channel tape drive
	UNIT=SYSCP	Any card punch
Model number	UNIT=2314	For a 2314 disk
	UNIT=3330	For a 3330 disk
	UNIT=2321	For the data cell
	UNIT=2400-3	For a 1600 bpi tape drive

Table 13.4 System/360 input/output devices and addresses in a particular installation

Unit		Address
1052	Console printer	01F
2540	Card reader	00C
2540	Card punch	00D
1403	Printer	00E
2311	Disk drive (left)	190
2311	Disk drive (right)	191
2403	Tape drive (left) 9-track	280
2402	Tape drive 9-track	281
2402	Tape drive 9-track	282
2401	Tape drive (right) 7-track	283

13.8 VOLUME, DISP, AND SPACE OPERANDS IN DD STATEMENT

The VOLUME operand in a DD statement specifies a particular volume or volumes occupied by the data set. If the volume is a direct-access one, the SPACE operand is needed to allocate space. The disposition operand DISP, briefly expressed in Section 13.5, expresses the status of the data set at the beginning of the job step and the disposition of the data set after the completion of the same job step. It also specifies what to do in case of abnormal termination of the current job step. Each of these three operands has various forms. We shall now discuss them.

VOLUME

Three common volume operands are:

1. VOLUME=REF=*dsname*
2. VOLUME=REF=*.*stepname*.*ddname*, or
   VOLUME=REF=*.*stepname*.*procstepname*.*ddname*, or
   VOLUME=REF=*.*ddname*
3. VOLUME=SER=*a six-digit serial number*

The *dsname* in the first volume operand refers to the name of an existing data set, already catalogued or passed in a particular volume. The new data set is specified to be located in the same volume. For example, the following operand

VOLUME=REF=SYS1.USERLIB

requests that the data set in consideration will be located on the same volume as the data set SYS1.USERLIB.

The second form of VOLUME operand (with its backward reference) is used to obtain the data set volume from the *ddname* of an earlier DD statement. As mentioned before, the *stepname* is omitted if the same job step is involved. Likewise, the *procstepname* is not necessary if no catalogued procedure is used.

The third form of VOLUME operand, VOLUME=SER=*a serial number*, specifies a volume with a particular serial number. For example, the following operands in a DD statement

UNIT=2311,VOLUME=SER=794972

request that the data set is to be located in a direct-access volume whose serial number is 794972 for a 2311 disk unit.

If this particular data set is very active (such as a FORTRAN compiler), we do not want to keypunch the following two operands over and over again for a large number of DD cards:

UNIT=2311,VOLUME=SER=794972

We can avoid this undesirable clerical work by putting these two items of information, together with the data set name, into the system catalog SYSCTLG (see Fig. 13.7). Once a data set is catalogued, the UNIT and VOLUME operands may be eliminated from its associated DD statement, but the data set name must be written. For example, consider the following DD statement:

//SYSLIB DD DSNAME=SYS1.FORTLIB

where only data set name is given. This tells the initiator that the required information of VOLUME and UNIT is in the system catalog SYSCTLG.

Other forms of the VOLUME operand include:

1. VOLUME=(PRIVATE,RETAIN,SER=*a six-digit number*)
   where PRIVATE ensures that a private volume will be mounted and RETAIN dictates that the volume remains mounted after its last use in a step.
2. VOLUME=SER=$(n_1, n_2, \ldots, n_n)$
   It is used for multiplevolume data sets, where n_1, n_2, $\ldots$, n_n are six-digit serial numbers of the volumes.

In general, the VOLUME operand is not required in the following cases: (1) If the data set is catalogued, (2) if the data set is placed on a scratch tape, and (3) if UNIT=SYSDA is used. VOLUME may be punched as VOL on a DD card. Also, a data set name is usually recorded on the volume containing this data set. The *dsname* is always the name by which this data set is referred to in the VTOC and in the catalog.

DISP

There are two different forms of the DISP operand. Let us first discuss the more common one:

$$
\text{DISP}= \left(\left\{ \begin{matrix} \text{NEW} \\ \text{OLD} \\ \text{MOD} \\ \text{SHR} \end{matrix} \right\} \left[, \left\{ \begin{matrix} \text{DELETE} \\ \text{KEEP} \\ \text{PASS} \\ \text{CATLG} \\ \text{UNCATLG} \end{matrix} \right\} \right] \right)
$$

The first subparameter is the status of the data set at the beginning of the job. The NEW and OLD, already discussed in Section 13.5, have the following meanings:

NEW: this data set is created in the current job step.
OLD: this data set existed before the current job step.

The MOD subparameter is used for a sequentially organized data set (such as the one on a reel of magnetic tape) which is already in existence. MOD means that new records are to be *added* to this already existing data set. If this data set cannot be found by the initiator or if no volume information exists for it, the system assumes that the data set does not exist and takes a status of NEW instead of MOD.

The SHR option is applied primarily in multiprogramming environment. It is used if the data set resides on a direct-access volume, and if it is part of a job whose operations do not prohibit simultaneous use of the data set by another job. If used in other than a multiprogramming environment, SHR is equivalent to OLD. Finally, if the first subparameter is omitted, the NEW option is assumed.

The second subparameter in the DISP operand informs the terminator what to do with a particular data set at the end of a job step. For example, CATLG indicates that the data set, NEW or OLD, is to be catalogued. On the other hand, UNCATLG is used to remove the name of an already catalogued data set from the directory, but the physical space is not automatically released. The DELETE and KEEP subparameters indicate that the data set is deleted or kept at the end of this job step. Note that the operand DISP=(MOD,PASS) is the same as (NEW,PASS) if the data set cannot be found, whereas KEEP is the default value of the second subparameter if the first one is OLD, MOD, or SHR.

The less common form of the DISP operand is

$$DISP=(S,D,C)$$

where the first two subparameters S and D stand for status and disposition as discussed before. The third subparameter C indicates how the data set is to be handled at the end of the job step if the step terminates abnormally; it may be UNCATLG, CATLG, KEEP, or DELETE. If this subparameter is omitted—and if the step terminates abnormally—the second subparameter D is performed.

SPACE

The SPACE operand allocates space on a direct-access volume when creating a new data set. The spaces may be allocated by cylinders, tracks, or in bytes.

The SPACE operands can have forms as follows:
1. For sequential data sets:

$$SPACE=(unit,quantity)$$

where *unit* indicates the basic unit in which the allocation is to be made; it may be one of the following:

a) TRK   if space is to be allocated by tracks,
b) CYL   if space is to be allocated by cylinders,
c) An integer   the average block length in bytes, if space is to be allocated in bytes.

The second subparameter *quantity* specifies the number of units to be assigned in the initial allocation, or the primary allocation.

For instance, the operand

$$SPACE=(1700,400)$$

requests space for 400 blocks, each of average length 1,700 characters. Similarly, the following operands

$$\text{SPACE=(TRK,16)}$$
$$\text{SPACE=(CYL,6)}$$

are used to request 16 tracks and 6 cylinders, respectively.

This format is often used when the exact number of either cylinders or tracks is known, or when the average number of blocks can be estimated.

2. For sequential data sets:

$$\text{SPACE=(}unit\text{,(}quantity\text{,}increment\text{))}$$

where subparameters *unit* and *quantity* are described in the first format. The third subparameter *increment* specifies the number of units to be added in secondary allocations if additional space is required. If required, up to 15 secondary allocations will be made on the same volume. For example, the space operand

$$\text{SPACE=(1700,(400,150))}$$

requests space for 400 records, each record containing about 1700 characters. Each time the specified space is exhausted, a space for additional 150 records is automatically allocated. This format gives more flexibility to the user in specifying the required space.

3. For sequential data set: The last subparameter in the operand

$$\text{SPACE=(}units\text{,(}quantity\text{,}increment\text{),RLSE)}$$

is used to release unused space when the data set has no possible future growth. If space is requested in units of tracks (or cylinders), space is released starting with the first unused track (or cylinder). The RLSE subparameter here is a regular positional parameter and may be written in a DD statement to release unused space at the end of the current step for a data set being created in the current step.

4. For sequential data sets:

$$\text{SPACE=(}units\text{,(}quantity\text{,}increment\text{),,CONTIG)}$$

will require that the space is allocated in contiguous tracks or cylinders. If the subparameter CONTIG is specified when requesting additional space to an existing data set, the new quantity is not necessarily contiguous to the original space. Note the two commas before the subparameter CONTIG.

5. For partitioned data sets:

$$\text{SPACE=(}units\text{,(}quantity\text{,,}directory\text{))}$$

The subparameter *directory* is the number of 256-byte blocks assigned for the directory of a partitioned data set. As a rough rule, one directory block is set aside for every five members of a partitioned data set. Note the two commas between the subparameters *quantity* and *directory*.

6. For sequential data sets:

$$\text{SPACE}=(units,(quantity,increment),,,\text{ROUND})$$

or for partitioned data sets:

$$\text{SPACE}=(units,(quantity,increment,directory),,,\text{ROUND})$$

where the last subparameter ROUND is used to round up to the nearest unit. The net effect is to enhance input/output performance at the expense of more space.

13.9 EXAMPLES—ALLOCATING SPACE AND CATALOGUING DATA SET ON DISKS

This section presents five practical examples to illustrate the application of job control statements to disk usage. Since each installation has its own data set naming convention and its JOB card requirements, let us assume that:

1. The name convention used in the remainder of the book is

$$\text{USER.A3141.P5926.}name1[.name2]$$

where

A3141 = account number or project number,

P5926 = programmer's number,

$name1$ = any name $\Big\}$ standard eight-letter convention.
$name2$ = any name

Note that .$name2$ may be omitted.

2. The JOB card has the following format:

```
//A710   JOB   (UNH,T117),KUO,MSGLEVEL=1,CLASS=G,TIME=5
```

You should check the above assumptions with the programming consultant in your computation center. Any changes to suit local conditions should be of rather minor character.

Two facts which relate to the disk usage cannot be overemphasized.

First, a user cannot refer to a data set by its name unless he has reserved space on a disk and has catalogued the data set.

Second, the necessary *index levels* must be created in the system catalog SYSCTLG (see Fig. 13.7) before its associated data set can be catalogued. If you use the recent release (release 21 and on) of OS/360, the system will *automatically* build the necessary index levels before cataloguing a data set. Otherwise, you must do it yourself.

Let us examine SYSCTLG more closely. Figure 13.11(a) and (b) shows its contents before and after the data set USER.A3141.P5926.TEST9 is catalogued. Arrows function as pointers. USER, the highest-level index, may contain a number of lower-level entries, one of which is A3177. Similarly, A3177 has an entry to P2331, the third-level index. Analogically, P2331 contains a lower-level entry to TEST7. Finally, TEST7 has an

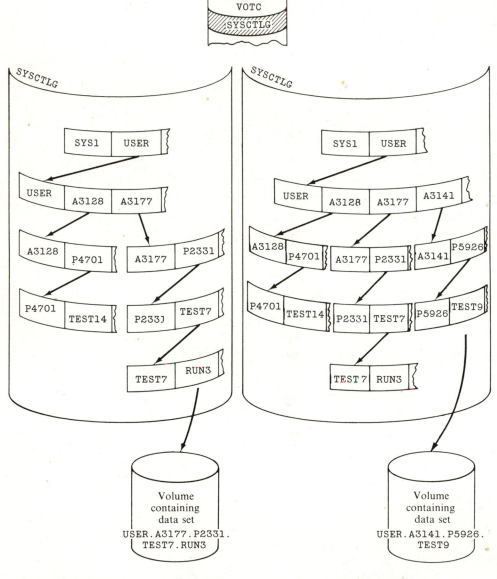

(a) Before data set USER.A3141.P5926.TEST9 is catalogued

(b) **After it is catalogued**

Fig. 13.11   Details of SYSCTLG.

entry to RUN3, the lowest-level index. The contents in Figs. 13.11(a) and (b), which each can be conveniently expressed in terms of an index structure, are shown in Figs. 13.12(a) and (b), respectively. As far as the index-level building for the data set USER.A3141.P5926.TEST9 is concerned, three levels are involved, ranging from high to lowest: A3141, P5926, and TEST9. The highest-level USER has already existed in SYSCTLG and there is no need to build it again.

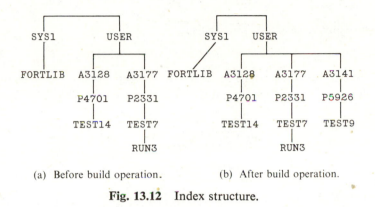

(a) Before build operation.   (b) After build operation.

Fig. 13.12   Index structure.

We are now in the position to present five practical examples in disk usage. The first three deal with the building of index levels, allocation of spaces, and cataloguing a data set. The remaining two are concerned with the converse problems: how to scratch the data set and delete the index structure.

Example 1

Prepare job control cards to build the three index levels for a partitioned data set USER.A3141.P5926.TEST9 in the system catalog SYSCTLG. [*Note:* If you use release 21 of OS/360, the required index levels will be *automatically* created before the associated data set is catalogued. It is superfluous for you to use this example to create the index levels.]

Figure 13.13 shows a set of job control cards for building the three index levels in the system catalog SYSCTLG. The IBM utility program IEHPROGM (the index-level builder) is used,† which requires a special control card BLDX. Its keyword parameter INDEX must contain a name identical to the data set in consideration, but the last qualification is omitted. For example, corresponding to the following data set:

DSNAME=USER.A3141.P5926.TEST9

† Comprehensive information on all utility programs can be found in the manual *IBM System/360 Operating System: Utilities*, GC28-6586, IBM Corp. The most common utility programs are IEBUPDTE, IEBGENER, IEBPTPCH, and IEHPROGM.

```
//A710   JOB   (UNH,T117),KUO,MSGLEVEL=1,CLASS=G,TIME=5
//EXAMPLE1 EXEC PGM=IEHPROGM
//SYSPRINT DD    SYSOUT=A
//SYSIN   DD    *
       BLDX INDEX=USER.A3141.P5926
/*
```

Fig. 13.13 Job control cards to build index levels before you can allocate space and catalogue a data set (for the release 20 or the earlier versions of OS).

the BLDX card should have the format:

        BLDX   INDEX=USER.A3141.P5926

Special control cards can start in any column except column 1 and cannot extend beyond column 71. Additional information, beyond column 71, can be put on the continuation card.

When the job control card deck (see Fig. 13.13) is run, the index levels for the data set are automatically built in the system catalog.

Example 2

In Example 1, the index levels of a partitioned data set were built in the system catalog. Now we wish to allocate and catalogue this data set on a 2311 pack, whose serial number is 111111. Prepare the job control cards.

```
//A710   JOB   (UNH,T117),KUO,MSGLEVEL=1,CLASS=G,TIME=5
//EXAMPLE2 EXEC PGM=IEFBR14
//DD1      DD   DSN=USER.A3141.P5926.TEST9,UNIT=2311,
//              VOL=SER=111111,SPACE=(1600,(10,1,1),RLSE),
//              DISP=(NEW,CATLG),
//              DCB=(BLKSIZE=1600,LRECL=80,RECFM=FB)
//
```

Fig. 13.14 Setup to allocate space and catalogue a partitioned data set.

A possible setup is shown in Fig. 13.14. The vendor-supplied program IEFBR14 is a *null step* or dummy program, which is used to
a) Allocate space on a direct-access volume,
b) Define the necessary data set attributes, and
c) Catalogue the data set.

The DD card serves (1) to request the space (by the SPACE operand); (2) to catalogue the data set (see the DISP operand); and (3) to define the attributes of the data set (by the DCB operand which will be discussed in detail in Chapter 14).

For a partitioned data set on disk, we suggest the following format for the SPACE operand:

        SPACE=$(n,(i,j,k),RLSE)$

Recommended values for n, i, j, and k are listed in Table 13.5. For example, if space is allocated to store a source program, we take the following values:

$$n = 1600 \text{ bytes,}$$
$$i = 10, \text{ or primary allocation takes } 16{,}000 \text{ bytes,}$$
$$j = 1 \text{ or secondary allocation takes } 1600 \text{ bytes,}$$
$$k = 1, \text{ or directory takes } 1600 \text{ bytes.}$$

A rule of thumb: For every five members in the partitioned data set, k increases by 1. For example, if a partitioned data set has 14 members, $k = 14/5$, or take $k = 3$.

Table 13.5 SPACE operand in disk usage

Suggested SPACE operand:

    For partitioned data set: SPACE=(n,(i,j,k),RLSE)
    For sequential data set: SPACE=(n,(i,j),RLSE)

Subparameter		Suggested value	Remarks
n	Data, source deck, object module or macro	1600	The same value must be used in DCB operand, if any specified. DCB operand is discussed in Section 14.3.
	Load module or subroutines	1024	
i	Source deck, object module, macro or data deck	$\dfrac{Number\ of\ cards}{20}$	1 card column = 1 byte (in EBCDIC) on disk.
	Load module	$\dfrac{Number\ of\ bytes}{1024}$	Number of bytes for a load module is shown at the end of link-editing step.
	Subroutine library	$\dfrac{Number\ of\ bytes}{1024}$	Number of bytes in each member of library is approximately equal to that in object deck.
j		$j = 0.1 \times i$	j-value may be up to $0.15 \times i$.
k		$k = 1$ for 5 members; $k = 2$ for 10 members; etc.	Used in partitioned data set only.

When the job control card deck containing this DD card (Fig. 13.14) is run, the space is automatically reserved and VTOC entry written. The data set USER.A3141.P5926.TEST9 is also catalogued (by CATLG subparameter in DISP operand). Once catalogued, the data set can be referenced by its name, not by its actual location on the disk.

Example 3

The data set USER.A3141.P5926.TEST6.RUN4 is a sequential one. Prepare job control cards to (1) build the index levels; (2) allocate and catalogue the data set on 2311 disk pack, whose serial number is 111111; (3) store the information on each of the 600 data cards in the reserved space as the card images. Do each of the three items in a job step.

Figure 13.15 shows a setup for job control cards, containing three job steps. IBM utility program IEHPROGM (the index-level builder) is used in the first step and a "null step" or dummy program IEFBR14 in the second. The third step is accomplished

```
//A710    JOB    (UNH,T117),KUO,MSGLEVEL=1,CLASS=G,TIME=5
//*
//*   THREE STEPS USED IN THIS JOB
//*
//STEP1      EXEC PGM=IEHPROGM
//SYSPRINT DD    SYSOUT=A
//SYSIN    DD    *
     BLDX INDEX=USER.A3141.P5926.TEST6
/*
//STEP2      EXEC PGM=IEFBR14
//DESCRIBE DD    DSN=USER.A3141.P5926.TEST6.RUN4,
//               SPACE=(1600,(30,3),RLSE),
//               UNIT=2311,VOL=SER=111111,DISP=(NEW,CATLG),
//               DCB=(BLKSIZE=1600,LRECL=80,RECFM=FB)
//STEP3      EXEC PGM=IEBGENER
//SYSPRINT DD    SYSOUT=A
//SYSIN    DD    DUMMY
//SYSUT2   DD    DSN=USER.A3141.P5926.TEST6.RUN4,DISP=OLD
//SYSUT1   DD    *
*************************************************
*                                               *
*                                               *
*                  DATA CARDS                    *
*                                               *
*                                               *
*************************************************
```

Fig. 13.15 Job control cards to (a) build index levels; (b) allocate space and catalogue a sequential data set; and (c) store information on 600 cards in the space. *Note:* The first step (shaded) may be omitted if you use release 21 of OS.

by using an IBM utility program IEBGENER. The IEBGENER program is a very powerful data set copier: it can copy a sequential data set or a partitioned member. It can also create a partitioned data set from a sequential data set. Finally, it can expand an existing partitioned data set by creating partitioned members and merging them into the parent data set.

The //* punched in Columns 1, 2, and 3 of the second, third, and fourth cards in Fig. 13.15 mean that the information in each card is a comment.

Note that each column in a data card takes one byte of the disk space. As suggested in Table 13.5, the SPACE operand in STEP2 takes the general format for a sequential data set:

$$SPACE=(n,(i,j),RLSE)$$

where i is equal to the total number of data cards divided by 20 (rounded off to an integer) or 30; and $j = 0.1 \cdot i$, or 3.

Example 4

As soon as public disk space is allocated to your data set, the rental charge begins. For this reason, a data set should be deleted if it is no longer needed. The complete work involves the following items:

a) Delete the data set on disk.
b) Remove the data set name from VTOC.
c) Uncatalogue the data set.
d) Delete the associated index structure from the system catalog.

Prepare the job control cards to do the first three items for a data set USER.A3918.P4959.EXAM4 which has been catalogued.

A possible deck setup using the dummy program IEFBR14 is shown in Fig. 13.16.

```
//A710   JOB   (UNH,T117),KUO,MSGLEVEL=1,CLASS=G,TIME=5
//EXAMPLE4 EXEC PGM=IEFBR14
//DD1        DD   DSNAME=USER.A3918.P4959.EXAM4,DISP=(OLD,DELETE)
/*
```

Fig. 13.16   Scratch and uncatalogue a catalogued data set.

The first two items are automatically accomplished by writing DISP = (OLD, DELETE) on the DD card which identifies the data set. The item (c) is also performed if the data set has been catalogued. Note that the setup in Fig. 13.16 does not perform the item (d).

Example 5

Prepare the job control cards to scratch and uncatalogue the data set USER.A3131.P6071.EXAM5. Also, delete the index structure of the same data set.

Two job steps are shown in Fig. 13.17. STEP1 performs items (a), (b), and (c) as listed in Example 4. In STEP2, IBM utility program IEHPROGM (the index-level builder) performs item (d). Note that special control cards DLTX are used; each DLTX card removes one level of index from the catalog. One should bear in mind that the index level intended to be removed must have no dependents. For example, the special control card

DLTX   INDEX=USER.A3131.P6071.EXAM5

deletes the index EXAM5. Similarly, the following card

DLTX   INDEX=USER.A3131.P6071

```
//A710    JOB   (UNH,T117),KUO,MSGLEVEL=1,CLASS=G,TIME=5
//STEP1    EXEC PGM=IEFBR14
//DD1      DD   DSN=USER.A3131.P6071.EXAM5,DISP=(OLD,DELETE)
/*
//STEP2    EXEC PGM=IEHPROGM
//SYSPRINT DD   SYSOUT=A
//SYSIN    DD   *
    DLTX INDEX=USER.A3131.P6071.EXAM5
    DLTX INDEX=USER.A3131.P6071
    DLTX INDEX=USER.A3131
/*
```

Fig. 13.17   Scratch and uncatalogue a catalogued data set. Also, delete the index structure.

deletes the index P6071. On the other hand, the control card

DLTX   INDEX=USER

would be invalid, since it has many other dependents—many other lower-index levels, say, A3132, A3133, and so on.

13.10 THREE LESS COMMON OPERANDS IN DD STATEMENT

We shall now discuss operands which are less often used in a DD statement—SEP, LABEL, and DCB. As mentioned before, not all the operands are used in all cases. You may skip the details of these operands in the first reading.

SEP

The channel separation (SEP) operand serves to optimize the channel usage. When the System/370 or System/360 in your installation has two or more selector channels, it is a good practice to specify separate selector channels for moving highly active data sets residing on different devices. For example, if two temporary data sets &&GO and &&GOSET(RPG) are associated with *ddnames* SYSLIN and SYSLMOD as follows:

```
//SYSLIN   DD  DSNAME=&&GO,UNIT=...
//SYSLMOD  DD  DSNAME=&&GOSET(RPG),UNIT=...
```

and if you wish to use a different selector channel for the data set DS1, one may write:

```
//SELCHSEP  DD  DSNAME=DS1,SEP=(SYSLIN,SYSLMOD)
```

If a second data set DS2 is to use a different selector channel than &&GO and &&GOSET(RPG), either of the following two DD statements will do:

```
//CHSEP   DD  DSNAME=DS2,SEP=(SYSLIN,SYSLMOD)
```

or

```
//CHSEP   DD  DSNAME=DS2,AFF=SELCHSEP
```

where AFF stands for affinity. It means that DS2 has the same channel separation from the two data sets, &&GO and &&GOSET(RPG), in exactly the same way as the data set DS1 described in SELCHSEP card.

LABEL

In Section 13.5, we discussed a volume and a volume label. A volume may be a disk pack or a reel of magnetic tape. In the case of a disk pack, the volume label is required at the beginning of the volume. In order to be compatible with OS/360, the volume label must always have a standard format (see Fig. 13.9) so that it may fit the data-management packages supplied by the vendor. On the other hand, a tape volume may or may not have a volume label.

The second type of label, called the *data set label*, mainly identifies each data set on a volume. On a disk pack, such label, known as the data-set control block (DSCB), includes the following information:

a) Name of the data set,

b) Track address of the beginning of the data set,

c) Data of allocation of space,

d) Earliest date the data set may be deleted,

e) Physical organization details.

The DSCB is a part of VTOC. A data set is considered *scratched* when its DSCB is removed from the associated VTOC.

In contrast, the data set label on a reel of tape contains rather limited information which includes the sequential order of data sets. When no data set label is used, the operating system assumes that there is only one data set on tape. If used, a data set label may be standard or nonstandard.

The LABEL operand in a DD statement is used exclusively for data sets residing on magnetic tape to indicate the relative position of a data set on the tape as well as the type of label. Its form is:

$$\text{LABEL} = (\textit{data set number}, \textit{type})$$

where the *data set number* on a tape must start at 1 and is sequentially incremented by 1. The subparameter *type* may be:

SL   for a standard labeled tape. If the status in the DISP operand is OLD, the DCB operand may be omitted from the DD statement. SL is the default value if the subparameter type is not specified.

NL   for an unlabeled tape. The DCB operand must be written in the DD statement.

BLP   for bypassing label processing. In this case, the DCB operand is required in the DD statement. BLP may also be used to a standard labeled tape.

The LABEL operand is discussed in greater detail in Section 14.2.

DCB

The data control block (DCB) operand describes the physical layout of a data set *at execution time*. It is required in a DD statement if (a) a new data set is being created, or (b) a data set on a reel of the unlabeled tape is being read.

The DCB operand has three forms:
1. DCB=*dsname*

    where *dsname* is the name of another data set from which the DCB information will be copied. This data set must be catalogued and placed on a mounted direct-access device, such as a disk.
2. DCB=∗.*stepname*.*ddname*

    where *stepname* is the step name of a previous job step and *ddname* is the name of a DD card from which the DCB operand is to be copied.
3. DCB=(*list of subparameters*)

    where the subparameters describe the arrangement of the information on the data media. The subparameters including RECFM, LRECL, DSORG, and BLKSIZE will be discussed in Section 14.3.

We shall now conclude the discussion of DD statement by commenting its name—*ddname*. First, a DD card must have a name, except in the case when more than one data set are used as a single data set. An example of this exception is shown in the following DD statements:

```
//INPUT   DD   DSNAME=FILE1,DISP=OLD
//        DD   DSNAME=FILE2,DISP=OLD
```

Here, the data sets FILE1 and FILE2 will be treated as one data set. This is known as *concatenation* of data sets. The concatenated data sets are normally read in the order of DD statements in the input stream.

In general, to concatenate several data sets, the *ddnames* must be omitted from all DD statements except the first in the sequence. The first DD statement should refer to the data set with the largest block size (BLKSIZE) of all the data sets to be concatenated. The remaining DD statements have to be arranged according to the block sizes, from large to small. BLKSIZE is discussed in Section 14.2.

Second, the *ddname* in a DD card does not represent a data set directly. A *dsname* serves as a linkage between a data set and a DD card (see Fig. 13.18), but the *ddname* merely connects a DD card with a DCB macro. A DCB macro, specified by a programmer, is used principally to describe a data set in a formal way; it will be discussed more fully in the next chapter.

Third, many *ddnames* are documented in IBM manuals and became standard names. For example, the SYSLIN DD statement defines the data set used by all compilers, except the assembler and Report Generator (RPG), to store the object module; while the SYSGO DD statement defines the one used by the assembler and RPG for the object module. Table 13.6 gives a fairly complete list of commonly used *ddnames*.

Table 13.6 Commonly used *ddnames*

Used by	DDNAME	Its associated data set
Compiler	SYSGO	Used by the assembler and RPG to store the object module.
	SYSIN	Defines the input for the compiler, or the source deck. The DD statement appears in the input stream.
	SYSLIB	Defines the library from which the compiler fetches the source code common to most problem programs.
	SYSLIN	Used by all compilers, except the assembler and RPG, to store the object module.
	SYSPRINT	Defines the system output writer used to print the compiler output.
	SYSPUNCH	Defines the system output writer used to punch the object deck.
	SYSUT1 SYSUT2 etc.	Defines temporary work areas used by the compiler.
Linkage editor and loader	SYSLIB	Defines the system library (in load and/or object modules) required by user's program.
	SYSLMOD	Used to store the load module.
	SYSLOUT	Defines the system output writer used to print the loader output listing.
	SYSPRINT	Defines the system output writer used to print the linkage editor output listing.
	SYSUT1 SYSUT2 etc.	Defines temporary work areas used by the linkage editor.
Execution	FT04F001	Defines a temporary disk area used by PLOT/CHAR routines.
	FT05F001	Refers to SYSIN DD statement in user's program to read cards.
	FT06F001	Defines the system output writer used to print output for a user's program.
	FT07F001	Defines the system output writer used to punch output for a user's program.
	FT13F001	Defines a temporary disk area available to a user's program.
	FT32F001	Defines a seven-track data set used by the PLOT routines.
	SYSPRINT	Defines the system output writer used to print output for a user's program.

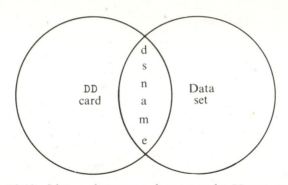

Fig. 13.18 Linkage between a data set and a DD statement.

13.11 EXAMPLE—COMPILATION OF A SOURCE DECK IN ASSEMBLER LANGUAGE

In this section, we shall study a complete set of job control statements used to compile an assembler language program.

A programmer must select an assembler and write its official name in an EXEC statement as follows:

```
//  EXEC  PGM=IEUASM
```

He must also list all input/output requirements for this job. They may include:

1. A printer used to list both the original instructions in source language and the results of compilation.
2. A 400-record space on any disk pack, the first area of the intermediate results from the assembler. The average record length is 1700 bytes.
3. Another 400-record space on any disk pack, the second area of the intermediate results from the assembler.
4. A third working area of the same space. For the data set in this area one has to use a different selector channel than in the previous two areas.
5. An on-line punch to yield the object deck, if requested.
6. A card reader to read the source deck.

In terms of job control language, each device requirement is implemented by a DD card (see Fig. 13.19a). The requirement 1, for example, is translated as follows:

```
//SYSPRINT  DD  SYSOUT=A
```

where the double slashes // in columns 1 and 2 indicate that this statement is meant for the reader/interpreter. The *ddname* SYSPRINT is conventional for an output from any output device. It is defined by the vendors because they wrote the program IEUASM. The operand SYSOUT=A specifies the required device as class A, or the printer.

```
//A710  JOB   (UNH,T117),KUO,MSGLEVEL=1,CLASS=G,TIME=5
//ASM       EXEC PGM=IEUASM
//SYSLIB    DD    DSNAME=SYS1.MACLIB,DISP=OLD
//SYSUT1    DD    UNIT=SYSDA,SPACE=(1700,(400,50)),SEP=SYSLIB
//SYSUT2    DD    UNIT=SYSDA,SPACE=(1700,(400,50))
//SYSUT3    DD    UNIT=SYSDA,SEP=(SYSUT1,SYSUT2),
//              SPACE=(1700,(400,50))
//SYSPRINT  DD    SYSOUT=A
//SYSPUNCH  DD    UNIT=SYSCP
//ASM.SYSIN DD    *
******************************
*                            *
*                            *
*          SOURCE DECK       *
*                            *
*                            *
******************************
/*
```
                              (a)
```
//A710  JOB   (UNH,T117),KUO,MSGLEVEL=1,CLASS=G,TIME=5
//FIG1319B  EXEC ASMFC
//ASM.SYSIN DD    *
******************************
*                            *
*                            *
*          SOURCE DECK       *
*                            *
*                            *
******************************
/*
```
                              (b)

Fig. 13.19 Two deck setups to compile an assembler language program. (a) Control cards for compilation of an assembler language program. (b) Use catalogued procedure ASMFC to compile.

The requirement 2 (400-record space on any disk) may be implemented by the following DD statement:

        //SYSUT1 DD UNIT=SYSDA,SPACE=(1700,(400,50)),SEP=SYSLIB

where SYSUT1 is the standard *ddname* for the first area of intermediate results of all compilers and assembler. The operand SPACE=(1700,(400,50)) signifies that 400-record space is requested, each record is about 1700 characters long. Each† time the space is exhausted, a space for 50 additional records is automatically allocated. The SEP operand requires that a different channel is used for data set SYS1.MACLIB which contains many system macros.

The final device requirement, a card reader to read the source deck, may be implemented as follows:

        //ASM.SYSIN DD *

where SYSIN is the standard *ddname* for an input on any input device, and ASM is the *stepname*. The asterisk tells the reader/interpreter that the cards following this DD

---

† A maximum of 15 times only.

card are the data cards to be processed by program IEUASM. Here, the so-called data cards are actually the source cards to be compiled.

The last card in Fig. 13.19(a) does not have double slashes // in columns 1 and 2; thus it is not meant for the reader/interpreter. This /* card is rather used to indicate the end of the source program, or the end of a data set in the input stream.

As mentioned before, the EXEC card and its following DD cards may be considered as a group. We then assign a name, say, ASMFC to such a group of control cards, and store them in the system procedure library as a member of SYS1.PROCLIB library shown in Fig. 13.7. This is then known as a catalogued procedure. When this is done, the user can follow the simpler deck setup as shown in 13.19(b) to compile an assembler language source deck.

It is possible to echo-print a member of procedure library SYS1.PROCLIB. Figure 13.20 shows a complete deck consisting of seven job-control cards and three utility-control cards. The EXEC statement requests the execution of the utility program

```
//A710   JOB   (UNH,T117),KUO,MSGLEVEL=1,CLASS=G,TIME=5
//COPY   EXEC    PGM=IEBPTPCH
//SYSPRINT DD    SYSOUT=A
//SYSUT1 DD      DSNAME=SYS1.PROCLIB,DISP=(OLD,KEEP)
//SYSUT2 DD      SYSOUT=A
//SYSIN  DD      *
         PRINT   TYPORG=PO,MAXNAME=5,MAXFLDS=5
         MEMBER  NAME=ASMFC
         RECORD  FIELD=(80,1,,20)
    /*
```

Fig. 13.20   Control cards and data cards to print the catalogued procedure ASMFC.

IEBPTPCH, whose whole purpose is to print or punch all (or a portion) of a sequential or partitioned data set. The three utility-control cards specified by a programmer, are used to control the functions of the IEBPTPCH. The operation field PRINT, MEMBER, and RECORD can begin in any column from 2 through 71. We shall now briefly explain each of the three special control cards.

PRINT   TYPORG=PO,MAXNAME=5,MAXFLDS=5

This special control card specifies that the data set is to be *printed*. The type of organization (TYPORG) of the input data set is partitioned (PO). MAXNAME specifies a decimal integer no less than the total number of subsequent MEMBER card, which is actually 1 in Fig. 13.20. MAXFLDS specifies a number no less than the total number of FIELD parameters appearing in the subsequent RECORD card(s). In Fig 13.20, the total number of FIELD parameters is 4.

MEMBER   NAME=ASMFC

This utility control card specifies that the member ASMFC of the partitioned data set SYS1.PROCLIB is to be printed.

```
RECORD  FIELD=(80,1,,20)
```

This card defines a record group to be printed. FIELD specifies the field procession and editing information. The first parameter (80) indicates that there are 80 bytes in each input card. The second parameter (1) specifies that the starting bytes of each input card is the first byte. The third parameter (conversion) is not specified in Fig. 13.20, which means that the input field is moved to the output area without change. The last parameter (20) specifies that the starting location in the output records is the 20th column.

　　We can also print out every member of the procedure library. It takes only two cards:

```
//A0033931  JOB    .....
//STEP1     EXEC  LIST,LIBRARY='SYS1.PROCLIB'
```

　　A typical SYS1.PROCLIB has about 200 members. Thus, the printout is about one inch thick.

13.12 A CATALOGUED PROCEDURE TO COMPILE, LINK, AND GO

The procedure library in every 370 or 360 installation contains a procedure which carries out three related job steps: compilation, link-editing, and execution of a program written in assembler language. (These three steps were discussed in Section 6.1, see Fig. 6.1). The procedure name is not standardized, but we shall call it ASMFCLG. A sample of this procedure is shown in Fig. 13.21. We shall now discuss its job control statements.

　　In terms of job control cards, an EXEC card and several DD cards are required for each step. Let us list the DD cards required in the first step ASM. They are: (a) three working areas on disks, (b) a printer, (c) a punch, and (d) a disk space for the results of compilation, the so-called object module. This output, a data set whose name is often given as &&LOADSET, is used as input in the second step, the link-editing. In addition, we would also need both system and users' macro libraries.

　　In LKED step, the vendor-supplied program IEWL is used. It needs (a) working space on any direct-access unit; (b) space for the result, the load module; and (c) a printer to list the cross-reference table and other output. The input data set, the object module, is passed to this step from the first step.

　　The third step GO executes the load module.

　　We shall now take a look at some statements which are known to be difficult for a beginner.

```
//ASM  EXEC  PGM=IEUASM,PARM'LOAD,NODECK',REGION=56K
```

The program IEUASM is an assembler, residing in the system library on a disk. The parameter PARM=LOAD requests an option: Put the result of compilation of a disk so that it may be used later in the second step. The device is specified in the SYSGO DD

```
//ASM        EXEC  PGM=IEUASM,PARM='LOAD,NODECK',REGION=56K
//SYSGO      DD    DSN=&&LOADSET,UNIT=SYSDA,DISP=(MOD,PASS),
//                 SPACE=(80,(200,50),RLSE),DCB=BLKSIZE=80
//SYSLIB     DD    DSNAME=SYS1.MACLIB,DISP=SHR
//           DD    DSNAME=USER.MACRO,DISP=SHR
//SYSPRINT   DD    SYSOUT=A
//SYSPUNCH   DD    SYSOUT=B
//SYSUT1     DD    DSN=&&SYSUT1,UNIT=SYSDA,
//                 SPACE=(1700,(400,50),RLSE),DCB=BLKSIZE=1700
//SYSUT2     DD    DSN=&&SYSUT2,UNIT=(SYSDA,SEP=SYSUT1),
//                 SPACE=(1700,(400,50),RLSE),DCB=BLKSIZE=1700
//SYSUT3     DD    DSN=&&SYSUT3,UNIT=(SYSDA,SEP=(SYSUT1,SYSUT2)),
//                 SPACE=(1700,(400,50),RLSE),DCB=BLKSIZE=1700
//LKED       EXEC  PGM=IEWL,PARM='XREF,LIST,LET,NCAL',COND=(4,LT,ASM),
//                 REGION=56K
//SYSLIN     DD    DSNAME=&&LOADSET,DISP=(OLD,DELETE)
//           DD    DDNAME=SYSIN
//SYSLMOD    DD    DSN=&&GOSET(PROGRAM),UNIT=SYSDA,DISP=(MOD,PASS),
//                 SPACE=(7294,(7,2,1)),DCB=BLKSIZE=7294
//SYSPRINT   DD    SYSOUT=A
//SYSUT1     DD    DSN=&&SYSUT1,UNIT=(SYSDA,SEP=(SYSLIN,SYSLMOD)),
//                 SPACE=(7294,(7,2),RLSE),DCB=BLKSIZE=7294
//GO         EXEC  PGM=*.LKED.SYSLMOD,COND=((4,LT,ASM),(4,LT,LKED)),
//                 REGION=56K
```

Fig. 13.21   Job control statements to compile, link-edit and execute an assembler language program.   (Procedure ASMFCLG.)

statement. NODECK means that no object deck is required. The required REGION is 56 k bytes.

```
//SYSGO  DD  DSN=&&LOADSET,...
```

The &&LOADSET is a temporary data set name for the compilation result, or object module. This data set becomes the input one in the LKED step.

```
//SYSLIN  DD  DSN=&&LOADSET,DISP=(OLD,DELETE)
//        DD  DDNAME=SYSIN
```

The substantial effect of this concatenation is that any input data sets in the input stream (for the LKED step) will be attached at the end of the temporary data set &&LOADSET, which was produced in the ASM step (see the DD statement with *ddname* SYSGO). If there is no such input data set available, this concatenation is ignored.

```
//SYSLMOD  DD  DSN=&&GOSET(PROGRAM),...SPACE=(7294,(7,2,1))...
```

The load module is put into the member PROGRAM of the temporary partitioned data set &&GOSET. The partitioned data set is reflected in the last subparameter, or 1, in the SPACE operand to allocate space for a directory.

```
//GO  EXEC  PGM=*.LKED.SYSLMOD
```

The third step is to basically execute the load module. Note that the load module is expressed in its backward reference.

13.13 EXAMPLES—APPLICATIONS TO DISK USAGE

In Section 13.9, we discussed how to build the index levels, allocate disk space, and catalogue a data set. Several examples were presented. In this section, we shall present eleven more JCL examples for everyday disk usage. FORTRAN programs are used for illustrations.

In these examples, we shall assume that the disk space has been allocated and the data set catalogued. We shall also use many procedures, and since their names are not standardized, we assume the following procedure names:

FORTGC	Compile a FORTRAN program	
FORTGCL	Compile and link-edit	
FORTGCLG	Compile, link-edit, and execute (three steps)	Use linkage editor
FORTGL	Link-edit object modules	
FORTGG	Execute	
FORTGCDG	Compile, link and execute (two steps)	Use OS loader

You should know the common procedure names used in your installation. A word of warning: Procedures having the same name do not necessarily consist of the same set of job control statements.

Through these examples, we shall illustrate how to override one or two statements listed in a procedure. An understanding of the effect of these changes on a given procedure is important. However, overriding a major portion of an existing procedure is not recommended.

Example 1

In Example 3 of Section 13.9, we showed how a sequential data set

USER.A3141.P5926.TEST6.RUN4

could be stored on a disk. We wish now to retrieve them and use them as input to a program.

Prepare job control cards and a FORTRAN source deck to read in 25 data card images in the space allocated for the data set

USER.A3141.P5926.TEST6.RUN4

and echo-print them. Each data card contains ten integers.

Figure 13.22 presents a complete deck ready for a run. The procedure FORTGCDG consists of two steps and is used to compile and load-execute (by OS loader). The following DD card in Fig. 13.22:

```
//GO.FT05F001  DD  DSNAME=USER.A3141.P5926.TEST6.RUN4,DISP=OLD
```

```
//A710    JOB     (UNH,T117),KUO,MSGLEVEL=1,CLASS=G,TIME=5
//EXAMPLE1    EXEC  FORTGCDG
//FORT.SYSIN   DD    *
              DIMENSION I(250)
              READ(5,14)I
              WRITE(6,14)I
      14      FORMAT(10(2X,I6))
              STOP
              END
/*
//GO.FT05F001 DD    DSNAME=USER.A3141.P5926.TEST6.RUN4,DISP=OLD
/*
```

Fig. 13.22 Execute a FORTRAN program with data already stored on disk.

```
//FORT        EXEC    PGM=IEYFORT,PARM='DECK'
//SYSLIN      DD      DSN=&&LOADSET,DISP=(MOD,PASS),UNIT=SYSDA,
//                    SPACE=(80,(200,100),RLSE),DCB=BLKSIZE=80
//SYSPRINT    DD      SYSOUT=A
//SYSPUNCH    DD      SYSOUT=B
//GO          EXEC    PGM=LOADER,PARM='MAP,LET,PRINT',COND=(4,LT,FORT)
//FT05F001    DD      DDNAME=SYSIN
//FT06F001    DD      SYSOUT=A
//FT07F001    DD      SYSOUT=B
//SYSLIB      DD      DSN=SYS1.FORTLIB,DISP=SHR
//            DD      DSN=USER.SSPLIB,DISP=SHR
//SYSLIN      DD      DSN=*.FORT.SYSLIN,DISP=(OLD,DELETE)
//            DD      OBJECT
//SYSLOUT     DD      SYSOUT=A
```

Fig. 13.23 Procedure FORTGCDG.

serves to override the following DD card in the GO step of the original procedure
FORTGCDG shown in Fig. 13.23:

$$\text{//FT05F001   DD   DDNAME=SYSIN}$$

The net effect: The input data come from the data set on the disk, not from the card
reader.

Example 2

A programmer has a source deck and wishes to place the output of its compilation
directly on a disk (as a member of the partitioned data set USER.N3141.5926.OBJECT).
The disk space has been already allocated for the partitioned data set and its directory.
This data set has been catalogued. No punched object deck is required.

A possible set of job control cards is given in Fig. 13.24. The procedure FORTGC
is used; its listing is shown Fig. 13.25. Note that the programmer will not get an
object deck, in spite of the fact that the DECK option is specified in the EXEC statement.
Reason: The SYSPUNCH output is directed to the member EXAM2 of the partitioned data
set USER.N3141.5926.OBJECT. The FORT.SYSPUNCH DD card in Fig. 13.24 overrides
the original SYSPUNCH DD card in procedure FORTGC:

$$\text{//SYSPUNCH   DD   SYSOUT=B}$$

which specifies a card punch.

```
//A710   JOB   (UNH,T117),KUO,MSGLEVEL=1,CLASS=G,TIME=5
//EXAMPLE2       EXEC  FORTGC,PARM.FORT='DECK'
//FORT.SYSPUNCH DD    DSN=USER.N3141.5926.OBJECT(EXAM2),
//               DISP=(OLD,KEEP)
//FORT.SYSIN    DD    *
***********************************
*                                 *
*          SOURCE DECK            *
*                                 *
*                                 *
***********************************
/*
```

Fig. 13.24   Deck setup to place results of compilation directly on a disk area.

```
//FORT      EXEC  PGM=IEYFORT,PARM='DECK'
//SYSLIN    DD    DSNAME=&LOADSET,DISP=(MOD,PASS),UNIT=SYSDA,
//                SPACE=(80,(200,100),RLSE),DCB=BLKSIZE=80
//SYSPRINT  DD    SYSOUT=A
//SYSPUNCH  DD    SYSOUT=B
```

Fig. 13.25   Procedure FORTGC.

Example 3

Same as Example 2 except that the program will be executed right after the output of compilation is placed on a disk area.

This can be accomplished by simply using the procedure FORTGCDG (instead of FORTGC) as shown in Fig. 13.26.

```
//A710   JOB   (UNH,T117),KUO,MSGLEVEL=1,CLASS=G,TIME=5
//EXAMPLE3       EXEC  FORTGCDG
//FORT.SYSPUNCH DD    DSN=USER.N3141.5926.OBJECT(EXAM2),
//               DISP=(OLD,KEEP)
//FORT.SYSIN    DD    *
***********************************
*                                 *
*                                 *
*     SOURCE DECK FOR EXAM2       *
*                                 *
*                                 *
***********************************
/*
//GO.SYSIN      DD    *
***********************************
*                                 *
*                                 *
*          DATA CARDS             *    OMIT IF NO DATA IS USED
*                                 *
*                                 *
***********************************
/*
```

Fig. 13.26   Place results of compilation directly on a disk area. Use OS loader to link and execute.

Example 4

You have source decks of a complete program, and wish to (a) compile and link-edit; (b) put the resulting load module on a disk area which you rent; and (c) execute the load module. Prepare job control cards.

A possible setup is shown in Fig. 13.27 where the procedure FORTGCLG is used,

```
//A710   JOB   (UNH,T117),KUO,MSGLEVEL=1,CLASS=G,TIME=5
//EXAMPLE       EXEC FORTGCLG
//FORT.SYSIN    DD   *
*******************************
*                             *
*                             *
*         SOURCE DECK         *
*                             *
*                             *
*******************************
/*
//LKED.SYSLMOD DD   DSN=USER.N3141.5926.LOAD(EXAM4),
//            DISP=(OLD,PASS)
//LKED.SYSIN   DD   *
*******************************
*                             *
*                             *
*         OBJECT DECKS        *     OMIT, IF NO OBJECT DECKS
*                             *
*                             *
*******************************
/*
//GO.SYSIN     DD   *
*******************************
*                             *
*                             *
*         DATA DECKS          *     OMIT, IF NO DATA CARDS
*                             *
*                             *
*******************************
/*
```

Fig. 13.27   Get the load module, put it on a disk area, and execute.

which has three steps: compilation, link-editing, and execution (see Fig. 13.28). The SYSLMOD DD statement in this deck setup overrides the SYSLMOD DD card specified in LKED step of the procedure FORTGCLG. Thus

```
//LKED.SYSLMOD  DD  DSN=USER.N3141.5926.LOAD(EXAM4),DISP=(OLD,PASS)
```

overrides the DSN and DISP operands in the following DD statement

```
//SYSLMOD  DD  DSN=&GOSET(PROGRAM),UNIT=SYSDA,...
```

in the LKED step of the procedure. As a result, the load module is directed to the member EXAM4 of the partitioned data set USER.N3141.5926.LOAD.

```
//FORT        EXEC  PGM=IEYFORT
//SYSLIN      DD    DSNAME=&LOADSET,DISP=(MOD,PASS),UNIT=SYSDA,
//                  SPACE=(80,(200,100),RLSE),DCB=BLKSIZE=80
//SYSPRINT    DD    SYSOUT=A
//SYSPUNCH    DD    SYSOUT=B
//LKED        EXEC  PGM=IEWL,PARM='XREF,LIST,LET',COND=(5,LT,FORT)
//SYSLIB      DD    DSNAME=SYS1.FORTLIB,DISP=SHR
//            DD    DSNAME=USER.SSPLIB,DISP=SHR
//SYSLIN      DD    DSNAME=*.FORT.SYSLIN,DISP=(OLD,DELETE)
//            DD    DDNAME=SYSIN
//SYSLMOD     DD    DSN=&GOSET(PROGRAM),UNIT=SYSDA,DISP=(MOD,PASS),
//                  SPACE=(7294,(7,2,1)),DCB=BLKSIZE=7294
//SYSPRINT    DD    SYSOUT=A
//SYSUT1      DD    DSN=&SYSUT1,UNIT=(SYSDA,SEP=(SYSLIN,SYSLMOD)),
//                  SPACE=(7294,(7,2),RLSE),DCB=BLKSIZE=7294
//GO          EXEC  PGM=*.LKED.SYSLMOD,COND=(5,LT,LKED)
//FT05F001    DD    DDNAME=SYSIN
//FT06F001    DD    SYSOUT=A
//FT07F001    DD    SYSOUT=B
//FT13F001    DD    DSN=&FT13F001,UNIT=SYSDA,SPACE=(TRK,(40,10),RLSE)
```

Fig. 13.28 Procedure FORTGCLG.

Example 5

If you have object decks of a complete program (main program plus its subroutines), and if this program is often used, it would save CPU time by link-editing these object decks and placing the resulting load module on disk. Prepare job control cards to (a) convert the object decks to a load module; and (b) add this module as a member in an *existing* partitioned data set, whose name is USER.A1879.P5653.LOAD.

```
//A710  JOB   (UNH,T117),KUO,MSGLEVEL=1,CLASS=G,TIME=5
//STEP1       EXEC FORTGL
//LKED.SYSLMOD DD  DSN=USER.A1879.P5653.LOAD(EXAMPLE5),DISP=(OLD,KEEP)
//LKED.SYSIN DD    *
*****************************
*                           *
*                           *
*        OBJECT DECKS       *
*                           *
*                           *
*****************************
/*
```

Fig. 13.29 Input is object decks. Add to an existing load data set. No execution.

```
//LKED        EXEC  PGM=IEWL,PARM='XREF,LIST,LET'
//SYSLIB      DD    DSNAME=SYS1.FORTLIB,DISP=SHR
//            DD    DSNAME=USER.SSPLIB,DISP=SHR
//SYSLIN      DD    DDNAME=SYSIN
//SYSLMOD     DD    DSN=&GOSET(PROGRAM),UNIT=SYSDA,DISP=(MOD,PASS),
//                  SPACE=(7294,(7,2,1)),DCB=BLKSIZE=7294
//SYSPRINT    DD    SYSOUT=A
//SYSUT1      DD    DSN=&SYSUT1,UNIT=(SYSDA,SEP=(SYSLIN,SYSLMOD)),
//                  SPACE=(7294,(7,2),RLSE),DCB=BLKSIZE=7294
```

Fig. 13.30 Procedure FORTGL.

Figure 13.29 shows a possible deck setup using procedure FORTGL. The resulting load module is directed to the member EXAMPLE5 of the existing partitioned data set. The procedure FORTGL is listed in Fig. 13.30.

Example 6

Prepare job control cards to execute the load module which we have already added on the disk (see Example 5).

```
//A710   JOB   (UNH,T117),KUO,MSGLEVEL=1,CLASS=G,TIME=5
//STEP1     EXEC FORTGG,PROG='USER.A1879.P5653.LOAD(EXAMPLE5)'
//GO.SYSIN DD   *
******************************
*                            *
*                            *
*          DATA              *    OMIT IF NO DATA
*                            *
*                            *
******************************
/*
```

Fig. 13.31   Deck setup to execute a load module.

A possible deck setup using procedure FORTGG is shown in Fig. 13.31. Note that the EXEC statement has a parameter PROG=, which indicates the data set name in consideration. The procedure FORTGG is listed in Fig. 13.32.

```
//LKED      EXEC PGM=IEFBR14
//SYSLMOD DD    DSN=&PROG,DISP=(OLD,PASS)
//GO      EXEC  PGM=*.LKED.SYSLMOD,COND=(5,LT,LKED)
//FT05F001 DD   DDNAME=SYSIN
//FT06F001 DD   SYSOUT=A
//FT07F001 DD   SYSOUT=B
//FT13F001 DD   DSN=&FT13F001,UNIT=SYSDA,SPACE=(TRK,(40,10),RLSE)
```

Fig. 13.32   Procedure FORTGG.

Example 7

You have the object decks of a frequently used subroutine package, consisting of a number of subroutines. This package is to be placed on a disk (as your own private library and as a partitioned data set) in the form of a load module ready to be executed. Required: job control cards.

Step 1. Punch a name card and place it at the end of *each* object deck. This NAME card has the following format:

Column	Contents
1	Blank
2 through 5	NAME
6	Blank
7 through 71	Name of the subroutine library

For example, the NAME card for the subroutine package named NONLINER is shown in Fig. 13.33.

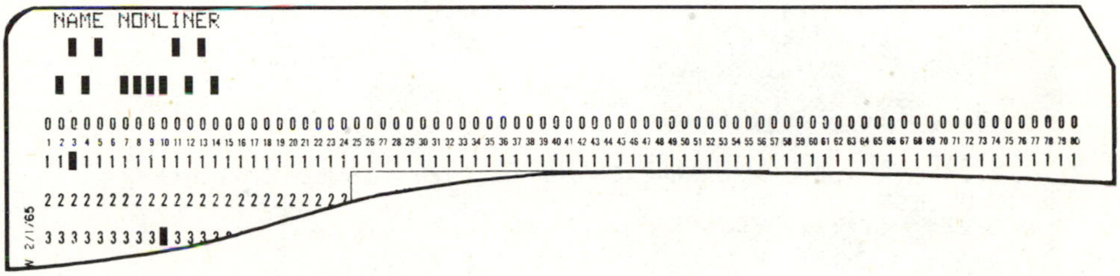

Fig. 13.33   Name card placed immediately after the object deck NONLINER.

Step 2. Prepare the job control cards as shown in Fig. 13.34. This job consists of only one job step.

```
//A710   JOB   (UNH,T117),KUO,MSGLEVEL=1,CLASS=G,TIME=5
//STEPA        EXEC FORTGL,PARM='NCAL'
//LKED.SYSLMOD DD DSN=USER.N3141.5926.MYSUBLIB,DISP=OLD
//LKED.SYSIN DD   *
*********************************************
*                                           *
*          OBJECT DECKS WITH                *
*          NAME CARDS INCLUDED              *
*                                           *
*********************************************
/*
```

Fig. 13.34   Deck setup to place your subroutine library on a disk area.

Example 8

In Example 7, we learnt how to place a subroutine library as a load module on a disk pack. Write JCL statements to compile, load, and execute a FORTRAN program. This program consists of several source decks and several object decks. It also calls several subroutines in your subroutine library already placed on a disk pack (see Example 7).

Figure 13.35 shows a possible job card setup. Note that a SYSLIB DD card is used in the load-execute step to access your own library already placed on a disk.

Example 9

Prepare job control cards to

a) Put card images of FORTRAN source decks on a disk;
b) Compile, load, and execute the program.

```
//A710   JOB   (UNH,T117),KUO,MSGLEVEL=1,CLASS=G,TIME=5
//STEP1        EXEC FORTGCDG
//FORT.SYSIN DD   *
```

```
****************************
*                          *
*                          *
*      SOURCE DECKS        *
*                          *
*                          *
****************************
```

```
/*
//GO.SYSLIB   DD   DSNAME=USER.M3141.5926.MYSUBLIB,DISP=SHR
//GO.OBJECT   DD   *
```

```
****************************
*                          *
*                          *
*      OBJECT  DECKS       *        MAY BE OMITTED IF NO OBJECT DECKS.
*                          *
*                          *
****************************
```

```
/*
```

Fig. 13.35   JCL statements to compile, load and execute a FORTRAN program. It calls your subroutine library.

```
//A710   JOB   (UNH,T117),KUO,MSGLEVEL=1,CLASS=G,TIME=5
//STEP1        EXEC PGM=IEBUPDTE,PARM=NEW
//SYSPRINT    DD   SYSOUT=A
//SYSUT2      DD   DSN=USER.A3301.P1206.SOURCE,DISP=OLD
//SYSIN       DD   *
./   ADD  NAME=EXAMPLE9
***********************************************
*                                             *
*       SOURCE DECK TO GO TO DISK             *
*            AS MEMBER EXAMPLE9               *
*                                             *
***********************************************
./    ENDUP
/*
//STEP2        EXEC FORTGCDG
//FORT.SYSIN DD   DSNAME=USER.A3301.P1206.SOURCE(EXAMPLE9),DISP=(OLD,KEEP)
//GO.OBJECT   DD.   *
****************************
*                          *
*                          *
*      OBJECT DECKS        *        OMIT IF NO OBJECT DECK
*                          *
*                          *
****************************
/*
//GO.SYSIN   DD   *
****************************
*                          *
*                          *
*       DATA CARDS         *        OMIT IF NO DATA CARDS
*                          *
*                          *
****************************
/*
```

Fig. 13.36   Put source decks on disk and load and execute.

The setup of control cards for these two steps is shown in Fig. 13.36. In the first step which directs source decks into a previously allocated and catalogued data set

USER.A3301.P1206.SOURCE

the IBM-supplied print/punch utility program IEBUPDTE is used. This program is very powerful and is often used to

a) Incorporate changes (e.g., addition, copying, or replacing) to partitioned members or sequential data sets.
b) Create and update a library of partitioned members.
c) Change the organization of a data set from partitioned to sequential or vice versa.

In using IEBUPDTE to add a member to a partitioned data set, the member name must be given; this is punched in a utility control card having the following general format:

./   ADD   NAME=*memname*[,LIST=ALL]

where *memname* is the member name of the source deck that is added to the partitioned data set. It may not exceed eight characters. The keyword parameter LIST=ALL is optional. If used as, for example, in Fig. 13.37, it demands that the output will include

```
//A710   JOB   (UNH,T117),KUO,MSGLEVEL=1,CLASS=G,TIME=5
//STEP1      EXEC PGM=IEBUPDTE,PARM=NEW
//SYSPRINT DD    SYSOUT=A
//SYSUT2    DD    DSN=USER.A5779.P1122.OBJECT,DISP=OLD
//SYSIN     DD    *
./          ADD   NAME=MYMAIN,LIST=ALL
****************************************
*                                      *
*                                      *
*             OBJECT DECK              *
*                                      *
*                                      *
****************************************
./      ENDUP
/*
```

Fig. 13.37   Put object deck on disk as member MYMAIN of a partitioned data set.

an echo-print of the newly added member as well as the job control statements used in its creation.

The ./ ADD special control card is placed in front of a member, forming a basic group. You may put any reasonable number of the groups, which must be followed by an ENDUP card:

./   ENDUP

As an added feature of the print/punch program IEBUPDTE, we may sequence the source decks as their card images are stored on disk. For example, if we wish to number the first source card as 0010, the second as 0020, and so on, simply place the following special control card:

$$./ \quad \text{NUMBER} \quad \text{NEW1=10,INCR=10}$$

right after the ./   ADD card (that is, right before the source decks).

Example 10

An object deck is to be placed on a disk as a member (MYMAIN) of the partitioned data set:

USER.A5779.P1122.OBJECT

Prepare the job control cards.

A possible set of job control cards using the print/punch utility program IEBUPDTE, is shown in Fig. 13.37. The setup is basically the same as that of the first step shown in Fig. 13.36, except that the name of the data set is changed.

Example 11

We have just shown in Example 10 how to place object deck as a member of a partitioned data set. Two such members already on the disk are a main program MYMAIN, and a subroutine ITSSUB1, called by MYMAIN. If MYMAIN also calls a second subroutine ITSSUB2 that must be compiled, prepare job control cards to execute the program.

A possible setup is shown in Fig. 13.38. It is a very simple one which needs little explanation, except perhaps that the special control card INCLUDE used in the link-editing step indicates that the object modules MYMAIN and ITSSUB1 should be included for the link-editing.

```
//A710   JOB    (UNH,T117),KUO,MSGLEVEL=1,CLASS=G,TIME=5
//STEP1          EXEC FORTGCLG
//FORT.SYSIN  DD    *
********************************
*                              *
*        SOURCE CARDS          *
*        FOR ITSSUB2           *
*                              *
********************************
/*
//LKED.OBJECT DD    DSN=USER.A5779.P1122.OBJECT,DISP=(OLD,KEEP)
//LKED.SYSIN  DD    *
       INCLUDE OBJECT(MYMAIN,ITSSUB1)
/*
//GO.SYSIN    DD    *
********************************
*                              *
*                              *
*        DATA CARDS            *    OMIT IF NO DATA CARD
*                              *
*                              *
********************************
/*
```

Fig. 13.38 Card images of two object decks are already on disk: MYMAIN (main program) and ITSSUB1 (first subroutine). MYMAIN calls another subroutine which must be compiled.

BIBLIOGRAPHY

Bender, G., D. N. Freeman, and J. D. Smith, "Function and Design of DOS/360 and TOS/360," *IBM Systems J.* **6**(1), 1967.

Cadow, H. W., *OS/360 Job Control Language*, Prentice-Hall, Englewood Cliffs, N.J., 1970.

Daley, Robert C., and Jack B. Dennis, "Virtual Memory, Processes, and Sharing in MULTICS," *CACM* **11**(5), 306–312, (May 1968).

Gibson, Charels T., "Time-Sharing in the IBM System/360 Model 67," *Proceedings of Spring Joint Computer Conference*, pages 61–78, (1966).

IBM Operating System/360 Primary Control Program (PCP), X20-1746, IBM Corp.

IBM System/360 Disk Operating System User's Guide Control Statement Techniques, Form C20-1685.

IBM System/360 Operating System Introduction, Form C-28-6534, IBM Corp., 1969.

IBM System/360 Operating System Job Control Language Reference, Form GC28-6704, IBM Corp.

IBM System/360 Operating System: Job Control User's Guide, Form GC28-6703, IBM Corp.

IBM System/360 Operating System Job Control Language Charts, Form C28-6632, IBM Corp.

IBM System/360 Operating System MFT Guide, Form C27-6939, IBM Corp.

IBM System/360 Operating System MVT Control Program Logic Summary, Form Y28-6658, IBM Corp.

IBM System/360 Operating System System Programmer's Guide, Form C28-6550, IBM Corp.

IBM System/360 Operating System Utilities, Form GC28-6586, IBM Corp.

Introduction to IBM System/360 Direct Access Storage Devices and Organization Methods, Form C20-1649, IBM Corp.

Katzan, H., Jr., "Operating Systems Architecture," *Proceedings of The Spring Joint Computer Conference* (1970).

Madnick, S. E., and J. J. Donovan, *Operating System*, McGraw-Hill, New York, 1974.

Rosin, Robert F., "Supervisory and Monitor Systems," *Computing Surveys* **1**(1), 37–54, (March 1969).

PROBLEMS

1. The utility UTGENER is used in an eastern university for listing and/or reproducing card decks. The example shown in Fig. 13.39 provides a listout of the input card deck.

```
//UTGENER JOB (accounting info),prgrmrname,MSGLEVEL=1
//A EXEC UTGENER
//SYSUT2 DD  SYSOUT=A,DCB=BLKSIZE=80
//SYSUT1 DD  *

            (input card deck)

/*
```

Fig. 13.39   Deck setup to list an input card deck.

a) Modify the JOB card to suit your requirement.

b) Is UTGENER a program or a procedure?

c) An EXEC card and its associated DD cards make a basic unit in processing. What is the name of this unit?

d) Change one operand only in one of the statements so that a duplicate deck of the input card will be *punched*.

2. In using the utility program UTGENER, multiple copies of listing and/or duplicate deck of an input card deck can be produced. The job control cards in Fig. 13.40, for example, will provide two separate listings of the input card deck and one duplicate

```
//UTGENER JOB (accounting info),prgrmrname,MSGLEVEL=1
//A EXEC UTGENER
//SYSUT2 DD DCB=(BLKSIZE=3200,LRECL=80,RECFM=FB),UNIT=2314,
//   DISP=(,PASS),SPACE=(TRK,(20,10)),DSN=&&T1
//SYSUT1 DD *

        (input card deck)

/*
//  EXEC UTGENER
//SYSUT2 DD   SYSOUT=A,DCB=BLKSIZE=80
//SYSUT1 DD   DISP=(OLD,PASS),DSN=&&T1,VOL=REF=*.A.UT.SYSUT2
//  EXEC UTGENER
//SYSUT2 DD   SYSOUT=A,DCB=BLKSIZE=80
//SYSUT1 DD   DISP=(OLD,PASS),DSN=&&T1,VOL=REF=*.A.UT.SYSUT2
//  EXEC UTGENER
//SYSUT2 DD   SYSOUT=B,DCB=BLKSIZE=80
//SYSUT1 DD   DISP=(OLD,PASS),DSN=&&T1,VOL=REF=*.A.UT.SYSUT2
```

Fig. 13.40   Deck setup to list the input card deck twice and also punch the same deck.

card deck. Basically, multiple copies may be generated by repeating the last three job control cards in Fig. 13.39 as many times as needed. (No DO loop is available.)

a) Modify Fig. 13.40 so that one listing and two duplicate card decks are produced.

b) Explain the meaning of *.A.UT.SYSUT2.

c) How many job steps are there in Fig. 13.40?

3. A possible set of job control statements to compile a PL/I program is shown in Fig. 13.41. DECK requests an object deck and NOLOAD has an opposite meaning of LOAD. The subparameter CONTIG following RLSE is coded to ensure that space is allocated in contiguous or adjacent tracks or cylinders. Explain each job control statement in detail.

```
//PL1D      EXEC   PGM=IEMAA,PARM='DECK,NOLOAD'
//SYSPRINT  DD     SYSOUT=A
//SYSPUNCH  DD     SYSOUT=B
//SYSUT1    DD     UNIT=SYSDA,SPACE=(1024,(60,60),RLSE,CONTIG)
//SYSUT3    DD     UNIT=(SYSDA,SEP=SYSUT1),SPACE=(80,(250,250),RLSE)
```

Fig. 13.41   Five job control statements for PL/I compilation.

4. To compile FORTRAN main program and its assembler language subroutine(s), link-edit and execute, two sets of deck setup are illustrated in Figs. D.1(a) and D.1(b) in Appendix D. One uses the procedure FORTASM, the other uses two steps involving the procedures ASMFC and FORTGCLG. In Fig. D.3, a possible deck setup is shown to compile PL/I main program and its assembler language subroutine(s), link-edit, and execute. Prepare a different setup to do the same thing. [*Hint*: Follow the idea used in Fig. D.1(b).]

5. Figure D.2 in Appendix D shows a possible deck setup to compile COBOL main program and its subroutine(s) written in assembler language, link-edit, and execute. Prepare a different setup to do the same job.

LABORATORY ASSIGNMENT

A minority of computer installations does not usually allocate "permanent" disk space to a student. In this case, you cannot build index levels or catalogue a data set. However, you can always use some temporary disk space for the following projects.

1. Prepare the complete job control cards for the following two steps:
   a) Use the utility program IEBGENER to copy ten data cards into a disk area as the temporary data set &&DATA (Refer to STEP3 in Fig. 13.15.)
   b) Use a procedure similar to FORTGCDG (Fig. 13.23) to compile, link-execute a main program in FORTRAN or other high-level language, which is used to read and echo-print the ten data cards (see Fig. 13.22).

2. Prepare JCL statements for the following two steps:
   a) Use IEBGENER to copy a source program in a disk area as the temporary data set &&TEMP.
   b) Use the utility program IEBPTPCH to echo-print &&TEMP.

3. a) Write a main program in a high-level language, and its subroutine SUBR1 in assembler language. Compile the subroutine SUBR1 and obtain the object deck.
   b) Prepare the JCL statements for the following two steps:
   Step 1. Use the utility program IEBUPDTE to add the object deck for SUBR1 in a disk space as a member of the partitioned data set &&TEMP1.
   Step 2. Use a procedure such as FORTGCLG to compile, link-edit, and execute. The object module for SUBR1 must be linked with that for the main program before the execution.

4. Given:
   a) A main program in a high-level language which calls two subroutines SUB1 and SUB2.
   b) Subroutine SUB1 is written in the same language as the one used in main program.
   c) Object deck of SUB2.
   Prepare JCL deck setup to put all object modules in disk spaces, link-edit, and execute.

5. Figure 13.42 shows a complete deck setup used to copy (with printer and/or punch) a given deck which may contain any job cards, including a delimiter card (/* in columns 1 and 2 and blanks in other columns.) The number of copies may vary from

1 up to 999. Note that the delimiter operand DLM='%%' in the job control statement

$$//GO.SYSIN \quad DD \quad DATA,DLM='\%\%'$$

makes possible to copy a /* card. Modify Fig. 13.40 so that the input card deck may contain /* cards. Change the name UTGENER, if necessary.

```
//A710   JOB   (UNH,T117),KUO,MSGLEVEL=1,CLASS=G,TIME=5
//STEP1 EXEC FORTGCDK
//FORT.SYSIN  DD *
        INTEGER ACARD(20)
CCC  NCODE.... 1=PRINT. 2=PUNCH. 3=BOTH.
        READ (5,100) NCODE
CCCC    N IS THE NO. OF COPIES NEEDED.
        READ(5,100) N
100     FORMAT(I3)
        READ(5,99) IEND
  99 FORMAT(A4)
10      READ(5,2) ACARD
2       FORMAT(20A4)
C   LOGICAL UNIT 13  FOR SCRATCH.
        WRITE(13,2) ACARD
        IF(ACARD(1)-IEND)10,50,10
50      END FILE 13
        REWIND 13
        DO 4 K=1,N
        WRITE(6,15)
15      FORMAT(1H1)
20      READ(13,2) ACARD
        IF(ACARD(1)-IEND)25,5,25
  25    IF(NCODE-2) 22,21,21
   21 WRITE(7,2) ACARD
        IF(NCODE-2) 22,20,22
  22    WRITE(6,3) ACARD
3       FORMAT(1H ,1X,20A4)
        GO TO 20
    5 REWIND 13
4       CONTINUE
        CALL EXIT
        END
/*
//GO.SYSIN DD    DATA,DLM='%%'
003
001
++++
************************************************************
*                                                          *
*                                                          *
*   DECK TO BE REPRODUCED, INCLUDING THE JOB CONTROL CARDS *
*                                                          *
************************************************************
++++
%%
//
```

Fig. 13.42   A deck setup to reproduce a deck which may contain any job control cards.

6. Given: A complete deck of cards as shown in Fig. 13.42, which is essentially a duplicator.

Required: Self-reproduction—JCL statements needed to reproduce the FORTRAN deck (the first shaded portion in Fig. 13.42).

[*Hint:* Use the following four steps:

Steps 1 through 3. Copy the contents of the three shaded portions in Fig. 13.42 as three separate temporary data sets, &&DATA1, &&DATA2, and &&DATA3.

Step 4. Use FORTGCLG procedure to execute the data set &&DATA1. The input data in this step should be the concatenated data set: &&DATA2 followed by &&DATA1, then followed by &&DATA3.]

CHAPTER 14

Input/Output Using System Macros

14.1 INTRODUCTORY REMARKS

One of the most difficult subjects in assembler language programming is input/output. In earlier chapters, main program written in a high-level language was used to handle this chore. In this chapter, we shall illustrate just how to take care of input/output using facilities available under Operating System/360 (OS/360 or simply OS).

Take, for example, a very simple output problem. To print a message "VOTE FOR ME", skip three lines, and print the same message again. A possible program† written in FORTRAN and that in PL/I are shown in Figs. 14.1(a) and 14.1(b), respectively. In contrast, a comparable program in assembler language is much more complex. As shown in Fig. 14.1(c), you rely on a number of system macros (such as OPEN, PUT, DCB, etc.) to control the input/output functions.

The key to the effectiveness of input/output programming is the intelligent usage of many input/output macros and subroutines. To learn how to achieve this is the main purpose of this chapter.

To lay the groundwork, a brief overview of the chapter is in order.

In Section 14.2, we shall introduce the additional terms and conceptions associated with a data set, which were not covered in the previous chapter. Section 14.3 deals with Data Control Block (DCB), a main-storage area containing detailed information of a given data set. Practical examples are given to illustrate how items of the information can be supplied through a DCB operand in a DD statement. The routine usage of magnetic tapes are deliberately stressed in Sections 14.2 and 14.3.

Many of the system macros for input/output are concerned with buffers. An example of a buffer is a main storage area to hold the input information temporarily

---

† In this chapter, the complete deck setup is shown for each program used. The job control statements are unshaded, whereas the statements used in a program (and data cards, if any) are shaded.

```
//A711   JOB   (UNH,T117),KUO,MSGLEVEL=1,CLASS=G,TIME=5
//STEP1 EXEC FORTGCLG
//FORT.SYSIN   DD *
C      IN FORTRAN
       WRITE (6,124)
  124 FORMAT(60X,' VOTE FOR ME'///)
       WRITE (6,125)
  125 FORMAT (60X,' VOTE FOR ME')
       END
/*
//
```

(a) A program in FORTRAN.

```
//A711   JOB   (UNH,T117),KUO,MSGLEVEL=1,CLASS=G,TIME=5
//STEP   EXEC   PL1LFCG
//PL1L.SYSIN    DD  *
F14_1B: PROCEDURE OPTIONS(MAIN);
/* IN PL/I */
PUT SKIP EDIT (' VOTE FOR ME')(X(60),A);
PUT SKIP(3) EDIT(' VOTE FOR ME')(X(60),A);
END F14_1B;
/*
//
```

(b) A program in PL/I.

```
//A711   JOB   (UNH,T117),KUO,MSGLEVEL=1,CLASS=G,TIME=5
//A EXEC ASMFCLG
//ASM.SYSIN DD *
VOTE       CSECT
           SAVE   (14,12),,*
           BALR   11,0
           USING  *,11
           OPEN   (OUTPTDCB,(OUTPUT))
           MVC    LINE+61(11),MSG
           PUT    OUTPTDCB,LINE
           CNTRL  OUTPTDCB,SP,2
           PUT    OUTPTDCB,LINE
           CLOSE  (OUTPTDCB)
           RETURN (14,12)
LINE       DC     CL133' '
MSG        DC     CL11'VOTE FOR ME'
OUTPTDCB DCB      DSORG=PS,MACRF=PMC,DDNAME=SYSPRINT,LRECL=133,     X
                  BLKSIZE=133,RECFM=FA
           END
/*
//GO.SYSPRINT DD SYSOUT=A
//GO.SYSUDUMP DD SYSOUT=A
//
```

(c) An assembler program.

Fig. 14.1   Three programs to print VOTE FOR ME.

until they are needed by CPU. In Section 14.4, we shall explore the input/output buffers and the buffer pool.

The software concerned with the input/output functions normally consists of two basic components: First, the Input/Output Supervisor (IOS) that communicates with the channel; second, the access method, also known as Input/Output Control

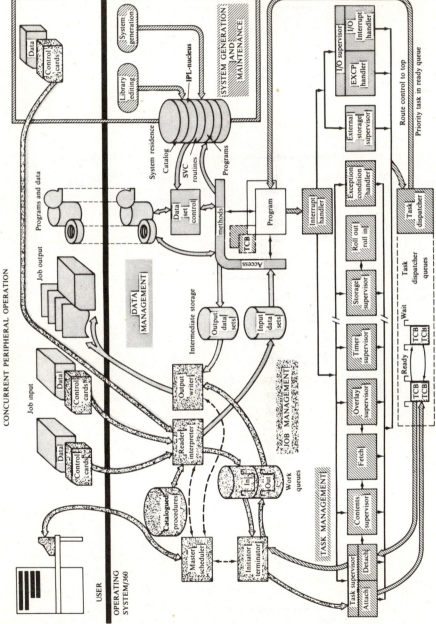

Fig. 14.2 Overview of Operating System/360.

System (IOCS), that communicates with the program. They are shown as two components of data management (data control) in Fig. 14.2.

Essentially, the requests of the system macros for input/output are performed by the input/output supervisor, a set of most complex routines in the operating system. However, the input/output supervisor does not deal with your program directly. When your program needs a piece of data or wants to write a message, you usually direct it to call another set of data management routines, the *access method* routine. This routine informs your program where in main storage the next input record for processing can be obtained, or where to put the next output record. We shall take a look at the access method routines in Section 14.5. The next five sections deal with the important input/output macros; they will be illustrated with many complete examples.

Note that Fig. 14.2 presents an overview of OS/360. To help consolidate the materials covered in Chapter 13, you should (a) compare this graph with the contents shown in Fig. 13.1, and (b) trace through the job management (job control) portion in Fig. 14.2. The recovery control routines are not shown in the graph.

A word of caution here: Assembler language programming is intimately tied to a particular type of machine. Furthermore, the input/output macros available to you in your installation reflect the options and parameters of a specific operating system. In this chapter, we do not attempt to provide complete discussion of features of all options for input/ouput control. Rather, we shall be concerned with a specific set of input/output macros under a particular access method. They are probably the easiest ones to start using.

14.2 BLOCK FACTOR, RECORD FORMATS, AND LABELS

In Chapter 13, we learned many basic terms which recur frequently in connection with a data set. This section will introduce additional important terms and conceptions.

To distinguish one driver from another, the information used in a state agency may contain the following items:

1. Name
2. Address
3. Date of birth
4. Sex
5. Height
6. Weight
7. Color of eyes
8. Color of hair

In computer jargon, each of the eight items in the above list is a *field;* the complete list is called a *record* or a logical record; and a collection of all related records becomes a data set (or a *file*). Thus, in the Motor Vehicle Bureau of this state, each driver's record consists of eight fields. The collection of updated drivers' records might be called the driver data set; its data set name might simply be DRIVER.

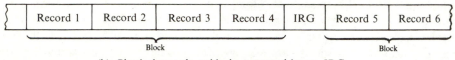

(a) Two logical records may be separated by an IRG .

(b) Physical records or blocks separated by an IRG .

Fig. 14.3   Logical and physical records.

A record may be placed on punched card(s), magnetic tape, disk pack, or data cell. For simplicity, let us discuss now the records on a reel of magnetic tape. They are organized sequentially; two adjacent records may be separated by an interrecord gap (IRG) as shown in Fig. 14.3(a). Physically, 0.4 to 0.75 in. long, each IRG is completely magnetized by the writing mechanism of a tape drive. During reading, the tape comes to a stop at the center of the next IRG.

In order to cut down the number of IRG, thus conserving the tape space and reading time, we can conveniently group a number of logical records into a *block*, also called a *physical record* (see Fig. 14.3b). Two adjacent blocks are separated by an IRG, or more correctly, an *interblock gap* (IBG).

The logical record length (LRECL) and block size (BLKSIZE) are both expressed in bytes. The following ratio

$$\text{Blocking factor} = \frac{\texttt{BLKSIZE}}{\texttt{LRECL}}$$

indicates the amount of information that may be recorded per unit tape-length.

Example 1

Information is stored on a reel of tape having the recording density 800 bytes/in. (b.p.i.). Each interblock gap requires 0.6 in., or 480 bytes. If BLKSIZE and LRECL are both taken as 80 bytes, find the number of cards whose image can be stored on a 2400-ft tape reel.

Since there are 480 bytes overhead for each 80 bytes of useful recording, the storage efficiency is

$$\frac{80}{480 + 80} = 14.3\%.$$

When stored on a reel of tape, each card takes 80 bytes. Thus, in a 2400-ft reel, the number of cards that can be stored is

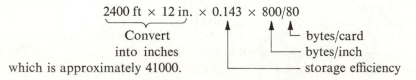

which is approximately 41000.

In the above example, each block contains only one logical record. If, on the other hand, several logical records were placed in one block, the storage efficiency would be different as shown in the following example.

Example 2

Same as Example 1, except that the block size is now equal to 1600.

The block factor becomes 20 and the storage efficiency rises sharply to

$$\frac{80 \times 20}{480 + (80 \times 20)} = 77\%.$$

The corresponding number of cards which can be stored on the same tape reel increases to 221,000.

Figure 14.4 shows the relationship between storage efficiency versus blocking factor. We see that the storage efficiency rises sharply in the initial stage, but tapers off when the value of block factor becomes large.

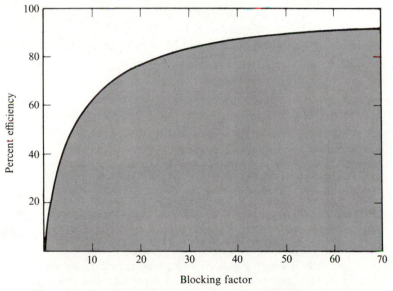

Fig. 14.4   Blocking factor versus percent efficiency for a tape.

The blocking of records not only increases the storage efficiency, but also saves the total *start-up time* and the total *stop time* of tape drive. Before we explain these two terms, let us first make clear a simple fact which is not commonly recognized: Each input command (e.g., a GET instruction discussed in Section 14.7) transfers *one entire physical record* from the tape to main storage.

Due to its inertia, a tape drive, like any other input/output devices, takes a fixed amount of time to get ready to transfer data after an input command is received, called start-up time. Similarly, due to its momentum, the tape drive requires a fixed amount of time to bring it to a complete stop after an IBG is sensed. For a given tape length, the greater is the block size, the less overall time is consumed for the start-up and stopping.

Example 3

Consider the tape described in Example 1. Find (a) the total number of input commands needed to read the complete reel of tape, and (b) the total start-up time in seconds if each start-up takes seven milliseconds.

Solution. In this example, each block consists of only one logical record.
  a) The total number of blocks in the tape reel is

$$2400 \text{ ft} \times 12 \text{ in.} \times 800 \times \frac{1}{480 + 80} = 41{,}000.$$

Thus we need a total of 41,000 read commands to read the records in the reel.
  b) The *number* of start-ups is also 41,000. As a result, the total start-up time is 41,000 × 7/1,000 = 286 sec.

Example 4

Same as Example 3, except that the tape reel is the one described in Example 2.

Solution. In this case, each block consists of 20 logical records.
  a) The total number of blocks is

$$2400 \text{ ft} \times 12 \text{ in.} \times 800 \times \frac{1}{480 + 80 \times 20} = 1{,}110.$$

Thus we need only 1110 read commands to read all records.
  b) The total start-up time is

$$1110 \times 7/1000 = 7.7 \text{ sec.}$$

Record Formats

The logical record length (LRECL) is taken as 80 in the above examples; this is the so-called *fixed* type of LRECL. Although simple to use, it is often very wasteful if each record contains items which are optional. For example, some drivers might have certain restrictions such as hearing aid, outside mirrors, or cars with automatic transmission only. It is uneconomical to contain all these items in every driver's record. In this case, one should use variable-length record. Reflecting these ideas, the data management routines (Fig. 14.2) enable us to use fixed-length (F) formats, variable-length (V) formats, or undefined (U) format. They include:

F: simple fixed-length format, commonly used for punched cards and printing output.

FB: fixed-length, blocked record format; normally used on disk, tape, etc.

FBS: standard-fixed length, blocked record format. This is the most efficient format for disk. By "standard" we mean that each block has the same number of logical records except possibly the last block, which may contain fewer logical records.

V: variable-length format; used to save space.

VB: variable-length, blocked format.

U: undefined format. Here the records are taken as unblocked.

A logical record of fixed length may contain either an ASCII† or a machine control character in its first byte, used to control printer-paper skipping or to select the stacker packet in a card punch. To reflect this control character, it is possible to suffix either A or M to the record format used. For example, FA stands for fixed length with ASCII control character; FBSM for the standard fixed-length format with machine character.

Tape Labeling—Labels Recorded on Magnetic Tapes

A reel of tape may be labeled or left unlabeled. However, a labeled tape is recommended because it helps process (1) the tape reel you want, or (2) the data set you want in a given reel of tape. Two standard labeling conventions are normally used: IBM standard (which we choose to use in the following discussion), or American National Standards Institute (ANSI) standard. Figure 14.5(a) presents the layout of IBM standard labels recorded *near the beginning* of a tape volume under OS. It consists of three types:

1. A *volume label* to identify the tape volume.
2. A set of two *header labels* for each data set.
3. A set of two *trailer labels* for each data set.

Each label is itself a record, 80 bytes long. The header and trailer labels are often collectively called *data set labels*.

The various fields used in a volume label, as shown in Fig. 14.5(b), are self-explanatory, perhaps with the exception the volume security byte which has the following meaning:

Zero = no further identification of each data set in the
        volume is required before its processing.

Nonzero = further identification is required.

The volume label is followed by a tape mark, which is a unique character. Unlike IBG, a tape mark is not used to start or stop the tape.

For each data set, there are two header labels, called the header label 1 (HDR1) and the header label 2 (HDR2). Their formats are shown in Figs. 14.5(c) and 14.5(d). They contain a large amount of information on the associated data set. *In particular, the record format, block length, record length, and printer control character (A or M) are included in the header label 2* (HDR2).

At the end of each data set, two trailer labels (end-of-file labels) EOF1 and EOF2

---

† The American Standard Code for Information Interchange (ASCII) and EBCDIC are two main ways to represent decimal digits, alphabetic, and other special characters in System/360. No ASCII is permitted in System/370.

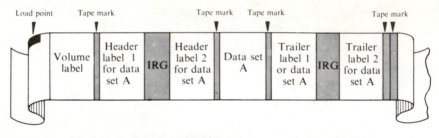

(a) Layout of IBM standard labels in a tape volume under OS.
Each label is a record, 80 bytes long.

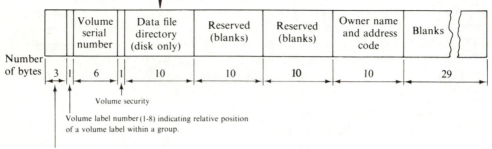

(b) Volume label format for tape *or* disk.

Fig. 14.5   Standard tape labels under OS.

are recorded. With minor exceptions, their formats are identical to the two header labels. At the end of the physical reel, two end-of-volume labels (E0V1 and E0V2) are also recorded.

Let us conclude by explaining the meaning of a new technical jargon: how to *initialize* a tape. Virtually all computer installations will do this for you on request.

The basic steps to initialize a tape are:

1. A serial number (e.g., CC0603) is assigned to the tape volume and written on an adhesive label placed externally on the reel. You can now use this serial number in the VOL operand of a DD card to specify the tape volume (e.g., VOL=SER=CC0603).

2. A small aluminium strip is placed, if not already there, about 12 feet from the physical beginning of the reel. This is called *load point* which signifies the beginning of the recorded surface.

3. A volume label and a tape mark are recorded on the tape right after the load point. The operator can readily accomplish this step by running a utility program IEHINITT. The volume serial number and, optionally, your name are placed in the volume label.

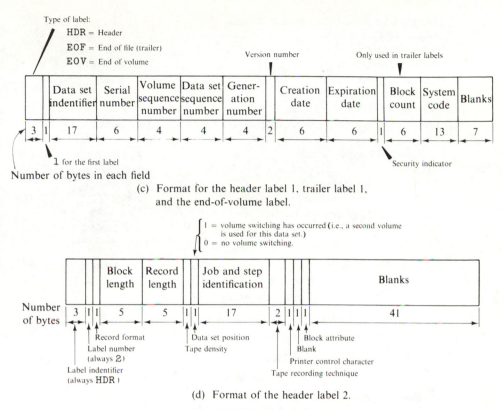

(c) Format for the header label 1, trailer label 1,
and the end-of-volume label.

(d) Format of the header label 2.

Fig. 14.5 (*concluded*)

4. You can carry the tape volume away, or you may get a permanent slot in the
installation tape library. The slot number is often the same as the serial number.

14.3 DATA CONTROL BLOCK (DCB)

Information about a specific data set is collectively stored in an area of the main
storage. This area is known as a Data Control Block (DCB) because this block of
information controls the input/output. For example, DCB of the data set OUT1 might
contain the items of information listed in Table 14.1. If you write programs in a high-
level language and use only card input and printer output, you do not have to deal with
DCB directly. However, if you use magnetic tape or write stand-alone assembler language programs, then you must supply detailed information such as listed in Table 14.1
from the following three sources:

1. A DCB operand in a DD card supplied at the execution time; and
2. A DCB macro specified in an assembler language source program.
3. If the data set is already residing on, say, a reel of tape, then several items
of information (such as block length and record length) can be supplied from the
header labels of the data set (see Fig. 14.5d).

Table 14.1 Information about a data set

Name of data set	= OUT1
Its organization	= Sequential
Output or input	= Output
Address of I/O device	= 00E
Number of buffers (discussed in Section 14.4)	= 4
Buffer technique used (discussed in Section 14.5)	= Exchange
Length of block	= 1000 bytes
Length of a logical record	= 200 bytes
Record format	= Fixed blocked
Address of next record	= 03142C
Address of current buffer	= 084630
Address of end of output data routine	= 00472C
Address of error routine	= 005144

In this section we shall illustrate a DCB operand in a DD card with three examples in routine tape usage, leaving the discussion of DCB macro for Section 14.8.

Let us first make the following assumptions:

a) All tapes are 9-track, 800 b.p.i., and have standard volume labels. The serial number of your tape is 001999.

b) Data set naming convention is

    DSNAME=USER.A3141.P5926.TEST6

c) The catalogued procedures used are as follows:

    FORTGCDG: FORTRAN compile, and load and go (see Fig. 13.23),

and

    FORTGCLG: FORTRAN compile, link-edit, and execute (see Fig. 13.28)

d) Your instruction of mounting your tape is done informally: a message written on the back of your JOB card. In some installations, this message is punched in code as a part of JOB card.

Example 1

The information of a deck of cards is to be copied on a reel of tape. This card deck may be a source deck, object deck, or just plain data. Prepare the necessary job control cards.

A possible deck setup is shown in Fig. 14.6, in which utility program IEBGENER (the data set copier) is used. The following DCB operand in TAPE DD card:

    DCB=(LRECL=80,BLKSIZE=1600,RECFM=FB)

means: The logical record length is 80 bytes; the block size is 1600 bytes; and each record takes the fixed-length, blocked format.

As discussed in Section 13.10, the label operand LABEL=(1,SL) has the following meaning: The input data set is stored as the *first* one on the tape, and the data set has IBM standard tape labels.

```
//A710   JOB   (UNH,T117),KUO,MSGLEVEL=1,CLASS=G,TIME=5
//STEP1     EXEC PGM=IEBGENER
//SYSPRINT DD    SYSOUT=A
//SYSIN    DD    DUMMY
//SYSUT2   DD    DDNAME=TAPE
//TAPE     DD    DSN=USER.A3141.P5926.TEST6,VOL=SER=001999,
//               UNIT=TAPE9,DISP=(NEW,PASS),LABEL=(1,SL),
//               DCB=(LRECL=80,BLKSIZE=1600,RECFM=FB)
//SYSUT1   DD    *
***********************************************
*                                             *
*      SOURCE DECK, OBJECT DECK, OR           *
*      DATA DECK TO BE RECORDED AS            *
*      FIRST DATA SET (FILE) ON TAPE          *
*                                             *
***********************************************
/*
```

Fig. 14.6 Deck setup to write source, object or data decks on a reel of magnetic tape.

The card image is written in EBCDIC on tape. Each card column takes one byte.

Example 2

It is required to (1) store the card image of a FORTRAN source deck on tape; and (2) compile, and load and execute.

```
//A710   JOB   (UNH,T117),KUO,MSGLEVEL=1,CLASS=G,TIME=5
//STEP1     EXEC PGM=IEBGENER
//SYSPRINT DD    SYSOUT=A
//SYSIN    DD    DUMMY
//SYSUT2   DD    DDNAME=TAPE
//TAPE     DD    DSN=USER.A3141.P5926.TEST6,VOL=SER=001999,
//               UNIT=TAPE9,DISP=(NEW,PASS),LABEL=(1,SL),
//               DCB=(LRECL=80,BLKSIZE=1600,RECFM=FB)
//SYSUT1   DD    *
***********************************************
*                                             *
*      SOURCE DECK TO GO INTO                  *
*      FIRST DATA SET ON TAPE                  *
*                                             *
***********************************************
/*
//STEP2      EXEC FORTGCDG
//FORT.SYSIN DD   DDNAME=TAPE
//FORT.TAPE  DD   DSNAME=USER.A3145.P9265.TEST6,DISP=(OLD,PASS),
//               LABEL=(1,SL),VOL=REF=*.STEP1.SYSUT2
//GO.SYSIN   DD   *
***********************************************
*                                             *
*         DATA CARDS, IF ANY                   *
*                                             *
***********************************************
/*
```

Fig. 14.7 Deck setup to record source decks on tape and then to compile and load-execute.

These two job steps are shown in Fig. 14.7. The first one, identical to the one in Fig. 14.6, puts source deck on tape. In the second step, the procedure FORTGCDG is used to compile, and load and execute.

Example 3

Prepare job control cards (1) to write compiler output of a FORTRAN source program on tape; and (2) to link-edit and then execute.

The procedure FORTGCLG is used in a deck setup shown in Fig. 14.8. Note that the *ddname* FORT.SYSPUNCH is the one really used during the execution time. This was discussed in the last paragraph in Section 13.6 (see page 392).

```
//A710   JOB    (UNH,T117),KUO,MSGLEVEL=1,CLASS=G,TIME=5
//STEP1          EXEC FORTGCLG,PARM.FORT='DECK'
//FORT.SYSPUNCH DD    DDNAME=TAPE
//FORT.TAPE      DD    DSNAME=USER.A3141.P5926.TEST6,UNIT=TAPE9,
//              VOL=SER=001999,DISP=(NEW,PASS),LABEL=(1,SL),
//              DCB=(LRECL=80,BLKSIZE=1600,RECFM=FB)
//FORT.SYSIN    DD  *
************************************************
*                                              *
*                SOURCE DECK                   *
*                                              *
*                                              *
************************************************
/*
//LKED.SYSIN    DD  *
************************************************
*                                              *
*                OBJECT DECK                   *      OMIT, IF NO OBJECT DECK
*                                              *
*                                              *
************************************************
/*
//GO.SYSIN      DD  *
************************************************
*                                              *
*                DATA CARDS                    *      OMIT, IF NO DATA CARDS
*                                              *
*                                              *
************************************************
/*
```

Fig. 14.8 Deck setup to write compiling result on tape and then to execute.

14.4 BUFFERS AND BUFFER POOL

A CPU can process data in the nanosecond range, whereas the electromechanical peripheral devices, such as disk and tape drives, work relatively slowly. Specifically, the ratio of speed (bytes per second) between the fastest magnetic tape drive and the slowest core memory is about 1/100. Much CPU time would be wasted if, say, a tape drive were attached directly to the CPU because the CPU has to wait for the following two events before it can get the records to be processed: (a) A READ or other similar instruction is issued, and (b) the tape passes over the read head in a tape drive.

To avoid this, we can read in the required records in main storage ahead of time. This temporary area set aside in main storage to be used as the intermediate storage of input records is a *buffer*. Similarly, a second buffer may be used to store output before transmitting to an output device for actual printing. An analog of this output buffer is a piggy bank. Instead of going to the bank every time you have some money to deposit, you put them in a piggy bank, wait till it is full, and then go to the bank.

Let us examine the buffer action more closely. If it is filled with the required records ahead of time (Fig. 14.9a), then CPU does not wait at all. As a practical detail, it is common to fill a buffer with a block of data, then *unblock*, passing out the logical

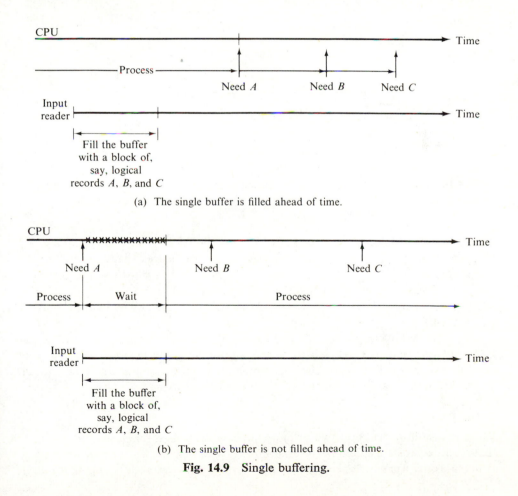

(a) The single buffer is filled ahead of time.

(b) The single buffer is not filled ahead of time.

Fig. 14.9 Single buffering.

records sequentially one at a time for processing or computing. Note that CPU processing overlaps in time with the buffer filling.

In the worst possible situation, this buffer is not filled with the required block ahead of time. Then the CPU must wait till the buffer is filled (see Fig. 14.9b), which means a waste of expensive CPU time.

It is often advantageous to use two or more buffers. For example, consider two input buffer areas in Fig. 14.10. Each block of the input data set consists of, say, four

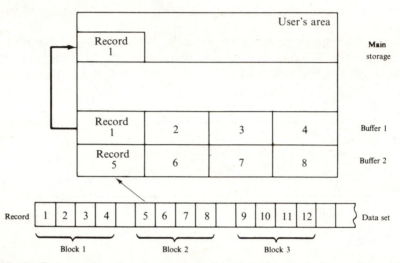

Fig. 14.10 Buffering action after the transmission of the first logical record from buffer 1 to user's area.

logical records. A block is now read into the input buffer 1. At the request of a user's program, the logical record 1 is transmitted to the user's area (work area). At the same time, the block 2, or the logical records 5 through 8, is transferred to the input buffer 2. Eventually, the input buffer 1 will be empty and released for a new block. In other words, the records 9, 10, 11, and 12 in block 3 will then fill in the input buffer 1 (see Fig. 14.11).

The double buffering described in Figs. 14.10 and 14.11 does not guarantee that CPU is always in active processing (i.e., no waiting for input record). In the case of possible waiting in Fig. 14.12, the input records are processed at an erratic speed. To eliminate this waiting, three or more buffers can be used.

Buffer Pool

We have just illustrated how two or more buffers can be used for *each* input device so that input records are stored in the main storage area before their turn for processing. A similar concept can be applied to output buffering. When many different input/output

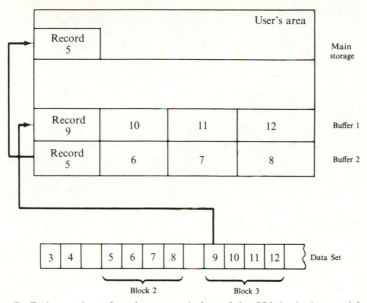

Fig. 14.11 Buffering action after the transmission of the fifth logical record from buffer 2 to user's area.

devices are used to transmit data, a large number of buffers is needed and a large area in main storage allocated.

In order to cut down this storage area, we allocate a buffer for use with *any* device. A collection of such buffers in main storage forms a *buffer pool*. When you request, say, four buffers, they are assigned after consulting the list of available buffers in the pool, containing also the address of each buffer. When a buffer is no longer needed, it is returned and added to the list of free buffers.

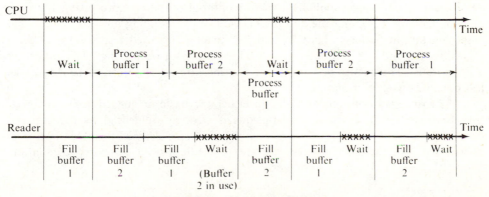

Fig. 14.12 Double buffering.

14.5 ACCESS METHODS, BUFFER PROCESSING MODES, AND BUFFERING TECHNIQUES

Earlier in the chapter, we mentioned briefly that the access method routines† have a very important mission: To tell the user's program where to get the next input record, or where to put the next output record in main storage. These canned routines simplify the programming of input/output operations and are very useful in debugging.

Under OS the access method routines exist in two major types: *basic* and *queued*; both are available to the programmer (see Table 14.2).

The basic access methods do not handle details such as buffering, and blocking and unblocking; they are best suited when you need flexibility to meet some unusual requirements. In this class, the READ and WRITE macros are the fundamental operations. When a READ macro is issued, a block of records is read into the specified locations in the main storage. This macro does not unblock, nor does it cause overlap of reading with processing as discussed in the previous section.

Table 14.2 Two major types of access method under OS

Access method \ Data set organization	Sequential	Partitioned	Indexed sequential	Direct	Telecom- munication	Graphic
Basic access	BSAM	BPAM	BISAM	BDAM	BTAM	BGAM
Queued access	QSAM	—	QISAM	—	QTAM	—

The queued access methods are more automatic; they take care of important details such as buffering, simultaneous action of input/output and processing, blocking and unblocking, assigning the address of each buffer, refilling an input buffer and emptying output buffers. The GET and PUT macros are used respectively to get a logical record and to put it in an output buffer ready for outputting. The important point here is: The queued access method routines are easier to use, since they make less demands from a programmer.

There are many options available in either the basic or queued access methods (see Table 14.2). The selection of options is strongly influenced by the required data set organization. The *Queued Sequential Access Method* (QSAM) option is probably one of the most popular ones for a medium-sized computer installation. We shall use it further in this chapter.

---

† Also known as the logical Input/Output Control System (logical IOCS).

A computer installation may adopt as many options as it sees fit, provided that its operating system supports the option. In general, BSAM and BPAM options are supported by OS/360; but many others—say, BTAM—are not. Whether an option is supported by an operating system or not is dictated during the system generation time. This decision is, in turn, much influenced by the available hardware components. For example, if a computer installation has no graphical output devices, then the BGAM option is definitely ignored.

Other access methods are sometimes used. One notable example is the Virtual Storage Access Method (VSAM). It is in part similar to BISAM and QISAM listed in Table 14.2, but it supports two types of data set organization: the key-indexed data set, and entry-sequenced data set. It is suitable for on-line applications, since it enables on-line creation and deletion of data sets, and sharing of data sets among various jobs and machines. It is the only method which takes advantage of the rotational positional sensing capacity of the disk drive 3330 and 2305.

In an assembler language program using QSAM for input/output, the buffer actions are carried out automatically. However, two important technical terms have to be explained here, since you often specify them in your program: *buffer processing modes* and *buffer technique*.

Buffer Processing Modes

In QSAM option, three buffering modes are available: in *move mode, locate mode,* and *substitute mode*. They are primarily associated with the extent of movement of a logical record. Let us review the buffer action discussed in Section 14.4. As shown in Fig. 14.10 or in Fig. 14.11, a logical record was actually moved: from an input buffer to your work area, or from your work area to an output buffer. In data management jargon, this is called the *move* mode of buffer processing.

There are two ways how to accomplish the same effect without actually moving the logical record between a buffer and your work area. First, we place the pointer to the next input buffer (or output buffer) in a general register, say, register 1. This record can then be readily located and processed (the so-called *locate* mode). This concept is simple to implement in assembler language programming. For example, if we wish to add the value of the first logical record in a buffer to the contents in register 8, we can use the following sequence of instructions:

```
LR   0,1
A    8,0(0)
ST   8,SUM
```

The sum will be stored in a fullword SUM.

Second, we interchange the pointer to the input (or output) buffer with the address of our work area (the so-called *substitute* mode).

To sum up: Each of the three modes of buffer processing serves to indicate how a logical record moves from its buffer (see Table 14.3).

Table 14.3 Modes of buffer processing

Mode	Does a logical record in a buffer actually move out?	Strategy used to avoid moving
Move	Yes	—
Locate	No	Place the pointer to the buffer in register 1. The record can then be processed *in place*.
Substitute	No	Interchange the pointer to the buffer with the address of user's area.

Buffering Techniques

For a QSAM user, there are two possible arrangements of logical records in a buffer: the *simple buffering* and *exchange buffering*. Figure 14.10 shows the simple buffering technique with all logical records contiguous in main storage and belonging to one data set. On the other hand, all records in an exchange buffering technique are not necessarily contiguous in main storage. In fact, they may not belong to the same data set.

Buffering techniques are closely linked with the buffering processing modes just discussed. In simple buffering, the move mode is most commonly used; whereas in exchange buffering, only the substitute mode has the utmost advantage. We shall illustrate these items on buffering with many concrete examples only after our discussions of some input/output macros in the next three sections.

14.6 OPEN AND CLOSE MACROS

We use OPEN macro to "open" a data set, or to make sure that the input or output device is ready for use. The I/O devices may include card reader, printer, card punch, disk drive, or tape drive.

In the case of a tape drive or a disk drive, the OPEN macro also performs an important function: It supplies additional information to a DCB by checking the header labels of the data set.

In the case of a reel of tape, the OPEN macro creates a set of standard header labels and trailer labels for *output* data sets. It also performs the specified control functions, such as rewinding or backspacing a tape.

After the execution of the OPEN macro the data set is available to a program. A typical OPEN macro for an output set is as follows:

```
START  OPEN  (DCB1,OUTPUT)
```

where DCB1 is the name assigned to the data control block (*dcbname*), and OUTPUT is one of several possible options available for the data set just opened. In short, this macro initializes the output device to handle the output data set, which is associated with the *dcbname* DCB1.

A more general format of the OPEN macro is:

[*label*] OPEN (*dcbname*[,(*2 options*)])

where square bracket indicates that the contents may be omitted.

The first option includes one of the following symbols:

INPUT = input data set.
OUTPUT = output data set.
RDBACK = tape reel is required to read backwards (magnetic tape volume only).
UPDAT = data set may be updated in place and/or records added (on a direct access volume only).

If no symbol is written in the first option (a default), it is considered as INPUT by the macro. The second option, normally omitted without writing a comma, indicates what is to be done in case that an end-of-volume is detected. The default value is DISP, which means the system will position the volume according to DISP operand specified in the DD card. In case that a labeled tape reel is last *read forward*, the second option can include one of the following symbols:

LEAVE = the system will position the tape following the tape mark which follows the data-set trailer label group.
REREAD = the system will position the tape preceding the data-set header label HDR1.

Example 1

OPEN (CARD)

or

OPEN CARD

This macro opens an input data set whose *dcbname* is CARD. Note that no parentheses are necessary, if there is only one operand in the OPEN macro.

Example 2

OPEN (CARD,,FIRST,OUTPUT)

This macro opens the input data set associated with the *dcbname* CARD, as well as the output data set whose *dcbname* is FIRST. Extra comma signifies the absence of the option INPUT, a default. In this macro, one input and one output data sets are opened. Up to 16 data sets may be opened by a single OPEN macro.

Similar to OPEN in syntax, but converse in action, the CLOSE macro causes disassociation of the data set from a program. In the case of magnetic tape and disk drives, the CLOSE macro has an additional function of checking the data set labels.

For example, it checks the trailer labels at the end of the data set, and then compares the following two items:

1. Number of data blocks from the last header label to the first trailer label. This information is contained in bytes 55 through 60 in a trailer label (see Fig. 14.5c).
2. Actual number of records read from the input data set.

If the do not agree, an error is signaled.

The CLOSE macro also can be used to rewind a magnetic tape.

The syntax of CLOSE macro for one data set is

$$[Symbol] \quad \texttt{CLOSE} \quad (dcbname[,option])$$

where *option* is used to signify the required positioning of the access mechanism of the device after the data set is separated from the program. There are three possible options: DISP, LEAVE, or REREAD; the default value is DISP. Several data sets can be closed with only one CLOSE macro:

$$[symbol] \quad \texttt{CLOSE} \quad (dcbname1[,option],dcbname2[,option],\ldots)$$

Example 3

$$\texttt{FINISH} \quad \texttt{CLOSE} \quad (\texttt{FIRST,,SECOND})$$

This macro closes two data sets; their associated *dcbnames* are respectively FIRST and SECOND.

Example 4

To rewind a reel of tape, the following instruction sequence may be used under QSAM:

```
OPEN   (DCB1,OUTPUT)
        ⋮
CLOSE  (DCB1,REREAD)
OPEN   (DCB1,OUTPUT)
        ⋮
```

Let us conclude this section by presenting the control macro CNTRL, which is used to skip lines or skip to a new page on an on-line printer. For example, in the following control macro in Fig. 14.1(c):

```
CNTRL  DCB1,SP,3
```

DCB1 is the *dcbname* associated with the data set, and SP,3 requests to skip three lines. In general, SP,j means skipping j lines, where the j-value may be 1, 2, or 3.

In another example:

```
CNTRL  DCB2,SK,1
```

SK,1 means skipping to the new page. In general, SK,j means skipping to a portion of this page ($j = 1,2,3,\ldots,12$). The programmer must consult his own computer installation for the details, since the skipping varies with the punched carriage tapes used in a particular on-line printer.

14.7 GET AND PUT MACROS

In queued access methods, the user issues a GET macro to get the required logical record for processing, which takes place either in your work area or in an input buffer. Before writing a GET macro, you must decide which mode of buffer processing is to be used: move mode, locate mode, or substitute mode. This is important as it affects the area address option in the following syntax of the GET macro:

$$[label] \quad GET \quad dcbname[, area\ address]$$

Most beginners use move mode.† In this mode, the *area address* is the symbolic address of your work area where the new record is moving to for processing.

Example 1

The following instruction segment is often used to read a card:

```
            GET   DCB2,WORKAREA
                    ⋮
WORKAREA    DS    CL80
```

The GET macro retrieves a logical record (a card) from the input data set (the card deck) ready for processing. The control is then returned to the instruction immediately following the GET macro. The record length and block size for the input data set are usually specified in a DCB macro (its name is DCB2) somewhere in the same program.

In the case of magnetic tape or disk, the first GET macro reads into the input buffer area the entire block of records. As shown in Fig. 14.10, the first logical record is then set aside from the block and made available for processing. From the programmer's point of view, it may seem that only one logical record is read because each subsequent GET macro will only make available the next logical record in the same block until all the logical records in the block are processed.

In general, the GET macro enables the queued-access methods to take care of blocking or deblocking; it also automatically uses the buffering technique (BFTEK) specified in a DCB macro.

For sophisticated programmers only: If the locate or substitute mode is used, the logical record in the buffer is not actually moved. By convention, the pointer to this buffer is stored in register 1. In locate mode, the GET macro for getting this buffer is simply

```
            GET   DCB2
```

---

† The mode you choose must be clearly stated in a DCB macro, which will be discussed in the next section.

A typical GET macro used in the substitute mode is as follows:

                        GET   SECOND,(0)

where (0) means register 0. In other words, the address of the work area (to be
exchanged with the input buffer) is stored in register 0. Complete examples dealing
with these modes will be given later in Section 14.9

Converse to the GET, a PUT macro prints or punches all logical records which have
been formed in the user's work area or in the output buffer. Its syntax is

            [*Symbol*]   PUT   *dcbname*[, *area address*]

where the area address depends on whether a move, locate, or substitute mode is
used, precisely as in the GET macro discussed above. A typical PUT macro using the
move mode is shown below.

Example 2

                      PUT   DCBOUT,OUTAREA
                                ⋮
            OUTAREA   DS   CL133

This PUT macro moves the logical records from the user's work area (OUTAREA) into
an output buffer and empties the buffer (meaning to print or take other output action).
The description of the data set, which contains the logical records, is given in a DCB
macro known as DCBOUT elsewhere in the program.

Consider now the output on magnetic tape; for simplicity, let us assume that the
blocking factor is 6. The first five PUT macros will put the first five logical records one
by one, into the output buffer. The sixth PUT macro will do the following:

1. Put the sixth logical record into the output buffer, thus completing a block.
2. Copy the whole block on the magnetic tape.

14.8 DCB **MACRO**

Let us now recall the basic features of a data control block we have discussed earlier.
Corresponding to each data set, there is a data control block (DCB) located in the main
storage which contains the data set information. The necessary information is supplied
from three sources:

1. DCB macro in your assembler language program before compilation.
2. The DCB operand in a DD card prepared just before the execution of the program
   (Section 14.3).
3. Data set label in a volume (Section 14.3).

Now we shall focus our attention on the DCB macro, a keyword macro. As
discussed in Section 9.4, the operands in a keyword-type prototype statement can be
written in any order and some may be omitted completely. In a DCB macro, however,

three operands must be present: DSORG, MACRF, and DDNAME. It is not unusual that a
DCB macro may have more than ten operands, each, in turn, having several options.
In view of this complexity, it seems convenient to first present a concrete example.

Example

In order to illustrate the overall picture of the DCB macro, we shall write an assembler
language program to read a card and echo-print on a printer. The read-print operation
continues until it is out of cards. Assume that the QSAM option and move mode are
used.

A possible program shown in Fig. 14.13 uses two DCB macros, each must have
its own *dcbname*: FIRST is used in connection with the card input, and SECOND deals
with the output data set. The OPEN macro opens these two data sets. By issuing this
OPEN macro, the unfilled items in each DCB will be completed at the execution time.

Let us discuss each operand in the DCB macro FIRST in Fig. 14.13.

```
//A711   JOB   (UNH,T117),KUO,MSGLEVEL=1,CLASS=G,TIME=5
//*  THIS IS FIGURE 14.13.
//A EXEC ASMFCLG
//ASM.SYSIN DD *
*  READ A CARD AND ECHO PRINT. USE GET MOVE-PUT MOVE.
CDPRT      SAVE   (14,12),,*
           BALR   11,0
           USING  *,11
START      OPEN   (FIRST,,SECOND,OUTPUT)
LOOP       GET    FIRST,MYAREA
           PUT    SECOND,MYAREA
           BC     15,LOOP
FINISH     CLOSE  (FIRST,,SECOND)
           RETURN (14,12)
FIRST      DCB    DSORG=PS,MACRF=GM,DDNAME=CARD,RECFM=F,               X
                  LRECL=80,BLKSIZE=80,EROPT=ABE,EODAD=FINISH
SECOND     DCB    DSORG=PS,MACRF=PM,DDNAME=PRTR,DEVD=PR,               X
                  RECFM=FA,EROPT=ABE,LRECL=133,BLKSIZE=133
MYAREA     DC     CL133' '
           END
/*
//GO.PRTR DD SYSOUT=A
//GO.SYSUDUMP DD SYSOUT=A
//GO.CARD DD *
        *******************
        *                 *
        *   INPUT CARDS   *
        *                 *
        *******************
/*
//
```

Fig. 14.13 Program CDPRT to read card and echo-print.

DSORG=PS

This operand specifies the data set organization. The PS signifies a physical sequential
organization as discussed in Section 13.5.

MACRF=GM

The macro-instruction and facilities operand. The G signifies that the GET macro is used; and M stands for the move mode, if you want the system to move the input logical record from an input buffer to your work area for processing. The general form of this operand may be expressed as

$$MACRF = \begin{cases} G \begin{Bmatrix} M \\ L \\ T \end{Bmatrix} \\ P \begin{Bmatrix} M \\ L \\ T \end{Bmatrix} [C] \end{cases}$$

where G = GET macro is issued to get a logical record;
      P = PUT macro is issued to put a logical record;
      M = move mode is used;
      L = locate mode is requested;
      T = substitute mode is requested (not S); and
      C = CNTRL macro is used to control the printer skipping and other functions. This is optional.

DDNAME=CARD

The *ddname* associated with this input data set is assigned as CARD. Once this is done, the programmer must also use the same name (qualified by GO) in the following job control card:

                    GO.CARD DD *

as shown in Fig. 14.13. Note that the GO step (the execution step) is the third step used in the catalogued procedure ASMFCLG (see Fig. 13.21).

RECFM=F

The record format used in the data set, as discussed in Section 14.2. The F indicates that records are of fixed length.

LRECL=80

   The length of record. For cards, use 80; for printer, 133. Note that the first of the 133 characters—the control character—is not printed.

BLKSIZE=80

The block size to be used. For the card reader, it should be an integral multiple of the record length; for the printer, it is same as the record length.

EROPT=ABE

The ERror OPTion operand specifies the action to be taken if incorrigible input or output error occurs. ABE, short for ABnormally End, indicates that, should this happen the task is to be terminated.

EODAD=FINISH

This is the end-of-data address. When a GET macro is issued to request a record, but the data set is exhausted and a record not available, two possible conditions exist. First, if this EODAD is given in a DCB macro, the control will branch to the specified address (such as FINISH). Second, if this optional operand EODAD is not specified, an abnormal termination will occur.

The operands used in the DCB macro SECOND are the same as those used in the DCB macro FIRST, except that the operand DEVD=PR is new. It stands for DEVice Description and specifies a PRinter for the output data set.

We have just explained many important operands used in a DCB macro. Three other common optional operands are BUFNO, SYNAD, and BFTEK. When the number of buffers (BUFNO) is not specified, it is automatically taken as two buffers. The buffer technique (BFTEK, *not* BFTEQ) has two possibilities:

BFTEK=S   for simple buffering

or

BFTEK=E   for exchange buffering.

Its default is BFTEK=S. Finally, the operand SYNAD stands for the symbolic address of a segment of program, which takes control in the event of an incorrigible error in reading or writing. When both operands SYNAD and EROPT are given in a DCB macro, the access method routines take the address in SYNAD operand first.

In summary, the DCB macro contributes information to a data control block for input/output operations such as follows:

a) Characteristics of the data set
b) Types of macro-instructions to be executed
c) Buffering choices
d) Device-dependent options
e) Exit addresses
f) Working storage used by access method routines.

The DCB macro must include at least three following operands: DSORG, MACRF, and DDNAME. The programmer must also assign a *dcbname* for the DCB in the DCB macro.

The DCB macro is usually placed near the end of an assembler language program. It must be placed at least 16 bytes from the beginning of a control section. It is not executable; an inspection of the statements generated from a DCB macro shows that

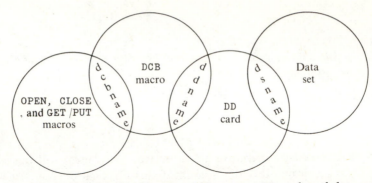

Fig. 14.14   Interrelations between I/O macros, DD card, and data set.

it consists of one DS instruction, two ORG instructions, and more than thirty DC instructions.

A DCB macro typically includes many operands, which requires two or more cards. Three common pitfalls in keypunching a DCB macro are observed; we now list the correct things to do:

1. On the second card and on, text must begin on column 16. See the last paragraph in Section 6.2.
2. A character, such as X, must be punched on column 72 (except on the last card).
3. With the exception of the last card, each card is usually ending with a comma, which separates two adjacent operand in a DCB macro.

Let us conclude this section by examining the interrelationship among (a) a given data set; (b) a DD card; (c) a DCB macro; and (d) I/O macros OPEN, CLOSE, and GET/PUT. As shown in Fig. 14.14, DCB macro and the I/O macros are united by their shared *dcbname*. The *ddname* connects the DD card with its DCB macro; and finally, the *dsname* is the linkage between a data set and a DD card.

14.9 EXAMPLES—SIMPLE BUFFERING AND EXCHANGE BUFFERING

In the example discussed in the last section (see Fig. 14.13), the move mode is used in connection with both GET macro and PUT macro. This is clearly indicated by the following MACRF operands:

> MACRF=GM   in DCB macro for the input data set

and

> MACRF=PM   in DCB macro for the output data set.

As a result, the following steps are taken: (1) A logical record is automatically moved from an input buffer to your work area; (2) it is processed in your work area; and (3) it is automatically moved to an output buffer. This process is known as GET-*move and* PUT-*move*. The technique used in Fig. 14.13 is simple buffering from default.

To cut down the excessive physical movement of a logical record to and from your work area, you can (1) process a logical record *in the input buffer* (thus eliminating your work area); and then (2) move it directly to an output buffer. This is known as GET-*locate and* PUT-*move.*

It is also possible to (1) move a logical record from an input buffer to an output buffer, and (2) process the record right in the output buffer. This is known as GET-move and PUT-locate.

```
//A711   JOB   (UNH,T117),KUO,MSGLEVEL=1,CLASS=G,TIME=5
//*   THIS IS FIGURE 14.15
//A EXEC ASMFCLG
//ASM.SYSIN DD *
*   READ A CARD AND ECHO PRINT.   USE GET LOCATE-PUT MOVE.
CDPRT     SAVE   (14,12),,*
          BALR   11,0
          USING  *,11
START     OPEN   (FIRST,,SECOND,OUTPUT)
*
* THE NEXT MACRO WILL LOCATE AND RETRIEVE A LOGICAL RECORD
* FROM THE DATA SET ASSOCIATED WITH FIRST.  BY CONVENTION,
* THE POINTER TO THIS RECORD IS RETURNED IN REGISTER 1 (BY
* SYSTEM.)
*
LOOP      GET    FIRST
*
* THE NEXT INSTRUCTION LOADS THIS POINTER IN REGISTER 0.
*
          LR     0,1
*
* THE NEXT INSTRUCTION PRESENTS A RECORD TO SUPERVISOR
* (FOR OUTPUTTING.)  THE POINTER TO THIS OUTPUT RECORD
* IS IN REGISTER 0.  THE SYSTEM THEN MOVES THE RECORD TO
* THE NEXT OUTPUT BUFFER.
*
          PUT    SECOND,(0)
          BC     15,LOOP
FINISH    CLOSE  (FIRST,,SECOND)
          RETURN (14,12)
FIRST     DCB    DSORG=PS,MACRF=GL,DDNAME=SYSIN,RECFM=F,          X
                 LRECL=80,BLKSIZE=80,EROPT=ABE,EODAD=FINISH
SECOND    DCB    DSORG=PS,MACRF=PM,DDNAME=SYSPRINT,DEVD=PR,       X
                 RECFM=FA,EROPT=ABE,LRECL=80,BLKSIZE=80
          END
/*
//GO.SYSPRINT DD SYSOUT=A
//GO.SYSUDUMP DD SYSOUT=A
//GO.SYSIN DD *
       ***************************
       *                         *
       *    INPUT CARDS    *
       *                         *
       ***************************
/*
//
```

Fig. 14.15 Program CDPRT to read card and echo-print. Using GET-locate and PUT-move modes (simple buffering). Processed in an input buffer and then moved to an output buffer.

```
//A711   JOB   (UNH,T117),KUO,MSGLEVEL=1,CLASS=G,TIME=5
//*   THIS IS FIGURE 14.16.
//A EXEC ASMFCLG
//ASM.SYSIN DD *
*  READ A CARD AND ECHO PRINT.  USE GET SUBSTITUTE-PUT SUBSTITUTE.
CDPRT     SAVE   (14,12),,*
          BALR   11,0
          USING  *,11
START     OPEN   (FIRST,,SECOND,OUTPUT)
*
          LA     0,MYAREA
*
* THE NEXT MACRO RETRIEVES A LOGICAL RECORD FROM THE DATA
* SET ASSOCIATED WITH FIRST DCB.  ITS SECOND OPERAND SPECIFIES
* THE ADDRESS OF A WORK AREA (IN REG. 0.)  THE POINTER
* TO THE NEW INPUT RECORD, BY CONVENTION, IS RETURNED
* IN REG. 1.
*
LOOP      GET    FIRST,(0)
* WORK AREA ADDRESS IS EXCHANGED WITH THE POINTER TO THE
* NEXT INPUT RECORD.
          LR     0,1
*
* THE NEXT MACRO PRESENTS A RECORD TO OS FOR OUTPUTTING AT
* EARLIEST CONVENIENCE.  THE (0) INDICATES THE ADDRESS OF THE
* INPUT AREA IS IN REGISTER 0.  THE RECORD IS PLACED IN AN
* OUTPUT AREA BY SUPERVISOR.  THE ADDRESS OF THE RECORD
* IS IN REGISTER 1.
*
          PUT    SECOND,(0)
*
* SUBSTITUTE THE ADDRESS OF THE CURRENT INPUT AREA WITH
* THE OUTPUT AREA.
*
          LR     0,1
          B      LOOP
FINISH    CLOSE  (FIRST,,SECOND)
          RETURN (14,12)
FIRST     DCB    DSORG=PS,MACRF=GT,DDNAME=SYSIN,RECFM=F,                        X
                 LRECL=80,BLKSIZE=80,EROPT=ABE,EODAD=FINISH,BFTEK=E
SECOND    DCB    DSORG=PS,MACRF=PT,DDNAME=SYSPRINT,DEVD=PR,                     X
                 RECFM=FA,EROPT=ABE,LRECL=80,BLKSIZE=80,BFTEK=E
MYAREA    DS     CL80
          END
/*
//GO.SYSPRINT DD SYSOUT=A
//GO.SYSUDUMP DD SYSOUT=A
//GO.SYSIN DD *
          *******************
          *                 *
          *   INPUT CARDS   *
          *                 *
          *******************
/*
//
```

Fig. 14.16 Program CDPRT to read card and echo-print. Using GET-substitute and PUT-substitute modes (exchange buffering). No actual movement of data.

Example 1

Modify the assembler language program and job control statements in Fig. 14.13 so that the following changes are made:

1. Change from GET-move and PUT-move to GET-locate and PUT-move.
2. Use SYSIN and SYSPRINT, respectively, as *ddname* for input and that for printing output data sets.

A new and more efficient program is listed in Fig. 14.15. As mentioned in Section 14.5, under the locate mode, the pointer to the input buffer is, by convention, placed in register 1. Note that the operand MACRF for input data set now reads MACRF=GL.

The program in Fig. 14.13 uses GET-move and PUT-move; whereas that in Fig. 14.15, GET-locate and PUT-move. Both programs are run under the control of simple buffering.

We shall now illustrate how exchange buffering can be used. Under its control, the logical record is not physically moved, which saves processing time. *There is no advantage in using exchange buffering unless the substitute mode is specified.* There are certain restrictions in using exchange buffering, such as:

1. Records must be in unblocked or blocked fixed format.
2. Input and output buffers must have the same size.
3. No unit record devices are to be used.

Example 2

Modify the program shown in Fig. 14.15 so that the following changes are made:

1. Use exchange buffering instead of simple buffering.
2. Use GET-substitute and PUT-substitute mode.

Figure 14.16 presents a possible program. When using exchange buffering, you have to specify an operand BETEK=E in the DCB macro. You must also define a work area comparable in size and alignment to a logical record in the buffer.

Although many beginners like to use the GM-PM mode, it is often more efficient (in CPU time) to use GL-PM or GT-PT mode. Based on a large number of computer runs for eight problems, our experiments have shown that the *average* CPU time for GL-PM is about same as that for GT-PT, whereas that for GM-PM takes about twenty percent more time.

14.10 EXAMPLES FOR INPUT/OUTPUT THROUGH THE OPERATING SYSTEM OS/360

This section illustrates the input/output techniques through the Operating System OS/360 with several additional examples. At this point, we no longer depend on the main program, written in a high-level language, to handle the input/output. We are now in a position to write a program in assembler language complete with its own input/output. The QSAM option is used.

```
//A711   JOB   (UNH,T117),KUO,MSGLEVEL=1,CLASS=G,TIME=5
// EXEC ASMFCG
//ASM.SYSIN DD *
ALONE1    CSECT
*
*   PART 1
*
          SAVE   (14,12)
          BALR   12,0
          USING  *,12
          ST     13,SAV+4
          LA     13,SAV
*
*   PART 2
*
          LA     2,1          PUT 1 IN R2
          LA     9,0          PUT ZERO IN R9
          LA     4,1          PUT 1 IN R4
LOOP      LR     7,4          PUT NUMBER IN REGISTER 7
          MR     6,4          SQUARE NUMBER
          AR     9,7          ADD SQUARED NUMBER TO TOTAL
          AR     4,2          ADD 1 TO NUMBER
          C      4,=F'11'     TEST FOR EXIT
          BNE    LOOP
*
*   PART 3
*
          CVD    9,ANS
          UNPK   SUM(4),ANS(8)
          MVZ    SUM+3(1),SUM+2
          OPEN   (PRT,OUTPUT)
          PUT    PRT,OTP
          CLOSE  PRT
*
*   PART 4
*
          L      13,SAV+4
          RETURN (14,12)
*
*   PART 5
*
PRT       DCB    DSORG=PS,RECFM=FA,MACRF=PM,BLKSIZE=133,LRECL=133,DDNAME=X
                 WRITER,DEVD=DA
ANS       DS     1D
SAV       DS     18F
OTP       DS     0CL133
          DC     C' SUM IS '
SUM       DC     4C' '
          DC     121C' '
          END
/*
//GO.WRITER DD SYSOUT=A
//
```

Fig. 14.17   Program to find the sum of the ten given numbers (Version I).

It is required to write a program in assembler language to add ten numbers: $1 + 4 + 9 + 16 + \ldots + 100$. A subroutine S410B in Fig. 5.24 (page 130) was written in the fixed-point binary instructions. We shall now modify it to become a single program complete with its own input/output in assembler language. Three versions are given below in the order of increasing complexities.

Example 1

Each of the ten numbers (1, 4, 9, . . ., 100) is to be generated in the program, and the simple output is as below.

SUM IS 0385

A possible program is shown in the shaded portion of Fig. 14.17, which can be subdivided into the following parts:

1. Save register contents used in the operating system and designate the base register.
2. Generate the number; perform the addition in fixed-point binary and store the sum in register 9.
3. Convert the binary answer to the unsigned unpacked decimal and print.
4. Return to the operating system.
5. Collection of DCB, DS, and DC statements.

Part 3 is important in that, without conversion, the fixed-point binary answer will be printed out in its hexadecimal equivalent 0000011D. When converted to its unpacked decimal (EBCDIC) equivalent, the answer will be printed out in decimal. The conversion is accomplished by the three instructions (CVD, UNPK, and MVZ) shown in Fig. 14.17. After the execution of each of these instructions, the contents of the field specified are presented in Fig. 14.18. The net effect: The four-byte field SUM now contains the unpacked decimal data. It will be printed out as 0385 *with* the leading zero.

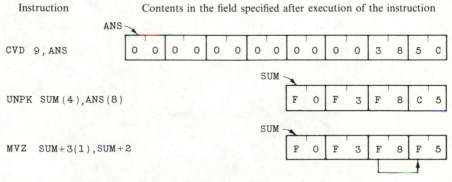

Fig. 14.18   Three instructions to perform the conversion.

In Part 5, the DCB macro has seven operands, of which DSORG, DDNAME, and MACRF must be specified. The DDNAME is specified in the DCB macro as WRITER, which has to be used in the last but one control card:

//GO.WRITER DD SYSOUT=A

```
//A711   JOB   (UNH,T117),KUO,MSGLEVEL=1,CLASS=G,TIME=5
//  EXEC  ASMFCLG
//ASM.SYSIN DD *
*
*   SUMMATION OF THE SQUARES OF THE INTEGERS ONE THROUGH TEN---
*   WITHOUT USING A MAIN PROGRAM IN A HIGH LEVEL LANGUAGE.
*
SUM        CSECT
           SAVE  (14,12),,*
           BALR  12,0
           USING *,12
           ST    13,SAV+4
           LA    13,SAV
*   LABEL THE OUTPUT
           OPEN  (OUT,OUTPUT)
           PUT   OUT,LINE1
*   PRINT THE SQUARES
           LA    7,SQRS               ADDENDS ARE IN ARRAY SQRS
           LA    8,0                  SET WORD COUNTER
           LA    10,10                SET LOOP COUNTER
           LA    9,LINE2              LINE TWO LISTS THE ADDENDS
           LA    9,1(9)               FIRST BYTE IS CARRIAGE CONTROL
*                                     CHARACTER
LOOP1      L     5,0(7,8)             LOAD A SQUARE INTO R5
           CVD   5,DNUM               CONVERT TO PACKED DECIMAL
           MVC   0(10,9),PATTERN      FIELD WIDTH IS 10.  R9
           ED    0(10,9),DNUM+3        CONTAINS FIELD ADDRESS
           LA    9,10(9)              GO TO NEXT FIELD
           LA    8,4(8)               INCREMENT WORD COUNTER
           BCT   10,LOOP1             OUT OF LOOP AFTER TEN WORDS
           PUT   OUT,LINE2
*   COMPUTE SUM OF SQUARES
           LA    9,0                  CLEAR R9
           LR    10,9                 SET WORD COUNTER
LOOP2      A     9,0(7,10)            ADD A SQUARE TO TOTAL IN R9
           LA    10,4(10)             INCREMENT WORD COUNTER
           C     10,=F'40'            TEST FOR END OF SQUARES
           BL    LOOP2                OUT AFTER TEN WORDS
           CVD   9,DNUM               CONVERT SUM TO PACKED DECIMAL
           LA    5,LINE3+14           BYTES1-13 CONTAIN LABEL
           MVC   0(10,5),PATTERN      FIELD WIDTH IS 10.  R5
           ED    0(10,5),DNUM+3        CONTAINS FIELD ADDRESS
           PUT   OUT,LINE3
           CLOSE (OUT)
           L     13,SAV+4
           RETURN (14,12)
SQRS       DC    F'1,4,9,16,25,36,49,64,81,100'
PATTERN    DC    X'402020202020202020'
SAV        DS    18F
DNUM       DS    D
LINE1      DC    CL28' THE NUMBERS TO BE ADDED ARE'
           DC    105C' '
LINE2      DC    133C' '
LINE3      DC    CL13' THE TOTAL IS'
           DC    120C' '
OUT        DCB   DSORG=PS,RECFM=F,MACRF=PM,BLKSIZE=133,LRECL=133,      X
                 DDNAME=SYSPRINT
           END
/*
//GO.SYSPRINT  DD   SYSOUT=A
//GO.SYSUDUMP  DD   SYSOUT=A
//
```

Fig. 14.20   Program to find the sum of the ten given numbers (Version II).

Example 2

Same as Example 1 except:

a) The ten numbers to be added are specified in a DC statement;
b) The required output is a little more sophisticated as shown in Fig. 14.19, where no leading zeros are permitted.

```
THE NUMBERS TO BE ADDED ARE
          1        4        9        16       25       36       49       64       81       100
THE TOTAL IS        385
```

Fig. 14.19   Required output.

A possible assembler language program together with the required job control cards is presented in Fig. 14.20. The EDIT instruction, which was discussed in detail in Section 11.4, suppresses the leading zeros.

Example 3

Ten numbers are *read in*, squared, and added together. Each data card contains a number, occupying the first three columns. The required printed output is given in Fig. 14.21.

```
        NUM           NUM**2

         1              1

         2              4

         3              9

         4             16

         5             25

         6             36

         7             49

         8             64

         9             81

        10            100

     THE SUM OF THE SQUARES IS   385
```

Fig. 14.21   Required output.

Figure 14.22 shows a possible stand-alone assembler language program, which performs input, carries out the computation in fixed-point binary, and converts the binary answer to EBCDIC for printing. The leading zeros are suppressed by means of the EDIT instruction. Note that GET-move and PUT-move modes are used. With minor modification, we can also employ GET-locate and PUT-move modes or GET-substitute and PUT-substitute modes.

```
//A711   JOB   (UNH,T117),KUO,MSGLEVEL=1,CLASS=G,TIME=5
//MANN EXEC ASMFCLG
//ASM.SYSIN DD *
ALONE3    CSECT
          SAVE    (14,12),,,*
          BALR    2,0
          USING   *,2
          LR      12,13
          LA      13,SAVE
          ST      12,4(13)
          ST      13,8(12)
          OPEN    (INDCB,(INPUT),OUTDCB,(OUTPUT))   OPEN ALL DATA SETS
          PUT     OUTDCB,OUTAREA1  PRINT COLUMN HEADINGS
          SR      4,4             ZERO R4
          SR      8,8             INITIALIZE THE SUM
          SR      10,10           SET COUNTER AT ZERO
LOOP      GET     INDCB,INAREA    INPUT A NUMBER
          MVC     NUMOUT,NUMIN    PREPARE NUMBER FOR OUTPUT
          PACK    NUM,NUMIN       PREPARE FOR CONVERSION TO BINARY
          CVB     5,NUM           CONVERT TO BINARY
          MR      4,5             SQUARE THE NUMBER
          AR      8,5             ADD THE SQUARE TO THE SUM
          CVD     5,SQUARE        CONVERT THE SQUARE TO DECIMAL
          MVC     SQROUT(4),PATTERN
          ED      SQROUT(4),SQUARE+6
          PUT     OUTDCB,OUTAREA2    OUTPUT THE NUMBER AND ITS SQUARE
          LA      10,1(10)        INCREMENT THE COUNTER
          C       10,=F'10'       CHECK TO SEE IF AT END OF LOOP
          BL      LOOP            IF NOT END, BRANCH TO LOOP
          CVD     8,SUM           CONVERT THE SUM TO DECIMAL
          MVC     ANS(4),PATTERN
          ED      ANS(4),SUM+6
          PUT     OUTDCB,OUTAREA3
          L       13,4(13)
          RETURN  (14,12)
*    END OF INSTRUCTIONS
*
*    START DC AND DS INSTRUCTIONS
*
          DS      0D              START ON DOUBLR WORD BOUNDARY
NUM       DS      D               DEFINE WORK AREA FOR NUMBER
SQUARE    DC      D'0'            INITIALIZE WORK AREA FOR SQUARE AT ZERO
SUM       DC      D'0'            INITIALIZE WORK AREA FOR SUM AT ZERO
*
INAREA    DS      0CL80           CALL THE INPUT AREA INAREA
NUMIN     DS      CL3             DEFINE AREA TO READ IN NUMBRRS
          DS      77C
PATTERN   DC      X'40202020'     DESIGN THE PATTERN
*
* OUTPUT FORMATS FOLLOW
*
OUTAREA1  DS      0CL133          AREA FOR COLUMN HEADINGDS
          DC      C'1   NUM        NUM**2'  HEADING
          DC      113C' '         BLANK OUT REST OF LINE
*
OUTAREA2  DS      0CL133          DEFINE STORAGE FOR OUTAREA2
          DC      C'0   '         CARRIAGE CONTROL AND INITIAL ZEROS
NUMOUT    DC      C'ZZZ'          OUYPUT AREA FOR THE NUMBER
          DC      10C' '          SPACING
SQROUT    DC      3C' '           OUTPUT AREA FOR THE SQUARE
          DC      113C' '         BLANK OUT THE REST OF THE LINE
```

Fig. 14.22 Program to find the sum of the ten given numbers (Version III).

```
*
OUTAREA3 DS      OCL133              DEFINE STORAGE FOR OUTAREA3
         DC      C'OTHE SUM OF THE SQUARES IS ' LABEL
ANS      DC      4C' '               OUYPUT AREA FOR THE SUM
         DC      103C' '             BLANK OUT THE REST OF THE LINE
*
SAVE     DS      18F                 DEFINE AREA TO SAVE REGISTERS
         LTORG
INDCB    DCB     DSORG=PS,MACRF=GM,DDNAME=READER,BFTEK=S,              X
                 LRECL=80,BLKSIZE=80,RECFM=F,DEVD=DA,EROPT=ABE
OUTDCB   DCB     DSORG=PS,MACRF=PM,DDNAME=PRINTER,BFTEK=S,RECFM=FA,    X
                 LRECL=133,BLKSIZE=133,EROPT=ABE,DEVD=DA
         END
/*
//GO.SYSUDUMP DD SYSOUT=A
//GO.PRINTER DD SYSOUT=A
//GO.READER DD *
  1
  2
  3
  4
  5
  6
  7
  8
  9
 10
/*
//
```

Fig. 14.22 (*concluded*)

A word of warning: If your program uses one of the input or output macros, you must provide a save area so that the contents of registers 0, 1, 13, 14, and 15 may be saved. This is true *even if your program does not call another subroutine of your own.* The reason is that these macros are expanded into calls on *system subroutines*, which reside in the supervisor.

14.11 SUPPLYING INFORMATION TO DCB AT THREE DIFFERENT TIMES

We conclude the chapter by discussing in more details the three sources of information for a data control block.

1. DCB macro (discussed in Section 14.8);
2. DCB operand in DD card (discussed in Section 14.3); and
3. Header label of the data set (discussed in Section 14.3).

Note that the operands DSORG, MACRF, and DDNAME must be specified in a DCB macro. The other operands may be left out from a DCB macro; but the missing items of information must be supplied by a DD card or a data set label. For example, if the block size (BLKSIZE) of a data set is not specified in a DCB macro, this information can be supplied later from a DD statement. Table 14.4 shows the alternate sources of information for various operands of a DCB macro.

Table 14.4 Sources of information for a data set

Operand in DCB macro	Meaning	Sources of information	Required (R) or Optional (OP)	Default value
DDNAME	Name of the DD card	Must be in	R	—
DSORG	Data set organization	DCB macro	R	—
MACRF	Macro and facilities		R	—
BFTEK	Buffer technique	Either in DCB	OP	Simple buffering
BUFNO	Buffer number	macro, or in	OP	2
DEVD	Device description	a DD card	R	—
BLKSIZE	Block size	May be in	R	—
LRECL	Logical record length	DCB macro, in	R	—
RECFM	Record format	a DD card, or in a data set label	R	—
EODAD	End-of-data address		OP	
EROPT	Error option	Only in a	OP	Abnormal termination
SYNAD	Symbolic address to take control	DCB macro	OP	

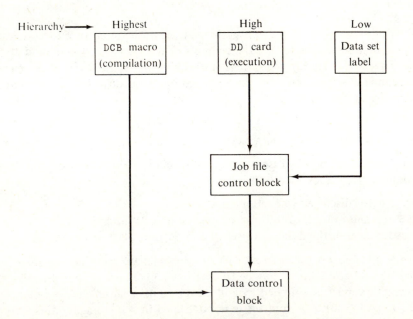

Fig. 14.23 Sources of information for data control block when the data set is already in existence.

It is interesting to see the sequence of filling up the data control block. As shown in Fig. 14.23, a job file control block (JFCB) is first formed from the information supplied from the DD card and the header label. This JFCB is identified by its *ddname*, which is the same as the one in the DD card. The contents of the JFCB must consist of at least a *dsname* or a device number. Together with the information supplied earlier by a DCB macro, they fill out a data control block.

The hierarchy of sources of information to complete the DCB is as follows

Highest	DCB macro in user's program
High	DCB operand in DD card
Low	Data set label

If an item has already been specified in a DCB macro in your program, it cannot be overruled by a DD card. If, however, it is missing in your DCB macro, it can be supplied later through a DD card.

Let us have a look at DCB from the standpoint of the collection times. A data set can be defined at three distinct times: assembly time definition, load time definition, and run time definition.

Assembly Time Definition

During the assembly time, a DCB macro specified in the user's program not only serves to set up the DCB, but also to supply the information of the data set to the DCB. At this time, it is necessary to give details, say, about the data set organization, but it is not necessary to give specifications on, say, physical record or input/output device.

Load Time Definition

During the link-editing time, a DD card may supply any additional information which was not specified in the DCB macro. In practice, this is not very often done.

Run Time Definition

During the run time, a DD card is often used to supply any remaining items of information about the data set. This helps preserve maximum flexibility and avoid the freeze of input/output devices to be used in your program. For example, you have a data processing program and the output data set is placed on a reel of tape. To allocate this *tape* volume, you can specify the necessary information through a DD card:

```
//DD    DD  DSNAME=USER.A1381.P7701.OUTPUT,
            UNIT=2400,VOL=SER=111111,LABEL=(1,SL),DISP=(NEW,KEEP)
```

If, say, the tape unit 2400 is down, but a 2311 disk drive is available, you can still run your program. Simply direct the output to this disk drive by replacing the above DD card by the following:

```
//DD    DD  DSNAME=USER.A1381.P7701.OUTPUT,UNIT=2311,
            SPACE=(TRK,(60,5)),DISP=(NEW,KEEP)
```

The important point is: your source deck(s) and/or object deck(s) remain undisturbed.

BIBLIOGRAPHY

IBM System/360 Operating System Data Management Services, Form GC26-3746, IBM Corp.

IBM System/360 Operating System Supervisor Services, Form GC28-6646, IBM Corp.

IBM System/360 Operating System Supervisor and Data Management Macro Instructions, Form GC28-6647, IBM Corp.

IBM System/360 Operating System Utility, Form GC28-6586, IBM Corp.

PROBLEMS

1. a) What is a record? a block? an IRG? a logical record? a physical record?
   b) Name six kinds of record format.
   c) Name four principal types of data set organization.
   d) Give an example of a partitioned data set.
   e) Is a member in a partitioned data set a data set?

2. Explain what each of the following macro instructions means.
   a) OPEN   (INP,INPUT)
   b) GET   INP,INAREA
   c) PUT   OUTP,OUTAREA
   d) CLOSE   (INP)
   e) GET   INP1,(6)
   f) CNTRL   DCB6,SP,3
   g) CNTRL   DCB8,SK,2

3. State in words each operand of the following DCB macro: ⌐──Col. 72
   a) CONTROL   DCB   DSORG=PS,MACRF=GM,RECFM=F,BLKSIZE=80,   ↓
                                                                       X
                         LRECL=80,DDNAME=SYSIN,EODAD=D
                         ↑
                         └──Col. 16
   b) INDATA   DCB   DSORG=PS,RECFM=FB,MACRF=GM,DDNAME=DATAL,   X
                         EODAD=FIN
   c) OUTP   DCB   DSORG=PS,RECFM=FB,MACRF=PM,LRECL=133,   X
                         DDNAME=SYSPRINT

4. Each output message of the program shown in Fig. 14.1(c) is printed near the center of a page. Which instruction must be changed so that the message will be printed starting with the second column?

5. Answer the following questions by referring to Fig. 14.13.
   a) How many input buffer areas are specified?
   b) In the SECOND DCB, what operand(s) may be deleted without affecting the final output?
   c) Explain the function of the job control card below.

   //GO.SYSUDUMP DD SYSOUT=A

6. In Fig. 14.19, each field of the second line takes ten columns in the output. Modify the program shown in Fig. 14.20 so that each field will take only six columns. How many instructions do you have to change? What are they before and after the change?

LABORATORY ASSIGNMENT

Write program in assembler language for each of the following projects. Run your program.

1. Print out the numbers 2, 4, 6, 8 in a row. Each number is six columns away from the next number.

2. Print out the following matrix:

```
 1   2   3   4   5
 6   7   8   9  10
11  12  13  14  15
16  17  18  19  20
21  22  23  24  25
```

3. Print according to the following format:

```
ROW 1
1  2  3
ROW 2
4  5  6
ROW 3
7  8  9
```

4. Same as project 2, except that the answers will be on punched cards.

5. Read a data card containing some commas and other characters. Count the number of commas on the card, and print out the answer. Repeat the process until the cards are exhausted.

6. Same as project 5, except that the total number of commas of all cards is also required to be printed.

7. Read a data card containing some apostrophes and other characters. Echo-print the card and then convert all apostrophes to minus signs. Print the converted message.

8. Read a data card containing four four-digit numbers. Echo-print the numbers. Subtract 2 from each number and print the result. If any of the numbers become less than zero, substitute it with a zero.

9. Read in 100 four-digit numbers. Echo-print them. Starting with the 100th entry (i.e., in reverse order), print out the first number it reaches that has a zero in the bit position 15.

10. Read in 60 two-digit numbers. Subtract 32 from each number. If any of the results is less than 0, add 1 to the result. Print the desired result.

11. Print a table of K, $1/K$, and K^2 for $K = 1$ to 100. [*Note:* Since $1/K$ is a fraction, $10,000/K$ is computed so that four digits are obtained in the fractional part.]

CHAPTER 15

Interrupts and Program Status Word

15.1 COORDINATING INPUT/OUTPUT PROCESSES WITH COMPUTING

Input/Output (I/O) devices in a modern high-speed computer are not connected directly to CPU; the three basic reasons are:

1. If CPU is used to control an I/O device, then CPU has to wait when the I/O device is in action.

2. There is a glaring difference in speeds between an I/O device and CPU. For example, an on-line card reader can read about 200 cards per second. In that time, a fast CPU would have performed about a billion arithmetic instructions. Moreover, the range of speeds of various I/O devices spreads rather widely, from about 10^4 to 10^7 byte per second.

3. All electromechanical I/O devices have trouble to get started (due to their inertia) or to stop (due to their momentum). For example, a tape drive does not allow starting and stopping for each byte. If CPU were connected with an I/O device, it would have to be able to accept the first byte before the arrival of the second one, or the first one would be lost.

To alleviate these difficulties, the following idea is used in System/370 or System/360: Process I/O commands separately from the instructions used in computing. To implement this idea, an additional hardware—the channel—is required.

We shall discuss two types of channels in the next section. A channel is basically a scaled-down processor; its main job is to interpret and execute all input/output commands—called channel command words (CCW's). The common CCW's will be discussed in Section 15.3.

To handle I/O operations, you can take one of the following options under OS (in the order of increasing complexities and flexibilities):

1. You use the canned access methods to communicate with the supervisor.

a) Use the queued access methods (logical IOCS) by issuing the GET or PUT macros (discussed in Sections 14.5, 14.7, 14.9, and 14.10).

b) Use the basic access methods by issuing the READ or WRITE macros (discussed in Section 14.5).

2. You decide *not* to use any canned access method.

a) Use the system macros EXCP and WAIT. The key features are:
   · You must construct CCW's.
   · You must ask CPU to wait until the execution of CCW's is terminated. This option is sometimes called "processing with the physical IOCS." We shall explore this option in Section 15.4.

b) Use the standard I/O instructions. We shall study these assembler language instructions near the end of the chapter.

Interrupt

The CPU and a channel have master-slave relationship. Take, for example, an output operation on an on-line printer. The CPU first tells the channel to start the output operation (point 1 in Fig. 15.1) and then continues its computations. At the end of this output operation (point 2 in Fig. 15.1), it is important to get another I/O device started on the channel immediately. To accomplish this, a signal is sent to CPU through the channel as a kind of door bell. This causes CPU to temporarily halt

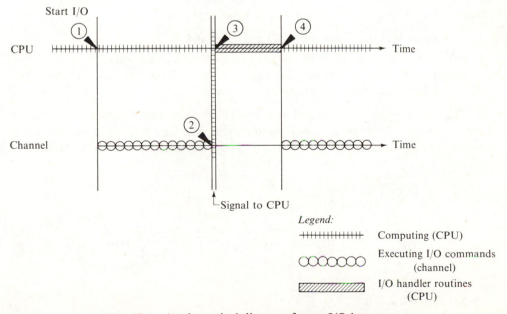

Fig. 15.1 A schematical diagram for an I/O interrupt.

whatever it was processing (point 3 in Fig. 15.1)—hence the name *interrupt*—and proceed to execute a totally different program located somewhere else in main storage. This program is a software package known as *interrupt handler routines*; It will pinpoint the cause of the interrupt (e.g., the end of printing or discovery of an error in the data) and take immediate actions. At the end of this set of interrupt handler routines, the control is returned to the user's program at exactly the point where it was interrupted (point 4 in Fig. 15.1). This whole process of input/output interrupt will be studied in detail in Section 15.5.

In System/370 or System/360, four other types of interrupts are possible: machine check, program check, supervisor call, and external; they will be discussed in Section 15.6.

At the heart of an interrupt is the Program Status Word (PSW). This is one of the storage elements in special part of CPU of the System/370 or System/360. It contains much important information about the status of program currently being run or just interrupted. In debugging a program (i.e., to determine why an interruption occurred), you must have a clear understanding of these valuable data in PSW. Two fields were already introduced in Chapter 4: the condition code (CC) and instruction address field. In Sections 15.5 through 15.10, we shall study the bit configuration of the remaining fields, and the significance and practical applications of each field.

15.2 MULTIPLEXOR CHANNEL AND SELECTOR CHANNEL

It is a common practice to put several low-speed input/output units (such as card readers or printers) on one channel. The reasons are:

1. A channel is an expensive piece of hardware; and

2. Such a low-speed device does not take much time for actual data transfer. (For example, the byte transfer time for a card reader is about three microseconds, but the waiting time between two bytes is about 500.)

The transmission of bytes are interleaved in time; and a channel, containing several registers for addresses and counters, can take care of several Input/Output devices *in rotation* (see Fig. 15.2). This way of transmitting bytes from different devices

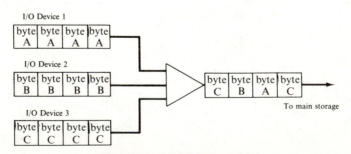

Fig. 15.2   Multiplexor mode.

on one single channel is known as *multiplexing* or in multiplex mode. The channel
itself is called the *multiplexor channel*.

On the other hand, a fast I/O device (such as disk or tape drive) needs a channel
of its own, a *selector channel*, which can be connected to several fast I/O devices,
but only one of them can be in action at a given time. In Fig. 15.3, a selector channel
transfers an entire record between the main storage and a device, or operating in the
burst mode.†

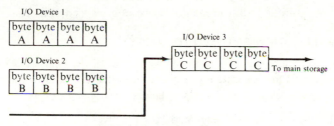

Fig. 15.3 Burst mode.

0	C	C	C	A	A	A	A	D	D	D	D

Fig. 15.4 12-bit address for a device.

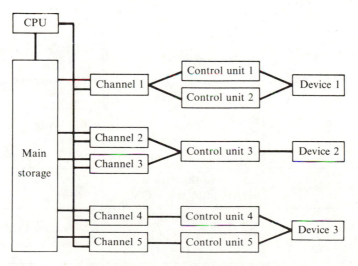

Fig. 15.5 A typical multiple path.

---

† A multiplexor channel can also operate in burst mode if it is connected to only one fast
I/O device. This arrangement is very inefficient.

Each I/O device is assigned a 12-bit device address (Fig. 15.4) where the three *C* bits signify the channel number (0 to 7); the four *A* bits represent the control unit (adapter) number from 0 through 15; and the four *D* bits stand for the device number from 0 through 15. They are usually expressed in hexadecimal. For example, the device 7B9 stands for the ninth device on the eleventh control unit of channel 7.

As a result, it is possible for an installation to have up to $8 \times 16 \times 16$ or 2048 devices. A possible setup in a typical installation is shown in Fig. 15.5. The address of device 1 can be either 111 or 121; and the address of device 2 can be 232 or 332. This concept of multiple path to reach a device offers speed and reliability.

15.3 CHANNEL COMMAND WORD (CCW)

As mentioned before, a channel is in reality a processor. Initiated by the CPU, a channel can interpret and execute input/output commands, called Channel Command Words (CCW's). A set of related CCW's makes a *channel program*.

Table 15.1. Fields in a Channel Command Word (CCW)

	Field	Bit positions	Purposes	Remarks
	Command code	0–7	Operation required	*Examples:* (in hexadecimal) For 1403, 1443, or 3211 printers: 01: Write, no space 09: Write, space 1 after print 11: Write, space 2 after print 19: Write, space 3 after print For 2400 tape drives: 01: Write 02: Read 08: Transfer-in-channel
	Data address	8–31	Address of the data area referenced by this CCW.	—
Flag bits	Chain data (CD) flag	32	The data area in the next CCW is to be used in this operation, if this bit is 1.	Known as data chaining (see examples in the next section).
	Chain command (CC) flag	33	The operation in the next CCW is initiated on normal completion of the current operation, if this bit is 1 and bit 32 is 0.	Known as command chaining (see examples in the next section).

Table 15.1. (*continued*)

Field		Bit positions	Purposes	Remarks
Flag bits	Suppress length indication (SLI) flag	34	It controls whether an incorrect length condition is indicated to the program (see Section 15.4).	The incorrect length indication is supressed, if SLI flag is one and CD flag is zero in the last CCW used. If both CC and SLI contain 1, command chaining always takes place.
	Skip flag	35	It suppresses the transfer of information to main storage.	The suppression takes place if the skip flag bit is 1.
	Program controlled interrupt (PCI) flag	36	It causes an interruption as Program Control Interrupt.	The interruption takes place if the PCI flag bit is 1 when the CCW takes control of the channel. If PCI flag bit is zero, normal operation takes place.
	—	37–39	Set to 000	They must contain zeros for each CCW except one specifying a transfer-in-channel.
	—	40–47	Ignored	—
Count		48–63	Length of data (in bytes) to be processed.	—

Each command is coded numerically and kept in the main storage. The command codes include Write (01), Read (02), Transfer-in-channel (08), Sense (04), and Control. Transfer-in-channel is an unconditional branch in a channel program. The Sense commands request information on the status of a device, and check abnormal operations during the last operation. Examples of Control commands are: rewind a tape reel, position the read-write heads to a given cylinder of disk pack, and skip to the top of a new page on a printer.

Note that these CCW's are stored in the main storage. Thus, *a channel works into the same storage as the CPU.*

If you use any one of the access method routines (discussed in Section 14.5), you do not have to write your own channel program. In this case, the remaining portion of this section, which deals with the details of CCW's, and the next section may be skipped in the first reading.

Each CCW is 64-bit long, and has four fields: Command code, data address, flag, and count. The detailed description of each field is listed in Table 15.1. For example, the command in Fig. 15.6 is used to read 80 characters of data from a card reader into locations 000A00 through 000A4F.

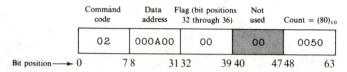

Fig. 15.6 A typical CCW to read 80 bytes from a card reader. (Bit positions 37 through 39 normally contain zeros.)

There is an assembler instruction CCW which may be used to generate an eight-byte CCW in machine language, aligned on a doubleword boundary. It has the following format:

CCW   *op code, data-address, flag, count*

where no operands may be omitted. A possible assembler language instruction corresponding to the CCW shown in Fig. 15.6 is as follows:

```
        CCW   2,INAREA,X'00',80
          ⋮
INAREA  DS    CL80
```

Note that the flag field (bit positions 32 through 36) was set to zeros in the above example. Actually, they can be manipulated to yield further important information about a channel program. We shall illustrate the usages of chain data bit (bit position 32) and chain command bit (bit position 33) in the next section.

15.4 EXAMPLES: DATA CHAINING AND COMMAND CHAINING

This section illustrates manipulation of the chain data bit and that of chain command bit in a CCW with four concrete examples. As noted before, a programmer writes CCW's to handle input/output operations only when he or she elects not to use any standard access methods.

Example 1

We wish to read a card into four separate areas in main storage:

Columns	Description	Main storage address	Length in bytes
1–9	Social security number	IDNUMBER	9
10–34	Name	NAME	25
35–69	Department	DEPT	35
70–74	Telephone extension	TELEXT	5

Figure 15.7 shows a channel program segment. The first CCW initiates the read operation. It reads the first nine bytes, as specified in the count field, into the IDNUMBER field in main storage. Now the content in the chain data (CD) flag bit (bit position 32) is checked. It is 1 because the flag field is specified as X'80' or B'10000000'. As a result, the read operation does *not* stop, but continues to read the data area specified in the next CCW. This procedure is known as *data chaining*. In general, when the CD flag bit is 1, *the data area specified in the next CCW is to be processed with the current operation.*

```
       CCW     2,IDNUMBER,X'80',9     DATA CHAINING
       CCW     2,NAME,X'80',25        DATA CHAINING
       CCW     2,DEPT,X'80',35        DATA CHAINING
       CCW     2,TELEXT,X'00',5       END OF READ OPERATION
                  .
                  .
                  .
 IDNUMBER  DS     CL9
 NAME      DS     CL25
 DEPT      DS     CL35
 TELEXT    DS     CL5
```

Fig. 15.7 Segment of channel program to read a card into 4 separate fields in a main storage.

Let us examine more closely the mechanics involved in a data chaining. When reading or writing a block of records, the contents in the count field of the current CCW are automatically reduced by 1 after each *byte* is read or written. When the count becomes zero and the records in the block are not completely depleted, then the chain data (CD) flag bit plays an important role. If it is on (i.e., 1), then the next CCW is executed as a continuation of the same operation (this is data chaining). If it is not on (0), then something is wrong with the data length. As a result, channel program will be brought to an end. (This is an error condition. This incorrect length indication can be aborted by turning on the Suppress Length Indication (SLI) flag, bit position 34 in the current CCW.)

There are three data chainings in Fig. 15.7. The read operation is terminated after columns 70–74 are read into the TELEXT field in main storage, because the CD flag bit (bit position 32) in the fourth CCW contains 0. (The flag field in the fourth and last CCW is specified as X'00'.)

Note that (1) the four consecutive CCW's deal with one card record; (2) the four contiguous fields in the card are read into four separate areas in main storage; and (3) the operation code 2 in the second, third or last CCW is not important and may be replaced as another number, say, 0. This is because, under data chaining, reading of the four fields is carried out in *one* operation. However, none of these operation code fields can be left blank.

Example 2

It is required to read three blocks of data into *an* input area in main storage. The three blocks, each containing an 80-byte record, are recorded consecutively on a reel of magnetic tape. The symbolic address of the 240-byte input area is INAREA.

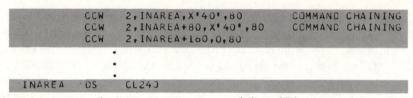

```
CCW    2,INAREA,X'40',80        COMMAND CHAINING
CCW    2,INAREA+80,X'40',80     COMMAND CHAINING
CCW    2,INAREA+160,0,80
         .
         .
         .
INAREA  DS    CL240
```

Fig. 15.8   Command program segment to read three 80-byte records into INAREA.

A possible segment of channel program is shown in Fig. 15.8, where the flag field of the first CCW is X'40' (or B'0100000'). This means the chain command (CD) flag bit (bit position 33) contains a 1. As a result, the next CCW is automatically executed on normal completion of the current operation, called the *command chaining*. Note an important point here: The command chaining in Fig. 15.8 enables three CCW's to read three separate blocks of logical records with one single tape movement. The second CCW and the third CCW each specifies a *new* read operation. In contrast, the three successive CCW's in a data chaining (see Fig. 15.7) deal with three different storage areas for the *original* read operation.

Example 3

Write a *complete* program to print 'VOTE FOR ME' twice (on two consecutive lines), skip three lines, then print the same message and skip two lines, and finally print the same message once more. The required output is shown in Fig. 15.9(a). Use CCW's (with command chaining) and other necessary system macros.

```
VOTE FOR ME
VOTE FOR ME


VOTE FOR ME

VOTE FOR ME
```
Fig. 15.9(a)   Required output.

A complete program together with the necessary JCL cards is shown in Fig. 15.9(b). Let us first focus on the four CCW's. The command codes 9, 19, 11, and 1 mean "write" with the following differences in skipping: 9 means skipping one line after printing; 19 means skipping three lines after printing; and 11, skipping two lines after printing; 1 has no skipping (see Table 15.1). The command chaining permits the initiation of the second write operation on the normal completion of the first one; it permits the initiation of the third write operation right after the completion of the second one; and so on.

Note that the program shown in Fig. 15.9(b) does not use any standard access methods, as no GET, PUT, READ, or WRITE macros are used. As a result, you must communicate with the input/output supervisor directly. Specifically, you must:

1. Write CCW's (channel program).

2. Build the control blocks necessary for the execution of CCW's:

   a) Input/output block (IOB) containing information about CCW's.

   b) Event control block (ECB) to house a *completion code* at the termination of the execution of a channel program.

```
//A711    JOB   (UNH,T117),KUO,MSGLEVEL=1,CLASS=G,TIME=5
//A EXEC ASMFCLG
//*
//* THIS IS AN EXAMPLE OF COMMAND CHAINING IN A CHANNEL PROGRAM.
//* THE PROGRAM PRINTS  'VOTE FOR ME' TWICE ON TWO DIFFERENT LINES,
//* SKIPS THREE LINES, AND THEN PRINTS THE SAME MESSAGE
//* AND SKIPS TWO LINES, AND FINALLY PRINTS THE SAME MESSAGE.
//* USE EXCP AND WAIT MACROS.  USE PHYSICAL IOCS.
//*
//ASM.SYSIN DD *
COMCHAIN CSECT
         SAVE  (14,12),,*
         BALR  11,0
         USING *,11
*
*    FOR EACH DATA SET, YOU MUST USE OPEN, CLOSE, AND DCB MACROS.
*
         OPEN  (OUTPUT,OUTPUT)
         EXCP  IOBLOCK        EXECUTE THE CHANNEL PROGRAM
         WAIT  ECB=ECBLOCK    WAIT FOR IT
         CLOSE (OUTPUT)       CLOSE THE OUTPUT DATA SET
         RETURN (14,12)
*
MESS     DC    CL12' VOTE FOR ME' MESSAGE
*
*    WE HAVE FOUR CCW'S.
*
CHANNEL  CCW   X'09',MESS,X'60',12   COMMAND CHAINING
         CCW   X'19',MESS,X'60',12   COMMAND CHAINING
         CCW   X'11',MESS,X'60',12   COMMAND CHAINING
         CCW   X'01',MESS,X'20',12   END OF COMMAND PROGRAM
*
*    YOU MUST DEFINE THE INPUT/OUTPUT BLOCK FOR THE DATA SET.
*    NEXT INSTRUCTION IS A USER-DEFINED MACRO.
*    IT IS USED TO DEFINE  THE INPUT/OUTPUT BLOCK.
*
IOBLOCK  IOB   CCW=CHANNEL,ECB=ECBLOCK,DCB=OUTPUT I/O BLOCK
*
*    THE NEXT INSTRUCTION IS TO DEFINE A FOUR-BYTE
*    EVENT CONTROL BLOCK.  IT IS A MUST.
*
ECBLOCK  DC    F'0'             EVENT CONTROL BLOCK
*
*    (E) IN THE NEXT INSTRUCTION MEANS THAT EXCP MACRO IS USED.
*
OUTPUT   DCB   DDNAME=SYSPRINT,MACRF=(E),DSORG=PS,IOBAD=IOBLOCK
*
         END
/*
//GO.SYSPRINT DD SYSOUT=A
//
```

Fig. 15.9(b)   Complete program using EXCP and WAIT macros.

3. Issue a system macro EXCP to pass the pointer to IOB to the supervisor.

4. Issue a system macro WAIT.

We shall now explore† these two system macros and the two required control blocks.

Execute Channel Program (EXCP) Macro-Instruction

This system macro requests the system to start the operation for a given input/output device. Its format is:

$$[\textit{name}] \quad \text{EXCP} \quad \textit{blockname}$$

where *blockname*, the only operand, is the name for the input/output block (IOB), or the pointer to IOB. The required device is first determined from an item in the IOB, and then the associated channel program will be executed if both the channel and device are available.

Input/Output Block (IOB)

For each I/O device used, you must construct an IOB by writing DC and DS instructions in your program. Its format is shown in Table 15.2. It is 40 bytes long for a direct-access device; 32 bytes long for the others. The unshaded areas in Table 15.2 are used by the system; they are usually defined as all zeroes.

You must supply the information for each of the five shaded fields:

1. Bit positions 0, 1, and 6 in FLAG1 field.
2. ECB address.
3. Channel program address.
4. DCB address.
5. Block count increment (usually a positive integer 1).

An IOB, constructed for our example, is shown in Fig. 15.10(a), which was actually generated from a user's own macro instruction IOB. A possible macro definition for IOB is shown in Fig. 15.9(b).

WAIT Macro-Instruction

This system macro is usually written right after the EXCP macro; it has the following format:

$$[\textit{name}] \quad \text{WAIT} \quad \text{ECB}=\textit{blockname}$$

---

† Comprehensive information can be found in the following two manuals:
  1. IBM System/360 Operating System: System Control Blocks, Form C28–6628, IBM Corp.
  2. IBM System/360 Operating System: System Programmer's Guide, Form C28–6550. IBM Corp.

Table 15.2 Input/output block (IOB) Format

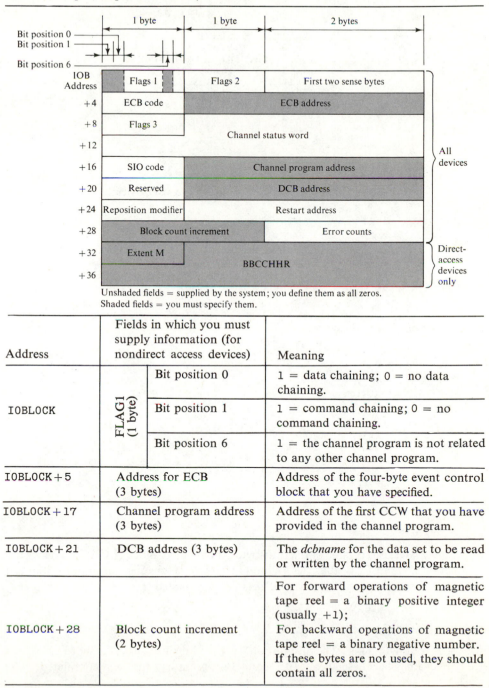

Address	Fields in which you must supply information (for nondirect access devices)		Meaning
IOBLOCK	FLAG1 (1 byte)	Bit position 0	1 = data chaining; 0 = no data chaining.
		Bit position 1	1 = command chaining; 0 = no command chaining.
		Bit position 6	1 = the channel program is not related to any other channel program.
IOBLOCK + 5	Address for ECB (3 bytes)		Address of the four-byte event control block that you have specified.
IOBLOCK + 17	Channel program address (3 bytes)		Address of the first CCW that you have provided in the channel program.
IOBLOCK + 21	DCB address (3 bytes)		The *dcbname* for the data set to be read or written by the channel program.
IOBLOCK + 28	Block count increment (2 bytes)		For forward operations of magnetic tape reel = a binary positive integer (usually +1); For backward operations of magnetic tape reel = a binary negative number. If these bytes are not used, they should contain all zeros.

```
+IOBLOCK  DS     OF
+         DC     X'42'    FLAG 1 FIELD
+         DC     X'0'     FLAG 2 FIELD
+         DC     X'0'      SENS0
+         DC     X'0'      SENS1
+         DC     X'0'      ECBCC
+         DC     AL3(ECBLOCK)      ECB ADRESS
+         DC     X'0'      FLAG 3 FIELD
+         DC     XL7'0'    ADDRESS OF FIRST CCW
+         DC     X'0'      SIOCC
+         DC     AL3(CHANNEL)  IOBSTART
+         DC     X'0'
+         DC     AL3(OUTPUT)   DCB POINTER
+         DC     A(0)      RESTR
+         DC     AL2(1)    INCAM
+         DC     XL2'00'
+         DC     XL8'0'    SEEK FIELD
```

Fig. 15.10(a)   Generated statements for I/O block.

```
IOBLOCK   MACRO
          IOB  &CCW=0,&DCBAD=0,&ECB=0,&FLAG1=42,&FLAG2=0,&FLAG3=0,        X
               &INCAM=1,&SEEK=0
.*
.*  THIS IS AN USER'S MACRO TO DEFINE AN INPUT/OUTPUT BLOCK.
.*
          DS     OF
          DC     X'&FLAG1'
          DC     X'&FLAG2'
          DS     X              SENS0
          DS     X              SENS1
          DS     X              ECBCC
          DC     AL3(&ECB)
          DC     X'&FLAG3'
          DC     XL7'0'         CSW
          DS     X              SIOCC
          DC     AL3(&CCW)
          DS     X
          DC     AL3(&DCBAD)
          DC     A(0)           RESTR
          DC     AL2(&INCAM)
          DC     XL2'00'        ERRCT
          DC     XL8'&SEEK'
          MEND
```

Fig. 15.10(b)   Macro IOB.

where *blockname* is the name of the four-byte event control block (ECB). It checks the completion code in ECB, thus determining whether the channel program, initialized by the EXCP macro, has terminated. If it is not terminated, the CPU must wait.

Event Control Block (ECB)

An ECB is four bytes long. The bit position 0 is called the *wait bit*. It is set to one if the WAIT macro has been issued, but the channel program has not been completed. The bit position 1, called the *complete bit*, indicates whether the channel program has been completed:

1 = the channel program has been completed.

0 = the channel program has not been completed.

The whole purpose of ECB is to post a completion code. The code, which includes the wait bit (always zero) and the complete bit (always 1), is placed by the supervisor in the four-byte ECB. Two typical completion codes, in hexadecimal, are

7F000000 = The channel program has completed without error; and

41000000 = The channel program has terminated with permanent error.

You must construct an ECB for each I/O device in your program, which is readily accomplished by writing the following instruction

```
ECBLOCK   DC   F'0'
```

Example 4

Its purpose is to show that data chaining and command chaining may be both present in one command program. However, data chain must take place within a command chaining.

In Example 1, we showed how to read four fields in *one* data card into four different areas in main storage. Suppose that (1) we have a deck of data cards of same format in the card reader; and (2) we wish to retain only the contents of the *last* card in the four areas in the main storage. Write CCW's to accomplish this.

A possible segment of channel program is shown in Fig. 15.11. The operation code 8 means transfer-in-channel, or an unconditional branch to HERE. A loop is thus formed in this channel program.

```
HERE       CCW    2,IDNUMBER,X'80',9     DATA CHAINING
           CCW    2,NAME,X'80',25        DATA CHAINING
           CCW    2,DEPT,X'80',35        DATA CHAINING
           CCW    2,TELEXT,X'40',5       COMMAND CHAINING
           CCW    8,HERE,X'40',5

                    .
                    .
                    .

IDNUMBER   DS     CL9
NAME       DS     CL25
DEPT       DS     CL35
TELEXT     DS     CL5
```

Fig. 15.11   Data chaining and command chaining.

We conclude this section by noting that a number of computer installations do not support the data chaining involving the unit record devices. They are usually operated under the operating system OS/360.

15.5 PSW AND ITS ROLE IN AN INTERRUPT

In System/370 or System/360, the heart of the interrupt mechanism is the Program Status Word (PSW), which is one of the storage elements in CPU and not a part of main storage.

In the medium and large models, the PSW is eight byte long. It has two distinct formats:

1. Format for Basic Control (BC) mode—used in System/360, and in models in System/370 involving no virtual memory operations.

2. Format for Extended Control (EC) mode—used in models in System/370 with virtual memory operations.

Prime attention of this chapter is devoted to the PSW for the BC mode which is divided into eight fields (see Fig. 15.12).†

System mask	Key	AMWP				Interrupt code
(Section 15.7)	(§ 15.8)	(§ 15.7)	(§ 15.7)	(§ 15.7)	(§ 15.5)	(§ 15.6)

Bit position → 0   7 8   11   12   13   14   15 16   31

ILC	CC	Program mask	Instruction address
(§ 15.6)	(§ 4.5)	(§ 15.7)	(§ 4.5)

32   33 34   35 36   39 40   63

Fig. 15.12 Eight fields in PSW for the BC mode (with section references).

In Section 4.5, two of these PSW fields were already discussed. One is the condition code (CC) field stored in bit positions 34 and 35; and the other, the instruction address field, containing the address of the next instruction to be executed, in bit positions 40 through 63. In this section, we shall examine the role the PSW plays in an interrupt.

Earlier in the chapter, we discussed the master-slave relationship between CPU and a channel. Let us study it more closely using a write operation on an online printer as a specific example.

In the user's program, a PUT or an EXCP macro is issued. As a result, the input/output supervisor will schedule the I/O request and issue a Start I/O (SIO) instruction to activate the printer. If everything goes well, a print operation is initiated by CPU as indicated by point 1 in Fig. 15.13 (which is essentially a reproduction of Fig. 15.1). This operation is initiated by using a Channel Address Word (CAW) which supplies

---

† Unless otherwise noted, we shall deal with the PSW using the format for BC mode in the remaining part of this chapter.

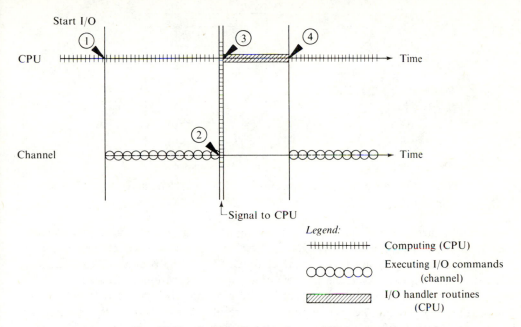

Fig. 15.13   A diagram showing an I/O interrupt.

the channel with the necessary pointer to the required channel program. The channel then takes over and executes each CCW in the channel program until, say, the whole printing operation is complete.

Now, a signal is sent to the CPU (point 2 in Fig. 15.13) to request next I/O operation so that the channel is always kept busy. In response, the CPU completes the instruction already started, and then let the following events take place:

1. The present contents of the PSW, the so-called *current PSW*, are loaded by interrupt hardware into a preset main storage area known as the "old" PSW (see Fig. 15.14). It cannot be overemphasized that the contents of the old PSW reflect the status of the system *just before* the interrupt. In this connection, the instruction address field (bit positions 40 through 63) in the old PSW contains the address of the instruction which would have been executed if the interrupt had not taken place.

2. The contents of "new" PSW, a doubleword at a fixed location in main storage, are loaded into the current PSW. This new PSW points to the first instruction of the Interrupt Handling Routine (IHR), a component of the complex input/output supervisor, whose purpose is to branch to the correct SVC routine. In other words, bit positions 40 through 63 in the new PSW contain the pointer to the routine which handles the I/O interrupt.

3. The IHR determines the true cause of the interrupt, whether it is due to the completion of an input/output operation, or whether it stems from a request of an input/output device. If, for instance, the interrupt is caused by the end of an input

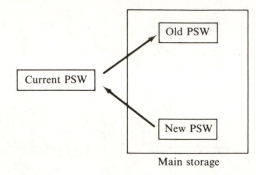

Main storage

Fig. 15.14   Interrelations among current PSW, old PSW, and new PSW.

operation, then another component of the input/output supervisor, called *channel end routine*, will be executed. Its main objective is to check whether there are any requests in waiting to use a particular channel. If so, the routine fulfills the next input/output request. As a result, a new input/output operation is initiated.

4. The last instruction of the interrupt handling routines is Load PSW (LPSW) which loads the old PSW into the current PSW. As a result, the execution of the interrupted program is resumed from the point of interruption (see point 4 in Fig. 15.13).

Despite their names, neither old PSW nor new PSW is physically located in the PSW; they are stored in two separate doublewords in the main storage. By convention, the address of new PSW due to an I/O interrupt is 000078, whereas that of old PSW is 000038. The Start I/O (SIO) instruction discussed above belongs to a class of instructions related to an I/O operation. The Load PSW (LPSW) instruction is a typical example of another class used to alter or load the PSW. These two classes of instructions are collectively called *privileged instructions*.

A privileged instruction can be executed only when CPU is in the *supervisor state*; this is only possible when PSW contains a 1-bit in bit position 15 (the so-called problem state bit). The opposite of supervisor state is known as *problem state* when bit position 15 in PSW contains a zero. The whole idea of the privileged instructions and supervisor state is to protect the status of CPU against any changes made by users deliberately or unintentionally. An attempt to execute a privileged instruction in the problem state is illegal and will be considered in Section 15.7.

The treatment of an interrupt is summarized below (see Fig. 15.15) in terms of supervisor and problem states: (Step numbers in Fig. 15.5 are encircled.)

Step 1. An interrupt has occurred during the execution of your problem program, in which no privileged instructions should be used. Your program has been executed in the problem state.

Step 2. The contents of the PSW from your problem program is copied into the old PSW.

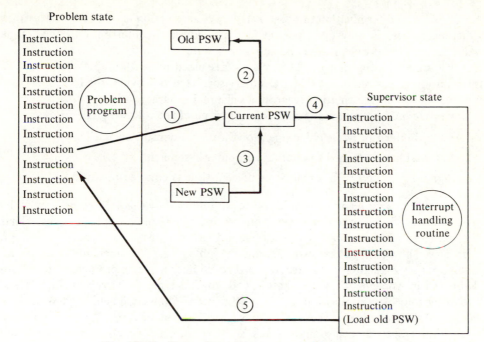

Fig. 15.15   Supervisor state versus problem state.

Step 3. The new PSW is copied into the current PSW, pointing to the beginning of the interrupt handling routine (IHR) of the supervisor.

Step 4. The IHR is executed. Privileged as well as non-privileged instructions are used in IHR. It can be executed only in the supervisor state.

Step 5. Return to the problem state and execute your problem program.

15.6 FIVE TYPES OF INTERRUPTS

So far in this chapter, we have illustrated the mechanism of interrupt with input/output processing. In System/370 or System/360, this interrupt mechanism applies equally well to a number of illegal or unusual conditions, such as 1. machine check; 2. program error; 3. supervisor call (SVC); and 4. external source.

A *machine check* interrupt is caused by machine error automatically detected by hardware in CPU. Typically, all storage units use *parity bit* as an error detection device. A *program check* interrupt, caused by invalid instruction or data for the instructions, may come from any one of the 15 different possible illegal conditions, known as exceptions (discussed in detail in Appendix C). The *supervisor call* interrupt is brought about by executing a SVC instruction. For example, the instruction

SVC   13

causes abnormal termination of the job step. SVC instruction is of RR format with a difference: there is only one operand field providing the interruption code. It is valid in both the problem state and supervisor state.

It is worth noting that the EXCP macro (discussed in Section 15.4) makes a SVC interruption to pass control to the I/O supervisor. It also provides the I/O supervisor with the necessary information regarding a channel program to be executed.

An *external* interrupt may result from any one of the following conditions:

1. Forced interrupt by machine operator through a console switch;

2. External lines attached to another computer system; or

3. Signal from the system timer as its present time is counted down to 0.

Right after an interrupt has taken place, an *Interruption Code* (IC) is automatically loaded, by hardware, into the bit positions 16 through 31 of an old PSW. The IC has five possible interpretations, each corresponding to a particular type of interrupt, which are shown in the last two columns in Table 15.3. Consider, for example, an interrupt due to an attempt to execute a privileged instruction in problem state. From Table C.1 in Appendix C, we see that the code for this type of interrupt is $(2)_{10}$. Thus, the lower four bits (bit positions 28–31) in the interruption code field of PSW contain 0010, and the remainder of the bit positions (16–27) are made zero. Secondly, consider an I/O interrupt. By inspecting the bits 21–31 of interruption code in the old PSW, the I/O check routine of the supervisor will be able to pinpoint which channel and device are associated with the present interrupt.

When an interrupt occurs, the so-called *instruction length code* (ILC) is *also* set in PSW. (ILC will be discussed presently.) Then the following actions are taken:

1. The contents of the current PSW are saved at a fixed location in main storage, known as an old PSW. The location of old PSW varies with the cause of an interrupt, as shown in column 4 of Table 15.3. For example, an attempt to execute an invalid instruction causes a program interrupt. As a result, the current PSW will be loaded into the doubleword at location 000028, the old PSW for a program interrupt.

2. A new PSW is loaded in the current PSW. This new PSW contains an address of IHR associated with the particular type of interrupt. IHR then decides what to do with this interrupt.

3. The last instruction in IHR is Load PSW (LPSW), which returns the old PSW into the current PSW. The CPU then resumes its interrupted processing. We now see that *an interrupt is essentially an automatic branch to a new sequence of instructions.*

It is worth noting that either new or old PSW has five possible addresses, each corresponding to a particular type of interrupt (see Table 15.3). Consequently, the address of either old PSW or new PSW is used to indicate, in a precise way to the supervisor, the cause of an interrupt. If, for instance, the new PSW is brought out from the storage address 000068, the supervisor is in fact informed that the interrupt

Table 15.3. New PSW and old PSW

1	2	3	4	5	6
				Old PSW	
		Address of new PSW (hexadecimal)	Address (hexadecimal)	Interruption-code field (bits 16 through 31)	
Type of interrupt	Priority			Bit positions concerned†	Its representation
External	3	000058	000018	24	Timer
				25	Interrupt key
				26	External line 6
				27	External line 5
				⋮	⋮
				31	External line 1
SVC	2‡	000060	000020	24–31	Eight bits for *R1* and *R2* in SVC instruction
Program	2‡	000068	000028	28–31	A four-bit interruption code for program interrupt (see Table C.1)
Machine check	1	000070	000030	—	—
Input/ Output	4	000078	000038	16–23	Channel address
				24–31	Device address

† Other bits in the interruption-code field are set to zeros.
‡ Interrupts due to SVC and program check cannot occur simultaneously.

was caused by the user's program. Secondly, the *specific* cause of a *program* interrupt is identified by the *interrupt code* in the PSW.

Before we turn to the next section to discuss how to prevent some interrupts, we shall digress to introduce the *Instruction Length Code* (ILC) in a PSW. Essentially, this field contains the length of the instruction which has caused the interrupt, expressed in halfwords. The field takes up two bits, bit positions 32 and 33 in the old PSW. For instance, if the instruction

$$\text{DR} \quad 4,7$$

causes an interrupt, the ILC field in the old PSW will contain 01, as this instruction is only one halfword long.

15.7 MASKING—INTERRUPT PREVENTION

In the previous sections, we discussed five types of interrupt: machine check, input/output, program exception, external source, and supervisor call. During the period in which one interrupt is being serviced, it is possible that other interrupt conditions come into being. This is not desirable because the contents in old PSW will thus be erased. It is therefore necessary that, during this period, other interrupts should be suppressed (but kept pending).

In System/370 or System/360, not all types of interrupt can be prevented. In this section, we shall learn how to use the masking technique in order to disable three types of interrupt; input/output, machine check, and *some* program exception interrupts.

Selective Masking of Each Channel

In order to control an input/output interrupt in a System/360 computer, a system mask, located at the bit positions 0 through 7 in the PSW, is used. As shown in Table 15.4,

Table 15.4. System mask field in PSW for the System/360

Bit position in PSW	Interruption source masked	Contents in each bit
0	Multiplexor channel	0 = interrupt prevented (This means the interrupt can be held pending, but not completely ignored.) 1 = interrupt permitted
1	Selector channel 1	
2	Selector channel 2	
3	Selector channel 3	
4	Selector channel 4	
5	Selector channel 5	
6	Selector channel 6	
7	External signal, interrupt key, or timer	

each bit identifies a channel; and its contents indicate whether an I/O interrupt is prevented or not. For instance, a 1 in bit position 3 simply means that any input/output interrupt involving the selector channel 3 is permitted. However, after the occurrence of such an interrupt, the bit position 3 is automatically set to zero which prevents further I/O interrupt involving this selector channel.

We shall further illustrate the usage of system mask by the following examples.

Example 1

In order to prevent any I/O interrupt originated from selector channels 2, 4, 6, and the multiplexor channel, we can use the system mask shown in Fig. 15.16.

Example 2

In order to prevent all input/output as well as the external interrupts, a system mask containing all zeros is required.

Bit position ⟶ 0   1   2   3   4   5   6   7

Fig. 15.16   System mask field in a PSW.

Example 3

In contrast to Example 2, a system mask field containing all 1's is needed to allow all of these interrupts.

Let us now take a look at the system mask field used in System/370.

The function of each bit in bit positions 0 through 5 of the PSW (for the BC mode) is the same as that for System/360. The function of PSW bit 6 is changed; it controls the interruptions from channels 6 through 31 in conjunction with control register 2. Control registers will be discussed later in this chapter.

A privileged instruction is available to set the system mask—Set System Mask (SSM). This instruction is of SI format (see Fig. 3.1), but the immediate operand (bit positions 8–15) is ignored. It copies the contents of a particular byte in the main storage to the system mask field, leaving the bit positions 8–63 in PSW untouched. The address of this byte can be readily computed as $D + C(B)$. For example, the instruction SSM HERE will copy the byte content at HERE to the system mask field in PSW. [Note: System masks may be set in a second way: Through a SVC interrupt or a Load PSW instruction, introduce a new PSW with the required mask bits.]

Machine Check Handling

Machine check interrupts can be prevented by means of another mask, the so-called *machine check mask*, located at bit position 13 of the PSW. If this bit contains a zero, machine check interrupt will be ignored. However, an operator can overrule this condition simply by turning on the CE switch on the control panel. If bit position 13 contains a 1-value, the machine check interrupt will be performed, regardless of the CE switch.

Program Mask Field

We see now that it is possible to suppress the input/output and machine check interrupts respectively by using the system mask and machine check mask. The third type of mask, the program mask, can prevent certain kinds of program exception interrupt. As listed in Table C.1 (see Appendix C), there are 15 possible causes for a program exception. We can only prevent program interrupts due to the following four causes: fixed-point overflow, decimal overflow, exponent underflow, and significance (see Table 15.5).

The program mask is located at the bit positions 36 through 39 in PSW. As with the system mask and machine check mask, the bit configuration has the following

Table 15.5. Program mask field in PSW (format for BC mode)

Bit position in PSW	Exception	Bit content
36	Fixed-point overflow	
37	Decimal overflow	0 = interrupt prevented
38	Exponent underflow	1 = interrupt permitted
39	Significance	

meaning: If the bit has a zero value, the interrupt will be prevented; if the value is 1, the interrupt is permitted. For example, a program mask of 0101 prevents the interrupts caused by any fixed-point overflow or exponent underflow.

A nonprivileged instruction—Set Program Mask (SPM)—is available to copy a program mask in the bit positions 34–39 of the PSW (the condition code and program mask fields). This instruction is of RR format but has its own peculiarities. The bit positions 2–7 of the first operand contain the prototype condition code and program mask; the second operand is ignored. For example, if the contents of register 7 are

$$B'00010101000000000000000000000000'$$

after the execution of the instruction SPM 7,0 the condition code field (bit positions 34 and 35) in PSW will contain 01 and the program mask field (positions 36–39), 0101. This instruction *simulates a computer system without automatic interrupts.*

Example 4

Write a segment of instructions (nonprivileged) to suppress interrupts on any fixed-point overflow or exponent underflow. Assume that the contents in the rightmost 32 bits of PSW are 800002F8.

The required program mask is B'0101' (see Table 15.5), and the program segment in Fig. 15.17 is a possible solution. The BALR instruction, first discussed in Chapter 4, loads the rightmost 32 bits of PSW in register 6. After the execution of the OR instruction, the contents in register 6 become 850002F8. As a result, the contents of program mask in PSW, after the execution of SPM instruction, become B'0101'.

```
        BALR    6,0
        O       6,CCPMSK
        SPM     6,0
          .
          .
          .
CCPMSK  DC      X'05000000'
```

Fig. 15.17 Program segment to suppress interrupts on fixed point overflow or exponent underflow.

There are in total eight fields in a PSW: system mask, interruption code, ILC, CC, program mask, instruction address, AMWP, and key field (see Fig. 15.12). We have thus far discussed the first six of them. In the remainder of the section, we shall present the AMWP field in detail, leaving the key field for discussion in the next section.

The AMWP field occupies the bit positions 12 through 15 in PSW. Each bit has its own significance. The bit position 13, already mentioned above, functions as machine check mask. Also, the bit position 15—the *problem state bit*—was discussed in Section 15.5. When it contains a zero value, CPU is said to be in the supervisor state; when it has 1-value, in the problem state. We shall now discuss the functions of the bit positions 12 and 14 in a PSW.

The PSW bit 12 in System/360 indicates the code used: EBCDIC or the ASCII code. The former was discussed in Chapter 10; the latter is a code adopted by the American Standards Association. Their difference lies primarily in the representation of the zone bits. When a zero value is inserted in bit position 12 of PSW, it signifies that the EBCDIC is generated internally; whereas a 1-value indicates that the ASCII code is used.

In System/370, the ASCII code is not used, and the associated meaning of PSW bit-position 12 is no longer valid. If the virtual storage operation is not involved the bit position 12 must be a zero, or a program interruption for specification exception will occur.

Let us turn now to the bit position 14 in the AMWP field, better known as the *wait bit*. If this bit contains a zero, a new instruction is fetched and executed in the usual manner. However, if this bit is set to 1, no new instruction is fetched or executed and CPU is then in the *wait state*. A typical case was discussed in Example 3 of Section 15.4, where the CPU must wait till the execution of a channel program is terminated. In general, when CPU is in this state, it usually waits for either an I/O or an external interrupt so that it may resume its processing.

In retrospect, the following four questions can be asked to determine the overall CPU status at a given time:

1. Is the CPU in problem state (represented by zero in bit position 15 in PSW) or in supervisor state (1 in bit 15)?

2. Is it in wait state (represented by 0 in bit position 14 in PSW) or in run state (1 in bit 14)?

3. Is it in masked state or in interruptible state? The system bits, the machine-check bit, and the program mask bits are used to reflect the masked state of the CPU for the particular interruption source.

4. Is it in operating state or in stopped state? This type of alternatives is effected only by manual intervention or by machine malfunction.

If we ignore the question number 4 (which is usually not of concern to a programmer), the other three questions relating to the CPU states can be shown in the three-dimensional diagram (Fig. 15.18).

To a beginning programmer, the problem-run-interruptible combination (shaded in Fig. 15.18) is of major concern, while the supervisor-wait-masked combination is important to a seasoned systems programmer in developing, say, an interrupt handling routine.

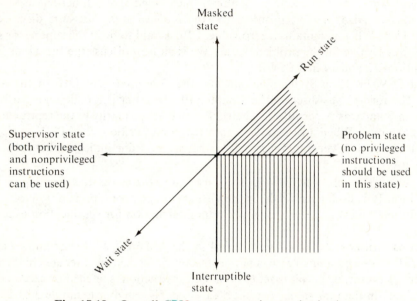

Fig. 15.18   Overall CPU status at a given point in time.

15.8 STORAGE AND FETCH PROTECTION

In the previous sections, we discussed seven fields in PSW. We shall now consider the remaining one—the key field—from the viewpoint of storage and fetch protection. First, we shall discuss how the contents in the main storage can be protected from accidental erasing. Lack of *storage protection* may result in, say, storing characters into a supervisor program area which can be extremely damaging. We shall then see how *fetch protection* may be accomplished. By fetch protection, we mean that the access to some predetermined sections of the main storage area is restricted, so that information of security value cannot be obtained by an unauthorized person.

The storage protection is available in all System/370 and only some System/360 models. The main storage is divided into blocks, each having $(2048)_{10}$ bytes. For example, a 8K main storage may be divided into four blocks as shown in Fig. 15.19; associated with each block is a five-bit storage key whose four leftmost bits represent a protection key number, ranging from 0 to 15. Figure 15.20, for example, shows a storage key whose protection key number is 4.

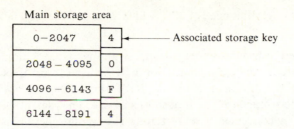

Fig. 15.19   Each storage key is associated with a block of 2048 bytes.

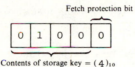

Fig. 15.20   Storage protection key.

Closely related to this protection key number is the four-bit protection key field (bit positions 8 through 11) in PSW. The contents of this four-bit key in the current PSW can be used to match the storage protection key associated with a block of main storage. Data are not permitted to be stored or transmitted into such block unless one of the following two conditions is met:

1. Two keys are equal; or

2. The contents of the protection key in the current PSW are zeros.

Failing that, a protection exception will occur, causing a program interrupt. Instructions which could cause protection exceptions include CVD, MVC, MVI, PACK, ST, STM, and UNPACK.

Example 1

Given:

1. Four storage-protection keys as shown in Fig. 15.19.

2. The bit configuration of the key field in the current PSW as shown in Fig. 15.21.

Find: Which block(s) in the main-storage area can store information?

Solution. There is only one block in which information may be stored: from location

Bit position⟶   8   9   10   11

| 1 | 1 | 1 | 1 |

Fig. 15.21   Key field in the current PSW.

4096 to 6143. Its key number is $(15)_{10}$ which matches the key field in the current PSW.

Two privileged instructions are associated with the manipulation of a storage key. First, the Set Storage Key (SSK) instruction may be used to set the storage key for a block of main storage; this instruction is of RR format. The first operand is a register which contains the storage key in bit positions 24–27. The remaining bit positions are ignored and may be conveniently set to zeros. The second operand is another register whose contents are shown in Fig. 15.22.

Ignored	Identification of storage block	Ignored	0000

Bit position ⟶ 0   7 8   20 21   27 28 31

Fig. 15.22   Contents of the second operand R2 for a SSK instruction.

Example 2

What does the instruction

$$\text{SSK} \quad 4,5$$

accomplish if the register contents are as follows:

$$\text{Register 4: 000000F0}$$
$$\text{Register 5: 0000A800}$$

Solution. The protection key number 15 (in decimal) will be assigned to the block of storage from locations 00A800 to 00AFFF. This is the twenty-first block (of 2048 bytes in decimal) since the bit positions 8 through 20 in register 5 contain 0000 0000 1010 1.

Example 3

Same as Example 2 except that the contents in register 5 are 0000A9E0.

Solution. The contents in register 5 address the same block (from locations 00A800 to 00AFFF). As a result, the protection key number 15 is assigned to the block. In fact, register 5 could contain any number from 0000A800 to 0000AFFF to address the same block.

Second, the Insert Storage Key (ISK) instruction is used to examine the storage key of a block of main storage. This instruction, which is the converse of the SSK instruction, it also of RR format. The second operand is a register containing the address of the block whose key is to be examined. For example, after the execution of the instruction

$$\text{ISK} \quad 4,5$$

the storage key of a block (from register 5) is inserted into bit positions 24–27 of register 4. The bit positions 0–23 remain unaltered, but positions 28–31 are changed to zeros.

We shall now turn our attention to the *fetch protection*. Not all System/370 or System/360 models have the fetch protection feature. If installed, it can be used to prevent one program from addressing either a second program or the supervisor routines. There is a close relationship between the fetch protection and the storage protection. If the former is in operation, the latter is automatically in operation. The converse is not true.

The rightmost bit in the storage protection key (see Fig. 15.20) is called the *fetch protection* bit. If it contains 1, both fetch and storage protection are in operation; otherwise, only storage, but not fetch, is protected.

Example 4

Given:

1. Associated with the block for storage locations 0000 through $(2048)_{10}$ is the storage protection key shown in Fig. 15.23.

Fetch protection bit

Fig. 15.23   Storage protection key for a block.

2. The protection key field in the current PSW is shown in Fig. 15.24.

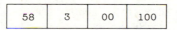

Fig. 15.24   Protection key field in PSW.

3. Load instruction to be executed is shown in Fig. 15.25.

| 58 | 3 | 00 | 100 |

Fig. 15.25   Load instruction.

Find: Is there any violation related to the fetch?

Solution. No, there is no violation to the fetch protection. The fetch bit in the storage protection key contains a zero; and as a result, the contents in the fullword, whose address is 000100, is loaded in register 3.

Note that, when the fetch protection bit is 1, both fetch and storage protections are provided if: (1) the keys do not match; or (2) the current PSW does not have a zero value.

Example 5

Same as Example 4, except that the storage protection key has the configuration shown in Fig. 15.26.

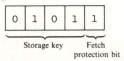

Fig. 15.26   Storage protection key for a block and the fetch protection bit.

Solution. The protection key field in PSW (Fig. 15.24) does not match the storage key for the block shown in Fig. 15.26. In addition, the value in the fetch protection bit is 1. As a result, no fetching is permitted at byte address 000100.

We conclude this section by noting that the address of the *first* CCW in a channel program is stored in a fullword (storage location 000048), called Channel Address Word (CAW). The format of the CAW is shown in Fig. 15.27. The bit positions 0–3

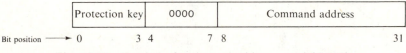

Fig. 15.27   Format of a channel address word (CAW).

contain a protection key. The channel uses the protection key to gain its access to main storage. It must either contain zeros or match the storage key of a block of main storage before a piece of data can be placed in the block. The protection key field in CAW is copied in the positions 0–3 in a Channel Status Word (CSW), which we shall explore in Section 15.10.

15.9 CONTROL REGISTERS AND THEIR ROLES IN MASKING AND MONITORING

In the IBM System/370, there are 16 *control registers* to supplement the PSW in controlling the system, principally for the masking. These control registers (numbered 0 to 15) are not to be confused with the 16 general registers. They are not addressable, but can be loaded and stored by two privileged instructions: Load ConTroL (LCTL) and STore ConTroL (STCTL).

Currently not all control registers are used. Also, not all bit positions in a control register are relevant to a particular 370 model. We shall now explore their usage.

Table 15.6 lists the functions of control registers 0, 1, 2, 8, and 14. Some control registers are used jointly with PSW. Take the control register 2, for instance. In BC mode, interrupts from channels 6 and up are controlled jointly by the I/O mask bit (PSW bit 6) and the corresponding channel-mask bit. Specifically, the channel 9 can cause an interruption only when the I/O mask is one *and* the bit 9 in control register 2 is one. In BC mode, the interrupts from channels 0–5 are controlled *only* by PSW bits 0–5.

As another example, consider the bit position 24 in control register 0. It is used jointly with PSW bit 7 (the external mask bit). Only when both bits contain 1, an external interruption due to the timer value becoming negative can occur.

The principal application of control register 8 lies in the *monitoring*.

During the execution of programs in time sharing, multiprogramming, or virtual memory environment, it is often desirable to record information at some predetermined places in a program. This is made possible in System/370 by inserting Monitoring Call (MC) instructions at these selected places.

The MC instruction is of SI format (see Fig. 15.28). The bit positions 8–11 of *I2*

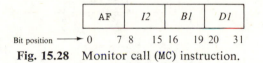

Bit position ⟶ 0   7 8   15 16   19 20   31

Fig. 15.28   Monitor call (MC) instruction.

field must contain zeros, and bit positions 12–15 of *I2* field contain a four-bit binary number (such as 0010 or 1110), one of 16 possible *monitoring classes* specified by a programmer. During the execution of MC instruction, a program interruption for monitoring is initiated if the corresponding monitor-mask bit in control register 8 is one (see Fig. 15.29). In addition, three operations take place:

a) The contents of *I2* field are copied in locations 148 and 149 in main storage. Thus the monitor class numbers are in byte 149.

b) The sum *D1* + *C(B1)*, not its contents, is stored in locations 157–159, and zeros in location 156.

c) Bit position 9 of the program interruption code is set to one, and the other bits of the code to zero.

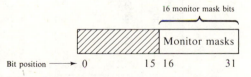

Bit position ⟶ 0   15 16   31

Fig. 15.29   Control register 8 is used as monitor masks.

For example, if the contents are as follows:

General register 9:   00000010 in hexadecimal

Bits 16–32 in control register 8:   0000010000000000 in binary

Table 15.6 Functions of some selected control registers

Control register	Bit positions	Name of field (bit description)	Used jointly with a PSW bit	Used for interruption	Type	Reason of interrupt
0	0	Block-multiplex mode	No	No	—	—
	8 9	Page size in virtual storage operation	No	No	—	—
	10 11	Segment size in virtual storage operation	No	No	—	—
	24 25 26	Timer mask Interrupt key mask External signal mask	Yes (PSW bit 7)	Yes	External	Negative value of timer. Pressing of interrupt key. External signals 2–7.
1	0–7	Length checking for segment table	No	No	—	—
	8–25	Address of segment table	No	No	—	—
2	0–5	Do not participate I/O interrupts in BC mode, but they do in EC mode	No in BC mode, but yes in EC mode (PSW bit 6)	No in BC mode; yes in EC mode	I/O	I/O from a channel.
	6–31	Channel masks	Yes (PSW bit 6)	Yes		

8 / 14	16–31	Monitor masks		Monitor	Corresponding to one of 16 monitor classes, the monitor mask bit is 1.
8	0	Hard stop	No	Yes	
			†		
14	1	Synchronous machine check Extended Logout mask	No		Machine check
	2	I/O extended logout mask	No		
	4	Recovery report mask	Yes (PSW bit 13)		
	5	Configuration report mask			
	6	External damage report mask			
	7	Warning mask			
	8	Asynchronous MCEL mask	Yes (PSW bit 13)		
	9	Asynchronous fixed log mask	No		

† A machine-check interruption caused by a hard machine check condition can occur only when PSW bit 0 is one. If it is zero, the subsequent action depends on bit 0 of control register 14: (a) bit 0 is 0, machine check condition is held pending, execution attempt is made; and (b) bit 0 is 1, processing stops immediately.

then after the execution of the following instruction in your program:

MC   4(9),B'00000101'

05 = one of 16 monitor classes

a program interruption for monitoring will be initiated, since the corresponding monitor-mask bit (bit position 21 in control register 8) is one. The location 149 in the main storage contain 05 (monitor class), and the locations 157–159 contain 000010 + 4 = 000014, known as the monitor code. (The locations 148 and 156 are set to zeros.) Thus this monitoring interruption is identified by a 24-bit code $(000014)_{16}$ in combination with the monitor class number $(0101)_2 = 5$.

The MC instruction becomes a no-op instruction if the *I2* field contains all zeros. For example, the instruction MC 210(9),B'00000000' will be identical to a no-op instruction. No interruption will occur.

Hardware malfunction in System/360 in reflected by the PSW bit-position 13 (machine-check mask bit). In System/370, the machine check handling has been greatly extended. The detailed information of location and the nature of the cause is supplied to the program. In addition, the system may either try some corrective actions, or circumvent the components which are not functioning correctly. The control register 14 is used for machine check.

The number of available types of machine check in System/370 varies with model number; they can be either *hard* or *soft* machine checks. When corrective actions or re-try attempts are not successful, it is called a hard machine check. On the other hand, soft machine-check interruption occurs if corrective actions are successful and an interruption is initialed to record the error condition.

During a machine-check interruption, a machine check logout is stored in bytes 232 through 511 in main storage. The contents of the first eight bytes (232 through 239) indicate the state of hardware when the interruption occurred. The logout automatically places the items of information concerning the state of internal circuitry into main storage. It may be either *synchronous* or *asynchronous*. If the logout occurs during the machine-check interruption, it is synchronous. By contrast, if it occurs without a machine-check interruption or if the logout and the interruption are separated, it is then asynchronous.

In addition to the logout area, a machine-check extended logout area (MCEL) is also allocated. Its starting byte address is specified by the contents of control register 15. The length is model-dependent.

15.10 CONTROL REGISTERS, DAT, AND PSW ASSOCIATED WITH VIRTUAL STORAGE OPERATIONS

In virtual storage operation, your job is loaded into the auxiliary disk area, called external page storage. Your program and data are arbitrarily divided into small blocks, known as *segments*. Each segment is further divided into *pages*. During processing, pages of instructions and data are transferred between external page storage and (real) main storage according to the needs of your job.

To implement virtual storage operations, several additional pieces of hardware are necessary. One of them is the Dynamic Address Translation (DAT). It has two basic functions:

1. To find the (real) main storage address when a page in real storage is referenced; and

2. To give a signal when a page must be brought into (real) main storage.

Some control registers are also used to support virtual storage operations. As shown in Table 15.6, the bit positions 8 and 9 of control register 0 are used jointly to indicate the page size; while bit positions 10 and 11 designate the segment size. Typical examples are shown below:

Bit positions in control register 0	Contents	Meaning
8 and 9	01	Page size is 2K
8 and 9	10	Page size is 4K
10 and 11	00	Segment size is 64K
10 and 11	10	Segment size is 1M

Control register 1 is used in conjunction with the DAT. The bit positions 0 through 7 indicate the length of the segment table in units of 64 bytes (used as a check).

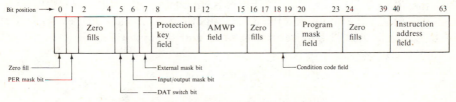

Fig. 15.30   PSW format for EC mode.

The remaining 24 bits designate the pointer to the segment table. Control registers 9, 10, and 11 control the program event recording (PER).

As discussed earlier in the chapter, the PSW has two formats: BC and EC. In virtual storage operations, the extended control (EC) mode must be used. As shown in Fig. 15.30, it is different from the BC mode format. The basic modifications are:

1. Condition code field is moved from bit positions 34 and 35 to 18 and 19.

2. Interruption code field (bit positions 16–31 in BC mode) is moved, expanded, and placed in various fixed locations in main storage (see Table 15.7).

3. Instruction length code field (bit positions 32 and 33) is removed.

4. The first six system mask bits (bits position 0 through 5) are removed. The functions of these six and additional 26 mask bits are performed in the control register 2.

5. Insertion of the Program Event Recording (PER) mask bit (in bit position 1).

6. Insertion of the translate control bit (in bit position 5).

The translate control bit must contain 1 before an effective address is translated in (real) main storage address by DAT. If it contains 0, then the effective address is treated as the real storage address.

15.11 CHANNEL STATUS WORD (CSW)

Just as the PSW mainly indicates status of CPU, the Channel Status Word (CSW) shows the status of an Input/Output device as a result of a preceding I/O operation. It is a doubleword stored at the fixed location 000040. The format of a CSW is shown in Fig. 15.31. Bit positions 0–7 contain a copy of the eight-bit contents (in the same positions) of the original CAW. Positions 8–31, the *command address* field, contain the address of the last CCW plus 8. Bits 48–63 contain the *residue count* from the last CCW used. If the number of bytes read or written agree with the count field of the

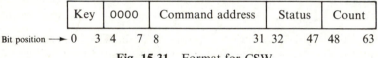

Fig. 15.31   Format for CSW.

CCW, then the CSW count is zero. Otherwise, it contains the difference between the count specified in the CCW and the actual input/output count. For example, if we wish to read the first 72 byte record on tape, and the count field in the associated CCW contains 80:

```
CCW  2,INAREA,X'00',80
```

Table 15.7. Permanent storage assignment

Address		Length in bytes	Purpose	Basic control mode (BC), extended control mode (EC), or both
Decimal	Hexadecimal			
0	0		Initial program loading PSW	
8	8		Initial program loading CCW1	
16	10		Initial program loading CCW2	
24	18		External old PSW	
32	20	8 each	Supervisor call old PSW	Both BC and EC
40	28		Program old PSW	
48	30		Machine-check old PSW	
56	38		Input/output old PSW	
64	40		Channel status word	

Table 15.7.

Address		Length in bytes	Purpose	Basic control mode (BC), extended control mode (EC), or both
Decimal	**Hexadecimal**			
72	48		Channel address word	
76	4C	4 each	Unused	
80	50		Timer (uses bytes 50, 51 & 52)	
84	54		Unused	
88	58		External new PSW	Both BC
96	60		Supervisor call new PSW	and EC
104	68	8 each	Program new PSW	
112	70		Machine-check new PSW	
120	78		Input/output new PSW	
128	80		Diagnostic scan-out area	
134	86	2	External interrupt code in EC mode	
136	88	4	SVC codes in EC mode	
140	8C	4	Program interrupt code in EC mode	
144	90	4	DAT interrupt address	
148	94	2	Monitor Call class	
146	96	2	PER interrupt code	
148	98	4	PER address	
156	9C	4	Monitor Call code	EC
168	A8	4	Channel identification from Store Channel ID command	
172	AC	4	I/O Extended Logout (IOEL) address	
176	B0	4	Limited channel logout codes	
186	BA	2	Input/Output interrupt address in EC mode	
216	D8	296	Maintenance logout data	
232	E8	8	Machine check interruption code	
240	F0	8	Unused	
248	F8	4	Failing-storage address	
252	FC	4	Region code	Both BC
256	100	96	Fixed logout area	and EC
352	160	32	Floating-point register save area	
384	180	64	General register save area	
448	1C0	64	Control register save area	

then there is a difference of eight bytes. As a result, the count field (bit positions 48–63) in CSW will contain 0008.

Ths *status field* of a CSW (bit positions 32–47) is conveniently divided into two bytes: Status information from the I/O device is stored in positions 32–39; and that from the channel, in positions 40–47. Let us examine these bit positions in detail.

The *I/O-device status byte* (positions 32–39), supplied by the I/O device and transmitted to the channel, is shown in Fig. 15.32. Bit positions 34, 36, and 37 are

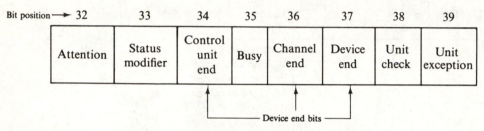

Bit position → 32   33   34   35   36   37   38   39

| Attention | Status modifier | Control unit end | Busy | Channel end | Device end | Unit check | Unit exception |

— Device end bits —

Fig. 15.32   I/O device's status byte in a CSW.

collectively called *device end bits*. A 1-bit in *each* of these three positions serves as a signal to CPU: The I/O operation for the unit is completed and a second I/O operation is now requested.

The *unit check* bit (bit position 38) signals an error from the control unit or an I/O device (such as reader "not ready" condition, or a byte on tape not having correct parity bit). The *unit exception* bit (position 39) signals an unusual condition, not necessarily an error. A typical example for a reader is end-of-file condition: all cards are read and transmitted to main storage. The *busy* bit together with the *status modifier* bit (position 35 and 33, respectively) indicate that control unit and I/O device are busy. Finally, the *attention* bit (position 32) reflects any operator's action at an I/O device.

The channel status byte, bit positions 40–47 in a CSW, gets the information from a channel (see Fig. 15.33). A 1-value in bit position 41 indicates that the number of

Bit position → 40   41   42   47

| Program-controlled interrupt | Incorrect length | Channel-detected errors |

Fig. 15.33   Channel status byte in a CSW.

bytes actually read or written does not agree with the count specified in the count field in the CCW just executed. You can prevent this bit from setting to 1 by using the SLI flag in the CCW (see page 477).

Secondly, if bit positions 42 through 47 contain any ones, it means that an error (either a machine error or a command error) is detected by the channel.

Finally, if an input/output interrupt is caused by the PCI flag in a CCW (see page 477), the bit position 40 of the CSW will contain 1. Typically, the contents of this byte should be all zeros if the I/O operation is normally terminated.

15.12 INPUT/OUTPUT INSTRUCTIONS

As mentioned earlier in the chapter, CPU and a channel have master-slave relationship. Although a channel can execute its own commands, it still has to be told by a CPU instruction as to (1) when to handle an I/O operation; and (2) which I/O device is to be used. For these purposes, four input/output instructions are available: Start I/O (SIO), Test I/O (TIO), Halt I/O (HIO), and Test Channel (TCH). They are all

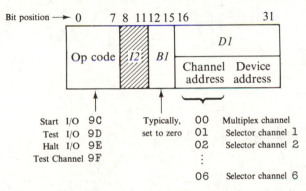

Fig. 15.34   Instruction format for 4 I/O instructions (privileged).

privileged and can be executed only when the system is in supervisor state (that is, when bit position 15 in PSW is zero). All four instructions are of SI format (Fig. 15.34), but have two important variations:

a) The immediate field is ignored; and

b) The sum $C(B) + D$ has nothing to do with main-storage address; instead, it indicates the channel and device address.

For example, the instruction 9C 00 040F means: Start the following I/O device; its channel address is 4 (selector channel 4) and I/O unit address is 0F (say, a tape drive). Note that the corresponding assembler language instruction is STO X'40F' where the first operand is omitted and the address (such as 40F) is specific to the individual installation.

The Start I/O (SIO) instruction starts an I/O operation such as read, write, control,

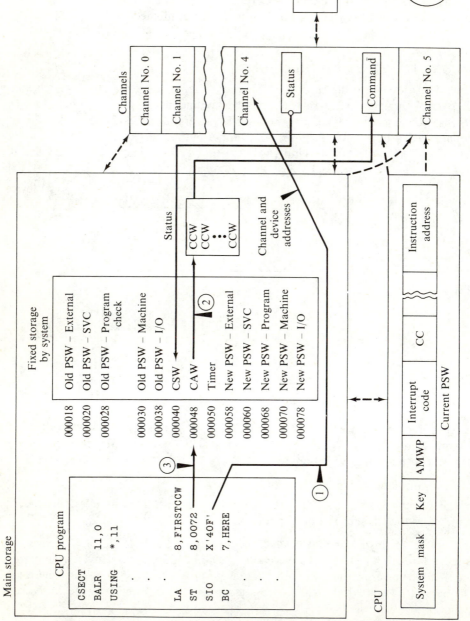

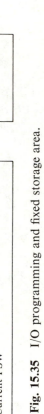

Fig. 15.35 I/O programming and fixed storage area.

and so on. Before the execution of this instruction, the designated channel must obtain
the following two items of information:

1. Complete address of the I/O device; and

2. The address of the first CCW to be executed.

The first item is readily supplied to the channel from the second operand of the SIO
instruction (see point 1 in Fig. 15.35); the second item, from the CAW (see point 2
in Fig. 15.35). You must put the address of the first CCW in CAW before a SIO
instruction is issued. A sample program segment to do this is shown in Fig. 15.36

```
            LA      8,FIRSTCCW
            ST      8,0072
            SIO     X'40F'
                    .
                    .
                    .
FIRSTCCW    CCW     2,INAREA,X'00',80
INAREA      DS      CL80
```

Fig. 15.36 Program segment to establish the contents in a CAW.

(also see point 3 in Fig. 15.35). Note that $(72)_{10}$ used in STore instruction is the fixed
location 000048 in main storage for CAW. The X'40F' used in the SIO instruction
specifies the channel and device address as three-digit hexadecimal number 40F.

An alternate way to establish the contents in a CAW is shown in Fig. 15.37.

```
            MVC     72(4),ADCON
            SIO     X'40F'
                    .
                    .
                    .
FIRSTCCW    CCW     2,INAREA,X'00',80
                    .
                    .
                    .
ADCON       DC      A(FIRSTCCW)
```

Fig. 15.37 Alternate segment to establish the contents in a CAW.

As a result of the execution of a SIO instruction, the condition code is set. (The
condition code settings for the four input/output instructions are listed on the next
page.) It is a common practice to use a branch (BC) instruction after a SIO one, as
shown in Fig. 15.38. For example, if an I/O device is started successfully, then CC is

```
            SIO     X'40F'
            BC      B'0111',ENDFILE
TEST        ...
                    .
                    .
ENDFILE     ...
```

Fig. 15.38 Instructions to start an I/O device.

set to 0 after the SIO instruction. As a result, the above BC instruction has no effect and control is passed to the instruction labeled TEST. If, however, the starting of an I/O device fails, then a branch is made to the instruction labeled ENDFILE.

The Test I/O (TIO) instruction checks the status of a device and sets the condition code (see Table 15.8). The branch (BC) instruction often follows the TIO instruction as shown below.

```
            TIO   X'00E'
            BC    7,*—4
```

Note that this pair of instructions forms a permanent loop if CC = 1 (device is busy), CC = 2 (channel or subchannel is busy), or CC = 3 (channel, subchannel, or device

Table 15.8. Condition code setting due to an input/output instruction

CC \ instruction	0	1	2	3
SIO	Operation is initiated. All goes well. (CAW gives the address for the first CWW to be executed).	Have some unusual conditions (e.g., interrupt pending, an end-of-file, an immediate operation, command chaining not specified). Status is stored in CSW.	Channel or subchannel is busy.†	Channel, subchannel, or device is not operational (no power or no such address).
TIO	Device and subchannel are available. No interrupts pending.	Device is busy; the device or subchannel has already kept an interrupt pending. When CC = 1, status is recorded in CSW.	Channel or subchannel is busy.	Channel, subchannel, or device is not operational.
HIO	Subchannel has an interrupt pending. Ignore the Halt instruction.	Details of the halt is in CSW.	An operation in burst mode is completed.	Channel, subchannel or device is not operational.
TCH	Channel is available.	An interrupt is kept pending in the channel.	Channel is in burst mode.	Channel is not operational.

† Subchannel represents the channel facilities required to sustain a single input/output operation. A selector channel has only one subchannel, but the multiplexor channel contains multiple subchannels.

is not operational). This loop will be broken only when the channel finishes transmitting the data (a channel end condition is present), or when CC = 0.

As shown in Table 15.8, the TIO instruction causes to store a CSW in the fixed main-storage location 000040, only if (a) the addressed device is busy, or (b) the device or subchannel has an interrupt pending. In other words, a CSW is stored only when CC is set to 1. This relationship has a practical application: it clears (or avoids) a pending I/O interrupt. We shall explore this topic in the next section.

15.13 EXAMPLES: INPUT/OUTPUT PROGRAMMING

This section will discuss two possible programs for the following problem. Read in a deck of cards and check the end-of-file condition of the card reader. The presence of an end-of-file condition means that the last card is just read. In the first example, we shall use a loop formed by TIO and BC instructions to *avoid* any input/output interrupts. In the second, the occurrence of an I/O interrupt is permitted, and the control is passed to Interrupt Handling Routines (IHR) as discussed earlier in this chapter.

Example 1

Write an I/O program to read cards and check for the end-of-file condition.

A possible program is shown in Fig. 15.39. The CSECT instruction defines a control section (Section 8.1). The BALR and USING instructions define a base register (Section 5.5). The LA and ST instructions are used jointly to set up a CAW (see Fig. 15.36). The SIO and BC instructions start a card reader (see Fig. 15.38).

```
          CSECT
**        BASE REGISTER(IMPLIED) IS REGISTER 11
          BALR   11,0
          USING  *,11
**        PREPARE CAW
          LA     8,FIRSTCCW
          ST     8,0072
**        START READER
OUTER     SIO    X'00E'
          BC     B'0111',ENDFILE
**        TEST READER
          TIO    X'00E'
          BC     7,*-4    LOOP TILL SUBCHANNEL AND DEVICE ARE AVAILABLE
          BC     15,OUTER
**        CHECK END OF FILE
ENDFILE   TM     68,B'00000001'
          BC     1,LOADPSW
          LPSW   ABNORMAL
LOADPSW   LPSW   NORMAL
FIRSTCCW  CCW    2,INAREA,X'20',80
INAREA    DS     CL80
ABNORMAL  DC     X'000200000000FF00'
NORMAL    DC     X'00020000000000FF'
          END
```

Fig. 15.39 Program to read cards and check the end-of-file condition.

Let us now examine, step by step, the effects of the TIO and other instructions shown in Fig. 15.39.

Step 1a. After the execution of TIO instruction for the first time, CC is set to 2, since the channel is busy (see Table 15.8).

Step 1b. The BC 7,*–4 instruction causes a branch back to TIO instruction, since CC ≠ 0.

The steps 1a and 1b form a "permanent" loop until the channel is free (that is, a channel end condition exists). If so, go to step 2a.

```
        CSECT
        BALR    10,0
        USING   *,10
HSKD    XC      24(52),24           SET UP I/O NEW PSW
        MVC     120(8),IONEW
INPUT   LA      4,RDCCW
        ST      4,72
        SIO     X'00C'
        BC      8,CCO
        TM      68,X'01'
        BC      1,EOF
        BAL     2,ERROR
CCO     LPSW    WAIT1               WAIT FOR I/O INTERRUPT CHANNEL END
IOINTR  CLI     59,X'OC'
        BC      8,CHSTAT
        BAL     2,ERROR
CHSTAT  TM      69,X'FF'
        BC      8,DUSTAT
        BAL     2,ERROR
DUSTAT  TM      68,X'02'            UNIT CHECK
        BC      1,UNCK
        TM      68,X'04'            DEVICE END
        BC      1,INPUT
        TM      68,X'08'            CHANNEL END
        BC      1,*+8
        BAL     2,ERROR
        LPSW    WAIT2               WAIT FOR I/O INTERRUPT DEVICE END
EOF     LPSW    WAIT3               0003 IN ADD LITES
UNCK    LA      4,SENSE
        ST      4,72
        SIO     X'00C'
        TIO     X'00C'
        BC      7,*-4
        LPSW    WAIT4
ERROR   STH     2,WAIT5+6
        LPSW    WAIT5
RDCCW   CCW     X'02',INAREA,X'20',80
SENSE   CCW     X'04',WAIT4+6,X'20',1
WAIT1   DC      X'800200000000001'
WAIT2   DC      X'800200000000002'
WAIT3   DC      X'000200000000003'
WAIT4   DC      X'000200000000004'
WAIT5   DC      X'000200000000005'
IONEW   DC      X'0000000000'
        DC      AL3(IOINTR)
INAREA  DS      CL80
        END
```

Fig. 15.40   I/O programming.

Step 2a. The TIO instruction is now being executed. Since the channel is free, CC is set to 1 and a CSW is stored to reflect the status (see Table 15.8). The busy bit (position 35) in CSW is turned on. (See Figs. 15.31 and 15.32.)

Step 2b. Same as step 1b. Steps 2a and 2b form a "permanent" loop until the reader completes its cycle. Then go to step 3.

Step 3. The reader now completes a reading, and informs the channel with "device end" message. Since both the subchannel and device are free, CC is set to 0 as a result of the execution of the next TIO instruction.

Step 4. Unconditional branch to the SIO instruction. Repeat step 1 through 3 until card input is exhausted (end-of-file condition). Then go to step 5.

Step 5. Reader now signals the end-of-file condition. After the execution of a SIO instruction, CC is set to 1 (see Table 15.8), since an end-of-file is considered as unusual condition. A new CSW is stored; its bit position 37 (the unit exception bit) is now turned on (having a 1-value) to reflect the end-of-file condition. The remaining steps are used to check this bit position.

Step 6. A Test under Mask (TM) instruction checks the byte 68 in main storage, the device status byte in a CSW. The mask field of 01 in the TM instruction is used only to test that the bit contains 1. If so, CC is set to 3.

Step 7. The BC 1,LOADPSW instruction tests for a CC of 3, finds it, and branches to LOADPSW, where a Load PSW (LPSW) instruction loads a doubleword at 000038 into the current PSW.

Example 2

In Example 1, all input/output interrupts were avoided by the TIO–BC loop. We shall now permit occurrence of interrupts. In this case, Interrupt Handling Routines will be used. A possible I/O program is shown in Fig. 15.40.

BIBLIOGRAPHY

General

Brown, D. T., R. L. Eibsen, and C. A. Thorn, "Channel and Direct Access Device Architecture," *IBM Systems J.* **11**(3), 186–199 (1972).

IBM System/370 Principles of Operation, Form GA22-7000, IBM Corp.

IBM System/370 Model 155 Channel Characteristics, Form GA22-6962, IBM Corp.

Padegs, A., "The Structure of System/360: Part IV—Channel Design Considerations," *IBM Systems J.* **3**(2) (1964).

Pierce, J. R., "The Transmission of Computer Data," *Scient. Am.* **215**, 144–159 (Sept. 1966).

Sutherland, I. E., "Computer Inputs and Outputs," *Scient Am.* **215**, 86–111 (Sept. 1966).

Virtual Storage and Virtual Machines

Denning, P., "Virtual Memory," *Computing Surveys* **2**(3), 153–190 (1970).

Introduction to Virtual Storage, Form GR20-4260, IBM Corp.

OS/VS1 Planning and Use Guide, Form GC24-5090, IBM Corp.

OS/VS2 Planning and Use Guide, Form GC28-0600, IBM Corp.

Introduction to Virtual Machine Facility/370, Form GC20-1800, IBM Corp.

PROBLEMS

1. If the PSW (of BC mode) printed in a dump is

   $$\text{FFA50033 } 4003D7A2$$

   a) during the last operation, was CPU in supervisor state or problem state?
   b) was CPU in wait or run state?
   c) which I/O channel was interruptible?
   d) what was the condition code in decimal?
   e) was the machine check mask *on* or *off*?
   f) was the fixed-point overflow interruptible?
   g) what was the storage-protection key?
   h) what was the address of the next instruction to be executed?

2. When the current PSW is copied into an old PSW (see point 2 in Fig. 15.15), only seven of the eight fields are copied exactly. The interruption code (IC) field, however, is changed to record the information about the interruption. Interpret the IC field of PSW used in Problem 1.

3. Write a *complete* program to read just one card into the main storage area MYAREA. Use EXCP, WAIT, and CCW instructions and write your own IOB.

4. Write a segment of six CCW's to read two blocks from a tape reel *in one tape movement*. Each block consists of only one 60-byte logical record, which is divided as:

Identification number:	1–15 bytes
Name:	16–24 bytes
Address:	25–60 bytes.

5. Assume that the CCPMSK field in Fig. 15.17 contains X'03000000'. What are the contents both in the condition code field and in problem mask field?

SUGGESTED COMPUTER PROJECTS

1. Write a macro definition IOB of your own for the input/output block as shown in Table 15.2.

2. Write a complete program to print three words of your choice, one word on a line. Use EXCP and WAIT macros as well as command chaining.

3. Write a program to read a deck of cards and echo print them on a printer. Use EXCP and WAIT macros.

4. Write a program to read a deck of cards and record them on a tape volume as an unblocked data set. Use EXCP and WAIT macros.

Number Conversions

The conversion of integers and fractions from one system to another may best be explained by a set of examples. Table A.1 illustrates these conversions between decimal, hexadecimal, and binary number systems.

Table A.1 Conversion operations

Operation: Hexadecimal to binary		*Operation:* Binary to hexadecimal	
Integers	Fractions	Integers	Fractions
Rule: Represent each symbol in the hexadecimal number by an equivalent four-digit symbol in the binary system as follows:	Rule: Represent each symbol in the hexadecimal number by an equivalent four-digit symbol in the binary system, beginning at the hexadecimal point as shown.	Rule: Divide the binary number into groups of four digits, beginning at the right, and convert each group to its equivalent hexadecimal form.	Rule: Divide the binary number into groups of four digits, beginning at the binary point, and convert each group into its equivalent hexadecimal form.
$(3F4)_{16}$ $(0011\ 1111\ 0100)_2$	$(.3951)_{16}$ $(.0011\ 1001\ 0101\ 0001)_2$	$(0011\ 1001\ 0100)_2$ $(394)_{16}$	$(.0110\ 0111\ 0001)_2$ $(.671)_{16}$

Operation: Decimal to hexadecimal

Integers	Fractions
Rule: Divide the decimal number by 16 and develop the hexadecimal number as shown below.	Rule: Multiply the decimal number by 16 and develop the hexadecimal number as shown.

Integers

Rule: Divide the decimal number by 16 and develop the hexadecimal number as shown below.

$(953)_{10} = (?)_{16}$

```
16 |953  Remainder  9  ◄
16 | 59  Remainder  11 |
16 |  3  Remainder  3  |
         0
```

The hexadecimal number is read as directed by the arrow. Thus
$(953)_{10} = (3B9)_{16}.$

Note: When converting from decimal to hexadecimal, it is easier to convert the decimal number to a binary number first and then to a hexadecimal number.

Fractions

Rule: Multiply the decimal number by 16 and develop the hexadecimal number as shown.

$(0.953)_{10} = (?)_{16}$

```
        0.953
      ×   16
      15.248
      ×   16
       3.968
      ×   16
      15.488
```

Only the portion of the number to the *right* of the decimal point is multiplied by 16. The answer in hexadecimal is made up of the single digits to the *left* of the decimal point, as directed by the arrow. Thus
$(0.953)_{10} = (0.F3F)_{16}.$

Operation: Hexadecimal to decimal

Integers

Rule: Multiply the hexadecimal number by 16 and add as shown below.

$(953)_{16} = (?)_{10} \quad (BA6)_{16} = (?)_{10}$

```
   953           11106
 ×  16              16
   144              66
 +   5              11
   149             176
 ×  16            + 10
  2384             186
 +   3            × 16
  2387            1116
                   186
                  2976
                 +   6
                  2982
```

$(953)_{16} = (2387)_{10}.$
$(BA6)_{16} = (2982)_{10}.$

Note: Change all alphabetic symbols to their decimal equivalents before performing the operation.

Fractions

Rule: Express the hexadecimal number as powers of 16, add, and divide as shown.

$$(0.953)_{16} = (?)_{10}$$
$$= 9 \times 16^{-1} + 5 \times 16^{-2}$$
$$+ 3 \times 16^{-3}$$
$$= \frac{9}{16} + \frac{5}{256} + \frac{3}{4096}$$
$$= 0.56 + 0.031 + 0.00073$$
$$= 0.59173$$
$$(0.953)_{16} = (0.59713)_{10}$$

Table A.1 (*continued*)

Operation: Binary to decimal		*Operation*: Decimal to binary	
Integers	Fractions	Integers	Fractions
Rule: Multiply the binary number by 2 and add as shown below. $(010110)_2 = (?)_{10}$ 0 1 0 1 1 0 $\times$ 2 / 0 $+$ 1 / 1 $\times$ 2 / 2 $+$ 0 / 2 $\times$ 2 / 4 $+$ 1 / 5 $\times$ 2 / 10 $+$ 1 / 11 $\times$ 2 / 22 $+$ 0 / 22 $(010110)_2 = (22)_{10}$	Rule: Express the binary number as powers of 2, then add and divide as shown. $(0.10011)_2 = (?)_{10}$ $= 1 \times 2^{-1} + 0 \times 2^{-2}$ $\quad + 0 \times 2^{-3} + 1 \times 2^{-4}$ $\quad + 1 \times 2^{-5}$ $= \frac{1}{2} + 0 + 0 + \frac{1}{16} + \frac{1}{32}$ $= 0.5937$ $(0.10011)_2 = (0.5937)_{10}$	Rule: Divide the decimal number by 2 and proceed as shown. $(301)_{10} = (?)_2$ 2 | 301 remainder 1 2 | 150 remainder 0 2 | 75 remainder 1 2 | 37 reaminder 1 2 | 18 remainder 0 2 | 9 remainder 1 2 | 4 remainder 0 2 | 2 remainder 0 2 | 1 remainder 1 0 The binary number must be read as directed by the arrow. Thus $(301)_{10} = (100101101)_2$.	Rule: Multiply the decimal number by 2 and develop, as shown below. $(0.821)_{10} = (?)_2$ 0.821 $\times$ 2 1.642 $\times$ 2 1.284 $\times$ 2 0.568 $\times$ 2 1.136 Only the portion of the number to the right of the decimal point is multiplied by 2. The binary answer is made up of the single digits to the left of the decimal as directed by the arrow. Thus $(0.821)_{10} = (0.1101)_2$.

EBCDIC Character/Numeral Sets

Table B.1

Graphic	Bit configurations	Hexa-decimal	Punched card code	Graphic	Bit configurations	Hexa-decimal	Punched card code
(Blank)	0100 0000	40	no punches	#	0111 1011	7B	8–3
¢	0100 1010	4A	12–8–2	@	0111 1100	7C	8–4
.	0100 1011	4B	12–8–3	'	0111 1101	7D	8–5
<	0100 1100	4C	12–8 4	=	0111 1110	7E	8–6
(	0100 1101	4D	12–8–5	''	0111 1111	7F	8–7
+	0100 1110	4E	12–8–6	A	1100 0001	C1	12–1
|	0100 1111	4F	12–8–7	B	1100 0010	C2	12–2
&	0101 0000	50	12	C	1100 0011	C3	12–3
!	0101 1010	5A	11–8–2	D	1100 0100	C4	12–4
$	0101 1011	5B	11–8–3	E	1100 0101	C5	12–5
*	0101 1100	5C	11–8–4	F	1100 0110	C6	12–6
)	0101 1101	5D	11–8–5	G	1100 0111	C7	12–7
;	0101 1110	5E	11–8–6	H	1100 1000	C8	12–8
¬	0101 1111	5F	11–8–7	I	1100 1001	C9	12–9
−	0110 0000	60	11	J	1101 0001	D1	11–1
/	0110 0001	61	0–1	K	1101 0010	D2	11–2
,	0110 1011	6B	0–8–3	L	1101 0011	D3	11–3
%	0110 1100	6C	0–8–4	M	1101 0100	D4	11–4
--	0110 1101	6D	0–8–5	N	1101 0101	D5	11–5
>	0110 1110	6E	0–8–6	O	1101 0110	D6	11–6
?	0110 1111	6F	0–8–7	P	1101 0111	D7	11–7
:	0111 1010	7A	8–2	Q	1101 1000	D8	11–8

(continued)

Table B.1 (*continued*)

Graphic	Bit configurations	Hexa-decimal	Punched card code	Graphic	Bit configurations	Hexa-decimal	Punched card code
R	1101 1001	D9	11–9	1	1111 0001	F1	1
S	1110 0010	E2	0–2	2	1111 0010	F2	2
T	1110 0011	E3	0–3	3	1111 0011	F3	3
U	1110 0100	E4	0–4	4	1111 0100	F4	4
V	1110 0101	E5	0–5	5	1111 0101	F5	5
W	1110 0110	E6	0–6	6	1111 0110	F6	6
X	1110 0111	E7	0–7	7	1111 0111	F7	7
Y	1110 1000	E8	0–8	8	1111 1000	F8	8
Z	1110 1001	E9	0–9	9	1111 1001	F9	9
0	1111 0000	F0	0				

Dumps

C.1 INTRODUCTION

A storage *dump* is a hard copy of the contents of all or a part of the main storage area. The dumps are often used to debug a program or examine the intermediate results of a program. During execution, your program does not start with the main storage address 000000. The starting point of your program in the main storage, known as the *relocation quantity*, is listed in the dump. The locations between 000000 and the first byte of your program contain mainly OS nucleus (see Section 13.2) and possibly other programs. You can dump OS nucleus and/or your program area.

This appendix deals primarily with the techniques of providing dumps and the steps to interpret them. We shall concentrate on the dumps under the MVT (multi-programming with a variable number of tasks) option of OS/360. The steps used to interpret an OS/360 MFT or PCP dump is quite similar to those for a MVT dump.

C.2 DUMPS UNDER MVT

When the rules governing the instruction formats and specifications are violated in an assembler language program, its execution will be abnormally ended (ABEND). This is known as an *interrupt* of the program due to a particular type of *exception*. Consider, for example, the division I/J. If $J = 0$, a fixed-point divide exception will occur with a code number 9. Likewise, if the operation code is not legal, an operation exception will occur with the code number 1. Table C.1 shows a complete set of interruption codes due to a program interrupt.

If we run the program shown in Fig. C.1† under MVT, a dump will be produced

---

† Fig. C.1 is a reproduction of Fig. 1.17 in Section 1.6.

```
//SAMPLE JOB T361-17,'S S KUO'
//STEP1 EXEC ASMFCLG
//ASM.SYSIN DD *
*     THIS IS A SAMPLE PROGRAM
*     FOR CALCULATING THE SUM OF TEN NUMBERS.
BEGIN     BALR  11,0
          USING *,11
          LA    9,CZERO LOAD THE ADDRESS OF CZERO IN REGISTER 9
          LA    8,10    LOAD 10 INTO REGISTER 8
          SR    12,12
LOOP      A     12,0(9) ADD A NEW VALUE
          LA    9,4(9)  UPDATE THE ADDRESS OF NEXT VALUE
          BCT   8,LOOP  LOOP FOR CALCULATING SUM
          ST    12,ANS  STORE ANSWER
DUMP      DC    X'82000000'  THIS INSTRUCTION CAUSES A DUMP
ANS       DS    F
CZERO     DC    F'1,4,9,16,25,36,49,64,81,100'
          END
/*
//GO.SYSUDUMP DD SYSOUT=A
//
```

Fig. C.1 Program to find the sum of ten numbers.

(such as shown in Fig. C.2). For convenience, we divide the following interpretation into four parts. In many cases, Part I is all that is needed to pinpoint the bug.

Part I

Its purpose is to find out when the ABEND occurred. This part consists of the following steps:

Step 1. From the first line in Fig. C.2(a) showing page 0001 of the dump, find the name of the step being executed at the time of the ABEND; it is the GO step (that is, during the execution).

Step 2. From the second line in Fig. C.2(a) showing page 0001 of the dump, get the task completion code. There are two possibilities:

a) The dump is invoked by the operating system. Read the meaning of the system completion code in Table C.1 or from IBM Messages and Code Manual (Form C28–6631).

Table C.1 Interruption codes due to a program interrupt

Interruption code (in decimal)	Interruption cause	Remarks
1	Operation	No such operation code
2	Privileged operation	The operation code can be executed only in the supervisor mode.
3	Execute	Misuse of the Execute instruction.

Table C.1 (*continued*)

Interuption code (in decimal)	Interruption cause	Remarks
4	Protection	See Section 15.8.
5	Addressing	Address is outside the limits of available storage on the computer used.
6	Specification	An operand specified in an instruction is invalid: a) Boundary alignment; b) Floating-point registers 1, 3, 5, or 7 through 15 is specified; c) Register operand address is odd in D, DR, M, and MR instructions; d) Branch to an odd address.
7	Data	When CVB instruction is used, the operand is not in the packed decimal format.
8	Fixed-point overflow	Result is too large to be expressed in 32 bits.
9	Fixed-point divide	a) Binary integer division by zero; b) Quotient too large to be expressed in 32 bits; c) Result from a CVB instruction too large to be expressed in 32 bits.
10	Decimal overflow	Overflow occurs in the addition or subtraction of two packed decimal numbers.
11	Decimal divide	Quotient in packed decimal is too large.
12	Exponent overflow	The floating-point result is equal to or larger than 16^{64}.
13	Exponent underflow	The floating-point result is equal to or smaller than 16^{-64}.
14	Significance	The floating-point operation yields an all-zero fraction.
15	Floating-point divide	Floating-point division by zero.

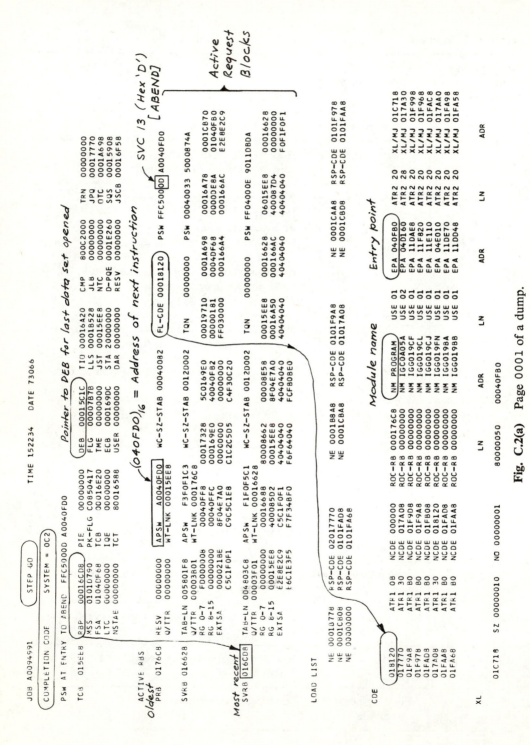

Fig. C.2(a) Page 0001 of a dump.

```
017A30    SZ  00000010    ND  00000001    800006A0    0004D160
01F998    SZ  00000010    ND  00000001    80000120    0011DAE8
01F968    SZ  00000010    ND  00000001    80000040    0011F820
01FAC8    SZ  00000010    ND  00000001    80000110    0011E110
017AA0    SZ  00000010    ND  00000001    80000078    0004E010
01FA98    SZ  00000010    ND  00000001    80000190    0011DE70
01FA58    SZ  00000010    ND  00000001    80000128    0011D048
```

Data Extent Blocks For Open Data Sets

DEB ← SYSUDUMP

Address of DCB   Start of DEB

```
015BE0                                                                                    *0S..............8.*
015C00   00000B06  0011E110  0000080B  00000000   00000000  00002BE0  0011F820             *...............Y*
015C20   10000000  C800000B  8F000000  01000000   7800000D  CF04E7A0  0601EFE8  33001E6C   *....H.......X...8.*
015C40   00010001  00000000  0000000D  C2C2C2C1   C6D5C3D1  020158F8  3D3C3C6  00000000    *BBBAFNCJCLCF....*
015C60   00000000  00000000  00000000  00000000   C3D3C3C6          8...8C0008129*
```

Address of next DEB (Last one since address = 0)

```
TIOT  JOB  A0094991  STEP GO            PROC  STEP1
      DD              14040140  PGM=*.DD      007E0D00  80001B7C
      DD              14040140  SYSUDUMP      00711600  80001E6C
      DD              14040100  SYSIN         00711B00  80001974
```

DATA MANAGEMENT CONTROL BLOCKS

```
MSS        ********** SPQE **********               ************** DQE ************** ******* FQE *******
           FLGS  NSPQE        SPID   DQE            BLK       FQE       LN       NDQE     NFQE      LN

010D790    00    01E298       251    013A3C8        00040800  0004E0800 0000800 0000000  0000000   00000780
01E298     00    01CC00       252    01D398         0004E088  0004E088  00017660 00017660 0004E088  00000718
                                                                                          0000000   00000010
01CC00     CO    000000       000    01CCB8         0004D000  0004D000  0000800  0000000  0000000   00000160
01CCB8     60    000000       000    01CCC8         0004D800  0004D800  0000800  0000000
                                                                                          0000000   00000730
```

```
D-PQE  0001E260  FIRST 0001C750  LAST 0001C750
PQE    01C750    FFB 0004D000    LFB 0004D000    NPQ 00000000   PPQ 00000000
                 TCB 0001A698    RSI 0000E000    RAD 00040800   FLG 0000

FBQE   041000    NFB 0001C750    PFB 0001C750    SZ 0000C000
```

QCB TRACE

```
MAJ  01EEA8   NMAJ  0001D380   PMAJ  0000A0C8   FMIN  0001EAE8   NM   SYSDSN
MIN  018200   FQEL  00018288   PMIN  000182F0   NMIN  000181E0   NM FF  SYS1.MACLIB
              NQEL  0001D6E8   PQEL  80018288   TCB   0001A698   SVRB 00016460
MIN  017EA8   FQEL  000180A8   PMIN  000181E0   NMIN  00018158   NM FF  USER.MACRO
              NQEL  0001C708   PQEL  80018A0A8   TCB   0001A698   SVRB 00016460
```

Fig. C.2(b)   Page 0002 of a dump.

```
MAJ 0175E8    NMAJ 00000000    PMAJ 0001D380    FMIN 000175D0    NM SYSIEA01
MIN 017500    FQEL 000175C0    PMIN 000175E8    NMIN 00000000    NM CO IEA
              NQEL 00000000    PQEL 000175D0    TCB 00015EE8    SVRB 00016CD8

SAVE AREA TRACE

INTERRUPT AT 040FD0
                       ← Contents in registers

( REGS AT ENTRY TO ABEND )

FLTR 0-6   0000000000000000   0000000000000000   0000000000000000   C1F0F0F9F7F2F8F9
REGS 0-7   FD000008  0004DFF8   00017328  5C0169E0   00019710  0001A698   0001CB70
REGS 8-15  00000000  0004DFFC   000169E0  4004DFB2   00000181  0004DF68   0000DE8A  0104DFB0
```

Register 12 contains the answer in hex. $(181)_{16} = (385)_{10}$

```
LOAD MODULE  PROGRAM        ← Instruction causing ABEND

040FA0   05804190  B0224180  000A1BCC  5AC90000
040FC0   41990004  4680B00A  50C0B01E  82000000   00000181  00000001  00000009
040FEC   00000010  00000019  00000024  00000031   00000040  00000051  00000064  00005880

LOAD MODULE  IGCOA05A

040160   41930D099  1B114313  0001A481  41330001   95FF3000  47806068  18EE18FF  18001811   *...........................*
040180   43E30030   43030001  8CE00004  88F0001C   8C000004  8810001C  1A2044E0  6070A1AE   *.T..............F..O..J...*
0401A0   41818001   44F06076  F84D0069  D069CC07   D0696CC6  41FFF001  44F0607C  418F8004   *.....0..8....0..-.0..J...*
0401C0   41353003   47F06010  41330001  47F060E2   D2008000  D2008000  D2008000  D2008000   *....0.....0.S.K..K..K..K.*
0401E0   D0695050   D08C5000  D12094FC  D1235800   D1201A10  5800D120  41110003  50100064   *.&....J.......J..J.......*
040200   54FCD067   D703D06C  18005D00  54006290   19014780  60BC1810  4010D06C  58100064   *...P....J...........J....*
040220   4A1DD0DC   1B005D00  66784000  D06A1211   47706110  4810006A  12114770  60E85850   *......J............J..Y..*
040240   D08C5860   D12407F5  41200121  45806236   58200120  413062C4  48A0D06A  48A0D06C   *J...J.5..J.....J..D..J..J*
040260   68A00002   45B0623E  46A06104  96400112   45506204  94BFD112  47F060DE  18A15810   *.......J..J..O..J..J.....*
040280   D1204810   D06C5010  D0704120  D07145B0   62364810  D06C8810  00011A31  58200120   *J....J...J..J..J.........*
0402A0   45B0623E   5020D120  9640D112  455062DA   94BFD112  4810006C  12114770  61984700   *..J..J.O..J..J.....J.....*
0402C0   6158411D   0001191A  47B061A6  D06E1211   10002000  D06C46A0  4810D006  4810D06E   *.....N...J..J..J...N.....*
0402E0   41110001   4010006E  41220020  50200120   46A0615E  47F061B0  18114410  D06C46A0   *.........&..J....J..J....*
040300   D0704120   D07148D0  D06E0610  12114770   58100120  4800D006  89000005  18105010   *.J..J..J..........M......*
040320   D20CD0AA   62229640  D1124550  62DA94BF   D120D701  D06ED06E  41306294  4580623E   *K....O.J....J.P.J..M.K...*
040340   6190D204   005F6290  41306297  45B0623E   9260D0AB  58100120  58106678  50100070   *.K....J...J..K......J..O.*
040360   41200071   4130629A  45B0623E  D2000DB2   62A247F0  61664130  62B04F0  65744180   *.J.....J..K...S.0...J....*
040380   D0995FFF   30004780  627C1800  43030000   1B114313  00011A80  44106284  F384D070   *.R....K....O.......K..3.J*
0403A0   C0700C07   D0702C2B  41111001  410628A   41330001  422000A4  47F06228  41330001   *.....J........F.....O.3..*
0403C0   07FB0040   D200D070  20000200  80000070   FFFFFFE0  0802FFFC  02FF1302  FFD3C905   *..K.J.......0.W...0...LIN*
0403E0   C5E24DE2   C1C4C540  C1E240C1  C2D6E5C5   0002FF09  03120318  03240330  03390342   *ES SAME AS ABOVE....K..K.*
040400   034303FF   0903FF12  03FF1803  FF2403FF   3003FF39  03FF4203  FF0998F0  D08012EE   *...0....K.....0....0..0..*
040420   4780310    D27CF000  D09441FF  007D50F0   08044441F  00701910  47006330  D08012EE   *.....K..O.K....0.....O..0*
040440   09902203   F000D090  41FE0004  50FD0084   41100048  92201005  58F10008  58F0F030   *K.........0....K.0..1..0.*
040460   05EF4110   D004858F0  10085BF0  E03405EF   41100001  4800D05C  9560D098  47406348   *..........0........0.....*
```

Fig. C.2(c) Page 0003 of a dump.

b) The dump is caused by the user's task through the execution of an ABEND or SNAP macro. Read the meaning of code from the user's guide or the documentation for the program. (SNAP macro will be explored in the next section.)

In our particular example, the dump was invoked by the operating system. The message SYSTEM = OC2 indicates that the interruption code number is 2, which means that a privileged instruction is asked to be executed in the problem state, an illegal operation.

Step 3. Take a look at the contents of each of the 16 general registers. The hexadecimal numbers represent the contents during the interrupt; they should be carefully checked. These contents appear just before the first load module (see Fig. C.2c, page 528 which presents page 0003 of the dump). Note that register 12 contains the correct answer $(181)_{16}$, or $(385)_{10}$.

Part 2

Its purpose is to locate what module was executed at the time of dump: Is it your program or a system code, such as a SVC? Under the heading of ACTIVE RBS (active request blocks)† on page 526 (i.e., page 0001 of the dump), check if it has the following three active RB's: PRB, SVRB, and SVRB. If so, then it is highly probable that the user's program has caused the ABEND. We shall assume this is the case in the following interpretation.

Step 1. In the first listed RB on page 526 (this is the oldest or the third most recent request block), find the flags and contents directory element (FL–CDE) field.

In Fig. C.2(a), the oldest RB is the PRB (program request block). The FL–CDE contains 018120, which is the pointer to the contents directory element (CDE on the same page) for the load module.

Step 2. The CDE contains the name (NM) field and the entry-point address (EPA) to this load module.

In Fig. C.2(a), the NM is PROGRAM and its entry-point address (EPA) is 040FB0.

Part 3.

The following two steps are used to determine what instruction in the user's program caused the ABEND.

Step 1. Look at the ABEND program status word (APSW) field of the PRB, which contains the right-half of the PSW at the time of the ABEND. This is the address of the next instruction to be executed. In Fig. C.2(a), it is 040FD0.

Note: In this step, the APSW address may be outside the range of the user's program or it may be 000000. In either case, some unexpected branch has taken place.

Case 1. APSW address is outside the range of the user's program, but not 000000. Examine

---

† A request block (RB) records the status of the interrupted module so that its execution can be later resumed on the return of the control. Whenever control is dynamically transferred to another module, an RB is automatically created.

```
LCC    OBJECT CODE   ADDR1 ADDR2   STMT   SOURCE STATEMENT

                                      1    *        THIS IS A SAMPLE PROGRAM
                                      2    *        FOR CALCULATING THE SUM OF TEN NUMBERS.
000000 05B0                           3    BEGIN    BALR  11,0
000002                                4             USING *,11
000002 4190 3022          00024       5             LA    9,CZERO  LOAD THE ADDRESS OF CZERO IN REGISTER 9
000006 4180 000A          0000A       6             LA    8,10     LOAD 10 INTO REGISTER 8
00000A 1BCC                           7             SR    12,12
00000C 5AC9 0000          00000       8    LOOP     A     12,0(9)  ADD A NEW VALUE
000010 4199 0004          00004       9             LA    9,4(9)   UPDATE THE ADDRESS OF NEXT VALUE
000014 4680 B00A          0000C      10             BCT   8,LOOP   LOOP FOR CALCULATING SUM
000018 50C0 B01E          00020      11             ST    12,ANS   STORE ANSWER
00001C 82000000                      12    DUMP     DC    X'82000000'  THIS INSTRUCTION CAUSES A DUMP
000020                               13    ANS      DS    F
000024 00000001J0000004              14    CZERO    DC    F'1,4,9,16,25,36,49,64,81,100'
                                     15             END
```

Fig. C.3   Assembly listing of a program.

the contents in register 14 listed just in front of the load module for the problem program. By convention (Chapter 5), this is the return address; the associated instruction has led to the instruction causing the ABEND.

Case 2. APSW address is 000000. Look at the third line on page 526 The rightmost six bytes of the PSW AT ENTRY TO ABEND contain the address of the instruction next to the one causing the ABEND.

Step 2. Obtain the relative address of this instruction:

$$\begin{array}{ll} 040FD0 & \\ 040FB0 & - \leftarrow \quad \text{From CDE or the loader map} \\ \hline 20 & \leftarrow \quad \text{Relative address of the next} \\ & \qquad \text{instruction to be executed} \end{array}$$

Step 3. Look for the instruction right behind the erroneous one which caused the interrupt. From the assembler listing (Fig. C.3), this instruction (at location counter 000020) is as follows:

                    ANS   DS   F

Step 4. The invalid instruction is then

                DUMP   DC   X'82000000'

and the bug is found: 82 is the operation code for a privileged instruction.

   Note: In Fig. C.1, the following job control card is used:

          //GO.SYSUDUMP   DD   SYSOUT=A

which does not give a dump of the nucleus area. If this dump is required, replace the above control card by the following:

          //GO.SYSABEND   DD   SYSOUT=A

The resulting dump will consist of nucleus area and the program area.

C.3 DEBUGGING WITH THE SNAP MACRO

In an assembler language program, the system macro SNAP can be written to help debug the program. The macro causes the control program to dump some or all of the main storage areas assigned to the current job step. Any portion of the control program can be also dumped. Right after the dump, *normal execution will continue.* In practical applications, many SNAP macro instructions may be scattered in one assembler language program.

   You should supply a data set to contain the dump. You must open this data set and specify a DCB macro for this data set. The following operands must be given in the DCB macro:

    DSORG=PS,MACRF=(W),RECFM=VBA,LRECL=125,BLKSIZE=882(or BLKSIZE=1632),
    DDNAME= any name except SYSUDUMP or SYSABEND.

```
//A711    JOB   (UNH,T117),KUO,MSGLEVEL=1,CLASS=G,TIME=5
//STEP1 EXEC ASMFCLG
//ASM.SYSIN DD *
SNAPSHOT CSECT
          SAVE    (14,12),,*
          BALR    11,0
          USING   *,11
LOC1      L       4,=A(THERE)
LOC5      L       6,=A(THERE-HERE)
          ST      6,LOC3
LOC2      ST      4,LOC4
HERE      OPEN    (SNAPDCB,OUTPUT)
*
* THE FOLLOWING MACRO WILL DUMP THE CONTENTS OF REGISTERS,
* PSW, AND YOUR PROGRAM.  IT ALSO PRINT ID NUMBER AS 1.
*
          SNAP    DCB=SNAPDCB,ID=1,PDATA=(REGS,JPA,PSW)
*
* THE FOLLOWING MACRO WILL DUMP A SECTION OF STORAGE OF THIS PROGRAM
* FROM LOC1 TO LOC2. IT ALSO PRINT ID NUMBER AS 2.
          SNAP    DCB=SNAPDCB,ID=2,STORAGE=(LOC1,LOC2)
*
* THE FOLLOWING MACRO WILL DUMP THE SYSTEM NUCLEUS
*
          SNAP    DCB=SNAPDCB,ID=3,SDATA=(ALL)
*
* THE FOLLOWING MACRO WILL DUMP THE CONTENTS OF ALL LOAD MODULES
* EXCEPT YOUR PROGRAM.  ID = 4.
*
          SNAP    DCB=SNAPDCB,ID=4,PDATA=(REGS,LPA,PSW)
*
* THE FOLLOWING MACRO WILL DUMP A LIST. THE STARTING AND FINAL
*  LOCATIONS ARE LISTED IN LIST1 BELOW.
*
          SNAP    DCB=SNAPDCB,ID=5,LIST=LIST1
*
THERE     CLOSE   (SNAPDCB)
          RETURN  (14,12)
LOC3      DS      F
LOC4      DS      F
* THE NEXT 4 STATEMENTS INVOLVE THE DUMP OF A LIST OF ADDRESSES
LIST1     DC      X'00'     X'00' INDICATES THE START
          DC      AL3(LOC5) START WITH LOC5
          DC      X'80'     X'80' INDICATES THE END
          DC      AL3(LOC2) ENDS WITH LOC2
SNAPDCB   DCB     DSORG=PS,RECFM=VBA,MACRF=(W),BLKSIZE=882,LRECL=125,    X
                  DDNAME=SNAPDUMP,DEVD=PR
          END
/*
//GO.SNAPDUMP  DD  SYSOUT=A
```

Fig. C.4   Applications of SNAP macros.

An example of the required DCB macro is shown in Fig. C.4. Its *dcbname* is arbitrarily taken as SNAPDCB.

If you wish to dump the contents of all registers, PSW and your own program, and you wish to identify the dump as ID=001, the following SNAP macro may be used (Fig. C.4):

```
SNAP  DCB=SNAPDCB,ID=1,PDATA=(REGS,JPA,PSW)
```

The time of the day and the date of execution are also printed.

As second example, the following SNAP macro will dump the contents of your own program from the symbolic location LOC1 to LOC2:

```
SNAP  DCB=SNAPDCB,ID=2,STORAGE=(LOC1,LOC2)
```

This dump will be printed out with an identification number ID=002.

As the third example, the following SNAP macro will dump the contents of the necleus area (a part of the SYSABEND dump):

```
SNAP  DCB=SNAPDCB,ID=3,SDATA=(ALL)
```

This dump is about 70 pages long.

As the final example, the following SNAP macro will dump a list of addresses starting with X'00', and ending with X'80' (see Fig. C.4):

```
SNAP  DCB=SNAPDCB,ID=5,LIST=LIST1
```

In Fig. C.4, the program is written in assembler language. The SNAP macro also may be used in an assembler language subroutine, which is called by a main program written in a high-level language. A typical example is shown in Fig. C.5.

```
//A711    JOB  (UNH,T117),KUO,MSGLEVEL=1,CLASS=G,TIME=5
//STEPA  EXEC ASMFC
//ASM.SYSIN DD *
SSNAP      CSECT
           SAVE    (14,12),,*
           BALR    11,0
           USING   *,11
           L       3,0(1)   POINTER TO VALUE I GOES TO R3
           L       4,4(1)   POINTER TO VALUE J GOES TO R4
           L       5,8(1)   POINTER TO VALUE IANS GOES TO R5
           L       6,0(3)   VALUE I GOES TO R6
           A       6,0(4)   SUM IN R6
           ST      6,0(5)   SUM GOES TO IANS
           OPEN    (DCBSNAP,OUTPUT)
           SNAP    DCB=DCBSNAP,ID=71,PDATA=(ALL)
           CLOSE   (DCBSNAP)
           RETURN  (14,12)
DCBSNAP    DCB     DSORG=PS,RECFM=VBA,MACRF=(W),BLKSIZE=882,LRECL=125,   X
                   DDNAME=SNAPDUMP,DEVD=PR
           END
/*
//STEPMAIN  EXEC FORTGCLG
//FORT.SYSIN  DD *
C       THIS IS A FORTRAN MAIN PROGRAM
        READ(5,11) I,J
   11 FORMAT(2I3)
        CALL SSNAP(I,J,IANS)
        WRITE(6,12) I,J,IANS
   12 FORMAT(3I10)
        CALL EXIT
        END
/*
//GO.SNAPDUMP DD SYSOUT=A
//GO.SYSIN    DD *
   5  7
/*
//
```

Fig. C.5   FORTRAN main program calls the control section SSNAP.

BIBLIOGRAPHY

System/360 Operating System: Messages and Codes, Form C28-6631, IBM Corp.

System/360 Operating System: Control Blocks, Form C28-6628, IBM Corp.

System/360 Operating System: Programmer's Guide to Debugging, Form C28-6670, IBM Corp.

System/360 Operating System: Supervisor and Data Management Macro Instructions, Form C28-6647. Complete description of the SNAP macro.

"Interpreting an OS/360 MVT Dump," Programming Procedures Series, No. PP-12, Information Processing Center, Massachusetts Institute of Technology.

Job Control Cards Used in all Examples

In order to run a program on an IBM System/370 or System/360, you normally submit the following three items:

1. Job control cards.
2. Source deck(s) or object deck(s).
3. Data, if any.

The detailed arrangement of these cards, known as the deck setup, is vital to a successful run. Table D.1 presents the required deck setup at a particular 370/360 installation to obtain final answers for each example used in Chapters 1 through 12. The catalogued procedure FORTASM used in Fig. D.1(a) is listed in Fig. D.4. If your installation does not have this procedure, you can use the alternative setup as shown in Fig. D.1(b).

The job control cards required for each example in Chapters 13 and 14 are shown in the text where the associated assembler language program appears. Note that some details may vary from one computer installation to another, as discussed in Section 1.7.

Table D.1 Deck setup for Examples used in Chapters 1 through 12

Assembler language program			The calling program in high-level language		Use the deck setup shown in	
Subroutine name or other identification	Figure number	Chapter and section	High-level language used	Figure number	Figure number	Chapter and section
Unnamed control section	1.17	1.6	—	—	1.20	1.7
Subroutine ARITH	5.20	5.6	FORTRAN COBOL PL/I	5.17 5.18 5.19	D.1 D.2 D.3	Appendix D
S410B S413B S413C S415	5.24 5.25 5.26 5.27	5.7	FORTRAN	5.23	D.1	Appendix D
FLOFIX	5.32	5.8	FORTRAN	5.31	D.1	Appendix D
SHUFFL	7.15	7.7	FORTRAN	7.12	D.1	Appendix D
ARITH1,ADD	8.7 8.8	8.6	FORTRAN COBOL PL/I	5.17† 5.18† 5.19†	D.1 D.2 D.3	Appendix D
RECORD, LENGTH	8.12 8.13	8.7	FORTRAN	8.10	D.1	Appendix D
S410B (Multicontrol sections)	8.15	8.8	FORTRAN	5.23	D.1	Appendix D
S410B, etc. (intermix)	8.16	8.8	FORTRAN	5.23	D.1	Appendix D
RECORD (internal linkage)	8.17	8.8	FORTRAN	8.10	D.1	Appendix D
S410B (using DSECT)	8.20	8.9	FORTRAN	8.18	D.1	Appendix D
Using macro SECTION	9.7	9.3	—	—	13.19(b)	13.11

Table D.1 (*continued*)

Assembler language program			The calling program in high-level language		Use the deck setup shown in	
Subroutine name or other identification	Figure number	Chapter and section	High-level language used	Figure number	Figure number	Chapter and section
Testing macro CONTROL	9.8	9.3	—	—	13.19(b)	13.11
Using macro SELECT	9.9	9.3	—	—	13.19(b)	13.11
SQBAL	9.13	9.3	FORTRAN PL/I COBOL	9.10 9.11 9.12	D.1 D.3 D.2	Appendix D
KEYMC	9.14(a) and 9.15	9.4	FORTRAN PL/I COBOL	9.16 9.17 9.18	D.1 D.2 D.3	Appendix D
Using macro EVAL	9.20	9.5	—	—	13.19(b)	13.11
Using macro LOOP1	9.22	9.6	—	—	13.19(b)	13.11
Using macro STORAREA	9.23	9.6	—	—	13.19(b)	13.11
Using macro MOVEBYTE	9.24	9.7	—	—	13.19(b)	13.11
Using macro FIBO	9.25	9.7	—	—	13.19(b)	13.11
Using macro BOOLE	9.27	9.8	—	—	13.19(b)	13.11
Using macro TRUTH	9.28	9.9	—	—	13.19(b)	13.11
Using macro TYPE	9.29	9.10	—	—	13.19(b)	13.11
Using macro LEVEL1	9.30	9.11	—	—	13.19(b)	13.11

Table D.1 (*continued*)

Assembler language program			The calling program in high-level language		Use the deck setup shown in	
Subroutine name or other identification	Figure number	Chapter and section	High-level language used	Figure number	Figure number	Chapter and section
Subroutine CONVER	10.5	10.4	FORTRAN	10.6	D.1	Appendix D
CHGST	10.9	10.4	FORTRAN	10.6‡	D.1	Appendix D
ISLAND	10.21	10.7	FORTRAN COBOL PL/I	10.17 10.18 10.19	D.1 D.2 D.3	Appendix D
ISLAND (version 2)	11.12	11.3	FORTRAN COBOL PL/I	10.17 10.18 10.19	D.1 D.2 D.3	Appendix D
EDIT	11.26	11.8	FORTRAN COBOL PL/I	10.27 10.29 10.28	D.1 D.2 D.3	Appendix D
ISLAND (version 3)	11.30	11.8	FORTRAN COBOL PL/I	10.17 10.18 10.19	D.1 D.2 D.3	Appendix D
CLOCK	11.32	11.8	FORTRAN	11.33	D.1	Appendix D
ISLAND (version 4)	11.36	11.9	FORTRAN COBOL PL/I	10.17 10.18 10.19	D.1 D.2 D.3	Appendix D
ILOAT	12.19	12.10	FORTRAN COBOL PL/I	12.16 12.17 12.18	D.1 D.2 D.3	Appendix D
SQAB	12.25	12.11	FORTRAN COBOL PL/I	12.21 12.22 12.23	D.1 D.2 D.3	Appendix D

† In the CALL statement in Figs. 5.17, 5.18, and 5.19, replace the subroutine name ARITH by ARITH1.

‡ In the CALL statement in Fig. 10.6, replace the subroutine name CONVEX by CHGST.

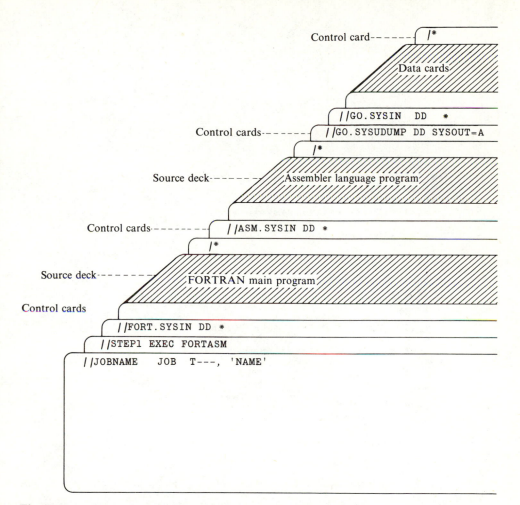

Control card ------ $/*$

Data cards

Control cards ------ $//GO.SYSIN$ DD $*$
$//GO.SYSUDUMP$ DD $SYSOUT=A$
$/*$

Source deck ------ Assembler language program

Control cards ------ $//ASM.SYSIN$ DD $*$
$/*$

Source deck ------ FORTRAN main program

Control cards
$//FORT.SYSIN$ DD $*$
$//STEP1$ $EXEC$ $FORTASM$
$//JOBNAME$ JOB $T---,$ $'NAME'$

Fig. D.1(a)   A sample set of job control cards for a FORTRAN main program and sub-routine(s) in assembler language. (*Note:* You can also use those shown in Fig. D.1b.)

```
//A711   JOB   (UNH,T117),KUO,MSGLEVEL=1,CLASS=G,TIME=5
//STEPA   EXEC   ASMFC
//ASM.SYSIN DD *
   ***********************************
   *                                 *
   *     ASSEMBLER LANGUAGE SOURCE DECK   *
   *                                 *
   ***********************************
/*
//STEPB  EXEC   FORTGCLG
//FORT.SYSIN DD *
   ***********************************
   *                                 *
   *        FORTRAN MAIN PROGRAM DECK    *
   *                                 *
   ***********************************
/*
//GO.SYSUDUMP   DD   SYSCUT=A
//GO.SYSIN DD *
   ***********************************
   *                                 *
   *    DATA  ( IF ANY)              *
   *                                 *
   ***********************************
/*
//
```

Fig. D.1(b)   Setup of control cards for FORTRAN main program and subroutine(s) in assembler language.

```
//A711  JOB  (UNH,T117),KUO,MSGLEVEL=1,CLASS=G,TIME=5
//STEP1 EXEC COBFC,PARM.COB='LOAD,NODECK,LIST'
//COB.SYSIN  DD    *
    **************************************
    *                                    *
    *   COBOL MAIN PROGRAM SOURCE DECK    *
    *                                    *
    **************************************
/*
//STEP2 EXEC ASMFCLG
//ASM.SYSIN DD *
    **************************************
    *                                    *
    * ASSEMBLER LANGUAGE SOURCE DECK(S) *
    *                                    *
    **************************************
/*
//* THE NEXT TWO CARDS ARE USED FOR FIGURES 12.17 & 12.22 ONLY
//LKED.SYSLIB DD DSN=SYS1.COBLIB,DISP=SHR
// DD DSN=ADMIN.COPYLIB,DISP=SHR
//* THE NEXT CARD IS USED FOR FIG. 12.22 ONLY
// DD DSN=SYS1.FORTLIB,DISP=SHR
//GO.PRINTER DD SYSOUT=A
//GO.SYSUDUMP DD SYSOUT=A
//GO.CARDIN DD *
    **************************************
    *                                    *
    *          DATA CARD(S), IF ANY       *
    *                                    *
    **************************************
/*
//
```

Fig. D.2   Setup of control cards for COBOL main program and subroutine(s) in assembler language.

```
//A711   JOB   (UNH,T117),KUO,MSGLEVEL=1,CLASS=G,TIME=5
//A EXEC PL1LFC,PARM.PL1L='ED,LD,L,NT,A,X,E'
//PL1L.SYSIN DD *
    *************************************
    *                                   *
    *     PL/I MAIN PROGRAM SOURCE DECK  *
    *                                   *
    *************************************
/*
//B EXEC ASMFCLG,PARM.ASM='LOAD,NODECK',PARM.LKED='XREF,LET,LIST'
//ASM.SYSIN DD *
    *************************************
    *                                   *
    *    ASSEMBLER LANGUAGE SOURCE DECK(S)*
    *                                   *
    *************************************
/*
//LKED.SYSLIB DD DSN=SYS1.PL1LIB,DISP=SHR
//GO.SYSUDUMP DD SYSOUT=A
//GO.SYSPRINT DD SYSOUT=A
//GO.SYSIN DD *
    *************************************
    *                                   *
    *          DATA CARD(S), IF ANY     *
    *                                   *
    *************************************
/*
//
```

Fig. D.3 Setup of control cards for PL/I main program and subroutine(s) in assembler language.

```
//FORT        EXEC  PGM=IEYFORT
//SYSLIN      DD    DSNAME=&LOADSET,DISP=(NEW,PASS),UNIT=SYSDA,
//                  SPACE=(TRK,(30,10),RLSE)
//SYSPRINT    DD    SYSOUT=A
//SYSPUNCH    DD    SYSOUT=B
//ASM         EXEC  PGM=IEUASM,PARM=(LOAD,NODECK)
//SYSGO       DD    DSNAME=&LOADSET,UNIT=SYSDA,SPACE=(80,(200,50),RLSE),
//                  DISP=(MOD,PASS),DCB=BLKSIZE=80
//SYSLIB      DD    DSNAME=SYS1.MACLIB,DISP=SHR
//            DD    DSNAME=USER.MACRO,DISP=SHR
//SYSPRINT    DD    SYSOUT=A
//SYSPUNCH    DD    SYSOUT=B
//SYSUT1      DD    DSN=&SYSUT1,UNIT=SYSDA,
//                  SPACE=(1700,(400,50),RLSE),DCB=BLKSIZE=1700
//SYSUT2      DD    DSN=&SYSUT2,UNIT=(SYSDA,SEP=SYSUT1),
//                  SPACE=(1700,(400,50),RLSE),DCB=BLKSIZE=1700
//SYSUT3      DD    DSN=&SYSUT3,UNIT=(SYSDA,SEP=(SYSUT1,SYSUT2)),
//                  SPACE=(1700,(400,50),RLSE),DCB=BLKSIZE=1700
//LKED        EXEC  PGM=IEWL,PARM=(XREF,LET,LIST),COND=(8,LE)
//SYSLIB      DD    DSNAME=SYS1.FORTLIB,DISP=SHR
//            DD    DSNAME=USER.SSPLIB,DISP=SHR
//SYSLIN      DD    DSNAME=&LOADSET,DISP=(OLD,DELETE)
//            DD    DDNAME=SYSIN
//SYSLMOD     DD    DSN=&GOSET(PROGRAM),UNIT=SYSDA,DISP=(MOD,PASS),
//                  SPACE=(7294,(7,2,1)),DCB=BLKSIZE=7294
//SYSPRINT    DD    SYSOUT=A
//SYSUT1      DD    DSN=&SYSUT1,UNIT=(SYSDA,SEP=(SYSLIN,SYSLMOD)),
//                  SPACE=(7294,(7,2),RLSE),DCB=BLKSIZE=7294
//GO          EXEC  PGM=*.LKED.SYSLMOD
//FT05F001    DD    DDNAME=SYSIN
//FT06F001    DD    SYSOUT=A
//FT07F001    DD    SYSOUT=B
//FT13F001    DD    DSN=&FT13F001,UNIT=SYSDA,SPACE=(TRK,(40,10),RLSE)
```

Fig. D.4   Procedure FORTASM.

Assembler Instructions

This appendix contains two tables of the assembler instructions, each in alphabetic order by the mnemonic codes. The first table lists the assembler instructions of most frequent occurrence. The second deals with these for special usage—in a macro definition or for a channel command word.

For each assembler instruction, an example is given to illustrate its usage. You should also consult the instruction description in the text for a particular assembler instruction. For your convenience, the reference section is also given.

Table E.1 Assembler instructions of most frequent occurence.

Name	Instruction op code	operand	Example and its meaning	Reference section
[sequence symbol]	CNOP	Two absolute expressions separated by a comma.	CNOP 0,4 It sets the location counter for the next instruction at the beginning of a fullword.	6.13
[sequence symbol]	COM	blank	COM It identifies and reserves a common area of main storage that may be referred to by *independent* assemblies that are linked and loaded for execution as a single program.	—
blank	COPY	a symbol	COPY ME It is used to copy source statements into an assembler language program, or to copy model statements and MEXIT, MNOTE, and conditional assembly instructions into a macro definition. ME identifies the section of coding to be copied from a library.	—
[any symbol]	CSECT	blank	ABLE CSECT It identifies the beginning or the continuation of the control section ABLE.	8.1, 8.8
[any symbol]	DC	one or more operands, separated by commas.	DC F'17' It defines a fullword constant; its value in decimal is 17.	6.10

Name	Operation	Operand	Description	Ref.
[sequence symbol]	DROP	one to 16 absolute expressions, separated by commas.	DROP 7,11 It prevents the assembler from using registers 7 and 11 for base addressing. They are no longer available to the assembler.	6.14
[any symbol]	DS	one or more operands, separated by commas.	DS 4CL10 It defines (reserves) four 10-byte fields.	6.12
set variable symbol or an ordinary symbol	DSECT	blank	USING INAREA,6 The dummy section INAREA : is written to generate INAREA DSECT addresses A and B using A DS CL10 register 6 without B DS CL20 allocating storage.	8.9
[sequence symbol]	EJECT	blank	EJECT It causes the next line of the assembly listing to appear at the top of a new page.	6.9
[sequence symbol]	END	[relocatable symbol]	END DECK3 It terminates the assembly of the program. When loading of the program is complete, the control is transferred to the instruction at DECK3.	5.5
[sequence symbol]	ENTRY	one or more relocatable symbols, separated by commas.	ENTRY EXPORT1,EXPORT2 It identifies linkage symbols EXPORT1 and EXPORT2 that are defined in this module but may be used by some other modules.	8.2

Table E.1 (*continued.*)

| Name | Instruction | | Example and its meaning | Reference section |
	op code	operand		
set variable symbol or an ordinary symbol	EQU	an absolute or relocatable expression.	REG7 EQU 7 The symbol REG7 is defined as a decimal number 7.	prob. 6.14(b)
[sequence symbol]	EXTRN	one or more relocatable symbols, separated by commas.	EXTRN IMPORT1, IMPORT2 It identifies the linkage symbols that are used by this module but defined in some other module of the same program.	8.2
blank	ICTL	one, two, or three decimal self-defining terms.	ICTL 20,80 It alters the normal format of a source program statement. Here, the column 20 replaces column 1 as the beginning column; column 80 replaces column 71 as the end column. It must precede all other cards.	—
blank	ISEQ	[two self-defined values separated by a comma]	ISEQ 73,80 It checks the sequence of input source statements. 73 and 80 are, respectively, the leftmost and rightmost columns to be checked. Checking begins with the first card after this ISEQ instruction; and terminates after an ISEQ instruction with a blank operand.	—
[any symbol]	LTORG	blank	LITABLE LTORG It generates all literals previously defined (but not generated) in the source module. The location of the first byte of the generated literal table is LITABLE.	8.8

Name	Sequence symbol	Operand	Description	Problem
ORG	[sequence symbol]	[a relocatable expression]	INAREA ORG *+DATA1+DATA2 — If the value of DATA1 is 60, the value of DATA2 is 80, and the current location counter setting is 1000 in decimal, this instruction reserves 140 bytes beginning at the location 1000. The location counter is set to 1140; the label INAREA is assigned an address 1140. You refer this 140-byte area by specifying INAREA-140 as an operand.	prob. 6.14(a)
PRINT	[sequence symbol]	one to three operands	PRINT DATA — DC XL131'00' — It requests all 131 bytes of zeros are printed in the assembly listing. Otherwise, only 8 bytes of zeros appear.	—
PUNCH	[sequence symbol]	one to 80 characters in quotes	PUNCH 'VOTE FOR ME' — It produces a punched card, with the message punched in columns 1 through 11. This card is in the object code output.	—
REPRO	[sequence symbol]	blank	REPRO — It reproduces the data on the following statement to be punched into a card. No processing of the data is involved.	—
SPACE	[sequence symbol]	a decimal self-defining term	SPACE 3 — It inserts three blank lines in the assembly listing.	—
START	[any symbol]	[a self-defining term]	BAKER START 100 — It defines the name of control section as BAKER, and sets the initial location counter as 100 in decimal.	6.4
TITLE	[symbol]	one to 100 characters in quotes.	BETA TITLE 'SECOND EDITION' — It provides the heading 'SECOND EDITION' for each page of the assembly listing. It also punches BETA into each output card (columns 73–76).	6.9
USING	[sequence symbol]	an absolute or relocatable expression followed by 1 to 16 absolute expressions.	USING *,7 — The assembler may *assume* that the current value of the location counter is the contents in register 7 at the object time.	6.14

Table E.2   Assembler instructions usually used in a macro definition or for a channel command word

Name	Instruction op code	Instruction operand	Example and its meaning	Reference section
blank	ACTR	a valid SETA expression	ACTR 50 It assigns a maximum count of 50 to the number of AGO and AIF branches executed with a macro definition or within the source program. ACTR stands for the conditional assembly loop counter.	—
[sequence symbol]	AGO	sequence symbol	AGO .CONTB It is an unconditional branch to .CONTB.	9.6
[sequence symbol]	AIF	a logical expression and a sequence symbol	AIF (T'&A EQ 'F').E1 If the type attribute of the symbol &A is the letter F, process the instruction immediately after the .E1 ANOP ANOP instruction.	9.6
sequence symbol	ANOP	blank		
[symbol]	CCW	code, address, flags, count	CCW 2,INAREA,X'48',80 Read in 80 bytes from a card reader into the main storage, starting the location INAREA.	15.3
blank	GBLA or GBLB or GBLC	one or more variable symbols.	GBLA &TYPE It declares that &TYPE is a global set symbol.	9.11

blank	LCLA or LCLB or LCLC	one or more variable symbols	LCLA &ABLE It declares that &ABLE is a local set symbol.	9.7, 9.11
blank	MACRO	blank	MACRO It indicates the beginning of a macro definition.	9.2
[sequence symbol]	MEND	blank	MEND It indicates the end of a macro definition.	9.2
[sequence symbol]	MEXIT	blank	MEXIT It terminates the processing of the macro definition.	9.8
[sequence symbol or variable symbol]	MNOTE	[a severity code and] a message in quotes.	.M5 MNOTE 'TYPE NOT H' It prints an error message as shown.	—
SETA symbol	SETA	an arithmetic expression	&A SETA 11 The symbol &A is set to 11.	9.7
SETB symbol	SETB	0, 1, or logical expression in quotes	&B1 SETB (L'&FROM EQ 4) The symbol &B1 is set to 0 or 1, depending on the statement is false or true.	9.8
SETC symbol	SETC	type attribute, character expression, substring notation, etc.	&C1 SETC 'ABCCBA' It assigns the character value ABCCBA to the SETC symbol &C1.	9.9

Detailed List of IBM System/370 and System/360 Instructions

This appendix contains a table of the machine instructions. It is in alphabetic order by the mnemonic codes. The extended mnemonic codes are not included as they are already shown in Table 4.5 (page 92). The notes associated with some of the column headings, the column for the condition code, and the column for the other pertinent information are as follows:

Explanatory Notes

1. Symbols used in an operand:
   - *R1*   The first operand is in a general register; it does not mean general register 1. *R2* and *R3* have similar meanings.
   - *FPR1*   The first operand is in a floating-point register.
   - *FPR2*   The second operand is in a floating-point register.
   - *S1*   The first operand is in main storage (specified by *D1* and *B1*).
   - *S2*   The second operand is in main storage (specified by *D2*, *B2*, and frequently *X2*).
   - C(*R1*)   Contents of the first operand (in a general register).
   - C(*R2*), C(*R3*), C(*FPR1*), C(*FPR2*), C(*S1*), C(*S2*) have similar meanings.
   - *I2*   8-bit immediate field of an SI instruction.
   - *M1*   4-bit mask field in an instruction.
   - PSW   Program status word in the format of basic control (BC) mode.
   - PSWEC   Program status word in the format of extended control (EC) mode.
2. The explicit operand format has its corresponding implicit format as follows:

Type	Explicit format	Implicit format
RR	*R1, R2*	—
RX	*R1, D2(X2, B2)*	*R1, S2(X2)*
	or *R1, D2(, B2)*	or *R1, S2*
RS	*R1, R2, D3(B3)*	*R1, R2, S3*
SI	*D1(B1), I2*	*S1, I2*
SS	*D1(L, B1), D2(B2)*	*S1(L), S2* or *S1, S2*
SS	*D1(L1, B1), D2(L2, B2)*	*S1(L1), S2(L2)* or *S1, S2*

3. *R1* ← C(*R1*) + C(*R2*) means "placement of the sum C(*R1*) + C(*R2*) in register *R1*."
   R1 ← C(PSW)$_{32-63}$ means "placement of the contents in bit positions 32–63 of PSW in register *R1*."
   → *S2* means "branch to the location *S2*."

4. Condition code settings

Condition code	0	1	2	3
Mask bits	8	4	2	1
a)	Answer = 0	Answer less than 0	Answer greater than 0	Overflow
b)	First operand = second op.	First operand is low	First operand is high	—
c)	Answer = 0; no carry	Answer ≠ 0; no carry	Answer = 0; carry	Answer ≠ 0; carry
d)	Answer = 0	Answer ≠ 0	—	—
e)	Answer = 0	Answer < 0	Answer > 0	—
f)	All inserted bits are zero, or mask is zero	First bit of the inserted field is one	First bit of the inserted field is zero	—
g)	First operand = second op.; or both fields have zero length	First operand is low	First operand is high	—
h)	Interrupt in a subchannel	CSW is stored	Burst mode is ended	Not operational
i)	First-operand and second-operand counts are same	First-operand count is low	First-operand count is high	No movement is performed due to destructive overlap
j)	Clock value is set	Clock value is secure	—	Clock is not operational
k)	I/O operation is initiated and channel is proceeding with execution	CSW is stored	Channel or subchannel is busy	Not operational
m)	Clock is in set state	Clock is in not-set state	Clock is in error state	Clock is not operational
n)	Channel ID is correctly stored	CSW is stored	Channel activity is prohibited storing ID	Not operational
p)	Available	Interrupt in channel	Operating in burst mode	Not operational
q)	All 1-bits in *I2* field match 0-bits in the byte tested or all mask bits are zeros	Some of the 1-bits in the mask match 0-bits in the byte tested	—	All the 1-bits in the mask have corresponding 1-bits in the byte tested
r)	All function bytes are zeros	Nonzero before the first operand is exhausted	Last function byte is nonzero	—
s)	Leftmost bit of byte specified is zero	Leftmost bit of byte specified is one	—	—
t)	—	Difference is not zero (no carry)	Difference is zero (carry)	Difference is zero (no carry)

5. Program interrupts:

A	Addressing	IK	Fixed-point divide
D	Data	LS	Significance
DF	Decimal overflow	M	Privileged operation
DK	Decimal divide	N	Monitoring
E	Exponent overflow	P	Protection
EX	Execute	S	Specification
FK	Floating-point divide	U	Exponent underflow
IF	Fixed-point overflow		

6. Available only if the protection feature is installed.
7. Available on System/370 only.
8. Available only if the decimal feature is installed; operands and results are in the packed decimal format.
9. Available only if the floating-point feature is installed; operands and the result are in floating-point form.
10. Result is normalized.
11. Result is unnormalized.
12. Long format floating-point instruction; each operand is 64 bits long (see Fig. 12.1b).
13. Floating-point instruction involving one or both operands using the extended-precision format (see Fig. 12.1c).
14. If the second operand is equal to zero, no branch takes place.
15. Only the rightmost six bits are used to define the length of the shift.
16. Condition code is loaded by the instruction.
17. Only the rightmost four bits in each byte are moved.
18. Only the leftmost four bits in each byte are moved.
19. The $R1$ and $R2$ fields each designate a pair of even-odd registers.
20. Starting with the control register $CR1$ specified by the $R1$ field and ending with the control register $CR3$ specified by the $R3$ field, the set of control registers is loaded from $S2$ field.
21. For details, see IBM System/360 Principle of Operations, Form GA22-6821.
22. For details, see IBM System/370 Principle of Operations, Form GA22-7000.

Name	Mnemonic code	Operands in explicit format[1,2]	Action[3]	Type	Numerical op. code	Cond. code	Exceptions[5]	Other pertinent information	Ref. section
Add	A	$R1, D2(X2,B2)$	$R1 \leftarrow C(R1) + C(S2)$	RX	5A	(4a)	P,A,S, IF		3.8
Add Double	AD	$R1, D2(X2,B2)$	$FPR1 \leftarrow C(FPR1) + C(S2)$	RX	6A	(4e)	P,A,S,U,E,LS	(9,10,12)	12.4
Add Double Register	ADR	$R1, R2$	$FPR1 \leftarrow C(FPR1) + C(FPR2)$	RR	2A	(4e)	S,U,E,LS	(9,10,12)	12.4
Add Floating	AE	$R1, D2(X2,B2)$	$FPR1 \leftarrow C(FPR1) + C(S2)$	RX	7A	(4e)	P,A,S,U,E,LS	(9,10)	12.4
Add Floating Register	AER	$R1, R2$	$FPR1 \leftarrow C(FPR1) + C(FPR2)$	RR	3A	(4e)	S,U,E,LS	(9,10)	12.4
Add Half-word	AH	$R1, D2(X2,B2)$	$R1 \leftarrow C(R1) + C(S2)_{0-15}$	RX	4A	(4a)	P,A,S, IF	(9,10)	3.10
Add Logical	AL	$R1, D2(X2,B2)$	$R1 \leftarrow C(R1) + C(S2)$	RX	5E	(4c)	P,A,S		prob. 7.16
Add Logical Register	ALR	$R1, R2$	$R1 \leftarrow C(R1) + C(R2)$	RR	1E	(4c)			prob. 7.16
Add Decimal	AP	$D1(L1,B1), D2(L2,B2)$	$S1 \leftarrow C(S1) + C(S2)$	SS	FA	(4a)	P,A, D, DF	(8)	11.2
Add Register	AR	$R1, R2$	$R1 \leftarrow C(R1) + C(R2)$	RR	1A	(4a)	S, IF		3.2
Add Unnormalized	AU	$R1, D2(X2,B2)$	$FPR1 \leftarrow C(FPR1) + C(S2)$	RX	7E	(4e)	P,A,S, E,LS	(9,10)	12.4
Add Unnormalized Register	AUR	$R1, R2$	$FPR1 \leftarrow C(FPR1) + C(FPR2)$	RR	3E	(4e)	S, E,LS	(9,10)	12.4
Add Double Unnormalized	AW	$R1, D2(X2,B2)$	$FPR1 \leftarrow C(FPR1) + C(S2)$	RX	6E	(4e)	P,A,S, E,LS	(9,12,11)	12.4
Add Double Unnormalized Register	AWR	$R1, R2$	$FPR1 \leftarrow C(FPR1) + C(FPR2)$	RR	2E	(4e)	S, E,LS	(9,12,11)	12.4
Add Extended	AXR	$R1, R2$	$[FPR1, FPR1 + 1] \leftarrow C(FPR1, FPR1 + 1) + C(FPR2, FPR2 + 1)$	RR	36	(4e)	S,U,E,LS	(9,10,13)	12.4
Branch and Link	BAL	$R1, D2(X2,B2)$	$R1 \leftarrow C(PSW)_{32-63};\ \rightarrow S2$	RX	45				(21)
Branch and Link Register	BALR	$R1, R2$	$R1 \leftarrow C(PSW)_{32-63};\ \rightarrow C(R2)$	RR	05			(14)	5.5, 8.3
Branch on Condition	BC	$M1, D2(X2,B2)$	$\rightarrow S2$ if $(MI)_{cc} = 1$	RX	47				4.6
Branch on Condition to Register	BCR	$M1, R2$	$\rightarrow C(R2)$ if $(MI)_{cc} = 1$	RR	07			(14)	4.6
Branch on Count	BCT	$R1, D2(X2,B2)$	$R1 \leftarrow C(R1) - 1;\ \rightarrow S2$ if $C(R1) \neq 0$	RX	46				4.7
Branch on Count to Register	BCTR	$R1, R2$	$R1 \leftarrow C(R1) - 1;\ \rightarrow C(R2)$ if $C(R1) \neq 0$	RR	06			(14)	(21)
Branch on Index High	BXH	$R1, R3, D2(B2)$	$R1 \leftarrow C(R1) + C(R3)$; If $R3$ is even, $\rightarrow S2$ if $C(R1) \leq C(R3 + 1)$ If $R3$ is odd, $\rightarrow S2$ if $C(R1) \leq C(R3)$	RS	86				prob. 8.13
Branch on Index Low or Equal	BXLE	$R1, R3, D2(B2)$	$R1 \leftarrow C(R1) + C(R3)$; If $R3$ is even, $\rightarrow S2$ if $C(R1) > C(R3 + 1)$ If $R3$ is odd, $\rightarrow S2$ if $C(R1) > C(R3)$	RS	87				prob. 8.15
Compare	C	$R1, D2(X2,B2)$		RX	59	(4b)	P,A,S		4.5
Compare Double	CD	$R1, D2(X2,B2)$		RX	69	(4b)	P,A,S	(9)	12.8
Compare Double Register	CDR	$R1, R2$		RR	29	(4b)	S		12.8
Compare Floating	CE	$R1, D2(X2,B2)$		RX	79	(4b)	P,A,S	(9)	12.8
Compare Floating Register	CER	$R1, R2$		RR	39	(4b)	S		12.8
Compare Logical	CL	$R1, D2(X2,B2)$		RX	55	(4b)	P,A,S	(9)	prob. 7.16

Name	Mnemonic code	Operands in explicit format[1,2]	Action[3]	Type	Numerical op. code	Cond. code	Exceptions[5]	Other pertinent information	Ref. section
Compare Logical Character	CLC	$D1(L,B1),D2(B2)$		SS	D5	(4b)	P,A		5.9
Compare Logical Immediate	CLI	$D1(B1),I2$		SI	95	(4b)	P,A		5.8
Compare Logical Long	CLCL	$R1,R2$	$C(R1,R1+1):C(R2,R2+1)$	RR	0F	(4g)	P,A,S	(7,19)	5.10
Compare Logical Characters Under Mask	CLM	$R1,M3,D2(B2)$		RS	BE	(4f)	P,A	(7)	(22)
Compare Logical Register	CLR	$R1,R2$		RR	15	(4b)	P,A		prob. 7.16
Compare Decimal	CP	$D1(L1,B1),D2(L2,B2)$		SS	F9	(4b)	P,A, D	(8)	11.2
Compare Register	CR	$R1,R2$		RR	19	(4b)			
Convert to Binary	CVB	$R1,D2(X2,B2)$	$R1$ (binary) $\leftarrow C(S2)_{0-63}$ (packed decimal)	RX	4F		P,A,S,D, IK		prob. 10.12
Convert to Decimal	CVD	$R1,D2(X2,B2)$	$S2_{0-63}$ (packed decimal) $\leftarrow C(R1)$ (binary)	RX	4E		P,A,S		10.6
Divide	D	$R1,D2(X2,B2)$	$R1 \leftarrow$ Rem. of $[C(R1),C(R1+1)]/C(S2)$, $R1+1 \leftarrow$ Quot. of $[C(R1),C(R1+1)]/C(S2)$	RX	5D		P,A,S, IK		3.9
Divide Double	DD	$R1,D2(X2,B2)$	$FPR1 \leftarrow C(FPR1)/C(S2)$	RX	6D		P,A,S,U,E,FK	(9,12)	12.7
Divide Double Register	DDR	$R1,R2$	$FPR1 \leftarrow C(FPR1)/C(FPR2)$	RR	2D		S,U,E,FK	(9,12)	12.7
Divide Floating	DE	$R1,D2(X2,B2)$	$FPR1 \leftarrow C(FPR1)/C(S2)$	RX	7D		P,A,S,U,E,FK	(9)	12.7
Divide Floating Register	DER	$R1,R2$	$FPR1 \leftarrow C(FPR1)/C(FPR2)$	RR	3D		S,U,E,FK	(9)	12.7
Divide Decimal	DP	$D1(L1,B1),D2(L2,B2)$	$S1 \leftarrow$ [quot. of $C(S1)/C(S2)$, rem. of $C(S1)/C(S2)$]	SS	FD		P,A,S,D, DK	(8)	11.2
Divide Register	DR	$R1,R2$	$R1 \leftarrow$ Rem. of $[C(R1),C(R1+1)]/C(R2)$, $R1+1 \leftarrow$ Quot. of $[C(R1),C(R1+1)]/C(R2)$	RR	1D		S, IK		3.9
Edit	ED	$D1(L,B1),D2(B2)$	$S1 \leftarrow C(S2)$	SS	DE	(4a)	P,A, D		11.4-11.8
Edit and Mark	EDMK	$D1(L,B1),D2(B2)$	$S1 \leftarrow C(S2)$. Reg. $1_{8-31} \leftarrow$ Addr. of 1st sig. digit	SS	DF	(4a)	P,A,S,		11.9
Execute	EX	$R1,D2(X2,B2)$	Execute instr. $C(S2)$, mod. by $C(R1)_{24-31}$	RX	44		P,A,S, EX		Lab.12.4
Halve Double	HDR	$R1,R2$	$FPR1 \leftarrow C(FPR2)/2$	RR	24		S	(9,12)	12.7
Halve	HER	$R1,R2$	$FPR1 \leftarrow C(FPR2)/2$	RR	34		S	(9)	12.7
Halt I/O	HIO	$D1(B1)$	Halt an I/O operation	SI	9E	(4h)	M		15.12
Insert Character	IC	$R1,D2(X2,B2)$	$R1_{24-31} \leftarrow C(S2)_{0-7}$	RX	43		P,A		prob. 5.11
Insert Characters Under Mask	ICM	$R1,M3,D2(B2)$	$R1 \leftarrow C(S2)$ for the byte positions corresponding to 1's in $M3$ field	RS	BF	(4f)	P,A	(7)	(22)
Insert Storage Key	ISK	$R1,R2$	$R1_{24-27} \leftarrow$ Stor. key of $C(R2)_{8-20}$	RR	09		M,A,S	(6)	15.8
Load	L	$R1,D2(X2,B2)$	$R1 \leftarrow C(S2)$	RX	58		P,A,S		4.2
Load Address	LA	$R1,D2(X2,B2)$	$R1_{8-31} \leftarrow S2$; $R1_{0-7} \leftarrow 0$	RX	41				4.4
Load Complement Double Register	LCDR	$R1,R2$	$FPR1 \leftarrow -C(FPR2)$	RR	23	(4e)	S	(9,12)	12.9
Load Complement Floating Register	LCER	$R1,R2$	$FPR1 \leftarrow -C(FPR2)$	RR	33	(4e)	S	(9)	12.9
Load Complement Register	LCR	$R1,R2$	$R1 \leftarrow -C(R2)$	RR	13	(4a)	IF		(21)
Load Control	LCTL	$R1,R3,D2(B2)$	$CR1, \ldots CR3 \leftarrow C(S2) \ldots$	RS	B7		M,P,A,S	(7,20)	(22)
Load Double	LD	$R1,D2(X2,B2)$	$FPR1 \leftarrow C(S2)$	RX	68		P,A,S	(9,12)	12.9
Load Double Register	LDR	$R1,R2$	$FPR1 \leftarrow C(FPR2)$	RR	28		S	(9,12)	12.9

Name	Mnemonic	Operands	Semantics	Type	Code	Note	Flags	Interrupts	Page
Load Floating	LE	RI, D2(X2, B2)	$FPRI \leftarrow C(S2)$	RX	78		P, A, S	(9)	12.9
Load Floating Register	LER	RI, R2	$FPRI \leftarrow C(FPR2)$	RR	38		S	(9)	12.9
Load Half-word	LH	RI, D2(X2, B2)	$RI_{16-31} \leftarrow C(S2)_{0-15}; RI_{0-15} \leftarrow C(S2)...$	RX	48		P, A, S		prob. 4.5
Load Multiple	LM	RI, R3, D2(B2)	$RI, ..., R3 \leftarrow C(S2)...$	RS	98		P, A, S		5.4
Load Negative Double Register	LNDR	RI, R2	$FPRI \leftarrow -|C(FPR2)|$	RR	21	(4e)	S		12.9
Load Negative Floating Register	LNER	RI, R2	$FPRI \leftarrow -|C(FPR2)|$	RR	31	(4e)	S		12.9
Load Negative Register	LNR	RI, R2	$RI \leftarrow -|C(R2)|$	RR	11	(4e)	S		(21)
Load Positive Double Register	LPDR	RI, R2	$FPRI \leftarrow |C(FPR2)|$	RR	20	(4e)	S		12.9
Load Positive Floating Register	LPER	RI, R2	$FPRI \leftarrow |C(FPR2)|$	RR	30	(4e)	S		12.9
Load Positive Register	LPR	RI, R2	$RI \leftarrow |C(R2)|$	RR	10	(4a)	S	IF	(21)
Load Register	LR	RI, R2	$RI \leftarrow C(R2)$	RR	18		S		prob. 4.4
Load Rounded (Extended to Long)	LRDR	RI, R2	$FPRI \leftarrow C(FPR2, FPR2 + I)$	RR	25		S, E	(9, 13)	12.9
Load Rounded (Long to Short)	LRER	RI, R2	$FPRI \leftarrow C(FPR2)$	RR	35		S, E	(9, 13)	12.9
Load and Test Double Register	LTDR	RI, R2	$FPRI \leftarrow C(FPR2)$	RR	22	(4e)	S	(9, 12)	12.9
Load and Test Floating Register	LTER	RI, R2	$FPRI \leftarrow C(FPR2)$	RR	32	(4e)	S	(9)	12.9
Load and Test Register	LTR	RI, R2	$RI \leftarrow C(R2)$	RR	12	(4e)	S		(21)
Load Program Status Word	LPSW	DI(BI)	$PSW \leftarrow C(SI)_{0-63}$	SI	82	(16)	M, P, A, S		15.5
Multiply	M	RI, D2(X2, B2)	$[RI, RI + I] \leftarrow C(RI + I) \times C(S2)$	RX	5C		P, A, S	(7)	3.8
Monitor Call	MC	DI(BI), I2	Causes a program interruption	SI	AF		S, N		15.9
Multiply Double	MD	RI, D2(X2, B2)	$FPRI \leftarrow C(FPRI) \times C(S2)$	RX	6C		P, A, S, U, E	(9, 12)	12.5
Multiply Double Register	MDR	RI, R2	$FPRI \leftarrow C(FPRI) \times C(FPR2)$	RR	2C		S, U, E	(9, 12)	12.5
Multiply Floating	ME	RI, D2(X2, B2)	$FPRI \leftarrow C(FPRI) \times C(S2)$	RX	7C		P, A, S, U, E	(9)	12.5
Multiply Foating Register	MER	RI, R2	$FPRI \leftarrow C(FPRI) \times C(FPR2)$	RX	3C		S, U, E	(9)	12.5
Multiply Half-word	MH	RI, D2(X2, B2)	$RI \leftarrow (C(RI) \times C(S2)_{0-15})_{16-47}$	RX	4C		P, A, S		prob. 3.12
Multiply Decimal	MP	DI(LI, BI), D2(L2, B2)	$SI \leftarrow C(SI) \times C(S2)$	SS	FC		P, A, S, D	(8)	11.2
Multiply Register	MR	RI, R2	$[RI, RI + I] \leftarrow C(RI + I) \times C(R2)$	RR	1C		S		3.8
Move Character	MVC	DI(L, BI), D2(B2)	$SI \leftarrow C(S2)$	SS	D2		S		5.3
Move Long	MVCL	RI, R2	$SI \leftarrow C(S2)$	RR	0E		P, A, S		5.11
Move Immediate	MVI	DI(BI), I2	$SI_{0-7} \leftarrow I2$	SI	92		P, A	(7)	5.2
Move Numerics	MVN	DI(L, BI), D2(B2)	$SI \leftarrow C(S2)$	SS	D1		P, A	(17)	11.3
Move with Offset	MVO	DI(LI, BI), D2(L2, B2)	$SI \leftarrow C(S2)$	SS	F1		P, A		11.3
Move Zones	MVZ	DI(L, BI), D2(B2)	$SI \leftarrow C(S2)$	SS	D3		P, A	(18)	10.7
Multiply (Extended)	MXR	RI, R2	$[FPRI, FPRI + I] \leftarrow C(FPRI, FPRI + I) \times C(FPR2, FPR2 + I)$	RR	26		S, E, U	(9, 10, 13)	12.5
Multiply (Long/Extended)	MXD	RI, D2(X2, B2)	$[FPRI, FPRI + I] \leftarrow C(FPRI, FPRI + I) \times C(S2)$	RX	67		S, E, U	(9, 10, 13)	12.5
Multiply (Long/Extended)	MXDR	RI, R2	$[FPRI, FPRI + I] \leftarrow C(FPRI, FPRI + I) \times C(FPR2, FPR2 + I)$	RR	27		S, E, U	(9, 10, 13)	12.5

Name	Mnemonic code	Operands in explicit format[1,2]	Action[3]	Type	Numerical op. code	Cond. code	Exceptions[5]	Other pertinent information	Ref. section
And	N	R1,D2(X2,B2)	R1 ← C(R1) AND C(S2)	RX	54	(4d)	P,A,S		7.3
And Character	NC	D1(L,B1),D2(B2)	S1 ← C(S1) AND C(S2)	SS	D4	(4d)	P,A		7.3
And Immediate	NI	D1(B1),I2	$S1_{0-7}$ ← $C(S1)_{0-7}$ AND I2	SI	94	(4d)	P,A		7.3
And Register	NR	R1,R2	R1 ← C(R1) AND C(R2)	RR	14	(4d)			7.3
Or	O	R1,D2(X2,B2)	R1 ← C(R1) OR C(S2)	RX	56	(4d)	P,A		7.4
Or Character	OC	D1(L,B1),D2(B2)	S1 ← C(S1) OR C(S2)	SS	D6	(4d)	P,A		7.4
Or Immediate	OI	D1(B1),I2	$S1_{0-7}$ ← $C(S1)_{0-7}$ OR I2	SI	96	(4d)	P,A		7.4
Or Register	OR	R1,R2	R1 ← C(R1) OR C(R2)	RR	16	(4d)			7.5
Pack	PACK	D1(L1,B1),D2(L2,B2)	S1 (packed dec.) ← C(S2) (zoned dec.)	SS	F2		P,A		prob. 10.10
Subtract	S	R1,D2(X2,B2)	R1 ← C(R1) − C(S2)	RX	5B	(4a)	P,A,S, IF	(7)	3.7
Set Clock	SCK	D1(B1)	Set the current value of time-of-day clock	SI	B2	(4j)	P,A,S,M		(22)
Subtract Double	SD	R1,D2(X2,B2)	FPR1 ← C(FPR1) − C(S2)	RX	6B	(4e)	P,A,S,U,E,LS	(9, 12)	12.4
Subtract Double Register	SDR	R1,R2	FPR1 ← C(FPR1) − C(FPR2)	RR	2B	(4e)	S,U,E,LS	(9, 12)	12.4
Subtract Floating	SE	R1,D2(X2,B2)	FPR1 ← C(FPR1) − C(S2)	RX	7B	(4e)	P,A,S,U,E,LS	(9)	12.4
Subtract Floating Register	SER	R1,R2	FPR1 ← C(FPR1) − C(FPR2)	RR	3B	(4e)	S,U,E,LS	(9)	12.4
Subtract Half-word	SH	R1,D2(X2,B2)	R1 ← C(R1) − $C(S2)_{0-15}$	RX	4B	(4a)	P,A,S, IF		3.7
Start I/O	SIO	D1(B1)	Start an I/O operation	SI	9C	(4k)	M		15.12
Start I/O Fast Release	SIOF	D1(B1)	Start an I/O device and subchannel	SI	9C	(4k)	M	(7)	(22)
Subtract Logical	SL	R1,D2(X2,B2)	R1 ← C(R1) − C(S2)	RX	5F	(4t)	P,A,S		prob. 7.16
Shift Left Arithmetic	SLA	R1,D2(B2)	Left shift bits 1-31, fill (with) 0's	RS	8B	(4a)	IF	(15)	7.2
Shift Left Double Arithmetic	SLDA	R1,D2(B2)	Left shift bits 1-63, fill 0's	RS	8F	(4a)	S, IF	(15)	7.2
Shift Left Double Logical	SLDL	R1,D2(B2)	Left shift bits 0-63, fill 0's	RS	8D		S	(15)	7.2
Shift Left Logical	SLL	R1,D2(B2)	Left shift bits 0-31, fill 0's	RS	89		S	(15)	7.2
Subtract Logical Register	SLR	R1,D2(X2,B2)	R1 ← C(R1) − C(R2)	RX	1F	(4t)			prob. 7.16
Subtract Decimal	SP	D1(L1,B1),D2(L2,B2)	S1 ← C(S1) − C(S2)	SS	FB	(4a)	P,A, D, DF	(8)	11.2
Set Program Mask	SPM	R1	PSW_{34-39} ← $C(R1)_{2-7}$	RR	04	(16)			15.7
Subtract Register	SR	R1,R2	R1 ← C(R1) − C(R2)	RR	1B	(4a)	IF		3.7
Shift Right Arithmetic	SRA	R1,D2(B2)	Right shift bits 1-31, fill $C(R1)_0$	RS	8A	(4e)	S	(15)	7.2
Shift Right Double Arithmetic	SRDA	R1,D2(B2)	Right shift bits 1-63, fill $C(R1)_0$	RS	8E	(4e)	S	(15)	7.2
Shift Right Double Logical	SRDL	R1,D1(B2)	Right shift bits 0-63, fill 0's	RS	8C		S	(15)	7.2
Shift Right Logical	SRL	R1,D1(B2)	Right shift bits 0-31, fill 0's	RS	88		S	(15)	7.2
Shift and Round Decimal	SRP	D1(L,B1),D2(B2),I3	S1 is shifted (Direction and no. of digits in S2)	SS	F0	(4a)	P,A,D,DF	(7)	10.8
Set Storage Key	SSK	R1,R2	Storage key of $C(R2)_{8-20}$ ← $C(R1)_{21-27}$	RR	08		M,A,S	(6)	15.8
Set System Mask	SSM	D1(B1)	PSW_{0-7} ← $C(S1)_{0-7}$	SI	80		M,P,A		15.7
Store	ST	R1,D2(X2,B2)	S2 ← C(R1)	RX	50		P,A,S		4.3
Store Character	STC	R1,D2(X2,B2)	$S2_{0-7}$ ← $C(R1)_{21-31}$	RX	42		P,A		prob. 5.11
Store Double	STD	R1,D2(X2,B2)	S2 ← C(FPR1)	RX	60		P,A,S	(9, 12)	12.8

Name	Mnemonic	Operands	Semantics	Format	Opcode	Note	Note	Flags	Ref
Store Floating	STE	R1, D2(X2, B2)	S2 ← C(FPR1)	RX	70			P,A,S	12.8
Store Half-word	STH	R1, D2(X2, B2)	$S2_{0-15} \leftarrow C(R1)_{16-31}$	RX	40			P,A,S	prob. 4.7
Store Multiple	STM	R1, R3, D2(B2)	S2 ... ← C(R1), ..., C(R3)	RS	90			P,A,S	5.4
Store Clock	STCK	D1(B1)	Store the current value of time-of-day clock	SI	B2	(4m)	(7)	P,A,S,M	(22)
Store Characters Under Mask	STCM	R1, M3, D2(B2)	S2 ← Selected bytes of S1	RS	BE		(7)	P,A	(22)
Store Control	STCTL	R1, R3, D2(B2)	S2 ... ← C(CR1), ..., C(CR2)	RS	B6		(7)	P,A,S,M	(22)
Store Channel ID	STIDC	D1(B1)	Location 168 ← Information for a channel	SI	B2	(4n)		M	(22)
Store CPU ID	STIDP	D1(B1)	S1 ← Information for CPU	SI	02		(7)	M,P,A,S	(22)
Subtract Unnormalized	SU	R1, D2(X2, B2)	FPR1 ← C(FPR1) − C(S2)	RX	6F	(4e)	(9, 11)	P,A,S, E,LS	12.4
Subtract Unnormalized Register	SUR	R1, R2	FPR1 ← C(FPR1) − C(FPR2)	RR	2F	(4e)	(9, 11)	S, E,LS	12.4
Supervisor Call	SVC	I	Interrupt; $PSW(old)_{21-31} \leftarrow I$	RR	0A				15.6
Subtract Double Unnormalized	SW	R1, D2(X2, B2)	FPR1 ← C(FPR1) − C(S2)	RX	7F	(4e)		P,A,S, E,LS	12.4
Subtract Double Unnormalized Register	SWR	R1, R2	FPR1 ← C(FPR1) − C(FPR2)	RR	3F	(4e)		S, E,LS	12.4
Subtract Normalized (Extended)	SXR	R1, R2	[FPR1, FPR1 + 1] ← C(FPR1, FPR1 + 1) − C(FPR2, FPR2 + 1)	RR	37	(4e)	(9, 10, 13)	S, E,U,LS	12.4
Test Channel	TCH	D1(B1)		SI	9F	(4p)		M	15.12
Test I/O	TIO	D1(B1)		SI	9D	(4k)		M	15.12
Test Under Mask	TM	D1(B1), I2		SI	91	(4q)		P,A	7.6
Translate	TR	D1(L, B1), D2(B2)	S1 ← C(S2)	SS	DC			P,A	Lab. 11.3
Translate and Test	TRT	D1(L, B1), D2(B2)	Reg. $1_{8-31} \leftarrow$ Address of Arg. byte; Reg. $2_{24-31} \leftarrow$ Function byte	SS	DD	(4r)		P,A	Lab. 11.4
Test and Set	TS	D1(B1)	S1 ← FF	SI	93	(4s)		P,A	(21)
Unpack	UNPK	D1(L1, B1), D2(L2, B2)	S1 (zoned dec.) ← C(S2) (packed dec.)	SS	F3			P,A	10.6
Exclusive Or	X	R1, D2(X2, B2)	R1 ← C(R1) Ex. OR C(S2)	RX	57	(4d)		P,A,S	7.5
Exclusive Or Character	XC	D1(L, B1), D2(B2)	S1 ← C(S1) Ex. OR C(S2)	SS	D7	(4d)		P,A	7.5
Exclusive Or Immediate	XI	D1(B1), I2	$S1_{0-7} \leftarrow C(S1)_{0-7}$ Ex. OR I2	SI	97	(4d)		P,A	7.5
Exclusive Or Register	XR	R1, R2	R1 ← C(R1) Ex. OR C(R2)	RR	17	(4d)		P,A	7.5
Zero and Add Positive	ZAP	D1(L1, B1), D2(L2, B2)	S1 ← C(S2)	SS	F8	(4a)	(8)	P,A, D, DF	11.2

Chapter 2

2.1. $(62,120)_{10}$

2.2. $(15)_{10} = (F)_{16}$

2.3. $(255)_{10}$; $(1196)_{10}$; $(20,512)_{10}$; $(65,530)_{10}$.

2.4.   000BF4; Yes.

2.5.   a) four bytes   b) 0101 1100 0010 0000 1011 0001 0001 1000
        c) 001A0F   d) 001A0C.

2.6.   0; 0; 0; 1.

2.8.   634; 8542; 110010; 011011.

2.9.   a) 0000 0000 0000 0000 0000 0000 0000 1100
        b) 1111 1111 1111 1111 1111 1111 1111 1000.

2.10. a) 1111 1111 1111 0101
        c) Error, overflow.

2.12. a) 1111 1111 1111 1111 1111 1111 1110 1101, no overflow.
        b) 80000001 in hexadecimal, overflow.

2.13. a) 0004126E,   b) 01050318,   c) 00FF8642,   d) 00057CD6,
        e) FF048C2C,   f) FEFF0F56,   g) 00FB73D4.

2.14. FFFFFFFD.

2.15. FFFFFA19 (sign extension).

Chapter 3

3.1.   Binary: 0001 1010 1101 0111; Hexadecimal: 1AD7; Symbolic: AR 13,7.

3.2.   a) eight bits.

3.3.   a) 1ACA or AR 12,10   b) 1A29 or AR 2,9.

3.4. $E = (001100)_{16}$. Yes, it is on fullword boundary.

3.5. $B = 00174C$.

3.6.   9EF13EEE.

3.7. 4A706100; 1A96; 5A947100.

3.8. AH 10,1042(5,2); AH 1,100.

3.9.
```
A   4,7            4         00000012
A   7,=F'256'      7         000000F6
A   7,J            7         003002A2
AH  4,J+2          4         000002C8
```

3.10.
```
S   4,J            4         FFCFFD70
S   10,=F'4096'    10        00009104
```

3.11.
```
MR  10,5           10,11     00000000 0001405A
M   6,=F'-2'       6,7       00000000 00000014
```

3.12. 00000074

3.13. 5C60C396; 1D69; 5D60C396

Chapter 4

4.1. $C(R12) = 00000002$; $C(R13) = 00000001$.

4.3.
```
L   5,DIVIDEND
M   4,=F'1'
D   4,DIVISOR
ST  4,REM
ST  5,QUO
```

4.4. $C(R3) = 00000004$; $C(R4) = 00000000$; $C(R5) = 00000010$.

4.6. a) 000002B8.
      b) LA 7,4(7).

4.8. 0000036C; 00002136; 00002136; 0000036C.

4.9. 1; 1; 0; 1; 2; 2; 1; 2; 2.

4.10. a) BC 15,400(3,2) or 47F32190
      b) 0010.

4.12. a) BR 7 or BCR 15,7.

Chapter 5

5.1. MVI 1500(9),X'A3' or 92A395DC.

5.2. MVI NUMBER,C'#'.

5.6. a) 01   b) 00.

5.7. They are the same if B and A are one byte long each.

5.8. 132 bytes: STAR through STAR+131.

5.9. a) MVI OUTPUT,C' '
         MVC OUTPUT+1(79),OUTPUT

5.13. 98ECD00C; 90E6D00C.

Chapter 6

6.3. 0011B0; 0011B4; 0010BA.

6.6. A1: 01A9
      A5: C1D6D2C1D6D2C1D6D2C1D6D2C1D6D2.

6.8. a) 00001776   b) doubleword
      c) 4 areas, each 80 bytes long.
6.13. The relocation factor plus 2.

Chapter 8

8.2. a) 0009A00C
      c) the address of the first byte in the save area of the calling program.
8.3. a) $C(R12) = 00014C00$ b) $C(00058070) = 00014C00$
      c) $C(SAVE+4) = 00014C00$.
8.4. a) $C(R14) = 000C4E0C$ b) $C(R15) = 0000A03C$.
8.8. a) $C(R14) = 004A16D0$ b) the return address.
8.12. a) Two control sections but one module   b) Yes.
8.16. a) 5 times; COMP actually is executed 6 times with INDEX varying 0, 2, 4, 6, 8, 10.
      b) 12.
      c) The program would take the next sequential instruction. The final value of
         INDEX = 2.
8.17. a) 25 times   b) 104   c) 24 and 100.
8.18. They count the number of times a branch on zero instruction is executed.

Chapter 9

9.1. Register 15 contains 000003FC.

9.2

```
PB          ADD       BETA,GAMMA,DELTA
+PB         ST        2,TEMP
+           L         2,BETA
+           A         2,GAMMA
+           ST        2,DELTA
+           L         2,TEMP
```

9.4

```
            SECTION   C,9
+SECTC      CSECT
+CBASE      EQU       9
+           BALR      CBASE,0
+           USING     *,CBASE
```

9.5(b)

```
            CONTROL   12,PART,A
+PARTA      CSECT
+PARTREG    EQU       12
+           BALR      PARTREG,0
+           USING     *,PARTREG
```

9.7

```
            HALF      12,9,146
+H12        DC        H(12)
+H9         DC        H(9)
+H146       DC        H(146)
```

9.8(a)   and   9.9

```
         LINKAGE BAKER                              HERE
+        L        15,A0001          +BAKER  CSECT
+        BALR     14,15             +       DC        A(PROB9)
+        B        A0001+4
+A0001   DC       V(BAKER)
```

9.8(b)

```
         LINKAGE BAKER
+        L        15,A0067
+        BALR     14,15
+        B        A0067+4
+A0067   DC       V(BAKER)
```

Chapter 10

10.7.   01.
10.8.   10.
10.9.   None.
10.11. F0F3F6F2C7.

Chapter 11

11.1.   In two bytes: 126C packed.
11.4.   Yes; yes; yes.
11.5.   Four bytes; 0000 0000 0000 0000 0000 0001 0111 1101.
11.6.   MINUS1   DC   PL2'−1'
        or   DC   P'−001'
                  DC   XL2'1D'
11.7.   BETA DC PL4'.007'
11.8.   ROW   DS   21CL4
        or ROW   DS   21XL4
        or ROW   DS   21PL4
        or ROW   DS   21ZL4
        and others.
11.9.   0012352C
11.10. 00 03 41 1D
11.12. ZAP DELTA,=PL3'0'
11.13. 10
11.15. No; no; yes.
11.16. 00364C2C
11.17. 000123456D
11.22. 0.
11.23. a) 20;   b) F0.
11.26. Pattern field: 40404040F1F6F7; S trigger: 0000111.

Chapter 12

12.3.   b) 14 hexadecimal digits, or about 17 decimal digits.
12.4.   a) and c) are normalized.

12.6.   a) 32; b) 64; c) 16; d) 4.
12.7.   No.
12.10. a) 160; b) 60.
12.13. X'42123456'
12.14. X'424824646'; yes; no.
12.20. Yes.
12.22. BE155555 55555555 in floating point register 2.

Index

Index

NOTE: Boldface page numbers indicate key references.